PUBLISHING

OMF International works in most East Asian countries, and among East Asian peoples around the world. It was founded by James Hudson Taylor in 1865 as the China Inland Mission. Our overall purpose is to glorify God through the urgent evangelisation of East Asia's billions, and this is reflected in our publishing.

Through our books, booklets, website and quarterly magazine, *East Asia's Billions*, OMF Publishing aims to motivate Christians for world mission, and to equip them for playing a part in it. Publications include:

- contemporary mission issues
- the biblical basis of mission
- the life of faith
- stories and biographies related to God's work in East Asia
- accounts of the growth and development of the Church in Asia
- studies of Asian culture and religion relating to the spiritual needs of her peoples

Visit our website at *www.omf.org*

Addresses for OMF English-speaking centres can be found overleaf.

English-speaking OMF centres

AUSTRALIA: PO Box 849, Epping, NSW 2121
Freecall 1800 227 154
email: omf-australia@omf.net   www.omf.org

CANADA: 5759 Coopers Avenue, Mississauga ON, L4Z 1R9
Toll free 1-888-657-8010
email: omfcanada@omf.ca   www.omf.ca

HONG KONG: PO Box 70505, Kowloon Central Post Office,
Hong Kong   email: hk@omf.net   www.omf.org

MALAYSIA: 3A Jalan Nipah, off Jalan Ampang, 55000, Kuala Lumpur
email: my@omf.net   www.omf.org

NEW ZEALAND: PO Box 10-159, Auckland
Tel. 09-630 5778   email: omfnz@compuserve.com   www.omf.org

PHILIPPINES: 900 Commonwealth Avenue, Diliman,
1101 Quezon City   email: ph-hc@omf.net   www.omf.org

SINGAPORE: 2 Cluny Road, Singapore 259570
email: sno@omf.net   www.omf.org

SOUTHERN AFRICA: PO Box 3080, Pinegowrie, 2123
email: za@.omf.net   www.omf.org

UK: Station Approach, Borough Green, Sevenoaks, Kent, TN15 8BG
Tel. 01732 887299   email: omf@omf.org.uk   www.omf.org.uk

USA: 10 West Dry Creek Circle, Littleton, CO 80120-4413
Toll Free 1-800-422-5330   email: omf@omf.org   www.us.omf.org

OMF International Headquarters:
2 Cluny Road, Singapore 259570

ISOBEL
KUHN

OMNIBUS

BY SEARCHING

NESTS ABOVE THE ABYSS

IN THE ARENA

OM
publishing

This Isobel Kuhn omnibus edition first published 1997 by OM Publishing

Reprinted 2000

06 05 04 03 02 01 00   8 7 6 5 4 3 2

OM Publishing is an imprint of Paternoster Publishing
PO Box 300, Carlisle, Cumbria, CA3 0QS, U K
Paternoster Publishing USA
PO Box 1047, Waynesboro, GA 30830-2047
www.paternoster-publishing.com

By Searching

First published in the UK 1957 by OMF
Thirty-five reprints 1957-1983
Second edition 1986

In the Arena

First published in the UK 1960 by OMF
Seventeen reprints 1960-1984
Second edition 1995

Nests Above the Abyss

First published in the UK 1947 by OMF
Nine reprints 1964-1983
Second edition 1988

ISBN 1-85078-261-X

Printed in the U.K. by Omnia Books Limited, Glasgow

ISOBEL
KUHN

BY SEARCHING

OM
publishing

CONTENTS

1. On to the Misty Flats   1
2. Slippery Ways in Darkness   7
3. What You should not Imitate   12
4. My Year in Arabia   23
5. A Pair of Shoes and the Firs Conference   36
6. Extinguished Tapers   43
7. J O Fraser of Lisuland   58
8. The Moody Bible Institute   68
9. Spiritual Prevision   82
10. At Sundry Times and in Divers Manners   93
11. Graduation and CIM Candidature   114
12. The Vancouver Girls Corner Club   126
13. "Let Us Go On!"   151

THE QUESTION THAT PIERCED THE MIST
"Canst thou *by searching* find out God?"—JOB 11:7

THE ANSWER
Ye shall *seek* me, and *find* me, when ye shall search for me with all your heart.—JER. 29:13

Jesus said unto him, *I am the way*, the truth, and the life; no man cometh unto the Father, but by me.—JOHN 14:6

Search the Scriptures ... they are they which testify of me.—JOHN 5:39

If any man will do His will, he shall know of the doctrine, whether it be of God....—JOHN 7:17

CHAPTER ONE

ON TO THE MISTY FLATS

> To every man there openeth
> A way and ways and a way.
> And the high soul climbs the high way
> And the low soul gropes the low
> *And in between on the misty flats*
> *The rest drift to and fro*
> But to every man there openeth
> A high way and a low
> And every man decideth the way his
> soul shall go.
>
> JOHN OXENHAM

"OF course no one in this enlightened age believes any more in the myths of Genesis and ..." But here Dr Sedgewick paused in his lecture as if a second thought had occurred. With a twinkle in his eye, he said, "Well, maybe I had better test it out, before being so dogmatic." Facing the large freshman class, who were hanging on his words, and pulling his face into gravity, he asked: "Is there anyone here who believes there is a Heaven and a Hell? Who believes that the story of Genesis is true? Please raise your hand," and he waited.

Up went my hand as bravely as I could muster courage. I also looked around to see if I had a comrade in my stand. Only one other hand was up, in all that big group of perhaps a hundred students. Dr Sedgewick smiled. Then as if sympathetic with our embarrassment, he conceded: "Oh, you just believe that because your papa and your mama told you so." He then proceeded with his lecture, assuming once for all, that no thinking human being believed the Bible any more.

Brought up in an earnest Presbyterian home (my grandfather was a Presbyterian minister and my father an ardent lay preacher) I had been carefully coached in the refutations of modernism before my parents had allowed me to enter the university. If it had been a case of arguing the claims of modernism *v.* fundamentalism, I do not think I would have been shattered in my faith. But there was no argument. There was just the pitying sneer, "Oh, you just believe that because your papa and your mama told you so," and then the confident assumption that no persons nowadays who thought for themselves, who were scientific in their approach to life, believed that old story any more.

On the way home from class I face the charge honestly. *Why* did I believe the Bible? The Genesis explanation of life's origin? Why did I believe in Heaven and Hell?

It was because I had been taught it by my parents and church from the hour I could understand anything. Was that reason enough for accepting it? No, I agreed with Dr Sedgewick that it was not a sufficient basis to build my life upon. We had experienced remarkable answers to prayer in our family life—didn't that prove the existence of God? But my psychology course taught that mind had a powerful effect over matter. If I had not been so gullible maybe I could have seen a natural explanation. Our twentieth century believed only when there was a test and a proof. We were scientific in our investigations; we did not swallow the superstitions of our ancestors just because they were handed to us.

Dr Sedgewick, Professor of the English Department in our university, was an ardent follower of Matthew Arnold's "sweetness and light" philosophy, and of Thomas Hardy's materialism. Yet he was so apparently patient and kind toward us whom he felt were still bound by our parents' old-fashioned thinking that he won our affection and respect.

At the end of my walk home, I came to the conclusion that I would henceforth accept no theories of life which I had not proved personally. And, quite ignorant of where that attitude would lead me, I had unconsciously stepped off the High Way where man walks with his face lifted Godward and the pure, piney scents of the Heights call him upward, on to *the misty flats*. The in-between level place of easy-going; nothing very good attempted, yet nothing bad either; where men walk in the mist telling each other that no one can see these things clearly. The misty flats where the in-betweeners drift to and fro; life has no end but amusement and no purpose; where the herd drift with the strongest pull and there is no reason for opposing anything. Therefore they have a kind of peace and a mutual link which they call tolerance.

I did not know that I had stepped down to the misty flats. I just was conscious of a sudden pleasant freedom from old duties. If there was no God, why bother to go to church on Sunday, for instance? Why not use Sunday to catch up on sleep, so that one could dance half the night away several times during the week?

Again, if the Bible was but a record of myths and old-fashioned ideas, why read it every morning? That took time and it was much easier to sleep in till the very last moment, getting up just in time for the first class at Varsity. Prayer, too, became silly. Talking to someone who maybe did not exist.

I would not call myself an atheist; because, well, there were those childhood answers to prayer still to be accounted for. But I called myself an agnostic—I frankly did not know if there was a God or not. It was a popular thing to be on the misty flats, you had plenty of company. And one was respected as being modern and intelligent to question the old faiths. Life drifted along so pleasantly—*for a while*.

My home training still had an effect upon me. Jesus Christ, now seen blurred in the mists which denied His godhead, is an acknowledged historical character. And His name was still as an ointment poured forth to me. He was like a perfume which haunts and calls so that one stops, lifts one's head and drinks it in wistfully. His name was the sweetest melody I knew and never failed to stir my heart, even though I had ceased to seek Him. His purity and holiness made me hate besmirching things.

And all this because my father and my mother had taught me so.

So when I broke with the old religious habits and frankly went into the world, I still was choosy in what I did. I never smoked. The tainted breath and stained fingers or teeth of the smoker revolted me. I told myself I was too dainty for such doings.

Neither did I drink. My father, broken-hearted at my callous turning-of-the-back on all my home training, still warned me as a medical man what drink would do to a girl.

"Drink affects men and women biologically, and under its influence girls can be led into sin that they would never consent to when in possession of their senses. Dr Hall and I have such come into our own rooms all the time. They never meant to, but there they are. Keep away from liquors and you can keep yourself pure, perhaps." So I did not drink. Also I had *signed the pledge* when twelve years old, and a certain whimsical loyalty to my childhood self kept me from breaking it.

So amid the group at the university I was considered *a good girl*, and even a Christian! But I knew myself: I wasn't.

In my studies I took the honours course in English Language and Literature which brought me much under the influence of Dr Sedgewick. But in my extra-curriculars I was mostly interested in the Players Club, the amateur theatrical club of the university. Apparently I had a gift for acting comedy parts, and in my freshman year I won life-membership in the Players Club, not usually attained by a first-year student. The staff patron of our theatricals was Professor H G C Wood, also a member of the English Faculty. He was a believer in God and Christ, and not an atheist like Dr Sedgewick, and his friendship helped to keep me from extremes. But the theatre was his hobby and soon became mine. Urgently my mother pled with me to attend the Young Women's Christian

Association. I went several times, but was frankly
bored, so dropped it. I loved the theatre and I liked
to dance and these occupied my spare time. In fact,
our Varsity 1922 year book has, as comment
opposite my picture: "And oh the tilt of her heels
when she dances!" No shadow of the missionary
there.

In my second year I was elected to be Secretary
of the Students Council; at that time the highest
position to which a woman student could be
elected. I met the leading young people of the
university and became secretly engaged to Ben,
one of the star rugby and basketball players.

Ben was a returned soldier from World War I,
several years older than I, not handsome, but six
feet two or three in height. He came of a good
Baptist family and my mother encouraged our
friendship. He even took me to his church on
Sunday nights! It made a nice inexpensive date,
for Ben did not have much money and when he
asked me to marry him said that our engagement
must be kept secret lest his "old man" be angry
with him for getting involved before he
graduated. I insisted that my parents be told, but
his never were. We went together for nearly two
years, and my path was perceptibly down-grade.

CHAPTER TWO

SLIPPERY WAYS IN DARKNESS

Wherefore their way shall be unto them as slippery ways in the darkness: they shall be driven on, and fall therein: for I will bring evil upon them, even the year of their visitation, saith the Lord. JER. 23:12.

AFTER the stretched muscles of climbing, to find oneself on the level is very relaxing and pleasant. Therefore the Misty Flats are attractive to foot, eye and palate *at the beginning*. There is no hint that the pretty mist will gradually close in in darkness. There is no suggestion amid the merry chatter of the populous throng that there are slippery places, which are going to bring hurt. In the boasted freedom of drifting whither you will, there is certainly no sign that one is being *driven on*, as Jeremiah so shrewdly perceived was the reality. And above all, there is never a hint that the end of the Flats is the visitation of the Lord and the judgment of sin. Yet all that is the real truth.

In my senior year there came a day when my college chum, Cora, shook my foundations with a sentence or so. "Isobel," she said, "I think I should tell you something, even though it may hurt. Everybody but you knows that Ben is not loyal to you. He is taking Reba out behind your back."

I turned a stunned face upon her, and her eyes filled with tears of sympathy, but with true friendship she went on: "You remember when

you were ill and could not go to his fraternity
dance?"

"Yes," I replied. "He took Reba in my place that
night; he asked me if I would mind and I said no."

"Well that was the beginning of it, I guess.
They've been seen together a lot. People are
talking and I can't bear that you should not know.
I don't think he's worth breaking your heart over,
Isobel," she said earnestly.

But it did break my heart. It was difficult to
believe and yet I knew he had not been so
attentive of late. My father had spoken to me about
it. "You let Ben get too sure of you, Baby," he had
said, using his tender pet name for me, the
youngest in the family. "Show a man all the love
you have *after you are married*, but keep it in
reserve while you are just engaged. The elemental
male *likes* to fight for a mate. What is the use of
chasing a street-car after you've caught it?"

So it was not all Ben's fault. I had been
inexperienced, I was still only in my teens. With
the promise to be his wife I had truly given my
heart to Ben and love struggled hard with "maybe
if I ..." and "perhaps I could still win him back."
But it was Ben himself who made it hopeless.

I met him one morning at the entrance of the
university; no one else was around, so I charged
him with taking Reba out behind my back. I
wanted to hear from his own lips that it was true,
for love rebelled at believing it. He drew himself
up to the full stature of his six feet two inches, and
I never forgot the curl of his lip as he said, "Isobel,
you're a softy. You don't suppose, do you, that
after we are married, I'm not going to take other
women out sometimes?"

"Then we part," I whispered, dazed as if stricken. I was on my way home from a class and have never forgotten the dull agony of that walk. I knew I could never marry a man with such standards. That was the trouble. They were just the standards of the Misty Flats. But I had known the Christ and I could not be satisfied with less than the ideals He had set me.

So I found myself in the slippery places of darkness. Pride wounded me; love wounded me; sleep departed from me. I had signed up for the honours course in English Language and Literature, which in our university entailed more work than a mere pass degree. I was working hard and needed to rest during sleep hours, but I couldn't.

My mother was distressed that I should break with Ben and kept saying, "If you would only take my advice"; but I could not bear to discuss it with anyone. I discussed it with myself night and day. My father was my greatest comfort. He knew enough to be silent and just love me. He even sensed I was not sleeping. One night when all the house had been asleep for hours and I was still tossing, I heard him come into my bedroom. He knelt down beside me and prayed God to help me, but it only made me irritated. "Thanks, Dad," I said wearily, "I know you mean it well, but it doesn't go beyond the ceiling, you know," and I never forgot the groan with which he turned from my agnosticism and left the room.

The climax came just before Christmas. My birthday is December 17 and I was to be twenty years old, but I do not remember if it was before or after that date. The Post Office clock on Main

Street had just struck 2 a.m. and I was still tense
and tossing. I was desperate. I knew I'd be ill in
the morning if I did not get to sleep. Then came
the Tempter.

"Of what use is life?" he whispered. "Ben is
only an average fellow. Probably all men are just
like him. You'll never find anyone to love you like
you want to be loved—your ideal is too high. And
you'd never be happy with a lower ideal of
marriage. Why go on with life? It has no purpose,
only suffering. This would be a good time to slip
out. There is that bottle in the bathroom marked
Poison. A good long drink and your troubles are
over." A good idea. The only sensible solution. I
jumped out of bed and started for the bathroom.
*Slippery ways in the darkness: they shall be driven on
and fall therein.*

My hand was on the door knob when a deep
groan, thrice repeated, broke the silence of the
dark. It was my father, moaning in his sleep in the
next room. I was not afraid, for I recognized
father's tones, but I was startled into
remembrance of him. I stood with my hand on
the knob debating. If I committed suicide, Daddy
would think I had gone to Hell. Of course, that
would not make a place called Hell, but how
terrible for Daddy to think so. He had been such a
dear, kind father to me all my life. Dare I make him
such a dastardly return? No, I couldn't be so mean
and selfish. In agony I turned and sat down on the
edge of my bed and faced the darkest moment of
my life. I didn't want to live and I couldn't die! Oh
the black despair of the *Misty Flats*. How little did I
know of the golden sunshine pouring on the High
Way above them. What a lot of heartache I might

have been saved if I had only been told that God
had already laid His Hand on one who was to be
dear husband to me, with the same ideals and the
same passion for God's highest purposes. But it
was necessary that first I drink to the dregs the
emptiness of the promises held out by the Misty
Flats: only then could I be freed from their lure and
subtle call.

And now a strange thing happened. That day I
had been studying Matthew Arnold's essay on *The
Study of Poetry*. (You remember, it was Sedgewick,
a disciple of Arnold, who had first pushed me off
the High Way?) In that essay he gives various
quotations from the classics as touchstones of
perfect poetry. One such was from Dante and ran:
In la sua volontade è nostra pace. From my knowledge
of Latin I had guessed the meaning: *In His will is
our peace*. Now that sentence wrote itself across
the dark of my bedroom. Dante believed in God.
What if there were a God, after all? If so, I certainly
had not been in His will. Maybe that was why I
had no peace? An idea struck me. No one was
watching to see if I were a fool or not. Sitting there
on my bed's edge, I raised both hands
heavenward. "God, if there be a God," I whispered, for I was not going to believe in what did
not exist just to get a mental opiate, "if You will
prove to me that You are, and if You will give me
peace, I will give You my whole life. I'll do
anything You ask me to do, go where You send
me, obey You all my days." Then I climbed into
bed and pulled the blankets over me.

CHAPTER THREE

WHAT YOU SHOULD NOT IMITATE

THE next thing I knew, it was morning and the golden sunshine of a December day in Vancouver was pouring into my bedroom. I lay there drowsily enjoying it when suddenly a thought startled me into full consciousness. I had been sleeping like a baby—how did it happen? Such deep relaxed slumber had not touched my pillow for many a long day. What brought it? Thought traced itself back to the experience of the night before. I had made a bargain with God. I had asked Him for peace and—*peace had come*. Oh yes, answered Reason; but that was easily explainable apart from God. That was not proof God existed. It was just the effect of mind over matter; I had committed my troubles to an imaginary being and that was why body and mind quietened down.

Restlessly I threw off the bedclothes and sat on the edge of my bed. I was not going to use religion as an opiate. I was going to be realistic or nothing; as a matter of fact, I believe I was born with "a flair for reality." But as I pondered the thought persisted, "You made a bargain last night. The Other Side kept His part ... there was no stipulation as to how peace should come, *and it came*. Nobody knows about it and nobody shall know, if this should prove to be foolishness. Why not continue your part of the agreement and see?"

But what was my part? To yield my whole life *if* He proved Himself. And in the meantime, why not try to seek Him?

Seek God? Where?

Can a man by searching find out God? Zophar had questioned Job, obviously not believing it possible. Job had tried to answer by pointing to God in His creative works. But the twentieth century had another theory for the origin of the earth.

Where does one go to search for God? Even as I asked myself that question, a picture from memory floated before me. It was at the Guelph conference of 1921 when the Student Christian Movement was formed. A young man was on his feet giving his testimony. "While I was interned in Germany as a prisoner of war," he said, "I got hold of a Bible and started to read it. *I found God through reading His Word.*"

I had been university delegate for the YWCA to that convention, but had apparently been unaffected by it. I knew there was a conflict on between the modernist students and the fundamentalists—this young ex-soldier was earnest for the old beliefs. I was still an agnostic and weary of religious arguments. I let them talk and did not let it enter my heart. But this young fellow was aglow with something real: he was the outstanding memory of that conference to me, yet I did not even know his name. Now in my own hour of need I could see him standing there,

radiant, affirming he had *found God*. And found
Him through the Christ of the New Testament.

Well, I had a Bible. There it was on my bookshelf,
unused, a bit dusty, but beautiful and new—a gift
from my father when I graduated from High
School. I pulled it down and looked at it.
Modernists said the Pentateuch was not written
by Moses; this was questioned, that was
questioned. Was there anything that wasn't
questioned? Yes ... the historicity of Jesus Christ is
beyond doubt. And the four Gospels are accepted
as a more or less authentic record of His teachings.
As authoritative as Plato's were of Socrates, at
least.

So I decided to search for God *through Jesus
Christ*; to read the Gospels only; to underline
everything and anything that Jesus said *to do* and
try honestly to do them. Also Jesus prayed, so I
would begin to try praying again; cautiously, of
course, and not really assuming that it went any
higher than the ceiling. With that decided, I arose
and dressed for another day's study at the
University of British Columbia.

And now began a life at two levels. An outer
level of study, worldly gaiety and pride, and an
inner level of watching, seeking after God—if
there was a God; always I added that.

God is not a puppet. Man may not pull strings
and expect Him to perform—not even doctrinally
correct strings, such as Balaam tried to pull. God is
not man's servant, that a puny atheist may shout a
challenge and He is bound to respond. Neither is
God a genie, that if man is lucky enough to find
the right combination of words, He will suddenly
pop out and reveal Himself. God is our Creator; all

powerful and dwelling in light unapproachable.
He demands reverence. But He is also willing to be
Father to such as come to Him by His ordained
road, Jesus Christ; and as a Father He tenderly
stoops to the immaturity of the babe in Christ.
This is the only explanation I have to offer of the
following facts. God answered prayers which were
unworthy even to have been brought before His
presence. If I prayed those same prayers today He
would *not* answer them. He responded then,
ignoring the selfish vanity of the request, simply
because of the honest seeking at the base. He
knew I meant it when I said I would give Him my
whole life. *The Father seeketh such to worship
Him—in spirit and in truth.*

For some three months after my "bargain" I
experienced nothing convincing. I read the
Gospels and prayed in private, but I never went to
Church or showed any outward interest in
religion. Then one day I was invited to a private
dance at the home of a girl friend, Jill. Jill had
moved away to a different part of town and
probably did not know that I had broken with
Ben, but as she did not inquire as to whether I
wanted him to be my partner, I had no
opportunity to tell her. She usually gave a dance
once a season and only invited Ben because he
went with me, her friend. She usually just invited
him and left it to him to arrange for my escort to
and from her house. So as I prepared to go, I
wondered if he would be there.

But on arrival he wasn't and I prepared to enjoy
the evening thoroughly, for it was a small home
dance with just our crowd, and I loved my friends
dearly. Jill's new house was centre-halled, so that

for dancing we had three spaces, parlour, hall and dining-room. I was dancing with Les (Cora's friend and long since her dear husband) when it happened. We had circled out into the hall when the doorbell rang. Jill opened the door and I beheld Ben, Reba with him, and he was ushering her into the house! I could hardly believe my eyes that he would have dared to do such a thing—it was like slapping my face publicly. And the dance was so small that there was no avoiding constant contact. I became completely unnerved. Trembling from head to foot, I began to walk all over Les's feet. Long hours of study, late hours of dancing, unhappy broken sleep had wrecked my nerves. I was undone; there was simply no escape from the humiliating fact. Les's look of respectful compassion did not help my chagrin. I could not fool Les as to the cause of my agony and the knowledge was too much for my pride.

"Les, I don't feel well—will you please excuse me?" and, stopping at the foot of the hall staircase, I fled up to the bedroom assigned as our dressing-room. Up and down the floor I paced in a rage at myself trying to use pride to whip my trembling body into control. It was perfectly useless—I shook like an aspen leaf.

Suddenly I remembered I was trying to prove if there was a God. With almost a sneer at such a ridiculous thing I nevertheless prayed. "Oh God, if You are, please give me p——" but I did not have time to finish the sentence. Something like an electric current struck me, shot through me and I tingled all over. *It had come from above; and from outside me.* But it left me completely poised and quiet. Incredulous, I stretched out my hand—it was steady and firm. Without stopping to say "thank You," marvelling inwardly, I turned and ran down the stairs. That same dance number was still on and Les was still standing at the foot of the staircase where I had left him.

"I'm all right now, Les," I said gaily. "Let's finish," which we did. A wonderful exultation, a feeling as if I had new life pulsed through me and continued all evening. Ben asked for a dance and made no effort to conceal his admiration. "You are beautiful tonight," he whispered, but I gave an evasive answer. Our ideals were too different; I must not let affection get involved again.

The evening was a triumph of gratified pride and vanity for me. But when I was alone in my bedroom, emotional reaction set in. Ben was a superb dancer, and the longing to float through life in perfect rhythm together would not be challenged by common sense. Sleep again departed from me and I tossed in agony until morning.

But the one fact stood out. I had cried to God for help, my lips twisted in sardonic unbelief that He even existed, but He had answered swiftly. This was no mind acting upon matter; the mind had had no faith at all. But help had come *from the outside entirely*. I was now convinced that some force outside me, intelligent, loving and powerful, was Up There trying to get in touch with me. Never again did I pray *if Thou art*. And now I wanted to know—how much could I ask of Him? Did He always answer prayer in Jesus' name? Morning and night I now prayed in faith. Those prayers were still all selfish and this is the part of my story where I do not want any young readers to try to imitate me.

Follow me in my pursuit of God—yes.

Like me, come to Him via the Christ of Calvary—yes.

Seek for the revelation of that Christ in the Bible—yes. But don't imitate my flounderings. I was pigheaded now in the matter of refusing all human advice, and my own level of living was so low that God could not meet me on a higher.

I wondered if God could answer seemingly impossible requests. For instance—get me invitations to certain balls and dances? It was our senior year and almost all our "gang" were paired off now, either engaged or going steady. There was no one who would be free to invite me, within the circle of my close acquaintances, unless I hinted—which I did not intend to do, ever. God answered wonderfully, causing my incredulity to marvel at His power to do it. I will just take space for one instance.

A neighbouring university had sent their football team to play ours and a *thé dansant* was to be given to the two teams after the match. It was purposely a small affair in honour of the teams, just the players and their girl friends and such team officers as the coach, manager, etc. Now Ben was one of the star players and I wanted to go; he had barged in on my party; now I wanted to go to this held in his honour to show that I was not dependent on him for a good time. A thoroughly low fleshly reason but also—it was hopeless to expect an invitation to such an exclusive party. Could God do it? I challenged Him.

The day before the match came. No one would ask me now—it would be an insult to ask a girl at such a late hour: sure proof she was only second or third choice.

That last afternoon a fellow student and I had arranged a rehearsal of a theatrical scene in which he and I were to act alone. George was a good friend of mine and engaged to a girl called Martha. He also happened to be on the manager's staff of the football team, but this I did not know then. He had come to my house for the rehearsal and after it was over and he reached for his hat to leave, he said, "Well, Isobel, see you at the *thé dansant* tomorrow afternoon after the match." Then I saw he did not know I had broken with Ben.

"No; I don't think you will, George," I said slowly.

He whirled around and shot me a keen look; then, gentleman that he was, he drew himself up and said with fine courtesy, "Isobel, last night Martha was called out of town unexpectedly. I thought I was going to have to 'go stag' to the *dansant*. May I have the pleasure of your company? I'll explain to Martha, I'm sure she won't mind."

It was just as simple as that. I was almost intoxicated with the wonder of it, and again the afternoon was a great triumph for me. I had more partners seeking me than there were dances, while Reba was more than once a "wallflower." In fact, while dancing with me, Ben had to excuse himself to go find her a partner!

Now, do I really believe that God was responsible for that? I am sure God gave it to me. Moreover, by piling on the triumphs He taught me a lesson I never forgot. I learned that pride and

gratified vanity could never bring me peace or
happiness. Underneath the gay triumphant
surface I was miserable. My heart was often like
lead even while my lips were chattering merry
nonsense. This kind of a life would never satisfy
me—I grew more and more unhappy and
disillusioned. And that was what God wanted. It
was as if He said, "If this is what you think you
want, dear, have some more." And He stuffed the
froth of life down me. Yet every time He got me an
invitation when humanly speaking it seemed
impossible, He proved to me again there was
nothing He could not do for me.

All during this time, my parents knew nothing
of my inward seekings. They sensed a change was
going on, but I still refused to go to church with
them and usually spent Sunday trying to catch up
on the sleep I had lost at dances during the week!
But there may have been a softening visible, for
Mother began again to try to help me.

"Isobel, I want you to come with me to hear
Professor Ellis. The meeting is just a Bible class,
not held in a church, but in a classroom of the
Vancouver Bible School. Just to please your
mother. Won't you do a little thing like this to
please me? I don't want to go alone."

And so I went.

I did not know that anyone else in that room
knew me. In fact, I did not look at the audience; I
had ceased to be interested in human beings. But
the speaker held my attention. Professor Ellis was
a very cultured, educated Christian gentleman. I
liked his quiet, refined manner of speech. He was

speaking that day on the Temptation of Christ,
and as he went on to give his message, he also
very frankly pointed out the liberal interpretation
of that passage. Without any belligerent
dogmatism, he courteously but deftly refuted their
arguments. I saw clearly that here was a scholar
who knew both sides of the argument. Here was a
real gentleman who would never stoop to nasty
remarks about an opponent. And, watching the
quiet radiance of his face, I instinctively knew that
here was a man who had *personal experience with
God*. I decided that this was the preacher for me; I
would come again.

Seated behind me was another Christian
gentleman. White-haired, shy and reserved, he
was known to me only as Mr Wright, a friend of
my father's. I forget if it was that first time I went
to Professor Ellis's Bible class, or on a succeeding
occasion, but at the close of the meeting he leaned
forward and spoke to me.

"Isobel, I'm glad to see you here. I've been
praying for you for some seven years," and his
eyes flooded with tears.

I was stunned. It was about seven years since I
had decided to dance and go in for worldly thing
against my father's pleadings. The yearning in
Christ which lit up Mr Wright's face stirred me to
the depths, for my soul still knew periods of
agony. With eyes as flooded as his own, I tried to
murmur "Thank you," then escaped quickly from
the building.

But every Sunday saw me back in that afternoon
service, and weekly I was fed and nourished in the
truth of God's Word. Professor Ellis's scholarship

and his expositional preaching combined with his gentle culture had won my full confidence and I was willing to learn from him.

And so, my head still befogged by the Mists of the Flats, my feet were once more planted on the High Way, prepared to climb, and my face steadfastly turned Godwards.

CHAPTER FOUR

MY YEAR IN ARABIA

IGRADUATED in May 1922, when I was twenty years of age. Because of my credits, I only needed to take five months' Normal School training in order to get a teacher's certificate. My ambition was to be a dean of women in some university and teach English. But as I was so young and inexperienced in teaching I had to accept an elementary grade school first.

I could have got a high school appointment up-country but my mother would not hear of it. She insisted I have a city school and so, being absolutely inexperienced, I had to accept a place as teacher of the Third Grade at the Cecil Rhodes School, Vancouver.

In the meantime my family had moved to Victoria, B.C. My father was roentgenologist to Dr Ernest Hall of Victoria, and mother sold our Vancouver home and purchased a chicken ranch just out of Victoria. This ranch was to be for my brother who had been a soldier in World War I and for whom employment must be found. He thought he would like ranch life.

So in February 1923 I found myself a "schoolmarm" in Vancouver and needing to find a

boarding-house. For the first time in my life I
would not live at home, but be "on my own," and
receiving a monthly salary for which I need
account to no one. The idea was distinctly
pleasing. But where to board?

Somehow I ran into the mother of a girl with
whom I had gone to Elementary School eight years
before. They were a Scottish family, and the mother
especially was a very superior person. Mrs Hunter
was a drinker, but, inbred with theosophy, had
fallen in with the idea that it was wrong to spank a
child. I have wondered if this was not the reason
her children did more as they liked than she liked.
The two youngest would not continue school, so
had to take employment below their family
cultural level. By the time I had my Arts degree,
Mrs Hunter was so reduced in circumstances that
she was trying to run a boarding-house and asked
if I would come to her. She was apologetic, for she
had lost her best furniture and could not provide
anything as comfortable as I had been accustomed
to; but she was very clean, an excellent cook and
her house was within walking distance of my
school. My mother knew her and felt at ease that I
should be with Mrs Hunter, who was as loving
and kind to me as if I were her own child.

So I found myself in this house—the only
Christian. The two daughters were both engaged
to sailors; the youngest child, a son, was a
policeman and had a wife and small baby. The
policeman's brother-in-law, whom we called
Laurie, was attending Normal School, hoping to
become a schoolteacher. As he was not yet
earning, he paid but a minimum, if anything. This

was the household among whom I became the ninth.

After graduation my particular clique scattered. Many went to other universities for further degrees. Some taught school, but went up-country, where they could get High School positions. In no time, I seemed to be alone and living in a different world. The young people of my boarding-house were very nice to me, but were all for the bright lights—I did not care to join them. We had little in common but our boarding-house. Surrounded with young laughter and noise, I was as alone as if I had been in the deserts of Arabia. For a year and a half, God shut me up to that aloneness, so that I have always called it *my year in Arabia*.

A young fellow we will call Mac had begun to ask me out. He was still studying and asked me to the various big dances of the university from time to time, but as he did not live in Vancouver our dates were not frequent.

I had begun to attend evening lectures at the Vancouver Bible School, but it was just beginning and I do not remember meeting other Christian young people. I was lonely.

F B Meyer points out that this is one of the planned training schools of God. "One symptom of being on that path is loneliness." He continues:

Nothing strengthens us so much as isolation and transplantation ... under the wholesome demand his soul will put forth all her native vigour ... it may not be necessary for us to withdraw from home and friends; but we shall have to withdraw our heart's deepest

dependence from all earthly props and supports, if ever
we are to learn what it is to trust simply and absolutely
on the eternal God.[1]

For one thing I found it hard to keep my prayer
times. The others in the house played cards and
danced or had what they called a good time until
long past midnight. I could not pray with those
noises in my ears. To get up early for it was not
productive either. Once up, my mind was rushing
on to my schoolteaching, which, by the way, I was
finding difficult. At last I hit on the plan of asking
the Lord to wake me up around 2 a.m., when the
house had settled to quiet, and then to arise for an
hour's prayer and Bible study. This worked
wonders. Always a sleepy-head, it was wonderful
to me to be awakened each morning, as I was, and
in the quiet of that still hour Christ became so real
to me that often I felt I could have touched Him, if I
but put out my hand. I was learning what Dr A W
Tozer calls "the awareness of His presence."[2] It
satisfied me as nothing on earth had ever done. It
filled me with a joy of communion that is
inexpressible. It was in my *Arabia*, as I called it,
that I learned fellowship with Christ, living
person-to-person fellowship which henceforth
became dearer than ought else in life to me.

The acute sense of His presence was not given
during the first few months I was at the Hunter
Boarding House. My head was still in the Misty
Flats and my feet too entangled with the world.

[1]*Abraham*, by F B Meyer.
[2]*The Pursuit of God*, by A W Tozer.

How I got lifted out into a clearer spiritual atmosphere is a story in itself, so I give it here.

It began with an angry disappointment.

But first I must explain that I was not happy teaching Third Grade (eight-year-olds). The children in my class fascinated me. It was my first real connection with children, for I was the baby of our family and we had early moved away from where small cousins lived. I was totally inexperienced with children and thought them "the cutest things." Even their little buttons of noses fascinated me. Needless to say, I had discipline problems! The small cherubs soon found out their teacher was a softy and she was given daily samples of what unexpectedly naughty things a cherub can think up—even without ever losing his angelic smile!

Then the subjects I taught were so elementary— spelling, arithmetic tables, simple nature studies and *drill*. Eight hours each day one's delightful mental life must be tied down to such boredom. I have often thought that if I had been allowed to teach High School English I might never have become a missionary—I would have loved it.

But now I hated teaching. I found the discipline so perplexing that I was afraid I was going to be a failure and became thoroughly alarmed. This was to be my life-work! I decided I must study teaching and so signed up for a Teachers' Convention in Seattle during—was it Easter holidays? I've forgotten.

Now, in Seattle there was a boy-friend who had corresponded with me since grade school, which we had attended together. I had not seen Donald for years, but when I wrote that I was coming to the Convention I got a letter right back saying I must stay at his house and he would be at the boat to meet me. So it was arranged.

I was just about to leave for the Seattle boat when a telegram was handed me. It read: HAVE ARRANGED FOR YOU TO STAY AT WHIPPLES', SEATTLE, LOVE. DADDY.

Was I annoyed! "Daddy, how perfectly mean of you. Oh, when will you and Mother stop interfering with my plans and realize that I am grown up?" Whipples'—who are they? Dim memory finally produced vague outlines. "Oh religious friends of Dad's. Yes; I remember now. So *that's* Dad's idea. Wants to have them talk to me about my soul, eh? Well, they won't find a porcupine more receptive. I'm just *not* going to be bossed like this. I'll telegraph I've made other plans." But a glance at the clock showed me I had no time if I were to catch the ship. Thoroughly provoked I went aboard and to my cabin. By morning we would be in Seattle.

Don was there all right and I explained my predicament. He was not put out. "Well, just sleep there," he suggested. "I can take you around from there," and so it was decided.

I don't remember anything of the Convention. I remember a nice supper with Don afterwards and an evening of fun—a dance perhaps. Anyway, I did not realize how late the hour was until we approached the Whipple house and found it in darkness. No; there was a dim light at the back. The door-bell ring produced other lights; then the door was opened by Mrs Otis Whipple herself. Don was introduced, invited in, declined, said goodbye, and I found myself in the sitting-room alone with my hostess.

I do not know the kind of person I was looking for, but it certainly was not the kind I met. Motherly plumpness, a cheery voice, Southern warmth of hospitality, geniality and culture were what greeted me. Culture is a form of beauty; beauty of a trained mind, and a heart trained to think of the other person's feelings. Beauty of any kind has always had power over me and I was drawn to her immediately. Instinctively I knew she was not one to barge into my inner sanctum without an invitation; as yet I did not know that there are other ways of soul-winning!

God and my soul were never mentioned. Just a charming talk about my home; their old friendship with my father; of a girl, Tony Black, to whom I was supposed to bear striking likeness. She spoke of a summer conference at a place called the Firs; and of her husband's sister, a missionary in China recently widowed who was to be at the Firs this summer of 1923. More and more I relaxed; better and better I liked her. So finally when I was shown to my room my porcupine quills were all safely laid flat.

The next day was Sunday. I had resolved to bend to decorum enough to go to church in the morning, then I meant to claim the rest of the day to do what I liked. I had a girl-friend in the city and I had an appointment to spend the afternoon with her, Mamie. Idly I wondered that Mrs Whipple had not as yet made any effort to get me alone and talk religiously. Little did I dream the truth, which she only told me years later. That first

night, after we had all gone to bed, she could not
sleep for the burden of *me*. At last she got up and
went on her knees asking God the cause? For over
an hour she battled in prayer that whatever was
the reason He had sent me to them, it might be
fulfilled before I left. Not before she felt she had
prayed *through* did she go back to bed. Having
committed the matter to the Lord, she did not get
anxious as to how He would accomplish it: *she did
not try to rush matters*, which in my case would
have been fatal. One of her pet sayings was
"Flexible in the hands of the Spirit," and she truly
lived it.

The afternoon visit to Mamie was very pleasant
(I had always loved her) until she asked me an
unsettling question: "Isobel, do you like
schoolteaching? Are you enjoying your work?"

"Oh, Mamie," I groaned in reply, "I'm not
happy at all. All my life I've planned to teach, and
now that I've graduated and am at it, I just feel like
a misfit. And yes, I just hate it. If only I had got a
High School position, I'm sure it would be
different. I'm still sure I would enjoy teaching
literature. But I'm only twenty-one, you know, and
so could not expect to get right into a city High
School, without any teaching experience. It's so
inane teaching spelling and arithmetic. I just
don't——"

"Isobel, I know what you need," struck in
Mamie earnestly. "You need to see a phrenologist,
and have your head read! He'd tell you what you
are fitted for. And it just so happens that a very
excellent phrenologist is in town, Dr X——. He is
a friend of ours and coming to supper with us
tonight. His charge is very high, but as a friend of

ours I'm sure he would do you for nothing. But you would have to come tonight, for he is leaving tomorrow."

"Oh, Mamie!" I cried, "How perfectly wonderful! There is only one snag. I'm staying with religious people, and they might be offended at a guest in their house going to see a phrenologist on *Sunday*. You know how particular some people are about keeping the Sabbath. Oh, if they will only consent! My hostess is really a dear and I just couldn't offend her. But I tell you—I'll go right back and ask her. If she says yes, I'll phone you and you make the appointment for me. Oh, it would be grand to be happy in one's work. It would be wonderful to know what one was fitted for in life."

"Well, Dr. X——will know, I'm sure of that. All right. Goodbye. I'll be looking for that phone call!" And we parted; I to return to the Whipples' home with beating heart. Was I about to lose the opportunity of my life because of old-fashioned religious scruples?

Arriving back earlier than expected, I met Mrs Whipple in the hall, and went straight to the point:

"Mrs Whipple, I would like to ask you a question. Would you object to my going to a phrenologist tonight to have my head read? I've not been very happy in my work and ..."

"Well now, dear," she said in her cheery, comfortable way, "let us go upstairs and discuss it. I'm not just quite sure I understand all that is involved. Here is Miss McCausland"—waylaying another guest who was crossing the hall at that moment. "Miss McCausland is a schoolteacher

herself, and maybe she can help us. Take her to the
little front bedroom, Margaret. I'll be there in a
moment."

I did not learn until many years later why she
delayed in coming. But she ran for prayer help.
Her young High School daughter, Lois, was in the
back of the house with two friends, all of them just
in their teens. It is interesting now to look back at
those three little maidens who were urged on to
their knees downstairs to intercede for the right
direction of phrenologist-seeker me upstairs. Lois
later became Mrs Nathan Walton of the China
Inland Mission. Evelyn Watson became her sister-
in-law, Mrs Eldon Whipple, whilst the third
young girl, Doris Coffin, became Mrs Willard
Aldrich, author of the well-known column, "Out
of the Mixing Bowl."[1] But at this moment the three
teenagers were just told, "Isobel has come to a
crisis in her life! Pray her through while I go up
and deal with her." So down on their knees they
went in prayer.

Upstairs Mrs Whipple was saying to me, "Now,
dear, tell us everything from the beginning so we
will understand."

So the flood-gates were unlocked and out
poured the story of my schoolteaching troubles
and disappointments; I spoke freely because I felt
an atmosphere of loving sympathy, and sensed a
poise about these two women which seemed to
say that *their* lives were satisfying. So I unfolded
this wonderful opportunity of having my head
read by a skilled phrenologist, and the supposed
snag—it was Sunday. With beating heart, I looked

---

[1] *The Moody Monthly.*

up into that kind, wise and lovely face and said, "Would you object to my going on Sunday?" No tremor of horror or shock crossed her face at all; just a look of deep thoughtfulness as if she were weighing the matter carefully. Then came her answer:

"Isobel dear, I don't think the matter of its being Sunday is the important thing. It's like this: *God has a plan for your life*. The Bible says that He has created us unto good works and *foreordained* that we should walk in them (Eph. 2:10). That means He has foreordained a useful life for you, and He does so for each of His creatures. The point as I see it is—to find out God's plan for your life and then follow it. If it is His will to reveal that plan through a phrenologist, going on Sunday would do no harm. But if it were not His will to reveal His plan through a phrenologist, *going any day of week would be wrong*."

I was struck with the common sense and logic of her words and thrilled through and through to hear that God had a plan for my life. Daughter of an elder in the church and granddaughter of a Presbyterian minister, I do not remember anyone ever telling me that before. I always had thought that God was a kindly, fatherly Being. Away off in the heavens somewhere we could call upon Him in trouble, but for the rest it was up to us to map out our own lives in good, honest work. Then we could ask His blessing and help from time to time. But that God was so minutely interested in *me*, that He would take the trouble to plan a career for me—plan it without my asking—the tender intimacy of a Love which could do that, just touched me to the breaking point. Hardly able to control my voice, I asked, "Well, how are we to find out His plan for us?

By this time I was kneeling at the bed on which Miss McCausland sat, Mrs Whipple in a chair beside me. She reached for her Bible and opened it in front of me saying, "Isobel, I've always found His will *through His Word*, this Book. His plan for us will always be in accordance with the Scriptures. And with me, it usually is from the Bible itself that I get my leading." At that moment the telephone rang and Mrs Whipple was called.

"Excuse me a moment, I'll be right back," she said. "Miss McCausland, will you tell Isobel what you think?" I do not remember what dear Miss McCausland said for I was thinking, "God's plan for my life is in that Book." Impulsively, I pulled it toward me. It fell shut and I reopened it at random with my eyes on Miss McCausland. Inwardly I was wondering what the Bible said about phrenology, when my eye happened to fall on the open page and there, unconsciously, my left hand lay with forefinger pointing at a verse. I read: "KEEP THEE FAR FROM A FALSE MATTER" (Ex. 23:7). It was as if a Voice had spoken to me and I was so startled at the directness of the answer to my inward question which no one had heard that my distressed heart collapsed with relief. I was weeping when Mrs Whipple re-entered the room; weeping terribly, simply rent with sobs.

"It is all right, Isobel," she tried to say. "He'll lead you."

"Oh He has," I cried. "Look at this verse," and I pointed to *Keep thee far from a false matter*. She too marvelled at such a quick, thoroughly complete answer. But the piled-up heartaches of a whole year and a half of searching after God had reached a climax, and I could only sob until exhausted. Very tenderly and lovingly the two ladies ministered to me. Dear Mrs Whipple never tried to pry; the privacy of the human soul was respected by her, and that was another reason we all loved and trusted her so.

I do not remember anything more of that visit, except that Mrs Whipple told me again of The Firs Bible Conference and urged me to attend that July as her guest. I was not interested. I still shrank from evangelistic meetings with their worked-up emotion and high-pressure methods. I did not intend to be high-pressured into anything.

"Thank you, Mrs Whipple," I said, "But I have already signed up to attend Teacher's Summer School in Victoria. Until God leads differently, I must earn my living and can only do it by teaching." And so we parted.

The Lord now wished to direct my thoughts into a channel where they would never have run of themselves. My life was about to turn a new corner, and strange to say, it all hinged at first, upon a pair of shoes.

CHAPTER FIVE

A PAIR OF SHOES AND THE FIRS CONFERENCE

"HERE, Julia," said Mrs Tom Cole to her sister-in-law, Mrs Otis Whipple. "The Firs Conference will soon open and you need a pair of shoes"—with a significant look at her—and she held out a five-dollar bill.

Julia Whipple was not one to neglect her personal appearance; in fact, to be well-groomed had been her lifelong habit, but of late funds had not been too plentiful. Julia and Otis Whipple had given their last earthly possession to the Lord, i.e. this honeymoon cabin at the Firs on Lake Whatcom, Bellingham in the State of Washington; and God used it to establish the yearly Lake Whatcom Bible and Missionary Conference which has been so blessed. 1923 was to be only their second attempt at a conference, and Julia Whipple was hostess. What would others think of her shabby shoes? But she had something else on her mind.

She had been praying that Isobel Miller would come to the Firs. She saw, as I had not, that here was one groping blindly toward God, and open to dangerous misleadings if not carefully grounded in the Word. As is a young person's weakness, I might be carried off my feet by some magnetic personality of one of the many "isms," if I chanced to meet such, at this stage. I needed grounding in the Scriptures and I needed Christian fellowship. I had had a small college debt to pay back and had only been earning a salary for six months—maybe money would be a factor in bringing me. At any rate, she waved the matter of new shoes aside, sat down and wrote me a letter urging me to come, and saying that the enclosed five dollars, she felt, was the Lord's provision for my boat tickets. Once I reached the Firs I was to be her guest—room and board would cost me nothing. Wouldn't I come?

I received it quite casually, not at all impressed with any desire to go. It was Mrs Whipple's kind heart, I told myself, and I was now forced to do something about it. But I felt my alibi would be easy. The conference came right in the middle of the summer school I had signed up for. I must get credit for this summer's study, and they would hardly give me full credit for six weeks' work if I ran off in the middle for ten or eleven days. So I made this my test, *and I prayed about it.*

"Lord, if it be Thy will I go, move the authorities to grant consent without reducing my credits, and I'll take it as Thy sign I am to go."

So the next morning found me before the Registrar of the Teachers' Summer Institute.

"I have been called to Bellingham on a matter important to me and I would like to apply for ten day's absence without reducing my credits. Could that be done, sir?"

He inquired my name, turned over a book,

pursed his lips a moment, then said, "All right,
Miss Miller. Just tell us when you leave and when
you will return."

I could not believe my ears. Just the day before a
fellow student teacher had applied for only a week
off and been flatly refused! I still do not know how
to explain it, but my full credits were given to me.

I came out of the office walking as if in a dream.
I inquired the boat schedule and sent word to Mrs
Whipple that I was coming, how and when, and
went home to pack my suitcase.

So it came about that one evening in July 1923
my boat arrived at Bellingham Pier. I had never
been there before and knew no one, but as I
looked eagerly around for Mrs Whipple, a smiling
young man and a sweet-faced girl stepped up to
me.

"Isobel Miller? We ve come to meet you. Eldon
Whipple and Evelyn Watson—do you remember
meeting us in Seattle? We've got a car here. Hop
in! We have to drive to the conference ground, but
it is not too far."

Their warm friendliness made me feel at home
immediately and soon we were whirling out over
curving roads with fragrant woods on either hand.
It was a twisting labyrinth to me, but finally we
turned into a path, drew up among tall fir trees,
and there was dear Mrs Whipple coming to meet
me. Her radiance, rippling laugh of joy, and
overflowing hospitality were something to cuddle
down into. I was duly hugged and kissed, then
shown into a big fire-lit room. Older people sat on
chairs, and the younger ones on the floor before
the big, crackling open fireplace of logs. The
flames threw a golden light over all faces and the

young people pulled me down on the floor to sit with them while the evening devotional service continued. Always shy and reticent with strangers, I was soon at home and filled with a wonderful content. The atmosphere was charged with the presence of the One whom I was learning to know and adore, and He was the centre of everyone else's attention too.

In the doorway I had been introduced to "my sister-in-law, Mrs Edna Whipple Gish, whose story I told you in Seattle. She is to be your cabin-mate," Years afterward I asked Mrs Whipple if this had been a premeditated arrangement, for it was to have a lasting effect on my life.

"I can't remember that it was," she said simply. "Edna's was the only cabin with a spare space, as I remember it."

After camp-fire service Edna led me through a woodsy path to the little cabin in the woods where she and I were to live. Before going to sleep she pulled out a little worn Bible from beneath her pillow and read a chapter with me, prayed, then at "Lights out" we settled down with the perfume of the fir trees soothing us into slumber.

I had just time to think back over Edna's story before losing consciousness.

"This is Ellis's Bible," she had said to me as she reverently took the worn much-marked volume from beneath the pillow. Then I had remembered what Mrs Whipple had told me in Seattle.

Edna met Ellis when he was on his first furlough, and found in him her ideal. He was a young man of deep devotion and consecration, and together they went to China to the South Gate section of Nanking city.

The next year they went for their vacation to beautiful Kuling, a famous mountain resort, where there is a pool and good swimming, also many lovely walks.

One morning they had decided on a swim—both were expert swimmers. As they left their tent they heard a cry from the pool. Ellis immediately ran and dived in to the rescue—a young missionary had caught a cramp and gone down. He was successful and saved her life, but he himself disappeared. Then Edna dived in to search for Ellis. As time dragged on and she could not find him, one can imagine the terror and anguish of her feelings. Theirs had been an ideal and wonderful union. Diving, searching, she did not notice that her body was being bruised and battered against rocks. Ellis—that was all she thought of. Finally, she saw his body washed up behind a little waterfall. Again she dived, reached him, dragged his body with her and got it to shore. But life had gone.

Exhausted she sank on a tree stump and covered her face with her hands.

A few minutes later she happened to look up and saw some Chinese coolies standing terrified with the dead man before them. Quickly she approached them and explained that the body on the ground was not her Ellis—that he was safe with God; and she preached Christ to them.

Edna's own body had taken such a severe beating that she was sent to the hospital and later advised to take a short furlough. Ellis's insurance money was enough to bring her to the Firs for the summer, and the Conference Council had asked her to lead the young people's meetings. We never knew what it was costing her to set aside her daily heartbreak and be our cheery, radiant Bible teacher. Years later Mrs Whipple told me how she would go to the Council and tell them she could not continue, but they would promise to pray for her, and back she would come to us.

She laid before us the Scriptural challenge to a consecrated life and to missionary service. I had never given the foreign field one thought up to that time. I was a very stay-at-home body by disposition and a veritable slave to physical comforts. Travel never attracted me, for it meant strange faces and strange ways—in other words, discomfort. Edna was the first to show me that I ought to be willing to give this up, if He asked me. When finally she gave a challenge to those who would surrender for foreign service, if He called, I put my hand up. I was surprised at how thrilled she was. To me it was a matter of course. That night I had made my bargain with God: I had promised Him my life. If He asked for it on the foreign field—why, of course, then I must go to the foreign field. It was not a question if I wanted to go. *I was no longer my own*. But then I had no clear indication it *was* the foreign field He wanted. I was willing, if it were, that was all. Why were they all so excited that I had raised my hand?

A much deeper blessing Edna had unwittingly brought me. Cabin life with her was my first encounter with a Spirit-filled life living in its daily routine habits. It was Edna *off the platform* who wrought most for me.

She sought the Lord's face before that of anyone else's at the beginning of each day. There was no wake-up chatter and pillow-flinging nonsense at dawn. This deeply bruised heart hungered and panted after the Lord, and her first waking thought was a longing for His fellowship and presence. And she kindled the same hunger in me. Remember, I had a bruised heart, too.

She read Philippians with me and Ellis's marginal notes.

"This one thing I do"—how it smote home because it was lived before my eyes. It got marked in my Bible, too.

"Rejoice always"—Edna had attained to that. How could I ever? I marked it, but decided to try for Phil. 4:11 as perhaps more within the possibility of attainment: *"For I have learned in whatsoever state I am, therewith to be content."* This became my life-verse for the next ten years or so.

"That I might know Him, and the power of His resurrection, and the fellowship of His sufferings, being made conformable unto His death" (Phil. 3:10). Great words that moved me to the depths of my being—they got marked down in my Bible. I was on that quest! But little did I know beyond that mere fact that my feet were on the High Way; I was in pursuit of Him.

> *And every man decideth*
> *Which way his soul shall go*

To such will come direction; there will come introductions to others of His family; there will come many helps which only One, on the outside of us (meaning a force which is not of us ourselves), could manipulate; and always He will also be within us for fellowship and love.

CHAPTER SIX

EXTINGUISHED TAPERS

> Who extinguishes their taper
> Till they hail the rising sun?
> Who discards the garb of winter
> Till the summer has begun?
>
> ANON

AND now it will astonish some adult readers (and perhaps make them shake their heads dubiously) to learn that all this time I was still indulging in theatres, dances and worldly things. My father had long years before urged me to separate myself from these amusements, but my mother felt he was "narrow" in his views on such matters, and she felt they did no harm if discriminately chosen. So I had gone with her viewpoint as the easier and more pleasant.

Occasionally I had wondered about it but had always fallen back on that old taunt, "You do this, or believe this, because your papa told you so." I was not going to give up any habit just because some human being told me to! If *God* told me to stop them I would obey; otherwise, I continued as I had been. These amusements were like the *taper* of our verse. They formed the light moments of my life—my *fun* as we Americans term it. I wasn't going to give up any *fun* just because some old religious fogey was prejudiced against it!

The first taper that I extinguished was card-playing. In McMillan's boarding house the young folk often played until past midnight, and if they had the wherewithal they put up some small stakes. I suppose the sailors thought a game inane that did not have the element of gain or loss to stimulate them. Of course, they called me in to play with them. I hesitated—more from reluctance to waste time and my precious pennies than for any other reason.

"Maybe Isobel doesn't think she should play cards, as she is religious," offered Jack gravely. Jack was one of the sailors, but very open to counsel. He even asked me to teach him the Bible at one time, and I believe he would have accepted the Lord if his wife and others had not pulled him away. I grabbed this offer of a legitimate excuse in order to get out of such invitations easily.

"Well, to tell the truth, Jack, I would prefer not to," I answered.

"Then we're not going to tease her into it," Jack informed everybody. "You play the piano for us, Isobel! We'd like some music while we play."

So it ended up. I loved to play the piano and I loved to play hymns better than anything else. Those young folk did not object to my religious selections, so the strange anomaly took place night after night. They played and gambled whilst I played from my hymn-book. Of course, this left me free to retire to bed as early as I liked and the arrangement pleased me well. But, having "given up" card-playing, supposedly for religious reasons, I must in consistency hold to it on other occasions. So I just did. It cost me nothing. I always thought cards were a tiresome waste of good mental energy—they acquired nothing for you but amusement, and I did not find them very amusing. So out went the taper of card-playing.

It was during the summer of 1923, perhaps before I went to the Firs, that I had to extinguish a second taper. This was quite a different affair and one of which no human being had even spoken to me. I was a voracious reader of romantic fiction. Novels just held me and were my favourite mental escape from my trials and difficulties, or from an evening which had to be spent alone. With a good love story I was immediately transported into another world, and if the drama was exciting I could not put the book down.

We were living with my brother on his ranch for the summer, and as there were no young people around I had to occupy many evenings, so a good novel was my first resort. This particular time, it was an exciting one and I could not lay it down. I might say that I never read the modern sexy novel; these were just clean, exciting love stories; but, like such, very often not really true to life. Life does contain moments of adventure, but they are interspersed with long periods of plain, unvarnished hard work. The real things of life are attained at these monotonous level periods, so to speak, more than they are at the high peaks of excitement. So that novel-readers who feed on the lurid and melodramatic are not prepared for the long stretches of routine work which fill every life. I believe this is partly responsible for the many broken marriages we have today. Young people think married life should be all moonlight and thrills and they baulk when they find themselves on the level stretches of plain, ordinary working together, which actually are the real life and backbone of a home.

Anyway, I was deep in the excitement of my

book. Midnight came and I was so near the end I could not stop. In fact, it was one o'clock in the morning before I finished the book and took up my Bible for evening devotions. But I got no blessing from it. Never had the Bible seemed so drab and dull; and when I tried to pray later, the Lord seemed far away. "It's just sleepiness," I told myself, and curled up for slumber.

But the next morning was little better. God still seemed far away and the Bible stuffy and uninteresting. Before the Teachers' Summer Institute opened I was clerking in a Bible Depot, which belonged to my father. It was a sideline with him, as his real work was roentgenology, but he had felt that Victoria lacked a good Bible store where reliable Christian books could be obtained as well as the Scriptures, and so he, supported by Christian friends, had opened this Bible Depot. I substituted for the clerk while she was on summer vacation, so I had to be in to the city by opening time. I went in by bus and had time to think. What had happened to me that the Lord seemed no longer real to me? And the Bible, which I had begun to read through from Genesis to Revelation for the first time in my life, had become insipid? I was alarmed. Sitting in the bus, I talked to the Lord about it in my heart.

"Oh Lord, what is wrong with me? Why can't I sense Your Presence now as I have lately? Why has the Bible become dry?" It seemed to me that He answered thus:

"When a child fills its stomach with ice-cream and soda-water, why does it lose its appetite for meat and potatoes?"

"Lord, do You mean the novel did that to me?"

"It excited all the fleshly part of your nature, didn't it? Did it do *anything* to help the spiritual?"

"Nothing, Lord. It kept me up so late. I'm tired this morning. Lord, if I promise to give up novel-reading, will You come back to me? Will the Bible come alive to me again?"

"Try it and see."

From that moment on, the Lord was real and present once more and the Word took on new meaning. My spiritual growth could have been traced by the markings in that Bible as I read it from cover to cover. I "discovered" verses that seemed to spring out of the page as His voice to my need at the moment. Unfortunately, that particular Bible was among our books which the Communists ordered to be burned, but one verse I remember was given me as particularly mine and, as such, I have claimed it through the years and it has been fulfilled to me:

Isa. 54:10: For the mountains shall depart and the hills be removed; but my kindness shall not depart from thee, neither shall the *covenant of my peace* be removed, saith the Lord that hath mercy on thee.

I need not say that the taper of novel-reading (which included magazine short stories) was extinguished from that day on. For about fifteen years I never permitted myself to read a love story. After that, when I had to be alone in Lisuland so often, with such problems pressing upon me, I used to read a bit at mealtimes; but they were, in the main, the old classics, such as Dickens, Thackeray, Brontë and Barrie. These I had read before so they had no "hold" on me to continue reading past mealtime, and they did give me a wholesome mental holiday for an hour, lifting me out of the canyon-world back into life among my own race.

Did I find it a hard denial?

> *Who extinguishes their taper*
> *Till they hail the rising sun?*

Does one begrudge candle-light when morning sunshine is pouring in the window? I was *richly repaid* for this self-discipline.

The next taper that the Lord touched was my dancing. Mac continued to invite me to the university big dances, and to some of the smaller ones occasionally. It was at one of the latter (was it a fraternity dance? I forget) that I ran into Marion A——in the dressing-room. Marion was a Christian girl in our year who had abstained all through her course from worldly amusements. We had both graduated now and here we met at a dance!

"Why, Marion!" I exclaimed in surprise.

"Well, you are to blame, Isobel Miller," she said with her merry frankness. "You're the reason I am here tonight. You are a Christian too, aren't you? And all through our four years you danced and had a good time and I got left out of everything. People say you are a good Christian, but you dance, so I decided to dance, too. This is my first dance."

I did not know at the moment, but it was my last. I do not know how Marion ended up; but I fear she drifted from the Lord.

Back in the dancing-hall, I had as partner, for one memorable dance, a tall, good-looking boy whom I had known since High School days. His name was Keith and he was a science major. As we were waltzing around he made some contemptuous remark about "old-fashioned fogies who believe in God." Ah, said I to myself, here is my chance to witness. I always felt if I kept in with the dancing crowd, it would afford me contacts for Christ with people who could not be contacted otherwise. So I started in eagerly, "Keith, why do you say that? I believe in God, and you used to."

"Oh, that was before I met Dr Sedgewick or studied science," he replied impatiently. "No one with a scientific approach to life believes that old stuff any more."

"Oh, but they do!" I cried eagerly. "I have been investigating God and have indubitable proof that He is!"

"What proof?" he scoffed. Then I tried to tell him, but he refused to believe. He got angry and we were arguing together hotly when a ripple of laughter brought us to ourselves. The orchestra had taken their seats. Just Keith and I were left; and we, unconscious that the number had ended, were waltzing round and round in the centre of the room obviously fighting over something.

"Better give up, Keith!" called out a pal from the sidelines. "A woman convinced against her will is of the same opinion still! They never give in and they don't know how to reason!"

When Keith saw what a laughing-stock we had made of ourselves he swore angrily, marched me to a seat and stalked off in high dudgeon. If there is one thing a man can't forgive, it is a wound to

his pride; a public humiliation I had caused him
and he "cut me dead" from that hour. My
testimony to him had not only been a failure; it
had left him more antagonistic than ever.

It was a very subdued and thoughtful Isobel
whom Mac saw home that night. Was this the
Lord speaking to me? I had led Marion A——
astray. I had further antagonized Keith. Was
dancing worth it?

A few nights later Mac telephoned me and asked
me to the Agricultural Ball—in April, I think it was
to be. "Mac, I'm not sure," I parried. "That is so far
ahead. Phone me a little later, will you?" and we
left it at that. I'd need to pray about it before going
to another dance. Was it just an accident or was
the Lord speaking to me about giving up the
dance?

I was in the throes of indecision when something lovely happened. The telephone rang one
evening and a cheery voice with a rippling laugh
called me from the other end. "Guess who is
speaking, Isobel!" Only one person had such a
contagious, delightful approach.

"Mrs Whipple!" I cried in joy, almost trying to
jump into the receiver. "Are you in town? Can I
get to see you?"

"That you may," was the answer. "We are here
on some business for just a day or two and we are
staying with Mrs Ernest Walsh. Can you come out,
or shall we come to you?"

McMillan's boarding-house was no place for
quiet discussion. "Oh, I'll come to you," I cried.
"Tell me how to get there." Inside of one hour I
was in the parlour of Mrs Walsh's nice home, and
seated on a stool at Mrs Whipple's feet. Oh, it was

the most wonderful feeling just to be near her again. Mr Whipple was one with her, but a shy silent disposition which took time and experience to appreciate. However, she often appealed to him for his opinion and it was always worth waiting for.

"Well, tell me what you have been doing since Conference," she said gaily.

"That is just what I want to do," I answered. "For I have a pressing problem. Just before you called, a boy-friend phoned to ask me to the Aggie Dance (Agricultural student's ball), and I put him off but told him I'd tell him definitely a little later. I'm all in a stew about it," and then I told her of my adventure with Keith. She probably was scandalized to see that the girl she thought had been led into full consecration was still deep in worldly amusements *but she never showed it*. To have looked shocked at my doings would have made me resentful— for wasn't I *honestly* seeking the Lord and His will? I was merely refusing to act on *Your papa and your mama told you so*.

She did give a significant glance at her husband, then answered me so sweetly:

"I can quite see that you are in a mess, Isobel. You are trying to serve two masters at one time and it always has painful results. Let's see what the Word of God says. I Cor. 6:12: 'All things are lawful unto me, *but all things are not expedient.*' You are comprising and that is fatal *whatever realm it occurs in*. Have you ever told Mac that you have become a Christian?"

"Oh, no," answered this product of the twentieth century. "Our set doesn't do that. It is a point of honour among us not to thrust our religious opinions upon the other fellow. I've never told anyone! It is my private life with God."

Poor Mrs Whipple. What a warped little human being to try and straighten out! But she was *full of faith and of the Holy Ghost.*

"Those are standards of your old life, Isobel," she said gently. "2 Cor. 5:17 says that if any man be in Christ he is a new creature: *old things are passed away*: behold all things are become new."

Oh, what a lovely verse—down it was marked in my Bible. Why, it sounded as if it had been written just about me.

"But look at 2 Cor. 6:14–17, Isobel," went on my dear spiritual mother, "'Be ye not unequally yoked together with unbelievers ... What communion hath light with darkness? ... *Wherefore come out from among them and be yet separate*, saith the Lord." That is the basis of our separation from things of the world and standards of the world. 1 Pet. 3:15 says that we should 'be *ready always* to give ... *a reason of the hope that is in you.*' I think it is your duty, under the standards of your new life with God, that you tell your friends about Christ and what He has done for you. You will be surprised at the spiritual blessing it will bring."

"But I did try to tell Keith," I wailed, simply terrified at this idea of witnessing.

"But look at the place you were in when you told him. You stood in the place of compromise and worldliness and then expected him to respect your testimony. No wonder he despised it. But now if you take your stand against dancing as belonging to your old life, but unsuitable to the new, I believe you will find Mac will have a different reaction."

"Well, I'll try," I said dully. Young people always think that the older folk don't understand their generation. Inwardly I felt this way at that moment and dreaded speaking plainly to Mac. He had been so fine to me; I shrank from offending him or rendering myself odious in his eyes as I had rendered myself in Keith's.

For the rest we had a pleasant time together and then I had to return home.

All the next day I dreaded that evening phone call, and when the moment came I went cold all over and was nearly paralyzed with fright. But I gritted my teeth and took up the receiver. It was Mac all right.

"Well, Isobel," he said. "What is the decision about the Aggie Ball?"

My throat was so dry I could hardly get my voice out.

"Mac," I answered, "I hope you will forgive me. But I have become a Christian lately and have decided to give up dancing altogether. I do not criticize the gang in this matter, but I have had some experiences which make me feel that God would not have me continue to dance. I'm so sorry not to have told you before—I was just undecided."

A long silence at the other end, during which my heart beat so violently I was afraid he could hear it. I was trembling from head to foot. At length Mac's voice came over the wire:

"Thank you, Isobel, for being so straightforward with me. I honour you for not playing with me about this. May I have the pleasure of your company to the Baccalaureate Service on Sunday instead?"

"Oh, thank you, Mac! Yes, indeed. I would be delighted to go with you."

"It's a date, then. I'll call for you at nine-thirty. Goodbye."

I staggered to my room and fell across my bed in the weakness of relief. Mrs Whipple had been right after all. Mac said he *honoured* me for being straightforward! And to prove it he had asked for another date immediately! Oh, how good of the Lord to let it happen that way. How did Mrs Whipple know? She knew the general principles of life; that compromise wins respect from no one, but a straightforward testimony does. Clean-cut action does, too. The older generation may not understand all the new scientific terms of the young generation but they know the principles of life which never change. And it is a wise youngster who will not discard her or his *inheritance of wisdom and experience* from those who have gone before.

So the taper of dancing was extinguished, and forgotten very quickly as the Rising Sun flooded my life with new and fascinating interests.

There remained but the one taper now, the theatre. I had only gone to good movies, an occasional opera (one of the classic ones) or wholesome family theatre acts. There could be no harm in such? And they taught one much of human nature.

The last one I went to was a sweet, harmless story; I think it was *Smilin' Thro'*. I enjoyed it very much, but as I went home, once more all the old longings for romance and story-book experiences flooded me. The music too, had stirred up the emotional side of me and once more prayer was a blank and the Bible had lost its savour. In vain I tried to push through to the Lord's presence. "*My Beloved had withdrawn Himself and was gone*" then was true of me as of the little bride. "*I sought Him but I could not find Him: I called Him, but He gave me no answer*" (Song of Solomon 5:6). Later when I read the Song of Songs and came to this incident, I knew what it meant perfectly. I had been there myself—this, for the second time.

"Oh, Lord," I prayed, "If You will but return to me I will never go to the theatre again. You may have that also."

It was but a little that ... I found Him whom my soul loveth: I held Him and would not let Him go.

Nothing was worth the loss of *fellowship* with Him. Then did the Sun of Righteousness arise in my heart with healing in His wings.

I remember only once being tempted to relight this last taper. Remember how alone I was, how young, how so accustomed to lots of friends my own age. It was an evening, perhaps in May, when everything in youth was calling for companionship and fun. The McMillan young folk were all going out together to see a movie and I would be left alone in the house.

"Oh, come on, Isobel," they teased, catching me by the hand. "It's a good clean movie tonight— can't possibly do you any harm. What does a young girl like you want to mope in the house for on such a lovely evening? Be companionable— come on with us!" They were a kind-hearted bunch and I was sorely tempted to go. The

perfumed May air called to me from the open
doorway. I was about to yield when I saw a
doubtful look in Jack's eyes.

"Don't press her to do what she doesn't feel is
right," he said quietly. That settled it.

"No, thank you," I returned. "Have a good
time!" and waved them gaily off; then turned to go
upstairs with a heavy heart. I entered my bedroom, drab, rather dark, with its cheap furniture,
and cried out into the silence of the empty house,
"Oh, Lord, is it to be so dull always? And I'm still
young? A girl looks her nicest at twenty-one or
two. Nobody to go with! Nothing to do but Bible
study! Oh Lord, speak to me!" and I pulled over
my Bible and opened it at random.

The words on the page sprang up before me.
John 6:67: *Then said Jesus unto the twelve, Will ye
also go away? Then Simon Peter answered him, Lord,
to whom shall we go? Thou hast the words of eternal
life.*

I sat there reading and re-reading that quiet
potent question. He did not refuse to let me go
back to my earthly tapers. He just wanted me to
think well before I did. Did I really prefer them?
Would I change places with any one of the three
girls who had just left the home? God forbid—I
shrank from such a thought. Did I want to go back
to Ben's world of loose loyalties? Again I shud-
dered. *Lord, to whom shall we go?* There was no
other road. The low road? Not for a moment. The
Misty Flats? God deliver me from ever again
drifting around there. Then there only remained
the High Way.

"Forgive me, Lord," I bowed my head in
contrition. "There is no one I want but Thee.

Please comfort me." Then the sense of His Presence so filled the room that it is too sacred to talk about. Suffice it to say, I never again looked back; but more and more I learned the value of communion alone with Himself. Dr Tozer has pointed out how our generation is in danger of missing this sacred joy. He says: "We have been trying to apply machine-age methods to our relations with God ... our thought habits are those of the scientist not those of the worshipper. We are more likely to explain than to adore." *Searching* is a scientific procedure, but we want to beware that it does not get into mechanical ruts. "We read our chapter, have our short devotions and rush away, hoping to make up for our deep inward bankruptcy by attending another gospel meeting, or listening to another thrilling story told by a religious adventurer lately returned from afar."

We need to worship and to adore as well as to analyze and explain. Mary of Bethany learned much by just sitting at His feet, listening to Him and loving Him. Our generation's greatest lack is just here.

By now the summer of 1924 had begun. Unknown to me, my year in Arabia was over. Mac had gone out of the city on a summer job. When he returned I was in Chicago at the Moody Bible Institute. We have never seen one another since. My Rising Sun had planned many things to fill the place of my extinguished tapers, but each was to be a separate and delightful discovery. Next on God's programme for me, was a contact which changed the whole course of my life.

CHAPTER SEVEN

J O FRASER OF LISULAND

WHEN Mrs Whipple lent me a book called *The Growth of a Soul*, at the close of the Firs Conference, 1923, she had no idea that for many years Dr and Mrs Isaac Page had been secretly praying that God would lay His hand on Isobel Miller for missionary service in China. She just rejoiced that in the life-story of Hudson Taylor, founder of the China Inland Mission, were experiences of searching for God and proving Him, which were parallel to some which were now mine.

Anyone who knows *The Growth of a Soul* will recognize the gold mine it was to me. Hudson Taylor went much deeper in his searchings, of course, and came out with definite maxims for life and conduct. "Learn to move man, through God, by prayer alone" was one of the many that I eagerly noted down, and it has blessed me all my life. By the time I had finished the book one thing was clear to me. I wanted to belong to the mission Hudson Taylor founded: I wanted to work with the group who daily proved God in that quiet, unostentatious fashion. Having finished *The Growth of a Soul*, I went on to read the second

volume, *The Growth of a Work of God*[1]—the
founding of the China Inland Mission. It was
while reading this that I received a call to the field.
Previously I had felt a call to the *Mission* regardless
where it worked. But as I read of the sorrows and
sufferings of Chinese women my heart was greatly
stirred. I knew now what heartache was. But when
I was groping for a way out, my Bible was on my
bookshelf. It was easy for me to find the way. But
what about those who had never heard of Christ?
No matter how willing they would be to follow
Him fully if they only knew of Him, and His death
for their salvation, they must perish unless someone went to them and told them. *How shall they
believe in Him of whom they have not heard? And
how shall they hear without a preacher*? (Romans
10:14). I knew I must go and tell them.

So when I arrived at the Firs Conference, 1924,
my decision to apply to the China Inland Mission
had already been formed. Needless to say, no one
needed to give up a pair of shoes to bring me to
conference for the second time! I had saved up,
during the year, and had also applied for the
position of waitress to earn my board while there.

I was simply thrilled to be back at the beloved
place. I ran, almost flew, from spot to spot of
hallowed memory. The cabin which Edna Gish
(now back in China) and I had shared; the spot in
among the tall fir trees where I had often prayed
alone; the open-air auditorium where our classes
had met; the original Firs cabin with the big
fireplace where we had had such blessed times of

---

[1]These two books are now combined as Biography of J Hudson
Taylor (Hodder & Stoughton).

testimony—I wanted to see them all. The cabin
was the last in my inspection tour and I dashed in
eagerly and was halfway to the centre of the room
before I could check my impulsive entrance. For it
was not empty. One lone occupant, a middle-aged
gentleman, was sitting there by himself; he smiled
at my surprise, and I tried to apologize whilst
backing out as speedily as I could.

"Some old bachelor," I told myself, and flew off
to look at the kitchen. How I knew he was
unmarried, I do not know. Maybe it was a certain
lonely, wistful look in his eyes. Anyway, I prompt-
ly forgot him in the joy of greeting other arrivals,
and getting into the swing of the waitress routine,
which was new to me. Little did I dream that I had
just met one who was to be a lodestar spiritually to
me and to the dear husband God was planning to
give me, but of whose existence I, as yet, knew
nothing.

It was not until the evening meeting that, to my
intense surprise, I found that the "old bachelor" of
the sitting-room loneliness was seated on the
platform, and being introduced as our principal
speaker for the conference! Mr J O Fraser[2] of the
China Inland Mission, was his name. I had never
heard of him, and apparently neither had anyone
else. Even Mr Whipple probably did not know at
this point that this young Englishman was an
honours graduate of London University in electrical engineering, and a brilliant pianist. He
appeared among us as a simple missionary, and

---

[2]Mountain Rain by Eileen Crossman (OMF) is J O Fraser's
biography.

never by word or action gave any hint of his extraordinary gifts.

When he got up to speak, he told us simply how the CIM had sent him to one of the furthest corners of China, to the border of Burma and Yunnan Province. There he worked among the Chinese for several years, but had frequently noticed a people coming into the market who were not Chinese at all. They did not speak Chinese among themselves and they did not dress like Chinese. Their costume was very colourful (especially the women's) and trimmed with cowrie shells and silver bangles. Also they wore turbans. They knew some trade-language Chinese and through this he discovered that they were the Lisu tribespeople who lived in the mountains of the Salween River canyon. They had never heard of the Lord Jesus Christ, and their language had never been reduced to writing—they were entirely illiterate. Moreover, they were not idol-worshippers, like the Chinese, but animists who worship demons directly. God called him to go to these people with the gospel; and since he had several evening hours at his disposal, Mr Fraser decided to divide up his work among the Lisu, taking a different phase each evening. For instance, one night he took us itinerating over those wonderful alpine mountains, climbing great heights to where small villages perched (precariously it often seemed!) at the edge of abysmal ravines. Another lecture he gave up to the language difficulties; how he learned it from living with them in their smoky little shacks; how he reduced it to writing; and how with two colleagues he was led to form what is now called the Fraser Script.

Another evening he gave over to the patience needed in teaching the older folk, illiterate from their youth. He was full of humour and his descriptions of the old ladies who declared they had no power of memory, and then were tricked by him into relating with detail what had happened to their children fifteen years ago, were simply hilarious—and touching. We learned to love those old women.

Another lecture was on the spiritual battle in the heavenlies. How he had roughed it, and laboured, and given them a written language and still there were so few converts and such as did come were not stable. Then he wrote his mother in England to gather in the neighbours and *pray*. It was only after this prayer group began to function in earnest that "the break" came in the Lisu tribe. At the same time he on the field had been led to resist in Christ's name the devil and his host who were holding this tribe enchained. As I sat listening I saw plainly that it was true the *Lisu church was born in prayer travail*, and I decided that I must employ this weapon of "all-prayer" too. It is attainable to any of us; it is obviously so effective. I received a life-pattern at that moment for which I have ever been grateful.

Another evening was given over to the joys of harvest. He took us on a trip with him, and his descriptions were so vivid we were simply transported out of America to the mountainous banks of the Salween canyon. We saw him (dressed in the costume of a Chinese coolie, lest better clothes distract attention from his message!) and a Lisu carrier or guide, climbing the steep approach to one of these high villages. He cupped his hands to his mouth and gave the Lisu call: "*Ma-pa chi la-o!*" (the male teacher is arriving!) at which all the dogs of the village rush out and down the path at them.

> Hark, hark the dogs do bark
> The ma-pa is coming to town!

Then the banging of doors and the shouts as the brightly coloured costumes of the women flashed back and forth and the men folk darted forward to drive off the dogs. The Christians line up to shake hands, and as the tall missionary goes down the line each woman has managed to stick an egg into his hand as she gave the welcome handshake! They had learned that he liked eggs! So he always had to carry a bag over his shoulder to hold the eggs (fresh and ancient!) which such a visit collected!

He told of the Prophet's Chamber behind the chapel, which the Christian villagers built for him, learning that queerest trait of the white man; that he liked privacy sometimes! Just imagine *wanting* to be alone! Eh, eh, how queer. Perhaps it came from the colour of his skin: but if he wanted it he should have it. So he had a little Prophet's Chamber of his own in each village.

Then would start the catechizing for baptism. He told of going to call the next candidate and finding the man on his face, prostrate in prayer, asking his new Saviour to help him to answer correctly, so that he might be adjudged ready for this solemn step. And so on. The last night he said he needed more missionaries—young men of consecration willing for the privations and loneliness such a life entailed.

Down in my seat in the side aisle my heart thrilled with love for the Lisu people. Inwardly I prayed, "Lord, I'd be willing to go. Only I'm not a man." Never did the vision of the Lisu tribe leave me. I dared not name it a *call*, but I believe that time has proved it was.

My father was with me at the Firs that summer. And as it happened, he was Mr Fraser's cabin mate. To my surprise, I found out that Father had invited Mr Fraser to come and stay with us in Victoria for a week, before he sailed for China in August. That summer we had rented a house at Oak Bay, near the beach, and had room for a visitor.

I was amazed at Father's temerity in inviting Mr Fraser without consulting Mother, because she and my brother at that time were both opposed to my going as a missionary to China. And Mother was not likely to be pleased at bringing a CIM missionary into her home when she was trying to influence me to be content with Christian work in America! But I was thrilled at the possibility of having a private talk with Mr Fraser about missionary service. I was hoping to go to Moody Bible Institute that autumn, but the obstacles in my way were so many that I sometimes wondered if they could be from the Lord. I was Mother's only daughter: how important was that? I had made up my mind, during those evening talks on Lisuland, that this unkown missionary was a great man of God. His gifts, apart from his platform ability, were still hidden and unknown to me, but the man himself was obviously walking closely with the

Lord. It was one of the thrills of my life in later years, to discover that many far more capable of judging such matters than I, also acclaimed him as one of the great spiritual men of his generation.

Come he did, and by his simple sincerity and kindly interest won the admiration of both my mother and brother. My mother had been a musician before her marriage. She composed music and often wrote the words too, and none of her pieces were ever refused by any publisher to whom she offered them. She just did not go on with it after marriage—that was all. It was in seeking for a contact with Mother that Mr Fraser suddenly revealed his brilliance at the piano. Mother was enthralled. They "talked music" and Mother knew the names of his teachers and said he had been taught by some of the best masters in London.

But I was watching for a chance to present my own problems; and it came later on in the week. Mr Fraser wanted to see the beach and I was appointed to take him down one afternoon. We were no sooner alone than I told him I had wanted a talk about my missionary call, so we sat down on the sands by a rocky bit of shore and I told him. I have never forgotten that session.

"Missionary life can be very lonely," he said quietly, and then he proceeded to unfold some of his own early sufferings. I believe now that he did it deliberately to sift me. If I was truly called of God, I would not be discouraged by plain talk of the cost. If I were not called by God, but just had romantic notions of a foreign land, the sooner my gossamer dream was pricked the better. But he little knew the unveiling of his own life that he

was unconsciously giving. In fact, as he re-
miniscsed he seemed to forget for a while that I was
present. His blue-grey eyes brooding out over the
sunny, sparkling ocean, he seemed talking to
himself. In the quiet of contemplation, as now,
they seemed to understand all the sorrows and
loneliness that human heart can know. *Acquainted
with grief*, they were sad eyes; knowing the victory
possible, they were *steadfast and patient*.

I told him of Mother's view and opposition to
my call. He answered with the slow drawl which
was his when thinking out a question—for none
could talk faster than he on occasion. "I have
sensed that Satan is opposing you and working
through your mother and your brother. We are
taught 'whom resist' when it comes to obstacles
produced by the devil. I think that should be your
stand. In prayer resist the devil, always remembering to be kind to those who are unconsciously his
tools at the moment (2 Timothy 2:24). I have a
prayer formula which I use on such occasions. It is
this: If this obstacle be from Thee, Lord, I accept it:
but if it be from Satan, I refuse him and all his
works in the name of Calvary. I have found that
formula works." I was to use it throughout my life
and never found it to fail when prayed with the
honest intention of obeying all it implied.

Again he brooded out over the ocean thoughtfully, then added, "I wonder if you will ever get to
China. You are very young and you have great
obstacles to face. Hm," and again he lapsed into
reverie. Then he began to talk as if he knew what
to say: "It is even conceivable that *after you get to
Moody*, Satan will attempt to get you away. For
instance, a telegram might come saying that your

mother was very sick and urging you to return home immediately. Now, if that should happen, you cannot leave the moment you get the telegram. You would have to pack your trunk, for instance, and buy a ticket, and so on. Is there any Christian in Vancouver or here whom you can trust to be unprejudiced and yet godly enough to discern such a matter for you?"

"There is Mr Charles Thomson, Secretary of the CIM," I answered.

"The very man!" he replied quickly. "If you get such a telegram, *immediately telegraph to Mr Thomson*, asking him to check just how ill your mother is. By the time your trunk is packed you should have his reply, and can then see more clearly the path the Lord would have you take."

I listened in awe, but would have been still more amazed if I had known how nearly that prophecy was to be fulfilled.

He *that is spiritual judgeth all things* (I Cor. 2:15).

It was an afternoon well spent. Upon the plastic material of a young life had been imprinted standards and ideals which were to last for ever. And a deep glimpse had been afforded me into the life that is hidden in God; the cost of it, the fragrance of it, and the power of it.

CHAPTER EIGHT

THE MOODY BIBLE INSTITUTE

SEPTEMBER 3rd 1924 found me in Chicago, enrolling as a student of the Bible-Missionary course at Moody Bible Institute. This was a most unexpected turn of affairs and not the product of my own planning. I was so very Canadian in loyalty that I would never have chosen to come to the United States for my training. And I admired Professor Ellis so much that I would not have thought of looking beyond the Vancouver Bible School for my missionary preparation. But the Lord took the matter out of my hands.

At the end of the school year 1923–4 I still lacked funds to put me through any Bible school, but outside of my parents and one other I told no one. God, in His wondrous workings, brought that one other person into contact with Miss Marjorie Harrison, whom I had met at the Firs. And it was at the precise moment when she was asking Him how to use some money she had saved that she inadvertently learned that I needed the where-withal to train for China. *It was Marjorie who chose Moody for me*, directed by the Lord, I am sure. Herself a graduate of the Bible Institute of Los Angeles, and knowing there was this small Bible

School right in the city where I was living, she still chose to send me halfway across the continent to Moody. It was the largest Bible institute in the country, and was rich in opportunity for many kinds of Christian work. This latter was what I needed more than I knew. Marjorie explained that her money was limited to that little savings account. She would buy my ticket to Chicago, but could not help me with the return fare! She would pay my board and room for one year, but had no money for my incidental expenses. And she could not help me after that first year. The Moody Bible Institute has an employment bureau which helps students find jobs for odd hours in safe places. For the rest, I must trust the Lord. Was I willing?

Fresh from reading Hudson Taylor's experience in proving God able to supply his need through prayer only, I was thrilled with the opportunity to go on *searching*.

My brother had to make a business trip to Chicago, staying only a few weeks, so I had company across the continent. Dr Isaac Page met us at the station and took me to MBI. Otherwise, I knew no one in that big, whirling metropolis. The Pages had but recently moved to Chicago themselves as deputation workers for the China Inland Mission in the Midwest.

That first day of enrolment, with its trips to this office and that, was bewildering and at the end I was truly weary. I was put into a double room (cheaper) with a strange girl who was European and spoke with a strong accent. The furnishings were very simple, but the house opened right off the street, and, being on the first floor front, people walking along the street passed right under our window. I had never lived in a house which did not have a front enclosure, and it gave me an "exposed" feeling to be so near a public street. This, added to weariness and loneliness, made me homesick. Could I stand it for two years? I was asking myself when a bus rumbled up to a stop at our corner. To sleep with your head just the other side of a wall from such public things seemed almost scandalous. But in another moment I was swung into the heavenlies. The bus was the MBI street meeting group, returning from their first evening's witness, and they had begun to sing:

> He makes the path grow brighter
> All along the way:
> He makes the journey lighter
> Every passing day.

Beautiful young voices in four-part harmony sung with a fervent faith in the words that came right from their hearts: it thrilled me through and through. Something in the traffic held them there while they sang it to a finish.

"Oh, Lord," I prayed in ecstasy, "Thank You! Thank You! That is to be *the other side* of this 'exposed' existence! Comradeship in the things of Christ and in the cause of soul-winning. And Christian friends who are my own age and who can sing like that? Oh, thank You, Lord!" I was truly transported into His presence where I nestled down in deep content and fell asleep.

But good things still awaited me. The next day I was called to the phone. It was the Dean's office. "Miss Miller, there is a girl called Lillian Billington, just arrived from Bellingham, who would like to room with you. What is your pleasure in the matter?"

"Oh," I cried, "has she really come? Yes, *please*. I would like so much to be her room-mate. I met her at the Firs Conference. She is a young schoolteacher."

"Yes; that is right," answered the office voice. "But you will have to change your dormitory. We have Miss Billington down for the third floor, Ransom Hall Building, Room 303. Would you kindly proceed to move there as soon as possible, and leave your present room in a proper state for a new occupant? Thank you. Report to us when the move is complete."

Room 303, Ransom Hall, was much larger, higher above the street, so more private, and in every way a happier arrangement to my taste. And best of all, I was to share it with *a girl from the Firs*. We had just met the summer before, but I liked her sweet face. "Billie" and I were happy room-mates for two years. Next door at 304 was a Scottish girl, Anne Barr (who, unknown to us, was to be namesake to my daughter!), and a very unselfish American girl, Ella Dieken, who was later to play a part in my life that the wildest dreams could never have conjured up.

What a meeting Billie and I had! And what fun to help her unpack and find that she had things I didn't—pretty curtains for our windows, cretonne drapes for our trunks, lacy dresser scarfs and so on. Soon our room was transformed into a real girls' bower, and my beauty-loving soul was deeply grateful.

Mealtime was an adventure. Hundreds of students all eating at once. Oh the noise of the talk, the clatter of the cutlery or dishes. The men sat on one side and the women on the other, twelve to a table. A senior and a junior student sat one at each end, but the rest of us changed seats each day. When you arrived at a certain seat you automatically became waitress for the table for that day. One waitress removed the dirty dishes; another had the duty of going early into the kitchen and bringing in the hot food, and must go for "seconds" when necessary.

I was waiting in line one day for the hot vegetables; as soon as the bell went they would be dished out to us, but there was still a moment before the hour struck. I was dreaming of Lisuland, when turning around suddenly I encountered the eyes of another dreamer—the young man who ran the dish-washing machine. It was one of those shock-encounters when you find yourself already over the threshold and into the other fellow's soul before there is time to knock for admission. Very embarrassing. Each of us looked away quickly and pretended not to notice, but it had happened. From then on I was conscious of that dishwasher! Whether he was full-time kitchen employee or student-help I did not know. The annoying thing was that I had become conscious of him. Now, I had made up my mind that I was not going to have any boy-friends at Moody. I had proved that they were distracting and I wanted these two years to be given to unhindered preparation for my life work in China. So I was extremely cross with myself to find that as soon as I entered the kitchen I looked to see if he was there or not. To discipline myself, I did not inquire his name or his status; but frequently I had to carry dishes past him and I felt sure he knew my name and all about me. And I was correct: he did. But he never tried to speak: I did appreciate that. I did not know that he had come to Moody vowing to have nothing to do with girls—lest they distract him from his studies. But he had made inquiries as to who the girl was who wore the green blouse trimmed with brown swan's down.

Shortly after my arrival, Dr and Mrs Page had invited me to supper in their apartment. He had long been my father's close friend and I had called him Daddy Page for years. After I had taken off my wraps, he thrust a bundle of photographs of Moody and Moody students into my hands, excusing himself while he went to help his wife in the kitchen. As I looked over them I came across one which greatly attracted me. It was a girl's face, and there was character as well as beauty there.

"Oh, Daddy Page," I cried. "Who is this? What a lovely face! Is she here at the Institute?"

He came in and looked over my shoulder. "Oh that," he said. "Yes, Isobel. She *is* a lovely girl. Her name is Kathryn Kuhn, but she has just graduated and gone on to Wheaton. I wish you could meet her. She has a brother here at the Institute."

"Oh yes?" I said politely and quickly changed the conversation. But inwardly I said, "Well, if her brother looks like she does, I'll stay away from him. Here's where you don't go to any mixed parties, Isobel Miller!"

And, apart from the Freshman Reception, I quietly refused invitations to any party or picnic where the other sex would be present—that is, during my first term. It was my second term before I found it had all been in vain.

It was months before I learned that the dishwasher in the kitchen was the brother of Kathryn Kuhn!

Of my studies during those two years and four months (I was ill and lost a term) I can only glance at the blessing they brought me. Dr James Gray was President then and I was privileged to have a class under him. Bible analysis under Dr Jaderquist was an outstanding joy, and I later passed it on to the Lisu church, analysing First and Second Peter with our Bible School Students. Those notes are still being used.

Dr Elbert McCreery taught me comparative religions and phonetics and was one of my favourite teachers. He was himself the blessing, with his gentle, Christ-like life.

Dr Robert Glover made me sit on the edge of my seat, week after week, as he presented the challenge of missions, and in another class taught the history of missions. His fire continually enkindled my own.

Talmadge Bittikofer taught us part-singing and conducting, which I was to use constantly with the Lisu church. We all loved "Bitti" and his solos stirred me to the depths. He sang his message right into your heart.

So one could go on, but I think the greatest thing Moody did for me was in the practical work assignments. Mrs F C Allison was in charge of these. Every student had to take one or more such assignments each week; and your assignments were changed each term, so that you got a great variety. Open-air meetings among the Jews would likely mean rotten eggs and tomatoes pelted at you, so you wore your oldest clothes (I was knocked off the pavement into the street once when my turn came for Jewish work). Sunday school classes and hospital or jail visitation were considered easiest and my kindly Lord started me off gently. A slip of paper from the Practical Work Department told me I was assigned to teach a Sunday school class and do visitation during the week in the Italian slums. I would work under senior student Miss Ethel Thompson, Room X, 830 Building, and would I please report to her immediately for instructions.

So behold a young Moody freshman climbing the stairs of the 830 Building and standing before a closed bedroom door about to knock. What would Miss Thompson be like? How could I ever do slum visitation? How my heart beat as I firmly knocked at that door. Once it opened, I was *in for it*; that is, I must plunge into soul-winning from which my shyness had always shrunk.

It was opened by a short, slim young woman, perhaps in her early thirties, who, when she heard my name, welcomed me quickly with a soft, southern drawl in her voice. After asking me to sit down, she began: "I suppose I had better tell you about our assignment. We are working under a Community House or Church in the Italian quarter. On Sundays we are in charge of the Primary Department and we have full liberty to preach the gospel there. They think we cannot hurt the little ones! Because, you see, the minister in charge is a modernist and he conducts dances on Sunday evening and so on. This is our big difficulty and the most discouraging feature.

"During the week we go into the homes— tenement houses, knock at doors and present our message. The people are poor, of course, and many of them Roman Catholics. But there have been a few decisions for Christ.

"Personally, I think the work needs prayer almost more than anything else," and she eyed this new freshman questioningly, wondering what the Lord had sent her in me.

Remembering Mr Fraser's lessons on the place of prayer in Christian service, I answered eagerly: "Oh, I believe in prayer too! I'd be happy to come over here to your room every day for a time of prayer together?"

"Would you?" said "Tommy" (none of the students called her *Ethel*. She was *Tommy* Thompson to us all) and her face lit up with hope and joy. "All right. I'm working my way through school here and so I am busy, but half an hour before noon each day—how would that suit you?" It fit in my schedule and became an important part of my life.

That first Sunday Tommy took me to the community centre and introduced me to the Rev. K—, the minister-in-charge, as her new helper. "Fine," he said. "How about having lunch with us today? I told the wife there would be a new worker and we ought to get acquainted—she's prepared."

That meant we stayed for the morning service and heard the usual liberal kind of sermon from Mr K—; something on courage or high ideals or one of such verbal essays; but nothing in it to bring new life to anyone.

At dinner afterwards, in their apartment, he said to us rather patronizingly, "You know, girls, I used to believe like you do. In fact, you may be surprised to learn that I am a Moody graduate myself. But after graduation I went into a seminary and there learned that no one nowadays believes in that old-fashioned stuff. I lost my faith, as you call it, at seminary. But somehow our liberalism does not energize people like the Moody teaching seems to, and so when I found out how dead the work here is, I asked for a couple of Moody students to be sent us (you work without salary!)"—this with a grin—"to stir up interest in the neighbourhood. You bring them in and we'll mould them into a good community!"

We ignored the comment that rose so quickly to our lips, and I said, "This is very strange, Mr K—. You have departed from the old faith and I have just departed from liberalism to return to the faith! I lost my belief in God in college, but I have done some personal investigation in the matter and I'm convinced that He is, and the only way to Him is through faith in the atoning power of the blood of Christ to bring forgiveness of sins and eternal life. You and I are a contrasting pair—you have entered the Misty Flats whilst I have just found my way out of them back on to the High Way again."

He was truly moved. His eyes sparkled and he leaned forward, plying me with questions; he was sarcastic, argumentative, but deeply interested. Tommy sat quiet, praying. She had never heard my story, but recognized instantly the working of the Spirit of God.

When it came time to leave, Mr K—was belligerent again. "You're too intelligent a girl to slip back into that old stuff," he challenged me. "We'll have to have some more talks about this! You girls will have to come to supper some night after your visitation work." And so we left.

On the long car ride home Tommy said, "I believe God has already begun to answer our prayers. Just think of His sending a worker who had been through all this liberal stuff that is binding this man from any power really to help change lives! I watched his face while you talked and many of your points went home, though he was too proud to acknowledge it. I've got faith now to believe that God will bring Mr K—back to the faith! Let us agree together on Matthew 18:19 and add this request to our daily prayers. Now, let's see—we go visiting in the homes on Thursday, is it?"

Tommy proved to be a most rare companion. She had a keen sense of humour, and droll wit simply poured from her. Visitation was in itself a grim experience for me. Those dark, dirty tenement houses, with broken stairs, bad plumbing which often made the place reek, whole families cooped up in one small room sometimes, would have terrified me. But Tommy always had a merry retort or comment for a stumbled toe or an offended nose; a remark so pungent in its truth and applicability that I was shaken with laughter as well as with distaste. Then it was always she who took the brunt of the first attack, so to speak. She was an artist at a tactful approach, and I sat at her feet and tried to learn. Over thirty years have passed since those days, so I cannot remember conversations or her delightful wit. But I remember one incident. In a long, dark hall of an old tenement house we went from door to door, seeking entrance and conversation. One was opened by a big brute of a man who scowled at us and shouted, "What are you after? What ya doin' here?"

"Brother," smiled up Tommy at him with her soft, southern drawl, "we're a couple of friends who are interested in seeing that you get a better deal. Won't you let us come in and talk a moment?"

"Ah, come on," growled the man suspiciously. "Nobody's really interested in helping us. What's your line? Salesman? Politics? Whatever it is, we ain't interested," and he moved the door as if to bang it in our faces.

"Now, brother," piped up Tommy plaintively, "a pair of poor tired girls can't hurt a big fellow like you. Won't you even offer us a chair a moment? We've been on our feet for hours and we did hope—" A woman's voice from within: "They can sit down a moment, Bill. I know what it is to have tired feet."

Bill cursed bitterly, but left the door open, turned and stalked to the far side of the dismal room. Then Tommy, with a droll remark about her feet, made the woman laugh and a conversation was soon under way. However, the Lord's name was no sooner uttered than Bill appeared in our midst again, eyes blazing with anger.

"So it's religious sluts you are! That's the worst of all! I'm not going to have any blankety blank"— he swore profusely—"whinings around here! I'm an atheist, I am"—and so on.

Tommy turned on her loving, merry humour. I do not know how she did it, except the Spirit of God was working with her, but she had him quietened and listening before we left. I think, too, his wife decided for Christ. Almost every visitation day, some soul made that decision. Dear Tommy, it was she who taught me that "loving folks" is the only way to approach them for the Lord Jesus.

In the Primary Department God began to work too. The children started to ask the Lord to come into their hearts. Mr K—was interested and indifferent by turns. Sometimes he would ignore us for weeks, almost as if antagonistic; then again he would come into our Sunday school, listen and watch; and invite us around for a meal.

How we laboured in prayer for him. Tommy with her cute remarks in the dark hallways of tenement houses was one person; on her knees praying for the salvation of souls and the reclamation of Mr K—was quite a different person; yet the two sides of her character blended into one another. If you only heard her jokes, you would never have guessed at her tears and her passionate pleadings for sin-bound souls.

In my second term I asked to be reappointed to the same assignment as both Tommy and I felt the Lord's work was not completed yet in that place. But that was the term when I fell ill and lost six weeks of study and of course could not go with Tommy. At the end of that term she graduated and left for Mexico. But there is one precious thing yet to record.

After I was out of the infirmary and just before Tommy left the Institute, we were both called down to the Reception Room one day. To our surprise, it was Mr K—. He was a changed man; his very face had that gentle, chastened look upon it, but there was also a light there we had never seen before.

"I just called you girls to tell you that the Lord has answered your prayers for me. I have come back to Himself. It has been a bitter fight, as you doubtless have watched and seen. Pride refused to be crucified for a long time. But it was weekly more evident to me that the Word you girls preached was the power of God unto salvation. Lives were changed through your ministry—my honesty had to admit it. Nobody was changed through mine. Maybe you don't know that I began to preach the Bible again as I saw how God used your Bible teaching. But nothing happened. Then I had to come to the place where I was willing to preach the Cross of Christ as the only way; the blood of the Redeemer as the only atonement for our sins. *That worked* — for me as well as for you. There has been an awful fuss. I made a confession in the pulpit and stopped the Sunday dances. My church filled for service, but the Committee got wind of it and were very angry." Tears came to his eyes. "They dismissed me, in short; but I have got a little country church appointment now and I'll be moving the family out there. And I can preach the truth there. My wife is wholeheartedly with me and we both feel we have to thank you two. God bless you. And *God bless the school that D L Moody founded.*"

Heartily, with tears in our eyes and awe in our hearts we said, "Amen." We never saw him again.

CHAPTER NINE

SPIRITUAL PREVISION

IT was in December 1924, that I received a letter from my mother saying that she was facing the possibility of an operation. It was discovered that she had a tumour and there was a choice before her; radiology treatments over quite a long period or surgery. She was inclined to have the latter as being less drawn-out; "get it over" instead of many long trips to town, which the radiology would necessitate. But I had not heard definitely what her decision had been when a telegram arrived saying she was with the Lord. She had chosen surgery and had died in the hospital. Father wired me lovingly, but said the funeral would be over before I could reach home, so I should not try to come.

This was a shattering blow to me. My mother had opposed my going to the foreign field because to her clinging love for me, her only daughter. In the agony of her pleadings with me she had said some bitter things which at the time I had not taken to heart, as I recognized they were the upflinging of violent emotion and not the result of considered thought. But one word had been: "You are praying to go to China and God answers prayer; but you will only go over my dead body." Of course, that word now came back to me and simply lacerated my heart.

I owe a great deal to my mother. She had deep affections, high ideals and was very conscientious. She sacrificed her musical career and many opportunities for a musical evening with other young people in order to baby-sit with her two children at home. She was married young and was still in her twenties when my brother and I were born: she had great ambitions for us and carefully watched over us. We were never allowed to "run the streets." She gave up her evenings to reading to us and planning to make home a pleasant place where our friends were welcome. She was a Christian, at one time a consecrated Christian, and always trained us to love the Lord and honour His Word. As we grew older she wanted us "to move in good society," and this was the temptation which had led her to compromise with worldly things. But at the root of it was her love for us. I had never known life without my mother. I took her affection for granted as I accepted the warmth of the daily sunshine, and in such careless security I had not shown her the gratitude which was her due. All these things came to me, now that she was gone: it was too late to express my thanks to her, and my heart was sorely torn.

During that Christmas vacation I took employment as a waitress in a restaurant.

School reopened in January. I do not remember the date, but one day in class a messenger went up to the platform and interrupted the teacher. He read it and said: "Will Miss Isobel Miller please go to the office of the Dean of Women? There is a telegram for you."

Perfectly astounded and wondering, I got up and sped toward the Women's Building. What could it be? I was trembling by the time I reached the office and from the Dean's face I knew it was bad news of some kind. I could only look at her in agony and beg that she tell me quickly and not prolong suspense. She did so. "Sit down, dear. The telegram reads: FATHER FATALLY INJURED IN ELEVATOR ACCIDENT. COME HOME AT ONCE. MURRAY. Who is Murray?"

"My brother," I choked. "Oh, but I can't stand it. Father too! Oh."

"Is there anyone we can call to help you, dear?" she asked tenderly.

Suddenly I was far away, sitting on a seaside beach beside a tall, strong man who was looking out over the breaking sea with brooding eyes, and he was saying, "Satan may try to get you away from the Institute. Is there anyone you know who can be depended on for godly, unprejudiced judgment?" In a flash I recognized that Mr Fraser's foresight had come true: he had just missed the instrument used, that was all. He had thought it would be Mother, and it turned out to be my brother who summoned me home. It steadied and quieted me.

Sitting up, I said, "Yes, please, I would like Dr Isaac Page to come and help me."

The Dean was relieved to be able to do something, and in a moment she was talking to him on the phone. I heard him say, "I'll take a taxi and be there immediately." I waited in the Dean's office until he arrived—my father's intimate friend.

"Daddy Page," I said, "Mr Fraser told me this might happen. He *also told me what to do if it did happen.* I will go and pack my trunk, but will you please do two things for me? Reserve a ticket for the train tonight, but don't buy it yet. Wire immediately to Mr Charles Thomson and ask if Dad is as bad as Murray said?"

"Excellent idea, Isobel," said Dr Page. "First reports of these accidents are often excited and exaggerated. Mr Thomson will know. I will go and do that immediately—there is no train going to Vancouver until this evening, anyway. And you? You will *trust and not be afraid*?"

"Yes," I said, much calmer now that a plan of activity was under way. "Thank you. Everyone here is so kind and loving to me. I will be all right."

"I'll come back just as soon as I have wired and made the train reservation," he said, and was gone.

Before supper that evening the answering telegram arrived. It read: FATHER IMPROVING SENDS LOVE AND SAYS STAY AT YOUR POST WRITING THOMSON.

Oh what a relief. The letter that followed told how the elevator girl had lost control and the cage had crashed four storeys on to a cement basement. Daddy was injured inwardly, and the jar began a trouble which did finally take his life, but he lived for nearly twenty happy years before that took place!

"He that is spiritual judgeth all things" (I Cor. 2:15).

How did Mr Fraser know? When God's child is living close to Him and perfectly yielded to His will (some phrase it *being filled with the Spirit*) it is possible for him to spread his mind out in the Lord's presence and catch the instruction of God especially if interceding for someone else. If there was no God this could not be. Satan can read man's thought and describe the past, he can use intelligence and *guess* at the future, but he cannot *know* the future.

This experience was followed closely by another special instance of the Spirit's operation.

The Otis Whipple family were, at this time, no longer in Seattle, but in China. Mr Whipple is a fine architect and he had been called to build a mission hospital in one of the big inland cities. He took his family with him, so it was some little time before Mrs Whipple heard of my sorrows.

One day I got a letter from her. It said something like this: "Isobel, I feel your mother was spiritually prepared to go home. It was very strange. I knew nothing of the possibility of her operation, let alone her danger, but the day of her death I was so burdened for her I spent a long time in prayer for her and had an assurance that she was at last yielded to God's will in all things.

"But now as I write I have another burden that presses upon me. It is for you, and *somehow connected with your father*. I am in much prayer for you, dear, and for him. I do not know what is happening, but God has called me today to intercede for you both and claim only His will to be done upon each of you."

I looked up the date. It was the very day of the telegram of father's accident! Mrs Whipple was in inland China, halfway around the world; she had no human knowledge whatever of that which had taken place. She could not possibly know (for I did not know myself for several months) that before she went to the hospital mother admitted that I had chosen the better course in pursuing the will of God. What had been worldly ambition in her life she confessed to Him and came back to her earlier consecration of all to her Lord, before she died. And who knows how much Mrs Whipple's intercession helped to win that battle?

Of course, I was deeply impressed. Wistfully I wondered if I would ever attain to the place where God could trust me with His counsels in this way. I did not know that God has these gifts in greater or less measure for all who are born again in the Spirit and living in obedience to that Holy Spirit. I was soon to learn.

Joy at Father's recovery was quickly followed by a new anxiety. Mother had been the business head in the family and it was she who had managed to make ends meet, and who had planned so carefully that I was able to get an education. Father was of Micawber's optimistic and gullible temperament. He was always going to "strike it rich" by investment in copper mines, silver mines, gold mines, etc. The fact that he had consistently lost all his life savings in these "promising" stocks never seemed to teach him. After Mother's death I was perturbed to hear that Father had given up his profession and gone in for stock-selling—a new invention which would make us all millionaires in a short time! Brother, too, had sold his chicken ranch, and apparently was not working at anything. Why start something new if you are going to be independently wealthy soon? They had rented a little bungalow in North Vancouver, sold some of our furniture and moved the rest in. These cheerful, wonderful-sounding letters only served to burden me: the higher Dad's expectations rose the lower sank my heart!

"Lord, is life to be always grim?" I whispered to Him. His answer was not long in coming.

It was in the General Missions class that Dr Glover repeated a previous announcement. "I have told you before," he said, "of the Foreign Missions Convention of the United States and Canada to be held in Washington, DC, January 28 to February 2. The Moody Bible Institute has been allotted eight delegates, but we only have six signed up to go. This will be a wonderful experience, since famous missionaries and converts from all over the world are coming. President Coolidge is to open the session. I am sure there are some in the student body who can afford to pay their own way. The time is getting short. I would urge you to sign up. Next week is the last opportunity, so get ready."

Delegate to the great missionary conference in the capital city! My heart reached out in longing to go. Suddenly I felt I was to go. It was as if the Lord said, "You've had a long enough siege of sorrow, dear. I'm going to send you to Washington for a little time of joy." I thrilled through and through and believed Him. Yet it was an impossible hope; I had not a cent I could put towards it. All week long I imagined the Lord sending me a huge gift of money and my trotting up to Dr Glover and offering to be a delegate; but not a cent came in.

The last day of opportunity arrived. At missions class that morning several student volunteers had been asked to speak three minutes each, telling why they felt they should go to the foreign field, and at the end Dr Glover again made an impassioned plea for one more delegate to the Washington Conference. The opportunity closed that night, he said. I left the class wondering: Had it been the voice of the Lord? Had I been deceived by wishful thinking? That noon there was a note in my mail box. *Call at Dr Glover's office immediately*, it read. With high-bounding heart I simply ran to the building where the Director of Missions had his office and, trembling with excitement, I knocked at the door.

"Come in! Oh Miss Miller, sit down." And Dr Glover beamed at me. "I sent for you to tell you that someone has offered to pay your way to the Washington Conference. Would you like to go?"

"Oh," I gasped. *"Would I*? But who could it be?" (Dr and Mrs Page? But how could they afford it. Oh, who could it be?)

"The donor wishes to remain unknown. I believe she is a stranger to you," he smiled. "She." Then it was a woman? "She has paid your fare, your hotel fees and meals and given an extra twenty for just fun. Here it is. The fare and hotel bill I'll pay for you. Now, you'll have to be ready to leave by tomorrow. Can you make it? I have already got permission for you from the Dean of Women."

It is needless to say I was able to make it!

But I would like to tell you how God worked this out for me, for the dear benefactress did allow me to know the story later on. She was a well-to-do Christian recently widowed. That Thursday morning she happened to be downtown on business near the Institute, and, glancing at her

watch, she saw there was time to slip in and listen
to Dr Glover's mission hour. As she slipped into a
seat among the students, I was called upon to give
my testimony. When I was through Mrs X whispered to the girl seated next to her, "Who was that
speaker?" We neither of us knew who that girl
was, but she not only told my name; she added,
"She has been going through deep sorrow. Her
mother died before Christmas and a few weeks
later her father was nearly killed in an accident."
The kind little widow's heart went out to me, her
own bereavement still fresh upon her; so when Dr
Glover arose to make a last plea for the one
remaining delegate, she felt instantly that she
would like to send me. "A change of scene,
inspiring messages, sightseeing around the
capital," she thought. "Just what that girl needs.
I'll give it to her, and incidentally MBI can have its
full quota of delegates." God bless His generous
stewards who live in the flow of His thoughts, so
that He can think and act through them.

Such spiritual premonitions I never had before I
found the Lord. From time to time I have had them
ever since. I believe they are given for the purpose
of comfort and to refresh our experience *that He is
there*, and that He cares. Only God could have
worked out that little forecast and fulfilment.

And so began one of the high peaks of joy which
tower up exultantly above the painful valley
experiences of my life. It was one that has always
been outstanding; and it moulded my life as I little
suspected it would have any power to do, for one
of the other eight delegates was John B Kuhn.

I had been formally introduced to him at last,
and it was at a mixed party after all! The occasion

was Daddy Page's birthday, when a group of the young student volunteers whom the Pages had at their home decided to give him a surprise party! I was told there would be boys present and also told that one of these would be that brother of Kathryn Kuhn, so I knew I was to meet him at last. But how could I get out of it? If it had been any staff member's birthday I could have found an excuse. But my own dear Daddy Page—I just *had* to go to his birthday party!

The group were to meet at Clark Street corner, where we caught the 7.30 p.m. street-car. We girls arrived first, and the moon was rising over the tall old houses when we saw the boys' group approaching. "Oh, here they come!" cried the leader of us girls. "Miss Miller, let me introduce Jack Graham and John Kuhn and ... " I heard no more. I found myself looking straight into the face of—the dishwasher from the Bible Institute kitchen!

I might add that it was a wonderful convention with world-renowned missionaries taking part. We heard them speak and met some of them personally. In between meetings we went sightseeing. We visited the White House and were presented to President Coolidge, shaking hands with him. And after it was over we all had a short trip to Mount Vernon to see the home of George and Martha Washington. Sitting together; eating together; sightseeing through snow-slushy Washington; laughter and teasing when we set out to buy Gordon Hedderly Smith some galoshes, only to hear one store say they did not carry such a large size!

How little we knew of the future years. That two

of the delegates would marry each other and serve Him in far off Lisuland; that Jack Graham would be in the same province, ministering to the Miao tribe; that Irene Forsythe would have a wonderful ministry in Shantung Province among the Chinese; that Gordon Smith would open up work among many new tribes in Indo-China. Friendships were formed during those delegate days that have sweetened the whole road of life ever since.

CHAPTER TEN

AT SUNDRY TIMES AND IN DIVERS MANNERS

WHEN is the Search ended? In one sense, it is finished when our hand, stretched out to God in the name of His appointed mediator Jesus Christ, feels the answering grasp and knows that He is there. But in another sense the searching never ends, for the first discovery is quickly followed by another, and that by another, and so it goes on. As I write it is dawning a new day. The far horizon has seen the bright spot of the rising sun, but heavy clouds soon covered it. However, these clouds have become illuminated and streaks of pink and gold beauty are breaking through chance rents in their filmy cover. One discovers glory after glory as the eye eagerly explores the heavens. And so it is with God. To find *that* He is, is the mere starting-point of our search. We are lured on to explore *what* He is, and that search is never finished, and it grows more thrilling the farther one proceeds.

Up to this point I have discovered that God is; and that He is mine by the mediatorship of Christ. I have discovered that He can and will teach me His way, or His plan for my life. I have found that He can overcome obstacles and that we do not need to arouse a great hullabaloo to get Him to do so. Hudson Taylor was right in his discovery: "learn to move man, through God, by prayer alone." By searching I have discovered that He has strange and sweet ways of manifesting Himself; at sundry times and in divers manners God is still speaking (Heb. 1:1).

This chapter will deal with the simple dry fact of finances. Elsewhere I have told how He provided, through Marjorie Harrison, for my fare to Chicago, board and room there for one year. Then came the autumn term of 1925, when Marjorie's money had all been used up and I was entirely dependent on my own earnings and God's care for the rest. But this involves the story of another life which had touched mine the previous spring.

It must have been about April 1925, that I was struck by a prayer request given in the evening devotions hour. A graduate student got up and asked prayer for "a girl-friend who has had a terrible tragedy happen to her, and she has lost her faith. She is coming to see me on a visit here to the Institute. Pray she may find the Lord again."

A girl, struck by heartbreak, pushed on to the Misty Flats and floundering bitterly—I saw it all with a sympathy that pierced my heart. "Lord, *give her to me*" I prayed inwardly. "Oh I can understand how she feels!" I felt He answered that He would. Humanly speaking, there was no likelihood of our meeting in the ordinary course of events. I was now working part-time as a noon rush-hour waitress, and the graduate student who had given out the request moved in a different circle from me. "The élite" we laughingly dubbed those students who were wealthy enough to go through Moody without working their way. They had plenty of leisure time and we had none; so "the élite" and "the workers" seldom met outside of classrooms. They had picnics and parties for which we could not afford the time and naturally each group clanned together. I could have pushed my way up to the graduate student and asked for an introduction; I would have been nicely received. But I decided if it were of the Lord, He must work it out His way, then I would know that it was not just my own impulsive wishing. But I prayed about it.

Now the strange thing is that neither Ruth nor I can remember how it came about! I have a dim recollection of a chance encounter in the post office. I, of course, was watching the élite set for the appearance of a stranger and so spotted her early. She was tall, slim, with light brown hair naturally curly, and the soft accent of a Southerner. But why she noticed me among the hundreds of unfamiliar girl-faces at MBI, I will never know. God answered my prayer and "gave" me Ruth— that is all I need to say.

Soon she was coming to our room for talks and pursuing me wherever she could catch this student labourer. I remember once encountering her just before the noon hour, when I was rushing off to be waitress at that restaurant (the employees' restaurant of a huge corporation nearby).

"I want to talk to you!" she said.

"Fine," I answered. "Can you come in tonight? I'm on my way to my job now and dare not stop—I'll just barely make it."

"No!" petulantly. "I want to talk *now*. I'll walk with you to your job—nothing against that, is there, ma'am?" (We had great fun over the difference in Canadian and Southern speech-forms. To me *ma'am* was the language of a servant to a mistress; to her it was the polite way to apologize. She laughed much, and mimicked drolly my "I beg your pardon?" and rubbed in her *ma'am* as often as possible with a teasing sparkle in her eyes.)

Now, I was just a little diffident about Ruth seeing me in that restaurant. I was servant to the servants there, so to speak, and the rush-hour girls had to take left-over apron uniforms, usually very ill-fitting ones. Ruth was the only child of well-to-do people, and cultured homes were native diet. What would she say if she saw me in that restaurant? But she was quick to notice my slight hesitation in accepting her escort, and nothing would shake her off from that moment. Right into the restaurant she came and saw it all; saw, too, my embarrassment, and mischievously determined to make the most of it.

Ruth was the twentieth-century counterpart of Mary Tudor—sister of Henry VIII. Charming, capricious, affectionate and utterly lovable, clever and nimble-witted, she was still untamed; or to use a more vulgar but more explicit word—*unspanked*. Her parents had spared the rod, and that always follows a child through the rest of life.

It was impossible ever to "handle" Ruth. She saw you tuck the handle under your apron just as soon as you moved your arm, and with an almost devilish mischief she would whisk it out and brandish it before your chagrined face and defy you. She was my superior in personality, brains, social culture—in everything but one thing. She did not possess the fellowship of the Lord Jesus or know Him as I did—and that was what I longed that she might. But I had not been with her long before I knew that I could never "deal" with her. She was too quick to recognize any such effort, and she had my own resentment at the invasion of her spiritual sanctum. She would open it up when and where she liked, but no one should knock it open. The only thing I knew to do was—to love her and pray for her.

Somewhere along the line (maybe an evening session, relaxed on her bed, talking in the dark) she suddenly opened up and told me her tragedy. She had become engaged to one of God's finest gentlemen; one who knew Him and served Him devoutly. But they had had a quarrel and Ruth had high-handedly broken their engagement. She had had an unfortunate experience with a religious hypocrite, and with her lightning-like petulance had said that she could not believe in God when a Christian would act like that. She had never meant to really break with Jack, she loved him too dearly for that. But she had conceived a pique against life for disappointing her and had to take it out on someone. The first overture Jack made, she would melt and be his own darling Ruth again—that was her inward thought. But no overture came. She did not know that even whilst she "tiff-ed" with him, he was going down with a fever. When she did learn it, he was already in Heaven.

Yes, it is better to have the rod when you are a child. When life must wield it against you, it is too cruel. Can you think what her agonies were? Not just to have lost him (their wedding date had been set) but to have him go before she was able to say,

"Oh, I did not mean it! I'm sorry. Please forgive."

Her kind, worldly father did the best he knew. He handed her his cheque-book and said, "Go to New York and have a good time. Forget the irrevocable." She went. And all the wild life she led I did not care to hear. Just one question was making my heart stand still: "Ruth, you did not *grope for the low road*?"

She was silent a moment. "I know what you mean. No. Somehow there has always been in me a hidden passion for chastity. But just everything else I did—I was wild."

I sighed a "Thank God!" "He had wallowed in fleshly things until his appetites had become fibrous"—that is what the low road does. Christ *can* save from it, as praise God our city rescue missions all testify, but it leaves scars. As for the hidden passion for chastity, I understood that too.

> Has thou heard Him, seen Him, known Him?
> Is not thine a captured heart?

Anyone who has ever really known the Lord, even only in reflection, can never again be satisfied with less.

"Did the cheque-book and New York's wildest—*help*?" I asked.

She withered me with a look. "You know it didn't."

How I prayed for this dear honest, if wilful, young life. I thought I had been able to help her out from the Misty Flats, but later she was sucked back in again. However, she is His now. In my Moody Autograph book (which is a large tome!) her autograph covers four pages, written in three instalments. The first is one of her nonsense poems, shrewd with perspicuity. (She has a literary gift, among other things. The élite publishing houses reach after her manuscripts! They do not even know that I exist.) But the third reads as follows:

Third Instalment.
Wonder if I'll ever finish this! Sounds like The Perils of Ruth in three instalments. What I've been trying to say for the last two pages is that I love you (just plain, unadulterated, simple-minded love). You have meant so very much to me—you, yourself—and you have meant infinitely more in that you have both *showed* me the way and *fought with* me during these hard hard days of decision. I can wish no greater thing than that you may mean just that to these dear folks in China.

I know that Ruth had been "sifting" me. When she caught a glimpse of pride wincing, she seized on it and walked right to the restaurant to see every bit of it. More than that, at a later date, without any warning, she brought a college girl-friend with her to that same restaurant to catch me as I was; which they did!

But she did more than just sift. Tenderly affectionate and generous, she discovered that I enjoyed beautiful things. Maybe it began by her getting permission from the Dean to take me out for a meal—so we would have that much more time to talk.

My frank delight in the harmonious drapes, shaded lights, soft classical dinner music amused Ruth. From then on she deliberately hunted up quaint, pretty tea-rooms and increased her

invitations! With her unfailing charm, she could
wangle a permission out of a Dean that no one else
would even dare to propose! And so she
"embroidered" my days.

But her careless use of money shocked me.
When away from Chicago she once sent me a
telegram, in lieu of a letter! When I remonstrated
(by two-cent post) I received a second telegram to
laugh at me! No, you could not "handle" Ruth!

But there came a day when, to her astonishment,
she found that someone else could be hard to
handle too. The summer of 1925 I spent in Canada
with my Aunt Nellie, mother's younger sister. On
returning to the Institute I now faced having to
support myself entirely, as said above. This meant
working three times a day instead of only at noon,
but I was highly favoured. I had obtained the post
of waitress at the faculty table in the Institute
dining-room. This meant being down a half-hour
before each meal in order to prepare the food
nicely, and it meant staying half an hour afterward
to wash up and to set the table, and then there was
the time consumed in having my meal when other
students were already through. But it was not too
strenuous; it was among Christians (no more
heathen Americans shouting at me!); It was
exacting, for you had to be there right on time, but
it was at no great distance away, such as the other
job had been. No time wasted in getting there.

One day I was in the act of preparing a meal
when in breezed Ruth! She had arrived unexpectedly with her parents for a short visit. "So this
is what we are now!" she teased. "Say, I've got
something to tell you." With an eye on the clock

hand which was travelling close toward my dead-line, I said, "Keep it, dearie, until tonight—can you? I'm dying to hear it, but my job has to come first. I've got to get this finished before the faculty arrive. I'm working full-time this term" (there would be no more meals out in pretty tea-rooms).

Ruth stood and pouted. "But I want to talk to you about my soul!" (Twinkle in her eye) "How important is *that*? And you stand there flaying radishes into rose-buds and say, 'Another time.' How do you know I'll feel like talking about it at another time? There is something wrong here. Something's got to be done about this," and then she had to leave as the faculty were beginning to arrive.

I felt very uncomfortable. 'Twas so. Ruth wasn't the kind that could open up the doors of her sanctum just at any odd moment. But then—I had to work, and surely the Lord expected faithfulness in my job? Inwardly I prayed for help and went on with the task in hand.

But Ruth was busy too. She arrived in my room that evening her old gay self. "I've got it all arranged!" she said happily. "No more table-serving for Little Pats!" That was her pet name for me. (Apparently I am addicted to short, quick movements when showing affection—many short, little kisses, and many little pats on the back in a hug. My children laugh at the former and Ruth declared she got homesick for the latter—the name has pursued me through the years.)

"I told my father about you, and he says he will be delighted to support you through the rest of your schooling here. Now then! Whenever Ruthie

arrives and needs talking to, she can have it. And
many others too. Don't you see the Lord's hand in
this—*ma'am*?"—with roguish delight.

But I didn't, and there was an awkward silence.
Ruth's father was a fine, clean man, *but he played
the races*, and gained his money in the usual
worldly ways. Hudson Taylor believed firmly that
God does not need, and will not use for blessing,
the money offered by unbelievers. He is able to
provide for His own children apart from help from
those who serve Mammon. "We can afford to have
as little as the Lord chooses to give, but we cannot
afford to have *unconsecrated money*," he once said.
But would Ruth ever be able to understand what I
meant by refusing on that score? Her eyes sparkled with mischievous delight when I said her
father's money was *unconsecrated*—she would
have a good time telling him that! But when she
saw that it really touched what was sacred to me,
she accepted quietly, for Ruth was a lady born.
When her visit ended I was still faculty waitress.

But I had not counted on Ruth's decisiveness.
After a week or so, I received a letter from her; I
wish I had it to quote now, for nothing reveals her
charm as much as her little notes. It simply stated
that she had got herself a job—teaching physical
culture at their local YWCA, and her monthly
salary was enough to pay my room and board.
Now, was that consecrated enough for me to
use—*ma'am*? Not a cent of her father's should taint
it! "Now, Lambkins, you know it will be good for
Ruth to have to hold down a job! Now don't you?
Just think of the good you are doing me by
accepting and thus making me an honest worker

in the hive of life, and not a drone? *Please* write and tell me you accept?"

And so you see, she had "handled" me after all. I never was able to handle her! But that is how the Lord sent me support for the term September-December 1925.

Christmas 1925, I was invited to the Harrison home for the holidays, Dr and Mrs Norman B Harrison were now living in St Louis, where he was pastor of the famous old Washington-Compton Presbyterian Church. They have a family of six talented children, and with two or three of us guests added we made an hilarious house-party. Members of his congregation invited us out to meals and helped to entertain us, but the most fun were the good times in their own home, where music and youthful antics embellished every day.

I arrived back at the Institute in January 1926, expecting to continue in my luxurious leisure. But a letter from Ruth was awaiting me. She had taken sick and the doctor forbade her to continue with her physical culture class! "*Please* let father support you until I get stronger?" was her little wail. But I could not consider it: it was not in the "pattern" which God had showed me. *See that thou make all things according to the pattern showed to thee in the mount* (Heb. 8:5) was one of my lodestar verses: I must follow it.

From the mountain-top to the valley in one swing! How often life does just that. One moment having all things and at the peak of "fun"; the next moment facing a grim poverty and hard work. For I must seek employment now and I had lost the comfortable faculty waitress job—it was never available for me again. Totally unprepared for this, I had not been careful in my spending, and now I anxiously marshalled out my funds. Just enough to pay the first month's board money (we paid in advance) and with something like eleven or twelve dollars over. I'd barely make it. I must go to the Employment Office immediately and see what jobs they could find for me. Humanly speaking, the nicer jobs would be all gone by this time, and more than that—friends had been told that I was being supported through school and no one would think to send me any extra gifts! But the Lord had not left me; it was another chance to *search* His powers; He was just asking me to be willng for the uncongenial work again.

As I sat looking at my accounts I suddenly saw something that made me go cold. In the Christmas rush I had forgotten to tithe my last income! What should I do? Let the tithe continue to slide for a while? I pondered a moment. What came first in my life anyway? "Oh, Lord, You come first," I whispered and resolutely set aside the tithe. That left me less than two dollars for a month's car-fare and incidentals—and I still had no job.

Well, the Employment Bureau found me two; noon rush-hour girl at that same old restaurant, and waitress for Evening School supper at MBI. I was now very busy indeed. The long walk to and from the restaurant, a later hour getting to bed at night from the Evening School began to tell on my health. Always thin, it was dangerous for me to lose weight, but I knew that I was doing so. By February my friends were beginning to notice that I looked haggard and tired and I myself felt that I was near the breaking-point. "Lord, is it Thy will that I have a breakdown?" I prayed in private.

One evening I was called over to the Reception Room—a visitor for me. There, tall and smiling and fatherly, was Dr Harrison! He was in the city on special speaking engagements and thought he would look me up. His keen eyes looked searchingly at me as we shook hands and he said, "How is it, Isobel? You look tired. Not working too hard, are you?"

"Perhaps I am," I answered. "When I returned here from your place I found that I must work my way again; the lady who had been supporting me since Marjorie stopped has been sick and can't do it any more."

"Well, Isobel," and the keen, kindly eyes again searched my face, "isn't it wonderful that *stop* isn't in the Lord's vocabulary? He never gets sick and He never forgets our needs and He is never at the end of His resources. Do you remember when you were at our place at Christmastime that you were invited out to dinner with Marjorie by a Miss Boyle?"

Oh, yes; that had been a real treat. Miss Boyle was a wealthy lady in Dr Harrison's congregation. She lived in an exclusive apartment hotel, the kind of place where an ordinary mortal scarcely dared to look, leastwise enter. Because of her love for Marjorie, Miss Boyle had included me in the invitation, but she had scarcely noticed me beyond the usual courtesy care of one's guests. But I did not mind that; it left me free to enjoy the exquisite appointments of the room, the table and the meal. How much the Lord did give me! "As having nothing and yet possessing all things." I was beginning to understand what Paul meant. But Dr Harrison was talking.

"I saw Miss Boyle just before I left and when she heard me say I was coming to speak at the Institute she said, 'Oh, by the way, I was thinking the other day that I have never donated anything to MBI. I feel I'd like to do so by way of that little friend of Marjorie's who came to my place for lunch that day.' And, Isobel, she handed me a cheque for two hundred dollars. I meant to give it you in small gifts, perhaps ten at a time. But maybe I'd better give it all to you now!"

Two hundred dollars—just like that. *At sundry times and in divers manners* truly!

"Oh if you did," I cried, "then I could give up one of my jobs and not have to work so hard."

"I'll see you get it tomorrow, dear," and that dear father-in-Israel went on his way.

So I was able to give up the evening work. The noon rush hour, though disagreeable, paid better for the time used, so I retained it. By this and the other gifts I managed to reach the summer.

When I returned for the last term (September-December 1926) I was once more faced with earning my way entirely, but I had left word with the Employment Bureau and they had tried to choose the best for me. For one thing, they had been in touch with Mrs Allison of the Practical Work Department, and she had given me a very special assignment for Sundays *which also paid a salary*! I was the Sunday pianist for St Charles Reformatory for Boys; the Government paid for a pianist. I gasped at that assignment and straightway sought out Mrs Allison.

"Oh, I can't play the piano well enough to hold down that job!" I expostulated. "I am largely self-taught, and always before this has been given to a music major student—isn't that so?"

"True," answered Mrs Allison. "But I have heard you play for evening devotions and I think you can make it. I'll ask Miss X to give you some tips on evangelistic playing and get permission for you to practise on one of the pianos here. The reason I chose you is that there is such a wonderful opportunity there for personal work, and the lady who has been in charge up to now is sick. A friend is substituting for her, but is quite inexperienced in bringing children to decisions. You know the Reformatory, don't you? Every kind of boy problem is there, from playing hookey from school to murderers. There have been some wonderful conversions and we don't want to see it slump. You are paid to play for the morning and afternoon services, but you are *allowed* to visit the boys who are sick in the infirmary and deal personally with them between services. You get two meals into the bargain, so it will help you financially."

With fear and trembling I accepted, and for four months each Sunday was a thrilling experience. "My strength encampeth on weakness" is one rendering of 2 Cor. 12:9. The substitute leader who taught the Sunday school lesson in the morning service was very conscious of her inexperience and the pianist trembled lest she be called on to give a piano solo, as sometimes happened. Truly we were weak, and therefore the Lord alone was exalted when scores of those boys decided for Christ. I could fill a chapter with all that took place at St Charles Reformatory; but this one happens to be on finances, so I must pass on and continue my theme.

Of course, Sunday piano-playing salary was only a mite. I had to take a major job besides that. The Employment Office felt they had a choice one for me. Again it was waitress (those hours fitted my schedule best), but at a very select tea-room near Michigan Boulevard. Noon and evening I was to serve and the salary promised was good. It was in a private house (one of Ruth's pretty, quaint tea-rooms) and the clientele were mostly high-salaried clerks or office-workers from the wealthy district around. Undoubtedly, I would get good tips in addition to the good salary. The proprietor was a widow, Mrs Mac; the moral conditions had been investigated and all was trustworthy. Now at last I ought to have plenty of money; in one's graduation term one needed extras.

I liked it very much. Mrs Mac was a middle-aged Southern lady, gracious and warm-hearted. The tea-room was pretty, the food delicious and the clientele were very nice to me. My tips grew. I was congratulating myself when a cloud appeared. At the end of the first month I walked in one morning to hear shouts and high words. The cook was swearing at Mrs Mac, and the latter was at the phone.

"Isobel, stay here in this room," commanded Mrs Mac, all flushed up. "This woman is threatening my life. I've called the police and I do not dare be left alone with her until they come here and put her out."

"No need for the police if you just give me my salary!" shouted the excited and irate cook. "This is a nice place for you to be in, Miss Isobel! She pays nobody! I've worked here two months and not got anything hardly. She owes the butcher, the baker, the ... "

"Shut up," cried Mrs Mac. "You lie ... " And then they were at it again when a tall policeman arrived at the door and the cook had to leave. My heart sank. That wonderful salary—would I really get it? Today was the end of the month. Just what was the situation, anyhow? Within a half-hour a new cook had arrived and the business of the day rushed on: but as I went from table to table my mind was also busy on this problem. Should I ask Mrs Mac for my salary? Or should I just pray that God would move her to give it to me? By the end of the day I had made a decision—I would speak if she did not offer to settle accounts. She made no offer nor gave any hint that she remembered my salary was due.

"Mrs Mac," I said as I put on my hat and coat. "Tomorrow is the first of the month and I must pay my board and room bill. Do you think you could let me have my salary tonight?"

She hesitated, then went slowly over to the till. "I had an unexpectedly big bill to pay today," she said. "Could you take just half now and I'll pay you the rest later?"

This was what I had feared; the dismissed cook had told the truth; Mrs Mac was not in the habit of paying her bills. Her promises were wonderful, but it was quite a different thing to get her to keep them. Again I was in a predicament. If told the Institute, they would recall me, of course, but at this late date what other jobs would be available? Here at least I got something from tips; in fact, my tips for the first month, combined with what she had just given me, made just about the sum of the promised salary, and this had given me an idea.

"Mrs Mac," I said earnestly. "I am a Christian and accustomed to ask God directly for what I need. I cannot serve you for nothing; but I am willing to keep track of my tips, and at the end of each week if you will make up what is lacking to the amount of the salary you promised the Insititute to give me, I will be content with that. Then we will just ask the Lord to move the clients to tip me as much as is needed."

She flushed a little. "But that is not right, Isobel. The tips should be yours as extra."

"But I am content and can make ends meet if I get what you originally promised me," I replied.

"It is very good of you," she said sadly, then opened up and told me her troubles. I do not believe she was deliberately crooked; she was just utterly undisciplined and improvident. She had no conscience about debt and spent freely what come in to the till. Each Saturday I faithfully reported my tips, which continued to be high, and as the weekly dole-out was not as high (she seemed to be better able to part with a small sum than a large one) she gave me her part. I believe now that I was the only worker she hired whom she paid regularly! Of course, I talked to her about trusting the Lord for her salvation. She liked to listen and often agreed with me, but that miracle of a new birth within her never took place, that I could see. I fear dishonest thinking had become a refuge from conscience with her. The new cook only lasted some six or eight weeks and then there was a scene similar to the first one. She would pay just a little bit on her big butcher's and grocery bills—just enough to keep the stores from suing her—but, of course, that could not go on for ever.

I believe it was December when one morning I walked in to find the tea-room empty—nothing cooking in the kitchen, nothing prepared for the lunch-hour clientele. I called Mrs Mac, but there was no answer. The upper stories of this beautiful old home had been let out to roomers and one of them heard me and came downstairs, dressed for departure.

"There has been a big blow-up here," she said in a low voice. "I didn't get it all, but I think the old lady has gone bankrupt. The cook made a furore about salary not paid and Mrs Mac said she wished she were dead. Do you think she can have hung herself in the cellar? Better go down and have a look. I'm going to my office. Goodbye." And I was left alone in the empty room.

There followed a nerve-racking experience. All was silent as the grave and imagination conjured up my going down a cellar and bumping into her dead body dangling from the rafters! I shook all over. I just couldn't get enough courage to open that cellar door and go down and look. I prayed for the courage to do so, but I did not receive it. I despised myself; I lectured myself; I asked the Lord how could I ever go to China if I did not have nerve enough to open a cellar door and go down and investigate? But I was petrified. I just could not do it.

At length after about an hour I heard a step on the verandah and ran forward eager to see another *alive* human being. It was Mrs Mac.

"Oh, Isobel," she said with a heavy sigh. "I forgot about you. There won't be any more tea-room. I'm bankrupt and the receivers are coming to take over the building. I've lost everything. I couldn't stand the silence, so I've been out for a walk."

"Mrs Mac, I do wish you would give yourself to the Lord!" and I tried again to help her, but nothing seemed to penetrate. She was appreciative, almost affectionate toward me; but in spiritual matters she was just vacant. She would not acknowledge she was a sinner and that is the first step toward knowing God: and so I had to leave her.

Again I was in a predicament—just a few weeks from graduation and no income! I remember only two details of those last days. Mother had left me her silver service and Father asked to buy it for fifty dollars—that helped a lot.

Then there was a day when a bill was due and I was five dollars short. I had been praying about it, but nothing had come in. The morning I had to pay it, I received a letter and in it was just five dollars. It was from an old Christian lady whom my father had visited, and when he told her I was working my way through Moody she decided to send me that gift. She had not given me anything before, and she never gave me anything afterwards; but the morning of my lack her five dollars arrived.

At sundry times and in divers manners, always the good hand of my God was upon me. He had wrought wonderfully for Hudson Taylor; but as I looked back over my two years and four months at the Institute I felt He had done just as wonderful things for little unknown Moody student me. *By searching* I had found Him able and faithful to supply my financial needs. And He will do so for any of His children who trust and obey.

CHAPTER ELEVEN

GRADUATION AND CIM CANDIDATURE

I FINISHED at the Moody Bible Institute in December 1926, and I was elected as the girl class speaker (MBI custom demanded two valedictorians, one from the women's side and one from the men's).

As I prayed for a message, thinking of our class as they would be going out into the world to represent the Christ, I was given the verse John 20:25 and took as my theme, *The Print of the Nail*. I chose Thomas's words: "Except I shall see in His hands the print of the nails and thrust my hand into His side, I will not believe," and I made it representative of what the unbelieving world is unconsciously saying to the Christian Church today. The heathen around us have not much respect or interest in a smug, ordinary Christianity. "If it costs you nothing, what proof have you that it has any value?" is their indifferent, shrugging attitude. But when they see in any life *the print of the nail*, they are challenged; and like Thomas of old, if they can be made *to see Him* at that moment, they will fall down and cry, *My Lord and my God*.

I felt this message deeply and wanted it to speak

to other hearts as it had to my own. But MBI required that the valedictory messages be memorized (they had, of course, to be careful that students represented correctly the teaching of the Institute). This bothered me a little. The memory work didn't, but I had never been able to pour out my heart unless given the freedom of extemporaneous wording. I did not know this then, for I had done comparatively little public speaking. I just knew that I felt hampered, somehow, at reciting a memorized text. But rules were rules and I fell in line, as I had tried to do throughout the Institute days.

My father came to Chicago for my graduation, and Miss Boyle sent me a white silk dress. She and I did not correspond; in fact, apart from the two hundred dollar gift at the beginning of that year, I had heard nothing from her. And certainly no one was told that I had no money to buy the required white dress for graduation! (Remember, I had lost my employment at Mrs Mac's.) Moreover, in those days MBI required that girl students' clothing have sleeves below the elbow and skirts nine inches from the floor! The 1926 year styles were worn shorter than that, yet when Miss Jackson measured the gift dress it fulfilled all requirements and did not have to be altered at all. (Miss Boyle's gifts to me ended here. I've never heard from her since.)

As we went up to the platform, I, on sudden impulse, gave the text of my message to Anne Barr, our Vice-President, just in case I got stage fright and needed prompting. (I had recited the whole thing more than that once before Mr Bitticofer, so it was not that I did not know it.)

When my name was called, I went forward and found that big audience. I did not feel as nervous as I expected and started in easily. But as I proceeded I felt that I was merely reciting, and not pouring out my soul; I found it was not going into their hearts and in my anxiety to give it the meaning it had for me, I forgot how the next paragraph started. It was only for a second and Anne behind me prompted quickly in a low voice that not everybody heard, but to me it was a catastrophe. I got through, went to my seat, hung my head and just waited until the end of the programme when I would be free to dash for my bedroom. Once up there (during my last term I had a room to myself), I fell on my knees in an agony of humiliation and failure. A pale December sun shone weakly through the heavy city atmostphere upon me, and then suddenly the Lord was there with me. I felt His love folding me around. "Never mind, dear," He was saying. "Failure or success it is all over now and My love is just the same."

"The beloved of the Lord shall dwell in safety by Him; and the Lord shall cover him all the day long, and he shall dwell between His shoulders" (Deut. 33:12).

The words were as if spoken, and the tenderness that engulfed me was balm of Gilead to my agonized soul. Slowly I quieted, relaxed, rested back on Him and drank deeply of His love. It was a wonderful experience and I was lifted up in spirit so that I no longer cared for any personal humiliation. I was deeply sorry I had disappointed the expectations of my class, but apart from that *I was beyond hurt*. I have never forgotten the outpouring of His love upon me that day when I felt such a failure.

After graduation came candidature at the China Inland Mission Toronto Home. Their yearly candidates' class had been in August, when Kathryn Kuhn and her brother John, with many others, had been accepted, and they had sailed for China that October (1926). I was the only candidate applying in mid-winter, and as I would be leaving for my home on the west coast, the Mission decided that I should come to Toronto immediately after graduation. As I was born in Toronto, we had relatives and friends there with whom my father stayed, waiting until he and I could travel west together.

Daddy Page came to the train to see us off. I do not know whether I was looking anxious or sad or just plain tired, but suddenly a tender compassion lit up his face and he leaned forward and said to me, "Don't be afraid, Isobel. There is nothing to dread in candidates' school. The CIM has known you from a child." I thanked him for this good cheer and for all his loving, fatherly care of me during my Institute days, and then the train pulled out.

Mr and Mrs Brownlee were in charge of the Toronto Mission Home, but Mr Seaman (the Seamans were on furlough and staying at the Home) was the one appointed to start me on the Chinese language study. Candidates learned to recognize the difficult radicals (roughly corresponding to the English alphabet and other sample beginnings). I was also to help and act as companion to the widow of one of the Mission donors; her bereavement had made her distraught and her family felt the quiet, prayerful atmosphere of the CIM Home might benefit her.

The Brownlees' son, Dana, was present, otherwise the only other young person I remember was Ida McInnes. I had met Ida at Moody (indeed, it was she who had organized Daddy Page's surprise birthday party and had introduced me to John) and learned to love her. She had graduated earlier and applied to the CIM, but did not pass the medical examination. China being closed to her, she became office worker for the Mission to Lepers but was allowed to stay on in the CIM Home until she could find a boarding-house elsewhere.

Ida was "the embroidery" to my candidate days. She was devoted to the Lord, and we were one in the things of the Spirit; but next to that her keen sense of humour was a safety valve for my youthful spirits. Quick, impulsive and day-dreaming, I had been an easy prey to *faux pas* all my life and I was not in the Home twenty-four hours before I had made the first one.

Knowing the Brownlees' reputation for perfect administration I am sure the fault was mine, but I did not know the daily schedule. Likely they had told me while I was day-dreaming! Conscious that this was more than likely, I felt shy to ask what the hours were, and decided to watch carefully the bells which summoned the household to meals and meetings. I got along well the first morning, but at 1.30 p.m. I was startled by a new clang. What did that call me to? I rushed to Ida's room, but she was out. A girl was dusting the corridor, so I asked her: "What was the bell for, please?"

She looked at me wonderingly, "It's the prayer meeting bell," she announced.

A prayer meeting? And the candidate not attending? That would look bad.

"Sorry," I said hastily. "I'm new here. Which room is it?"

She told me, indicating the office buildings, and I rushed over. The door was shut, but a murmur of voices within settled it for me. I knocked gently and opened it. In my excitement, I did not notice that only staff was present!

"Excuse me for being late," I murmured and sank into a seat. They received me politely, albeit a little blankly, and that day the staff prayers were very general! After the meeting Mrs Brownlee came to me and told me gently that the 1.30 p.m. meeting was for the staff only and that my presence would not be required!

How Ida laughed when I told her. "They probably *discuss you* at that meeting!" she teased, and from then on there were many pointed remarks as to when my presence was required and when it wasn't! We had hilarious times in her room.

I was there some three or four weeks, and then I had to meet the Council. That is a formidable occasion and I was nervous, as I am not quick at thinking on my feet. I always do better with preparation and time to consider the best answer. However, the meeting came and went one afternoon and that evening after supper I was called in to the sitting-room by Mr Brownlee to hear the verdict. He said something like this:

"The Council was quite satisfied with your

answers today, and we in the Home have enjoyed your presence. But the Council has asked me to speak to you upon a very serious matter. Among your referees there was one who did *not* recommend you. The reason given was that you are proud, disobedient and likely to be a troublemaker. This person has known you for some years and the Council felt they could not ignore the criticism."

"Who was it?" I asked quickly, simply dumbfounded.

"The CIM does not betray the confidence of referees. We write to those who have had business associations with you as well as to the referees you yourself give — and we promise to keep all reports in confidence. I cannot tell you the name, but I would like to discuss with you what havoc such characteristics can cause on the field." He then proceeded to do so. At the end of an hour of earnest exhortation, he pronounced the verdict: "The Council decided to accept you conditionally. There is an anti-foreign uprising in China just now which is very serious and we dare not send out any new candidates. That will be our public statement on this matter. For yourself alone, and we hope you will not spread it around, during your waiting period the Vancouver Council will be watching to see if any of these characteristics show themselves. If you prove that you have conquered them, you will then meet with the Western Council and be accepted fully, and sent out with the first party that goes. As we anticipate your victory in these matters, it was voted to pay your train fare to Vancouver, as *en route* for China. I can assure you I have not found it easy to say these things." And indeed his face was sad and tired. I felt sorry for him even with the misery that was numbing my own heart.

"Good night." And I went up to bed, but, as you can readily believe, not to sleep. Who could the unknown referee be?

Proud. Disobedient. A troublemaker. This was the third time the adjective proud had been attached to me. The first time was by Daddy Page himself months ago: he had read me an anxious lecture on the subject, to my extreme surprise, for pride was one of the human frailties of which I felt I was not guilty. I would have taken Daddy Page's lecture to heart if he had not ended it by holding up to me, as one example to emulate, a certain fellow-student. That particular student stood high in the regard of the staff, but I happened to room near her and I knew that secretly she broke many Institute rules; also she lied about her age to her boy-friends, and so on. I was sure if Dr Page knew what I knew, he would never have held her up to me as a pattern of conduct. So I concluded he just did not know either of us and brushed the accusation aside. China was later to be a painful revelation to me of my own heart and frailty. From this distance I now know that Dr Page had indeed sensed a real flaw in my life; he had just got hold of the wrong label, that was all.

I was selfish. I had whimsically divided the world into two classes, people who interested me and people who did not. I felt I was not proud, because the people who interested me were often among the poor or the uneducated, but when it was so, my friendship for them was still as warm as for those who had had advantages.

Towards the people who did not interest me, I must have appeared proud. I cold-shouldered them and brushed them off me as time-wasters. This, of course, was a serious flaw for a missionary, but I fancy its basis was selfishness rather than pride.

The next point was—disobedience. How I did get indignant! MBI had had many rules which were difficult to keep (they have since revised them, and it is no longer so), but I had been meticulous in obeying simply because I had signed a promise to do so, and I felt honour bound to keep it. Just the little matter of laundry, for instance. We had washbowls in our bedroom, but their use for laundry was forbidden—one pair of stockings a day was allowed, no more. Ransom Hall had then no laundryroom: I had to waste many weary steps going to another dormitory to do my laundry and waste more minutes because it was required that each time I get permission from the Matron to do so! — and I could not always find her. This was my most galling trial. The girl who had been held up to me as an example washed all her lingerie and sometimes even night clothes right in her bedroom at hours when she knew the inspectors would be busy elsewhere, and dried them on her radiator! "The rule is unreasonable" was her only answer when I remarked on it. But I has *promised to obey*, and so I dragged my weary self over to the other building every week. And now the CIM had been told I was disobedient!

I had been told not to spread around this second condition of my acceptance by the CIM, but I did write a few friends. They wrote back quickly, indignant and sympathetic, and I was somewhat mollified. All but one. That one was Roy Bancroft, a music student with a beautiful baritone voice and a consecrated heart. We had asked Roy out to St Charles Reformatory to sing to the boys there and to help deal with them. I happened to be writing to him those days and impulsively told him. A letter came back quickly and I opened it with a smile of anticipation, thinking that Roy too would be indignant on my behalf. But I got a shock.

"Isobel," he wrote, "What surprised me most of all *was your attitude in this matter*. You sound bitter and resentful. Why, if anyone had said to me, 'Roy B. you are proud, disobedient and a trouble-maker," I would answer: 'Amen, brother! And even then you haven't said the half of it!' What good thing is there in any of us, anyway? We only have victory over these things as we bring them one by one to the Cross and ask our Lord to crucify it for us."

These words "stabbed my spirit broad awake." Faithful friend he was, not afraid to *season his words with salt* even as he did not forget to speak *with grace* also: I was on my knees in no time asking the Lord to forgive me.

I arose from my knees with a different attitude. Instead of resentment there was alertness to watch and see if these three horrid "Diabolitians" (pride, disobedience, rebellion) were really lurking in my camp. The town of Mansoul should not protect them, if detected. This brought me into peace, even though I always shrank from the memory that I was to be watched for their appearance in my life.

Subsequently it so happened that in a most

unexpected way I learned of my detractor's identity and then I knew the reason for her hostilty. It will suffice here to say that she was a teacher in a school which I had attended. She wished me to assist her in spying on my fellow-pupils. I felt that was unworthy and so had incurred her displeasure by refusing. When I learned this I was tempted to clear myself with Mr Brownlee and the Western Council. But should I? I seemed to hear a voice say: "If that had been said of me, I'd answered 'Amen, Brother! And then you haven't told the half of it!'" Dear old Roy—he was right. Why try to make the Mission think I was lily-white? They'd have personal experience before long as to just how earthly a person I was!

"No Lord!" I whispered. "I won't bother the Mission with it. But how princely of You to let me know—it is like a miracle. Only You could have done it."

For the Lord is always kind
Be not blind.

Kind? To let me end up at Moody, where I had striven so to be faithful, under such a cloud? To let me begin with the CIM under such a stigma? *Kind?*

Yes. You see, the Lord foreknew there was a work to be done in Vancouver before I sailed for China, and if I had ended up Institute life with great *éclat* I would quite possibly have wrecked that work at the very outset. My *self-confidence* needed to be thoroughly jarred before He dare put this delicate affair into my hands. And He had jarred it all right. My Master is thorough, "no one worketh like Him." But He had also been meticulously kind—just as soon as He dared, He had showed me why. And that after-graduation ceremony experience of His enfolding love has blessed me all my life.

Only by *searching* can we find out what He is.

Again to jump ahead of my story, but to complete this little matter, when the door did open for China again, Mr Thomson wrote me a letter. I cannot quote it verbatim, but it ran like this: "I have never mentioned to you that little condition of the Toronto Council. From the first, both Professor Ellis and I felt there was a mistake somewhere, and I want you to know that so thorough was our confidence in this that I have not felt it even necessary to call the Western Council together. I phoned each one of them, and we want you to know that you are accepted by the CIM *unconditionally and unanimously*. Every one of them said that. And our loving prayers and blessings go with you."

I bowed my head over that little letter and wept tears of gratitude. Yes, my Master is thorough. He wounds, but He *binds up*, and His balm of Gilead heals without stinging; it cools, refreshes and restores in every part. He gives the garment of praise for the spirit of heaviness, and brings beauty out of our ashes.

CHAPTER TWELVE

THE VANCOUVER GIRLS CORNER CLUB

FATHER and I travelled on the train together from Toronto to Vancouver, and there my brother, Murray, met us at the station. It was strange to be together without Mother, and still stranger to find myself going across the ferry to North Vancouver in order to get *home*.

Father and Murray had rented a small four-room bungalow on Twelfth Avenue. Dad had one bedroom, I was given the other, and Murray put up a cot in the sitting-room at night and slept there. The fourth room was the kitchen; a bathroom separated the two small bedrooms, and a good big basement took in my trunk and suitcases. We three just barely fitted in the little place. Inside was more familiar, for there was Mother's piano, the well-known parlour chairs, equally familiar bookcases and a big fireplace—just like the one we had had in the old home. It was good to be back and I came to love that little house on the hill. From the front porch I could see the harbour and the waters of Puget Sound, beyond which lay—China.

There now faced me the need for employment. I must earn my living until the door to China reopened. Was I to go back to school teaching? I would have to sign a contract and then would not be free to leave if the way opened before the contract date expired. I felt great reluctance in my spirit to do this. God had led me *out* of school teaching. I felt it would be like sending Abraham back to Ur of the Chaldees to return to it. While I was praying and pondering I received an invitation to speak to the Vancouver Girls Corner Club (VGCC) at their evangelistic service on the next Tuesday night. Yes, I replied; I would be very pleased to be their speaker; then, on leaving the phone, I asked my father who the VGCC were?

"Christian business girls banded together to try to win other business girls to the Lord," answered Father. "The Club was founded by Mrs Neff, lady worker in the big French E Oliver evangelistic campaign held here when you were in your teens. Don't you remember? Well, when the meetings were over they had a final supper with the converts, and some of the business girls got into a corner to discuss how they could keep together and keep going on after the campaign ended. They decided to form a club and to hold a weekly meeting to bring in unsaved friends. 'Here we are in a corner,' said one jokingly. 'Let's call it the *Corner Club.*' And that is how it started and how it got its name. It's a fine work. I am glad you are going to speak to them."

The next Tuesday evening Father took me downtown to the Club rooms. They had a big lounge overlooking Granville Street (one of the busiest streets of the city), a small office for their Superintendent, and a big dining-hall where we went for supper. On Tuesday evenings a good supper was furnished for only fifteen cents a person; the dessert was always cake, and these delicious cakes were baked and donated by the women's societies in various churches, thus enabling the supper price to be low.

After supper the tables were cleared, pushed back and the chairs arranged for the meeting. A platform and piano were at the end of the long room and a bright evangelistic service was conducted for an hour. Christian business girls themselves led this meeting, and it was an enjoyable time, I thought.

In less than a week I received a second phone call. It was from the girls' President of VGCC, and she astounded me by an invitation to be their Superintendent! I had not noticed that the position was vacant, but apparently they had been without one for some time. "We feel shy to ask you to take it," said the President, "because we can't afford to pay you the salary you deserve, or even as much as we have paid in the past. Corner Club is run down a bit, having gone so long without a Superintendent. We can only give you eighty dollars a month to start with. As the work picks up we would hope to increase it, but your hours will not be heavy. You do not need to be in the office until 10 a.m. each day."

When I asked what were the duties of the Superintendent, she replied, "Well, to lead and direct the work. Every day at noon tea, coffee and milk are sold in the dining-room. Business girls bring their bag lunches there and enjoy getting hot drinks to go with them. You will circulate among these girls, get to know them and try to lead them to the Lord. Every Tuesday evening you will be in charge of the evangelistic service and will speak. The Corner Club has had to draw speakers from various churches in the city during this period without a Superintendent, and we would like to pay back our debt to them, so to speak, by having you speak at any of their young people's societies who invite you. This would also advertize the Club. And maybe you yourself will create some new activities. Remember, our motto is *The Other Girl*." I asked time to pray about it and a date was set for my answer.

Nothing else offered, and as I waited in prayer I felt the Lord wanted me to accept; and so it came about that I became Superintendent of the Vancouver Girls Corner Club for the year 1927 and the early part of 1928. I had stipulated that the moment the door to China opened, I should be free to resign and that was agreed upon.

I now entered upon a fascinating period of my life. Corner Club was run by a Girls' Board, a Women's Board (representatives from different churches and different denominations in the city), the Superintendent and a business manager.

The business manager was a godly middle-aged woman whom everyone called Mother Fitch. Mrs Fitch was one of those energetic saints who are described as *full of good works*. She had not enjoyed higher education but she had been taught of the Spirit and she simply lived for the glory of God and the winning of souls. There was no big evangelistic effort in Vancouver but Mother Fitch had a hand in it somewhere. The city missions were enriched by her prayers and practical services. Realizing that God had not trained her for platform work, she humbly accepted any mund-

ane service—cooking, serving or even scrubbing—
and prayed it into a ministry of blessing. Every
Sunday she went to the jails to preach and during
the week she ran the kitchen department of the
Corner Club. Needless to say, I found in her a
kindred spirit, although she must have been more
than twice my age. We were a queer-looking team,
but always a united one.

The Girls' Board were elected by the members of
the Club. I was only twenty-five years old by now,
and most of the Girls' Board, I think, would have
been a bit older than that, but our times together
are among my happiest memories. I have always
felt that my Corner Club girls were among the
loveliest young women that God ever made. They
were ready for any venture that would win souls,
but they were also a very merry group, and the
Club rooms resounded with laughter and gay
banter in between the earnest prayer meetings
and discussions.

I did not meet the Women's Board immediately,
and Mother Fitch laid hold of me early in that first
week with a warning.

"Isobel," she said, "I would like to suggest to
you that you do away with the Women's Board.
They are not spiritually-minded like the Girls'
Board, and I think they may be a drag on you. I
believe God has sent you here for a red-hot
soul-winning campaign and I am behind you one
hundred per cent. You preach and I will cook! I
know my place. The Women's Board won't allow
you to give a call to decision on Tuesday nights,
and I'm afraid you will meet with other restric-
tions. It is true the Club does get support from
their churches and they would cut it off if the

Women's Board were removed, but I am willing to live by faith like Hudson Taylor, and I am sure you are too. I think you could talk the girls into agreeing, for they are anxious to give you a free hand to direct things as God leads you."

Now, this was the delicate affair I referred to previously. I was young, inexperienced, and the words *red-hot soul-winning campaign* thrilled my soul. To give up a salary and live like Hudson Taylor would be heroic—just the strongest kind of appeal to me at that period. It was many years yet before a quiet article in the CIM's private *News Bulletin* alerted me to the danger of *missionary heroics.* The article pointed out that just because a line of action is difficult, painful or dangerous does not necessarily prove that it is the will of God. As a very simple instance, a call for medicine comes in the middle of a missionary's meal. She jumps up and leaves her food half eaten and rushes off to answer. That may seem noble and sacrificial on the surface; in reality, it is foolish and harmful. Of course, I am not referring to life-and-death emergencies, when promptness is a duty. I mean an ordinary medical call. The messenger has probably dilly-dallied several times already and an extra ten minutes' wait until the nurse's needed nourishment is properly masticated will hurt no one. As I read the article, I recognized my own photograph with deep chagrin. I was not given to breaking up my meal period, but I had been guilty of other extremes of conduct. Some natures are more open to this temptation than others, and mine is one. So at this time of my youth, Mother Fitch's suggestion appealed to me as quite possibly the highest line of conduct. I was cautious, however, and told her we must pray much before doing anything so radical.

I believe it was that very evening when I met the President of the Women's Board. She was a warm-hearted Scottish lady who shook hands with me, giving me a hearty welcome to Corner Club. Then she added: "You are a candidate of the CIM, aren't you? I'm good friends with the Charles Thomsons, and he told me to keep an eye on you and let him know *how you got on here*!" And she beamed at me cordially, perfectly unconscious that she had just brought a whip-lash down over my shoulders with a sting!

I never for a moment doubted that Mr Thomson had betrayed our secret to her. Charles Thomson was a godly Scotsman, the soul of honour and common sense. I was sure that Mrs Mc—did not know the full implication of what she had said, but I saw in a second that I was in no position to begin my Superintendent's career *by dismissing her*! Some gentler method must be found, and so the Lord used this "whip-lash" to guide me on to a better road. I told Mrs Fitch that I felt we should go slowly and try what prayer could do first. She sighed, but never refused a challene to pray. The day was to come when the President of the Women's Board would kneel beside me in the little office, and with tears thank God that He brought me to Corner Club. And I (likewise with tears in my heart) thanked Him for keeping me from the precipitate action which would have wounded this dear life and hindered the accomplishment of His purposes.

As I gradually met with other members of the Women's Board I found a group of women very different in temperament, but gifted, reasonable and co-operative. They did ask that I issue no calls to come forward for decision; they felt that the business girls would prefer more decorum and dignity in the Tuesday night service than the usual "penitent form" method, but they too were desirous to see people converted.

God blessed the Tuesday night meetings in a quiet way. Not many made an open profession of Christ (which troubled me), but the attendance grew by leaps and bounds. No one knew how difficult I found those services. I was tormented by fear of stage fright again; of my mind going blank like it had during MBI graduation ceremony. Many a Tuesday night as the girls were gaily putting out the hymnbooks I slipped down the corridor to the bathroom (the only place where I could be sure I'd not be seen) and, leaning up against the wall, cried to the Lord for the nerve to go back and on to that platform. But He never failed me: the stage fright never came back seriously, and gradually I began to count on His help and speaking grew easier.

Invitations to the churches began to come too. Finding that several of the girls had beautiful voices, I organized and trained a quartet (following the teaching I had received at MBI in such). One of the younger members of the Women's Board had a bell-like contralto voice suited to sing bass, so the quartet represented both the Girls' and Women's Boards and was a real success. "Miss Miller and the Corner Club Quartet" began to get calls from all different denominations, and our opportunities to witness for the Lord multiplied. Often we took our suppers to Club and ate them

before leaving as a team for the church of the
evening. Then it was that the empty dining-room
rang with laughter, for all four had a keen sense of
humour and the relaxation from their office work
prompted an ebullition of youthful spirits. But
always the evening's work was brought before the
Lord in earnest petition before we left. I began to
see what a power a Christian Business Girls' Club
could be. Through its interdenominational character, it was quietly reaching out and challenging
young people's societies in many denominations
throughout the city.

And even into the business life of the city there
was an influence going out. A lawyer asked what
had caused the change in the life of his stenog-
rapher and her answer had an effect on him. I saw
more and more the wonderful potentialities of the
work when first things were kept first. There have
been corners clubs in other cities, but the temptation is to let them sink into merely social service
efforts. Young life must have an outlet, and I soon
saw that. So we had picnics, seaside corn-roasts,
hikes on Saturday afternoon and in the winter we
had a "Stunt Night"—girls only. This was one of
the most hilarious evenings I ever spent. The
stunts were all wholesome fun and revealed much
brains and talent. I myself had opened it, dressed
up as the cartoon version of an old maid schoolmarm, and I announced that the students of my
boarding school were about to put on a programme for their relatives and friends. Most of the girls
had never seen me lay aside the dignity of my
office just for fun, and it tickled their fancy to find
I could enjoy a joke as much as the next one. That

"Stunt Night" broke the ice between me and a certain girl for whom I had been fishing in vain for weeks. It was only a short time afterward that she accepted the Lord in my office. But all our parties were threaded through with the love of Him and a deadly earnestness that others might find Him too. I think that is the secret. A merely social club helps nobody very much, for it does not offer any solution to the problems of life.

My noontime circulating among the lunchers was to me the most difficult part of my work. Always shy about meeting strangers, I also had this unfortunate background of having so fiercely resented personal work in my own earlier days, so that it made me timid to barge in on other lives. I always felt I was a failure in the noon contact side of the work. A gifted evangelist could no doubt have reaped a big harvest from those opportunities. But I made friends and had their confidence. The sins and temptations which gradually opened up to me were appalling and led us into many unexpected adventures. I will just take space for two.

Edith was a clever young girl who had come out from England to get work in Canada and she lived with an aunt while doing so. She met and fell in love with a young man, and we followed her joy through the day she appeared in the lunch-room with her new diamond ring to the time when she said goodbye to office work and invited us all to her wedding. She had her dress and trousseau, had resigned her job, the wedding day was set and the invitations had all been mailed. A night or so before the actual marriage her telephone rang.

Edith heard a strange woman's voice on the wire.

"Is it true that you are to be married to Mr So-and-So in two days?"

"Yes," answered Edith, wonderingly.

"I am very sorry, but I must tell you he is already married. I am his wife. I have our wedding certificate here."

Can you imagine the shock to that young English girl? The shame? The heartbreak, for she had given her love unreservedly. But you cannot imagine the worst. Her aunt, humiliated at having to cancel the wedding invitations, in a towering rage ordered her out of the house. She would have no such thing of shame under her roof, she said.

Edith out on the street, homeless, wild with grief and heartache—where could she go? Her church? They were her aunt's type; probably would have the same views. *Corner Club*. She crept in broken, distraught—then found herself clasped on Mother Fitch's broad bosom. Corner Club protected her, loved her, found her a home and *led her to the Lord*. She proved to be an exceptionally gifted girl, and it was only a year or two before she had earned enough money to go back to England, where her own mother still lived. It was a soul saved and a young life saved, as well.

The most exciting story perhaps was that of Faye. A knock on my office door came one afternoon and I opened it to see a fashionably dressed woman standing there.

"Miss Miller? May I have a word with you? I have been to your Club rooms several times and admire the work you do very much. And in my boarding-house there is a young girl who needs help. May I tell you?"

I led her into the lounge and we sat while she talked. "She is a nice young thing from the prairies. Her mother is a widow, I believe, and sent Faye to Vancouver to study to be a nurse. She is a pretty girl and seemed to have a lot of dates with young doctors, you know, and I guess she neglected her studies. Anyway she failed her year, is out of the hospital, has no money, and I'm just anxious that the temptations of a big city do not suck her under. Do you think your Corner Club could help her? I told her you were very nice, despite—ahem—your long hair, and—ahem— your long skirts"—this with an eye to each. The fashions in 1927 had shrunk skirts until they barely reached the knees, and although I had shortened my dresses I still felt that modesty required that the knees be covered. My hair should be long for the China of those days, so I had never cut it.

I was much amused at her two "ahems," but boldly ignored this little difference of opinion between us, and answered, "We would certainly do anything we could to help her. We are not an employment agency, but ... "

"But you do have dishes to wash and dry?" urged the lady. "I thought if you could employ her here it would give you a chance to talk to her and perhaps steady her."

"I will consult our business manager," I replied. "Leave me your telephone number and I will call you. We do have dishes to wash, but our help is voluntary; our budget does not allow of much paid labour."

Mother Fitch, of course, was enthusiastic about taking in another young life to influence for Christ and it was agreed to employ her for a week or so whilst we sought to get her regular employment. So Faye was brought to us.

She turned out to be a gay little chatterbox. Most of the time she was busy in the kitchen, of course, but there came an hour when I was able to have her alone in the office and presented the claims of the Lord Jesus for her heart and life. She listened with the tears running down her face and acquiesced in everything. When she had left Mother Fitch came in to inquire about the result.

"Well," I answered slowly, "I am not satisfied. She was certainly touched and willing to follow me in prayer and accept Christ as her Saviour. She wept; but somehow I cannot believe she is born again. Something did not seem to click—if you know what I mean."

Although not an employment agency, and certainly not a "rescue work," still it was possible at Corner Club to announce to the girls that a certain one needed work and to ask that the members keep their eyes open for a suitable vacancy. This we did, and Faye was not with us long before a noon-hour girl named Helen came to my office.

"Do you suppose, Isobel," she said, "that this girl Faye would be willing to take a poorly paid job until something better turned up? My mother has had a stroke and is completely paralyzed—cannot even turn in bed. I am only an office worker and cannot afford a trained nurse to care for her during the day while I am away. But Faye has had some training; I would give her her room and board and a little for pocket money, if she would come and care for Mother?"

We called Faye in, and she accepted. She would

be free every evening and we urged her to come to our Tuesday supper and service, and said good-bye. As our life was full of unexpected cases, it was not possible to follow up Faye very closely.

Summer came, and I was to have two weeks' vacation, which I chose to spend at the Firs Conference, very naturally. It was just a few days before I was due to leave when I got a telephone call from Helen.

"Isobel, have you heard about Faye?" she asked.

"No, not a word," said I in alarm. "Please tell me."

"Well, she is in the hospital. She began to act and talk strangely here and one evening she had a sort of spell so that I called in a doctor. He sent her to her old hospital and now he says she is insane! I don't believe it myself. In fact, I think she is acting a part to get away from here. It was a bit quiet for her, I guess. I feel she's been accustomed to hit the pace, you know. Anyway, I wish you'd go and see her. Her doctor might believe you. He won't listen to me. Here is his name and telephone number."

. I was staggered at this news, but promised to go and see her. Helen hung up and I called the doctor's number. A crisp, professional voice answered.

"Doctor, this is Miss Miller, Superintendent of the Vancouver Girls Corner Club. I believe you are treating Faye—?"

"Yes," shortly.

"Well our Club is interested in Faye, and I have been asked to go and see her at the hospital if you ...."

"It would do no good, Miss Miller," came the answer quickly. "She would not know you. She recognizes no one, and I've had to put her in Ward X. She is violent."

"Well, Doctor, the friends with whom she was staying feel that she is just acting a part...."

An exclamation of anger stopped me. "Miss Miller, I have been a specialist in mental cases for many years. Do you presume to tell me I cannot recognize insanity?" He was clearly insulted.

"No, Doctor. I beg your pardon. But for the sake of her friends could you not give me permission to visit Faye? My pronouncement would quiet them."

He gave an exclamation of impatience.

"All right. Be at the hospital on Saturday afternoon at 2 p.m. I'll give orders for you to be admitted," and down went his telephone.

So down went mine too. And up went my heart to the Lord.

"Now, O Lord, I'm in for it! I've got a new search on now. Can you control the high-strung bunch of nerves which is me, and enable me to face an insane person?"

I think that most people have a private horror, a "phobia," some one thing. Most women fear snakes. I've known a big strong man just about go to pieces at the news that *a rat* was near. One famous scholar of our generation admits to a phobia as regards insects. Now my own private fear has always been insanity. I don't like snakes or rats, but they do not set my nerves a-jingle like the word *insane*.

"Lord," I prayed, "when I felt I should go down into that cellar to see if Mrs Mac had hung herself there, I asked You for the nerve to go *and I didn't get it*. Of course, You knew she wasn't there and that I did not need it. But still—can You nerve me to face insanity? Saturday afternoon will be my proving time."

I was to leave on Saturday night for the Firs: so I was all packed and ready for the train. Leaving my baggage at the Corner Club, I proceeded to the hospital at 2 p.m., and inquired for Ward X. It was in the basement. Across the corridor were heavy, locked doors and in front of them, at the side, was a desk with two nurses seated there. Above the doors were the silent words, *Ward X*. From behind the doors someone was singing a ragtime at the top of her lungs.

I went up to the nurses and said, "Please may I see the patient, Faye—"

The nurses looked at one another. "I'm sorry," said the older. "It is against the rules. No one is allowed to see her."

"But I was told that I might, if I came at this hour." Again they exchanged glances, then the younger said to me, "She is violent. That is her singing now!" The youthful voice was rollicking on.

"Dr—told me he would give orders to let me in," I protested. That was a magic word. "Oh," they scrambled through some papers on the desk. "Yes; there is an order for a Miss Miller."

"I am Miss Miller."

"All right. Step this way."

The younger nurse took a big bunch of keys and opened the corridor door, ushering me into the corridor on the other side. Small cells lined this corridor on either hand and each door was locked.

Each cell was beneath the ground, but had one iron-barred window high up near its ceiling, and level with the earth surface outside.

My heart was beating so violently I felt dizzy and sick, but before I knew what was going to happen the nurse had unlocked a cell, *pushed me in alone* and I heard her lock the door behind me!

Faye stood with her back to the door, looking up through the little barred window and shouting her song. She was in a dishevelled mess that it would not be kindness to describe. At the sound of the door key she whirled around like a wild animal about to spring on its prey, but as soon as she saw me, she went limp, blinked stupidly a moment, then said, "Miss Miller!"

"Yes, Faye dear," I answered. Going forward and taking her in my arms, I kissed her. "I've only just learned that you were sick. I've come to see you. Get into bed, dear, and then we can talk."

Like a lamb she climbed on to her cot and I sat at the foot of it, as there was no chair in the cell—nothing else in it but the iron bed. I talked about the Corner Club, trying to draw her memory back to quiet scenes and to the Lord. She answered each question intelligently and only once did she exhibit anything strange. I was telling her of some little Corner Club incident and said, "Mother Fitch—you remember who she is, Faye, don't you?"

"Yes," replied the young face on the pillow. Then there came an expression of cunning, "*And I know you*," she cried emphatically. I went cold all down my spine, but ignored it, continuing on in my quiet chit-chat. I told her to trust in the Lord and that I would write to her mother. Also that I was going on my vacation, but would come and see her as soon as I got back. I suppose I stayed about fifteen minutes. Then I knocked loudly on the door, hoping the nurse would hear. She came at length and I left—Faye still quietly lying in bed.

When I got back to the Corner Club I phoned the doctor. "Yes," he said. "Well, how did you get on?"

"She knew me immediately, Doctor, and called me by my name."

There was a staggered silence at the other end, then to himself: "Well, I'll be d—d." To me, "Miss Miller, please tell me exactly what happened, right from the first." After I had done so, he said:

"How soon can you visit her again?"

"I'm leaving in a few hours for my vacation, Doctor. I will be gone two weeks, but I will call you as soon as I return."

"You do that!" he said earnestly, and we hung up.

Of course, I felt that Helen must be right—Faye was playing a part for some reason. If I had known it was so important, I would have given up my vacation to attend her, of course, but I didn't. In my next telephone conversation with the doctor on my return from the Firs he told me she had been sent to an insane asylum outside Vancouver. He was quite indifferent whether I visited her or not, saying, "This time she won't know you," but he gave permission for a visit with her.

Viewing the matter after nearly thirty years have passed, and after having had more than two decades of experience with devil-worshipping mountain tribes, I am inclined to think it was demon-possession. The Devil has hoodwinked educated America into thinking he is a myth, and he is working havoc unrecognized. My reason for believing this is twofold. First, I found that *the mere presence* of a consecrated Christian in a demon-haunted house was enough to force back those powers. My entrance into that hospital cell brought with it the power of my Master and the demon force was temporarily quelled. Second, that look of cunning when she affirmed (unasked!) that she knew me, was the very same that I have seen on the face of a demon-possessed tribesgirl just before that demon was cast out: and the compulsion to confess recognition is similar to what took place in our Lord's day. But as Superintendent of the Corner Club, I knew as yet nothing of these matters.

Now I felt I must visit Faye in the asylum. Again I was terrified at the thought, but as God had taken care of me in the hospital, He would surely help me in this second step. So one afternoon found me arriving by bus at the famous institution which I had never dreamed I would ever see.

It was a huge place several stories high, and as I approached the large entrance, men patients behind the iron bars of a veranda screamed out to me and thrust their arms through the bars as if trying to reach me. Not very soothing to the nerves! Inside I was ushered first into the office of the resident physician. He was a young man, and as I advanced to his desk he exclaimed, "Why, it is Miss Miller!" It was my turn to be astonished.

"Isobel Miller of Arts 22, University of British Columbia, isn't it?" he repeated, shaking hands cordially.

"Why, yes. But how on earth do you know?" I queried. He laughed.

"I was an undergraduate, a year or so behind you. What have you been doing since?"

And so we had a little chat. My work at the Corner Club brought up Faye. There must have been several thousand patients in that place, so I asked, "Would you know Faye—?"

"Would I?" he returned. "I'll never forget the night they brought her here. It took four strong men to hold her!"

"What do you think? Is she incurable?"

"No-o," He answered thoughtfully. "This type is brought on by dissipation and with the use of modern drugs we can often effect a cure. Did she talk very much? That is the first sign it is coming on—extreme talkativeness. She'll be here two years at least, though, and then there is likely to be a recurrence later on."

"My Club would like to help. Of course, we believe that prayer will help her, but is there anything else you could suggest?"

"Yes," he answered. "She has got run down through late hours and the life she led. If your Club could send her nourishing food, extra protein values, meats and broths, etc., that might hasten recovery. The ordinary food here is good, but she needs extra meat and such, which a Government institution can hardly provide."

I promised that we would do our best, and he rang for an orderly to show me the way to Faye's ward.

"They must prepare her to see you," he warned, "so you will have to wait a while."

Again I was taken to a corridor with a locked
door in it. But also a lounge-room opened off at the
side where harmless patients were sitting around,
some embroidering, some reading, one playing
the piano, and a nurse at a desk was obviously in
charge. A bench was opposite the locked door and
I sat there to wait. Up tripped a young woman
who asked me boldly, "Who have you come to
see?"

"Faye—" I replied, rather wonderingly.

"Oh yes, a nice girl, I know her!" This with a
loud voice, with her eyes on the matron at the
desk. Then behind her hand in a whisper to me:
"She is no more insane than I am."

"I've brought her some chocolates. Do you think
she'll like them?" I asked more to make conversation than anything else.

"Oh, yes. The food here is fine!" This in a loud
voice toward the Matron, then behind her hand in
a whisper, "It's awful. They starve us. Bring her
lots of chocolates!" And so she went on—
compliments in a loud shout Matron-ward, com-
plaints in a whisper behind her hand to me. It was
all I could do to keep my face straight, but
evidently she was known to them, for after a few
minutes the Matron quietly lifted her head and
ordered, "K—, you come back in here."

"See our bondage!" whispered the woman,
making a wry face to me, but she obeyed.

At length a nurse came with a key and I was
again ushered in behind the door to where a
second nurse had brought Faye, then (to my
horror) both nurses left me alone and locked me in
with the patient.

I would not have recognized Faye. She was so

thin she was the mere shadow of herself. The "preparation" they had given her was to drug her into stupidity, then immerse her, hair and all, in a bath to clean her up. She stood before me swaying unsteadily, her damp hair clinging to her like a drowned rat's, and she obviously did not know me. I told her my name and she repeated it, but with no sign of recognition. I proferred the chocolates and she opened them eagerly, popping them into her mouth one after the other rapaciously. Within five minutes, I knew that conversation was useless. It was true, she did not know me nor could she follow my thoughts.

Then the effect of the drug began to wear off. She had been brought to me in a corridor, off both sides of which were rooms.

"I want to go back!" she said suddenly, and started staggering down the corridor, hunting for her own room. As I did not know it, I knocked and banged on the locked door to call the nurses back. At length one came and took Faye to her place. But by this time Faye had evidently come to. She turned fiercely on the nurse, swore and cursed her. A glimpse into the room showed me why they had had to drug her and bathe her before allowing any other human being to see her. Obviously she was living like an animal. Heartsick, I turned away and came home. It was an experience I would not care to have often, but the Lord had strengthened me to go through with it.

At the Corner Club I did not describe the above; merely gave the doctor's advice to send her nourishing foods. I told how emaciated she was and asked for prayer. I also wrote to her mother and the result was that a sister was sent to

Vancouver to visit Faye and care for her needs.

Prayer was made constantly for the poor child's recovery and cartons of jellied chicken, home broths, jellies and other good foods were sent by the girls and the Women's Board. Still we were not prepared for our dear Lord's *abundantly above*.

Within *six months* Faye was dismissed cured! After asking the Lord to do this daily, I was taken aback by His speed! I received a telephone call from a stranger one day which ran something like this: "Miss Miller, you do not know me, but I am Mrs X—, neighbour to Faye—'s mother on the prairies. My husband and I are on this trip to the coast and Mrs—asked me to bring Faye home with me when we return. You know she was dismissed from the hospital a few days ago? No? Well, she was. She is living with her sister, but would like to come in and see you before she leaves and thank you for what you have done for her. May I bring her this afternoon? We leave by the evening train. Thank you. At three o'clock, then."

I sat back in my swivel chair and gasped. Then bowed my head and thanked the Lord.

I awaited three o'clock with a little trepidation. I had met two very different Fayes already. Which one would this one resemble? The gay chatterbox? The doped animal? Could she really be normal? The third Faye was the real Faye and a distinctly different person still. She had gained weight to a pleasing plumpness, but she was so shy and quiet I could hardly recognize her. She thanked me prettily and sincerely, but when she was gone into the kitchen to salute Mother Fitch I turned to their neighbour and said, "My, she is quiet! Do you think she is afraid of me?"

The lady widened her eyes with astonishment. "Oh, no. Faye never did talk much. She was always the quiet one. She is just like she used to be. Her mother will be delighted."

And so we parted. But my story isn't ended.

Nine years passed and now I was back at Corner Club as a missionary on furlough, as a married woman and as a mother. What a welcome they gave me! But before the first message, which they asked me to give at the old Tuesday evening hour, I had had a telephone call.

"Isobel, I wonder if you will remember me; Faye—?"

I nearly jumped out of my skin "Faye! You back in Vancouver?"

"Yes. But I'm married now. Oh Isobel, the Lord has been so good to me. I want to tell you all about it before you meet my husband. Will you take supper with me downtown, just we two alone, and then I will go with you to the meeting. My husband is coming to the meeting tonight—I got permission to bring him, since John, another man, will also be present. But I want you to hear my story first."

I wonder if you can understand my joy? No one can who has not mothered spiritual children. No one can who has not stood and watched the brand blazing in the fire, and then shrunk from the heat which almost scorched the hand stretched out to snatch it from the burning!

That evening in a little cubby-hole of a restaurant we sat face to face once more. She was still sweet-faced Faye, her quiet manner lit up with heartfelt gratitude. "Yes; I have a good husband and two darling children. *And I've never had a recurrence.* I'm sure the Lord won't let me now. And, Isobel, I want my children to be brought up in the Church. My husband and I are agreed: we want a Christian home."

Just one little peach from a year's harvest at the Corner Club. What potentialities lie in such work—leading business girls to Christ.

Often, on furloughs, I have heard the impatient remark: "Why go to the foreign field? There is lots to be done at home here!" There most certainly is. And there are lots of Christians at home—are they doing it?

By searching for Him, He makes us conscious of the need of others, and helps us cut channels by which He may be poured into their lives. In no time we find ourselves His fellow workers, and life is rich.

But I must come back to my tale: for by now the door to China was opening again.

CHAPTER THIRTEEN

"LET US GO ON!"

IT was the spring of 1928 when the China Director of the CIM, Mr Gibb, paid Vancouver a visit. I was called in to meet him and well remember the searching look of concern he gave me. "My dear girl," he said, "you look worn out. Are you well enough to go to China?"

"Oh, yes. Physically I am sound. But I am very tired," I admitted. Our home on the north side was so far away from the evening church appointments. Late at night the ferry did not run so frequently and if I just missed one there was a long wait before the next. Often it was midnight before I got to bed, and 6 a.m. was my rising hour if I was to have a quiet time, get the house chores done and catch the 9 a.m. ferry.

But I think most of it was emotional fatigue. Mentally I knew the way of victory. I had read of Hudson Taylor's experience, *The Exchanged Life*, when he rolled all his burdens on the Lord. I had heard Keswick teaching expounded at the Firs and seen it lived in lives there. But how to transmute it into experience was beyond me. I secretly worried about things. My father's Micawber-like attitude toward business appalled me. Where would he end up? Now I knew my mother's secret trial and how much we all owed to her sound judgment and carefulness.

I worried about my own failure at the Corner Club. I did not have the gift of evangelism. Young lives were constantly being cleansed, rededicated and built up in Him, but I did not see that. I looked just for souls to take the initial step of salvation. Pentecostal girls were urging me to seek the baptism of the Spirit. One of them was a gifted evangelist, a golden-haired, angel-faced girl, and I fell into the snare of comparing myself with others. Peggy had something I didn't. Was it really the speaking in tongues? Inwardly I fretted. But the Lord was carefully holding me. I asked Peggy and Dorothy (another who kept at me) to describe what happened when they were "filled with the Spirit." Their most vivid descriptions were no more than what I myself had often experienced when alone with Him and the awareness of His presence would flood in. I had never spoken in tongues, but I seemed to have had everything else they claimed to have experienced. This kept me.

I always felt there was a peril in just seeking an *experience* from the Lord. The temptation is to think *the experience* has sanctified. It hasn't. These uplifting times in His presence, provings of His faithful care, *enrich us*, add to our joy, but they do not sanctify us. They do not make us stronger Christians; they do not make us holier than our fellows, as I was to learn to my shame. But they make us richer in our knowledge of Him, and they give us joy that addeth no sorrow to it. The only way to be holy is daily to hand over to the Holy Spirit what Dr Tozer calls "the hyphenated sins of the human spirit ... self-righteousness, self-pity, self-confidence, self-admiration, self-love and a host of others like them ... can be removed only in spiritual experience, never by mere instruction. As well try to instruct leprosy out of our system. There must be a work of God in destruction before we are free. *We must invite the Cross to do its deadly work within us. We must bring our self sins to the Cross for judgement.*"[1] The Holy Spirit will crucify these things for us, as we hand them over to Him, and then we must just accept the suffering involved, rejoicing in the knowledge that His resurrection life will be the final outcome.

And so with all my rich experience of answered prayers, I still was full of worry, self-pity and many other ugly things: but I was not acutely conscious they were there.

Mr Gibb was really perturbed. By now I wore an engagement ring, and John Kuhn was already in China and being used of the Lord there. If my health broke, would that bring John home? He consulted Mr Thomson, and they both ordered me to resign from the Corner Club and take six months' complete rest before sailing in October (1928). Mr Gibb intended to give instructions that I be put on Mission remittance in order to do this, but, most unusually for him, he must have forgotten. I waited and waited, but the CIM sent me nothing. And I felt I should not petition for it. Hudson Taylor would have just prayed.

Mr and Mrs Whipple heard of the order for me to rest and invited me to spend the five or six

---

1   *The Pursuit of God*, by A W Tozer.

months at the Firs. I could help in cleaning cabins and getting the Conference grounds ready, but first I was to have a full month of just rest— breakfast in bed! and so on.

I had been able to save no money, for I had felt I should pay my father's debts. It was clear to me that the next invention would never bring him in an income, and I was right. So I landed at the Firs with about thirty-six dollars, all the money I had left.

Maybe one reason my heart longed so for a home on the Crescent where I could give rest to tired business girls was due to my own experience. No one can know what it meant to me to be taken in by dear cheery Mrs Whipple and be given the upstairs porch which they were fixing up as bedroom for their own daughter, Lois, when she should return from the Bible Institute of Los Angeles, where she was studying. Two sides of the room were without full walls and the scented, tall fir trees were its screen. Mrs Whipple had procured some old cement sacks; she bleached them, stencilled a pretty fleur-de-lis pattern on them, and hung them up in lieu of walls. When Conference would bring many people around and the fir trees might not afford privacy enough, these could be drawn. But when I arrived the scented green needles were the wall, and I loved it. To wake up in the morning just when you had slept to the full, no pressure of schedule upon you, to hear the birds carolling and the sun trying to peep at you through the green foliage was like living with God in Eden. I can never forget it.

I knew that Whipples were "living by faith," but

had no idea that when they took me in that first night they were down to rock bottom financially. I just felt I would like to give them my thirty-six dollars. Before going to bed, I handed it to her, saying: "I want you to take this. It won't pay for all I'll eat these months, but I'd feel happier if I felt I'd given something."

I remember Mrs Whipple flushed a bit and tried to refuse, but I insisted and then the matter left my mind. She told me years afterward that that was one of the hardest things she ever did—to take my money. But the milk bill was due in the morning and she had nothing else with which to meet it! And I myself would need milk. My money fed us until a gift of sixty dollars came in; and from then on there was no shortage. This is just a glimpse as to how the Whipples lived; although gifts had been few, they did not hestitate to invite me to live with them for six months! And I do not need to say how God blessed them.

They had returned from China to find that the Firs was the only home they had. With funds low and the need to make and furnish a bedroom for Lois (and me!), they were put on their mettle. From the attic of a relative they obtained some old furniture free, and this they sand-papered and repainted a pretty green for Lois' bedroom. When the stencilled curtains were hung, it was as dainty a room as a girl could wish—and I had learned lots about how to convert old things into new!

The Conference that summer (1928) was the most blessed I had ever known. The special speaker was Dr Arthur Harris of Wales, and the Spirit of the Lord was powerfully among us. For one thing, Mrs Whipple had prayed that every young person attending the Conference should yield to the Lord before going home. One evening during the service she was impelled to go to the girls' dormitory, and there she knelt by each bed, claiming for Christ the occupant of that bed! Needless to say, every evening there were decisions made. Toward the last evening there were a few who still hung back from full surrender, so the staff called us leaders of the young people to pray all during the evening service. I can never forget that prayer service. The Spirit of the Lord came down upon us as in apostolic times, and we all started to pray simultaneously out loud. As for myself, I was not even conscious of the others. So lifted up into the Lord's presence and so burdened for the souls that were hanging back, that it was not till a break came that I suddenly came down to earth and realized that we had all been praying out loud at the same time. From the upper room where we prayed, down through the tree tops, we could see the open-air auditorium. As we prayed, one after the other of the recalcitrant ones got up and went forward in surrender. The very last, a girl for whom I had had little hope, has now been for decades a most faithful missionary on a foreign field. Very truly it was the work of the Spirit of God.

Conference over, I needed to go back to Vancouver and get my outfit ready for China. There were still no funds sent to me by the CIM, but a love-gift from my brother paid my fare home. (As he, Murray, saw the invention was not likely to make Dad rich, he set about getting a job.) But where would the next come from? To add to the perplexity came a letter from Marjorie Harrison saying that she was travelling in our party and would like to stop off and see us! When I answered with a cordial invitation, I did not have enough money to pay her car-fare from the station to our home, let alone feed her.

Then I got a call from Mr Thomson to come to his office, as there was some money waiting for me. "At last!" I said jubilantly to myself. "Mr Gibb has remembered his promise!" But it was no such thing. It was much more wonderful than that. It was fifty dollars from my own dear John in China! I think it was the remainder of a bank account he had left over from his earnings in preparation for Moody. "I want to have a share in your outfit," he wrote, "but it has no strings on it: you may use it for any need." And the first bit of it fed Marjorie!

From then on I had no difficulty. Corner Club girls gave me "showers" and a beautiful outfit, which included the money to buy a portable organ! That little organ went with us to the Salween mountains and brought much joy to Lisu as well as missionary for many years: and it must still be there.

I prayed much about my final message at the Corner Club. I did not know (though I shrewdly suspected) that some of those dear girls were going to prove prayer warriors for whom I would thank the Lord all my missionary days. And it has been so now for twenty-eight years. God laid on my heart a message for myself as well as for them from Heb. 6:1, *Let us go on*. The search is not ended. We have only begun to explore our eternal

unfathomable God. "Let us leave behind the
elementary teaching about Christ and go forward to
adult understanding. Let us not lay over and over
again the foundation truths. ... No, if God allows,
let us go on," paraphrases Phillips. And that was
the burden of my message.

On October 11, 1928, I sailed for China. There
was quite a large party of us (one being the little
American girl who roomed next me in Ransom
Hall at Moody. Ella Dieken was engaged now to
Jack Graham and we were to be room-mates at the
Language School in China). My father had got
permission to sail with me on our boat as far as
Victoria so that the emotion of parting from him
did not take place at the Vancouver Wharf. It was
about the noon hour when the ship was due to
pull out and the Corner Club girls forgot their
lunch and flocked down to the wharf. They made
such a crowd that a stranger asked my brother,
"Who is the girl who is getting this send-off?" Just
an unknown missionary going out for the first
time, was certainly not the answer expected. But
God can give special things to His unknown
children when He wants to.

At last a bugler climbed up to the highest bridge
of the *Empress of Russia* and began to play Queen
Liliuokalani's beautiful farewell song "Aloha Oe."
It is, of course, the sad parting of two lovers. It
breathes passion, but no certitude of hope. It is
earth doing its best to reach out for cheer, but
failing mournfully. I am so glad that Christian
words have been set to it for such moments. For it
is only Christians who dare to say, "We never part
for the *last* time." As the bugle notes poured forth

on the noisy air of the wharf, there gradually grew
a stillness over the crowd,

> In these the closing days of time
>   What peace this glorious thought affords
> That soon, O wondrous truth sublime,
>   He shall come, King of Kings and Lord of Lords.

> He's coming soon, He's coming soon
>   With joy we'll welcome His returning
> It may be morn, it may be night or noon
>   But oh, He's coming soon.

But "the gospel must first be published among all
nations" (Mark 13:10).

> And we, who living yet remain
>   Caught up shall meet our faithful Lord.
> This hope we cherish not in vain
>   But we comfort one another with his
>   this word.

The last notes quavered sadly on the high air.
The unbelieving in the crowd, grasping the only
best they knew, whispered, "Alohe Oe." The big
anchors rattled as they were pulled up, the paper
streamers began to tear as the mighty ship slowly
drew away from the wharf. Beloved girl faces were
working with emotion, and one or two were
crying. "Lord," I whispered, "give me a last word
they won't forget." A thrown voice could still
reach the wharf. I leaned over the side and called
out slowly, *"Let us go on!"*
The light of heaven broke through the tears of
earth on some faces, so I knew they had heard.
They waved their hands in a signal of assent and

then the *Empress of Russia* turned her stately head
slowly toward the Narrows, Puget Sound, the
Pacific Ocean and—China.

But there was one more step. At the city of
Victoria, on Vancouver Island, my father said
goodbye and disembarked. After he had left, the
purser brought me a telegram. It read simply, "WE
WILL GO ON—YOUR CORNER CLUB GIRLS."

Tears of gratitude rained in my heart. Twenty-
eight years have passed—a good, long testing
period? Corner Club is still operating. Most of
those girls have gone on. There are people in more
than one country of the world who rise up and call
some of them blessed. One of them on the wharf
that day had unconsciously been leaning on me
rather than on the Lord Himself, so she sprawled
spiritually when her human prop was removed.
But on the whole they kept their promise.

And now, as reader and author part, I can find
no better words to us than just these same, *"Let us
go on."* Go on searching and exploring the greatness and the dearness of our God.

He has no favourites. He has said, "Ye shall find
me when ye shall search for me with all your
heart" (Jer. 19:13).

Notice that last phrase, for it is the only
condition. There must be inner honesty and
undivided loyalty—that is the only stipulation.
"The man who trusts God, *but with inward reserva-
tions,* is like a wave of the sea carried forward by
the wind one moment and driven back the next.
That sort of man cannot hope to receive anything
from God, and the life of a man *of divided loyalty*

will reveal instability at every turn" (Jas. 1:6–8—Phillips thus paraphrases it).

But—"He is a rewarder of them that diligently seek Him" (Heb. 11:6).

Said Susanna Wesley, "He is so infinitely blessed, that every perception of His blissfully presence imparts a gladness to the heart. Every degree of approach to Him is, in the same proportion, a degree of happiness."

So—*Let us go on* — SEARCHING.

ISOBEL
KUHN

NESTS ABOVE
THE ABYSS

OM
publishing

FOREWORD

O ne evening in the spring of 1942 the peace of
our quiet Szechwan town was rudely shattered by the appearance of a large convoy of trucks
and jeeps as a unit of the RAF. Though newly
arrived in China, they were already obliged to
move house in face of the Japanese advance from
Burma. With them, dusty and worn, came a dozen
or so Yunnan missionaries, and amongst them the
author of this book. That was our first introduction
to Isobel Kuhn. I shall never forget her as she
valiantly endeavoured in those days to adjust herself to low-lying Szechwan! The proverbial "duck
out of water" wasn't in it! She tried to find a quiet
spot, but alas! Our badly weeded and cramped
garden was such a contrast to the beauties and spa-
ciousness of the Yunnan mountains, and the Szechwanese to whom she spoke were so different from
the simple, approachable Lisu people. From the
second or third day she was eating her heart out to
get back! And the reason? Why, she had given her
heart, her love, her life to those laughter-loving
people of the hills of west Yunnan. Privation, loneliness and fatigue, though hard to bear for one of
her physique, could not keep her away longer than
necessary. As soon as conditions were easier in
Yunnan, off she went on a truck, accompanied only

by a young Chinese girl, to make the long, arduous journey back to the West.

It is impossible not to be impressed with the price that had to be paid to bring the Gospel to the Lisu of the Upper Salween Valley in west Yunnan, both by the Lisu from other districts and the incoming missionaries. Experience has shown that the best way of opening up new work is, where possible, first to send well-grounded Christian nationals to introduce the new message and life. In this way many prejudices are broken down and many preconceived ideas of Christianity are avoided. In 1919 J. O. Fraser wrote concerning the need of this area: "This district must be evangelized, but I want to find suitable natives to go first." It was a tremendous thing to ask the untravelled evangelists from the Lisu Church of the South to venture forth some sixteen days' journey into a land where food, dress and even speech were dissimilar, and dangers seen and unseen lurked round every corner. They responded for Christ's sake and the account of what they suffered is humbling indeed and brings forth afresh praise to the Lord who gave such enabling grace.

To follow up this opening amongst the Lisu of north-west Yunnan, in 1934 Mr and Mrs Kuhn left the last vestige of civilization on the Paoshan plain, and went to live amongst the mountain people of that region (until the Mission withdrew from China due to Communist pressure). Here amidst sin, squalor, poverty and darkness they have radiated the glory of the Master, and shown the redeeming and reclaiming power of the Cross, as these pen portraits reveal. That Isobel Kuhn was able to write so vividly about the doings of the

Lisu people is because she lived amongst them and, more still, lived with them; sharing with them their spiritual battles, big and small, and by her understanding sympathy entering into the very thoughts of their hearts. Mrs Kuhn did not gloss over sin, nor did she omit the failures of one or another, and yet she wrote with a note of triumph as she traced the growth downward and outward of some of the Christians.

The chapter on "Unseen Missionaries" places prayer in its right perspective to the missionary programme. For the experienced prayer warriors there is much here to encourage, while for the uninitiated in this realm of Christian warfare there is the challenge to undertake for the Master a prayer ministry which is perhaps even more precious and difficult, if properly executed, than going to a foreign land.

ARNOLD J. LEA

CONTENTS

Foreword

1.	The Munition of Rocks	1
2.	Beautiful Feet Reach the Canyon	16
3.	A Tree Beside the Waters	43
4.	Nest for Singing Bird	100
5.	A Rock in a Weary Land	121
6.	The Prey of the Terrible	163
7.	The Soul-seedling Patch	189
8.	A Thief Who Laboured to Give to Others	219
9.	The Unseen Missionaries	246
10.	"Jes' Pebbles"	269

Chapter 1

THE MUNITION OF ROCKS

SATAN has a stronghold–isolated and unchallenged for centuries–a great mountain canyon in West China. Its river takes its source in Tibet and its banks rise to the height of eleven to fifteen thousand feet. The tiers of mountain peaks, flung around chaotically on either side as far as the eye can see, are separated from each other by deep ravines and abysmal chasms. Impossible as it may seem, this canyon is inhabited by human beings, for everywhere you look the canyon sides are checked like patchwork quilt with little hamlets and · villages, and these almost perpendicular mountain sides are cut up into little squares or oblongs of farmed lands. Human homes, human nests, have been built on little knolls or jutting ridges that offer a scarce foothold–even over a dizzy drop down the bank. You may see them in such precarious positions that you almost hold your breath lest, even as you watch, they slide over the edge and disappear.

Anyone coming to the canyon must prepare to live perpendicularly as long as he stays; he must prepare to sweat and toil up and down steep mountain trails; he must prepare to live isolated from the rest of the world, from civilization with its medical, intellectual, and social comforts; he must prepare to have nature laugh at the feeble speck he is, and to have Satan hurl at him the fury of the hitherto unchallenged, unconquered lion faced in his own private lair. Surely this canyon is Satan's place of defence; here we will find his munition of rocks.

Are the Lisu tribespeople, who have built their nest-homes all over these mighty rocks where Satan reigns, enjoying the peace and happiness of living "the natural life?" (For some have said, "The heathen are happy: why disturb them?") Yes, they are just as happy and peaceful as fledglings in a nest built on a ledge of jutting rock over one of these mountain abysses, when the monsoon winds sweep like a hurricane through the canyon, and pine trees over a hundred feet tall are uprooted and hurled into space as easily as a child knocks down a twig in his sand pile. What chance has a little nest against such a strength? That wind is one of the munitions of rocks, and, as it hurls itself against the little dove's nest, with the dark gulf yawning beneath, what are the feelings of the poor little nestlings as they cling to the straw and sticks? They are a picture of the so-called "happy heathen" when one of the Sharp Winds of life strikes him. These Winds hit from many directions.

There is the *Wind of Physical Nature*. In the Rainy Season, when the soil is softened by constant drenching, an animal higher up may dislodge a boulder with his foot; that boulder is hurled down into the ravine and woe betide all living things in its path! I had pointed out to me one such that had killed a woman standing in her doorway and had smashed her shanty home. In 1935 a Lisu Christian was sleeping alone in a hut in his cornfield when, some time before dawn, a rock as large as a dining table (they said) got loosened from the heights above and crashed down. It hit his hut, struck the end of his bed, and bed and occupant were shot out of the door and a hundred feet down the mountainside. He was knocked unconscious, but came to out in the open, in the dark, with the rain beating on his face. His hut of a moment before was nothing but a wreck of splinters.

Another young man, going out early to plough after a heavy rainfall, was struck by another such rock and cut in two at the waist. His oxen ran home frightened at the sight of his mangled corpse. Abyss of physical destruction! When will the Sharp Wind hit?

Not only do landslides terrify the little nest, but earthquakes come just as unannounced. In May 1941 we were eating the midday meal in a Lisu shanty, when suddenly the shanty shook violently and we heard a great roar. One called out, "Thunder!" but the sun was shining brightly. Another shouted, "Aeroplane!" and we all rushed out to the edge of the high plateau to see. No aeroplane was visible, but before us lay a sight such as I had never seen in all my life. The whole opposite mountain range seemed to be belching smoke and clouds of dust everywhere. My first thought was that it had turned into a hundred-headed volcano. Then, however, I noticed that the fires were probably caused by the friction of the earthquake. Soon the whole opposite mountain range was hidden by a barrage of smoke and dust. It was a literal picture of Psalm 104:32: "He looks at the earth, and it trembles; he touches the mountains, and they smoke."

It did not clear until the next morning, for through the afternoon and long into the night again and again we heard the ominous roar of land sliding. Later we learned the sad details of that terror. Just one will illustrate. Forty Lisu were planting corn on a perpendicular field. The survivors said that all the intimation of danger they heard was when the earth shook; they heard a roar, looked up and saw the top of the mountain descending on them! When the dust and shock were over, of the forty persons only seventeen were to be found.

Sharp Winds from a Bitter Height! There is *the Wind of Merciless Heathendom*. In 1938, just thirty or forty miles to the south of us, a young heathen girl killed her husband and eloped with her lover. According to Chinese custom, she had been married (I suppose) against her own will, and when her true love came she eloped with him. They were caught and she was punished by being skinned alive. She was only eighteen years old. Poor little wind-torn nest! What a horrible abyss that is! Contrast with that this other little nest, hit by the very same Wind.

Going out along Sunset Trail one evening, I met a fellow-villager climbing up laboriously. She was carrying a babe tied in a sling in front of her bosom so that it could nurse easily. On the mother's back was a tall basket full of corn on the cob. The basket was so tall that it towered above her head. As she saw me descending, she rested her load against the hillside and her face lit up with a smile. "Ma-Ma," she said softly, calling me by my Lisu name. "S...!" I replied, greeting her by name. I was deeply moved and said, "How do you come to be carrying such a load? Don't you know that your body is not back to normal yet? This could give you life-long weakness. Where is your husband?"

"Oh, he's at home. But, Ma-Ma, you know him. He never does any work—just lives for the opium pipe. There was no food in the house and the little ones were hungry, so my mother gave me this load, but I have to carry it myself from Pine Mountain." (Pine Mountain is five miles away.)

I was very indignant, for her husband is a big, husky young fellow. "How did you ever come to marry such a man?" I asked.

"Why, Ma-Ma, it was arranged for me. You know our old heathen custom." She went on to tell me of the disappointment to find that the husband chosen for her was almost a devil. He was an opium-smoker, a thief, and would even sell their house furniture when she was absent in order to get money to buy opium. Yet in the telling of this her face was not bitter. There was a sweet peace upon it. As we parted she again thanked the Lord for meeting me and said, "Ma-Ma, take some corn out of my basket; they taste good roasted by the fire. I'd like to give some to you!" But I could no more accept that corn on the cob than David could drink of the water from the Well of Bethlehem. As I left her I thanked my Lord that He can bring an inward peace that passes understanding, that though the body is suffering, the spirit may dwell with Him in heaven. This little Nest had found the Cleft of the Rock hewn out for her, and when the Sharp Winds blowing upon her were too awful to bear, she could find peace in that Cleft.

Very pitiful times are they when the raw *Wind of Sickness* blows upon them. Knowing nothing of germs, they attribute it to the bite of demons and are terrified and helpless. They think it necessary to make animal sacrifices, and they must pay the wizard or witch also. For such a simple thing as malaria (for which the Salween canyon is notorious) all the livestock, one by one, may be killed off, and the family reduced to dire want. How can they plough such mountainsides without an ox?

Their poverty adds to their misery. I saw a man dying of cancer. His big emaciated frame was just skin-covered bone, yet he had to lie on a bare board day and night with no pillow to ease his pain. When he coughed up spittle they wiped it off with coarse straw paper which scratched his fevered lips mercilessly.

When a really dreaded disease like smallpox comes, they often desert their sick and flee into the fields. The needless sufferings of the sick are indeed a raw Wind. This very thing is one reason why they vie with one another to have the foreigner establish his home in their villages, for he brings his medicine and "unthinkable" ways of easing pain. Who can dare say, "The heathen are happy: leave them alone"?

There is a little Wind, not comparable with the monsoon, but it blows bitterly on some. It is the *Wind of Helpless Ignorance*. In the canyon a few Chinese schools have been established by the government. They are so isolated that they are not often inspected and the teachers soon become such opium-sots that even the heathen Lisu thinks it useless to send his children to sit under them. For this reason they are illiterate people. Until the missionary came and reduced their language to writing they had no books and could not of course write letters. When one's friend moved to another village, even though only a few miles away, it was like death. Possibilities of meeting again, or of any kind of communication were slim, especially for the women, who seldom travel. Yet when the Lisu are taught, they prove to be as intelligent as the other races. The Christians are keen to learn. An American, looking at a young Lisu Bible student once said, "That is a bright-looking boy. Just under-privileged, that's all." That same under-privileged one once sighed and said to me, "Ma-Ma, you white people are very fortunate. No matter what you want to study—farming, medicine, music, stones or stars, it seems there is someone who can teach you about it. We Lisu have no one to teach us anything, no matter how much we yearn to know."

A Lisu evangelist, being introduced to some American solders said, "All that we Lisu have, we owe to the white man." It is sweet to be needed and to be able to share.

But we are not through with these Winds. Daily there blows *the evil Wind of Sin*, blowing softly, wooingly at first, but most destructive of any in its end. Wide yawns the waiting abyss when this Wind blows.

With no shops, no radio, no books, no pleasures to break the humdrum monotony of their farm life, Satan knows the children of men must have some excitement, so he offers wine-drinking, quarrels, gambling, and immorality. When they have gambled away their money, they will often stake their children, their wives, even their own bodies as slaves. So in one night a whole family can be gambled away into life-long slavery.

I said the Wind of Sin blows softly at first. The Lisu are naturally singers and love music; and Satan and sin have given them a set of licentious yodel songs which they call, "Try-to-say-it." On the surface, I understand, it is nature-talk, as of birds, or the meetings of streams, but each is a metaphor so vile that no Christian Lisu will translate it for you or even repeat it. This suggestive metaphor is often composed spontaneously. At dusk the young men will melt on to the high trails and, as they slip along through the shadows, they will sing a line of challenge, yodelling it at the end. Their voices are carried down the mountainside by the clear air to a group of girls in a village, perhaps, or sleeping in a cornfield to guard the grain from wild animals, and these will answer back. This is where the Try-to-say-it comes in. There are time-used phrases, but if you are clever enough to make up a new one, he must find an answer to it. "Make up a harmless one, for an example," I once asked a Lisu evangelist. So he gave the following:

"I'd give the wide world to have you!" might come yodelling down the mountainside in a strong, young masculine voice.

A girl will take it up and yodel back, "My father's a good shot. You wouldn't dare come near our house!"

And so the musical word-combat, the Try-to-say-it gets under way. In the darkness the singer's position is hidden, indicated only by the direction of the voice. But urged on with home-made whisky, and a humdrum or unhappy day, one can understand the attraction of the unknown, unseen, offered love-call.

One night in a Lisu shanty, all the village around silent and dark, I was awakened. From far up on the high mountain peak towering above us, through the stillness, a chorus of yodels was coming. The clear, strong voices, full of youthful vim, were attractive, and they kept getting nearer and nearer. I understood nothing, discerned no words, but as I lay there unable but to listen, that musical young call lilting through the night made my flesh tingle. And then I knew the power of this "munition" from the Rock Height, and I prayed, "Oh Lord, keep your own tonight if there be any who must hear this. Oh, if I were a heathen girl with no Christ in my heart to quieten me, that call would entice. Thank you, Lord, that I am in you." And cuddling well into the Cleft of my Rock, I prayed on for younger ones upon whom that Sharp Wind was blowing. Not a voice from the village responded, so after about a half-hour of yodelling, the adventurers passed on and left us. But from then on, I knew why there are practically no pure young Lisu among the heathen. I heard a pretty heathen girl once boast, "There isn't a man in the valley can beat me at Try-to-say-it!" and her husband endorsed her proudly. That it was vile, licentious language in which she was so adept meant nothing to him.

But it is an abyss of destruction that awaits the little falling Nest. The unseen singer by daylight loses his glitter and often proves to be worse than the husband deserted for him. Homes are broken up; deformed children are born; and social diseases take their toll, and other unmentionable miseries perhaps, prove into what an awful pit the little Nest has fallen.

But the Cleft Rock (I Cor. 10:4) is making a difference. I once asked a handsome young Christian, "Do the girls ever yodel after you?"

"Sure they do—often from a cornfield as I go by," he replied.

"What do you do then?" I inquired curiously.

"Run down the road just as fast as I can!" he answered firmly. I could hardly keep my face straight at the picture thus conjured up, for this particular laddie was noted for his courage and valiance—yet in my heart how happy I was for his answer. He had been studying the scriptures and knew that God says unhesitatingly, more than once, "*Flee* youthful lusts" (2 Tim. 2:22; I Cor. 6:18). And God has rewarded. Three years ago He gave this young runaway a sweet little Christian wife, one whom an American soldier claimed was "the prettiest girl in the district."

One more Sharp Wind from the Bitter Height. The worst of all Satan's munitions of rocks is the *Wind of Death*; the spiritual hopelessness of the heathen Lisu, which, though pushed to the edge of his daily consciousness, every now and again sweeps in upon him with terror and horror.

A little bamboo hut on the mountainside. It is evening and the family is gathered around the central fire which blazes up and throws a golden light into every cranny of the simple primitive dwelling. Grandparents, father, mother and several children all are concentrating their attention on the little five-year-old son, who is lying on the wooden bed screaming.

"You shouldn't have told him!" expostulates one of the adults. "He is quite small yet. Too bad." (The speaker had no need to mention the death of their neighbour, whom the little boy had dearly loved. It was in all their thoughts.)

"Well, you can't keep it from him," retorts the oldest son. "He's heard the villagers talking about her. And besides he ought not to continue to run to her house the way he does. Her ghost" (in a lowered, fearful whisper) "might get him. She loved him so!"

"Yes, yes," says another, turning pale. "We all have to face this sooner or later. But it was early to tell him that some day he'd be put in the grave. He's only five years..."

"I won't! I won't!" shouts the child hysterically, sitting up and looking around. "You can die if you like; I'm not going to!"

"Who're you that can help it!" sneers his big brother. "Everybody has to..."

"Shut up, will you?" snaps their mother savagely; then, turning to the child, she tries to put her arms around him. "No, of course you won't, A-bi-rao; you..."

"You're a liar!" screams the child. "They say all of us have to die," and again he goes off into hysterical wails.

This is a typical scene, and that little child is the hero of one of the following pages. He told me the essence of that childhood terror, and how the Lisu have no hope beyond the grave, saying that for years after that awful introduction to the fact of death he could not come upon a grave on the mountainside without getting cold all over.

Another young evangelist, in quite a different part of Lisuland, told me he was six years old when he first learned of death, and cried so hard and so long that he was ill for days. Sharp Wind

from a devilish height! The Wind may scare the
nestlings, but it is nothing to the terror of looking
over the side and seeing the gulf yawning beneath!
And as for loved ones who must bury their
dead–they sometimes weep themselves blind, and
some go out of their mind. The Lisu have told me
of such.

The wizard of the village may be asked to perform *Ma-mu*. This is an incantation for calling up
the dead. Animal sacrifices are offered; the wizard
goes through his rites and becomes possessed. He
says his soul is wandering up the canyon to the
north, searching for the dead one. He will tell what
he sees in his search; local places known to all,
places farther north known but dimly. Then he will
"find" the dead one. When that occurs, the dead
man or woman's voice will come through the
wizard's mouth and talk to the family. The voice is
identical with that of the dead one and makes the
relatives sob with excitement. Sad reminiscences of
past days or loving greetings to this one or that are
accompanied with no word of peace as to the
present state of the departed. When the incantation
is over, no comfort has been obtained, grief and
loss have been newly stirred up, and that is all that
a Lisu wizard can achieve. After some years (if I remember rightly) the dead man's spirit cannot be
traced...he is "gone". No wonder a loving heart
grieves itself blind or mad. And other hearts
harden themselves. I heard a heathen mother tell
of the death of a darling girl of twelve or thirteen.
"I was grieving myself ill, so..." She laughed
lightly. "Forget her! Make an end of it!" She had
hardened her heart and become so shallow that no
call for pity or thoughtfulness could evoke a

response in her.

"Once you were not a people, but now you are the people of God; once you had not received mercy, but now you have received mercy," (I Peter 2:10).

The great heart of God yearned over these lost ones, over these little nests hopelessly perched above the mouth of the awful abyss, and now Lisuland has a Cleft in the Rock wherein to hide when the cruel Wind of Death blows by.

I remember a wooden chapel on a high mountainside. It was packed to the doors for an evening meeting. The speaker was the five-year-old boy mentioned above, now grown up and well-known evangelist among them. He was relating that story, and went on to tell of a later year when he heard Leila Cooke speak on "I am the resurrection, and the life: he who believes in me will live, even though he dies."

"As she explained that verse," he said, "suddenly the truth of it broke in on my understanding, and the fact of *eternal life*, a life after death, a hope beyond the grave, shone before me. I was thrilled through and through; faith and acceptance of the Saviour were born right then in my soul. It was that verse on the resurrection that brought me to Christ; and I have a feeling that I am not the only Lisu to become a believer because of this truth. All of you who were led to become Christians by the resurrection doctrine, hold up your hands!" And all over the building hands shot into the air and the glowing joy on their faces told its own story.

I have heard the wail of the heathen for their dead and my heart could hardly stand the hopelessness of their agony. But praise God for the

refuge of the Cleft Rock, when the Wind of Death
sweeps down from the Bitter Height.

One evening as I was viewing the lovely sunset
from our front garden, a servant came around the
corner of the house, and with a grave face said,
"Ma-Ma! Cha-fu-yi is dead. He was drowned in the
ravine stream this morning. His parents are just
carrying his body home on their backs now."

"Oh, no!" I cried out, for Cha-fu-yi was the
darlingest Lisu youngster that I knew, and the
pride of his parents. As I hurried up the hill to
their house, memories of the wee fellow crowded
in on me.

He was always so plucky. When he was very
small he had taken sick and my husband was
called upon to give him some bitter medicine; so of
course, baby-like, he thereafter viewed the big
White Man as an enemy who put nasty stuff in
your mouth! One day in playing he unconsciously
wandered into our front yard and, looking up,
suddenly saw John standing on the house platform. Scared, he started to cry and retreat as fast as
small legs could take him. John called out to him
not to be afraid, but, thinking that was a subtle
snare, the little lad was all the more upset. His
daddy had taught him to protect himself from
dogs by throwing rocks at them, so, as John again
called out to him, he stooped down and picked up
a big stone to guard himself from the White
Monster. He looked so sweet, so baby-brave, the
tears rolling down his small nose, the big stone
tightly clutched in tiny fist, and the chubby legs
trying to run fast in retreat. Valiant-hearted to the
last gasp—that was little Cha-fu-yi. What could one
say to comfort his parents at such a loss? As I ran

toward their house, I prayed in my heart for words, but I had no need for them.

As I came up to the sad scene–the little six-year-old figure was laid out on a plank of wood, Daddy, Mummy, and neighbours all weeping–his father turned to me and said, "It's all right, Ma-Ma. If he had grown up he might have gone into sin." And then we talked of heaven and the joy of the reunion there.

The stories that succeed this are all of little nests, perched always over the mouth of the abyss, but with a Cleft Rock that follows them through all their storms.

Chapter 2

BEAUTIFUL FEET REACH THE CANYON

How beautiful on the mountains are the feet of those who bring good news, who proclaim peace, who bring good tidings, who proclaim salvation, who say to Zion, "Your God reigns!"

Isa. 52:7

"**M**AMMA! Mamma!" cries of delightful terror bought small children running to their mothers to bury their heads on the familiar shelter of the blue apron, while one ear was kept free to hear the exciting talk of the older ones.

"Yes, truly, he is *white-skinned!* My husband told me—he is down there in Li-yi-gwey-pa's house, looking at the creature. I'd love to go too, only I dare not! It must be a demon. Who else would have human shape, yet a white skin? And they say his eyes are not black, but the colour of the river and..."

"Then *of course* he's a demon! We all know the demons can take human form. No, I wouldn't dare go either, and I'm so glad the children are afraid to go. Demons steal children," and the speaker embraces tightly the small, excited form buried in her apron.

"But they say he's awfully nice! Such a kind smile, and he talks Lisu and also speaks Chinese.

He has other people with him too, that talk the same sort of funny Lisu and they are black-haired, black-eyed and olive-skinned like us. They say they are Flowery Lisu from down the tail of the canyon. That could be true; you know we are called Black Lisu and..."

"Are we?" pipes up a young girl. "Why? We aren't any blacker than the Chinese."

"It isn't our skins, daughter," speaks up an old granny condescendingly, "it's our clothes. We wear this navy blue, but those Flowery Lisu! You should see what they wear"—in a tone of contemptuous disgust—"all red and green and white checks, with cowrie shells to trim the borders of their aprons, and red, blue, and white leggings, and..."

"How do you know, Grannie?" demands Miss Inquisitive. "Where did you see them?"

"When I eloped with A-fu-me-pa—that time we ran off to Burma until the old folks' wrath was appeased. The Lisu across the mountains from here still dress like that. But to go back to this white man—haven't you girls heard the old tradition that a White Lisu is going to come some day and be our king? If he has Lisu with him, maybe this is..."

At this point a twelve-year-old boy who has stalked up to the group breaks into the gossip and exclaims proudly, "I've *seen* him!"

"Oh, have you? What's he like?" eagerly from the now swelling crowds of timid yet enthralled females.

"He has a nose *this* high," says young Show-off, exaggerating, boy fashion, and carving a nose for himself out of the air, that makes the girls scream.

"Oh, how awful. That's a demon, sure! They have noses like beaks; they're part bird, some of them," and thus the conversation swayed back and forth, palpitating with excitement and fear.

The women and children were terrified and would not go near him. The men and some boys of about twelve were bolder and even gathered to converse. They were afraid of his white skin, blue eyes and the high nose we foreigners all have. He stayed only one night and never came again, but the old people still talk of it.

The "Munition of Rocks" was first entered for Christ by James Outram Fraser, whose life is told in the book *Behind the Ranges*.[1] But the strangeness of his white-man appearance so monopolized interest that no one remembers his message. J.O. Fraser was not slow to learn a lesson. This is one of the reasons why he laid down the rule that Lisu heathen should be evangelized by Lisu Christians, the foreigner staying in the background to inspire forward movement, to pray, and to teach the churches when established.

Five years passed, and Fraser with his colleagues were still busy establishing the Flowery Lisu church and caring for a new movement southward. The Munition of Rocks is to the north of their original work, and continued in its darkness, but a yearning God once more brought them to the pioneer missionary's attention. In 1919 Fraser wrote, "Last market day I met some Lisu from the Upper Salween. They were carrying tremendously heavy loads of betel-nut to sell. 'Come up to our village and teach us,' one of them said–his village is about sixteen days' journey away. 'We will give

---

[1] Now out of print, but Fraser's story is told in *Mountain Rain* written by his daughter Eileen Crossman (OMF Books).

you food—rice and pork—as much as ever you want.' Though he meant it sincerely, he was too busy to do more than just invite me. That district *must* be evangelized, but I want to find suitable nationals to go first."

Such were not easy to find. There were many dear Christians capable of being sent, but it was a tremendous thing to ask of any. The Upper Salween was at that time almost unknown; it was fourteen or more days' journey away from the mother church. It was peopled by Black Lisu, which meant difference in dialect, food, and customs. The postal system in the canyon is so negligible (only one post office in a six-day stretch, and that post office received mail only once in ten days) as to reckon none at all in Lisu eyes. There was no medical aid to be had anywhere, and those who had accompanied Mr Fraser on his exploration trip, in addition to calling it "a wild, inhospitable region," must have added stories of its famous fevers. A scholar's recent book declares it "The most malarial spot in the world", and quotes this US Army account of it: "Apparently well men, trudging along the mountain passes, would suddenly flush, complain of the fire in their heads, then die." The author's own trip to the Salween he calls "flirting with death," and he would have entered with pack mules of medicine, comforts, and protectives. Lisu evangelists take only what they can carry on their own backs. And with the easier southern field just opened up to the gospel and calling for volunteer preachers, it is not surprising that by 1922 (when Mr Fraser had to go home on furlough, never again, as unexpected events proved, to be free to give all his time just to

Lisu work) the Munition of Rocks was still Satan's unchallenged stronghold.

Yet, God had written their faces on a loving faithful heart which never forgot "the people waiting, accessible, and in desperate need," which his trip of 1914 had revealed to Mr Fraser. In leaving for the homelands, he must have referred this burden to Carl Gowman, who, with Mr and Mrs Allyn Cooke, were his successors in the work. The Cookes were vitally linked up with the evangelistic spread southward, and so we find Carl Gowman taking up the burden of the Upper Salween thousands, with a valiance of faith and passion of vision that would not be defeated.

How long he tried to get an opening, I do not know; but about 1927 Mr Gowman was writing to the Lisu church, "We need preachers for the Upper Salween!" One young heart felt that call. He who had been the missionary's goatherd, small in stature, badly disfigured with pockmarks; he who had been the most stupid student in the class learning Chinese—this one wrote to Mr Gowman and offered. "I know that originally I am a Black Lisu, and that my forefathers came down the canyon from up there, and God has given me a sign that He wants me to go for Him."

I wonder how Carl Gowman felt, when, in mind's eye, he saw his first candidate for the Munition of Rocks! Had I been there, I know I would have been disappointed. I would have been hoping for a big fellow, "a man of presence," a walking photograph of Great Heart! It is a land of giants—giant peaks, giant winds, giant disease, giant spiritual forces. But, "God does not look on the outward appearance," and Mr Gowman accepted the goatherd. He accepted that first one but he wisely waited for the Christmas festival to present the challenge.

A day or so before the birthday of Christ, every Christian Lisu village is making its preparations to send a contingent, young and old, everyone who can go, to the Christmas celebration. The poorer women are washing their clothes in the approved Lisu manner, treading them with bare feet under the flow of some nearby stream. But if at all possible, new garments are prepared, so the needles too are flying busily. Then each person must bring a certain amount of grain, salt and pork for the feast, so the foot mills are busy pounding out the corn, and the early morning hears many a pig give its final squeal, as abundance of pork is what makes a Lisu meal into a feast!

Then, early on the appointed day, all over the mountains, a delegation from each village set out. Merry holiday laughter and teasing ring out as they file out along the trails, all converging gradually toward the missionary's home of Stockade Hill. Before they have come in sight of the village, *Bang! Bang!* goes a gun over their heads, and the long file all turn to nod and smile at one another, knowing that the lookout party has spied them, and that the gun's reverberations are to wake up the welcoming committee! So up the hill they toil (or down the mountains, for at Stockade Hill many guests would be descending from the top of the mountain range) and as soon as the village slope is sighted, they come upon a floral arch with smiling faces peeking at them from underneath. Here they must halt while the other side tunes up.

"One-three-five (doh-me-soh)," sings out the leader of the reception committee. "Let it come!" And voices in four parts rise up from behind the flowers.

Christmas guests are at the door!
   Let them in.
It is duty to receive them,
   Let them in.

That of Jesus we may think,
   His Great Day that we may keep;
Praise to God, we come to greet.
   Let them in!

Then through the arch they come, shaking hands with each of the long line of singers, after which they are free to check their food supplies and seek out a place to sleep. Singing groups and sports fill in the time until the big evening service.

It was at one of these evening meetings that Carl Gowman gave out his challenge. Jesus' birthday! A chance to give to Him who gave us so much. On winter days, Lisu farmers are free, and the Lord's harvest is waiting to be reaped. "Over thirty men are needed to volunteer for evangelistic work," Mr Gowman said, "and of these, four men are wanted to go for Christ to the Upper Salween! One of those four has already offered; three more are needed to go with him!"

After that service, around the different home-fires, there was much discussion of that challenge.

"I'd like to go to the Upper Salween," says one fine-looking young fellow of about twenty-one years of age, hands clasped around his legs, chin on knees, eyes brooding into the flames.

"Go on with you!" anxiously thrusts in his

mother. "That's no job for a married man! And you've a child, besides a wife. Volunteer if you must, for the south country! Mr and Mrs Cooke are there; they'd look after you, give you medicine if you get sick, send your letters on to us. Pastor needs more men for the south than he does for the north—he said he wanted some thirty!"

"That's because he had no hope of getting so many for the north," comes the quiet answer. "He'll get thirty for the south—that's not very hard. But he may not get four for the north, that's why I'd like to go there. Thousands of Lisu are there," he said. And again the dark eyes brooded into the fire with a gleam in them that set his mother crying.

"*A-eh! A-eh!* He's going to volunteer for the Upper Salween and I'll never see him again. He'll die there of those awful fevers! *A-eh*. We'll never hear what's happened to him, for there's no mail up there. *A-eh*."

"Be quiet!" orders her husband. "Son, be careful what you do. Don't throw your life away. Remember you don't know the customs of the Black Lisu. They might not receive the gospel like we did. And if what your mother says is true..."

"It's not all true. Pastor Payne at the city of Paoshan has promised to keep an eye on us, and forward mail and supplies to us; and besides, there can be no harvest for Christ in those parts until someone takes a risk. Job, the goatherd, is going; he needs a partner. I'm going to volunteer." Then started the wails of the women and expostulations of relatives. Job told me, years afterwards, that not one of the four found it easy to say yes. The above arguments and more were anxiously poured upon

them. But on the last night when Carl Gowman
gave the final call, three more men stood up one by
one: Andrew, Wa-si, and twenty-one year old La-
ma-wu. I am sure the eyes of the Christian men
shone with pride as they looked up into those four
determined young faces, and I am sure their
mothers swayed back and forth on the benches,
weeping. Never had four Lisu evangelists faced
such an unknown, distant and bleak parish. "You
may get sick and die!" cried more than one
anxious-faced relative, and not without ground for
their fears, for of the four that went, only three
returned. But more of that anon.

Our next picture of the little band with beautiful
feet is after seven days' travel over strange country
into Chinaland. One day they appeared, dusty and
bewildered, in the courtyard of Mr and Mrs
Talmadge Payne, who were living at that time in
the Chinese city of Paoshan. The thrill of their
adventure would once more be brought back to
them in the joyous welcome the missionaries
accorded them. Seven days of tramping through
unfamiliar and indifferent country can take the
glow off any enthusiasm. You don't realize how
long is the road from home to your destination
until you go over it foot by foot, money diminish-
ing each day. I wonder if their faces, as they came
in the courtyard that day, were not a little
woebegone and anxious. One thing I am sure
of—they did not look like "heroes of the faith"
about to push into one of Satan's most impreg-
nable strongholds. Maybe they looked more like
children who have wandered away from home,
dazed and wistful, yet determined not to cry.
Having seen other such Lisu missionary parties

arriving in Chinaland, I know they appeared poverty-stricken and ill-at-ease, suddenly conscious of bare feet and mountain manners. I heard one such boy say something like this, "When I saw the fine houses of the Chinese and how they live, I felt myself to be like a monkey just dropped down from the tree-tops."

But those dear, devoted missionaries saw them as they were in the spirit–God's beautiful feet, sent to carry the news of salvation to His lost one, and they welcomed them as such. And I would like to say here (for these days some are emphasizing the use of national workers to a degree that outrules the missionary) these four would never have accomplished their mission, if it had not been for the earnest, loving backing of Mr and Mrs Talmadge Payne. As you will hear soon, again and yet again, the little band fell back fainting in spirit, to be caught up in the strong arms of Mr and Mrs Payne's faith and almost thrust into the canyon afresh.

Their second encouragement (the first would be a season of sweet fellowship at Jesus' feet) was to hear Mr Payne say, "I have supplies for you. From now on, I am your base of supplies. When you need money just come to me." A few dollars to buy some rice for present need clinking merrily in their pockets, the four start out for the town, and the excitement of a Chinese market. In their lonely hillside hamlets was nothing comparable to this rendezvous from the point of wares, numbers of people, or noise. It is like a mountaineer walking down Fifth Avenue or Piccadilly with the roar of a big city around him. Everything glitters and looks wonderful; the things you cannot afford to buy are as much fun to look at as the choosing of a bit of pork for dinner.

And then the people! To some Lisu the throngs of human beings were more fascinating than the tables of merchandise. Mostly Chinese farmers attended Paoshan Market, but frequently Lisu from the Munition of Rocks and even Tibetans brightened the spectacle with their varied costumes. On one such occasion, the four, hearing a Lisu sentence behind them, turned around to see a band of Black Lisu closely grouped together and talking to one another. Excitedly La-ma-wu and his friends accosted them and the Chinese farmers turned to stare at this large circle, blocking the traffic and babbling in a strange tongue—but only for a moment. "Earth people!" they say contemptuously, lose interest and press on.

"Where are you staying? Can you understand us? We're Flowery Lisu from the Burma border. We want to come to your parts. We'd like to talk to you—where are you staying?"

"Oh," with a wild boisterous laugh, "where do Lisu stay when they come to town? You'll find us out on the city wall tonight after the stars appear."

The writer remembers meeting just such a group at the very same market; and then that night, searching for them on the wall. Too poor to pay inn-fare, and children of the open always, there they were, cosily encircling a wood-fire; the flames leaping up brought their turbaned heads, beaded necklaces, and strong handsome faces into the light. Above their heads the stars shone brilliantly, and behind them in dark shadow, stretched out the almost unlit streets of the Chinese city. A Lisu campfire? La-ma-wu would be entirely at home, and pulling a loose stone over for a seat, the band of four would soon be lost in thrilling conversation.

"Yes, I can understand you, though your talk is funny," says one big fellow with a loud laugh, shifting his long knife to a more comfortable position at his side. "We're Black Lisu, but we don't come from the Salween canyon, we come from the Mekong. Eh?... ... Oh, the Mekong river runs parallel to the Salween–you can cross over to the Salween from our parts, one good long day's journey. But there are lots of Black Lisu in the Mekong. Why not come back with us? We'd like to hear your story. We're going back tomorrow, I think. We brought coffin boards down to trade for blankets–see?" pulling a new scarlet one around his shoulders with evident satisfaction. "Can't get such things up in the mountains."

They talked well on into the night. Lisu love to chat around the fire, and knowing no such thing as "hours," it is often very late before they retire. Going to bed is a simple thing to the Lisu traveller. He simply buries his fire for breakfast's use, curls up in his blanket and–he's asleep.

The four consulted Mr Payne, for it was the Salween Lisu they had been asked to evangelize (and for whom there had been years of prayer) but might not God want them to go to the Mekong first? Here were guides all ready to take them! So it was decided to go back with these Mekong Lisu.

Money for food along the way was supplied by Mr Payne but Lisuland is different from Chinaland. The magnificently beautiful mountain giants are cold and indifferent to the human speck who tries to live along their sides, so the human specks, recognizing a common struggle for existence, are banded together in necessary loyalty. No Lisu of the Munition of Rocks, heathen or otherwise, charges a traveller for lodging or food. Free hospitality is a point of honour among them, so money for food after they reached Lisuland had not been given to the four.

This produced a difficult situation, for the Mekong Lisu turned out to have a different custom. Their guides were good to them in a way, but too full of thoughts of displaying their market spoils to the home folk to care about the message of the cross. When the party arrived, La-ma-wu and his companions were shown into the home of one of their guides. Almost immediately they sensed a different atmosphere. Their welcome was not very cordial. Their southern dialect was openly laughed at. When at length the market chatter finally wore out and they were given a hearing, it was not a friendly one.

"It's a strange story; we've never heard it before.It wouldn't be convenient," with a yawn, "for us to change our customs. Why don't you try going over to the Salween canyon? Maybe they'd like to be Christians over there."

Clearly there was no response of faith and no interest was shown. Remember that there had been no special prayer preparation for this field. La-ma-wu would easily discern, moreover, that extended hospitality was not going to be given cheerfully; so one morning, with courteous "Thank you's" (which the Black Lisu just gaped and laughed at–it not being the custom to say thank you up there), the little band started off into the unknown–down, down the mountainside until, a little knoll affording a resting place, they stopped for a word of prayer and to encourage each other.

"Should we try going to the Salween?" questioned Andrew. "I hear there are no villages anywhere the whole journey across—it would be easy to get lost," said Wa-si.

"And we know the way back now, from here, but we would have no notion of the way out of the Salween canyon," offered La-ma-wu.

"I think so too," put in Job. "Look, you can see Lisu villages all over these mountains. We've tried only one village in this canyon so far. Let's go on, I say. Folks are praying for us, don't forget."

"Don't know about you fellows," piped up La-ma-wu, "But I'm still hungry. *Eh-eh*, I wish we could buy some rice. I just can't eat enough of this corn to get filled. But can't the Black Lisu stow it away, though! I counted nine bowls one of those chaps ate this morning. By the time I'd got four down I felt stuffed to the eyebrows—yet I didn't feel satisfied."

"Me too," said Andrew. "I've felt hungry ever since I've been here. They didn't serve us rice once, not once. I do hope some of those other places have rice!"

But no. In those northern reaches, corn is the staple diet. All the four were accustomed to eating rice, just like the Chinese, and it takes a considerable period to get adjusted, so they were hungry all the time, Job told me. Heartache was added to hunger pangs. Village after village did they climb to, only to be laughed at, argued with, and sometimes shown the door.

"We'd drop in at the first house of the village," they related later, "and not only the gospel was refused, but lodging and food also. 'Try the house above,' they'd say. We'd climb up there, only to be pointed to the house above that. Sometimes we'd go through the whole village, and arriving at the highest house, have them point us back to the bottom house which had already shown us the door. It was heart-sickening.

"Once we missed the road, and for a day and a half had nothing at all to eat. I'll tell you, that was tough," and there was a silent pause, as memory brought back the horrors and spiritual testings of that experience. "You'll never come back alive..." that wail of heart-anxious loved ones must have recurred often during those thirty-six hours without food, lost on the strange, wild, inhospitable mountains. When at length a village and a road were sighted, it is no wonder that the courage of one of the four faltered.

"I've had enough," said Andrew. "I'm going home. It's no use. These folk up here don't want the gospel. We don't know the country nor the trails and—I think we'd better wait until someone who knows more about the place can come with us. A foreigner could hire guides. Mr Fraser didn't get lost. I think we're wasting our days to stay on."

"Go back with not a single soul won for Christ? That's not satisfying to me. And we've never even been to the place we started out for—the Salween Canyon!"

The four argued back and forth. Lonely, heartsick, discouraged and hungry, they finally decided to go back to the missionary at least. He stood to them for fellowship, comfort, counsel and—not one would dare to mention it, but each would think of it!—a square meal of rice! But all the way back to

Paoshan the hearts of three of them were unhappy.
Volunteers for the Upper Salween! They could hear
Mr Gowman's stirring call, could see the faces of
their fellows glow with joy and pride as they four
stood up to volunteer; and now—sneaking back
empty. Thank God, there was a white missionary
near to cast strong loving arms of courage and
faith around them at that time! And like the true
"Big Brother," as they called him, he went a second
mile.

"I'll take you into the Upper Salween myself," he
said earnestly. "Not even Andrew is going back
home now, not until you've been where you were
called!"

That is how, after a few days of rest and refreshment, the beautiful feet started out again, this time
on a new road in every sense. The Lisu tribes
people are simple and childlike in disposition.
Through God-given wisdom, Mr Fraser established
an indigenous church—self-supporting, self-governing and self-propagating; but all the Lisu I have
ever known, never work so happily as when there
is a "Big Brother" somewhere near for fellowship
and counsel. I'm sure Mr Payne's escorting them
into the canyon played no small part in the harvest
which ensued. Like a mother's hand smoothing the
brow of a child in feverish sleep, it just did
something to the four.

Through twisting ravine and over mountain-top
the beautiful feet of God's messengers came nearer
and nearer the Munition of Rocks. Late afternoon
of the fourth day as they came on to a little
mountain promontory, the panorama of the
Salween canyon lay before them. Giant twisted
convulsions of rock lie, contortion upon contortion,

in every shape and form as far as eye can see; with a green ribbon of "the river-without-a-bottom" crawling in and out at their feet. Right before them the mountainside sloped in grassy sward to the river's brink, and across the river on another velvet slope lay the little fortified hamlet called Six Treasuries, glistening white against the green grass and trees.

Feudalism still reigned in the Munition of Rocks. The owner of one of those white castles told me he had purchased a whole mountain for six hundred Chinese dollars, and automatically all the Lisu on that mountain became his serfs. His personal servants (that is, those who "ate his rice" every day) numbered one hundred, and he showed us the huge pillars of his courtyard, each a whole tree trunk, felled from his own land by Lisu servitors. He also took us upstairs and showed us the fortifications of his castle. Brigands had attacked and destroyed the hamlet some years previously, and when he rebuilt he had gun-turrets made, and could now hold it against several hundred attackers, so he believed. He also showed us a roll-top desk, an organ and many other beautiful pieces of civilized, hand-carved furniture, made by the carpenters which he had brought all the way from Shanghai for that purpose.

Doubtless all this was shown to Mr Payne also, for this feudal laird liked to entertain strangers, and was the only enterprising laird I ever met. And thus the gate to the Canyon was entered.

"Are there many Lisu in these parts?" received the answer, "Many? Thousands. Everywhere, both sides of the river!" So, using the laird's home as a base, the four were sent out. Horse-Grass-Level was the place first visited. As Mr Payne was with them, we may be sure there was much prayer made unitedly before they set forth, but even so the Lisu encountered were slow to accept the message. Hospitality, however, was generously offered, and some said they would believe "when the wine was all drunk up." When the time came for Mr Payne to return to his wife at Paoshan, he could sense the four were losing courage.

"Andrew, you go up the canyon a way. Try a few more places and I'll wait until you come back." Then, at what seemed the eleventh hour, God gave the increase. On a steep mountainside, in the little hamlet of Falling Timbers, fifteen families accepted Christ, and promised to throw out their demon altars. One other family, where there was a young girl named Homay, nearer to the Chinese laird, had also promised to turn, so Andrew hastened back with his glad news and sent for the other three.

With what a thankful heart the five missionaries gathered in that first little home (Homay's) to tear down the demon altar and proclaimed Christ as Saviour and Lord! He had not failed their faith. he had not wasted their sacrifice. A great harvest was awaiting them, urged Mr Payne, and they must be bold in faith and push on. But homesickness must have been written on the faces of the four, for Mr Payne did a very wise and strategic thing.

"It's not time for all to go home now with victory just beginning. You stay here and cover as many villages as you can, and in one month I'll be back. I'll return myself, after a month, and we can then see what God has done, and again consult together."

Andrew, though, had reached the end of his endurance. "If you're going back, Pastor, I'm going with you," he said; and no pleadings could shake him. But the other three were willing to stay. *Stop, when the first fruit had just been gleaned?* They would never be satisfied all their lives if they did that. No, it must be a month's more hardship, a month's more eating corn (for corn is the staple food of the Salween too) and toiling up these mountainsides much more precipitous than in their home mountain country. Andrew would take word back of how difficult the task was, the mother church would pray, and they could send letters by Andrew, and—send for help! Maybe some other of the young fellows would come in and relieve them, now that a way in was cleared. Yes, hope shone a little brighter, and when Mr Payne and Andrew said goodbye, the three watched them go with happier hearts.

> Give me the love that leads the way,
>   The faith that nothing can dismay,
> The hope no disappointments tire,
>   The passion that will burn like fire.
> Let me not sink to be a clod,
>   Make me thy fuel, Flame of God.
>   AMY CARMICHAEL.

Now up the canyon go the beautiful feet—not flying with winged sandals, but plodding painfully in the hot and weary dust. The new believers were not stable—that is, not all of them; but here and there an earnest young face gladdened their hearts—that girl Homay, for instance. And up past Homay's house, on a high promontory commanding a magnificent view of the canyon, was a village called Deer Pool, where the most promising group of all had already built a chapel. In fact, Mr Payne said that he and his wife were going to move in and live for a while right at Deer Pool, which news created much joy and excitement. Almost unnoticed among the worshippers on Sunday was a young girl of about fifteen, the Leah of the following pages.

And up the canyon by the main road (a trail too narrow for an automobile) the village of Pine Mountain impressed them as large and important. The harvest reaped there seemed large at first, though in reality it proved shallow. Nevertheless, Old Big, whose story is told in our last chapter, was one of the firstfruits of that village.

Higher up the same mountain to an altitude of some eight thousand feet is the village of Plum Tree Flat: you will hear of little Amos after a while; that is his village. So the work spread.

North of Pine Mountain the message was not received so easily at first, but across the river on the west bank of the Salween Squirrel's Grave, Sandalwood Flat, and Village-of-the-Olives yielded fruit that was to remain. Gad, of whom you will read, was from Squirrel's Grave.

But as the three travelled up and down mountainsides they kept hearing of Luda Village and Shangpa, said to be six or seven days' journey up the head of the canyon. The Lisu up there were quite different in dialect. Another tribe, called Nosu, was to be found there also. Eagerly Job laid before Mr Payne the need to push farther on, to carry the Good News as far as human foot could take it.

By this time the Paynes were in residence at Deer

Pool (a pioneering effort whose hardships and sufferings were to tell on his dear wife, and was one reason they could not continue on in Lisu work), and Andrew's return to the mother church had produced the hoped-for results. Reinforcements arrived. As soon as possible (for the work in Oak Flat district badly required teachers) Mr Payne gave the longed-for approval, and suggested that one of the new volunteers, Luke, should go northward with Job.

That trail up the canyon has been described by an experienced pioneer as "the hardest travel in China." Certainly that was true of it in the old heathen days. A considerable section of it we call "The Robber District," for obvious reasons, and those hold-up men kill to rob. But it was not only fear of evil men; those inner parts of the canyon afford a bare living and food was scarce. Often the boys were hungry and had to tighten their belts as they pushed on, but the passion of conquest was on them.

> Then with a rush the intolerable craving
> Shivers throughout me like a trumpet call,
> Oh, to save some!...

You can imagine, then, their feelings as one day, five days north of Deer Pool, they came upon an old man on the road.

"Boys, are you travellers in these parts?" he addressed them, eyeing their Flowery Lisu costumes and book bags.

"Yes, we are teachers, come to tell you of a life after death," replied Job. He said he always preached the resurrection everywhere he went.

"*A-bo!* Isn't that wonderful!" exclaimed the old

man, sitting down on the earth bank of the trail. "We'd heard rumours that teachers who could tell you of those things had come into the canyon, lower down! And I've been longing to hear; I have been on the point of sending my two sons to find you! *A-egh! A-egh!* This is a wonderful day for me. You'll stay at my house tonight, of course! Come, let's go there now. You will be thirsty and hungry." So, talking excitedly, he led the way up a near trail to his village.

"I just knew my urge to come to these parts was not an idle one!" cried out Job ecstatically as they followed the old man. And that night saw the beginning of a new harvest, that of the Luda District Church, numbering to-day some two thousand Christians.

By 1932 missionaries of other missions had entered the canyon north of Luda; still farther beyond them, in later years, the Tibetan-Border Mission opened a station; so that the Munition of Rocks was at last invaded.

That stronghold of Satan, for so many centuries even unchallenged, has not "fallen"—oh, don't think that! Nor is the fight for it ended. A keen price of suffering and lives has been paid. Three white missionaries and one Lisu home missionary lie buried in the Luda district alone; and two Lisu home missionary graves keep solemn watch in the Oak Flat (Deer Pool) district.

Job and Luke were a month teaching the new converts when a call from Mr Payne brought them back. On hearing the grand results they had witnessed, Mr Payne suggested that Luke return, with La-ma-wu as companion, Job being needed elsewhere.

It was many long months now since Job and La-ma-wu had left home, but both were still pressing the battle to the gates. Several months in the Luda district brought in more families won to Christ; then the two young evangelists started back for Deep Pool, La-ma-wu hoping to go all the way home to his little family in Stockade Hill.

As they approached Oak Flat, La-ma-wu said he was not feeling well. But Deer Pool was only a day away, and then they would see their beloved white missionaries and get some medicine. So the two lads pressed on. It is a long and stiff climb, up from the Oak Flat ravine; over two thousand feet they had to ascend. Unknown to them, the virulent fever of the Salween had laid its death fingers on dear young La-ma-wu, for, as they reached the high level where the trail crosses that mountain, with the village of Deer Pool almost in view, La-ma-wu fell, like a shock of corn under the sickle.

He was only twenty-three years old: and what bitter grief to the comrade who had to bury him there by the roadside, away from wife, child, and even human habitation, the wild mountain trees and grasses waving over him while the Salween River moaned nearly eight thousand feet below.

It was Easter, 1938, before I learned the above story. My first Easter in Lisuland, it was, and we wanted to teach the growing church the importance and wonder of that celebration.

"Has the church no dead around here?" I asked Job, who happened to be back in the canyon, ministering again. It was then Job told me about La-ma-wu. My heart was stirred within me.

"Has there never been any monument put up there, Job?" I asked earnestly.

"Lisu don't use monuments, Ma-Ma," he replied, "But there isn't even a proper grave. It is sunken into the mountainside and in a few more years even I won't be able to find it. Guess I'm the only one around who knows where it is. I've thought more than once, as I passed, that we ought to do something, but we're all so busy..."

"No, not too busy to reclaim the resting place of God's corn of wheat, who gave his young life that the gospel might enter the canyon! The Lisu church ought never to forget La-ma-wu! And it will be grand and fitting that their first Easter service should be held at his grave."

And so it was planned. Easter morning found us in the village of Border Mountain, which is the nearest Christian village to La-ma-wu's grave. Four o'clock in the morning found Job, his wife Rhoda, Dorcas (a Nosu girl) and I, slipping out through the shadows of the sleeping village to stand on a rock there, and awaken them all with singing *Christ the Lord is Risen Today!* At first all was cold and dark, the surrounding mountain peaks dim and black against the breaking dawn of the sky. But as we sang on, the light came over an eastern ridge and lit up deep ravine, towering rock, shaggy pine trees and flimsy Lisu shanties. Just so had our dear Corn of Wheat preached the resurrection message among the cold darkness of heathenism; just so had he seen light begin to break through, thrusting back the shadow of heathendom and bringing into clear view souls here and there who were destined to yield fully to its warm life-giving glow, and who were to carry on his work after he fell.

As we went on to sing *I Know That My Redeemer*

Liveth, dim forms, hastily buttoning on jackets, stole out from the various sleeping huts and joined us. It was a great thrill, a great parabolic picture of how just that same thing, spiritually, had happened to La-ma-wu. By the time he died, Me-do-me-pa, Leah, and many others had turned to Christ—had joined him, so to speak, on the Rock, and were singing with him the song of the redeemed, bathed in that light which was breaking over the mountainsides in every part of the canyon. Hallelujah!

At the close of our song we were fourteen, and all went into the little rustic chapel, knelt together and had a worship-prayer service, then dispersed for breakfast.

After the morning meal, another Easter service was held, to which a greater number came, when we announced our purpose of honouring him who had given his life that the gospel might be brought to them; and we invited as many as were able to join with us in building him a good grave.

So noon found us trailing over the mountainside single file, as is habitual in the canyon, while the younger ones darted up or down the mountain to pluck scarlet and white rhododendrons, which were still in bloom.

By the side of a very high trail, skirting the banks of the Salween, Job stopped and began to look around. "It's somewhere near this pine tree," he said. Then he found it, quietly sunken into the wild grass so as to be almost obscured. Immediately our party dispersed to look for rocks and started to build it up in the common Chinese fashion. After the little mound was pronounced finished, we women took our lovely scarlet rhododendron blossoms and placed them upright in the centre, in the form of a cross, symbolic of the cross he died to proclaim; then all around it by the sides of the grave, we stuck in the lily-shaped and delicately fragrant white rhododendrons. It looked lovely. As Job had been La-ma-wu's comrade, I asked him to give the message as we reverently gathered in a circle. A copy of the Lisu New Testament in manuscript had just reached us, and so Job chose his text from I Cor. 15:53: "For the perishable must clothe itself with the imperishable."

When he finished we sang the Lisu hymn for those who have gone on before us, *Sleep on, Beloved–*

Although we Christians die,
There will be an awaking from sleep:
Because the Saviour died for our sins,
When Jesus returns we shall meet again.

And as we left to go home, the strains of the chorus drifted back over the mountain trail to that lonely grave,

When Jesus returns we shall meet again.

In September 1944, as my husband, baby son and I left for our furlough, we had to come out over that high trail; and as we came to the one little mound under the pine tree, I stopped to look back, and say goodbye to Lisuland. It was a sunny day, the blue heavens flecked with white clouds which curled lovingly around the necks of the tall peaks, and cast little shadows on the mountain sward beneath. A more wonderfully beautiful spectacle could not be seen, and everywhere I looked–at the

opposite bank of the canyon, or where both banks
became indistinguishable in the winding, tortuous
gorge of mountain knees, ridges, shoulders,
peaks—everywhere I looked, I could see little
villages clinging to ridge or shoulder, little "nests"
above the abysmal ravines, nests that I knew were
now Christian. We were leaving a church roll of
some twelve hundred, not including catechists,
and I turned to the lonely grave beside the road
and whispered "Goodbye, laddie! *Already* it is, not
a hundred, but a *thousandfold*."

Chapter 3

A TREE BESIDE THE WATERS

A DARK little shanty that looks like a junk shop, dusty cupboards, two big iron pots unwashed pushed up against them, a low bed by the central fire which pours forth smoke and soot over everything, and a group of anxious-faced Lisu squatting around the fire and poking it occasionally. From the low bed a moan pierces through the smoke, and a restless, feverish turning of the figure stretched on it, tell its own tale.

"It's no use, Dad," says one of the young men. "It's because we turned Christian. The demons are angry with us. Why, even the white man was in the party of teachers who cast out the demons! If this Jesus they talked about is so powerful, why did he let the demons bite mother? She was in good health until that happened. I say—throw it all over and go back quickly to our old ways. Sacrifice to the demons, call in the village wizard, before it is too late and mother dies!"

A young girl of seventeen years, sitting among them, looks anxiously from face to face, then dares to put in a word: "The teachers said that Jesus healed sick people when He was on earth. They say sickness is not from the bite of a demon, and that if we got sick we were to pray to God in Jesus' name!"

"Well," says the older brother, turning angrily upon her, "you *did* pray, didn't you? I saw you kneel by mother's bed a while ago. A lot we know how to pray! And where's the teacher to tell us? The white man has gone back to Paoshan, and the three Lisu have gone up the canyon–who knows where they are!" Another series of moans piercing the dark makes all turn to the restless figure on the bed. "Dad, make up your mind! She's very sick."

The old father shifts his position uneasily. "It wouldn't look nice to backslide. We were the *first* family to turn Christian; and the foreigner is coming back, he said. He is to move into Deer Pool village just up the road. He'll bring lots of medicines, he said."

"That won't be for a few months yet," puts in the second son. "Ma will be gone if you wait that long. Everyone in the village is talking about you for not calling in the wizard. If she dies..."

"All right," cries out the old man, pushed to extremity and fearing public opinion. "We'll have to backslide, then. But you boys call the wizard. I won't."

At that word one of the sons arose quickly with a "Sure. I'll go!" and disappeared while the young girl buried her face in her hands and waited there, motionless.

Blessed is the man who trusts in the Lord, whose confidence is in him. He will be like a tree planted by the water that sends out its roots by the stream. It does not fear when heat comes; its leaves are always green. It has no worries in a year of drought and never fails to bear fruit. (Jer. 17:7, 8).

On the outside a quiet little figure; on the inside

a raging, scorching fire.

Was it all going to be lost now–this new-found joy and freedom? She had thrilled to the resurrection story, but even more (we must be truthful) to the answer that the Lisu teacher had given her. "Yes, it is for women too. Women learn to read and write just as much as the men." Blessed Christ, who brings emancipation to women of all lands! How her heart had surged with hope. Only seventeen years old, but she had chafed inwardly at all the checking which her bright mind had received. "Go to school and learn Chinese? Oh, no! That is for the men. Don't hanker for what you can't have. Women's part is to farm, weave cloth, bear children, serve the men. You'll get into trouble if you try for anything more than that!" Always restrained, held down, pressed into the old female mould, reminded that she was a mere chattel belonging to the men.

Face buried in her hands, her hot heart communed with itself, with her past, trying to reach out to the future, but every direction was dark, hopeless. When the roots of our inward being reach no farther than our own thoughts, they find but dry ground. "*That sends out its roots by the stream.*" She was not yet aware that the Fount of Living Water was already within. She had not learned to "send out her roots," to reach forth in the spirit and touch the throne of grace. Poor little sapling! So newly planted. Many another has been uprooted, when the same sharp Wind blew. But searching within her own heart she found a ray of hope. Mr Payne had said he would move in with his wife, and live, perhaps, at Deer Pool! That was only some four miles away! She could steal up

there and learn. No. She wasn't going to backslide.
The vision of a new and wonderful life had opened
up before her. *Go back into dark heathenism, with its
virtual slavery? No. Better die first.* Her underlip set
firmly and she raised her head, for the wizard was
being ushered in the door.

I do not know how she escaped taking part in
the incantation which followed. A chicken, or pig,
or cow (depending on how important the sickness
was) would be killed, its blood offered with
incantations, its meat cooked, and a big meal
prepared. She would be called upon to cook that.
Her only chance of escape would be—absence. If
she were not home and did not return until all was
over, she would be free. But she might have to take
a beating for neglect of such an important occasion.
I have seen women who had been beaten—saw one
so bruised that she could not stand on her feet for
several days afterward; and I saw another who had
been hit on the head, and suffered periodically all
the rest of her life from frightful headaches.

Years later when the young girl of this story had
become one of the best readers and writers in the
Lisu church (men included) I asked her, "Homay,
how did you do it?"

"They punished me if they found me going to
chapel at Deer Pool," she said simply, "so I used to
reckon the days and make my firewood hunting on
Saturday evenings and Sundays." (Of course the
heathen do not count time by weeks so they would
lose track of the Christian worship day). "Then I'd
hunt it on Deer Pool mountain! Slip in and enjoy
the Saturday night prayer meeting, and the three
services on Sunday. Of course now and again
they'd find out and I'd have to pay for it, but on

the whole it worked fine! I'd go back with a big load of firewood on my back."

Her application for baptism, however, was turned down. Do not blame the Lisu teachers too much. Remember their disappointment when they heard that the very first family to turn Christian in the canyon had gone back. Of course no one paid much attention to the carelessly added, "except the oldest daughter." What does a girl reckon anyway, in oriental thinking? And who was near to see whether Homay partook with the family or not? In the beginning of a work it is good to be very careful whom you baptize–they set the standard forever after. And so this young Sapling felt the keen Wind of Humiliation. She was up for catechizing with the other candidates for baptism. She could answer all the questions, better and quicker than most, yet they would be accepted and she told "to wait till her affairs were clear." She endured that for two and a half years.

Even more than her family were involved–she was married. A few months before the gospel feet reached the canyon, her parents had held a drinking-wine affair, which is the Lisu heathen name for wedding, and her husband was supposed to enter her family as son. He was just a chit of a lad and Homay never liked him, and would not go near him (that is why I do not include him when speaking of her "family"). He did not seem to mind, for he was not at all faithful in staying with her parents. The marriage had been arranged for by the two fathers, and though the bridegroom would be consulted to some extent, he did not need to be enthusiastic over it. He also had turned Christian, with the coming of Andrew, but just as easily backslid when the others did. Homay never lived with him, and at length, when he eloped with another girl, she was secretly praising the Lord for such a deliverance. But her family were insulted and very angry. They had paid a big price to his parents for the privilege of having him enter their family (and do their farm work) and now that money was lost; at least, it would take a lawsuit to get it back, as his family excused his conduct on the grounds that he had not bargained for a "Christian" wife. Bitter words were her portion day and night; very bitter they could be, for her mother had died, and the wizard said it was because they had called him too late, so that also was added to the abuse poured on her head. A divorce had been obtained, however, and once more she was free. "We'll marry her to a heathen who will knock this nonsense out of her" was a threat which toned down her exaltation; earnestly and quietly she strove to win her father's pity by faithful work at home and obedience to him in all but that one thing.

Now she was learning to use her "roots." Up there at Deer Pool, Mr and Mrs Payne had lived for many months, and during that time she had the privilege of hearing them preach in chapel. She learned that she had "roots"–that she had the power, in the secret chamber of her spirit, to reach out and communicate with God. Her roots had "sensed" the river, and though outward conditions remained dry, and even antagonistic, down in the secret place her roots were reaching out thirstily, eagerly for the *living water*! She found that God answered her prayers in Jesus' name. Why He had allowed her mother to die, she could not understand. She discovered too that her prayers were not always answered immediately, and very frequently not in the way she had expected, but always sooner or later there *was* an answer. What an elation was hers! That she had a secret power with which she could overcome, and often change adverse circumstances, a power which her father and brothers were helpless to combat. She felt free, liberated! Gratitude made her decide to be His slave, for love's sake. As she went quietly about her work her heart talked with itself. When she saw the other heathen girls angered with injustice, chafing at their bondage, she said to herself, "I am different from them. I have eternal life. I have it now, within me, and it *works*!" Gently she would try to tell them about it, too.

At this time two big things were uppermost in her prayers. The matter of her marriage, and the longing to be free to worship. Daily she slipped up her secret stairway and laid these two matters before her new Father. Then one day a man from Deer Pool came into their shanty with a smirk on his face and asked for her parent. When the latter came, this man opened up the subject of Homay's marriage to a Deer Pool boy (whose name, later, was Philip). I do not know all the details of that transaction. Christian Lisu do not pay money (called a dowry) for their wives. The dowry was a heavy bondage in heathendom. Young men often cannot afford to marry because of it, or are all their lives burdened with the heavy interest and unable to get it paid off. The Lisu church has decided to give its daughters free of charge, and of course no Christian may marry a heathen with the church's consent. Philip paid some money for Homay.

Whether it was the costs of her divorce, or whether he had not yet publicly turned Christian, I do not know; but it seemed like God's answer to her prayers. True, Philip was not particularly attractive to her, but he planned they both should be Christians, so once again it seemed that she had conquered her family by remaining quiet and submissive on the surface, but warring valiantly and earnestly in the spirit. The marriage was delayed, however, so she still had to pray on for freedom to worship.

The answer to this was unexpected. She had been blessed and filled with joy at a visit from another woman missionary. The Paynes had gone on furlough, and Mr and Mrs A. B. Cooke (successors to Mr Fraser in the Lisu work) had volunteered for the Upper Salween. All Lisu loved Leila Cooke. Her kindly radiant spirit shone through her face, and just to be with her was a blessing. I once heard one of their servants say, "No wind ever blows under the Cooke wing." Although on this occasion Leila was just passing through on her way to Pine Mountain village, a long day's journey north, Homay felt the comfort of that "wing." After some months had passed, a note came for her from Mrs Cooke, and she was all prepared to obey whatever it said. It told her that the Cooke family were again on the move, but that Mr and Mrs John Kuhn were coming in to the Oak Flat district. Leila Cooke ended with, "Mrs Kuhn will have no servants to help her and I am sure she would be grateful if you would cook for her. Do you think you could?"

Cook to the missionary? I am sure she giggled at first and said, "*Ma srghe!*" (meaning "I don't

know"), for they all do. No Lisu likes to be a
servant. Poor as they are (and we always try to
house and feed them better than they would get at
home) they love independence. But the more
Homay thought of the new proposition, the more
attractive it became. To work with a foreign
woman might not be too bad; certainly not with
Mrs Payne and Mrs Cooke. And then there would
be the freedom to go to chapel services any time
she liked. And every evening there would be a
service, probably, where she could learn more.
Learn to sing! How she loved to sing the hymns,
and she had discovered she could learn even the
men's parts, tenor or bass, quite as accurately as
they themselves! And the missionary's home was
the centre of activity, with the evangelists coming
and going, and all that. It would be fun. Would her
father allow it? Well, there was the oriental way of
doing that. Luckily it was December, the slack time
of the year. Farm work had ended. The women
were spinning and weaving cloth for the family
clothes. Weave a bit later at night, and a bit earlier
in the morning, and she would get it all finished.
Then just tell her father, "I'm going up to Pine
Mountain to help the new Ma-Ma for a few days"
and–off she'd go. As the "days" lengthened
out–well, a nice gift out of her salary would be the
most potent argument to silence Dad! So again she
was victor over her circumstances through prayer
and faith alone. What a good God to plan this
wonderful salvation, a saving grace that is useful
every day of one's life, let alone its consummation
at death! And so this young Sapling was drinking
deeply of the river of life, and shooting up straight
and strong.

I was perfectly unconscious of the good things God was planning for me, when, on our entrance into the Munition of Rocks, my husband stopped our carriers before a sprawling little Lisu village. "Belle," John said to me, "there's a nice Christian girl in one of these huts and we're going to have lunch with her. Be nice to her; she stands alone and needs comfort. She can speak a bit of Chinese too, so you can talk to her" (I had not yet learned any Lisu). Mrs Cooke had written to me, "It is hard to get Lisu servants and in this mountain land you cannot live without help. Pray for some, even before you come in." But as I curiously picked my way past the pigsty, trying to manoeuvre my three-year-old daughter into the Lisu shanty, servants were nowhere in my thoughts. The little Lisu girl who needed comfort, and lunch (clean, if possible, please?) were uppermost. There she was—a short, plump little person running out to greet us; face slightly "dour" when in repose, but now lit up with a joyous smile as she cried, "Ma-Pa! Ma-Ma!" Then remembering that I had not yet had time to learn Lisu she changed it demurely to the Chinese greeting, *"Yang-si-mu, ping an?"*

I liked her the moment I saw her. I noted her tidy dress, how carefully she was washing her rice, and the air of ability which was hers, despite slow movements. I had not had a chance to inspect many Lisu girls, and she noticed my careful observation and laughed with embarrassment; so I said, "Don't be afraid if I look too hard. I haven't seen many Lisu girls before!" I never dreamed that she thought I was inspecting my new cook! She was so lovely with Little Daughter, too—saw that she had the softest rice to eat, washed out her bowl again, even though it was already clean, supplied her with a warm seat beside the fire, and so on. It was a happy meal, but we had to push on.

I thought I had said goodbye to her, when, the next day at noon, didn't our little hostess of the day before appear at our lunch stop, a roll of bedding on her back and all prepared, apparently, to go on with us!

"Do you think she is going to come with us?" I asked John. He too, was puzzled, but came nearer guessing it. "Wonder if she is not planning to be your helper?" he suggested. Hardly able to believe such good news I essayed a question, "Are you going to come with us and–stay?" Whereupon she laughed and said, "If you want me!"

The story of our arrival that night is told elsewhere.[1] But thus she became one of us, and from now on, our little Sapling was free to deepen her roots, and drink in her living water, with nothing to hinder. I think maybe you would like to get glimpses of her from our circular letters, because they were written down, not in the light of what happened afterwards, but "uncoloured," just little home things, but very revealing. They will incidentally give you glimpses of what composed the missionary's life during those early days. In our first circular, dated December, 1934, we wrote:

I lift up mine eyes to the hills
For my help comes down from the height,
Lord, Thy strength is the strength of the hill
And I cradle my heart in its might.

[1] Precious Things of the Lasting Hills

Here we are at last--in the mountain fastnesses of
West Yunnan, with the stillness of God's country
all around us, broken only by the surly roar of the
rough Salween River hundreds of feet beneath us,
or the musical tones of Lisu voices drifting over
from some unseen place on the steep mountain
side.

Come with us on our evening walk along this
narrow path that skirts the edge of Pine Mountain.
Let's stand beneath this old tree for a moment and
lift up our eyes to the hills. Did you ever see such a
chaos of mountain peaks? There is the highest
topmost range, a jagged line piercing the blue, and
thrown against it to right and left as far as the eye
can reach are masses of sharp crests, precipitous
pinnacles, queer knobs, slim pine-wooded ridges,
round dumpy foothills, and at their base, the
Salween River cutting its snake-like path through
and around the solid rock. Wonder and awe fills
the heart at first, and then joy comes; joy that the
Creator of all this has said, "And I will walk
among you, and will be your God, and you shall be
my people."

One evening as I was walking here with Homay,
I heard a voice that sounded very near. I looked up
and down (there is only up and down here, no
level spot) but could see no one. Then Homay
smiled, and pulling my sleeve, pointed way, way
down, a hundred feet or more beneath us where a
second path crawls along the hillside. "It's Pu-fu-
si-pa praying," she said simply. My unaccustomed
eyes gradually made out a figure in the middle of
the dusty road. This dear man had been trying to
carry a heavy load up to his home, and being
weary, he had set it down by the roadside and he
himself was kneeling in the dust of the path,
talking to his Lord. The mountain wind had
brought his voice up the slope until it sounded

quite near Yes, you may pray in Lisuland–
wherever you like; and if anyone does happen to
meet you, they accept the fact simply and pass on.

Now we must go back. See! the sun is finally
withdrawing from those highest peaks, the cold
grey-blue mantle of winter twilight is falling
around them, and we must hurry back home.

Home? Oh, you don't see anything like a home
on this wild mountain side. Look keenly–clinging
to the hill in front of us, can't you see three or four
little brown shanties? Here we are!–walk in.

Our Lisu house has only braided bamboo mats
for a floor over the earth, so we live much like
kittens in a basket. The roof is formed of wooden
stakes laid on the beams and held down by logs.
There are no nails used in the building, everything
being tied together with bark.

It's true, the walls are rather porous and, as a
matter of necessity, the weather is a member of the
family, coming and going out at will. One morning
at breakfast, a little white cloud walked in our
door! It vanished the next second–guess we scared
it away! The clouds up here are a continual marvel
of beauty. I have seen them go coasting down the
mountain side like gleeful children or fairy beings.
Sometimes they coax and cuddle around the shoulders of the great smiling peaks or tumble merrily
down their sides, or rise in still soft beauty from
their feet, as the sun draws them with his hot
magnetic rays. The human children of these mountain fastnesses are much like them–clinging with
tender hearts to those who love them, but delight-
ing too in a good romp, play, or something to
laugh at! However, they also have their still
moments, when the heart of them reaches out
yearningly toward Him they call their "Sun of
Righteousness."

The Christmas festival engaged our thoughts for the next month, but after that it was decided that the missionaries should change their place of residence from Pine Mountain Village to Oak Flat Village. The Christians at Pine Mountain had proved shallow and the deacon body felt they were unworthy of the presence of a missionary. Mr Cooke had heartily approved the change, so our next letter describes it.

January, 1935.

And now for our "flitting"! About three miles crawling up the southern trail, and still on the Pine Mountain range, the path comes to a kind of huge knoll, dotted with old gnarled oak trees. The rock cliffs, with here and there a lacy pine tree to add colour, lift abruptly above this high little tableland, and scrub-tree covered mountain sides sweep steeply down from its edge. Here is the village of Oak Flat where Me-do-me-pa, "The Shepherd," lives and where Pade-John has a log cabin home. The latter also owned a large field at the lower edge of the knoll, but when he learned that Ma-Pa Cooke thought Oak Flat a desirable centre for the missionary, Pade-John came forward with his sunny smile, and said that he would like to give this piece of ground for Ma-Pa to use free of charge, as long as he wished. So in January we moved to Oak Flat Village.

About this time an incident occurred which changed Homay's life. One late afternoon I was about to give Little Daughter her evening bath, when Homay came running into the room, flushed in face and excited. She was followed by the laundress who laughed and said, "Homay's fiancé has arrived!"

I had not known she was engaged to be married, so, hastily leaving Kathryn in the tub to be washed by Homay, I went to the back door, and saw Philip for the first time. I did not like him—at least not for my beloved little cook. I thought he looked shallow and mercenary, and indeed since then he has justified those doubts. I returned and looked at her.

"Homay, you are not engaged to him?"

She flushed and giggled nervously.

"My child, you must not marry that fellow! Don't you know that if you marry a man who is not as spiritually minded as yourself that *he* will pull *you* down? 'Do not be yoked together with unbelievers' means spiritually, as well as Christian to unbeliever."

"I have already said yes to him, Ma-Ma," she answered quietly. "We are engaged; what can be done about it?"

"Oh, break your engagement!" I cried hastily. I did not know then that a Lisu engagement is like the old Hebrew engagement, almost as binding as marriage. "If you marry that fellow you will wreck your service for God! Anything but that!"

She was silent, and I said no more. Later I was afraid I had said too much, as indeed I had, so I never mentioned the matter again. But I had sown a seed, and I believe it was of God. Outwardly she was the same, but the secret roots were reaching out in question to her *Fount of Living Water*. One day she asked me for permission to go home. She was gone for several weeks. I had forgotten about Philip, but when she returned to us, others told me that she was now free, the engagement had been broken. I asked her about it, but she was not inclined to talk. Yes, she was free; her father was furious—money must be paid back to Philip's family.

"Father always calls me—introduces me, now, to others as his 'Dry Daughter,'" she said to me, so quietly that I was not conscious of how deeply the reproach stung her. "A dry tree" is a barren woman; in the Lisu mind it is a stigma much more dreaded than actual deformity, I think. "A dry tree"—for Christ's sake? The little Sapling's roots must have clung desperately when that hurricane Wind of Temptation struck. To her dying day she never ceased to wince inwardly at the sting of that name, even after its use was impossible.

Now for more extracts from the old circulars.

June, 1935.

Homay is developing. She has twice brought messages at our local services, quite a departure for a woman. I asked Lisu teacher John what was the hindrance to there being Lisu Bible-women as well as men teachers, and he said, "None, except there is no woman fit for it." Let us pray Homay into fitness.

One day Ah-sah-me-pa came to ask Ma-Ma for help. A deacon of Spirea Flat Village had had his leg torn open to the bone by the kick of an animal. There was only one thing to do—summon Homay (always delighted to go trotting along behind), pack some medicines and go. (My husband remained with Little Daughter.) Despite its pretty name this village leaves the impression of just steepness and gravel. It is in a fold of the mountain, and its only view is the other side of the "fold"; although lower than Plum Tree Flat it is even steeper.

Arrived, I cleansed the wound (with a houseful

of people watching me of course), and then asked where we were to sleep. Ma-fa-tsai-ma looked around the little hut. There was the bed her sick husband lay on, and opposite was the one her children slept on; at the head of this latter stood two square wooden cupboards. "Oh, you and Homay can sleep on top of the cupboards!" she said. Well—I looked at Homay's short fatness, and she looked at my long thinness, and our vote was unanimous. *Us for the chapel:* Our rejection of the proffered sleeping quarters gave no offence, and when we went to service that evening, we found two big planks already set on the benches in preparation for our night's repose; so I had the unique experience of participating in Sunday evening service, sitting on the top of my bed!

On the way home, travelling on a high trail, whom did we stumble over, resting in the middle of the path, but Pu-gia-me! (She was the third of the three servants who came to help us at the first, but her conduct did not approve itself to the Lisu church, so they had asked us to dismiss her and then word came that she had really left the Lord and this was the first time we had met her since.) Now here she was, all togged out with the big silver earrings and ornaments of a heathen girl. She looked abashed at seeing us, but there was no escape. As my Lisu is insufficient I left her with Homay and the last I saw, Homay had taken her in her arms and was weeping over her—but Pu-gia-me remains obdurate.

However, those tears were not wasted, for the very next circular records this:

Some weeks later Pu-gia-me unexpectedly returned and announced that she wished to come back to the fold. As she gave due warning, they

were ready for her. That was a time when I was ill,
but John said that it was splendidly arranged. She
was made to confess to all the church, and then in
audible prayer to the Lord. They put her through a
kind, but very firm cross-questioning. (The Lisu
believe in apostolic discipline and offenders have
no easy time. But Pu-gia-me took it as if she really
was sorry and meant her repentance.)

Homay was my dear companion in trips among
the villages. She looked after Little Daughter (who
loved her devotedly) when I was occupied with
preaching and ministering to the Lisu, and my
heart could rest about it, for she was chaste and
dependable and I knew little Kathryn would be
safe.

In July 1935, we went as a family on a tour of
some of the northern villages. We had some
blessed experiences, but little Kathryn became
infected with malaria. From then on John and I felt
that we must be willing for separation. It was a
pale-faced, thin little girl whom we brought home,
so we decided travelling in that country was not
suitable for white children, and that while one of
us went, the other must stay at home with
Kathryn. John always has declared that the Munition of Rocks is not a woman's country, so the one
to itinerate was mostly himself.

However, more than Little Daughter had found
the above trip too much physically. We learned
from this experience never to try to itinerate in the
Rainy Season. It takes such a toll of health that it is
not worth while, unless God definitely leads to put
aside this rule. This was one of the reasons which
led us to hold our long Bible schools in the
summer, when rain made itineration impossible

for the foreigner.

John's next trip was to Goo-moo, the story of which will be related later on; but it was while he was away in Burma that I became sick with a disease unknown to me, later diagnosed as erysipelas. The circular of this time records that Homay was called back to her own home because of the sickness of her father. He died, and she returned to me just a day before I was compelled to go to bed. I was six days' journey from the nearest white person, many days away from a doctor, and my husband "somewhere in Burma," beyond communication. So you can know what it meant to me to have Homay back. She, like all Lisu, knew nothing of caring for the sick. It was that experience which taught me what the Lisu suffer when they are ill. I had high fever, felt sticky and dirty and longed so for a bath. Day after day passed in that condition—I was much too weak to wash myself. At last I asked Homay if she would not try to wash me. She was all love and pity, but when I asked her to bathe me she looked completely baffled. She went and got a basin of hot water, dipped her hands in it and rubbed her wet hands over me—that is all she knew how to do, and I was too weak to direct her, though the tears came with disappointment. How much enlightened countries owe to Christ! He is the origin of those studies which bring alleviation to the suffering; in every land the first hospital is always founded by Christ's messengers, the missionaries. We ought to think how much we owe Him, and those who brought Him to us and be willing to share our knowledge! "We are debtors."

The Lisu came every night to sing and pray for

me, but as I was obviously getting worse, Job
(again evangelist in those parts) decided to go for
help to the distant Chinese city of Paoshan. In two
weeks time he was back with Nurse Kathleen
Davies and Miss Winifred Embery, and from then
on I was properly cared for. But medical orders
were adamant—I must go out to Chinaland for a
while, where I could get better food.

I asked Homay if she would go with me and stay
with me, so I could continue my Lisu studies with
her. She gladly consented. The circular of October,
1935, says:

> Homay's father has died. Legally now she be-
> comes the chattel of her brother, and we are told he
> intends to get money for her. He has the power to
> sell her as a bride into a heathen family or even sell
> her as a slave; pray for her. We would like to buy
> her ourselves and let her work out her redemption
> gradually by serving us, but there are difficulties.

So all was not easy for our dear little cook. But I
remember on the way out, as all of us were
gathered about an inn fire one evening, our Lisu
carriers started to sing hymns. I heard one young
evangelist whisper to Homay who squatted next to
him, "Sister, sing bass with me!" She could sing it
better than he, and he wanted to learn the bass
from her!

We were out in Chinaland for three months, and
I tried to have prayer in Lisu with Homay each
day; first to practise my Lisu and secondly to
encourage her to pray daily for the other members
of the Lisu church. One evening as we were
kneeling together at my bed I felt urged to pray for
a dear deacon at Small Hemp. But I could not

remember his name exactly and, hunting through my mind for it, I was praying something like this, "And bless dear old *A-va-ni*-no. *A-va-tse?* No. Oh, *Va-chi-kya-pa!*" Whereupon Homay fell back upon the floor, opened her mouth and simply howled with laughter. I felt she was too excessively merry when I was merely reaching around in my mind for his name, when I was brought to remember what his name *meant*. All their names have meanings even as we have Mr White, Mr Baker, etc. And Lisu use their names without thinking of their meanings. However, my feeling around for this man's name had brought its full meaning back to Homay. In her ears I had said, "And bless dear old *Pig-Dirt*, no—*Pig-Grease?*—no. Oh, *Expel Pig-Dung Man!*" And it had broken up our prayer meeting!

I might say here that the heathen Lisu give their children these horrible names in order to deceive the evil spirits into thinking the child is refuse, like its name, and thus they will not "steal" it; in other words, that it might not die. But such names are so repugnant that we often give Bible names in their place, if the Christian proves earnest. Homay was given the name "Phoebe," but almost no one used it; because we had come to love her as Homay, I believe, and Homay means simply Ho-girl.

Those days in Chinaland, Homay watched over Little Daughter, did our laundry and was by no means idle, so at the end of the month I handed her the salary of five Chinese dollars, as usual. She stood looking at it in her hand as if dissatisfied; at last she picked out half of it and returned it to me. "Take this back, Ma-Ma, please. I am not doing a full day's work and my conscience would not be happy if I took money for full time labour."

I record this little incident so that you may see what lovely fruit was growing on this little Tree. I know of no keener test for any Christian, of any race, than his reaction to the greed for money. I would like to testify that Homay is not the only Lisu Christian we have found to be pure from this taint, but let us not pass over it lightly. Those days she went to the Chinese market where she beheld hundreds of useful pretty nicknacks she would have loved to own, but could not afford to buy.

Another little incident from old letters gives a picture of the tenderness of this young Lisu heart. We were able to get back into Lisuland in time for Christmas.

January, 1936.

Going into the kitchen last Sunday morning I was brought to a halt by the sight of Samuel, head between his knees, sobbing; Job at his right hand weeping audibly; Homay at his left crying into her dishpan; and Me-do-me-pa trying to look as if he were not going to be next.

"What are you crying for?" I whispered to Homay.

"Because Job is crying over Sam's affair," sobs Sister Sympathy.

Sam's affair (of which you will hear more later) is this. He was married to a girl, Philip's sister she was, whom he said he did not love, had not lived with, and so wished to get rid of; he had intended to reveal this by flying off to Luda, as a sort of ultimatum. That morning Job had gone to him and told him that this might not be, and the big young fellow took it so hard that all in the kitchen were dissolved in tears with him. As one knelt beside the lad and sensed the furious tide of hot youth, one felt utterly impotent to stem it, and could only cry in one's heart, "Oh God, you alone are sufficient to bend this strong young neck to the yoke!" And it was an hour or so before the gentle Lord of Calvary got possession of that vigorously resisting young nature. But as he arose to his feet quieted, we tried to prepare him for the loneliness of cross-bearing—no one can help us bear our cross but Jesus; it is one thing to surrender among tender sympathetic friends, but quite another to go back alone to the hut and its unwelcome presence. Homay knew so well what that struggle was. Knew how she herself had felt tied to a heathen; remembered her bondage to Philip, and though she had experienced God's power of deliverance, her tears flowed for the agony of this struggle. It was not always the missionaries in their study room that helped the church. The kitchen, where there was a Lisu Tree-Beside-the-Waters, was felt, somehow to be a place of power; and what the mistress sometimes might not be able to accomplish, the cook had ability to perform!

During these days Homay was sharing with us another experience. The little old Lisu shanty in which we had now lived for a year or so was considered unhealthy, and it was suggested that we build a better home. All had to be done from the standing tree on the mountainside, and the February, 1936, circular tells a bit of it.

There is a bare spot on Sunset Ridge where some thirty noble and beautiful trees have given up their lives that the missionary might have a safe dwelling in Lisuland. Day after day it was—

Anon a sound appalling,
   As a hundred years of pride
Crashed, in the silence falling,
   And the shadowy pine trees sighed.

Day after day, "out of the copse the stroke of the iron axe," accompanied by the *chip-chip* of long Lisu knives that had to hack off the bark, and turn the round trunk into square beams, with the nasal *sizz-sizz* of the great saw which further converted them into joists or beams. Noontide brought Ma-Ma, Kathryn and Homay down the hillsides with baskets, and soon beside a pine-chip fire a picnic lunch was spread out. Then a long, hard afternoon; and dusk saw Daddy wearily climbing the trail homeward, perfumed like a pine forest and covered with shavings!

After three weeks of such preparatory work, we were told that the day had arrived when we must flit. Up behind the Shanty was a rickety, black-sooted little log cabin, the only empty house in the village. So we attacked it with brooms, hung up some cheery texts and pictures, brightened it with our old but still gay travelling rugs, tucked into it those indispensable comrades, the baby organ and our dear books (arranged on cretonne-curtained shelves hastily shaped out of packing cases!) and the cabin looked so cosy that we quite fell in love with it.

It was a sad day when the beloved though leaky old Shanty had to be torn down, but joy returned when a solid, sturdy framework began to rise in its place.

But before the walls were up, the February rains descended on us black and relentless. Allyn and Leila Cooke were scheduled to arrive on a certain date and we were all to hold a Bible school for the

Lisu. As the day approached we had only a wall-less but roofed-over house, no kitchen, and rain still descending. John was laid low with a very bad tooth, his face terribly swollen, and too ill to stand on his feet, let alone superintend the weaving and nailing up of the bamboo walls. Homay had to cook meals with only a lean-to roof over her mud stove, and the ground beneath her feet a constant puddle. How she ever did it I never knew, but she was so sweet and serene with it all that she was a benediction to us. I quote from the March circular:

"They will never be able to make it, Ma-Ma. It's been raining for days, you know, and the roads are too bad in such stormy weather. You need not expect them this week." The little group of Lisu women, shivering in the cold drizzle, nodded their heads to confirm Ah-be-pa's words.

"Well, but they said in their letter that they would arrive tonight or tomorrow, and we cannot but prepare for them, can we? Let's get the bedroom completed anyway, and as much of the dining room as we can accomplish, and let the rest of the house go."

Lisu do not usually work in such weather, but the faithful little group agreed, and despite their thin garments, and the penetrating damp chill, they threw themselves into valiant effort, Homay cheering them on, occasionally with cups of hot tea, or steaming honey water. And by Saturday night the two rooms were walled and ready for occupation. Then, as we were in the midst of finishing touches, a cry came echoing over the knoll—"They're coming!" and John (now better) came running in upon me, "Belle! Cookes are here! Cookes are here! Just climbing the hill now!" The next moment we parted as if a bomb had burst us asunder–he to the right to welcome our guests, and I to the left to the bedroom to pull out dresser scarfs and linen that had been packed away from the building dust.

Up through the thin drizzle, our beloved friends plodded. "Why, none of us thought you'd *ever* get here today!" we cried, as we shook hands. "Well, we had promised we would," was the simple answer that covered the two nights they had had to sleep with insufficient bedding, for they had become separated from their coolies, and the hard bitter day, up before daybreak, pushing on through biting cold and wet, not even stopping for lunch, and all because they had "promised." Allyn and Leila Cooke are a never-ending inspiration to us, a joy and comfort for which we continually thank God. Before going on to Luda they had said they would join us in holding a short term Bible school for the Oak Flat district Lisu, and God rewarded their faithful sacrifices by pouring out unusual blessing during the week's session.

But all through those hard days, the little cook, so serene and thoughtful of others on the outside, was carrying a secret heartache. Her brothers were threatening her, anxious to turn her into money whether it be by selling her to a heathen for wife or as a slave. So once more the little Tree was shaken by the Sharp Wind from the Bitter Heights. And once again her only strength was to send down her roots, secretly, deeply to draw on her Living Water.

> There is a viewless, cloistered room,
> As high as heaven, as fair as day,
> Where, though my feet may join the throng,
> My soul can enter in, and pray.

One hearkening even, cannot know
When I have crossed the threshold o'er,
For He alone who hears my prayers
Had heard the shutting of the door.

                                        AMY CARMICHAEL.

And once more there came an answer. Evangelist
Joseph proposed to her and was accepted. That
story is told in *Precious Things of the Lasting Hills*
and Homay is the girl there called "Heart's
Desire." How her brothers were prevailed upon to
give her to him, I do not know.

And now we were called upon to separate, for
the Kuhn family was needing to go on furlough.
John had been out ten years and I, eight.

Before we left, however, Leila Cooke had written
to me, "Would you be willing to lend Homay to me
until you come back? I do not know her equal and
I would like to have her with me in Luda so as to
be an example to the other Lisu girls up here, who
are far from attaining to Homay's spiritual position." Of course both Homay and I were delighted
that she should be under such a safe wing until the
day of her marriage to Joseph, and so we parted.

Furlough brought us the new delight of Lisu
letters, and among others was this one from
Homay herself.

You-who-have-gone-back-to-the-foreign-country–
Ma-Pa, Ma-Ma, and Kathryn,

Ma-Pa, Ma-Ma and Kathryn whom I love, whom
I never can forget, whom I deeply regard in Christ
Jesus, whom I long to see. Oh dear. I think of you
three and send you a handshake on paper. After
we parted I wanted to see you, loved you, and
many tears came out. When we came to Luda from

Oak Flat, Sunday we paused at Lu-mu-teh and were there three days. The following Wednesday we went to Luda. The (Chinese) laird at Lu-mu-teh wants to hinder the building of the chapel and put two of the villagers in jail; Saturday they were imprisoned and Tuesday they were freed. Sunday early, Mr and Mrs Cooke, the villagers and many others of us before breakfast prayed (for them) and God answered our prayers. Tuesday, toward evening, they were released, thank God!

By God's help I was enabled to walk all the way from Oak Flat to Luda in peace. Ma-Pa, Ma-Ma, you three, I would like to know if you arrived safely at the foreign country. Oh dear. Ma-Pa, Ma-Ma and Kathryn I thank you; we lived together over a year and by God's grace (during that time) there was nothing happened to be regretted. I thank you. I learned how to study a little, while I was with you, and learned how to do a few things. I am so glad. Oh dear. Ma-Pa, Ma-Ma and Kathryn I can't tell you how I long to see you and touch your hands a little, and take you, Kathryn, around a little. I can't forget your faces; it's as if I hear your voices in my sleep. Oh dear. When you get to your foreign country, don't forget us but pray for us all the time, thank you—please forgive any mistakes I've made in writing this; thank you. The writer Homay Phoebe who loves you and will never forget you.

Her letter was enclosed in one from Mrs Cooke which tells that Homay's engagement may have to be broken. She says, "We are sorry to hear that Homay's younger brother wants to make trouble. Homay feels that it is not so much that he wants a bridal price, as that he wants her to marry the blue blood instead of an ordinary Lisu. She says the folks in her village like to claim they are not Lisu but Chinese, and they want her to marry one of the same class. They all think her brothers would be satisfied if she decided to remain single all her life, and she is quite willing. But Job does not feel that she had better tell her brother that as yet, and Moses feels the same. It is difficult to know what to say about it. I am sure you are praying. I feel sorry for Joseph, for she is the second one he has sought for a wife."

Always the dread fear of the "dry tree" life following her! But it caused her roots to go all the deeper; and by fall (1936) her third hope of a husband and family were gone—but in a most unlooked-for way.

While we were at Orcas Island, a letter came from Andrew giving the heart-breaking news that our dear Joseph was with his Lord. He was returning from Goo-moo, where he had been teaching, and was on his way home to get his bride, dear Homay, when he was drowned. The day was hot and he and his companions decided to have a bath; Joseph could not swim and got out of his depth. Samuel and Lysias were with him at the time, and they buried him and carried his things back home for him.

When John first read this out to me, it just seemed as if I could not allow it to be true. It was so hard to have lost one beloved teacher the year before, and Joseph was one of our priceless ones—a pure spirit, absolutely devoted to his Lord. He could have been a farmer like the rest, but he left it all to carry the gospel message to others of his own race. For a year's labour he received merely his board and lodging and fifteen local dollars for clothes. Poorest of the poor, he was rich in another kind of goods–"as poor, yet making many rich."

One of my last memories of Joseph is of the testimony meeting one Christmas. The testimonies were a blessing to us all and Joseph kept quiet as long, doubtless, as he could; then he sprang to his feet, and with his face so radiant it was almost glorified he cried out, "I haven't anything to give to God, but all that I am and all that I have, I give back to Him." And now God has gathered in the complete offering.

Our hearts wondered about dear Homay, and how she would receive this sad solution to her problems. A letter from Mr Cooke told us she received it bravely. After a while they heard her singing softly in the kitchen, *Have Thine Own Way, Lord*, and *Looking This Way*. Then after a time she went out into the little house where Miss Ward had died, and had prayer. Brave little Lisu sister, what are God's plans for your life now? Back to the old place where she is, humanly speaking, unprotected.

Lisu-like, her next letter never mentions it:

Ma-Pa, Ma-Ma, you three–
Whom I love and can never forget, whom in the name of the Holy Spirit of the Trinity I behold in my heart all the time, I send you a hand-shake and greetings on paper. Oh dear. Are you happy now in your own country? We love you and long to see you beyond expression. Oh dear. Ma-Pa, the letter you wrote to me has come, and I received it October 15, and my happiness knew no bounds. Oh dear. Ma-Pa, thank you for that letter. You said you had arrived at Grandpa Miller's home, and we thank God. Are you now also in peace? You said

you had been to a summer conference where you received much spiritual food, and I thank God. You had received three letters from me; now Ma-Pa, did you really and truly cry when you read them? Oh dear. I truly long to see you more than I can express. Since I have been at Luda my physical strength has grown, pray for me that my spiritual strength may increase also. Oh dear Ma-Pa, I am in much prayer that you will come back to us; we at Oak Flat would be delighted if that were God's will. Now Mr Fraser arrived at Luda on November 5, we do thank God.

Oh Kathryn [I had guided the little girlie's hand in writing Homay a note, and also stuck in a part of the snap on which Kathryn appears and apparently one of my own feet]. So happy I was to get your letter, and also for the picture. Ma-Ma, I can see your foot but not your head; this is not satisfying! Oh dear. Ma-Ma, have you forgotten Lisu words? Please write me a Lisu letter, I long to read one from you. When I think of you I weep and love you very much. Oh dear. Ma-Ma, the writer is the one who wants to see you, thinks of of you, and to whom you gave the name of (Homay) Phoebe. Oh dear. Ma-Pa, Ma-Ma, and Kathryn, dwell in peace!

But we see by this that now the pioneer of the Lisu work, our provincial superintendent, Mr J. O. Fraser, had arrived at Luda where Homay was staying. He and the Cookes were working on the revision of the Lisu New Testament. Inevitably he got to know Homay. In that northern district where the tribes are farther away from the Chinese civilization, and so are cruder in the living, Homay's neat capable cleverness must have shone like a diamond among rough pebbles. Her fiancé's death having been noised abroad, proposals of

marriage began to flow in! The great, brilliant
superintendent at the translator's desk, and the
little Lisu housemaid...what connection could there
ever be between such? But it was part of his
greatness that he always had time and loving
sympathy for the humblest life near him. He heard
of those proposals and was greatly amused. As
they began to mount up in numbers and passed the
fifty mark (if I remember rightly) he suggested
jocularly to the Cookes that they have refusals of
marriage printed for Homay–it would save her so
much time and letter-writing! But he was pondering what he knew of the strange movings of
Providence in this young life, and one day he
called her to him.

"Homay, have you ever thought that perhaps
God is calling you to a single life, in order that you
may serve Him in a sphere new to Lisuland? You
know the Lisu church has few Bible-women. All its
evangelists and teachers are men. Yet men cannot
reach women like a woman could. Would you
consider giving yourself to the Lord for His
ministry?"

With all his spiritual penetration I do not think
that Mr Fraser knew what a knife he had plunged
into Homay's heart. Outwardly she was always
serene and quiet–she had schooled herself for so
many years to keep her inner thoughts from
showing on the surface, that she had wonderful
control of herself. She would not appear to have
been "stabbed," and he of course did not know of
the stigma-name of "Dry Tree," and that it had
been a horror to her all these years. Even if he had
known, he would have put the question, for he
never feared to face-up any soul to God's highest

demands; and I have often wondered, would Homay's story have had a different ending if she had accepted his advice? But Homay had never seen a woman single for Christ's sake—her Lisu white missionaries were married, why couldn't God use her, married? I do not say she was unwilling; but her answer was, "If God asked me to remain single I would do so; but I cannot now promise never to marry."

She must have left his presence with a hurricane in her heart. Was it necessary to be a "dry tree" physically, to bring forth spiritually? And there was such a handsome, consecrated young evangelist now casting eyes upon her. Mrs Cooke had written to us of this boy, Daniel:

> Daniel has given his life to the Lord's work. Please thank the friends at home who have been praying for him. God has answered prayer in the breaking of his engagement to the heathen woman to whom he was betrothed in childhood. It was a real fight with the powers of darkness, but God made Daniel victorious. Daniel's heathen brother said he would kill Daniel rather than let him free from the engagement. Daniel ought to have had plenty to pay back the bridal price but the father and brother refused to let him use his share of the property. For one year's wages as evangelist David received twenty-five dollars. When the father saw Daniel would not be forced to marry the girl, he asked Daniel to give him twenty dollars to get rid of her. Daniel gave it to him and of the five dollars left of the whole year's wages he handed me fifty cents to help pay the coolies to carry (Teacher) Moses when Moses was too sick to walk.

But a new and exciting page of experience was

about to be turned for Homay. Cookes were asked
to go on a long journey south to investigate the
field of Bana, which had been offered to the China
Inland Mission. And they had invited her to go
with them! What fun! A long trek through
beautiful Lisuland. Then (thrill of thrills) a motor
bus ride into Burma, along the Burma Road.
Homay had never seen an automobile in her life.
After that a train ride—and she had never seen a
train before! Then an exciting day in the city of
Mandalay—her first glimpse of modern civilization.
Then once more familiar trail-trekking, and the
mission station of Bana was reached, where several
other tribes beside the Lisu were being evangelized. But amidst all these thrills, in the Secret Place
she was wondering about the bearing of fruit for
God. In her next letter Mrs Cooke wrote:

> Homay is here with us and is a constant joy to
> us. The other day I found her out in the kitchen
> counting the kernels on one ear of corn. She asked
> me to help her and we found 538 kernels on one
> ear. She wanted to know the number so that she
> could glorify God for His power in making so
> much out of one grain of corn. Then another day
> she was looking at some caterpillars, and when I
> came along she said, "Isn't it wonderful that these
> can all turn into butterflies?" And then another
> day I was telling her about the verse in Hosea
> where it says, "I will be like the dew to Israel" and
> she said Teacher John (the Lisu evangelist who
> died in 1935) said, in preaching, "We must not feel
> that God forgets us, for He does not even forget
> the little leaves, but sends a portion of dew for
> every little leaf." I often find Homay off in a quiet
> place with her portion of the New Testament and a
> pencil. And at night after she is in bed I hear her

softly repeating scripture verses before she goes to sleep. As you think of Homay you will pray that God will provide His own escort to take her home from here when we leave for furlough. She is about thirty days' journey from home. Her sister and three Lisu men are here to return with her, but as it is necessary to sleep out in the open while travelling, we feel it would be more to the glory of God if she had an older man or a missionary to escort the party.

Into these thoughts walked the postman, with a bunch of Lisu letters from Luda. Among them was one from Daniel to Homay! Evidently she had been expecting this proposal, and had made up her mind, for the return mail to Luda took her acceptance of his offer of marriage. Mrs Cooke said that Homay's reply to him was very sweet, and that she had said, "I am sure that I love you, but wait until there are no doubts in your own mind about your love for me." That, of course, was just a bit of coy teasing!

However, the happy little acceptance note arrived in Luda station where Mr Charles Peterson was living alone at the time. As he read it, he sat filled with grief and bewilderment. For he had just been bowled over in spirit to hear that Daniel, their shining splendid Daniel, had fallen into sin. A period of idleness at home had brought temptation. Laziness, even if under the guise of "rest," is no preparation for overcoming, and Daniel had fallen. Of course, had Homay known this, she would never have said yes; so what should he do? Thinking it might touch and revive Daniel, Mr Peterson took it to him, but Daniel read it with darkening face. He knew of course, that he now

was not worthy of her, and that his fall had cancelled this sweet little answer. And so ended *this*
engagement of Homay's also. Of Daniel's reclamation, largely due to the earnest intercession of a
faithful prayer partner in Seattle, you will hear
later. But when Homay and we met again, she was
still single and free.

We were back in Lisuland (from furlough) four
months and then, on April 21, in the afternoon, a
cry came, "The Bana party is arriving! They are
coming up the hill now!" How we dropped
everything and ran. There being neither telegraph
nor telephone and almost no postal service in the
canyon, expected loved ones could not announce
their arrival beforehand. Yes, there was my dear
Homay, not seen for two years now, but she was
plump as usual, and her laugh and hug were as
warm as ever. Along with her came Luke, A-che,
another Luda Lisu unknown to me, and her sister
Ruth. We took their picture to let others see the
Bana party almost as we saw them.

You can imagine how Homay and I hugged one
another, each of us conscious of the absence of a
little form who had never swerved in her devotion
to "Big Sister Homay," and who remained always,
as Homay's precious white baby (Kathryn had
gone to school at Chefoo). Almost immediately,
with tears flooding her eyes she asked, "What is
the latest word of Kathryn, Ma-Ma?" And so I
shared with her the latest letters from Little
Daughter.

And now we found that our Homay was too advanced for her old position as cook. She had
learned to use the Lisu typewriter, and of the three
Lisu whom the Cookes tried out in typing the

manuscript of the Lisu New Testament, Homay was the most accurate. So she became a sort of secretary to us. She oversaw the housekeeping, the buying in and measuring of the year's supply of grain, charcoal, salt, potatoes, etc., but she gave half of each day to typing out copies of the various New Testament Books for the Bible students, of whom you will be hearing anon. (It was half a year before the printed New Testament reached us.) At the month's end, when we went to give her her small salary, she again handed half of it back to us saying. "Ma-Pa, Ma-Ma, I would like to contribute the half of each day to working for the Lisu church by typing, as my gift to God. I will do that for nothing. The other half of each day, we will reckon as working for you, and for that I will take wages, if this is agreeable to you!"

It touched us very deeply–as you may imagine, but we have long learned the truth that God is no man's debtor. To be rich toward God is to be rich eternally; and so we accepted her offer.

And now we faced the coming true of a vision given to us while on furlough, but before I mention that, I want to quote from the circulars again, so that our station personnel, when referred to, will be intelligible to you.

A NEW MISSIONARY

We had brought a Christmas gift to the Lisu on our return in December 1937, in the person of a new missionary, Victor Christianson. He worked with Earl Carlson among the Chinese over a year ago, and when he heard of the latter's death he felt that God had asked him to take up the fallen torch, among the Lisu. I think I can best describe our new comrade to you by a picture. Our first day out was

very long, and dark overtook us while we were
still on wild mountain tops. The end of the stage
was a very long steep and rocky descent, the last
miles of which were made by feeble moonlight.
Indeed three of the Lisu carriers did not reach the
village at all, but had to spend the December night,
huddled supperless, in the middle of the road.
Those of us who managed to get to the inn were
very weary, and I was not slow in getting to bed.
Victor had to sleep in the main room, a very public
place. As he was having his devotions, an old
(Chinese) lady in the house asked him about the
Book he was reading, and tired as he was he
started to teach her. As I lay there on the other side
of the thin partition I heard the kindly voice going
on and on patiently explaining the way of salvation, regardless of his personal fatigue and a waiting bed–she had never heard before and very
probably might not again, so it was told her in full
before he slept. And in my heart, as I lay and
listened, I praised God for His missionary in lonely
mountain places.

Then another worker was brought to us, but
before I quote concerning that, reference should be
made to a young missionary hero who laid down
his life while serving the Lisu in the northern field
of Luda. While the Cookes were at Bana, and later
when they went on furlough, the Luda station was
in charge of Mr Charles B. Peterson and Mr Earl
Carlson. This book is about *Lisu* "Nests" and so I
do not feel free to interject missionary biographies,
but one might well be written about the noble
young life which Earl Carlson laid down in that
far-distant corner of the mission field. He was
smitten with typhus fever (we think it was), taken
while toiling unremittingly among the Lisu vil-

lages. There was no doctor to tend him. One was sent for, but he arrived too late. And so Mr Peterson had to see his chum laid to rest on the little knoll outside his kitchen door. Mr Peterson continued on alone, but the Mission felt it was too precarious, so the following quotation will explain itself.

OUR FAMILY ENLARGES

On January 15 we had the glad privilege of welcoming Charles Peterson to Oak Flat. Charles is one of "our own" boys; we use that designation only of those young missionaries who spent their initial days in Yunnan in our home, as language students, in years past. So Charles is no new friend. If I had to describe him in one word I think I would choose "faithful." No matter how trying his post, you cannot tempt Charlie away from it until he feels the Lord has said, "Go." Both the superintendent and fellow missionaries urged him to take a holiday after Earl's death, and "come out," but he quietly refused.

However, it has been decided to vacate Luda temporarily as a main station, and work it by visits, as an outstation of Oak Flat. Under such advice Charlie moved, and so we are the wealthy possessors of two other workers, Charles and Victor.

To go back to our "vision"; it was that of holding a Rainy Season Bible School (RSBS) for three months, June through August, of each year. The main purpose was to teach the Bible to the Lisu evangelists. We had soon discovered that these dear zealous young fellows were really ignorant of the scriptures–much too ignorant for their work. Of course they had never read the

whole New Testament, and they had done the best
they could with the four Gospels and Acts, which
they possessed. To win heathen to Christ, one does
not require much more knowledge than the plan of
salvation and John 3:16. But to *build up a church*
after they are won is a different matter. There were
now many babes in Christ waiting to be shown the
next step, and since the Lisu New Testament was
available in manuscript form at least, we felt the
need for a prolonged session over the Word. Mr
Fraser was delighted, and urged us on. A full-time
Bible school was an impossibility; we had the
oversight of a field four days' journey in length,
and more if you counted the outstations. The Luda
district, just committed to our oversight, was six
days' journey away. The pastoring of hundreds of
believers, steadily increasing in number, demanded
visitation. And we were the only medical help
anybody had within the radius of three or more
weeks' travel, at that time. We could not possibly
spend all our time at a Bible school.

We chose the Rainy Season for this purpose as
our experience, related in previous pages, had
taught us that it was dangerous for us to travel at
that time of the year. Also, the summer being the
farmers' busiest time, the Lisu teachers had then
much less to do. People lived in their fields to
protect the growing grain from birds and animals,
and the villages were partly empty. So we chose
June to August for Bible study. Of this work I hope
to devote a whole chapter later on. Just now, its
effect on Homay is all I will relate.

We began that first school with a session of
heart-searching and cleansing. Although it was
mainly for men, a few girls attended it at first, and

Homay always took in as many classes as she had time for.

One of those first days, John and I were seated at our table, deep in work when Homay came slowly up to us and stopped, waiting for an invitation to speak. Her face was so grave that John said immediately, "What is it, Homay?"

"Ma-Pa, I have a confession I must make to you." As she spoke tears began to well up in her eyes.

"All right, don't be afraid," her pastor answered kindly.

"Before your furlough, when we were building the house here, I–I lied to you once, Ma-Pa," and at that word the flood gates broke and the tears streamed so that it was hard to get the rest of the story.

"I found a penpoint on the ground, after everything was torn up, and I did not ask if I might have it, but just took it–I knew you'd give it if I asked; and I found a twig and made a stem for it, and it worked as a pen quite nicely. But one day when I was using it, you came by and said, 'Where did you get the pen, Homay?' and I was scared and before I thought I had answered, 'Mr Cooke gave it to me,' and then you walked away. I was not happy afterwards, but I always too ashamed to confess it to you. You might have thought I was in the habit of telling you lies and I've never lied to you in anything else." By this time she was shaking so with sobs that we tried to stop her. But she had more to say.

"Then you left for furlough, and we went to Bana; but always in the services, when sin was mentioned, that penpoint came up before me. I confessed it to the Cookes, but still I got no relief. Then I told Teacher Luke, and he thought it was too small a matter to worry about, but still I was not happy.

"And then on the way back from Bana, we stopped at Paoshan where Miss Anna Christensen was holding meetings, you remember, and she spoke of unconfessed sins, and said even little things might keep us from God, and so I made up my mind to tell you about the penpoint."

By this time all of us were weeping, but I hope this little story will speak to some reader, who has been told by the Holy Spirit to confess a sin, perhaps a seemingly unimportant one, and you are not obeying, because Satan tells you it is too small a matter. There is no path to peace or blessing until you confess. Confessing to other people than the ones involved, like Homay tried, is the devil's own snare to keep you in bondage. And the fear of confession is his delusion also. After confession was all over, and the tears dried, what joy and lightness of heart! And her Ma-Pa against whom she had offended, and whom she deeply loved, only cherished her all the more because of her obedience to the Spirit in the little thing, and her great desire to be a clean vessel for God to use.

And now we have a surprise for you. The circular of August, 1938, recording the end of our first RSBS, has this paragraph.

WEDDING BELLS
That busy day before closing day, about four in the afternoon, Job performed a ceremony which made Thomas and Homay man and wife for life. I do not know how it came about, but feel it was more of a

comfort marriage than a hot love affair. She is the best to be had in Lisuland, as Thomas well knew, and Homay was conscious that she could not say yes to a more faithful or finer Christian, so I think that was how it happened; but happiness seems to increase in their hearts every day. Homay was dressed in a combination of orange silk and dark blue cotton. Rhoda was her bridesmaid (and a very pretty one) and Luda-Peter was best man.

I played Lohengrin's *Bridal March* as they entered and left the chapel, and the whole ceremony was holy and quiet–a memory. Thomas is to be kept in this district for a while at least, and they live in a little house right next to ours, for Homay continues to help us in typing and in the house work. (Dorcas has gone home to her family in Luda.)

Thomas is a Stockade Hill boy. A deep sorrow in his life (one that need never have happened if he had not obeyed his conscience before the promptings of his heart) made an evangelistic trip away from home seem attractive to him. And so he was sent to the Munition of Rocks, and worked most of his time in the Luda district. As a strange providence had it, he paid one evangelistic trip to Goomoo, and while there heard of dear Joseph's drowning and was asked to conduct Joseph's funeral. So as it turned out in the end, the one to bury Homay's fiancé was the one who married her! As the Luda district was temporarily under the Oak Flat district, the Luda evangelists were all summoned to RSBS and thus Homay and Thomas met.

Both were very nervous. Thomas lost ten pounds between the date of the engagement and that of the marriage. And our usually serene Homay, when asked by Job (at the wedding ceremony), "Are you pleased to take this man as your husband?" opened her mouth to answer, "Pleased," but only a wheeze came out! Her mouth was so dry with nervousness that she could not get her voice to work. Astounded, Job said, "What?" whereupon, her eyes beseeching him in agony, again her mouth opened, and again only a wheeze emerging, Job was loyal. "Oh yes, she says, *Pleased!*" he announced to everybody, and proceeded.

Then when the bridegroom was to put the ring on her finger, his hand shook so, that he could not pick up the ring; so again Job silently came to the rescue, and put the ring on her finger in lieu of the bridegroom. But these are small matters–the Lisu consider it went off very nicely.

Their honeymoon (which Lisu do not take) was a trip to Goo-moo, Burma, which will be recorded in the story of Goo-moo. The Goo-moo Christians loved the pair of them so much, however, that when the time for our departure came (Homay and Thomas had gone with us) they begged us to leave the newly-weds with them to teach them the Bible for six months; and we gladly consented. They were given the little house which the Goo-moo Christians had built for us, and six happy and useful months were spent over there in Burma.

In the beginning of 1939 a shadow passed over their sunshine. The February circular has a note–

> Thomas has been incapacitated for work by a strange illness giving him acute pain. It sounds like a serious hernia, but we really do not know. His valuable ministry is being hindered–pray.

And now 1939 RSBS was coming upon us.
During the time that the Cookes were on furlough,
the Luda teachers came down to study with us,
and this time, to our joy, Daniel appeared with
them. He had returned to the Lord, and felt the
need of studying the Word. His deacons had
recommended him, so were glad to receive him
along with the other students from Luda. Their
arrival is told in the following circular:

And another delightful reunion was the following Monday night–a cry from the kitchen sent me
flying through the doorway. It said, "Teacher Job
has returned!" As I came up to his humble doorway I asked, "Didn't Rhoda come too?" and a
meek "Yes" from the direction of the garden revealed the lassie herself, braids hanging down her
bosom, coming from the vegetable patch with
something for supper. She got a kiss on the spot
and then Homay pulled my hand and whispered
with a meaning smile, "Daniel's in there!" thrusting her chin (native fashion) in the direction of the
hut. She did not seem the least embarrassed, in fact
I think she was secretly pleased that she could now
show the one who had been faithless to her, just
what a fine husband God had eventually given her.
I hurried into the crowded shanty (for everybody
was there to welcome them) and was happy to see
Job's face once more, and sure enough, there in the
corner, hanging back as if ashamed, was Daniel–he
has come for the Rainy Season Bible School and is
doing odd jobs before it begins. He is paying his
own way for these three months of study. He
listens to the messages very earnestly and one can
see why the Cookes loved him so much. The next
evening, when a little group of them including
Homay were present, Daniel apologized to her in

front of them all—she herself told me so with
shining eyes—and once more I thought how God
works out all things, even the heartbreak of
unfaithfulness to the one who loves and cleaves
unto Him.

"You must learn, you must let God teach you,
that the only way to get rid of your past is to get a
future out of it. God will waste nothing."— *Phillips
Brooks*

But Thomas's trouble did not clear up. He was a
good student usually; in fact in 1940 he led the
whole student body. But this year of 1939 seemed
to be going to be a failure. The August circular
says:

I had no sooner spoken of Thomas' glowing face
in last month's issue, than the Enemy put a blight
upon it. Praise God he could only touch the outside, but he did hit hard. Thomas got severe pain
in his head and around the left eye, and then after
about a week of suffering, the pain passed, but left
the sight impaired. The right eye has now become
affected. Do pray for him—he is only twenty-six
years old and he and Homay are expecting a little
gift from God in December.

I remember well those days. We could not diagnose his trouble; as a matter of fact, it was double
hernia, but at the time the whole pain was in his
eyes and he seemed to be going blind. Now
blindness in a mountain land, where everything is
perpendicular, is an awful affliction. Well that
Homay had learned to send her roots out to the
Living Water! Yet even so, when such a storm hits
a young tree, the upper part of it can be badly
shaken. And one morning I shall never forget. I

was called to see Thomas again–he could see out of neither eye and was in severe pain. I could do nothing for him, and felt my uselessness. So I just put my arms around the anxious little wife and whispered, "Don't worry, dear. God is faithful and remember you are a daughter to us. You and Thomas will always have a place in our home." She broke down and wept, which was most unusual for her, who had such wonderful outward control.

In answer to prayer, Thomas was healed sufficiently that he was able to finish RSBS, but at the end of the school, it was plain that he must seek medical help. In Burma there was a mission hospital where they were very kind to the Lisu, and Thomas knew that if he could only get to that faraway place he would receive attention free of charge. That autumn and winter we itinerated a lot and were seldom home, so I do not remember when Thomas left. I only knew that later I discovered that his little wife had given all her savings to pay his expenses there and back. Here I would like to say what a good wife Homay was. She was a very nimble seamstress and I think she had secretly made up her mind that her husband was to be the best dressed and best cared-for of all the evangelists. Living still in our home, she was at the source of supplies; when cloth or books came in, to be sold to the students, she made the first selection and bought the very best for Thomas. I once teased him, "Don't you know what a lucky man you are, to have such a wife?"

"I sure do," he replied with such a happy laugh that I felt he was not being spoiled, and I was glad that happiness had come to them both.

It was a regret to me that I could not be present when her first-born arrived. No longer a Dry Tree! God knows how to lighten our loads. How joyfully she prepared for that baby. Lisu do not usually make any preparation for a coming child, except, perhaps, to sew it a hat! "Why, you can't tell whether it is going to live or not!" they will say when you suggest a few garments to welcome the wee newcomer. Such a thought shows how high infant mortality is, and is expected to be. Over half their babies die. But Homay had lived with missionaries and had learned some hygiene; so an array of knitted bonnets and small clothes were carefully being added to as the months rolled on.

Baby was to come in December. Thomas was still away and no letters were possible. Then Kuhn family had to leave on a long three months' trip to Village of the Three Clans, but fellow workers were present to carry on the work of Oak Flat district. Mr Peterson was on furlough, but Mr Christianson had married Miss Cath Galpin, and she promised me to do all in her power to help Homay when her time came. I knew she would, but at the same time, she was a stranger to the lonely little mother. But my duty called me north and I had to go.

When I learned that Homay and Thomas were expecting a little one I wrote and told Kathryn that God had promised to give Homay a baby for Christmas, but had not said whether He would give a boy or a girl. Her reaction was the following letter to Homay which so amused us that I copy it here.

Chefoo.
October 31, 1939.

My dearest Homay:

I think of you a lot and pray for you too.

I cannot speak Lisu now except yes. I hope you will teach me some Lisu when I see you again, because it is fun learning other languages.

Mummy has told the secret that God told you, and I think it is a very nice secret. I will love the baby. I will tell you a name if it is a girl–Kathryn–not because its my name because it is the gift of God, and if it is a boy–John–that is only to help you.

I love you very much.

I am having a good time at school am learning very much it is only twenty-eight more days till the holidays.

With love from,
KATHRYN K.

Homay was thrilled that her "white baby" should want to name her own real baby, so when a son appeared she named him John. Though that was his legal title, she herself always referred to him as "Oldest Hemp" (Thomas' surname is Hemp). I could not understand it, until I "thought Lisu" and saw that she was looking forward to many more little Hemps; and then I realized how the name "Dry Tree" had stung, all through the years. Always she referred to her baby as "Oldest Hemp" with a smile which spoke of the secret hope that there would be many others.

When we returned in March, 1940, baby John was already quite big and very cute, but cried a great deal. He just cried night and day, and Homay was exhausted long before he was. Germs of a serious illness were already working her body, but this we did not know. Homay had been the healthiest Lisu I have ever met. Every other helper had periodic hours in bed with malarial headaches at least, often more serious diseases, but not Homay. Plump and flourishing, she seemed immune to everything, so when we came back and Cath Christianson told me that Homay had moved out of our house and was living in a room off the Lisu church kitchen, and that she never seemed to have time to do anything but look after little John, I was worried. A baby takes a lot of time and young mothers can easily fall into the habit of letting the baby steal their quiet time with God–and that is fatal spiritually. I sought out the little mother and watched her for some days. She seemed lazy–so unusual for the energetic girl of the past; she disliked to haul water to wash John's baby clothes and would sit by until our laundry girl had finished and then beg for the wash water.

Then in April, one evening as the Infant Brigade (of whom you will hear later) were in the midst of their singing lesson, a gunshot rang out through the dark. Immediately we were all out of the room and into the night. Pushing up the trail, I could just discern other villagers emerging from their huts. A white horse was coming with someone leading it! Job! and behind him Luke, Andrew, their wives, and–Thomas! I believe that was our first word that he was even alive, after the hospital treatment. Here he was, cured–and anxious to behold the baby he had never yet seen.

After joyful greetings we all hurried back to Luke's house where, snug and cosy by the fire, we felt at leisure to ask questions. Thomas was entirely healed! How we thanked the Lord and how mystified we were to hear that an operation for hernia was what fixed him up, eyes and everything!

Of course little John was hauled on to his Daddy's lap for much inspection and hugging. There were the other teachers who also had stories to tell, so that Thomas and his little family were able to slip away to the privacy of their own room next door.

Events followed one another and it was RSBS, 1940, before my attention was drawn particularly to Homay again. Thomas appeared one evening and said, "Ma-Pa, I'm concerned about John's mother" (the oriental way of mentioning one's wife). "She has had no appetite for a long time, and her legs are swelling. Do you think you have any medicine that would help her?" He looked very anxious about symptoms that seemed unimportant to me. Homay had always had fat ankles. I examined one medical book, but none of the diseases attendant on swollen ankles seemed to fit. From then on I watched the little mother as closely as possible in a busy life that did not often, now, touch hers. She looked all right, but was so lethargic and sluggish that I began to think that maybe it was a spiritual problem and wrote the American prayer helpers to pray for her. I had her in for an interview, too.

"Homay, are you reading the Word and praying, like you used to?"

"No, Ma-Ma," she answered immediately. "There isn't time now and I have not the strength. Baby cries so at night that I am too tired in the day." She had a sort of "What's the use" attitude,

that it made me anxious for her. Never having
known her to be sick, I did not dream that a dread
disease had already laid fast hold upon the still
plump little form. She knew herself to be ill, yet
she was not in actual pain, so that no one but
Thomas took it seriously. I myself thought it was a
spiritual matter and exhorted her to remember that
the spirit needs food as much as the body. Poor
little Nest; it was a sad wind blowing upon it.

At the end of each RSBS the Lisu teachers are reappointed to districts where they usually remain
for the following twelve months. Thomas was sent
to Village of the Olives, across the river from us,
and the Christians there had prepared a nice little
house for him and his family. Homay was reluctant
to leave us, although no medicines we had given
her had helped her. I urged her to go, thinking that
some active testimony for the Lord might be her
greatest help. So we parted rather sadly on each
side.

For the next few months I had many important
things to take my mind off Homay's "lethargy," as
I thought of it. Mrs Christianson had become
seriously ill, her life was in danger, she had to be
taken out to a hospital, and eventually she and her
husband had to return to America. We ourselves
were called upon to make a long trip south to
Stockade Hill district, there with the parent church
to hold one of the first Bible studies since the New
Testament came into their hands—for they had had
no missionary for many years, and at present
writing still have none. This was important work.

So it was Christmas before we returned to Oak
Flat and I found a lot of Lisu letters awaiting me,
among them one from Thomas which said some-

thing like this: "I hope you will forgive me for not travelling around my field here. Homay is so ill that I cannot leave her. I fear it is a destroying sickness. But I teach every night in this village."

Then it was I became alarmed, and as Leila and Allyn Cooke were expected back from their furlough, to arrive soon after Christmas, we sent one of our mules to Village of Olives for Homay to ride, and urged Thomas to bring her that Leila Cooke might try to diagnose her case. Homay came, outwardly a little thinner, but that was all that was apparent. Inwardly she seemed back at the place of victory. Her face had once more that quiet peace upon it.

I had no opportunity to talk with Homay personally that time, so I do not know when it was that the Little Tree awoke to the fact that the one thing needful is to spread out our roots unto the river. Then, "it does not fear when heat comes; its leaves are always green."

Homay's "leaf" was so green that neither Leila Cooke nor I thought it was "a destroying sickness." We proposed her going out to a Chinese hospital and offered her our mule to ride, but as I remember it, she refused, saying she had not the strength to make such a trip. "I always thought that horseback riding was restful," she said with a smile, "I never imagined that it can be as tiring as walking, until I had this trip over from Village of the Olives." And I laughed too, recollecting the many bone-aches of a whole day in the saddle through such a country—and how the Lisu expect you to be quite rested after "sitting all day," at the end of such a trip!

So back they went and we prayed for her daily,

but with no special concern until February, when Orville Carlson (who had now joined us, to take his dead brother's place in the Lisu work) made a trip to Village of the Olives to conduct a Bible school. He brought back an enthusiastic report of the growing little church there, but added that he was burdened for Homay. "She does not complain of pain, but seems to have no strength to do anything. Just crawls out into the sunshine in the morning and lies there hour after hour. It is pitiful. We ought to pray for her."

From then on, we did, very earnestly, and yet a faith to claim healing never came to us. I was really alarmed now, and the next month, after conducting Bible school in a neighbouring village, I came over and spent a weekend at Village of the Olives. I was shocked at the sight of Homay. She has simply wasted away. She said she had no pain, but daily diarrhoea (medicines for this had long ago been given her without effect); and it was plain to see that death was stamped upon the thin, wan face.

Deeply moved at her obvious condition, I probed for the most important thing–the health of the spirit. And I can still see the light that sprang on to her wasted features as she smiled and answered, "The Lord's will be done, Ma-Ma; I'm happy to accept His will." Tears came with the smile, but did not overflow. Neither of us mentioned what we knew caused them–namely, the question, "What will happen to Baby John?" I did not dare offer to take him, for I was committed to a life in which travelling occupied most of the year. And at that time we had no dependable woman working in our home, only three irresponsible boys, The

Infant Brigade, of whom you may hear later. So the question had to remain unanswered.

As the earthly vessel was wearing thin, the treasure within was shining out. All of her Christian life one of Homay's favourite hymns was, *Have Thine Own Way, Lord*, and now that the supreme test was being put to her, those words were always her answer. The Christians there told me that Homay was simply a marvel to the heathen women of the village. They used to come just to see and talk with the young teacher who was not afraid to die, nor even rebellious. The Tree Planted by the Waters..."has no worries in a year of drought and never fails to bear fruit." The little group culled out of heathenism during that year of dying were among the choicest of the Munition of Rocks.

As for ourselves—we had work calling for us, and could not stay to see her through the Valley of the Shadow, except in spirit. Our circular letter, telling of the gathering of RSBS students for 1941, has this paragraph:

THE DISTANT TRIUMPH SONG
Among all our wonderful forty we missed Thomas' face. "Homay is too ill for me to leave her," he wrote, "and I can hardly bear to look at her" (she was so wasted). "My heart is breaking to see the others going off to school and I must stay behind, but there is no help for it."

Then one night after those weeks of heavy rain, as I was about to open the evening service, someone said to me, "Thomas has come! He came in just now, carrying his little son on his back." The news, though long expected, pierced with the sharpness which only the last enemy to be destroyed can inflict. Thomas' coming meant only one thing.

Hardly able to speak for tears, I asked, "When did Homay pass away?"

"Sixth of the sixth moon," was the answer. Then I had to go in to prepare for service.

The next day our Thomas was in class. He is very brave, but when opportunity afforded I asked him to tell of Homay's last days. He said her faith was triumphant to the end. Spiritually she seemed to grow stronger as the body grew weaker. There was never a murmur against this decree of her Father's, although she was only about thirty years old. Fellow villagers say her patience under suffering made the heathen marvel. But when it came to telling her last words, which were ones of pity for himself and little eighteen-months-old John, Thomas broke down; so I said, "Write to me." With no one to care for baby, Thomas had at first said he would go back to his relatives and his own old home, but the pleadings of the flock in Village of Olives made him hesitate. Here is his note:

"Ma-Ma, I want to answer you now. I wanted to answer you when we were talking together, but I couldn't, because of grief. First I said I was going back to my home, but that was for sorrow of heart. Now I would like to say this, if God shows me the way, I will go back to Village of the Olives. The brothers and sisters there were not satisfied that I should not, and neither am I. For they are more to me than my own people–all in that district are. But I cannot forget Homay; before RSBS I cried all day–not for her, but for myself and for Baby John. Homay's last words were, 'I cannot eat. If God is going to take me I will go, but it will be hard for you and baby.' After that her speech was not clear; she felt so sorry for Baby John."

Asked to speak at the Sunday main service, Thomas chose I Thess. 4:13-⁊ and used it as a testimony to his faith in the resurrection. "We sorrow not as others who have no hope," he quoted. Then we held a memorial service for her who is rejoicing in her Saviour's presence. Since turning to Him, Homay's life among her fellows was without reproach. She went to Him having no cause to be ashamed—what a glorious finale!

Thou wast their rock, their fortress and their might;
Thou, Lord, their Captain in the well-fought fight;
Thou, in the darkness drear, their one true Light.
        Alleluia!

And up in Heaven, her old friend, Mr J. O. Fraser, pioneer missionary to her tribe, he who had given up a brilliant career in the homelands that these poor despised "earth people" might know the way of salvation, was already there to greet her. I would like to ask you, dear reader, what of the many other tribes' girls, just like Homay (for there are many more) who would love to accept and follow this Saviour, *if only they knew how!* What of the many other little Wind-blow Nests, who seek desperately for a Cleft in a Rock to shelter them, but cannot find Him, if you and I do not go and point out the Way?

What of the thousands of young Saplings who wither up and perish under the scorching fires of Life, because no one has told them of the River, and the secret path their roots may take, to drink of its coolness?

Friends, let us live and work for eternity.

Chapter 4

NEST FOR SINGING BIRD

> *What a God, who, out of shade,*
> *Nest for singing bird hath made.*
>
> AMY CARMICHAEL.

WHEN Homay was just a new believer, struggling to worship God at Deer Pool chapel under the cover of fuel-hunting, another young girl was also entering into the joy and emancipation of Christ's salvation.

Deer Pool Village is one of the most magnificently beautiful village sites in the canyon. The trail climbs gently up from a deep ravine until it reaches that face of the mountain which banks the Salween, and there, some eight hundred feet high, it runs on level around the neck of the mountain until it has to curve back into another abyssal drop. And below this level pine-needle-carpeted path are the tiers of little Lisu shanties. There are two mountain knolls side by side on the trail which make a natural divide, so that the village is in two parts, and in between, by the side of the level trail, a little chapel has been built. I wonder if Homay and Leah first met there? I know that the heathen Lisu women do not usually travel; many of them never visit even neighbouring villages until they become Christian. So it is quite possible that as Homay left her wood basket at the door and slipped in on to one of the women's benches, she often found herself beside Leah, who was only a year younger than Homay.

But such a contrast the two young lives presented! Both girls were in earnest and both became outstanding Christians; both loved to sing and became good singers. But the one had to believe in secret, surrounded every day by heathen talk and heathen habits; and the other was one of a fine family, free to go to the uttermost for God. Leah, as she sits in chapel beside Homay, can reach out and touch her mother, one of the most devoted Christians in the community, and two dear little sisters are sitting beside her eagerly trying to learn. Across the aisle is her father, partially blind but with a light from heaven on his face, and in his arms is a baby boy who grew up to be a sturdy little Christian. Lucky Leah, easy to be a Christian under such circumstances, isn't it? Yes, but wait. This little family Nest is already built well into the Cleft of the Rock, it is true, but the Evil Spirit, so long ruler of the Munition of Rocks, has plans laid to dislodge that Nest.

In the meantime let us share the joys of those early days. The Lisu teachers told us that the Christians in the canyon were not stable, except those at Deer Pool, who became a joy and inspiration so sweet that it gave courage and hope to push farther in. "God is a rewarder of those who diligently seek him,"...so to Deer Pool Village was given the honour of becoming the first mission station in those parts. Mr Talmadge Payne and his wife moved in from Chinaland, and made their home in one of the Lisu huts, with a tent pitched at

the side. I wonder what were the feelings of the
first white woman to enter the canyon of the Upper
Salween! I can but record my own impressions
when, some years later, I followed in her footsteps.

By the time we had climbed the long trail the sun
had set, and we were ushered into a tribal shanty
where we were to spend the night. But I had
caught a glimpse of the breath-taking scenic beauty
of this village site, so, setting down my hat and
things, I hastily went outside to view the panorama before darkness hid it from me. The back of
the shanty rested on the ground; the floor, to make
it level, was supported in front on stilts, and as
Lisu have no nails the floor boards were just laid
loosely on the stilts. I stepped gingerly on the
warped planks which wobbled at each of my steps,
for underneath me was just air–the ground beneath
was a steep cornfield which dropped away from
under the house like a gigantic tobaggan slide of
someseventhousandfeet, to the Salween river, unseen, far below. I crouched there nervously afraid
to look down again at that disappearing slope, but
enthralled with the beauty around and above. I
seemedontop of the world. The high peaks opposite appeared to be just on my own level, while
beneath us many lower peaks and ridges spread
themselves north and south; in either direction one
could see the twisting canyon for many, many
miles–in fact for two or three days' journey–and all
was sinking gradually into the black shadows of
night. Such beauty I have never seen surpassed.
Up there close to the heavens God seemed very
near, and worship was an unhindered joy.

But one cannot live on scenic grandeur, so I had
to turn at length and find my way back into the

shanty, where around the crackling cosy fire a hot
meal was ready for us. They had cooked rice, meat,
and vegetables Chinese style, which was really
enjoyable; then after supper a copper gong's
mellow *boom! boom!* drifted through the night air,
calling the village to chapel service. Our Lisu host
led us over the pine-scented trail, and other forms,
each holding a flaring pine-torch to light his way,
loomed out of the darkness. The chapel was of
their own building—earth floor, backless benches,
and a huge elevated flat stone, up at the front, on
which burning pine chips were piled to give light.
Men sat on one side, women on the other, all
peering at the new Ma-Pa and Ma-Ma, and smiling
happily, if self-consciously, as their look was
returned. I could not understand Lisu then, but we
were all on common ground when the singing
commenced. They in Lisu and we in English
together could sing—

> I'm tired of sin and straying, Lord,
>   Now I'm coming Home;
> I'll trust Thy love, believe Thy Word,
>   Lord, I'm coming Home.
>
> Coming Home, coming Home,
>   Never more to roam,
> Open now Thine arms of Love,
>   Lord, I'm coming Home.

or perhaps it was—

> What a friend we have in Jesus
> All our sins and griefs to bear.

Whatever the colour of our skin we all had the
same testimony, the same experience. As the

flames leaped up, every face stood out clear and shining with joy, and as it waned, shadows stole forth and framed their faces softly. Through the crevices of the crude wall a pine-scented mountain wind sighed gently in. I thought of how far we were from home and civilization. I thought of the bitterly rugged road we had come over, and I was filled with exaltation and joyous thanksgiving to God that He had allowed me to be one of His messengers to the ends of the earth.

I imagine Mrs Payne's experience was much the same. And the Lisu, on their backless benches, gazing at the foreign woman, marvelling at the colour of her skin and the height of her nose, trying to picture her natural background but quite in vain–what were their thoughts? Grace Payne was the first white woman ever to enter the canyon, and as Leah and the others watched her that first evening of their arrival I wish we might enter their thoughts. Of one thing I know for sure–gratitude and love were uppermost. One of the questions inthe Lisu catechism is, "Why should we be grateful to the foreign missionary?" and the answer tells clearly of the cost of leaving home and loved ones. And the Lisu do not forget it.

"You are the one who brought us salvation," they will exclaim, and pat your hand lovingly. And as Leah watched the missionary and remembered that she had left father and mother, brothers and sisters to come that long journey just to help earth people, a fount of love and gratitude sprang up in her heart that was never to die. In heaven they will see what it cost even more fully perhaps, and the love tie between us will be eternal.

"I'll pray for her every day," vowed the young

heart, in all probability, for that is what our spiritual children do.

And then how enthralled they must have been to hear her sing! Grace Payne was a lovely soloist in the homelands, and the Lisu script, being based on our own English letters, is easy to master. We all learn to read (and hence to sing, if the tune is familiar) long before we can talk.

"Isn't it funny?" whispers one of the girls to Leah. "When she sings I can understand what she says, but when she talks, I can't!" Not realizing that the "talk" was, as yet, English!

"Her voice is different from ours," says another. "When she sings it touches my heart and the tears come out!"

No wonder, through those precious months when Paynes were at Deer Pool, that lonely little Homay loved to slip in at the back of the chapel and listen. It was worth a scolding when she got home.

But to happy Leah they were the most wonderful days of her life. All day long while she herded the cattle on the wild mountainside, or hoed corn with other villagers, or spun cotton for the family clothing, she would think and talk of nothing else.

"Did you hear of Ba-shia-nyio-pa?" someone would say to her. "He wants to be a Christian, you know, but he is so tied to his opium. And when he broke it off to believe, Ma-Ma gave him medicine to help when the craving comes on, and dandy stuff to drink that she calls *coffee*—I drank some; he let me have a sip. My, it was good! Just imagine anyone being so kind as she is! She pities us so."

Mrs Payne is a trained nurse, and the village has never forgotten her loving ministry among them.

Mr Payne could already speak some Lisu, and was quite eloquent in Chinese. Leah loved the evening services when the white man opened up the Word of God to them. He had the whole Bible, while at that time all the Lisu church had were the four Gospels, Acts, a catechism, hymn book, and a small book of abbreviated Old Testament stories. Mr Payne felt that the catechism alone might give an impression of legalism, and so he preached ardently on the grace of God, on the uselessness of man's doing anything to save himself apart from accepting that grace, and one young heart at least caught the vision of our heavenly Father's marvellous love and condescension–caught it so vividly that all the storms and trials which were waiting on the path ahead of her were unable to shake her faith in God's kindness.

But the hard life of privations was telling on the foreign woman. I myself slept one night in the shanty that had been given to the Paynes for a home. The rats held carnival over my head and down the sides of the walls. Scared at their boldness, I wrapped myself tightly up in my bedding with only my nose sticking out in order to breathe, and part of my forehead. But there was no escape–a rat walked right over me–I could feel the coldness, on my forehead, of tiny feet sauntering across! But Grace Payne's trials were much greater than mere rats. The rainy season had begun. Day after day the tent and miserable hut were swept by torrents: clouds and drizzle veiled the grand scenery. All was just cold and mud and wet.

"From Sunday morning until Saturday night, I never had my galoshes off, except to go to bed," she told me.

But in addition to this, the work had spread so rapidly that Deer Pool was no longer the centre and so Mr and Mrs Payne felt the time had come to move on, to build a little shanty somewhere else that would be healthier and more central. The Village of Pine Mountain was chosen. How Deer Pool villagers lamented! Of course the missionaries would only be a day's journey away, but that is far when a loved one is sick and needs medicine.

And after they had gone? How empty the beautiful mountainside seemed. The shanty they had used was still there, but no loving forms to cheer and help them; and somehow in chapel even, everything seemed desolate; a cheeriness, a fellowship had gone.

"I don't want to go to chapel any more; it makes me cry," someone would say.

"But God is still with us," urged young Leah, "and He will hear if we pray in Jesus' Name. We must keep on worshipping."

There she was always at service time, near the front seat, and her clear voice leading in the hymn singing cheered on many a disconsolate neighbour.

Loss of her missionaries was like a brisk breeze which foretells the coming of a storm. For some time now Leah's eyes had been itching. Knowing nothing of hygiene, she rubbed them, of course, when they itched, unconscious that her hand was not clean. Lisu homes are ventless, hence very smoky and sooty. In her person Leah was always remarkably clean and neat, but in cooking every Lisu has to handle sooty pots and hands cannot remain white. Little wonder, then, that dread trachoma had laid hold of her eyes. Her father was almost blind from it already, but, not understanding the danger of infection, Leah had not been careful in contacting him. Trachoma victims are everywhere in Lisuland.

Whenever anyone was going to Pine Mountain Leah would ask them to buy for her "a little eye medicine," and after using that, sight would be clearer for a few days, and so she was not alert to her danger.

My attention was first called to Leah when in 1935 I took sick, as mentioned in Homay's story, and Nurse Kathleen Davies came in to attend me. She and Miss Embery had stayed one night at Deer Pool, and Miss Davies was impressed with Leah.

"There is a young girl up here with eye trouble," she said. "Ingrowing eyelashes is a part of it, and she asked me to pull them out for her, but her eyes are really very bad. I noticed her at Deer Pool that time we stayed there. She was sitting in the sun, practically sightless, but *singing*–singing away like a little bird. Extraordinary, to be so happy under such an affliction."

> What a God, who, out of shade,
> Nest for singing bird hath made.

Life was to be an ever-deepening "shade" experience for Leah; yet through it all the testimony of those who knew her was that she was full of song, full of stout testimony as to the Lord's goodness. How could such a thing be? As mentioned above, the canyon contains many blind Lisu, but I never once, in all my ten years of travel there, saw a blind heathen with a song in her heart! They are the most wretched of the wretched unhappy ones. And lest you think that Leah's was just a chance case of cheerful temperament, let me testify that she was not the only blind Christian who had an inner joy that upheld.

I knew another woman, almost blind, eyes continually running pus, but who had light in her face. Her daughter, in the early twenties only, was really blind—could do no work. Her sister-in-law, who lived with them, was totally blind and totally deaf and dumb. She, with her suffering eyes, had to farm and work for these afflicted ones, yet it was a blessing to meet her. I once asked her what made her happy. She answered, "It is the thought of Heaven, Ma-Ma. The Lisu teachers have told me what a wonderful place Jesus is preparing for me. There is no sickness up there, no blindness, and things that even good eyes have never seen or can imagine for beauty and wonder are being kept for us. God is going to wipe away every tear from our eyes. I like to talk and think about it."

Yes, in the sad shade of blindness, God has made a nest for singing bird! He only can give songs in the night. When outward eyes fail, if the heart reaches out after Him, He will open the eyes of the spirit and lift the inner man from earth's drudgery to sit in heavenly places with Himself.

It was 1942 before I had much contact with Leah. I knew her only as the Blind Singing Girl of Deer Pool Village. But in February, 1942, we started a new venture: a month's Bible school for girls only. Lisu women were always the hardest to reach. Their husbands and brothers said with a laugh, "Oh, they can't learn!" so when a Bible study week was planned for a village, the audience was mainly men. At such a time the farm work was thrust upon the sex that "couldn't learn." And of those that did attend Bible classes, I must say that it looked as if the men had spoken the truth. At any attempt to make them recite scripture or study in the simplest form, they would dissolve into giggles and silliness; to try to get them to pray in public was to ruin your service hour. It seemed hopeless. Yet there were Homay, Leah, and as these pages proceed you will meet with others, here one and there one, who seemed an exception to the general rule, which made us hope that, with patience, work among the women also might be accomplished. When the Rainy Season Bible Schools began, a few girls also would come and sit on the back row—mention of them will be made later. But we gradually saw that the mixed education was attracting the wrong type of girl, and endangering our boy students, so we had to forbid their coming.

That is why we decided to try a school for girls only. But, if there were no boys present would any girls come? We did not know. The right kind would come, we hoped. Another serious question was, *when* could they come? Lisu men were free as soon as the year's harvest was over. Lisu women were never free. When farming ends, spinning, weaving, and sewing the year's garments for all the family commenced. Even the deacons were not much in favour of trying for such a thing as a girls' school, but one young evangelist said, "Except at Chinese New Years'! Everybody is more or less free then. If the school were in February, and those who planned to come were to weave cloth a little later at night and a little earlier each morning during January, they could get it all done and be free to come for February!"

Some shook their heads dubiously; others agreed it was a possibility. None thought that teaching the girls would amount to much, but they hated to disappoint Ma-Ma! So at Christmas time,when the great crowd from all over the district was present, we gave notice that a girls' school would be held the next February, and asked the applicants to sign up for it. Not everybody was invited. We had rules of admission:

1. The girl student must be a saved Christian, not just a professing one.
2. She must have a recommendation from the deacon of her village that for the past year at least, her conduct has been irreproachable.
3. She must be able to read and write. (In later years this rule was cancelled.)
4. She must be at least seventeen years old; no limit after that.

A great deal of talking, girls' heads bowed together in whispering circles, and of course giggling, followed the above announcement. Only about six signed up; but the Lisu evangelist mentioned above said to me, "Don't be discouraged, Ma-Ma. More than that are planning to come. They just don't know what 'sign up' involves and are afraid to sign lest later they are hindered from coming."

We had to make preparations for them in faith and prayer. You can imagine our joy on the day of assembling, when twenty-four students arrived and enrolled! Two had to be turned away because their deacons would not recommend them. But some of these girls came a day's journey from north in the canyon, south in the canyon and from across the river. And from the south came—Leah, with two other women from Deer Pool. Her chum

Tabitha came forward, that afternoon, while Leah hung back shyly and nervously, and Tabitha said, "Ma-Ma, the rules are that every student must be able to read and write. Well Leah used to be able to, but her eyes won't admit of it now. Still she'd like to come and listen; will you allow her?"

"We surely will!" I cried out most happily, reaching out for the blind girl's hand and patting it. "That rule is only to weed out girls that could not follow the meaning of the lectures, which does not apply to Leah. She is very welcome indeed." And how the sightless face beamed with happiness!

Then the little band of three went off cheerfully to find a dormitory where they could all be together. The Chinese school had kindly lent us their little dormitories, as it was New Year's holidays and their students had gone home. These dormitories are merely shacks with wooden planks for beds, earth for floor, and three rocks for a fireplace!

Before school commenced, it was the custom for the teachers to interview each student personally and alone, as to their salvation. When Leah came into my study, we went through the usual procedure of questions, even though I knew she was an exceptional Christian.

"Well, Leah, here you are at our first girls' Bible school. I want to know just what each of you understand about God's Word, before we begin to teach you. So I have a few questions to put to you. Are you yourself a born-again Christian?"

"Yes, Ma-Ma. I am born again from above."

"What does 'born again' mean, Leah?"

"It means to have eternal life as well as physical

life, doesn't it?"

"That's right. And when were you born again, Leah?"

"When I took Jesus as my Saviour, who died on the cross for my sins."

"Why do you want to study at this school, Leah?"

"Because I want to know the Holy Book better. I have not been able to read for some years now, Ma-Ma."

"How old are you, Leah?"

"About thirty years old....I don't know exactly."

"Well, we are very glad to have you, Leah, and if I can help you in any matter, you just come to me."

A shy twisting of her hands betokened there was just such a matter right now.

"What is it, Leah?"

"I'm told that this girls' school is to be conducted just as nearly like the men's RSBS as possible."

"Yes, we are going to try and give you just what we give them."

"Then there will be weekend preaching assignments for the girls each week?"

"That is our plan, but..."

"Ma-Ma, I'd like to ask a favour. When you send me out, could you please send me with Tabitha and Abigail? I can see a wee bit, but I cannot walk quickly over strange trails. My friends are accustomed to that and don't mind it; but if I had to go with girls I do not know, they might not..."

Tears were in my eyes. I had no thought of sending a blind girl out over these high and perilous paths, but the stoutness of her courage shamed me. If she was willing to go, who was I to say it was too much?

"Leah, set your heart at rest. You will never be
asked to go with strangers. I am delighted that you
are willing to go, and I am sure God will use you. I
will arrange that Tabitha, Abigail, and you will
always be on the same team." Her smile of relief
betokened that her one dread in coming to school
had been allayed. Now all before her was one
sweet enjoyment.

In the classroom, Leah was given a seat at the
front, near the speaker, of course, and her quiet,
attentive, sightless face was an inspiration. It was
on the first morning that she, and most of the
others, received their Bible names. Heathen names
often have such a polluted meaning, as I have
explained before, but it is mostly to help the
praying friends at home that we give the Bible
students a Bible name. Leah, for instance, is much
easier to remember than *Sah-me-nyio*.

At that first year of girls' Bible school, each
evening I gave a talk on one of the women of the
Bible. Biographies of the saints are rich in practical
application to all our lives, but especially to the
lives of women in the East. When we came to Leah,
I tried to point out (as does Dr Edersheim) how
God was Leah's ally all throughout.

As we told the story, outside the little shanty the
night wind howled and moaned bitterly. But inside
a radiance rested on the young faces uplifted to
mine. God taught us all precious lessons in those
evening hours together. And the blind girl saw
things as they really are, and was comforted and
strengthened to accept the trial which is but for a
moment and which worketh a far more exceeding
weight of glory.

Another evening stands out in memory. It was when the story of Abigail was told. Leah's chum, Abigail, was also going through deep waters those days. It was she who had married Philip, when Homay broke with him, and he had definitely backslidden, deserted her and their unborn babe for a heathen girl; and just before Abigail came to Bible school she was told that Philip had carried off her corn—her store of food for the winter. We named her Abigail purposely; for the Bible character of that name also was married to a churl, a son of Belial. The fact that the Abigail of old was very clever and beautiful only made her plight the more pitiful—and incidentally when that little matter of beauty was mentioned in class, there were many girlish grins and nods in Lisu Abigail's direction, which provoked a wan smile from the grim young face. Then the story unfolded; hopelessly tied to a man who did not deserve her and with whom there could never be any fellowship, Abigail must have faced the inevitable temptation of a woman in such a position—the temptation to take matters into her own hands, and run off with someone else more attractive. Lisu heathen readily do that. The only other alternative is to bank your all on God, and leave it for Him to work out. That Abigail did this latter is evidenced in the way she pleaded with David to do the very same thing, when the temptations to use force had swung David off his spiritual balance.

And then the wonderful "end of the Lord." When she proved that her own lesson was humbly and faithfully learned, God suddenly worked for her. Within a few weeks the churl had been removed, and she was wife of—a *king!* And of

David, at that. Abigail ended her days as wife of a king. Someone has said it is not fair to judge a thing while it is in the making; wait until the product is finished, then we may pass judgment. And so we should never judge our lives and our trials, until God has completed in us what He is trying to do for us. When we see His finished product, we will be satisfied.

Friend, can you not see what the Word of God has for a torn young life which *longs* to do what is right, if it only knew the way? Can you feel the suffering of Abigail's little nest until the shelter of the Cleft Rock was pointed out to her? Can you know the gladness of the missionary, when at the end of that evening, at the close of the lesson, her hand was grasped and held, while two earnest young eyes looked into hers and said, "Thank you, Ma-Ma. That helped me so much!"

And yet, as we stood there with clasped hands, both of us safely out of the danger of the sharp blast that blew towards the Abyss, how many were, *and are*, battling hopelessly against that Wind and that Abyss, with no knowledge of the Rock, Christ Jesus, nor of His way of salvation, because no one has gone to them. Always it presses on my heart....Those others that would so gladly take Him as Saviour, if only someone would go and tell them the way!

At the end of school, although it was only of a month's duration, to encourage the girls, we held closing exercises and gave out certificates to those who had passed. The results were good, considering not one of the girls had ever been to school before, and had never studied to take an examination in her life. But only one girl got first-class honours. And who do you suppose she was? The blind girl, Leah! She had had exactly the same examination questions as the other girls had, only we took hers orally. They had written down notes from which to review, she had none. Always part of every examination was the recitation of scripture passages, and Leah could not read, yet she alone passed with first-class honours. I asked her how she did it. Her face glowed with pleased embarrassment as she answered. "Well, I could hear the other girls in my hut going over their notes and scriptures in preparation for the exams."

We were very proud of our twenty-two Lisu maidens as they marched into chapel to the music of the little portable organ, and separated in simple form to their designated seats. One of them conducted the singing for the whole service, and two of them gave valedictory addresses! One of them was chairman, and they had closing day songs and music just like the Rainy Season Bible Schools. Many of the boy students had come, some a day's journey, to "escort sister home" or some such excuse, but really to see what good the teaching of girls could ever accomplish. At the end of the service one such boy student exclaimed with beaming face, "Why, wasn't it nice! It was almost as good as ours." Complacent male! I thought it was quite as good.

After all was over and as the happy, excited girls were rolling up bedding and clothes to go home with their proud brothers and friends, I called the three from Deer Pool aside, and, little dreaming what the future was to hold for them or me, I said something like this:

"Now you girls are going back home, and for

none of you is life easy. I want you to promise me
not to forget the *power of prayer*. I want you to
promise me to meet together regularly and *pray
through* your problems. You know Deer Pool
Village is not now what it used to be, spiritually.
The craze to make money by trading has been used
of the devil to cool off many, and some of the first
believers who were so consecrated are now dead.
Is that not so?"

"Yes, Ma-Ma," they answered sadly. They promised to pray and not to faint, and we parted.

I never saw Leah again. A severe toothache and
other ills warned me that I had better go out to
Chinaland to seek dental aid. John had been
attending a conference in Chungking and as I had
not seen him for three months I hoped we might be
able to come back together. But in the spring of
1942 the Japanese were walking up Burma as with
ten-league boots. By the time I was physically fit to
return, they had already reached Lisuland, and I
was evacuated out of the province by the British
Consul. Six months elapsed before I was able to get
back to the Munition of Rocks. When I did arrive,
and had time to inquire into my dear girl student's
affairs, this is what I was told of Leah.

Shortly after she got home from Bible school her
young brother, the only son of the family and a
fine Christian, died of tuberculosis of the leg bone.
One of her younger sisters had died of a fever the
year before. And within a few months, Leah herself
was laid low of a fever, probably typhus. Up to
that time she and Tabitha and Abigail had been
faithful in holding their prayer meetings. But not
long after she took sick, Leah knew that God was
going to call her Home. She asked the family (then

only mother, father and one married sister) to gather around her bed, and they said the strength with which she was able to talk was wonderful. "I know I am going back to God," she told them. "And my one concern is for you folk, *lest your faith fail you*. You have been afflicted much this last year; we none of us can understand why these troubles come, but two things we know; that is, that *God loves us* and that *God is faithful*. Everything that happens to us is for our good and some day He will show us why it had to be. You must not wail for me–I am going to the land of Happiness and Light, and where Christ is. But what concerns me now is lest you dishonour Him by complaining, because He is taking me! Dad, promise me you won't! Promise that you will go on believing and not doubt God's goodness!" And they said that with her last strength she pleaded that God's honour should be defended by the ones she left behind. Who can account for a spirit like that, except it be, even as Christ said, "Born from above"?

So they laid their third child in the grave and, as tears flowed, they strove as a family to follow out her injunctions and not let other people suggest that God was too hard on them.

But still the Sharp Wind from the Bitter Height continued its onslaught. The mother, one of the most faithful of the Christians, was ill with an unknown and very painful disease. I think it was cancer. Within a year she too had gone to be with the Lord; so the old sightless father and the married sister were left alone. But the words of their dead Singing Bird were constantly with them. "Promise me that you will not complain!

Promise me you will believe on!" And they followed in her faith. "The Lord gets His best soldiers from the Highlands of Affliction," some-one has said. One little picture, as told me by a Lisu evangelist who was ministering at Deer Pool for a few weeks, will show the faith and trust which was their life.

"We had an exciting experience of fire while I was at Deer Pool," he said. "One or two of the huts were aflame, a keen wind was blowing and we were afraid the whole village would go. I was on top of David's house, spreading wet blankets over it to save the roof from flying sparks, and everyone was running around hauling water, etc., when I happened to look up, and there in the middle of the road was Leah's old blind father. His house was right in the path the flames were taking, but he had no one to help him now, of course. And there he was, lifting his sightless eyes up to the sky and praying. There he stood, and even as he prayed the wind began to veer around and his house was saved. He, a layman, old and afflicted, was *committing*, and I the preacher, was rushing around *working* to save the house in which I was guest. He surely taught me a lesson. I came down from off that roof and went on to my knees. And the wind carried the flames out toward the wild mountainside, and no other house was harmed."

Friends, there is a blessed shelter in the Cleft of the Rock for you and me. Blindness is a cruel Wind from a Bitter Height, but a blind girl had her inner eyes so opened that her vision of faith lived on and enlightened others, long after her physical voice was silenced.

Chapter 5

A ROCK IN A WEARY LAND

A TALL young figure clattered over the loose boards of the narrow veranda and plunged into the semi-darkness of the Lisu hut.

"Mamma!" he called out, "Have you heard the news?"

An equally tall lean woman, sprawled on a bed near the fire, face streaked with soot, a dirty turban wound around her head from which the hair had all been shaven off, sat up, pulled a long pipe out of her mouth, and answered, "What news? Ain't heard nothing."

"Well," answered her son, and as he talked he was hunting through the dim light of the shanty for his crossbow and arrow sheaf, "Dad's gone and run off with Nyio-Er-Me, curse her!" and a string of profanity filled the air.

Then it was the woman's turn to get excited. Every other sentence a filthy curse, she ranted on, working herself up into a passionate rage.

"What's he done that for? Haven't I been a good wife to him? I've given him sons! There isn't a pair of fellows on this mountain that can touch my two for stature or strength. And a daughter besides, have I given him. What's he want to run off with that..." and more profanity.

By this time her tall son had found his bow and

arrows and slung them over his shoulder. A
dangerous knife, some three feet long, was fastened at his side. As he stretched himself up to
adjust the weapons, he was a splendid-looking
figure, despite uncombed hair and dirty face.
About six feet tall, with broad shoulders, he was
well-proportioned, and the comeliness of fine
straight features was manifest in spite of dirt. His
face was fierce with excitement.

"Give me a drink of wine, Ma!" he cried. "Don't
you worry!" And with a turn and a fling, he was
clattering back over the loose boards and on to the
trail above the house. The old mother, left alone,
cursed and wept alternately as the sore evil which
all Lisu women dread and fear loomed up on her
horizon.

Up through the mountainside plunged the two
young men, talking excitedly and laying their
plans. Somehow they had learned which was the
village where the eloping pair had decided to
spend the night, and which family was befriending
them. Of the capture details, I do not know. Being
only sons, they could not force a separation, and
this the father knew well. But of the fierceness and
cleverness of his eldest son he had reason to know
also, and likely he did not dare bring home his
second wife immediately. Their persuasion was
impotent to change his mind: his passion had
fastened on Nyio-Er-Me and she knew how to hold
him her slave. She was truly an evil woman. So
with what lying promises he held off the wrath of
his two formidable sons we do not know, but
return home alone, he did not. To run off to Burma
for a year or so had often proved successful for
others, but he had aroused a strong character

against him, one who did not forget. That oldest son—well, everybody dreaded him when he got into a fury. Give him a present of opium? Yes, that probably was the most potent way to calm things. Opium will destroy any character, if taken over a sufficiently long period. And because it soothes pain it is greatly prized. His oldest boy was already an opium addict at the age of twenty.

But as the father and his evil companion were laying their plans, the oldest son was also laying his. It was time he was being married, anyway, and he had already started out to build his own house. When that was finished, and his bride brought home, his mother could come and live with him—and then her face would be saved and his father could do what he wanted.

In the deep ravine was another village named The Village of Tree Roots, and there he found a girl more or less to his liking. She was not pure, but then, who was? That does not reckon as important in heathen thinking.

"What do Lisu look for in a wife?" I once asked one of them.

"Oh, some want good looks," was the answer. "Others want to marry into a rich family; and still others want a wife who is hospitable. It's humiliating to a fellow if his wife does not want to entertain strangers, and some women don't."

One or other of these motives influenced Lao-Ta, and the engagement was made. He must pay a lot of money for her—perhaps two hundred dollars in silver. Her family reckon they have had the expense of bringing her up, feeding and clothing her, and once she is married she is lost to them as a farmhand, so they reckon that the ones who get the

benefit of her abilities should pay for what she has
cost. This is called "dowry money" and its various
items are amusing. The mother will charge for
having nursed her, i.e. a "milk bill" is sent in. Then
sometimes there is a charge for *Jwa-jwa-chwa*, that
is, the labour of premasticating her food for her
when she was a baby! (The mother chews the corn
or meat, and then with her own lips puts it into the
baby's mouth.) And so on. To wed is expensive in
Lisuland. For this reason the Lisu church in our
parts has voted against the dowry, and no
Christian may pay it. But we are discussing the
days before the gospel arrived; for our hero was
already married and a father, when he first heard
of Christ.

Time heals all wounds. Ten years later we see
Lao-Ta and Lao-Er both married and living in their
own house, and tilling their separate farms in the
Village of Oak Flat. The father and his second wife
live in the original homestead, and now have a
son, and a daughter, Susanna. Father and sons
have long forgotten their anger, and work and help
each other happily, but the two wives never forget.
Bickering, jealous quarrels continually upset the
peace. The first wife has been offered a home with
her eldest son as he promised, but love for her
husband probably drew her back to him after a few
years. When the gospel came, and her husband
wanted to become a Christian, however, a final
break was made, and she came permanently into
the home of her oldest boy.

That boy had now seen his first-born, a little girl,
whom he named Me-do-me, and so his own name
is changed for the rest of his life. Lisu practice
teknonymy; that is, the father takes the oldest

child's name and *pa* (man) added to it, and the mother takes the same name, only with *ma* (woman) added to it. So automatically the family is now Me-do-me-pa and Me-do-me-ma and little Me-do-me. From now on their fellow villagers must address them as such; to call them by their childhood name is to insult them.

Now we must go back in thought to 1932.

One evening, up the long winding two-thousand-foot ascent from the ravine stream, climb two or three Lisu men of a slightly different costume. They stop at Cha-Lao-San's shanty and ask if they may spend the night there. Welcomed cordially, they sit down on the big low bedboards which inevitably act as fireside seats in the daytime, and take out *books* from a small bag slung over their shoulder.

"Oh, you read Chinese?" asks Lao-San curiously.

"No," said the visitors, "these are Lisu books."

The effect is electric. Everyone in the shanty turns around and amazed attention is riveted on the speaker. He is, of course, Job, with that little band.

"Lisu books? Didn't know there were such! Do you mean to say that those leaves speak *our* language?"

"Well, I'll read some and you judge for yourself," says the speaker casually. Whereupon the Book is made to tell its own message. Job's favourite was the story of the resurrection of Lazarus, but sometimes the Catechism was used. Its first question, "Who made the earth and everything upon it?" is arresting.

Then the interest swung around from the books to the message and soon the shanty is filled with amazed questions and thrilling answers. Finally, someone says, "Better go call Me-do-me-pa!" for our hero had now become the political headman of his village, and it is not convenient to do anything "different" without consulting the headman. So Me-do-me-pa was summoned.

He enters, tall and matured now into young manhood, perhaps thirty-two years of age. But being a heathen he is still dirty, a wine-bibber and an opium-smoker. There is the gleam of a keen mind in his eye, nevertheless, as he listens to the story of Calvary.

As all wait for his verdict, he says, "I'd like to have eternal life–who wouldn't? But it's never been followed in these parts before. What do you do to get it? Could a Lisu receive it?"

"You must believe in God," was the Lisu evangelist's answer. "Jesus died for your sins. You must cast out your demons and turn to God. You must stop unclean sinning, and so forth."

This was shock. The only excitements and pleasures of a heathen life are those just named! Immediately some voices were raised against it. But not so Me-do-me-pa. While the others clamoured that that was too much to expect of human mortal, he was thinking. A glimpse of something that answered a long-felt heart cry was holding him. Every now and again he shot a keen question into the hubbub, and always it brought a silence while all listened for the answer.

"Have you done all this?"

"Yes," was the sturdy reply. "We cast out our demons over fifteen years ago; hundreds of Lisu have done so in our parts, and nothing has happened to them. Jesus is stronger than the demons.

And as for worldly pleasures, God gives you other things in their place. We have wonderful songs to sing; happy fellowship in worship services. Once a year we all gather from all over the canyon and hold what we call the Christmas Festival. It is lots of fun. I would not go back to heathen life for anything. And in your own district here, the people of Deer Pool have already cast out their demon altars and accepted Christ."

Long into the night the discussion waged. By that time most of the men of Oat Flat Village would be in the crowded little hut, listening to the new doctrine. At the close Me-do-me-pa stood up.

"I want to believe. Come to my house tomorrow morning, teacher, and cast out my demons. And have breakfast with me!"

Up stood Cha-Lao-San. "And you must cast out my demons for me also," he cried. "I'm going to believe in God, too."

And so the work began at Oak Flat Village. Word soon spread over the mountain. "Teachers have come with a strange doctrine. They say we should not worship demons but should believe and trust in God. The headman of Oak Flat and some others have cast out their demons!" And so as the teachers pushed on they found their way prepared for them. Joseph of Dried Fungus (later engaged to Homay) joined the little band of Christians. At Tree Roots Me-do-me-ma's brothers turned to God. At Pine Mountain, old Big and Pufu-si-pa. Plum Tree Flat turned as a village. At Spirea Flat a fine young man and his wife took their stand and became the nucleus of a church there, and so on.

Finally, word came to the Feudal Laird at Place-of-Action, and he was easy to stir up against the new movement. They whispered to him: "This new doctrine is not Chinese. It was brought by the white man. It is a ruse he is using to steal your land. Better stop it before all your people go over to the white man. Me-do-me-pa, of Oak Flat, has already joined them." Of course it was all lies—the devil is the father of lies—but the Laird thought it was true, so he sent forth word that his people were not to accept the new doctrine. Such messages are taken to the headman of each village, who, in turn, is responsible for conveying it to each member of his village. Undoubtedly it came to Me-do-me-pa.

What conflict must have waged in that Lisu heart! He was quite a favourite with the Laird. It meant much to be a favourite—no taxes, partiality in law suits, and innumerable other advantages. And to *disobey* him! Well, wealthy men who had done so had gradually been reduced to poverty. And some, who had wilfully disobeyed, had been tortured. He knew what the Laird could do, if he wanted to. I think it went this way.

Cha-Lao-San came running in the door.

"Oh, Me-do-me-pa! I hear that runners from the Yamen have come with orders that we are not to turn Christians. Is it so?"

"Guess so," was the grim reply.

"Well, are you going to send the notice around to all of us?"

"No." A gasp from all who were listening.

Cha-Lao-San asked slowly, "What will he do to you, if you don't?"

The tall Lisu lifted his head and looked the questioner in the eyes. "Whatever he does can only be done to the outside of me—he can't take away the eternal life God has given to me. This morning I was reading Luke 12:4, 5. "I tell you, my friends, do not be afraid of those who kill the body and after that can do no more. But I will show you whom you should fear: Fear him who, after the killing of the body, has power to throw you into hell. Yes, I tell you, fear him."

Silence reigned in the little huts, now nearly full of villagers. Then Cha-Lao-San spoke again softly. "It is like an answer, isn't it? Well, I won't turn back either, then."

The word went around like wildfire, "Me-do-me-pa is not going to turn back!"

It was a crucial moment in the forming of the little church. Friends at home were praying that God would raise up a leader, a Rock-man, to steady the weak little group of new believers sure of persecution. We have known many other similar cases where the villagers all turned back to heathenism because the headman decided to backslide. It is a weary land where you cannot do what you long to do, and believe is right to do. But if there is *one man* who is willing to take the punishment on his own head, many others will shelter under his shadow and stand with him.

I would just like to ask the reader one question. *What made that man* WILLING?

Willing to lose all his lands and physical comforts, perhaps. At the same time he must give up all his popularity, his wine, his opium—everything that had spelled pleasure to him before. And gain what? A nebulous "eternal life?" This man was no dabbler in philosophy; he was an illiterate farmer. Moreover, he was unusually marked out by

common sense. You would never catch him making a poor bargain. Then *what* made him gamble
his all, for Christianity? The only answer is in Rom.
8:16, "The Spirit himself bears witness with our
spirit that we are God's children." 1 John 5:10.
"Anyone who believes in the Son of God has this
testimony in his heart." This earth person (as the
Chinese slightingly call the Lisu) *knew*, though he
could not explain it, that he was contacting God
through faith in Christ. He *knew* that whole worlds
of undreamed-of joys and privileges were opening
up to him. And he *knew* that he was only at the
weak ignorant beginning of new life, and he was
so thrilled that none of the old pleasures of the
flesh could compare with it any more. They might
go, but this new life with God, he *must have*. So he
stood, and everybody waited to see what punishment would ensue.

Days passed without anything happening, but
Me-do-me-pa was not deceived. He too was
oriental, and knew the ways of the Laird. One day
he was driving pigs to market. He had to pass
Place-of-Action; a retainer from the Yamen came
out and laid his hand on Me-do-me-pa's shoulder,
"The Laird wants you!"

Ah, it had come, then. All right. He followed
quietly into the Chinese courtyard which began,
likely, to fill up with onlookers. The Laird was
standing there in a great rage, apparently.

"What are you doing, driving pigs to market
when you had orders to be building the road?" he
shouted. There was no use answering that there
had been no orders. Everyone present knew it was
but an excuse to hide the real reason. Legally
China recognizes religious freedom.

"Tie him up to the whipping post and give it to him!" cried the Laird, and feudal hands reached out and grasped the strong frame which did not resist. It was done. Lash upon lash. What a beating that must have been! One of the strongest Lisu in the district, he was beaten so that he could not walk for three days. When the miserable punishment was over the tall form lay senseless on the ground. Word had gone as fast as human foot could take it to Oak Flat Village; his fellows dropped their work and with grim faces sped to the scene, knowing they would have to carry him home. They wondered if he would live—if he would ever be the same physically again, and the little group of Christians whispered together and trembled. Would it be done to each? Or was Me-do-me-pa, like his Master, only in a small way, to bear in his wounds "the chastisement of our peace?" Perhaps they had all better backslide? No, word came that the suffering man was recovering. He had spoken! He had said it was all right and that he was *going on in the faith*! Days passed and no other Christian was touched. "A man shall be as a rock, in a weary land." Spoken of his Master, it was true in a sense of the followers. The anxious, frightened believers gradually rallied, and, as usually happens, others joined them! What was Me-do-me-pa getting from Christianity that he deemed it worth such a beating? It did the cause good.

Dr Jowett has said, "The man who is sure and restful in the conscious companionship of his Lord has about him the strainlessness and inevitableness of the oceantide, and gives off bracing influence like God's fresh and wondrous sea."

And the Laird? He had beaten his loyal hench-
man in ignorant suspicion, and for some time tried
by heavy taxation to discourage the new doctrine.
But gradually he began to notice things. He noticed
that the Christians were prospering in a material
way. That they were well-behaved. That their
obedience to him was just the same, if he did not
step on their religious toes. And after some eight
years, he ended up by proclaiming openly that the
Christians were his best citizens; and as they gave
up opium and became physically strong enough to
work their fields properly, their tax returns were
actually netting him money! (The taxes are a
percentage of the harvest, so the more harvested,
the more grain is given to the landowner.) This
man never became a Christian, but like Felix of
old, he used to call the deacons in and ask them to
preach to him. Perhaps he planned to believe at the
last hour, but it was not granted him. A sudden
fever laid him unconscious and he passed away
without repentance.

Now the church in Oak Flat district was an established thing, but evangelists to carry the Good
News afar were few. La-ma-wu's partners went
home to Stockade Hill; some others came in their
place, but always too few to meet all the demand
for teachers, so the responsibility of personal
witness fell on the shoulders of the new believers.
A long day's journey to the south and across the
Salween River on the west bank was the Village of
Horse Grass Level. Among the first to hear the
gospel, they had been slow to receive it, but now
they wanted teachers, so Me-do-me-pa volunteered
to go down there and give his testimony.

"How did your wife take all this?" I asked him

one day, as he was telling me this story. "Did she believe along with you from the very first?"

"No, she didn't, Ma-Ma," he said with a broad smile, "and she caused me no little trouble. She resented having to give up heathen pleasures, and made such stormy scenes that I just got sick at heart with it all."

"Well, she is certainly one with you now!" I replied. "What effected the change?"

"I got to my wit's end over her," he said, a twinkle of reminiscence in his eye, "so I decided to pray about her. For instance, she did not want me to leave home and go preaching, as I had volunteered to do, but I found that as I prayed regularly and faithfully for her, she began to change. She kept on changing as I kept on praying, until now she never objects to anything I want to do!"

I might say right here, that as long as he lived, Me-do-me-ma seemed the model deacon's wife. She was faithful at prayer meetings, testified and exhorted others until, a full day's journey away, I heard of her being the means of effecting peace between another headman and his wife! After her husband's death she lapsed into girlhood weaknesses, but that does not change, only heightens the fact that his prayers had made a different woman out of her.

At Horse Grass Level, Me-do-me-pa's quiet, common-sense witness bore much fruit, and a steady little church grew up there. Now we approach the days when my husband and I moved into Oak Flat Village, into a house just beneath Me-do-me-pa's and where we had many neighbourly touches. I would again like to quote from the circulars written during these years.

I first saw him in the spring of 1934 while we were visiting Mrs Cooke at Pine Mountain Village, before we actually moved in as a family. It was Sunday and Mrs Cooke was pointing out some of the main men of the church as they arrived for Sunday service. Pointing to Me-do-me-pa (easily discerned because of his height) she said, "That big Lisu I call The Shepherd because he has such a heart of love and care for the rest of the flock." Then in December, 1934, the Cookes moved up to the Luda district and we moved in as a family and took charge of the Oak Flat district. March, 1935, has two references to Me-do-me-pa.

> One of the snares in our Lisu work is the matter of lawsuits, quarrels over land, etc., referred to the heathen Chinese Laird for settlement. We had a grave discussion about it on Sunday afternoon, for Pade-John (Cha-Lao-Shan) and Me-do-me-pa were among the guilty parties; in the evening when the testimony meeting was thrown open, the dear "Shepherd" was the first to stand up, and he confessed his fault before the flock. His face was so shining and modest as he talked, that one could not but love him.

The Lisu church, being founded on indigenous lines, was self-governing. The missionary gave advice when asked, and likewise preached only when invited. In each Christian village there was one elected as service leader, and this one wrote down on the blackboard the names of those he wished to preach during the coming week. If the missionary's name did not appear, he did not preach but sat in the audience while the selected national Christian officiated. In those early days, before I could speak Lisu, I was in the audience one night when Me-do-me-pa was the speaker. Not knowing much of the language, I could not follow his message, but I knew enough Lisu to find the text he had chosen. It was John 12:1-9, the story of Mary's alabaster box of ointment poured forth at Jesus' feet. As I listened and saw the glow of inspiration on the Shepherd's face, and felt the hush in the audience, I wondered just what in that story had spoken to this farmer's heart. He had received very little Bible teaching up to that time, but he was gifted with keen spiritual insight, and Mary's costly offering ungrudgingly lavished on the Master had touched and blessed him. There was a kinship of feeling with that Hebrew maiden of old, on this Lisu man's face. "There is neither Jew nor Greek, slave nor free, male nor female, for you are all one in Christ Jesus" (Gal. 3:28).

From the circular of July, 1935, comes this paragraph demonstrating that although the foreign missionary was present, the matter of discipline was left in the hands of the local church.

That night in the evening service, Prodigal got up and said he wanted to return to the Lord, that he realized it meant salvation and happiness. When he sat down, teacher John grunted, "You didn't say enough!" And then, Me-do-me-pa and Pade-John went after him. "What about your sins? 'Return to the Lord' and not a word about repentance? God is not to be treated that way!"—it was good to hear them hot after their Lord's honour. No, once we forfeit His "well-pleased" there is no path of self-complacency back to it. The church has accepted Prodigal's confession and is giving him a second chance to believe, and allowing him to shake hands again—a sign, not of church membership, but of fellowship.

In September it became necessary for Little Daughter and me to go out to Chinaland for a few months' physical recuperation as has been told in Homay's story. We got back in time for Christmas, and the circular that month tells of our arrival.

We had a wonderful welcome back to Oak Flat on December 16. Halfway down the mountain John met us, accompanied by Ye-Chia-me (Kathryn's playmate), Gu-fu-chee (banging the chapel gong) and Mark. The rest of the crowd was ordered to be in ceremonial line farther up the hill, but on hearing our voices Plum Tree Flat-ers could not contain themselves and came pelting down on us, led by Caleb with his big boyish laugh and gripping handshake. One old man said half to himself, "Thank God—He wouldn't allow us to be separated"—an involuntary little word that nestled down softly into the missionary's heart.

Farther up was the reception line—Job, Pade-John, Me-do-me-pa, Keh-gee-sen, and others. On our approach they began to sing, but in their excitement suddenly forgot the words and all came to a stop. There was a blank and awful silence for a second, and then Job said, "Oh, let it go! Let's shake hands."

Our dear Lord is a magnificent giver; He knows how to add the tiny little extras which make a pleasure perfect. Among those who ran forward most eagerly and shook hands most warmly were some we had long been praying for as "cold-hearted."

We had a happy three months with them before

having to come home on furlough. I am glad that
the furlough circulars contain a letter from Me-do-
me-pa, because, although it is not a remarkable
one, it is his own voice speaking.

Oak Flat Village.
March 14, 1937.

Big Brother and Sister:

Whom I yearn for, cannot forget and continually
long to see, in the name of the Father, Son, and the
Spirit I send you a handshake. Now Big Brother
and family, are you dwelling in peace?

There is nothing wrong with us and because of
the help of the Lord we are all well. Won't you
pray very much for me? Also pray much for the
deacons of the surrounding districts. Thank you
very much.

We are earnestly praying for you to come back
and teach us. Won't you do so?

The photo you three had taken, came in the early
part of March; we were unspeakably happy to get
it. Now there is going to be another period for Oak
Flat of "no missionary"—sheep without a shepherd
once more! I am wondering whom God has for us
in the future?

The writer is one who loves you, the servant of
Jesus Christ.

ME-DO-ME-PA.

Reading it in this respect, one is struck by that
simple little question, *I am wondering whom God has
for us in the future?* because the answer to it
involves the biggest storm that ever struck the
Rock-man. He little knew what he was asking.

For some months after our departure, Oak Flat
was without a missionary; and then one whom the
Lisu named Brother Two volunteered to go in and

help. It is not the policy of the China Inland Mission to put new workers on a station alone, without the counsel and help of experienced seniors, but sometimes in an exigency, when no senior has been available, this has been done. And the following story is the result of such an emergency.

Brother Two was a very zealous and devout young missionary, and one with brilliant gifts. He picked up the Lisu language quickly, and his indifference to personal hardship and suffering was a blessing to us all. His arrival was heralded with joy and satisfaction by Me-do-me-pa and everyone else, and his quickness in learning their tongue elicited their admiration.

However, the Lisu language is a very ambiguous one, which even an experienced missionary can misunderstand. And later, the Lisu told us, "There were times when Brother Two thought he had understood us and he had not; we could tell by his answers." Let us keep this in mind as the story unfolds.

With no experienced senior missionary present to explain matters as they cropped up, and full of zeal to see the Word spread and multiply unhampered, Brother Two gradually began to take exception to the way the Lisu church conducted certain things. Mr Fraser had given them a catechism, which long experience with various tribal attempts at catechisms has made us value because its simplicity makes it easy for the beginner to master, and thus encourages him to further study. But Brother Two felt that the catechism, with its simple question and direct answer, had a tendency to produce a "do-this-and-thou-shalt-be-saved" effect on the Lisu mind. In other words he feared legalism for the Lisu church. He was much strengthened in these misgivings to hear that Mr Payne had feared the very same thing.

Brother Two decided to step out and combat legalism, and began to take exception to the way the church was handling cases of church discipline. This of course, brought him up against Me-do-me-pa, who was the head deacon and in charge of all such decisions. Hitherto the missionary, as already pointed out, had let the church do its own disciplining in its own way, only giving the word of advice now and again, the purpose being to strengthen them as an indigenous church; but here was a white man who wished to sit in on their consultations, seemed to want to take charge, and was insisting that methods taught them by the mother Lisu church were wrong. Me-do-me-pa objected to such an abrupt change, without being able to consult Mr Fraser or Mr Cooke who were experienced in all the districts of the Lisu work. Brother Two was a newcomer; Mr Fraser and Mr Cooke had long ago proved and approved themselves to the Lisu mind and heart, and both had sanctioned the methods Me-do-me-pa was using. It was very painful, very upsetting and very bewildering, for Brother Two held to his opinions and pressed them with all the zeal of youth and the in-experience of a novice in oriental matters.

Samuel Rutherford in a mellow old age said, "Satan has a Friend-at-Court in the heart of youth," and commenting on his own past added sadly, "Often my zeal was mixed with my own wildfire." This was a case in point, but neither side was able, as yet, to discern it as such.

Matters came to a head, finally, over young Samuel of Deer Pool, whose dislike for his wife had made Homay weep.[1] In order that the case might be more clear to the reader we must go back and see what happened to Samuel.

The exhortation by Job and Me-do-me-pa to take up his cross and accept his wife had held Samuel to the Narrow Way for a few months. But Sam was never one to "spread out his roots by the river" as Homay did. He just would not take time to read his Gospel portions and pray, so when the Sharp Wind from the Bitter Height struck him he was easily upset. After we had left for furlough, Samuel had met with a crisis and definitely, wilfully left the Lord and had gone into sin. There was nothing bad that he had not done, they said. His old father, believing it to be because of the unloved wife, took her to the heathen laird at Six Treasuries and bought a divorce. Now Samuel was a very attractive young Lisu, tall, broad, open-faced, and with a sunny smile; we all liked him. Moreover, Brother Two had misunderstood part of his case—thought that his wife had been married, without himself being consulted, in the heathen days; whereas in truth Sam had had a Christian wedding. It was noticeable that none of the deacons was making any effort to get Sam back; Brother Two evidently did not know that Me-do-me-pa had spent much time and loving exhortation in trying to keep the boy from going into sin. "You do not even try to reclaim sinners!" said Brother Two with heat, and went after Samuel himself, prayed with him and earnestly urged him to return

[1] *See page 64*

to God. Much flattered by the white man's personal interest, Samuel at length confessed his sin and consented to return. Brother Two was naturally overjoyed, and expected everybody else also to open wide their arms and receive the young sinner jubilantly. But it was not so.

"We are glad he has confessed his sin and wants to come back," said the Lisu deacons. "He went into sin wilfully–it is not our custom to receive such back immediately to the Lord's table. We would like him to be suspended from handshaking and the Communion Table for a period, that he may prove his repentance is sincere."

Again, Brother Two gave out opium as medicine, and when told that Lisu Christians were not allowed to have anything to do with opium, replied hotly that "there is nothing in the New Testament which says that one may not use opium! Nothing to say you may not smoke tobacco or drink wine either!" This was an awful shock; and some of the weak Christians made his words an excuse to go back to old sins. And always Brother Two quoted the New Testament–a book which Me-do-me-pa and the others had heard of, but never been able to read, as the translation was not yet finished. Mr and Mrs Cooke were working on it at the time.

And so a definite schism broke the Lisu church. One need not go into the details, but some followed Brother Two and the others stood by Me-do-me-pa. Never had such a Sharp Wind ever blown upon the Shepherd or the little flock. The beating from the Laird was nothing to this; that had been from the outside but this was from the inside of the body of Christ! Fearfully and weakly they talked together in the desolate chapel. Was there any use in going on?

Then it was that Me-do-me-pa again became a Rock-in-a-weary-land. "I know what we must do," he said sadly. "We must write to Mr Fraser, and ask him if we are wrong, ask him what to do. If we should have let Brother Two rule us, we can confess it—God knows we only want to do His will. But Sam never looked sorry for his sin as far as I could see. He confessed it to please Brother Two, to my mind. What will happen to the church if they are allowed to drink, smoke, handle opium?..." Everyone groaned thinking of the misconstructions already put upon Brother Two's words by some. And so that letter was written and mailed. But it would take some three months to get an answer from the superintendent who was away off in the east of the province. In the meantime there was the split church to face every day, and the jeers of the heathen.

One day this came out from Brother Two's followers. "Brother and Sister Kuhn are back in China, but they are not coming back here. They are to work at Paoshan. If you don't accept Brother Two he will leave, and you will have no missionary ever!"

This was a hard blow. It was true that we were back from furlough and had been designated to Paoshan city; our own letters gradually arrived and ratified it. Then the Wind blew its fiercest. "We had better write to the China Inland Mission Headquarters to leave Brother Two here," said some of the deacons anxiously. "We can do as he says! It is better to do that, than to have no missionary!" And they drew up a letter to the Shanghai Council asking that Brother Two be left with them. Only Me-do-me-pa refused to sign.

"I did not refuse lightly, Ma-Pa," he said to us, in relating it afterwards. "Keh-teh-seh-pa and I stayed up all one night praying; all night we cried to God to show us what to do. But I could not sign."

His refusal shook the deacon body. But finally, after they had swayed back and forth, now going to send it without his signature, now not daring so to treat one who had always proved wise and loving to them; finally, they rallied around the Rock-man... "All right, then we won't sign either," they said sadly. And at that point, help came.

A letter from Mr Fraser arrived, expressing tender sympathy and telling them to stand their ground; that Brother Two had misunderstood some things, and that he, Mr Fraser, was coming in to discuss these matters with Brother Two himself; then all would be talked through and cleared up. "You have not been wrong in your stand," he had written. Oh, how those words comforted! "God has answered our prayers!" Me-do-me-pa cried, almost weeping for gratitude.

After that it was easier to wait with patience. Finally, word came that Mr Fraser was too busy to come so far, but that he was coming to Paoshan, and that Brother Two was to go out and meet him there; and in the meantime, Mr and Mrs Kuhn were being sent in to visit them and, he trusted, "comfort their hearts." Joy and sadness!

Joy to think of seeing the missionaries who had lived among them in 1935-6; sadness to see Brother Two packing up, still maintaining he was right, and saying that he would never return to them–for the Lisu love their missionaries more than they do their own parents, and although Brother Two was vexed with them, they remembered that he had come all that long way from his own country, had parted with his loved ones, and had made many sacrifices in order to bring the gospel to them, despised earth people that they were. So it was grief to see him go without a reconciliation.

In about a week's time, a runner arrived to say that Brother and Sister Kuhn were coming up the hill that afternoon probably. As Me-do-me-pa waited behind the Welcome Arch a few hours later and saw his loved missionary coming towards him, something within him seemed to crack; all that weight of decision as to what was wrong and what was right, might be shifted now on to familiar shoulders. It was too much for the dear Shepherd; when he saw my husband he just threw his arms about John's neck and let the tears run. It was a moving sight, for he said nothing at all, he criticized no one, just clung and wept silently. And in the long interview which followed, I never heard Me-do-me-pa say one word about Brother Two that was angry or "nasty." All was just grief.

That very night the Shepherd had a severe attack of pain. It was the beginning of strange seizures, which finally settled down into the constant pain and symptoms of cancer. But for over a year, though the loved deacon would have one of these attacks every now and again, we never dreamed he was in danger.

We must say a word of the meeting of Mr Fraser and Brother Two. The latter had told the Lisu before he left, that he was severing his connection with the China Inland Mission; so sure was he that he was right, and that Mr Fraser could never convince him of anything but that. Truth to tell, none of us had much hope that the meeting could result in anything satisfactory, but we prayed anyway. December 31 of each year the members of the China Inland Mission set aside for prayer and fasting; and as the year was drawing to a close John invited the Lisu to join in keeping the last day thus. Me-do-me-pa and some ten others gathered with us that afternoon on the open hillside. Of course the matter of the meeting in Paoshan city was uppermost in the minds of all of us. As my husband led, in a little preliminary talk, he said something like this: "Now in our prayers, I do not want to hear anyone telling the Lord about the faults of Brother Two. God knows them already. This prayer time is to confess *our* sins, and get *our* hearts right with God. After doing that, we can ask Him to help Mr Fraser and Brother Two get reconciled."

The prayers that followed were among the most precious I have ever heard. The dear Lisu did just what their Big Brother had asked. Not a word that was not loving was said of Brother Two, but many confessions as to anger, hardness of heart, etc., went up to the Throne of Grace.

> And if your hand or foot offend you,
> Cut if off, lad, and be whole;
> But play the man, stand up and end you,
> When your sickness is your soul.

There was "cutting off" that day in Lisuland, and way off down in Chinaland, God worked beyond thought and expectation. The result was, gradually, a letter from Brother Two to the Lisu church came; it asked forgiveness for disrupting them and

for anything done or said wrongly. He did not say
that he had been entirely wrong. To the end he
believed the Lisu church discipline was wrong; but
Mr Fraser was too big a man to ask a sincere
opinion or conviction to be changed. All the
superintendent wanted was that unity of heart be
restored. So although their individual convictions
regarding church discipline and the catechism
continued unchanged, their fellowship as members
of the same Body was re-established. The same
mail brought a letter from Mr Fraser, one of the
sweetest I have ever read, in which he told us that
they had been reconciled as brothers in the Lord;
and he added, "Now I never want to hear Brother
Two's mistakes mentioned again by anybody! As
regards myself, they are already forgotten—he is a
brother beloved. And I order and exhort you also
to receive him as such, and urge the Lisu
Christians to do the same! 'Love covereth.'" And I
believe it did.

Years later, Old Big (of the following pages) was
watching me open some mail. "Ma-Ma," he said,
"where is Brother Two now? I know there were
some things happened when he was here," with a
twinkle in his eye, "but he healed my foot when it
was badly cut, once, and I can never cease to be
grateful to him. I love-long after him!" Brother
Two was sent to another part where the China
Inland Mission was working; and the last I heard,
he was in the British Army, and winning many
souls to Christ.

And now to our joy, permission was given to us
to stay on in Oak Flat, and in addition to ourselves,
the two fellow-workers previously mentioned were
granted to us. Then, as summer approached, the

dream and vision of our furlough was laid before
the Lisu church—a three months' Bible school (the
RSBS) for Lisu evangelists and laymen whom the
Lord might choose to send.

The deacons were pleased with the idea, but
when John told them that the expenses (food of the
students, chiefly) were to be paid for by the Lisu
church (indigenous principles), they were in consternation.

"Ma-Pa"—they approached the objection anxiously —"food for fifteen or so for three months
takes a lot of corn! Where can the church find so
much? It's never been done before in Lisuland, has
it? Not for such a long period? Not even in the
parent church of Stockade Hill? To feed fifteen
students for three months!"

Me-do-me-pa was church treasurer. He, the man
of ingenuity, also looked grave. "Ma-Pa, I think it
would be fine, but I do not know how it would
work out. There are many difficulties..."

"Well, Me-do-me-pa," answered John, "suppose
we start out and try to feed them and teach them
for three month. I'm sure God will supply the
corn,but suppose we just say we will holdthe
school for as long as He does supply corn?" On
that basis the deacons were comforted and plans
were made. The story of the RSBS will be told in a
later chapter,but sufficeit tosay herethat the results
gratified all so much that a vote was taken to
continue the same thing the next year, and it was
unanimous.Thus it became a yearly institution.

As told before, we began that first school (and
subsequent ones) with a time of heart searching,
and I notice from the circulars of those days that it
touched more than the students—I quote from June,
1938:

THERE ARISETH A LITTLE CLOUD

In looking over prayer partner letters I came upon this sentence–"We are led of the Spirit to pray for a general revival among the Lisu Christians." We rejoice that the Lisu have people praying for them who are led of the Spirit. Like Elijah's servant on Mt. Carmel, sent up to look for the prayed-for showers, we would like to tell you that "there ariseth a little cloud...like a man's hand." From the first days of our arrival there have been individual confessions of sin–some every month–and in a few cases the ones who sought cleansing were touched directly by the Spirit Himself; that is, not through a human medium. It is always a peculiar joy to see God work all by Himself. He uses us to give us that pleasure, but He does not have to use us.

Sunday, May 1, was the day the little cloud arose. The first Sunday of the month is always communion here, and that day John led the service. He spoke on "Go, and sin no more," then before administering the sacrament, he asked if there were not some who wished to make things right before partaking. Immediately Me-do-me-pa was on his feet. He is church treasurer among other things, and some time ago in making up accounts he found $1.50 more than was necessary, so he decided it must be on his own money and pocketed it. During prayer in his own home, thinking of something quite different, the Holy Spirit brought that $1.50 to his mind and told him he should have given the church the benefit of the doubt. Me-do-me-pa had already confessed it to Job, but now wished to tell the church. His lead made it easy for others. I cannot relate all here, but will pick out some I think might interest you most.

Va-ci-me-pa is the brother of our Joseph who is asleep in Jesus. This boy has had further affliction;

their father died a few months ago, and by the
way, on his death-bed he said he saw Joseph in
heaven leading the singing! Then just lately Va-ci-
me-pa's house burned to the ground through his
wife's carelessly leaving the flax too near the fire.
They lost everything, and in his shock and grief,
Va-ci-me-pa beat his wife. He arose that day to
confess to all and publicly shook her hand before
us. Dear boy—he seems to have the same tender
heart that Joseph had, for he broke down and cried
and cried.

Rhoda, Job's wife, had a quarrel with Pade-John
and the two of them were not on speaking terms.
They both confessed and shook hands.

Then Pade-Peter came forward. First he confessed to having stolen a pencil from us three years
ago; then to having ill-treated his old parents. At
this point Me-do-me-pa, from his own seat on the
penitent form, looked up and ejaculated grimly,
"Yes, you had better say that!" Both old people
were in the audience and both broke down and
cried and started to flood us with miserable details
of how unfilial the boy had been, so that the Spirit
was quenched and no more confessions followed.
Job closed with prayer saying, "Father, there must
be many more and greater sins in our midst. Please
cleanse us." Altogether we were four hours in
chapel that Sunday.

One of the rare qualities in a Rock-man is the
ability to say no. Many a leader has spoiled his
career, and failed to attain greatness, when he met
this seemingly simple test. But Me-do-me-pa had
that ability to be upright at any cost.

As spring of 1939 advanced, the Kuhn household
began to run low in corn. We often bought the corn
which the Christians had donated to the church,

and which had to be sold. We paid the regular market price, of course, but it was convenient to get it from next door, instead of having to have it hauled from a distance. So John asked Me-do-me-pa, as church treasurer, to sell him some of the church corn. To his surprise Me-do-me-pa refused! He did it very graciously and explained his position thus, "If I sold any of the corn which is in this village now, Ma-Pa, there would not be enough left to feed the Bible students through RSBS, and the church should not pay to have corn hauled, when there has been enough stored here, to start with."

My husband was slightly nettled at first, then we saw that properly we should rejoice, "Just think how he has shouldered the responsibility of feeding the students! He is thinking and planning carefully that the school may be run without hindrance. If anyone is to be bothered with hauling corn, it should be private people like ourselves. After all we can afford it. What a gift, to have a man who cares about the interests of the church whether it makes him popular with his neighbour or not!" And truly after Me-do-me-pa was gone, we had a succession of worries over that very thing. The Lisu who later took charge of the corn (a true Christian himself, but unable to say "No" to friends and relatives who want to "borrow" or otherwise use church corn) was embarrassed by many a shortage which should never have been. It was not due to dishonesty, but merely to that lack of courage in not daring to become unpopular.

As RSBS (1939) was approaching, Pade-John presented himself as a candidate for entrance. He applied to Me-do-me-pa, saying that he now intended to do the Lord's work, and so expected the church to feed him free. But Me-do-me-pa refused him free board, saying it was against the rules. Now Pade-John is a relative of Me-do-me-pa's, and in the East it is customary to wink at rules if the applicant is your blood relative. But the dear deacon knew that there was just enough corn for the teachers, and to admit a layman free would be to run short for the evangelists. Pade-John certainly never expected to be refused,and he was quite upset. The kind Shepherd looked at the disconsolate young fellow, and said, "John, have you no money of your own to buy corn?"

"Yes, about three dollars; but the cost of three months' food is five dollars."

"Well," said Me-do-me-pa, "you use that three dollars and I'll add a fourth!" Whereupon a guest in the home piped up, "And I'll give the fifth!" and so the boy got his study expenses and the church did not suffer. This is a small incident, but it is revealing. For the good of the majority, Me-do-me-pa had to stay by "the law"; but he tempered it with "grace" out of his own pocket! That is why his reputation for integrity and yet for kindness and ingenuity, spread for many days' journey up and down the canyon.

It was now becoming clear that an incurable disease had laid hold of our beloved Rock-man. We sent him to a Chinese doctor at Paoshan city, but though they put him through many tests, some very painful ones, they could not diagnose the trouble. Perhaps if they operated they could find out, they said. But at that he refused and elected to come back to his beloved mountain home.

A little incident stands out in my memory, but I

cannot place its date. However, I give it here. Charlie Peterson had just returned from the district of Luda, where he evidently had spent some time. It was Sunday morning at breakfast.

"Who is slated to speak this noon?" he asked.

"Me-do-me-pa's name is up," I replied.

"Me-do-me-pa!" he exclaimed, sitting back in his chair. "So I am going to see and hear the celebrated Me-do-me-pa! Well I tell you frankly, *I am prejudiced against that fellow!* What a time I have had with the deacons up there at Luda! No matter could be brought to a decision. Just as it seemed to arrive there, someone was sure to say, 'Well, let's wait awhile and see what Me-do-me-pa will say about it.' Me-do-me-pa, six days' journey away, and who does not belong to their district at all! What has he got to do with Luda affairs, anyway? What is he? A Lisu pope?"

At that time I did not know of the Shepherd's reputation for godly wisdom and I was alarmed lest something had been going on which I did not know. So I just answered, "I don't think he is like that. But, anyway, you will hear him yourself this noon. You can ask him anything you like then."

That noon service as the dear Shepherd stood up to break the Word of God to us, his face aglow with the light so often there, I soon forgot the suggested accusation, in listening to his humble, sweet message. It touched my heart and I did not think of the matter again until at the close of the service I suddenly saw Charlie Peterson rise from his seat, and go forward with both arms outstretched as if he would embrace the Shepherd. But he planted those hands on the big Lisu's shoulders and said, "Thank you, Brother. That message was a blessing to my own heart." And the Lisu deacon blushed with pleasure like a schoolgirl. Charlie Peterson was one of his faithful friends from that hour onward.

Our next circular said:

> Our beloved Shepherd Me-do-me-pa is likely dying of cancer. Pray that he may end triumphantly. He has had to resign from all church work and the church is in a flutter. In fact I am so grateful for the privilege of being here at so critical a time–if there were no missionary here I don't know what would happen–likely there would be difficulty in having any Rainy Season Bible School at all. As it is, the deacons insist that there is food for only one month's supply. Perhaps they are to have a lesson in faith. Perhaps God has other plans for this summer, but pray that if the RSBS is God's will for these months Satan may not be allowed to hinder supplies getting through.

But though he "resigned," Me-do-me-pa was not allowed to lay his burdens down. People flocked to his sick bed with their problems. The following extract will be a sample:

May 23, 1940.

THE VALLEY OF THE SHADOW

It was Sunday evening, May 12; the sun had just set quietly behind the opposite mountains. No glorious streamers of gold and crimson has he displayed for a long time now; he merely wraps himself in a mantle of grey cloud and silently drops over the edge. Was he trying to match the grey tenor of my days, I wondered? Or was he also grieving for the emaciated suffering one, up there in the little shanty in Oak Flat Village, whose feet are painfully threading the unlightened path of the valley of the shadow? Me-do-me-pa is not far from any of our thoughts, as the following little story will tell.

Dusk in Lisuland. Although I was still alone and the days still heat-misty I rejoiced in this hour. Everything then is settling down for the night's rest; grey though the sky is, it is peaceful and serene; twitter of drowsy bird and happy hum of contented cricket or cicada, the quiet of God's holy places seems to brood over earth and sky. I was strolling back and forth over the rock platform which made our shanty home level, drinking in all the stillness and the nearness of the Other Land, when my solitude was interrupted by Papa Peter coming jauntily down the hill and seating himself near the edge of the stone foundation work, evidently intent on having a conversation. After a while it burst out.

"Ma-Ma, there is a wind-word has reached my ear"—with many grimaces and gesticulations without which Papa Peter would be as unable to talk as a Frenchman.

"And what did it say?" I asked, smiling and stopping in front of him.

"It is said that when Me-do-me-pa goes up to heaven the Big Fellow is going to leave too."

I was puzzled. Lisu is a most ambiguous language which often leaves much to the imagination. Other Lisu had appeared and were grouping themselves around us. "He means," said La-fu-si-ma with a smile, "that when Me-do-me-pa dies you white folk will go away too." "Yes-s," groaned Papa Peter expressively; "and that is why everybody's heart is cold. Oh, when Me-do-me-pa goes I won't dare to live on the earth any longer, for when evil men abound and try to steal my fields, what shall I do? Even sick as he is now, he always has some place or idea to help me out of a trouble. I'm a fool; I have no ideas to combat anybody. I'll just be a helpless victim when he is gone!"

His woebegone face made me smile, but the tears were very near the surface. Memory flew back to a Sunday years ago when Papa Peter had brought some iron to church (he is the village blacksmith) in order to bargain for the coming week's work with a certain heathen or some such thing. The heathen came before the service was over and called Papa Peter in the middle of the meetings. When Me-do-me-pa saw that the old man had actually brought the iron to chapel and was hiding it under his bench, he seized it and threw it outside. Whereupon there was a hot argument afterwards, and the Shepherd said, on our trying to make peace, "I was wrong to get angry, but there is no one gives me more trouble than that old man. He is a continual trial to me!" And here was Me-do-me-pa's "Continual Trial" sitting before me with a gloomy countenance telling me that he would not dare to live after the Shepherd dies!

But I saw in a trice that Papa Peter was the voice of the ignorant part of Lisu church. So I pointed the obvious lesson. "But, Papa Peter, the Lord is not going to leave us, nor is your white pastor." (How grateful I was at that moment that I had stayed behind. My very presence was a living testimony that the wind-words were not true and need not be feared.) "Don't you suppose the Lord Jesus has ideas too, and can defend His own from evil? Is your trust in Me-do-me-pa or in Christ? Perhaps this is the reason that Jesus is taking Me-do-me-pa from us, so that His children will learn that He is their true Leaning-Place. Haven't you heard Mr Yang's story of how the Lord took care of him some months ago? He was on his way to Luku market when his horse ran away at the top of the mountain as they were about to descend. He had to chase back after it, but when he caught it and finally reached the river bank he found a heathen fellow bleeding and wounded. Robbers had been waiting there, and because Mr Yang's horse ran away the heathen man reached the robbers first, lost all that he had with him, and had his arms badly cut, or perhaps broken, besides. Could Me-do-me-pa have done that? Isn't the Lord Jesus a safer trusting place?"

Papa Peter was impressed—he had not heard that story. "That's so. You've comforted my heart, Ma-Ma. Thank you," he said slowly. Then...does it ever fail?..."the fowls of the air devoured it"; the "fowl" this time being Abel who said with a light laugh, "Oh, but Mr Yang is a preacher; you and I could not expect such attention!" Do not the devil's lies make you angry? But aren't there some Abels at home who say just the same thing? "Oh, that life of faith is all right for the missionaries. God has a special love for them"—and so on. Yet all the time the Word tells us that Peter said, "I now realize how true it is that God does not show favouritism, but accepts men from every nation who fear him and do what is right." The only conditions to such acceptance with God are faith, the love that fears to sin against Him, and the life that in no point has been consciously disobedient to Him. But I do not know whether "the seed" was wholly devoured or not; the group broke up and the conversation ended.

But I have told you this so that you may see how to pray. In every church there are spiritual and carnal Christians, and in every church practically the same class predominate. Are you harshly judging Papa Peter and his crowd? My mother died when I was twenty-two years old—old enough to stand on my own feet—but I can never forget that awful sense of desolation. I had never known this world without mother to run to when in trouble, I did not know that God had a dear husband all planned for me. Well, the Oak Flat church has never known Christian life without Me-do-me-pa to run to when in trouble. They are shaking and trembling; that is, the carnal ones—our spiritual Christians are not afraid. But I sympathize with Papa Peter. I have had experience of the Lord's love and power. I know he can raise up some one, something to make life livable again—in my case it was my husband, but always it is something. Those who live after the flesh have no such experience to bolster them and they are needlessly afraid. But we are not told to cast them out because their faith is not enough... "accept him whose faith is weak." Put your loving arms of prayer about these doubting ones, that they may *see*, later on, the glory of God.

Amy Carmichael says that the words, "No one is indispensable. God will give you another Me-do-me-pa" are not true. She says, "No, it is not *by giving us back what He has taken* that our God teaches us His deepest lessons, but by patiently waiting beside us till we can say, 'I accept the will of my God as good and acceptable and perfect of loss or gain.'"

When is the time to trust?
  Is it some future day,
  When you have tried your way,
  And learned to trust and pray,
By bitter woe?

Nay; but the time to trust
  Is in the moment's need,
  Poor, broken, bruised reed!
  Poor troubled soul make speed
To trust thy God.

And now the Wind of Death was blowing bitterly upon the dear Shepherd. It was his "time to trust." At first when he realized recovery was hopeless, the "why" of it bothered him. One afternoon as I was sitting with him, he turned to me almost weeping and said, "Ma-Ma, I have searched and searched my heart and I cannot find any sin big enough to have brought this upon me!" And then, as I went over the story of Job and showed him how suffering is not always caused by sin, is not always a punishment, he was comforted, and from then on he seemed to enter into peace of heart, although bodily pain was on the increase.

At this time Homay was still alive, so she and I took the guitar and climbed the hill to Me-do-me-pa's house to sing to him daily, and try to be a comfort. He loved it and would ask for his favourite hymns. *The Great Physician* he wanted at first, then nearer the end it was *My hope is built on nothing less than Jesus' blood and righteousness, When I survey the wondrous Cross* and *Jesus keep me near the Cross*. I felt myself near the borderland of Heaven those days. Once he asked for "that hymn which says, 'this is the victory that overcomes.'" After we sang it, I read to him the fifth chapter of I John, then said to him, "Isn't it good that it says the victory is our *faith*, not our power to endure?" How his face lit up with joy at that thought, for his sufferings were beyond human endurance. "Ma-Ma," he answered, "I believe now what I always have, that Christ died for my sins and rose again, and I know He is going to reward me."

June is the rainiest time of the whole year at Oak Flat. It is the beginning of the Rainy Season and often for several weeks we did not see the sun—just rain, day and night. That year it was especially bad. On June 8, about one o'clock in the morning I was awakened by a knock at the door. I instinctively knew what it would be. "Yes, Ma-Ma," was the answer to my inquiry, "Me-do-me-pa is going and he has sent Job to ask if you will come to him." Hastily I threw on a heavy coat over my pyjamas, got into rubber galoshes and started out into the night. Me-do-me-pa's shanty is only about a hundred yards above ours, but the ground was so soft with the long wetting that my feet sank into it at each step and I had to have two Lisu, one on each side, pull me up the incline, for we had to climb through the mire of a cornfield. Meanwhile, the rain was drizzling gently down on our heads.

I had brought with me some medicine to be given when his pains were most severe. On arrival we found the shanty filled with people, some sleeping on the floor, some standing, some sitting. Almost to the end, people had persisted in taking their problems to him. In vain he pleaded to be freed from their worries. He even pleaded to me, "Ma-Ma, can't you ask the church to free me from these matters? I'd love to help the folk still, but I am so weak, and when they come with their long stories it wearies me so, can't you help me?"

I could have wept. He was so emaciated that his big bones stuck through the dry skin—just a living skeleton, and yet the people still sought his advice. He had been a rock in a weary land so long to them that it seemed as if they could not let him go—they were afraid he would die before they got the benefit of his counsel. I issued stern orders, and I think from then on he was freed. But they still surrounded him. The crowd that night were, at last, not thinking of themselves, and a reverent awe was in the atmosphere as I picked my way through and over them, to the little inner room where the dying man lay.

The death rattle was in his throat; he could not speak, but he knew I had come. I took his so-thin hand in mine, and it returned my pressure lovingly. So I knew he was conscious and I asked Job to read John 14:1-6. I felt the Lisu voice might be understood better than mine. After Job finished, Me-do-me-pa gathered himself together for a final testimony. I saw he was trying, so I administered the medicine I had brought, with an eye-dropper (he was too far gone to drink). Then suddenly he began to talk. His speech was so thick that I lost the first part of it, but it went on like this, "I believe what Pastor Job read just now and by His Cross I...Ma-Ma, pray for me, that God's will, whatever it be, may be accomplished." That last was remarkably clear. And so I prayed, committing him to the One who had died to redeem him. As I finished he said in his old natural voice, "Thank you," turned his head and seemed to have fallen into a light slumber. I knew the opiate might do that, and not sure when he would arouse, I left some of the medicine for him and went back home and to bed.

RSBS was in full swing, those days; there were just two of us to teach, and already I had a very bad cold. With so much depending on me I felt I must not go out into the wet without necessity, and I had left word that they should call me if he roused. It was eight the next morning when we heard a soft sound of weeping, up the hill. Before I could get galoshes on to go, the voices of Job, Luke and others started to sing the Lisu funeral hymn, *Sleep On, Beloved*, and I knew the dear suffering one was with his Lord.

They said the end came too quickly to call me. He slept on until about eight, when he awoke and asked the women to leave the room, "Now your uncle is going to leave you," he said to the men, "Don't make a wailing, but look for me"...and while he was speaking he was lifted over the ford.

> Deep is the stream and the night is late,
> And grief blinds my soul that I cannot see.
> Speak to me out of the silence, Lord,
> That my spirit may know
> As I forward go
> That Thy pierced hands are lifting me over the ford.

The funeral was hastened on. All guests who choose to come before the burial must be feasted, and he was so widely known that they feared too great expense for the widow, so he was laid in the grave that very afternoon. His married daughter, Me-do-me, was then nineteen years of age. Thaddeus was ten, and little Philip five.

The Rainy Season Bible School students dug his grave. They wrapped the body in native sheets, tied it to carrying poles, then friends carried it to the graveside, where the heavy coffin was waiting. He was enclosed and lowered, the grave being dug as I had never seen a grave dug before. Above the cell for the coffin which was twice its height, ledges on each side were dug; after the coffin was lowered, the space above was kept empty, but huge slabs of rock, heavier than two men could carry, were placed on these ledges, thus covering completely the coffin cell. Above the rock slabs earth was heaped, and rocks on top of that. Later I planted flowers. On an upright slab of smooth stone is carved a cross and "Me-do-me-pa, Forty-one years, Oak Flat Village, Deacon of the Church." Then on the horizontal part of the cross it reads, "He being dead yet speaketh." The site is in the curve where Sunset Ridge joins Oak Flat Mountain, and is right beside the path out to the main road, over which we all pass so often, so that his memory will yet be testifying to his fellow villagers.

Altogether Me-do-me-pa had been a Christian only about nine years. As a heathen he was little known beyond the precincts of his own village. But after yielding to Christ, he became loved and revered and a power for God, for many days' journey up and down the canyon. How account for that, except for the declaration of scripture, "For God, who was at work in the ministry of Peter...was also at work in my ministry." "Now to each one the manifestation of the Spirit is given for the common good. To one is given through the Spirit the message of wisdom."

Friend, if God could do so much for an earth person, in nine years' time, what might He not do with you–if you yielded yourself fully to His power?

Chapter 6

THE PREY OF THE TERRIBLE

THE scene changes. No longer the deep canyon of the Salween river, but the mountain land of Upper Burma, about seven days' journey straight west from Me-do-me-pa's home. We have been thinking so much of the Nests that found refuge in the Rock, that I wonder if we have forgotten the Abyss? This chapter is to remind us of the evil power which has always claimed the Munition of Rocks as his own. And he still does.

A small village on a hill, under a big tree. Before we get close, the loud clatter of loose floor boards and rough foot-tapping ring out far down the trail. A spirit seance is going on! Two women and a man are calling down the evil spirits. Beating a copper gong the while, they began a backward and forward foot dance, much like our Sailor's Hornpipe, and all the time they are calling out, "Come down! Come down! Come down!" Suddenly the clattering stops, the dancers are "possessed," their eyes become glazed as they go unconscious,[1] and a voice absolutely different from their own comes through their lips. This day the message is extraordinary.

"Worship God," they shriek, "He has a Son

---

[1] Just one in the village retained consciousness while possessed.

named Jesus and two daughters. They live in the stratosphere above the clouds. Cast out your demon altars. God will give you eternal life. He will raise the dead and the old shall be made young!" No such message had ever been heard before in those parts. The onlookers drop their jaws in open-mouthed amazement.

Then the man's demon turns on the two women and scolds them for not completely healing the sick one, in whose cause this seance is being held. Whereupon the two women, still possessed, turn upon the man, and scold his devil, using this new name, Jesus. This was in 1923; fifteen years later I personally visited these people and investigated this story. I thought that perhaps they might have heard that Name in a market and their subconscious mind retained it, but all declared emphatically that it was not so. Never had they heard that Name until the demon seance related above.

After haggling back and forth, the onlookers beat the gong. The demon-possessed ones stagger, come to, and the seance is over. An animal is then slain and offered to the demons.

The demon-possessed ones did not know what had been spoken through them, so when they asked the onlookers, there was a great babble of talk as to what this strange message could mean. One thing had stood out in everyone's mind; all three demons had said from now on they were not to worship ordinary demons but to worship one, Jesus. Knowing nothing more, they thought that Jesus must be a demon who wished to be their special protector. Very much interested, they decided to hold another seance the very next day, and this time definitely and exclusively invite

Jesus to come down.

So the two women and the one man again went through the seance just like the day before, except that it was Jesus whom they invited. And the same thing happened. Again the strange voice proclaimed, "Worship God and Jesus. The old will become young and the dead will become alive." Then there followed new instructions, "When you pray to Jesus, take off your turban, close your eyes and bow your head."

The man's devil again said, "Don't worship demons. Repent of your sins!" Whereupon the two women's devils cursed him and for three years he could not get possessed—his familiar spirit seemed to have left him. But others in the village tried, and got possessed. They could tell it was the Jesus—demon by his catch word, "Worship Jesus and the old will become young...." And new revelations flowed in.

"One day in seven you must rest—don't work your farms."

"Don't drink wine, smoke opium or commit adultery. Be good people."

"Don't thieve."

"Don't give false witness."

"Honour your parents" (a thought utterly strange to all Lisu; Christians of our parts have to be taught this from the Scripture).

As far as I could find out, all the Ten Commandments and some of the old Levitical law was given them, from time to time, by demons. The proof that it could not have come from any subconscious mind is that, although Christianity reached Upper Burma, the people were evidently not taught Christian separation from the world, and to this

day the tribal Christians in surrounding parts
drink, smoke, and do not observe the Lord's Day.
This village of the demon revelations was named
Goo-moo, and they were the only Christians who
tried to live a separated life, as a church. So the
thought of such separations from old pastimes was
absolutely, utterly, "out of the blue" to them.

Now, I have deliberately picked out, from all the
revelations given, those which affect our thinking;
but these were not the only revelations. Oh, no.
Satan uses the Word of God, but never without
mixing some folly and falseness up with it. So
there was talk of one, "God's daughter," very
vague it was; but most interesting to Goo-moo
were the gifts of this demon. He would say, "Go to
such and such a place in the mountains, and you
will find a bear." They'd go, and lo! a bear was
there and the village had meat to eat. In this way
they were enticed into bondage to the demon. All
his promises did not come true. For instance, he
said, "Build cow-sheds and pig-pens and God will
give you cows and pigs." (Lisu usually keep their
animals underneath their houses, among the stilts
on which the house rests.) But of course it took
years to find out that there was no increase in
cattle when the demon's order had been obeyed.
So it came about that the whole village threw out
their demon altars, rested one day in seven, and
started to worship Jesus.

Two or three months later, a visiting official of
the government noticed that they no longer had
demon altars in their homes and asked the reason.
On hearing their story he reported it to his superior with the result that Goo-moo villagers received an order to report to the government official

at Tow-gow, two days' journey away. There they were told that there was a school-teacher at Fort Pien-Ma, who had books about this Jesus, and that on December 25, a great festival was held at Fort Pien-Ma in honour of Jesus. To that festival they went and made themselves known, I suppose, because later on (which year I do not know) the school-teacher visited them and the third day of his stay the Jesus-demon came upon the two women, mentioned above, and through them said, "Don't study his books. They are dog books, monkey books." So no one was interested in the catechisms he had brought along. However, one thing impressed them—he had taken the gong out of the hand of one of the possessed women and said, "You must not do this!" whereupon she came out of her spell—the demon left her. The villagers were too intrigued with this new way of living, however, for it was in the early days of their bondage, when to be promised meat by revelation was thrilling to them; so the Christian school-teacher left them, baffled.

I have been asked why did Satan introduce the name of Jesus to these people? I feel it was because he saw that the gospel was inevitably going to reach them, and so he tried to make the name of Jesus and the outward forms of Christianity (the Ten Commandments, etc.) familiar to them under a system which was really worship of himself. We see that he had succeeded in his subtlety up to this point in the story.

But it did not continue so happily. Once thoroughly ensnared, the inevitable trickery began. One day the two women's devils gave forth a message. "The earth is going to be burned!" they

said. "Jesus is coming to earth! And all unbelievers
will be burned. You, believers, go to a certain place
in the mountains and wait for Him! When He
comes He will give you animals and money."

The whole village packed up. Left their farm
work unattended, and retired to the directed place
in the mountains, where they fasted, eating only
once a day, and waited a week without anything
happening, of course. Fooled, chagrined, and
anxious now for the unwatched crops left behind,
they returned to their homes. This happened four
times in nine years and once the whole village
almost starved because of it. The prey of the
terrible. Some began to wish to get free from this
demon.

One day a Karen teacher came for a night or so.
As he left the next morning, a demon came upon
one of the villagers and said, "He won't reach his
home–he is going to get sick!" And that night the
teacher truly, nearly died–a strange fever seemed
to be burning him up. "The demons were very
intelligent and knowing," the Goo-moo folk told
us, and so obedience gradually became that of fear
and terror. Then when the fourth revelation of
Jesus' coming was given, it was accompanied by
the order, "Don't plant your fields this year."
Should they obey? Dared they not obey? There was
one young boy in the village who had never
become possessed–he had cried, but the demons
would not come upon him, the only one in the
whole place on whom they would not come–and it
was through him, in the end, that deliverance
came.

"Dad," said this boy, as the family conference
whether to plant or not to plant was waging, "I

don't believe that Jesus is coming. Has he not told us that three times already and each time fooled us? We will starve if we do not plant our fields. What I'm thinking is—I'd like to find out the truth about this Jesus. The Karen teacher worshipped Jesus, but he did not go through seances like we do. And he does not get fooled either. And years ago that Pien-Ma school-teacher had books about Jesus, don't you remember? I'd like to take a trip out to where that Karen teacher lives and ask him to come back and teach us!"

"I think so too," said his father. "Take a friend and the two of you go." So the two boys set out.

But at the sight of them the Karen teacher become terrified. "Go to your village? Never!" he cried. "Your village is full of demons. I would not dare go to the other side of Schoolhouse Mountain!"

"We were wrong," pleaded the boys, "when you came that time. We did not listen then, but now we are tired of these demons and want to learn the truth. Please come!"

But the Karen teacher would not hear of it, so the two laddies had to return home, sad and troubled. No one to deliver them! However, Mark's father (later the boy was named Mark) had decided. He was going to have food, demon's wrath or not; he was going to plant! A few other families in the village followed them; the rest left their field unplanted, constantly expecting that Jesus was coming and would miraculously feed them, as demons did so often in directing them as to where to find game in the mountains. But as time went on—when planting was too late—and the Jesus-demon had not come, wan and thin faces besieged

Mark's door, pleading for food. But there was not enough to share with so many. Mark's face grew more grim each day. To be enslaved to such a deceitful, malicious master was intolerable.

Then, one day, into his house walked two fellow villagers who had gone to the Salween canyon to trade.

"Books!" they cried out, waving two Lisu catechisms under Mark's nose. "Lisu books about Jesus! You know we went away over to the market at Sandalwood Flat Village, and while trading our things we saw a Lisu selling these catechisms. They are Lisu books—he could read them so as to make them speak our language, and he was preaching about God and Jesus!"

Great was the excitement in the village. As news spread, more and more people gathered around the two young traders, and many times they had to repeat their story. They had met Andrew, one of the lads that followed La-ma-wu with the gospel evangelization, in the canyon.

Mark was fingering the books with a tremendous thrill in his heart. "Can you read them?" he asked eagerly.

"Oh no. We did not have time to stay long enough to learn. But other Lisu were learning to read them; Teacher Andrew was teaching them how. Bright fellows learn in two weeks, they say."

"Well, why didn't you bring teacher Andrew back with you?" cried out Mark, exasperated at so wonderful a chance thus slipping away.

"Oh, he couldn't come," they answered. "He could not cope with all the invitations he was getting from people who live nearby. And to our place is a journey of five days—seven days soon, for snow will be closing the pass, and he would have to go around Fort Pien-Ma."

"Well, I'm going," cried out the boy. "If I can't get teachers, I'll stay until I can read the books for myself. Dad, may I?" The decision was made, but there was still the Master of the Abyss to deal with. Not lightly would he lose such slaves to his every whim. Twice Mark started out with a comrade and was beaten back. The first time malaria nearly killed him. How the evil one must have laughed as the wan, pale boy staggered into his father's home—defeated, and nearly dead. That was May, 1933. In October he essayed to go again. A different route he and companions took, but before they got over the high pass (Mountain of Suffering, the Lisu had named it) his comrades became terrified and again he had to return home, still without knowledge of the way of escape from their terrible master.

But by March, 1934, Mark could stand their cheated, terrified bondage no longer. On consulting with his father, they decided, "The devils have led us astray. If there are people who know the truth and can reach us, we must reach them; better to die trying, than to go on as we are." Mark persuaded his brother-in-law and a neighbour to accompany him, and the little band of three started out for the unknown canyon, over a partially unknown road, and one which involved crossing the great Pien-Ma Pass (11,000 feet high) at a time when there was snow on the ground and new snow was likely to come down and obliterate the trail. A Chinese traveller whom they met told them they could get from Pien-Ma Fort to the Salween canyon in one day, so they got up before dawn the

next day, and started. Up, up, the air getting
freezingly cold. Snow everywhere on the ground;
so deep was the snow that they noticed the tops of
trees sticking through the crust they were treading
underfoot. Snow, tree-high! Up, up to the lonely
pass where no human habitation ever is. Snow
blew in their faces. They could not breathe for the
wind and the biting cold, so they buried their faces
in their turbans and sleeves and tried to get their
breath that way. Single file they walked and in
utter silence, but praying to the *unknown* Jesus (the
good Jesus whom the demon had tried to counter-
feit) to bring them through to where they could
find the truth about Him. As they felt their blood
chilling, they bit with their teeth into the flesh of
their own arms to increase circulation. Sometimes
they would fall through the snow crust and get
separated—they could not see their fellow in front
of them plainly because of the blowing snow. And
then—over the pass—and the descent on the China
side. Oh, praise to the unknown Jesus—no snow on
the China side!

Hope renewed, how fast the young feet now
sped over that rocky descent, through those miles
and miles of uninhabited, wild-grass mountainside; then at dusk—a village! Coming in the door of
a house, the man there looked up at them and
asked, "Where did you come from?" When they
answered, "Over the Pien-Ma Pass!" the whole
house of people exclaimed, "Oh, don't lie! You
could not get over the mountain in this snow!" But
they had. Wonderful joy of accomplishment.

But where were the Jesus-teachers?"

"Oh, there are white people in the canyon, teaching now," was the unexpected answer. "Their

name is Cooke, and they are living across the river at Pine Mountain Village. You will have to go up to Place-of-Action Ferry to get across."

All the next day they travelled beside the roaring Salween, and at night slept in rice-fields by its bank. Early next morning of the third day saw them at the crossing edge waiting for the first ferry boat. A young Lisu with a book-bag slung over his shoulder got out of the ferry as it drew up and hooked on to the rocks of the bank. "Who are you?" he asked, eyeing their different costume, for the Burmese Lisu are Flowery Lisu.

"We have come from Burma to get a teacher of the gospel," they replied.

"Oh," he said with interest. "I am the missionary's servant. I am on my way to collect their mail. Mr Cooke isn't home just now, but Mrs Cooke is there, and the night before last Mr and Mrs Kuhn arrived. Go on up. The road is easy to find. See you tomorrow!" and he sped on and left them.

And now I want you to change your point of view, and see things as we saw them, knowing nothing of all that I have been relating to you. My husband and I were on a trial trip into the canyon. Mr Fraser always feared that my health could not stand the rigorous life of the canyon, but when we heard that two districts had turned Christian, and that to care for each, Mr and Mrs Cooke were having to separate and live six days' journey apart, then we volunteered to move in and take over one district. So Mr Fraser proposed this trial trip, to see if I could stand it.

There being no mail service quick enough, we could not announce our arrival, so we walked in on Leila Cooke unawares. It had been about a year

since she had seen another white woman, so how
warm a welcome we received! And from now on I
will quote from the letter written right at that time.

> The second morning after we arrived as we were
> sitting in conversation together, through the open
> doorway walked three strangely clad but hand-
> some Lisu.
> Mrs Cooke urged them to take chairs, but they
> stared as if they had never seen such things before
> in their lives, and indicated that they much pre-
> ferred the safety of the shanty floor where they
> squatted down in front of us, a picturesque group
> with their white clothing and red turbans. As Mrs
> Cooke questioned them politely and listened to
> their rather lengthy answers she became visibly
> thrilled and began to drop to us short translations
> of the story told above. "They have come seven
> days' journey over those mountains yonder,"
> pointing to the craggy peaks with sparkling crests
> of snow which loomed up across the canyon
> through the open doorway. "Said they had to bite
> their way through the snow of the pass....Say
> they've come until they can take back teachers
> with them, no matter how long they have to
> wait....They've brought their own food to keep
> them....They have worshipped God and Jesus for
> eleven years without knowing anything more
> about it...This is their third attempt to get teach-
> ers."

When the conversation came to an end, the three
Goo-moo boys were introduced to Pastor Moses,
who led them off to his own house. Mrs Cooke
turned to us and said, "And just think, we have no
teacher to send with them!" How sad our hearts
felt; nay, even rebellious. I knew a town in Amer-

ica with only four thousand population, yet it had nine churches. And here these brave laddies had walked seven days' journey to learn the Way of Life and there was no teacher to send back with them. Every Lisu teacher in the immediate area had his hands too full already. Word had just come from Mr Cooke that now, if the Kuhns had arrived, would Mrs Cooke please come up and visit him for a while! And we could not talk Lisu, just Chinese,which the Burma men could not understand; so we were out of the question, anyway, though my husband burned to go.

"Well," said Mark, "we have brought food and money. We will just stay until there is someone, and in the meantime Pastor Moses can teach us." So day by day they pored over their books, waited and prayed for a teacher.

A month passed. Teacher Simeon arrived on the way home to Stockade Hill. He had fulfilled his promise of one or two years of evangelization and now wanted to get back and be married. Mrs Cooke had laid the call before him. It was a hard struggle, for he was already homesick. "But I can't go alone very well," he said. Lisu evangelists usually go out two by two, in case of sickness or other sudden need. The young lad who had gone for the mail stood by listening to this point, but surprised us all by crying out:

"I'll go with him! I'll go! Oh Ma-Pa let me go. I don't know much to be sure, but I can teach them to read and pray and sing a few hymns. Oh, do let me go!" And so it was arranged. In Lisuland we almost take it for granted that if a boy proves to be a good servant, we will soon lose him from the kitchen into the ministry. It has happened so often, and of course there is no question of whether we can spare him—the Lord's call comes first. It had happened again. Teacher Simeon postponed his longed-for trip home for a full six months, so when the three inquirers returned to Goo-moo something over a month after they had left, it was to show their fellows two Lisu teachers. With great joy, the whole village started in to learn of Him who was manifested that He might destroy the works of the devil, and deliver them who through fear of him had been in bondage.

During those happy six months, and the year that followed, the Kuhn family moved into Lisuland, and by September, 1935, John was free to follow his never-forgotten longing to visit Goo-moo.

John had the most wonderful time at Goo-moo. His party arrived on a Saturday after dark, and the villagers were all at chapel. Of course the visit was unannounced and unexpected, but as the weary band climbed the mountainside (at the end of seven days' travelling) grateful that the long, hard trek was nearly over, through the dark there came a sound of singing, and as they listened, they heard these words floating down the trail to greet them, like a heavenly welcome:

Have you been to Jesus for the cleansing power?
Are you washed in the Blood of the Lamb?
Are you fully trusting in His grace each hour?
Are you washed in the Blood of the Lamb?

"Before we saw their faces, we heard their testimony!" said John, touched to the heart. Then came the delight of surprising them by walking in the door. How they shouted his name, laughed and wept with joy—the first white missionary the village had ever seen. The man who had been possessed by demons could not resist kissing John—took his face reverently in his hands, and kissed him—much to my husband's discomposure! "There won't be any sleep for us this night, to think that Ma-Pa is here!" cried one. And so on. It was a happy time. Twelve were baptized, this making a total of twenty-five baptized believers and more catechists; for other villages were hearing the Good News and wanting to be taught. At length when the time came to part, there was true weeping and grief. In loving gratitude they insisted on acting as John's carriers, free of charge, on the return trip, and even provided chickens for his meals, though very poor themselves in this world's riches.

Three or four of them made the long journey to the Munition of Rocks at Christmas, for they had heard we were going home on furlough. When that happy festival was over, and it came time to to say goodbye, knowing it would be years before they saw us again, both men and women broke down and cried. I was deeply stirred to hear Mark's, "Oh, Ma-Pa!" as he broke from John's embrace and turned to the trail, sobbing.

So when furlough was ended and we were once more back in the beloved canyon, we made plans to go and visit that faraway little village in Burma, and see how they had been faring. Lisu teachers had continued to go from our district to teach them, so they had been growing, but I myself had never been there and wished to investigate their story. The account of our trip was written in the

November, 1938, circular–the year that Homay and Thomas were married.

LOSS AND A DREAM COME TRUE

"My heart is on it," said Homay to me with happy eyes. "That is what we Lisu say when we can hardly wait for something. I can hardly wait to start for Goo-moo!" That is how we all felt as we waited for the return of the mule, Jessie, and those who had escorted Mr Peterson and Mr Christianson to Paoshan. They arrived a day earlier than we expected for their hearts too were "on it," but they brought with them news that simply levelled us to the earth. Charlie Peterson, who in 1937 had buried his beloved comrade, Earl Carlson, arrived in Paoshan just in time to bury our beloved and indispensable superintendent, Mr J O Fraser.

I say "indispensable" for we still feel that way. After the first shock of the news there was a forlorn feeling, that, speaking of human fellowship, "there is no one now to work for." *How Mr Fraser will enjoy hearing about this*, was always a first reaction to any joy or blessing, and we still have found ourselves thinking that very thought, only to come to ourselves with the desolate realization that he is no longer here.There was no one else on earth who had such a complete knowledge of the details of our problems and so no one who could share so perfectly in our joys and sorrows. And he never disappointed us in that sharing. He was more than superintendent to us: he was our missionary ideal; a continual rebuke, challenge, and stimulus to maintain at any cost the apostolic methods of missionary work. His brilliant gifts, united to unfailing humility and a sympathy motherlike in its tenderness and thoughtfulness made him our refuge at all times of perplexity and need. To win a smile of approval from him

was worth any extra effort. It is one thing to be
praised by a person who has no experience of your
work; it is quite different to win a "well done"
from one who himself is a master in that very line.
We have lost a great stimulus as well as an
indispensable counsellor.

The Lisu of Oak Flat district asked for the privilege of paying the twenty dollars which the digging of his grave cost.

With the passing of our beloved superintendent,
John and I have, perforce, to enter an entirely new
epoch of our lives, for life can never again be quite
the same without him. But life does not stop for
heartache, so on the morning of October 2, a
beautifully clear morning after days of rain, we
started out to follow the road which had been
covered four years ago by that historic journey of
Mark and his two friends–a story we told again
and again while on furlough. Our party consisted
of Ah-be-pa, Luke, Thomas, Homay, Simon, Lucius, A-che (the Cookes' cook who is now cooking
for us), Abel as mule boy, three carriers, and then
just almost at the last moment the Lord set a seal
on our going, by bringing us haphazard into
contact with two of the Goo-moo church Christians
who had come into the canyon on private business.
They were needed as guides and interpreters as we
came to Kachin country and needed to buy food,
etc.

At the end of a good long travel, the first
evening out still found us in sight of our house. We
slept at Luchang, from which, across the canyon,
we can just barely make out the roof of "The House
of Grace," our shanty.

The second day we had to go over the great
pass, some 11,000 feet high. Up, up through valley-
sides, ravine-sides we climbed. Before noon we
had left the edge of habitation and for a long time

travelled through forest, dark overhanging, shut-
you-in forest, not a human soul or house in sight.
Mid-afternoon brought us out to bare rocks smitten
with a wind that made you shiver although snow
time had not yet come, and about four o'clock we
came to the narrow slit between peaks and shouted
with joy. At our back the great canyon of the
Salween and beyond it China's sea of mountain
peaks; before our eyes Burma and another monster
net of mountain-tops. We had still quite a little
walk over the high cold trail, before the earth fell
away from us and we beheld a panorama of
unrivalled beauty–the valleys of the Upper Irrawaddy, the sun setting behind the peaks that
guard those valleys, peaks that seemed in the
sunset to tower higher than those we had left
behind and made even the Lisu gasp with surprise;
then, as our eyes fell from the glory of crimson sky
and jagged silhouette, far beneath us on a little
knoll stood the British border fort of Pien-Ma with
its neat array of sepoy barracks–like a silent handshake from civilization. It was dusk before we
reached them, only to find them deserted–fighting
between the tribes people and the Buddhists of
Burma had caused the fort to be dismantled for
lack of soldiers. We slept that night in the middle
of the road, having travelled from daybreak until
eight in the evening.

Early on the third day we ran into a teacher of
the American Baptist Mission, which has work in
Upper Burma, and we travelled with him until
dusk. He brought us to a village of the A-Chia tribe
where we slept, but first held a service, John speaking by interpretation. This day began our travelling through a canyon of gorgeous beauty, scenic
falls every little while, a river of surging foam
banked by precipitous rocks with trees which were
full of orchids.

The fourth day everyone was so tired that we decided to sleep at Tawgaw although it was only two in the afternoon when we reached there. This is the post office town (mail once a week), a beautiful little place with red-roofed bungalows built foreign style; here there is a district superintendent, a garrison of twenty-six sepoys, a Government doctor, a Kachin school with three teachers (all of these officials, of course, were natives) and a few stores where we were able to buy canned milk and coffee! It used to be quite a town, but a severe earthquake has lessened its population to several hundred.

The schoolmaster made us welcome in his own house, and in the evening we were visited by three superintendents, one of whom had an excellent knowledge of English. They urged us to stay over a day so they could give us a dinner party, but our answer you will readily guess. They spied my guitar and asked for some music, so we had the Lisu sing for them, and they were delighted, calling for piece after piece. The Lisu tribe is despised in these parts, the Kachin being considered *the* tribe, so we were ever so pleased to show off our dear group.

The fifth day is made memorable by monkeys above and leeches beneath. Wooded cliffs towered above us and from these the monkeys kept us a sort of heavenly chorus–I presume warning each other of our approach. High above our heads in the tops of the huge trees which lined our mountain path we heard their "Oo-a-la! Oo-a-la!" like an antiphonal choir, but not a one did we see. Not so the leeches; underfoot, the little black wrigglers were legion. They stood on the dead leaves of the path, standing upright on their tails and waving back and forth in the air, for a foot to attack, hang on to, and suck. The mules' legs were blood-streaked that day and our dear barefoot band suffered equally. The vegetation too was distinctly different. I saw tree ferns for the first time—long, straight, unbranched trunks, unfolding at the top into beautifully graceful arms of fern each about ten feet in length. Other trees were tremendous, over a hundred feet high, and trunks big enough to contain an auto. That night we slept out in a ridge near a Kachin village with the canyon to our right, over whose jagged walls of rock the moon peered and then sailed majestically on high. We thought we would again have a good night, but we were to make the acquaintance of a minute fly which stings like a mosquito; a net is but a tracery of open doors for it. Goo-moo abounds with these tiny pests, much to Homay's misery, for her plump, bare ankles made good eating!

The last day was the hardest of all—my, what a day! We started on the road at seven in the morning, stopped for lunch at noon by a sheet of waterfall, the water running gently over a bare face of rock some fifty feet in height, then we pressed on through hot sun and black leeches to the river brink which we reached in the late afternoon. Early we had sighted the big tree by the Goo-moo chapel, high on the mountain of the opposite bank, but it was a different matter to get there. Here man battles Nature with only the most primitive of weapons. There was no bridge across the river and only a raft made of bamboo poles tied together with bark. It was so flimsy it could only take two passengers at a time and even then sank into the water; and there are two currents in the river to cross. When we arrived, the raft was on the other side of the river. Some Kachin rowed over with it, but they had come for a pal and refused to take even one of us, so we had to sit there and just look at the raft. We were four hours in getting across a stretch of water only about two hundred feet in breadth. Word had been called across to send a message to Goo-moo for raft-rowers and at length three men arrived and began the trips. What delayed us so long was getting Jessie and Jasper across, and a horse and a colt that belonged to our interpreter. We tried making them swim, but when they struck the first current they turned back. By that time half of us were on one bank and half on the other, dark had fallen and the rocks in the river bed made it too dangerous, so we had to wait for the moon to rise. Finally, by dim moonlight the animals arrived: tied to the raft by tail and one man holding their head, they had been made to swim for it.

We had no food with us and had eaten nothing since lunch. Goo-moo was still two thousand feet above our heads and that climb before us which is too steep to ride and where the traveller must go up holding on to the mule's tail. A drink of coffee all around and then we began. The trail was through dense vegetation twice our height—I could see nothing beneath my waist; my hands holding onto Jasper's tail were all that was within vision, except for a silver-laced gleam overhead where the moon was trying to penetrate the tropical canopy over us. I could not see where my feet were treading—we had seen big snakes that day and I thought of the leeches, but I was reminded that Christians walk by faith, and, throwing my cares on Him in all that stiff climb, I stepped on nothing to alarm me. The heat was oppressive, perspiration simply streamed off me and and we thought how merciful that it was only moonshine, not sunshine, overhead!

We came out to a Kachin village (toward the end of the climb we were able to ride a bit), where a black-clad figure sprang out of the shadow and in an ecstasy of delight ran to John, then to me, greeting us. We peered through the dark at him, that attractive smile and those beautiful teeth were familiar--Mark! Our precious Mark; he had not heard of our arrival in time to come to the river side and others of the Christians were lining the roads above our heads. It was a wonderful welcome and two tired but thoroughly happy missionaries that midnight lay down in the little whitewashed chapel with prayers of thanksgiving that another dream had come true and we were actually in Goo-moo!

> Come tell Me all that ye have said and done,
> Your victories and failures, hopes and fears.
> I know how hardly souls are wooed and won;
> My choicest wreaths are always wet with tears.

WATERING HIS GARDEN AT GOO-MOO!

We arrived on Saturday night, and Monday morning our boys scattered over the hills to surrounding villages, to announce our arrival and that we would hold a short-term Bible school beginning the next Sunday. Goo-moo villagers came night and morning to us for teaching and also set about building us a sleeping house and a cooking house. It is interesting to watch a Lisu shanty go up: not a nail was in the building of our curly-headed house--I call it that because I have slept under slate, tin, tiles, shingles, thatch, and canvas, but this was my first experience under a roof of leaves. They thatched it entirely with the long silver green leaf of the banana tree the ends of which tore and curled back, giving it the tousled appearance of a curly-head just out of bed and not yet reached by mamma's careful comb. Tousled heads are in the majority in Lisuland, so the house quite fits the country. Then began the Bible school, and I stop to wonder how to tell you about it. God gave us Isa. 58:11 as our verse for that session and then wonderfully fulfilled it: "The Lord will guide you always." There were weeds in His Goo-moo garden: strife, self-love, uncleanness, and day by day up to and including the very last day, sins were confessed and matters put right. Husbands and wives were reconciled. Our own dear Mark was greatly blessed. In fact, he said to us that our coming this time had been salvation to the little church here.

The last evening we had testimonies and Mark surprised us by staging a little play of his own inventing. He came on the platform and said, "I am an unbeliever and I have two friends whom I love very much. Come my friend," and beckoned to Sa-mu-ye-pa. On Sa-mu-ye-pa's chest was a placard: UNCLEANNESS.

"Do people listen to their beloved chums?" asked Mark.

"Some," replied his audience.

"Well, what do you say to me, my friend?" Mark asked, turning to Sa-mu-ye-pa.

"I say, 'Do unclean things; think unclean things!'"

Mark: "And I have to listen to my friend. But I have a second friend–come!" And A-che slipped on to the platform with a placard: HATRED.

Mark: "And what do you tell me to do, my dear friend?"

A-che: "Love yourself–don't pay any thought to your neighbour. This is hating him." Then Thomas comes quietly up with a chest placard: JESUS.

Mark: "And who are you? What do you offer me?"

Thomas: "I offer you eternal life and a heavenly inheritance, but to receive these you must break with your two former beloved companions."

Mark: "Teacher Kuhn, what shall I do? I've lived all my life with these two friends."

John (from the audience): "Take the advice of Him who offers you eternal life."

Mark: "All right—off with you!" (and Sa-mu-ye-pa with A-che slink from the platform). "But, Jesus, what will I do for a friend now? Must I live all alone?" (Simon comes on to the platform with a placard: THE HOLY SPIRIT.)

Thomas: "No, dear friend; here is a companion who will never leave you, but will abide with you always and be your counsellor."

Mark: (throwing his arms around Simon): "Thank you, Jesus, I accept Him—now, friends, this is my testimony and I want to ask you this question. Who are your friends? And what is your choice?"

The effect of this strange testimony was solemnizing. We got a new impression of our dear, precious Mark this time; the gentleness of his sweet smile is misleading. He is a very strong and forceful character. Just twenty-six years old, this leads him into difficulties with the church as he is apt to be a bit tyrannical and self-righteous in his governing of them. He is upright himself and he expects others to be just as consecrated and does not realize that babes in Christ require more patient handling. His self-righteousness he confessed before them all that week; his "strong hand" I do not think he realizes yet. He needs the epistolatory teaching and is going to make every effort to get to the Rainy Season Bible School.

Luke's and Thomas's messages were wonderful. We see more and more that the RSBS is already producing wonderful fruit. Goo-moo was soaked this time with the teaching on the second birth and we hear from all over the field of our boy students (the Ma-pa-ra) of last summer preaching this foundational truth.

After the school at Goo-moo we went to Sa-mu-ye-pa's village for the harvest festival. We got a wonderful reception—an aisle of flowers as well as an arch had been made for us. And a little house prepared as our dwelling was so filled with mountain blooms that their fragrance attracted the animals at night who tried to get in to eat them, and caused John some practice boot-throwing, for the door was far from stable.

Parting was, as usual, mournful. The Goo-moo Christians wept so that as we dropped down the mountainside from them, it sounded like the wailing for the dead, and I was relieved when they finally changed it to calling to us like monkeys, after we were too far beneath them to communicate otherwise.

Mark came to RSBS twice, in different years, but each time could not stand the discipline of it. Strange as it seems, he was much slower to grasp doctrines than his fellows, which hurt his pride, for he was by now accustomed to leadership. He was ashamed when he did not make excellent grades, and got so homesick that each time he stayed only a month or so, and then went home, taking his fellow Goo-moo students with him. The result is that none of the Goo-moo students were well-grounded in the truths of the New Testament.

During the war, the Japanese occupied Upper Burma. Goo-moo again appealed to us for teachers—with the Japanese at Tawgaw and spies everywhere, a little band of them worked their way through to us, and pleaded for Lisu evangelists! One of our young student teachers responded, and at the peril of his life went back with them. We just received one letter from him, in which he said that they were reaching out after another tribe which lives in their neighbourhood, and Mark was learning that tribal language in order to lead them to Christ! But he also told how Mark and Sammy-pa were quarrelling, and the church inclined to split over them. Had Satan been gaining an advantage? The Master of the Abyss will never forgive the fact that they were delivered from his clutches, and he has more than one way of enslaving men. Pride of heart is a Wind from the Snow Height which ignorant Christians may not recognize as heading them toward the Abyss; Satan has used that Wind to render useless more than one promising young disciple. The Sharp Wind from the Bitter Height is still blowing.

Chapter 7

THE SOUL-SEEDLING PATCH

N OW, in thought, we must go back to the canyon of the Upper Salween, to the station of Oak Flat. So much has been said of the Rainy Season Bible School, that it might be well to tell of those sessions now.

Brother Two's criticism that the Lisu church was becoming legalistic, was not without foundation. But side by side with that fact one should put this–that the church did not then have the New Testament, and its teachings on law and grace were not understood. John felt deeply that the time had come to do something definite about this general ignorance, and so the vision of our furlough had been a regular, prolonged season of Bible teaching, with the New Testament in manuscript before the students, if necessary. The Books of Galatians and First Corinthians and some others had been completed by that time. We were able to bring back with us a Lisu typewriter (a portable arranged to type Lisu script), so our very first summer in Lisuland, we began. Mr Fraser wrote us that he was delighted; he felt that nothing was so needed as a prolonged, continued time of Bible study.

And now I think that quotations from the circulars will be more vivid, for they tell of events just as they happened.

THE SEEDLING PATCH

Picture a great rocky mountain on a lone range. Up
through its wild grass and pine-tree studded sides
threads a yellow-brown trail. Three-quarters of the
way up to its crest the trail slims on to a small
brow where some tiny huts are planted, with a
long weather-beaten thatched bamboo shanty at
one corner perched above a deep drop. Around the
great wrinkles of the mountain, about three miles
up the ravine's abyssal sides is another collection
of huts. Of what importance to the world could
such far-away isolated poverty be? Why talk about
it! Write every month about it? The world may not
care–and indeed it does not. However, Heaven is
watching that wild mountain brow with joy and
brooding love, and it is Heaven's interest that
makes us talk of this place to you. Those little
shanties are Oak Flat Village, of course, and
Heaven is interested because there is a Soul-
seedling Patch here–the Rainy Season Bible School.

I told you before how at the end of May each
year, the Soul-seedlings gathered from all parts of
the canyon. Such insignificant, barefoot, coarse-
clad laddies, climbing these steep wrinkles on
Mother Nature's brow, perspiring yet laughing,
tired yet hopeful, crawling in here from north,
south, east and west like so many minute flies! A
passer-by would never dream that there had been
a stiff fight in the heavenlies, before some of those
little "flies" were set free to come. Yet it was so.
Prayer was the only thing that opened some of the
their barred pathways. And as they came trudging
over the muddy trails, their bantering talk lets
loose, perhaps, the flash of an angry eye here, or a
carnal word drops there, or the lagging steps of
that one betrays a tendency to laziness, and we

realize each one of them is a son of Adam the First.
Did that discourage the angels, I wonder? No, I
think the angels are more patient than we. I think
the angels were looking with eyes of gentle happiness at the book-bag slung over every shoulder.
Inside that little cloth bag was a Book which has
turned the world upside down–a Book which tells
of a last Adam, who has redeemed all that the first
Adam wrecked, and whose we may become by a
New Birth. They are not on the Seedling Patch long
before they are questioned whether they have
experienced that New Birth; because there is no
hope of growth where there is no life. But they all
have, they say–only they do not know how to appropriate or use that inheritance, so here they are

Before that first three-months' RSBS we held a
week's Bible study as a sort of "try-out." Those
eleven who attended did not all turn out success-
fully, but they are very typical of the ordinary
RSBS student body. Friends enjoyed that early
circular about them, so we reprint it here.

OUR VERY FIRST SEEDLINGS
"Belle, what are you grinning at, there in the
corner with your paper and pencil?" asked John,
looking up from a moment's lull in his dictation
class.

"I'm jotting down some impressions of your
pupils, for our prayer partners," was the explanation.

Eleven black heads were studiously bent over
books around the long stretch of table at the head
of which sat John. The table was composed of one
round one, plus one square one, plus two square
cupboards all placed end to end, and the students
were the Ma-pa-ra (which being interpreted means

the Small Teachers, or, as we have called them, the
evangelists). Our idea has been to call them all in
once every seven weeks for Bible study, so that
they have one week of study followed by six weeks
of preaching in the villages–putting into practice,
we hope, what they learned during study week.
Some of the eleven were Ma-pa-ra for whose board
the church pays; others were laymen who pay their
own expenses. As this little band will be the core of
our Rainy Season Bible Classes, I thought you
might like to meet them individually. The "grin"
was at various boyish characteristics, which I fear
cannot convey to paper.

JUNIA
A stripling, looks seventeen but is really twenty.
Lives at Spirea Flat and has been a believer for
eight years. Slight, eager, intense, he is the one
who started out after the February Bible school "to
do God's work," taking nothing, not even a hat. He
got bad headaches from the sun, and returned with
another Lisu's old cast-off hat, a wreck of felt
which was too large and sank down over his
eyebrows, giving him an eclipsed appearance.
Dear Junia–went off radiant and excited and returned under an eclipse, but only as to his
head–his heart was still happy. This is very typical
of him. When we were leaving for furlough Junia
had an attack of measles, but refused to let that
keep him from our farewell service. Hot with fever
and speckled like a leopard he walked the five
miles to and five miles from Oak Flat; I got quite a
shock when I saw that measly fact, rapt with
attention, in the middle of our audience!

SILAS
Twenty-three years old, from near Horse Grass
Level. Had believed for three years. At first we

thought he was stupid. The dictation lesson finds Silas laboriously working his pencil. He writes a few words then sits back scratching his head to look at them as if he wondered how he did it; bends to the task once more, carves out two more scraggly words and again stops, tugging at his collar to loosen its grip. Writes two more and then stands up and looks around to see how the others are conquering. When he happens to answer a question correctly he is the most astonished member in the class, which is saying something. But we later discovered that he can surprise everyone by remembering accurately some minor point that nobody else got; alas, that is characteristic. He has a talent for doing the wrong thing. What he should remember, he doesn't; but the complicated point that we expect will make no permanent impression on any one is faithfully registered on Silas. In other words, it is not that he can't study, but because he is incurably lackadaisical.

For practice preaching the class was told to prepare a message on the resurrection as Easter was approaching. All did so but Silas, who when his turn came gave a thoughtful résumé on the death of Christ. John expostulated, "But when I asked you to preach on the resurrection, why didn't you, Silas?"

Silas did not know why he didn't—and neither did anyone else.

In another dictation class John said, "Where have you got to, Silas?" (They were copying Philippians, which John taught that week.)

Without looking up from his book the lad replied, "The tenth chapter." There was a roar of laughter.

"But Philippians only has four chapters!" suggests someone. Oh, well! maybe it was the tenth

verse Silas was copying; anyway, he was copying
something. Dear boy, it is a shame to laugh at him.
He has a sweet disposition, never gets angry and
takes all the embarrassment with a smile.

LUCIUS

Twenty years old, comes from Village-of-the-Olives, the only child of Christian parents and supported by them in these study groups–not a Ma-
pa-ra yet. He is quick as a flash, sits next to the
bottom of the class, but leads it. John says, "He
stretches his long neck around the corner of the
table–and misses nothing." Quick of mind, his
thoughts outrace his tongue so that his words often
come forth on the stampede. Has the shyness and
high-strung mettle of a thoroughbred colt.

LUDA-PETER

Twenty-five years old, lives at Luda, has believed
for nine years. Some would say he is the handsome
one of the group, has suave manners with a graceful poise. A good speaker and an excellent song
leader; has a splendid knowledge of the portions of
the Bible already translated. Is a pleasure to teach,
he is so bright, but one has indefinable feeling that
these points are but an attractive shell and that the
centre is hollow. This lad needs prayer or something. He has not been dismissed from the ministry
because he gave a testimony of blessing after the
February Bible School, after which he was sent to
the backslidden village of Water Buffalo Mountain
and won three families back to the Lord. It may be
there is a spiritual revival in store for him.

NATHANAEL

Twenty-two years old and a Christian for two and
half years only. Lives at Horse Grass Level. Is
stocky, pleasant-looking, with a broad forehead

and an open countenance that begets trust. Study does not come easily to him; he ranks next to Silas, whose right to the bottom of the class, however, is beyond dispute! Nat has good solid qualities and surprised us by his sermon which was thoughtful and well delivered.

JOB

Thirty-two years old, comes from Stockade Hill district, has believed for eighteen years; is the man who first brought the gospel to these parts. Small, slight, pockmarked, undignified; with his hat often stuck on a side corner of his head looks more like a horse jockey than an evangelist. Perhaps the most insignificant-looking member of the class, but as far as we know, the greatest soul-winner Lisuland has yet produced. Job has so few natural gifts, and yet has been so used of God, that he is a monument of what God can do with any man who brings Him nothing much more than a heart of purposeful devotion. Now I am going to tell you something...just lest you think that we are all saints here and sit with halos around our heads! Job is not a "glowing" listener. Nay, he is the very opposite; I do not suppose there is one in the group who nettles his teachers (we all testify to this) with inattention as Job does. He is not really inattentive, as you will learn to your surprise some day when you hear him giving that message of yours to which you thought he had not listened! But he is just incurably restless. You spread your very best prepared eloquence before him and—he picks his teeth, or fiddles with his ear; he squirms and wriggles and finally turns around and stares at each of his neighbours. If perchance your subject should really require his thought, then he is less inspiring than ever; back goes his head, his jaw drops wide open, his eyes roll up to the ceiling—the most vacant of faces, you would never guess that this is Job thinking hard. But it is. You have to know Job. When you know him you love him—and love makes allowances.

CHO-A-TSEH

Twenty-two years old, from Goo-moo in Burma; acted as Job's escort home, but we pressed him to stay for this week of Bible study. He has a very affectionate, almost girlish manner. Simply adored John, laughed hilariously at all his jokes, and was never happier than when holding his hand and exclaiming, "Oh, Ma-Pa!" The week's study made a bigger change in him than in anyone; all of a sudden the "gush" seemed to leave, and he became thoughtful and quiet—gave the most satisfactory testimony (to my thinking) of any, in the last night's testimony meeting.

ARISTARCHUS

Twenty-two years old (cousin to Gaius) from San-dalwood Flat. Has believed for five years. Has a very shy, super-sensitive nature; lips that twitch and work like a rabbit's. Goes around with an awkward and self-conscious manner, even sometimes has a hang-dog look and a furtive glance as if always expecting life to hit him a blow. But when he stands up to preach, all that falls from him like a cloak; he speaks fearlessly, directly and with a quiet insistence that his audience understand his point. Has probably the deepest prayer-life of any in the group, but is so unobtrusive and quiet with it that few know. This boy left a position where he got his food and sixty dollars a year for the ministry where he gets his food and sixteen dollars a year! This is the wage for the Ma-pa-ra; Job, Luke and Andrew get more for they are "teachers," i.e. "Ma-Pa." The missionary is Ma-pa-da-ma or Big

Teacher,but to his face usually called merely Ma-
Pa.

RUFUS
Tall, thin, pockmarked. Twenty-three years old
and a believer for four years. Reminds me of a
cowboy. No shyness about him; willing to try
anything once, and frequently quite pleased with
his "try." Alert in mind but not much sign yet of a
spiritual mind. Capable, willing–"One thing thou
lackest."

JONAH (Sah-gwey-chee)
Twenty-two years old, from Village of the Olives; a
believer for six years. In temperament he is the
Simon Peter of the class. Warm-hearted and impetuous, he is the most appreciative and respon-
sive, as far as words go, of any in the group.
Resourceful and energetic, he is a natural leader,
but has the Peter-weakness of acting first and
thinking afterwards! Deep-voiced, a rapid speaker
with a bright mind. Jonah (and Titus) keep Lucius
on the qui vive for first place.

TITUS
Twenty-two years old, younger brother of Andrew,
comes from Stockade Hill, is a layman supporting
himself. Has believed for sixteen years, but declares he was only "born again" this spring of 1938.
He is a marked contrast to Jonah; as coldly
calculating as the other is affectionate and impulsive. Titus is usually alone, Jonah is often found
hugging a pal. Jonah receives the doctrine with
bursts of appreciation; Titus says little, but a gleam
in his eyes and a certain quick intaking of breath
reveal his interest. They sit together, not because
they are attracted to each other, but because they
want to get as close to the teacher as they can.

Titus has a shrewd, sharp business sense
and–dimples. He knows "where he is at" (which is
not true of Jonah) and his artistic impulse covers
all his books with drawings. He has another
gift–the loveliest tenor voice I have heard in
Lisuland. John said, "When Titus sings it touches
the heart, somehow brings the tears, doesn't it?"

Now I have told you about our boys, and I wonder if you have been able to see them–really. I
wonder how much you have noticed. That they are
all very different, yes? That they are very young?
But then youth has enthusiasm and heroic loyalty
to offer to its King, very often; Robert M.
McCheyne did most of his work before he was
thirty, did he not?

These extracts from circulars throughout the
years are not given in chronological order, but we
have been consistent in always giving the same
name to each character. When we got more than
one "John," for instance, we numbered them; we
actually had First John, Second John and Third
John at one school! Just plain John, of course, is my
husband!

And now for our first RSBS when Homay and
Me-do-me-pa were still with us, and the church
just recovering from the bewilderment of Brother
Two's days. Those days had done some good–the
church's self-complacency was shaken, and they
were willing to listen to the answer to the question,
"What is wrong with us?"

May 28, 1938, was a great day. On that day the
students for the Rainy Season Bible Classes arrived
in groups at intervals all day long. Those from the
south came first, among them was Aristarchus
returning from a trip in Horse Grass Level district

where he reported thirty converts from
heathenism. The party from Luda district arrived
next; among them was a new believer–so new that
he did not even know how to read, but had carried
his own food supply for the three months' study
and came prepared to learn. He bought books immediately on arrival, and the next day I found him
drifting about our house, his books hugged to his
bosom, his mouth wide open, and his eyes the
same, as he investigated how these white people
live. We nicknamed him "Brand-New."

"YOU MUST BE BORN AGAIN"

This has been our central theme. Opening day was
given to prayer and fasting, with some good results. Mrs Yang made a confession with tears, and
the consecration service at night saw some young
lives given over to their Master's use.

But before and after this, Charles Peterson and
John spent time in interviewing privately every
student with definite questions on their own regeneration. With the exception of Brand-New, there
was not one who did not give a satisfactory
answer, and it was surprising to me to see how
many of them date their "New Birth" to our April
study week when Job gave a message on John 3
that stirred everyone. We decided the Lisu church
leaders (for, as you remember, this is mainly an
evangelists' Bible school) need to be saturated with
this foundational doctrine, so every day in practice
preaching class each student, as his turn came, had
to give a message on the New Birth. I wish you
could have heard Job, Luke, Aristarchus and
Nathanael.

As if this were not enough, Mr Peterson gave a
message on the same subject every night for a
week, so it has been quite uppermost in Lisu

minds. Each weekend the student body scatters
(girls included), going into the villages on this side
of the river. Some of our boys must walk over
twenty-five English miles, take three services, walk
back the same distance, and do it all between
Saturday morning and Monday morning when
classes start. Not one of them has failed us so far.
Our hearts have been touched by their weary but
happy faces as they run in to shake hands early
Monday morning, having just completed such a
journey. Every week but one they have had to do it
in the rain, and Lisu don't usually have raincoats
or umbrellas. No wonder the missionary learns to
love his Lisu until he can say with Paul, "It is life
to me now, if you stand firm in the Lord." The first
weekend our students reached about five hundred
Lisu; the next over seven hundred; and this last
weekend a still greater number. Between the early
classes on Monday we have Report Hour when
each gets up and tells his experiences. Don't you
wish you could listen in?

But to go back to our first week: June 1-4 were
days of heart preparation messages. Then on
Saturday Andrew walked in. It was a crowning joy
and there is evidence that prayers for him had not
been in vain. He arrived a sick boy, with a heavy
cold which developed a strange puffy rash all over
his body, but he said quietly, "I have never been
sick since I've been up there, and now when I come
to study God's Word I get ill! I believe it is an
attack of the devil," and he steadfastly refused to
be downed by it; he not only continued to come to
classes but at the end of the week he led everybody
in the examination on 1 Corinthians.

LISTENING IN
How we have wished we could share with you
some of the glimpses into these Lisu hearts. The

only way I could think of was to jot down a few sentences from their prayers, now and again as I heard them.

"Lord, I'm not worthy to be your slave and you have made me your friend. I am worthy of death, and you have given me eternal life."

"Your name is written on my heart and my name is written on your hands, so we cannot be separated."

"Lord, you are my refuge; if I had not you I would have no hiding place."

"I used to pray to you, Lord, just for what I wanted; I never thought or cared if you wanted anything. But oh, that was wrong, please forgive me. Now I desire what you want."

"Lord, give strength to our teachers; help them so that when they teach, we may see the face of Jesus."

"Let your name be always in our hearts. Let it be as a perfume there."

For mankind all, Thy love is shown,
Yet seems't to be for me alone;
I claim Thee for my very own,
My Jesus.

Doesn't this verse–spoken probably by a foreign voice–find its echo in these Lisu heart cries?

We have some little notes slipped to us now and again. Here is an extract from a boy who had just had a talking to, on putting the will of God before his own will; "If ever you have any exhortation for me, please give it quickly. I won't be offended. If there were nothing in me to correct, I would not be in here."

This from one who regularly failed in every examination, but who showed by his preaching that he was assimilating the new truth: "I would like to

say a few words to you by the Blood of the Lord
Jesus and in His Name. I have no ability to study
the doctrines of God and the Lord Jesus. Although
I study in the school, I cannot think up the
answers, Big Brother Kuhn. But although I can't
memorize I have received the truth that Jesus
Christ died for me on the Cross. Now all that I
have, my spirit and body, are His, I have given up
all to Him. I can never forget His Cross. You have
taught me much, Big Brother, and it has brought
joy in Christ. Thank you so much. Although I
cannot memorize His doctrines, because His Blood
was poured out to purchase me, I must always be
happy."

In the days of 1938, Homay was still with us, of
course, so her name appears in the circulars.

BEHIND THE SCENES
If you were able to pass through the House of
Grace between hours, you would behold in the
large living-dining room, in one corner near the
window, a little Lisu lady bending her turbaned
head with an anxious expression over a large book
of loose manuscript leaves and with pretty plump
little olive hands, typing away earnestly at a typewriter which was bought in Lancaster,Pa.! This is
Homay, and without her and her typewriter this
Bible school could not possibly have been held. She
types out twelve copies of each Book we teach, so
that as we teach these new and strange Epistles the
students are able to read with us–if they could not
do that, they would never understand, for the
Pauline letters contain many expressions which the
Lisu language does not possess and which have to
be coined and carefully taught. Lately I have had
to teach "fellowship"and"example." When we first
said *"ja-la-ko"* no one (but Homay, Luke and Job

who had previously learned it)knew what we were saying; we had to explain not only that *ja-la-ko* meant fellowship, but what "fellowship" really is.

This reminds me of Trench's book, *The Study of Words.* He calls attention to the fact that no people can have a word before they have the experience which the word illuminates or describes. He says, "There is no such witness to the degradation of the savage as the brutal poverty of his language–rich in words which proclaim their shame, poor in these which attest the workings of any nobler life among them." He had doubtless never heard of the Lisu, yet this is true of our people too. Words to express sin in various forms are plentiful–they tell you with gusto how to skin a human being alive, but if you asked them what holiness was, they would not know, they had no word for it. Their language had no word of course for *redemption*, or *justification*, or *grace*, but it also had no word for *religion*, nor for *exaltation*, nor for *conscience* nor many other things. Just yesterday I had the word for *humility* on the board and Lucius asked what it meant. He said he had never heard of it before. And when we gave a message on conscience even Homay came to us and said she had not understood what that word meant in the scriptures, and did not know that she herself possessed a conscience. Yet the Lisu language had a word for God i.e. *Wu-sa*. They knew *Wu-sa* but they do not worship Him, and there seems to me to be evidence that the Lisu race once had a higher knowledge of life.

I want to slip in another picture from the weekend evangelism as it is so typical of many things Lisu.

"THE FATHER IS ALWAYS WATCHING"
It was communion week-end, and A-che and

Lucius were commissioned to take that service at
Squirrel's Grave Village. As the Salween is now, of
course, swollen, they had to cross by rope bridge.
There was quite a party to cross, for other Ma-pa-
ra were going to take services elsewhere on the
west bank, and also Juliet with two girl friends
from Runaway Horse Ascent had to be helped over
too. Those three girls studied with us the whole
month of July, paying their own way. Altogether
there was such delay at the rope bridge that the
two boys around which this tale hangs, could not
make their destination that day, but decided to
sleep at a Chinese hamlet where there is a Christian Lisu family. But by the time they arrived
there, dark had fallen and as robbers have
abounded this year, the Lisu family had closed and
barred their door and were all inside. Approaching
the house they were stopped by a clear call, "Stand
or we shoot!" As the Lisu poisoned arrow has to
prick the skin in any point to bring death they
"stood" very quickly and obediently.

"Don't be afraid of us!" they called back. "We
are only two Ma-pa-ra on our way to Squirrel's
Grave Village to take the communion service. We
want to sleep with you tonight."

"Humph!" comes the retort from mine host.
"Ma-pa-ra eh? Maybe you are and maybe you
aren't. How do I know?"

"Well," calls out Lucius, who knew them personally, "Pu-ra-pa, you ought to know me. I am
Born-on-the-Road from Village-of-the-Olives."
(Some of you thought I made up Lucius' heathen
name myself; I did not. His uncle named him that
in fun over the event, and the name stuck. More
people know him by that name than any other.)

"Oh, yeah?" came sarcastic drawl, this time
from the roof of Pu-ra-pa's house, where mine host

had climbed up better to protect his family. He was armed with a huge bow and poisoned arrows, a big knife and a long spear. "It is very likely that young Born-on-the-Road is in this place at this time of night. Quite handy to borrow a good fellow's name, it is." (Lucius had not visited this family for years.)

"Let's run for it," whispered A-che, "and sleep in the bush to-night."

"No," answered Lucius. "If we run he will think for sure we are robbers and shoot, and just one prick...you know!" Then patiently our laddie tried again.

"I am Born-on-the-Road all the same, and my pal is A-che from Luda and we are on our way to preach."

"Hm. If you are Ma-pa-ra then you can sing. Tune up a hymn and perhaps we will believe you." So out in the dark, hungry and weary, our two laddies sang *The Holy Spirit is with me*. But from inside the house comes a girl's voice. "Dad, there are a lot of backsliders nowadays that can sing hymns too; you had better be careful."

But just then the mother of the house had an inspiration. There was a peek-hole near their door, so she stuck a pine torch through it, causing the light to fall on the two boys' faces. "I know Born-on-the-Road," she began, then changed quickly: "Why it is he, sure enough! Come down, Dad. It's all right! My, my, my..." and then the doors were thrown open and welcome and cordiality flooded the tired pair. What laughs they had telling us of it! But more than one Lisu thief has died this summer from the poisoned arrow of a stout hearted crop-defender. That in none of the weekend preaching excursions was any student harmed is a matter of thanksgiving to God.

I hope you have not forgotten that this is still a story of little Nests above a dark abyss, but with a Rock-shelter who "follows" them.

ODDS AND ENDS

Our youngest student was informed just the evening before, that through the unexpected sickness of the one previously scheduled to go, he alone would have to be responsible for the weekend services of Knoll Village. He had never had such a responsibility to shoulder by himself before, and the next morning before breakfast he dashed into the bedroom of our bachelor missionary (blessed haven to the anxious student heart) and planted before that astonished gentleman his Lisu Gospel, a paper and pencil. "Write me a sermon outline on 'Seek first the kingdom of God'!" was his graphic order, whereupon he disappeared to go eat his breakfast, happily confident of the results, just like any American boy who slips a nickel across the drugstore counter and orders a cone to be ready in five minutes—and neither was our Lisu laddie disappointed. When he dashed in to get it and go, there was an outline ready for him!

From another circular:

Our "Baby" sits next. Lucius is taller than I am, and a splendid athlete, but in years he is our baby. He is responsible for the ringing of the gongs, and we persuaded him at night to take charge of John's gold watch. He was very reluctant to put his strong, inexperienced fingers on that delicate, ticking gold disk. Then sure enough—the worst happened. We heard his shuffling step in the next room one morning when I was combing my hair and a concerned young voice came through the bamboo mat wall—"Ma-ma, the watch has died! It doesn't go now."

Quickly remembering that we had neglected to wind it the night before, I told him not to worry, but to put it on the desk. Later a few twists and the familiar tick-tick came back. I immediately sought out our worried Baby. "Lucius, the watch has come back to life!!" My, what a smile. If only that watch will continue to live, Lucius' burdens will be light.

Our strongest (one who has carried my two-hundred-pound husband on his back through the rain down a slippery mountainside) stood baffled before the problem of how to remove a paper-clip. He had been asked to help me to rearrange some exhibition writing samples which were clipped to a string, and I was quite unconscious that paper-clips were a new thing in this young life. I turned to find him earnestly doing his very hefty best to unwind the wire spirals, which was the only way he could see to get rid of the thing. He had it well on the way to wreckage before I saw him and cried out, "Oh, that isn't the way! See!" and in a second I had whipped off the neighbouring clip before his astounded gaze. "*A-geh!*" he exclaimed in disgust at the ease with which things can be done if only you know how!

Our cleverest (as far as examinations are concerned) had desired to find him a private nook where he could practise the conducting of our newest musical attempt, which you shall hear about in a moment. He chose the corner between his cabin and the pig-sty, quite unconscious that he was in view from Ma-Ma's window. I happened to look out and there, singing and waving his hand, he stood, leading the pigs with unction and fervour in Handel's *Hallelujah Chorus*!

This sounds impossible (perhaps the pigs still think it is), but Mr and Mrs Cooke while at Bana

translated this wonderful piece of inspiration into
Lisu, taught it to Luke, Homay and A-che, and sent
it back with them. Luke is now teaching it to us of
the Bible school and though I have heard it more
than once in America, it has never so thrilled me
as when our Lisu sing it. They love it and sing it
with all the passion of their hearts. "The kingdoms
of this world are become the kingdoms of our Lord
and of his Christ'—oh, how that rolls out! how the
soprano sinks, then lifts! how the   bass climbs
up to meet it and the tenor like a bird swoops
under and then soars over. It is inexpressibly
grand—praise God.

Jonah had been teaching in Goo-moo, Burma,
earlier in the year, and came home all enthused
with the reverence and order of the service of
Mark's leadership. Lucius has just been elected
Village Service Leader; the two boys are second
cousins, so Jonah was not long in inspiring the
other to join him in an effort to maintain the same
order in the chapel at Village of the Olives. John
spoke at the big noon service, and shortly after he
began I noticed Jonah slip to the back of the chapel
and take his stand near the door with a long stick
in his hand. When any youngster in the audience
began to get audibly restless he received a stern
poke in the middle of the back by the aforemen-
tioned rod. It was a silent but vigorous reminder
that if he did not listen he might later have to deal
with the broad-chested young man at the other end
of the stick. And he listened.

Up at the front Lucius was seated. A husky
young farmer near him grew tired at the unusual
inactivity of listening and decided to sprawl his
limbs over the empty bench in front of him. As the
first brown leg was casually journeying through
the air, it received a sharp tap from Lucius and
quickly withdrew like a frightened snail into its

proper place and was not seen to wander again.
What we had always considered impossible–order
in a Lisu service–had been accomplished by these
two determined youngsters.

Memories of August seem to be marked by
sunset scenes; the first is trivial but illuminating.
The village of Oak Flat was not directly on the
banks of the Salween River, but rather perched on
the mountain wall of a tributary which runs into
the Salween. To reach the real bank of the Salween,
however, was but the matter of five minutes' walk
to the west over a path which curves, zigzags and
then drops down to a slender wooded ridge which
we long ago named Sunset, for there we would go
at the cool of the day to keep tryst.

One evening in early August we went down to
Sunset Ridge for a school-family picnic supper. We
missionaries took rugs and cushions to sit on, but
these children of the hills did not seem to notice
their lack of such possessions for they merrily and
quickly pulled each a heap of soft leaves from
nearby bushes and sat themselves down on the top
of their thrones. In the centre were black sooty
iron pots containing boiled corn and chunks of
boiled pork, and the extras–the dainties and
decorations–for our feast were well supplied in the
sweets of loving smiles and cheery banter, and by
the matchless panorama of the sun as he entered
the mountains of the western bank, spreading out
his canopies of gold, then pink and finally twilight
silver. As the latter fell softly around us, Titus and
some pals, the first to finish eating, gathered at our
right and sang to us, *Hallelujah, what a Saviour!*
Hallelujah, what a Friend! One by one the others

joined in and the falling dusk was filled with the
melodies of our favourite hymns, for at the end of
each they turned to us to make the next choice.

The next memory is quite different. It was the
evening of August 18. I had been feeling slightly
discouraged, wondering if we teachers were not
too ordinary in our own spiritual lives, wondering
if the boys' hearts were being penetrated with the
Word the way we wanted them to be, and so on. At
sunset time I slipped out for the usual tryst, but
this time decided to go up the mountain instead of
descending to Sunset Ridge. The evening wind was
blowing cool and sweetly in my face and I turned
to the upward path which cuts across a ploughed
field first, and suddenly turning a corner I came
upon Junia and Lucius who were descending,
apparently from the same errand on which I was
bound. They passed me in smiling but self-
conscious silence, and I was reminded that those
two were scheduled to take between them the
weekend services at Village-of-Knoll the coming
Saturday. We had continually urged our boys to
"keep tryst" and to pray about such things, but
who did, and where they did, I had no notion.
These two, being such youngsters, had evidently
felt their weakness and I had stumbled upon their
effort to fortify themselves.

Pleased and gratified, I continued to climb, when
I heard a voice on the trail above; wishing for
solitude I decided to avoid him so turned and
broke through the wild bush to a place higher up.
The mountains were a darkening grey flecked with
white clouds, the passion of sunset colour had long
passed and the cold, steady beauty of night seemed
to steel one's heart to fresh strength. The One I had

come to meet was not absent, but I might not tarry, so after a while I arose and returned to the trail; I feared the bush at that hour, and perhaps the student had left. But no, before I came in sight I could hear his voice clear and strong, "O Father God, help me to learn this Book..." and then I knew he was praying. I tried not to listen and glided more swiftly and carefully onward, but a curve of the path and I saw him, kneeling before the open scriptures, his face right down on the grass even with his knees and his voice cutting the still air with all the freedom of one who believes himself to be entirely alone in the woods. He did not see me at all, so occupied was he, but my first glance drew a second, for I could hardly believe my eyes were telling the truth, and as I stopped to look I heard him say distinctly, "O Father God, I hand over my whole body, soul, and spirit to you—do with me as you will," then with thrilled heart I turned and fled down the path out of sight and sound. What I could hardly believe was this, that praying lad was not our Aristarchus, nor any of the spiritual leaders of the student body, but that boy alone on the mountain consecrating himself to his Maker, was our dear little Brand-New.

The third scene is that of our consecration service at Sunset Ridge the evening of August 26. Our last week we were to have guests, as you shall hear, so the preceding week we viewed as the last we would spend together as a "family," and the last night of that week we betook ourselves to the open for a bonfire service.

Though that was in the rainy season, never had there been a kindlier one; especially was August

wonderful—heavy rain at night and in the early
morning, but clear and sunny hours through the
day. We had prayed beforehand and asked our
dear Giver of all good gifts if He would not add a
starlit night on August 26 to His list of generosi-
ties, and He was pleased to do just that! As we set
out for the spot at sunset, I thought I had never
seen the heavens above so beautiful. The mountains were a jagged line of dark blue and scattered
over the pale upper hemisphere were clouds
which had caught and held the last fire of the now
invisible sun. Our world was a dusky mass of jade
topped with pearl and rose, which shifted and
paled as if it were breathing and then all quietly
melted away to give place to a slight moon and
faraway stars. Night comes swiftly in those parts.

Soon a different scene held our eyes, a tent-
shaped tower of flaming boughs which cast light
and shadow on a wide circle of dear faces, all
tender with the thought that this was our last
family night together, and all grave with expec-
tancy as my husband John arose and came forward
to give his message on "Sacrifice." At its close he
called for all those who wished to consecrate their
lives completely to God from henceforth to come
forward and kneel with him, and one by one they
came. As far as we could see—for some were in the
shadow and one might not pry on such an
occasion—every one of our beloved students sooner
or later joined the inner circle. Hearts were then
poured out to God in prayer, and afterward on
happy risen feet they gave glad testimony. From a
letter written at that time:

And now the evening is far spent—my watch

has stopped but the pale moon has journeyed far across the sky. The word comes to stand and form a friendship circle; fresh boughs are heaped on the low fire and the flame soars and sings with joy as it reaches upward, casting its golden light on a great circle of fifty faces, glad smiling faces, while our Youngest tosses his head with rapture and calls out "*Ka-chi* (Joy!)" at the beauty of the scene. A hymn or two, the benediction, and we break up, but memory has still a last gift for us. Pine torches are lit to find us our path back to Oak Flat, for the moon is a mere curved wisp in the sky; as we climb the trail and reach its highest level we stand a moment, turn and look back and there behind us, flickering through the pine boughs like living golden jewels is the string of pine torches flaring out bravely into the dark and suddenly lighting up beloved faces which lift themselves laughingly toward us, and then as we turn once more to the path the music of dear voices pursues us lovingly through the night to our very door.

At the end of each Rainy Season Bible School, we held closing day exercises. The students elected their own chairman, song-leader, and valedictory speakers. They marched in to music, and at the close of the service, each received a certificate with his rank on it (honours or just pass, etc.). Here is an account of Closing Day, 1939-that summer the Tabernacle had been taught.

ONE CLOSING DAY
"Homay-y-y! Oh...are those flowers for your own room? Say, don't forget to pick some for the boys, will you?" The broad little figure laughed up at me.

"Just like last year, Ma-Ma?"

"Yes—everybody must wear a flower." Then, as I passed Brand-New on my way to the chapel–"Don't forget to go to the House-of-Grace and get a posy for your buttonhole!" brought a smile to his well-scrubbed countenance. Brand-New was looking quite civilized now.

The chapel floor was strewn with fresh pine needles—a fragrant joy which elicited an exclamation from one young Lisu girl, "Isn't it nice to have a celebration!" Up at the front was a temporary platform for the student body, at one side the portable organ, and opposite at the other side a table with a small model of the Tabernacle on it, which Job was putting in position preparatory to explaining it briefly. Caleb and Simon were flitting excitedly around, recalling memories of last year when they were both in the Hallelujah Chorus. Sickness kept both of them from attending more than one week this season, much to their sorrow.

"Caleb, give me the signal when they get close so I can start the march," I requested, and met with a quick, smiling assent, followed later by a briskly waved hand, and then the twenty-three young people, single file, with measured step came slowly up the aisle. Thomas, handsomely attired, after having passed Homay's careful scrutiny, led the procession; each was well groomed with a bright zinnia tucked in somewhere and there was an impressive and pleased silence as Chairman Christianson motioned them to sit down.

But alas! dignified occasions have been hitherto unknown in this land of the mannerless. I was just enjoying the solemnity of it all, when Luke, who was song-leader for the day, started out of his seat in consternation, "Where's my song book?" Then turning, he shouted at some invisible person in the audience, "Did you bring it?"

"Of course I did," came a female answer from the middle of the women's side. "Here it is," in tones of wifely indignation that he should doubt her faithfulness in public. It was handed up the aisle, and our dear song-leader, unconscious that he had ruined the dignity of the occasion, sat back in his seat with a sigh of satisfaction that now he was equipped for what lay ahead.

Titus was the first valedictory speaker. He was resplendent in black sateen with white anklets climaxed with pink shoes. The young monkey had coloured some white tennis shoes with beet juice (he is on good terms with our cook!) and appeared before us red-footed if not red-handed. He spoke on "The Dragon"—tracing Satanic appearances through the scriptures, but especially in the book of Revelation. He was good.

Job came next with the model of the Tabernacle. He got along well until he came to the coverings which he had been warned beforehand not to attempt to expound. But, seeing so much interest in his audience, he felt buoyed up and (like some of the rest of us) plunged in, with the expected result. "And this," says he, holding up the white curtain with easy assurance, "was made of goat's hair," But goats are not white in Lisuland. A sudden fear smote him. In horror, he turned and called over his shoulder in a stage whisper to Ma-Ma,"*Was it?*"Whereupon his congregation grinned.

Andrew was the other valedictory speaker, and with his usual quiet composure spoke on the "Lamb of God," tracing that doctrine from Genesis to Revelation. Cath Christianson thought he was the best of the day.

A recess for lunch was followed by the afternoon meeting when the rest of the student body were to give five-minute testimonies as to the different books studied this summer—John being chairman. Apart from Lucius, who was confined to bed with a sore foot, each one spoke a few words. Nosu-Mary and one or two others were quite perspiry, but got through safely. Junia's was short and simple; he could not afford to perspire, he had too many clothes on. He evidently had decided to put on all the respectable garments he possessed, so as to be sure he had selected the right one.

Luda-Peter, who, unknown to himself (for we publish only general results), led the whole school with a percentage of 97 3/5, got so nervous he began to pull the bark off the low beam over his head and wandered considerably from what he had promised Ma-Ma he would keep to, with the consequence that he mixed up shittim wood and almond wood, but otherwise made no heresy.

The Rainy Season Bible School for boys asked for the *Hallelujah Chorus* again this year, so they are practising it these evenings. Much of the success of this noble oratorio depends on alert and instant obedience to the leader. If this is missing you will find yourself singing, "Ha..." with lusty enthusiasm all alone while your neighbours bury their noses in their sleeves and snicker; and you have a miserable feeling that public prominence is not what you covet after all. For who could sing the *Hallelujah Chorus* without enthusiasm? *"The kingdoms of this world are become the kingdoms of our Lord and of his Christ....King of kings and Lord of lords—Hallelujah!"* Why, to know that we are actually going to see that accomplished some day, it sends the blood fairly racing through one's veins, with the joy of it. Ah, but if you "Ha" at the wrong moment—like Rhoda did last year on closing day, just because she was in the front row and too self-conscious to lift her head and watch the leader—it rather takes the glory out of it. Alert, instant obedience, that is what makes team work such a thrill.

May none of us have to hang our head on *That Day* because we were not ready to obey!

Chapter Six gave a glimpse of the Abyss and its Master. This chapter has shown the Nestling and how it cuddles down into Shelter of the Cleft of the Rock, when that Shelter is pointed out to its bewildered ignorance. The dangers of legalism are best combated by teaching "the word of his grace, which can build you up, and give you an inheritance among all those who are sanctified" (Acts 20:32).

The stiff Wind of Legalism–it blows in the West too. Christians sink so easily into thinking that to follow Christ is just a set of *do's and don'ts*. Our RSBS students carried the message of grace everywhere over the mountains. John could only be physically in one village at a time, but through the RSBS students, the message was preached in ten or twenty different villages on the same Sunday. And throughout the whole year, all over the field, the students continued to preach grace and tried to point out legalism. Quietly, sweetly, the transformation came about. Not that the church was now perfect–far from it; for that Wind also seems to blow where and when it listeth–but the trained evangelists and the whole deacon body changed in their attitude, from set laws for set offences, to consideration of each case on its separate deserts. And throughout, striving to get the mind of Christ on each matter.

As you paged through the story of the Seedling Patch, have you sensed what a privilege it was, to be a participant in God's work there? And as you continue to read, and see how far-reaching the lives of some of those humble, barefoot laddies became, do you not think that to lay before them God's full plan of salvation is a great joy, a worthwhile use of one's life?

One furlough I met a lady who said to me, "I have no interest in anything but my house and my garden. My house and my garden are my life." I thought how pitifully poor she had confessed herself to be; even though hers was a large expensive home and mine a mere shanty on the wild mountainside. For in imagination, I saw the uplifted faces of our Hephzibah classroom; thought quickly through the years of study and companionship with them; saw the dull empty look of ignorance change into that of shining radiant possession. And my heart cried out, *What a waste for her to spend that human life and sympathies on a wooden house and a dirt garden, when God's spiritual house is calling out for living stones and His garden has Seedlings of Eternal Destiny that need to be trained!* But the West is full of human beings (church-goers, many of them) who live just for things. When that lady dies, she must leave behind her house and her garden—everything that spells life to her by her own confession. When I die, I know I shall see again my "living stones"; and I shall comrade with my precious Seedlings throughout eternity.

> The angels from their home on high
>   Look down on us with pitying eye,
> That where we are but passing guests,
>   We build such strong and solid nests;
> While where we hope to dwell for aye,
>   We scarce take heed one stone to lay.
>   UNKNOWN

Chapter 8

A THIEF WHO LABOURED TO GIVE TO OTHERS

"Let him...steal no longer"
EPH. 4:28

Youth, O Youth, can I reach you,
  Can I speak and make you hear,
Can I open your eyes to see Me,
  Can My presence draw you near?

Is there a prophet among you,
  One with a heart to know?
I will flash My secrets on him,
  He shall watch My glory grow.

For I, the God, the Father,
  The Quest, the final Goal,
Still search for a prophet among you
  To speak My word in his soul.

And He does reach them; conquer them; captivates them until they yield to Him that valiant and glorious self-abandonment which belongs so markedly to youth.

S UNDAY. The big noon service had finished and I hastened down to House of Grace to get behind the dispensary table. The Lisu come to the Sunday noon service from many miles around, and so it is an opportunity to get medicine for their sick ones. As I measured out ointment and pills I was conscious that Luke and another were hanging around in the background of the crowd. At length, the last medicine-seeker satisfied, I turned to see what was wanted.

"Ma-Pa and Ma-Ma," said Luke briskly. "This fellow wants to confess his sins!" Then, turning to the young man, he added, "Now go ahead."

The repentant sinner was not an attractive Lisu. He had stubby hair and a hang-dog, on-the-defensive manner. This was all the more empha-sized at the present moment by the embarrassment of his situation. But, pulling himself together, in a low guttural voice, he began.

"Ma-Pa, Ma-Ma, I have sinned against you. The second Christmas you were here, I came to the festival to see what it was like. But I wasn't born again then, and..." Here it was hard going, but he straightened up and went on doggedly: "I saw a pretty bag hanging on your wall and I stole it. I want to be a Christian now, a born-again one, and I wronged you in something else too. I got some medicine from you once, and instead of returning the bottle to you, I sold it, and kept the money. Here is the price of it and I will pay you for the bag when I can get the money, later on." And he put a half-dollar in my hand, his feet shuffling nervously and his face sad and ashamed.

"Well, friend," we replied, "we are glad to see that the Holy Spirit has been working in your heart. When you start in to follow the Lord Jesus, it is good to clean up your past as much as you are able. So we shall accept this money. But this is what is called 'conscience money' and we do not keep such ourselves. We do not exhort you to repentance in order to get things back from you." So, putting the money in Luke's hand, "We shall give this to the Lisu church. And we hope you will study God's Word so that you may grow spiritually. Where do you live?"

"At Squirrel's Grave Village," Luke replied for him. "Across the river there!" and he pointed west through our open doorway.

"Well, you talk with him, Luke," we suggested, for Sundays always saw many Lisu wishing to consult with us on different problems, and we could not spare much time to any one person. Later this boy was named Gad, so we shall just call him that from now on.

A few weeks later I was pleased and surprised to hear that Gad had gone off on a preaching trip with Jonah! The latter needed a companion, and the self-confessing thief offered to accompany him (and incidentally get lessons in reading and writing), and so it was arranged. Gad carried Jonah's load and helped in small ways, and in his spare time pored over his scripture portions.

Each April, before RSBS began, we called in the evangelists for a week's Bible study, and to hear reports of their work. When Jonah arrived, lo and behold Gad was with him, and in his customary shamefaced manner asked to be allowed to study too. He appeared very dense in class, and I would have regarded him as hopeless if it had not been for his industry. Being new he was very slow at writing and copying the Bible notes we gave, but after classes, when the other students rushed off to the athletic field, day after day, Gad was to be found sitting before the blackboard laboriously copying all the notes he could find. Once I reprimanded him, "Gad, it is recreation time now. You ought to be down on the playground with the other students. You'll get too tired writing for such long hours at a time."

He looked up at me. "Ma-Ma, please let me finish. I'm slow because I'm new, you know." I had not the heart to discipline him for it. The willingness to labour hard in learning the Word of God is not very common. I dared not quench it. So I left him to copy, and copy, and copy until long after dusk had fallen.

In all Bible schools, even shorter ones, we endeavour to have one class a day in practice preaching (Homiletics being too high a name for the results!) and my husband and I have never forgotten Gad's first attempt at a sermon. He was such a babe in things spiritual that he really had nothing much to say, and embarrassment drove out any idea that he might otherwise have had. But we must all begin some time, so we would not excuse him, though he begged we would.

"All of us here know that you are a new believer and have not had time to learn much, but get up and try, anyway."

So, with his hang-dog look and deep guttural voice, Gad rose to his feet and tried. A most painfully boring succession of platitudes followed. He was, like other beginners, trying to remember what his Lisu teacher had last preached, and reproduce it. The result was incoherent and unconnected, but every now and then his fact lit up and looking at us earnestly he would say, "And we must not sin! We just mustn't sin." That far his face was filled with inspiration, but at the next step, panicky at his empty thoughts, he would make a desperate grab after memory and scramble on with more muttered platitudes, only to bring up again the one fact that he was sure of. "We must not sin! We must not sin," he would say again with that earnestness in his face. As a sermon it was ridiculous; but at least the one thought that was his own, he had driven home.

"Well," was our judgment upon it, "Gad has evidently learned one important thing, and that is, that sin comes between man and God. And that if man wants fellowship with the Father, he must first deal with the sin question. He was not able to put it so clearly, but he left that feeling with each of us, did he not? So, as a first attempt, his sermon is not a total failure! Now learn one thing from this. *The part of God's message which will be most potent from your lips is that which comes from your own personal experience of it*. Gad has learned what sin can do, and his earnestness on that point was a blessing. It is always so. What has blessed our own hearts is sure to have a message for others."

> For he that serves his Lord, must holy be,
> And he that labours must be free from guile,
> And he that sows be filled with purity;
> And he that speaks the message of the Word
> Must first receive the fulness of the Lord.
> M.B. WHITING.

Gad flushed with pleasure, for he had expected the worst, in criticism, and nothing but the worst. And I think everyone else had too, so it was a good thing for all.

At the end of that week, when we were discussing where each evangelist should go until RSBS brought them back to us again, Junia spoke up, "Ma-Pa, may Gad go with me? He says he'd like to!" I turned then and really looked at Gad. Could it be possible that one so shortly out of sin had a secret hope to become a preacher of the gospel? Though he would not dare voice it, so early, that hope evidently was already in his heart, and at the close of the week he and Junia trotted off happily together.

June, 1939, circular tells this part of the story:

> Earlier in the afternoon Junia and Gad had arrived—the latter with mumps! They were merely on their way to teach the new inquirers at Squirrel's Grave. Gad looked so funny with his great swollen jowls, but he never thought of stopping work as long as he could speak (for, of course, he had no knowledge of infection until we told him). Squirrel's Grave was his home, but he meant to testify there; he could read and write now and thus teach others. And this was typical of Gad.

A few weeks later:

> Titus, Jonah, Gad and Junia arrived last Saturday night and all are busy today getting a schoolroom built—last year we met in a part of the church but it was most inconvenient, so this year a school house, or rather bamboo Bible school is going up—the first Bible school building the Lisu have ever built, at least in these parts.
>
> Later: We have a brand new building this year, with seating accommodation for thirty and it has been filled so far. It is nice to have room enough to go around and inspect their work. This was not possible last year. Our Bible school building is named "Hephzibah" and I suppose it is the poorest little Hephzibah in the world—just bamboo mats for walls, bamboo mats for roof, and earth for floor. It has no need of windows, for mats do not reach to

the roof, and it possesses no door—everything nice and airy. The "desks" are crude slabs of rough wood held up by tree boughs driven into the earth, so they don't wobble! I love it. Its poverty does not worry me in the least—in fact I have been thanking God these last few months for the privilege of being asked to minister among the poor. If their lives were not so drab and ugly, so toilworn and uninteresting, Jesus and His messengers might not mean so much to them.

And now we must leave Gad starting in with his real book work, to trace a development which was later to affect Gad himself.

We must go back to the end of our first Rainy Season Bible School, and let us watch how God began, almost immediately, to use this study of His Word not only to tell the Lisu tribe, but also to reach out toward other parts of the country where His Name was not yet known.

Two weeks' journey to the east of us (over the high Mekong mountain range, and a sea of other mountains to the faraway, famous gorge of the Yangtse River) lay a great unopened tribal territory which we called Yongpeh. At the close of our first RSBS in 1938, a letter from Mr Andrews, a missionary labouring near Yongpeh, reached us. The circular of January, 1939, tells of it.

Some time ago we received a request from a missionary north of Tali, asking for evangelists to be sent to him, as he felt there were Lisu in his neighbourhood who would respond if appealed to in their own language, and he wished to start a Lisu work there. Our beloved superintendent wrote us, in almost his last letter, saying he hoped the church would give heed to this request from another mission, and so we laid it before them as a solemn trust from the one who has gone to heaven. They replied by sending Aristarchus and one other younger Christian named Secundus. We have requested that they be sent back to us by June, so as to continue their studies in the Rainy Season Bible School.

The next month's letter contains a report from the two young evangelists themselves.

They spent twelve days in arduous overland mountain travel in order to reach their base of operations. Part of Aristarchus' first letter here reads something as follows:

Sometimes we walked up into the night, and other times we were on the road at the cock's crow. We were tired and and cold and my partner almost cried. And just now they are pressing men into the army. For this cause, while we were on the march an army officer told us to become soldiers. But we answered them that we did not care to be soldiers. We were bound for the country of Lichiang, where the Pastor lives. However, the officers nearly forced us into the Army. On the other hand, God did not allow them to touch us, neither were the two of us given into their hands. Exceeding and unending thanks to God! This little experience, however, is not worth mentioning as suffering.

The writer is a Christian,
ARISTARCHUS.

April, 1939, brought us the following report from the two.

Yongpeh City.
To the Christians in the church of Oak Flat:
To the church at Oak Flat which we love and wish mutually to behold, Aristarchus and Secundus in

the name of the triune Father, Son, and Holy Spirit greet all you Christians with a letter. Are you Christians of the church at Oak Flat all safe and strong, dwelling peacefully in the Lord Jesus? We would like very much to know and we thank all the brethren for praying for us.

As Secundus and I came from Oak Flat country to Ya-pi market we saw some Lisu homes and people. But leaving Ya-pi on our journey to Lichiang we crossed much country where we saw no Lisu homes or folk. Eight days after arriving in Lichiang we went with the missionary and two evangelists from the Lichiang church into the country round about to teach. Leaving Lichiang without accident and travelling peacefully in the Lord we reached Yongpeh country, thank God. It is three days from Lichiang to Yongpeh and we had to cross a mountain range. From our Oak Flat to this place is some little distance! Yongpeh is a city like Paoshan, with a big market and the people around are all Chinese. There are lepers also in the city.

There was no preaching of the gospel there, so we pity them. Therefore the Lichiang missionary borrowed a house and now they have services. On the evening of January 30, the gospel began to be preached in this church. Please pray for the Chinese of this place.

Also on Chinese market day countless Lisu come. A half-day's journey from the Chinese city brings you to the Lisu villages and there are so many Lisu you cannot describe them! Moreover, the men and women resemble the Lisu of the Luda district. Many of them have a knowledge of Chinese. Please, brethren of the Oak Flat church, village by village all of you, pray more and more for these Lisu of Yongpeh.

My companion Secundus and I on February 2

went to the villages where the Lisu live. We went to village by village and preached the gospel. When we taught them they said, "We have never heard this story before nor seen any kind of Lisu book. Please pray for us!" Their words and our Lisu words are about one-third different. Kindly pray for us while we are in this country that we may walk in the Spirit and sow the seed of God's doctrine. Now there is another thing; in this country the money we formerly used we never see here. There may not be any traffic in opium. People have been killed for planting it. Over a thousand soldiers have gone from this place but none has ever returned home. How is our Oak Flat country now?

Now there is one more thing with which I would like to acquaint you brother Christians. In the middle of this Yongpeh district there is a people called the Lolo, over one hundred thousand of them. They are like wild people and steal and rob all the time. More than this, when they seize Lisu and Chinese, man or woman, along the road, they lead them away and make them slaves in their own country. None of the Chinese officials dare discipline these people. Pray that these folks may cease to be robbers and their hearts become tender—and constantly pray for us two, please. Now that is what we have to say. We are well and strong in the Lord. Many thanks to God.

The one who walks and writes to you is the Christian.

ARISTARCHUS

I was perfectly thrilled over that last paragraph, for he had undoubtedly come upon the *forbidden territory*—that tribe of Lolo which the Chinese have never been able to conquer and for which prayer has gone up in our Mission since before I came to China, at least.

RSBS, 1939 (when Gad first came), did not bring the two boys back to us as we had asked. Mr Andrews wrote us the reason.

Requests for a teacher had come pouring in on Aristarchus and Secundus. To cope with the spread of the work, they had separated, but still there were calls they could not answer. To leave at such a time with no one to replace them seemed disastrous. As it was, all they could do was to make clear the way of salvation, teach a simple prayer and perhaps a hymn, then pass on to others. How they longed really to establish the church in the truth. When their backs had to be turned on the new believer, Satan would send out his sharp Winds from the Bitter Height, and if they had not been taught how to shelter in their Rock, how would they ever stand? So of course we wrote our consent that they wait at Yongpeh until reinforcements could be sent to relieve them.

Mr Andrews paid the little infant church a visit and wrote to us of the happy time he spent there. "How they hunted the mountains for idols!" he said. "Some thirty-five families have cast out their demon altars...this means that about two hundred have confessed Christ as Saviour. It was a blessing to see how they came to the meetings and to hear their singing. Seeing a Lisu with his Catechism, I asked him to read it to me, which he did with such liberty and joy that the tears came to my eyes as I sat and listened. Wonderful indeed. 'As soon as they hear of me they shall come; and thy people shall be willing in the day of thy power.' The Lolo also have asked the evangelists to come to their villages and teach them."

In this way began something which we hoped

would grow—the Lisu tribe reaching out to evangelize other tribes. The missionary cannot hope
always to be in China; the national church should
be trained to care for and evangelize its own
countrymen.

Now to go back to Yongpeh. The very first of
these thirty-five families to turn Christian was a
local official, Chiu Teh-tsi by name. His is a
wonderful and rare story of a heart prepared. It I
remember rightly, the two evangelists were having
rather a lonely and defeated time of it, when they
"happened" upon this man, who, immediately he
heard the gospel, was thrilled with it. He invited
them into his own home and questioned them
eagerly, and with great intelligence; then made his
decision telling Aristarchus that he had long been
seeking after the truth. Upon casting out his idols
and ancestral worship, this dear man wrote us his
testimony in Chinese. A quotation from a circular
will introduce another from him:

"AN HANDFUL OF CORN...UPON THE TOP OF
THE MOUNTAINS"
Twilight—the day's responsibilities over—I turned
once again to the orange-brown path which slips in
and out among green foliage until it falls away into
Sunset Ridge on the banks of the Salween. There,
at the end of the day, I like to keep tryst. The ridge
is growing old...just as I am. Its rounded youthful
form has been stripped of so many trees and
bushes that it is thin and spare now, but it is still a
quiet spot and it possesses a forward look which is
incomparable in grandeur and never fails to silence
the soul into worship. As I sit on my favourite grey
stone, the opposite bank of the river towers up
before me into jagged peaks, navy blue in the

falling dusk, but with soft wreaths of pure white
cloud wistfully clinging to their great shoulders.
Peak behind peak–they trail away into the steel-
grey skies with an enticing lure–Come, find me!
Come, find me! and you feel quite sure that heaven
and the Prince of Glory and all the host of loved
ones gone on ahead are just over the border, and so
in the quiet of the evening you feel close. That's the
time and place to lay all the day's ruffles out
before Him and ask His dear hand to smooth them
out. And when the inner peace is matched to the
outward, I sometimes ask Him for a word, and
often, so often–with unfailing kindness He has
given it. He knows just what word will mean most,
and that evening He opened the Book for me and
pointed to Ps. 72:16 (KJV)–"an handful of
corn...upon the top of the mountains...the fruit
thereof shall shake like Lebanon."

"An handful of corn"–it just described them.
Our little handful of corn-kernel students who we
hope will fall into the ground and die to self and
bring forth a harvest of other kernels for Him. But
the handful of corn was getting slimmer every
day–how could one believe that its fruit would
increase until it was like the great trees of Lebanon?

Do you remember we told you of an official in
the Yongpeh district who had turned Christian
under Aristarchus' exhortations? Well, the very
next letter from there told that this dear "firstfruits" had passed the border country, and now is
with the Lord. As I sit and look at that sky trail,
and in the evening dusk feel "close" to those on the
other side, I remember that Mr Fraser's last request
to us before he went Home, was that we would try
to send a messenger of Christ to Yongpeh district.
And now he and that new convert have shaken
hands–isn't it wonderful? We aren't so very far

separated, are we? We never know when it will be our turn to slip heavenward. A letter from that new convert is a voice, now, from beyond the sky trail.

May 20, 1939

To the Oak Flat Church:

The two teachers you sent to Yongpeh, namely Aristarchus and Secundus, are now in the Sha-pa village teaching *God's clear road*. We are very fond of one another. In the Lord Jesus we have peace.

These two are working very hard for God, changing our superstitions and lifting us up to walk the *great clear road*. Up to now there are over forty families trusting Jesus and of men and women over two hundred are studying the books. But then there are still a few thousand who do not believe in Jesus. These unbelievers are all in the hands of the devil; please pray to God for them.

That everything is in God's hands is our great joy. (They say he died with his testimony still on his lips.) Thank God and thank you.

I would like you to announce to the church that the most important thing in this note is that Aristarchus and Secundus are going home in a short time. We have only escaped from the devil's hands a few months; and we of Yongpeh do not know anybody who can read Lisu characters and we cannot do without them. We thank you because you have been expending your hearts in order to bring us into the faith.

CHIU TEH-TSI.

The following is an extract from Aristarchus' letter announcing Mr Chiu's decease:

...Now among the brethren who have believed there are some Lisu but most are Lolo...of individuals about two hundred and fifty. They are now at this time working on building a chapel. They have already finished two chapels of about thirty feet in length. Thank God.

Moreover, after they had believed, the Lisu official (the one whose letter is above) and another Christian went home to God. But the believers were not saddened. In fact, it was the duty of Secundus and me to comfort their hearts from the scripture, but some of them comforted us saying, "Don't feel badly." This is a sign to us that we have cause to thank God.

Another thing, the believers here are meeting with trial and seduction from some people Satan is using. This country where Secundus and I are, is close to that governed by Szechwan. And in that place, here and there robber bands are continually stealing people. Seven years ago about seven hundred of them (Wild Lolo of the Forbidden Territory!) came to this village where we are now, and burned their homes. They drove before them their cattle and many of their young men and women.

Needless to say, we did not request that Aristarchus and Secundus come home immediately; still it was not wise to let them continue on without Bible study under a competent teacher, so all during 1939 RSBS we were hunting in our hearts for the two students whom we should ask to go and relieve Aristarchus and Secundus to come back to us.

Again the 1939 circular gives a description of each member of the student body, but as repetition becomes wearisome we will quote only what relates to our story.

...And next to him sits a young fellow, face lowered, looking up at you with such a black scowl you would think he was planning your murder. Oh, no, dear friend, this is just poor Gad trying to concentrate. He reminds me of Aristarchus—such an unattractive surface, a slow working mind behind it, but, we trust, a sincere desire to do what is expected of him. I hope some of you take a liking to Gad—a prayer liking.

The women's bench is over at the back next door—right next to Gad. Gad is not the type to distract a girl's thoughts. (Is that naughty? I'm sorry. I really like Gad, even if the girls don't.) Homay, Dorcas, Rhoda, Elizabeth, come as they can, and women visitors also but the only enrolled females are Mrs Yang and Nosu-Mary.

RSBS, 1939, was a happy school. I quote from the circular which reviewed it at the close.

Quite without our intending it, last year's RSBS held the keynote "regeneration," and quite without our planning it this year's one had a keynote also—it was "identification," our union with Christ in His death and resurrection. Many were the testimonies of what a blessing this study had been to our dear laddies. I listened to them with gratitude but with no excitement, for I know full well that to learn it in the classroom and to experience it alone on the field are often far apart. They do not need to be, but they often are. After a class on Rom. 8, Andrew said to me, "Ma-Ma, are there Christians nowadays who remain carnal all their lives?" Blessed innocence; may it always be that to learn a truth is to practise it, in their lives. But to put identification into practice necessitates suffering—there is no easy path to dying to self and living to God. My prayer for them is—may they recognize the opportunity to die, when it comes. I was myself blessed by these few sentences in a letter from our revered Miss Frances Brook: "Brokenness is the place of blessing. Broken personalities letting the fragrance of Christ out; broken purposes meaning power; broken plans meaning life; broken periods meaning glory. The corn of wheat breaks when it has let itself go to the ground and the embryo is free."

As I sat listening to the closing exercises I thought how much we had for which to thank the Lord. No student failed. Brand-New, Levi and Mrs Yang did not write examinations and so were not "graduated," but of the other twenty, ten got over ninety-four per cent. There were no spectacular ones, this year, but several little incidents made us feel there was real progress. For instance, there was not one dissension between the students, large enough to come to our ears; last year there were three. We had no worries about misbehaviour; there was only one exhibition of temper on the playing field, Rufus the culprit. And with many there was a gradual growth which has been a quiet joy to us. I would like to mention Gad, Ephraim, Pade-John, Daniel and A-che as gladdening our hearts, these in addition, of course, to those who have been an undiminished joy all along. This summer A-chu won a woman to the Lord on Water-Buffalo-Mountain Village and telling us of it later she said, "Now that's a fellow who loves folk." Little things like that show us the study of His Word is not in vain. Also we would like to praise the Lord for the safe journeyings made every weekend through stormy and dangerous weather, yet not a student was hurt by falling rocks, of which there were more than usual. Can you not see how God has been answering your prayers for us? And not least was the way the food supply kept up. In fact, I fear the "shepherds" were better fed than the flock, this summer.

Heading the list of unexpected joys was Gad! And now the designation of evangelists, their work and field for the coming year, was before us. Who were to be the exchange teachers with Aristarchus and Secundus?

Tall, good-looking, clever Luda-Peter had led the school that summer in marks, and my husband suggested him for Yongpeh.

"He is expecting to be married this winter," I demurred.

"Oh, that is an American thought, not a Lisu one," answered my husband impatiently. "I don't think he'd mind in the least. Any of our boys would be thrilled to go. Whom did you think to ask?"

"I thought of Daniel and Gad," I replied quietly.

"Gad! Why he's only a beginner! What on earth! Why, I want to send our very *best* to that great field! You know it was just about Mr Fraser's last request before he died, that we should respond to that call for help. Gad! Humph." And in some disgust John turned away.

But I had been noticing the once-upon-a-time thief–noticed how hard he worked, how blamelessly he tried to live. Life is a powerful testimony, more powerful than clever words. Gad's daily life impressed me more than Peter's.

The next day my husband approached me with a rather sheepish grin. "Guess you win, Belle! I suggested Yongpeh to Peter yesterday. His face fell and he answered slowly, 'If it is God's will, I'll go, of course...' but his face told enough for me.

Daniel, on the other hand, is glad to go. So I think I'll send for Gad and sound him out."

Gad limped in, and stood looking with a hang-dog expression from one to the other.

"Don't be afraid, Gad," cheerfully assured the missionary. "Nothing wrong. We've just called you in to ask if you would like to go with Daniel to Yongpeh for this next year?"

It was like pressing an electric button. His form straightened and his face flooded with light. "Oh, I'd like to *so much!*" he cried. But I had noticed his limp as he came in, and on inspection saw that one leg was just a row of ulcers from knee to ankle.

"How can you go, Gad, with a leg like that! There are twelve days of hard mountain walking before you get to Yongpeh, you know!"

"Oh," says Gad, looking down at his leg, "it will soon heal up. We don't have to go immediately, do we?" and he turned from kill-joy Ma-Ma to scan anxiously Ma-Pa's face.

"Oh, no," was the answer. "Job has to escort you and he is not going for a month or so yet."

"Well, I will be all healed by then," he replied with great relief. "Thanks ever so much!" And he limped off joyfully to communicate his good fortune to the others. The circular merely records:

> To exchange with Aristarchus at Yongpeh: Daniel and Gad. Job will escort them over there, as they must pass through Chinese territory and neither speaks much Chinese; then Job will remain to give the new believers a month of study before returning to his post at Luda.

One fine autumn day, the little band of three set out on the long trek to a pioneer field, where many

of the people were of a different tribe. "Go forth,"
He said.

I do not possess copies of any of the correspondence that ensued during that year of hard, faithful
labour. Up and down the mountains the two
plodded, teaching little groups of inquirers here
and there, or entering heathen villages to proclaim
their wonderful Word of Life. There was no hand-
clapping or praise of men to urge them on, or
comfort when the way was hard and lonely. They
must adjust themselves to a different dialect,
different food, and different customs, and all without any human help, except what they could give
one another. And the field was so large that more
often than not they had to separate in order to
meet the calls for service. We, on the other hand,
were so busy with a very full programme that we
did not write to them as frequently as we would
have liked to, and as they deserved.

Now back to the circulars. May, 1940, says:

> The safe return of Gad and Daniel from
> Yongpeh brought the news of over a hundred more
> souls won to Christ there, and one of them was
> coming along for teaching—Yongpeh James. There
> are now some six hundred Lisu in the Yongpeh
> area who have turned to Christ. Isn't that wonder-
> ful? In your joy do not forget that this is a mass
> movement....God will start His winnow going
> some day, but let's not be afraid of that—even in a
> mass movement all is not chaff.

That summer of 1940 we had four different tribes
represented in our RSBS: Chinese, Lisu, Nosu, and
two Lolo, one of whom Gad brought back with
him, and all had to study the scriptures through

the Lisu language![1]

There were three from Yongpeh: John and Peter have already been mentioned, so there is only James to describe. He was one of the newest converts–out of heathenism only about nine months. He could read but had not yet learned to write very well. He was only a laddie of twenty years, with a rosebud mouth and, the first few weeks a very worried brow. To ask him a question, even the simplest, was to petrify him. Poor laddie! He was a picture of Atlas–in Lisuland–with all the world on his shoulders. It was a joy to see the care smoothing out and smiles beginning to come. He sat next to Luke, whose duty it was to mother him!

Gad was with us all that summer, and it was easy to see that the year's preaching and testing, so far from home, had done him good. His hang-dog look had largely disappeared, and when it came to his turn in practice preaching, although he never was an outstanding speaker, he had something to say.

The end of RSBS came, and again the evangelists were allocated for the year. To Gad fell the honour of a field to himself. Previously he had always been just a cadet-evangelist; now he himself was to be in charge. He was sent to Hollow Tree district, about four days' journey to the south, a large area containing Shan and Lolo, as well as Lisu. We like to send the evangelists two by two, but this time there were not enough to go round. As always, Gad was quite happy to be given the difficult place.

1 All had previously learned it, of course; many of the tribes are bilingual.

"Don't worry," he said, smiling. "I don't mind. I'll be all right." Knowing how plucky he had always been, we let him go.

> Yet not in solitude if Christ anear me
>   Waketh Him workers for the great employ!
> Oh, not in solitude–if souls that hear me
>   Catch from my joyaunce the surprise of joy.

Gad was hoping for this kind of companionship, and we felt if once he got there, God would surely give it to him. Nevertheless, he was going far from home, so our "alone-boy" was much on our hearts.

That winter, we ourselves hoped to visit Little Daughter in Chefoo. As we must pass near Stockade Hill, we had decided to stop off there and give a short time of Bible teaching. That district had been given no teaching help since the New Testaments arrived, except the school at Longchiu conducted by Mr Peterson and Mr and Mrs Crane. It had been a good school and appetites were whetted for more study. We could give them only three days, but one hundred gathered from all over the district. One result was that Claude, a Lisu who had received a good Chinese elementary education, offered to go into the Lord's vineyard. We immediately told him of Gad's need of a companion, and off he went to Hollow Tree. Little did we dream how much Gad would need Claude, as soon as he arrived.

"GOD'S COUNTRY" FOR CHRISTMAS

It was a crisp, fresh December morning when very early we started out from the dark little Lolo hut where the past night had been spent. It was cold, riding muleback on that high mountain-top before the sun was up, but there was the hope of reaching home that day, and when the pale yellow beams glinted on the great quiet peaks across the canyon from us, warming the grey rocks and tinting the tree-studded sides into genial colour, we thrilled and were glad to be alive. Our path took us over a great cap of mountain whose fawn grass velvet sides dropped down from beside our feet some two thousand feet to the green, winding Salween River below. Everywhere the beauty of God's country, its meditative quiet, its kindly hospitality, its open-trailed freedom was spread around. I took a deep breath of the untainted air and said to myself, Back in Lisuland! I feel as if I could write a circular again! For I had a slightly guilty conscience – I had not written from Chinaland that last month. Somehow the noisy rush of city life, with its conferences and truck-travelling in between, had left my pen dry. There had been blessing, but somehow no leisure to think out its record. But during that early morning ride I knew what that exiled Israelite of long ago meant when he cried, "How shall we sing the Lord's song in a strange land?" Back in God's country the desire to chat with prayer helpers about Him and His work once more flooded my heart.

But why Christmas in Lisuland when we had planned to spend it with Little Daughter at the coast? War conditions, including the bombing of a bridge on our route out, seemed to close the door. Though heart-strings tugged for little girlie, trusting the wisdom of His faithful love who has never failed us in the past, we came back to spend the day with our Lisu children, and their love and welcome certainly comforted us. God is always so good to us—Charlie Peterson had reached home just a day and two nights before we arrived, but he had cleaned house, unpiled stored-up furniture and boxes, spread his own lovely new bedspread and other fresh-from-furlough possessions all throughout our rooms—well, the only rooms that had not been dressed up to welcome us nor fixed in any way were Charlie's own! Then we had brought a grand present for everybody in the person of Orville Carlson!

"All our joy is touched with pain," someone has said. Christmas Eve, as the line-up from the south-Horse-Grass-Level Village and Hollow Tree district—waited to come under the arch, I eagerly looked for Gad. Claude, I saw, and so thought for sure Gad would be there too, but I could not see him. So when all the greetings were over, I asked where Gad was. A quiet fell over them, then they answered, "Gad has gone home to God. He died around the first of December." (Probably, as I learned after, from relapsing fever.) The news was an awful shock, and could not be forgotten. As he was the first of our Rainy Season Bible School students to fall asleep we held a memorial service for him on the morning after Christmas. Orville Carlson had been appointed to speak by interpretation at that meeting and it was particularly fitting, for two of Gad's brothers were present. One, at least, had come purposely to meet Gad, not having seen him for over a year, and the news made him very bitter against the Lord at first.

Orville had been through the same thing. His first arrival in Yunnan had been filled with joy of an unexpected meeting with his loved brother Earl, only to be met with the news of Earl's Homegoing at Luda. As Orville movingly recalled his own grief, questionings, and how the Lord tenderly met them, there were many wet eyes in the audience and I am sure Gad's brothers got an answer to their *why*?

After Orville Carlson, Gad's fellow students and workers one by one gave short testimonies of different things in his life that had blessed them. Some of them have already been recorded in this chapter–his confession of stealing a book-bag from us and the restoration of the money, which began a new life for him. His fearless and faithful work at Yongpeh were mentioned. Rather an austere, very exact and unemotional character though he was, his faithfulness to his appointed task was almost everyone's testimony.

Claude had been with him at his death. He said, "Gad knew he was going. Many of his people came crowding in to see him and he spoke to them, gave instructions as to the disposal of his things and then said, 'I know for a certainty that I am going Home to God. All of you behave as you should,' and with that he fell unconscious, and passed away." Wasn't it lovely that he died exhorting men and women to walk in the light of Calvary's sacrifice? It was typical of him that he could not put it beautifully. He was not a gifted teacher, but one of the testimonies concerning him was that his fellows grew to know that he never was flippant–he always meant what he said, and he said it.

The last letter we ever had from Gad, not thinking it would be his last, we did not keep, but it ended on a note that none of his letters had ever had before. He never exhibited affection, yet this letter had a love-longing phrase at the end, a non-translatable Lisu love-sigh which means, "Oh, you dear ones." Then after it he wrote, "The writer is the least of those you love—Gad." One of the reasons the news of his departure brought tears was that I never had showed him how much his faithfulness and willingness for hardship were prized. But there is One with him now, who will see to his reward. In thinking of Gad I am reminded of a verse my grandmother loved and wrote in my autograph album:

> A noble life is not a blaze
> Of sudden glory won.
> But just an adding up of days
> In which good work is done.

What is love to Christ? F B Meyer says, "You would like to love with a strong, undying flame—but perhaps you fail to distinguish between love and the emotion of love. They are not the same. We may love without being directly conscious of love....*They love who obey.*"

Gad never could gush. Even if he felt "a strong, undying flame," he would not have known how to put it into words, or even into manner, *but he did know how to obey*.

Gad died, trying to "give to him that needeth." The great Abyss of Sin had once made him shudder, and the tender shelter of the Cleft Rock (the forgiving grace of the Lord Jesus) never ceased to comfort his soul. But comfort was not all he desired. He was ashamed of that past; he wanted to express gratitude. With that thought in his heart, Gad set his face towards service. The raw Wind of Sickness whipped against him but did not stop him. The moaning Wind of Loneliness made him shiver but it also taught him to snuggle into the Shelter of his Rock. Thus when unexpectedly (he was still in his twenties) that bleak Wind of Death came whistling over the Abyss, he was so disciplined to self-forgetfulness that it failed to produce any terror, just concern lest the younger nestlings around him, who had had less opportunity to study their Rock, might be needlessly overwhelmed.

Chapter 9

THE UNSEEN MISSIONARIES

" **B**ELLE!" My husband looked up from a letter he was reading. "We shall have to go to Luda after this RSBS is over. Here is another letter from Mr and Mrs Cooke" (they were on furlough then–it was 1939) "asking us again to give their Lisu a little oversight. I'm just ashamed we have not gone yet. And it is such a wonderful field. I've always wanted you to see Luda; you know that."

"Well, my dear"–I sighed a little–"you know we tried to go last year, but the rains drove us back. I'll go now if you want me to, but you know what Mr Fraser said once, that that trail up the canyon is the hardest travelling in all China. I could never walk it."

"You don't have to walk it–we have Jessie and Jasper!"

"But the Cookes say you can't use a mule on those mountains!"

"That is because they are both such splendid walkers. I don't believe they have ever tried to use an animal much. Probably felt safer on their own feet. But I've been up there too, and I believe our Jessie and Jasper can do it!"

"All right, I'll go then," I agreed.

"Three cheers!" exclaimed Friend Husband, jumping up enthusiastically. "Then I'll go over and talk with Luke, and we shall arrange a grand party of deacons and Christians to go with us. The last letter from Job said that Village-of-the-Three-Clans is split with quarrelling, and it is having a bad effect on the community. Cath and Vic Christianson are here now, and they can look after Oak Flat. Do you agree?"

"All right," was the answer given more cheerfully. And now I'll let the circulars of those days tell most of it.

December 12, 1939.

Let Him lead thee blindfold onwards,
  Love needs not to know:
Children whom the Father leadeth
  Ask not where they go.

TERSTEEGEN.

"BLINDFOLD ONWARDS"
We thought we were going to Luda for just three weeks. It happened that five of our Ma-Pas had to go back to their home in the Stockade Hill District for one reason or another: Luke to take his little daughter to school there; Job to be present while his dead father's estate was divided; Andrew, Titus, and James for other reasons. It seemed just the time for us all to unite in giving the Luda district a bit of help—a shower of love and grace—before going our separate ways for the winter.

One bright November morning we started out with the best evangelistic party we could assemble—Luke and Lucius, and two of our best deacons. Job also was to meet us at Luda. So, full of hope that God was going to give us revival blessing, we began the trip.

For six days we travelled, with adventures every day, but I will quote mainly those parts of the narrative that touch the problem at Three Clans.

THE RECEPTION

The last morning a happy, long, serpentine tail of us wagged along the river road. Rock formation was entrancing. At one point was a huge wall as smooth as if the missing part had been sliced off with a cake knife–a cake hundreds of feet high. At its feet approaching us was a little band with a gaily bedecked horse. "What is this–a wedding party?" I asked Peter.

He smiled knowingly and said, "No; not a wedding party." Then the supposed party began to shout and wave to us, and here if it was not a reception committee from Three Clans Village! Their service-leader A-ge-tsi and many others–and the red-trimmed horse was for us to ride, if you please!

But this was not all. Farther along we met someone else, who handed John a written invitation for the evening meal! Still farther on was a shout and along came the famous A-deng, who had paid forty cows to redeem his wife so he could marry her. With a bamboo tube in one hand, a tea kettle in the other and a grand smile on his face, he invited us to drink out of the kettle's spout–honey-water, but cold.

"Oh, take a good drink, Ma-Pa," he said. "I've plenty more here!" patting his long bamboo tube. Still farther on were some more Three Clans folk with hot honey-water–much more palatable, for the Lisu do not strain off the wax, and cold wax bits were sticking in my mouth. At the riverside, before the ascent to Three Clans Village, they had made a second raft (for at that time of the year we did not need to go over by rope bridge) to get us all across quickly, and on the hither bank were still more folk waiting to greet us with hot tea! At the top of the hill was an arch of wild orchids and a long line (Lucius counted over a hundred and then lost tally) for Three Clans is a big village, "the New York of Lisuland," says John.

We never had been given such a reception before, but our elation was short-lived. Alas! it was not all affection (though some undoubtedly was), for Three Clans had an axe to grind. The three main clans in this village were at loggerheads over some mountain plots left them by their ancestors, on which valuable wormwood had been discovered, and they all were in hopes that John would settle the dispute. Each relay of the reception, then, was not the lovely thought we had imagined, but a different clan trying to gain our favour. One side would not come to meet us with the other side, and each was afraid the other side's attentions would outdo theirs! Alas and alack for the missionary who takes things at surface value!

We had not brought Luke and party just for pleasure. They scattered over the hills to give a loving ministry, but before doing so they assisted John in the long and tiresome discussion meetings over this wormwood. More or less all day and late into the night our party pleaded with those dear folk to be forgiving and generous toward one another, and to accept the church's decision rather than take the disagreement to the heathen official for settlement. Though respectful and loving (I want to say that for them), they simply would not listen. John refused to make a decision–in fact, Ah-be-pa and all said that it was impossible–so they "went to Egypt" for aid, with the result we had expected.

The Chinese official came to inspect the disputed fields. They had to carry him on their shoulders

free of charge, kill a pig and feed him royally, and
then he went back home and sent them this word:
"First tax–for weariness of feet"–the trouble of
inspection, but the title amuses me, for his precious
feet never touched the ground, so to
speak–"$220.00; after this is paid me I will give
judgment," which means the tax for that, and the
tax for writing out the document, and other incidental charges will be made later after he received
the Weariness-of-Feet Tax! Result–the quarrellers
are sitting around holding their headaches and
groaning. Now my husband will say that is an
exaggeration, but it just describes the woeful coun-
tenances I have looked upon. The devil surely is a
hard master, but men won't believe it until they
feel his blows.

Three Clans was only one out of many villages in
that great Lisu district, so John decided that we
had better change our plans and stay three months,
instead of three weeks, and tour the whole district.
In the meantime, word of the seemingly hopeless
condition of Three Clans could be sent home, and
the Lisu prayer partners could get under its
burden.

With that decision made, we entered into the
Christmas festivities.

December, 1939.

GOD'S CHRISTMAS GIFT
We had not expected any gifts this year. Notice
from the Chinese post office said that after last July
all parcels from abroad containing–(then followed
pages of forbidden imports which seemed to include everything that a missionary uses)–would
not be allowed to cross the Chinese border, so we
concluded all gifts for us would accordingly be

confiscated. Nobody knew we were to be in far off
Luda for Christmas anyway, so the possibility of a
private celebration never entered our mind. We set
our hearts to forget what Christmas used to be like
and to make it a happy day for the Lisu. But His
Name is Wonderful and part of the wonder of Him
is revealed (to those with eyes to see) in the way
He thinks and takes care of even very little things
which add to happiness.

But the first was not a little thing. Some weeks
before Christmas we had heard most astounding
news–that Mr Morrison, a missionary of another
mission to the north of us, had already received his
Lisu New Testament! A little later we received a
note from him, asking if we could spare him some
of our Lisu hymn-books. Very crafty were we. We
immediately sent him a load of them with the
request that he lend us some of his New Testaments! He was most kind and gave us all that he
had left–not as many as we had hoped but enough
for us missionaries to have one each–and we were
able to send one to Job and one to Luke. Oh, the
joy of owning a copy–it has not left me yet! I felt as
I turned its pages that God had given me all the
Christmas gift I needed to make me happy, but He
had yet more in store. The evening of Christmas
Day, carriers from Oak Flat unexpectedly walked
in with mail, and in their bag was our girlie's
Christmas gift to us–a new photograph of herself;
and also two small packages from America (containing things forbidden to cross the border! Was
the postal examiner asleep that day?) In one of
them was some candy, so we had a foreign
Christmas after all. In those days of China's
turbulance, no one but God could have timed mail

to arrive like that!

Job, very busy as all Ma-Pas are during the festivity, wrote us later: "I got the New Testament you forwarded, Big Brother; thank you. I was very pleased to get it. That evening the festival was on, so I was too busy to do more than glance at it. All night I was so happy I could not sleep, so at midnight I got up and studied it. I am ever so delighted. Thank God."

The time had come for Luke and Job and the others to bid goodbye to us and start on their long trek to their homes in the south. As our little band of dear comrades dropped out of sight down the steep mountainside, and we turned back to the missionary shanty, it seemed cold and desolate. I noticed a watery look in my husband's eyes, and I could hardly keep the tears of loneliness out of my own. Leila Cook had once written from that very same house, "I feel as if I've jumped off the edge of the world," and now I knew what she had meant.

We felt sorry too, that the evangelistic party which had come to Three Clans with us with high hope that God would use us, had to return with the knowledge that all our labours, exhortations, and teaching had seemingly been in vain. But there remained one hope. The returning party carried with them letters to America and England, *to the prayer partners of the Lisu Church* and when those faithful, *unseen missionaries* got to praying, things might happen. We had explained the Three Clans problem and had given details of the need. Keep this in mind as the story unfolds to you just as it unfolded to us. We saw nothing, felt nothing, but turned our attention to the large district, full of villages, around the village of the Three Clans. We left the latter to the Lord, and to the *unseen missionaries*; for we had done all we could without them. Now I quote:

The evening of December 30, returning from prayer meeting, we heard voices in the servants' shanty. Peeking in, who should we see but Simon, Caleb, and another Plum Tree Flat boy—Joshua. The little bamboo hut rang with shouts of mutual joy, and the loneliness which had haunted us since arriving here seemed to melt away before the warmth of their comradeship. They had come, not for themselves, but to give several months to the Lord in either forward evangelism or teaching. Everyone is food-conscious these days, and most young men are making strenuous efforts these winter months to make money by trade or other work, with the hungry future in mind. Seth, Simon, and Caleb are all married men, each with a little one to care for, yet they are putting His Kingdom first, for they know there is a spiritual dearth in Lisuland worse than its physical need. Seth we did not see, for he had been retained in Oak Flat District in the absence of Luke, Thomas, James and Job. I wish I could pray down some special blessing on those three and their brave wives, but it comforts us to realize that the Lord is more careful to reward faith than we could ever be.

Sitting around the wood fire, John said to them something like this: "Well, Mr Fisher of Lanping" (an independent missionary) "has asked for teachers to evangelize the Lisu around his district, but our own Luda field is in such sad need of teachers that I'd like to split you three—find a partner for Joshua and send them to Lanping, keeping Simon and Caleb here in this field to go around the villages and teach." Hugging their knees, the boys looked up and said, "Anything you decide is all

right with us. We want the Lord's will, that is all."
A young Luda Christian was present, and the next
day John asked him if he would be Joshua's
partner–he knew the road across the mountains
and could act as guide and helper in general.

"I have to be back to plough in March, but I will
be glad to go until then," he answered. So we
named him Thaddeus, and he and Joshua left early
on New Year's morning to mine for Christ in the
mountains around Lanping, a Chinese city some
five days' journey east of here.

NEW THINGS WITH THE NEW YEAR AT LUDA

To reach the missionary's home at Luda you must
first prepare for a terrible climb, perhaps two
thousand feet up from the banks of the Salween.
Luda Mountain is gracefully knobby, and the village itself is spread over these tiers of knolls. It is a
village of over four hundred souls and, as you
climb, to right and left and in front of you are these
rounded swells of the mountain with Lisu homes
perched on their flat tops. Daniel's family live
toward the bottom, so you may perhaps first meet
his pretty little sister shyly waiting at the roadside
to shake hands, as we did.

After this breath-taking ascent you follow a
bamboo-trough water-course around the side of
the knoll on which the chapel is built, and above
you on the next mountain knob are two native
bamboo shanties at right angles to one another.
The one facing you is marked on the door "Mr and
Cooke" and the right-angle one is marked similarly
"Charlie," only, of course, in Lisu. As you pant up
through the hillside garden to Cookes' front door,
you notice a big tree down to your right and
beneath it a roughly fenced enclosure. That is
God's garden, where two precious grains of wheat
have fallen into the ground to bring forth fruit

more abundantly. Weather-worn wooden crosses are roughly carved "Sylvia Ward" and "Earl Carlson," with texts which I do not remember. Significantly, opposite the large tree which shades their sleep is a huge old stump.

"That was a devil-tree in the old days," said John to me. "The people used to worship it, and when they turned Christian they were still afraid of it, so Job said, 'I'm not afraid of it! Bring me an axe and I'll cut it down!'—and that is how it fell."

Up behind the simple shanties winds a road to further mountain tiers, where Peter and Dan live, and crowning all is a precipitous mountain peak out like a gingerbread loaf. I looked everywhere, on arrival, and inquired for Leila Cooke's waterfall which she had so enticingly described in her circulars, but saw none, and no one seemed to know of it. Then one day it was revealed, and this is how it happened: it snowed. Lucius was hoping it would, for in all his twenty-one years he had never seen it snow. From the low-lying Village-of-the-Olives, when the clouds cleared after a rainstorm, he had seen that the opposite peaks were white, and once only someone had shown him a wee bit of the white stuff brought down from the heights but that was all he knew of snow. One morning early, toward the end of the Bible school, I heard Lucius go out the kitchen door; then came a great yell, "Ma-Ma! It's snowing! A-bo! A-bo! (Oh my!) It comes down just like the rain does! A-bo! A-bo!" An hour later an excited laddie was showing us a snowball.

"Is this what you used to throw at one another when you were a little girl in America, Ma-Ma?"

"Yes, Lucius; only do not pack them too tight or they will hurt."

"I'm going to put mine on the stove and see what will happen," and away he trotted, while

John and I exchanged grins, but allowed him to
make his own experiment. Soon he reported. "Yes,
it turned into water. They had told me you could
cook with snow, but I did not believe them." Well,
he himself had to cook with melted snow for some
days after, for it continued to storm and the water
ceased flowing. Gradually the snow turned to rain,
and it was then, in the quiet night that we heard a
steady, thunderous sound. It was the waterfall!
Dry weather had turned it into a mere dripping,
but the storm had brought it back to life. It falls in
tiers down the ravine which faces Cookes' house
and can be heard but not seen from there.

In January, 1940, we toured the district of Luda,
and   in the course of events came to the village
where Mary of the Nosu tribe lived: we called her
Nosu-Mary.

IN THE HOME OF NOSU-MARY

These are Yunnan's golden winter days–a chill nip
in the air, but until February, clear skies and little
fear of rain or snow. This is the time to travel, so
on the second of January we set out to visit the
southern part of this field, with Nosu-Mary's home
particularly in mind. We visited eight villages,
holding service and sleeping in six of them, and
also held a baptismal service in one of the cold
mountain streams. It was an exciting journey for
we rode Jasper and Jessmine, though many folk
said animals could not possibly go over those
trails. Undoubtedly little horses would have been
of small use and how grateful we constantly were
to friends at home for their gift of our big mules. In
several places, we had to say to those begging for a
visit, "Fix the road for our mules to pass and we
will come." One place was a rock ascent where we
could not even "ride by tail," for the mules had to

spring up it at a run. Another place was a face of rock about thirty feet high broken three times by earth ledges some ten feet apart. Against the rock leaned the now familiar knotched-sapling ladders. Truly no animal could climb them, but they found a detour through dense growth which "Jas" and "Jes" could traverse after having all harness removed.

What a difference a frame makes to a picture! Mary against the frame of her dainty cousin last summer had seemed so loud and unattractive. But up here among her own wild mountains, and especially against the frame of her own mother, Mary shows up quite golden. I think, of all the women I have met who have loud, piercing voices, Mary's mother ranks among the three most outstanding. (One was an elevator girl in Canada, one is a Chinese woman in a poor, mountain-top village, and the third is this little Nosu lady!) I heard her about fifty yards away before ever we met. "Eh-eh, now isn't this just awful? They told us you weren't coming till Saturday, so we have no flower arch made to welcome you. It's perfectly dreadful, but there was nobody home to make it, and we can't help it; you will have to forgive us," and so on, was shouted in a continuous stream as we appeared around the curve of the road and came toward her. But oh, what a kind heart–she had prepared a nice room in their long bamboo shanty, killed a pig for us, and evidently searched the mountainside for food, for nowhere were we given such a variety of vegetables as in that generous house. Tall, jagged, most quaintly picturesque peaks encircle the little dell where Mary lives; and a full, happy, gurgling stream at the bottom, night and day seems to testify that a person has to talk loudly if she is to be heard above its chatter.

Like most husbands of talkative females, Mary's

father is a silent partner, but he listened to our messages with such a glowing countenance, and at parting put a leg of pork into my hand, a practical token that he was one with the rest of them in good deeds. Mary is the oldest child; she is followed by two brothers and a sister. One of the boys was very ill some years ago and all expected him to die. Later Job heard of him. "Why, is that fellow still living?" he exclaimed. "He ought to be called Lazarus!" And the name stuck. So Mary and Lazarus live together in the house by the rushing stream. Lazarus now is twenty-one, plump, healthy, and a very keen student.

The village is a small one and the chapel one of the tiniest we have been in, but those who worshipped there were among the best taught and the most interested we have met in this district. Isn't that a good testimony for Nosu-Mary?

A gladness greeted us shortly after our return to Luda Village. Aristarchus, Secundus, and a new convert named Yongpeh-Peter arrived from Yongpeh! Tired, thin and worn, our dear Aristarchus is just the same as ever. When John asked him to give a word about the work at Yongpeh at the Saturday Prayer Meeting, he got up in the old awkward way, with the same old awkward "Ahem...Ahem," and then sailed into his testimony. "Now this is *not* the work of Aristarchus, nor is it the work of Secundus. This is the work of God." After plainly emphasizing that, he went on to tell of four hundred and thirty-five adults and children in Yongpeh who now own the name of Christ.

Another great joy on our return to the Cookes' shanty was the arrival of the Lisu New Testaments, packages and packages of them—enough for everybody!

"Now we really must have a February Bible School!" cried John, and at the following chapel service in Three Clans Village, he stood up and said something like this: "Now that the New Testaments are here, and the missionaries are here temporarily, we really must have some teaching on the Word of God. I am going to send word out all over this district and invite *anyone who wants to come*, to join us in study for the month of February. We go back in March. Now you folk at Three Clans were a heavy disappointment to me in the Big Matter, when I asked you *for Jesus' sake* to rather suffer yourselves to be defrauded than to dishonour Him by quarrelling in front of a heathen judge. You did not do it, and my heart is sore." Here there were many nods and tears in a few eyes, in the audience. The Three Clans believers were not individually hard-hearted; it was just that they were in bondage to the law of the clan and did not know how to get free. "Now I am going to ask one other thing of you. Don't say *no* to me. I am going to ask you to entertain the students of the February Bible School—one family to feed one student, or even two students, for one month. Now that is not a lot. Hands up, those of you who will promise hospitality to one student for the month of February!" And hands went up all over the chapel. Dear souls, they wanted to do right. They were just enslaved to wrong and had not the courage to break away. So the Bible School was held. I quote from the circular:

The February Bible School was just ending. It almost failed once. It is hard for people who have lived an active outdoor life and never been to

school all their days to keep their noses in books
for a month on end. By the middle of the month
numbers had dwindled somewhat. A delegation of
Nosu interviewed John on that rainy, cold, miserable day.

"We must go home. Dan's sister-in-law died of
typhus last night and we daren't stay," they announced. It was true that the typhus epidemic then
raging in other parts of the canyon had reached
Three Clans Village, but only in Dan's home,
which is the very highest in the village and so
easily segregated, and it proved later that his
sister-in-law had not died. John pleaded with them
to trust the Lord and not go, but they shifted
uneasily, and it was plain they meant to leave.
There was only one thing left to do. John and I
went into our bedroom, shut the door, and asked
the Lord of Calvary once more to vindicate His
victory there, over Satan and all his powers. We
said no more to the students, but not one of them
left, and the school finished the month triumphantly. Oh, how well we know that it is not we
who do the work; feeble little us-lings whose best
arguments were but as empty air to those restless,
frightened students. And in the blessings poured
out finally, we had to stand and just look on and
marvel; like Jannes and Jambres of old we must
admit, "This is the finger of God."

Bible school teaching days are very difficult ones
in which to write circular letters. Although thrilling to the teacher, they make poor "copy" for the
writer. Every day is just the same in events, and it
is impossible to appraise the work justly. Often the
student who gives the most brilliant testimony of
blessing received, does not turn out afterward so
satisfactorily as the lame-tongued one who could
not put anything into words—so that the writer

does not know what to record. Many of the students of that February Bible School could not even read properly, and to judge from appearances some learned practically nothing all month. Yet experience has taught me in Bible teaching not to walk by sight: His is the Word of Life and somehow it does bring life, though it may fail to do so in certain individuals. After the school had closed there seemed to be an epidemic of quarrels and fleshly outbreakings that seemed to betoken that the study had produced no results. But the last two days, March 11 and 12, without any explanation that we could discover a sudden and astounding change took place.

Before we tell of that astounding change, I must announce that the February School ended with wedding bells! A double wedding took place, A-che to A-nyi-ma, and Aristarchus to–whom do you think?–to Nosu-Mary! Feeling he needed a wife, and hearing that one girl had come all the way from Luda to Oak Flat to enter the RSBS, he concluded, without knowing more of her, that she must be the right material for a preacher's wife, and he proposed on the strength of that! We do not recommend to all and sundry this way of getting a wife! but merely record it.

Great were the preparations. The mud chapel was decorated with pine needles and wild rhododendrons, and to endeavour to instil decency and order into the service, Caleb and Lucius were posted at the doors to refuse entrance to anybody after the ceremony had begun. A bench was placed in front of the officiating minister, and on it the two wedding couples with their attendants were to sit.

All went beautifully, in tribal eyes. The brides,

according to Luda custom, entered the chapel with an old skirt or blanket over their heads, so that they could hardly be seen at all, and stood thus beside the bridegroom until asked to be seated by the minister. At this crucial and breathless moment the calamity happened. Caleb and Lucius, anxious not to miss the ceremony (the bride is frequently too nervous to answer properly and it is often fun), forgot the doors; and a young fellow, knowing he must be be late, but eager to see the evangelists' wedding, broke through. Before anyone could stop him or even realize his entrance, he had dashed up the aisle searching for an empty seat, thought he saw one in front, and planted himself hopefully on a corner of the bridegroom's bench! With one simultaneous cry of wrath and horror, the bridegroom's bench arose, two stalwart and indignant doorkeepers dashed down to the front, and before the luckless guest knew what he had done, five pairs of hands fell upon him, and he was evacuated bodily to a place of less honour.

Decorum having thus been restored, the ceremony proceeded. A-nyi-ma shook so much that I went close to her in case she collapsed utterly while Mary refused to answer anything at all-she just tittered. But then, if the brides did not do anything unusual Lisu weddings would not be any fun. To the Lisu the pork feast afterward was the most important, anyway. And so they were married.

Now we were coming to the last days of our stay at Three Clans and the most significant part of this story remains to be told. In fact, I would not have told any of it, if it had not been for this last part. *For the whole material of this book is dependent on the truth I want now to emphasize.* That truth is this–the slaves of the Munition of Rocks could never be freed by so feeble a thing as missionary witness and effort. They are held under a Tyranny of Darkness so strong, that only God is stronger! Only tremendous spiritual forces, working on the ground of the Atonement of Calvary, can bring Light to those sightless eyes. That spiritual force is *the prayer of many.* The prayer of one or two missionaries or converts is *not enough* to break such bonds.

We had reasoned, we had opened up the Word of God to the Three Clans, until their souls shivered with conviction, *but they still could not see the way out,* still they could not muster up the courage to break the custom of years. But by March the friends at home had received our appeal for prayer, and had gone to their knees in intercession. Then, and then only, this little corner of Satan's kingdom began to shake. We felt it. Notice again how that last circular read. "The last two days... *without any explanation that we could discover* a sudden and astounding change took place." When I wrote that in April, 1940, a letter with the explanation was already written and on its way, *but had not reached us yet.* And the letter was written in human ignorance of how the victory had come.

Those last two days we sensed that the atmosphere of the village was softening, was changing, and the night before we left to return home, my husband got an inspiration. I will let the circular now tell the rest:

The last night before we left to return to Oak Flat

we held a service in the chapel. John had decided
to make a plea for the abolishing of the "law of the
clan." That law was, that if any member of the clan
gets into trouble whether he is guilty or not, all the
rest of his clan must back him up financially or
otherwise. So if one man decided to steal a plot of
farm land, his whole clan would have to help him
steal it. If any man fail in this loyalty, when his
time of legitimate trouble comes, he must face it
alone—the clan will not help him.

John had prepared a set of paper arrows. On one
set was written, "I have no desire to practise the
law of the clan"; on the other set was written, "I
desire to practise the law of love." That last service
together John very simply drew their attention to
how Satan was binding them to sin by the law of
the clan, and though it would be costly to break
away from it, followers of Christ are bound to the
law of Christ which is love—love toward all men,
not just your own clan.

"Now I am going to ask all who henceforth will
break free from the law of the clan and follow only
the law of Christ to come forward, take the clan
arrow, and burn it in the fire here. If you do this, I
will give you a love arrow to keep always." Then
he waited. There was no excitement, no play on
emotion, but deliberately and slowly, one after
another leaders of the various clans came forward,
took a clan arrow and burned it, giving at the time
a short testimony, received a love arrow and returned to his seat. Some twenty did so—all the
important leading fighters but one man. (I always
myself remember his name as "Lamb" because
the word, with the exception of tones, is the same
as the Lisu name for Lamb. The change in tone
gives it another meaning of which I am ignorant,
so I will just call him the Luda-Lamb for our
convenience although never was there a worse

misnomer.)

Lamb sat silent, head down, looking up at John through shaggy eyebrows. My husband ignored him for the moment and turned to some famous old quarrellers. He publicly named the disputants and asked them to stand, seek each other's forgiveness and shake hands before us all. They did so. I myself have never been present at such a scene as God gave us to see that night. Two brothers who had not spoken civilly to one another for twenty-six years were among those reconciled. Then John quietly sprang a surprise. "Now, a certain man present has held a quarrel with the Oldest Brother" (of the two just mentioned) "and I noticed that he did not burn a clan arrow. Luda-Lamb! Are you going to be the only one in the village to refuse the law of love?" The old woman sitting next to me sat up and whispered excitedly, "Oh, yes, yes—those two!" But the Lamb sat silent and obstinate. He is one of the most powerful personalities in the community and was at the bottom of all the wormwood fighting. I whispered to the woman, "Pray for him! Pray for him!" and while we did so John said sadly, "Well, I am afraid we must say of Lamb like that one of old, 'he went out from us because he was not of us.'" Then, just as John was about to close the meeting, suddenly Lamb stood up and clearly and definitely made a public apology to his long-hated enemy, who likewise apologised, and they two shook hands.

Luda-Lamb then came forward, plucked a clan arrow and burned it in the fire and took away an arrow of love. It was wonderful. Only God could have done it, and only God can maintain it, but He has decreed that you and I must help Him by putting our spirit with the Holy Spirit in "groanings that cannot be uttered," which is the travail of intercession.

That night, after we had returned to our shanty, I said to my husband, "John, that was more than your own inspiration. I'm going to note this date down and see—I'm sure someone in the homelands has been very specially praying for us." And the date went down in my diary.

We returned to Oak Flat. Some two months passed. Then one day when the mail had come, I called out to my husband, "John, read this, while I go and get my diary!"

It was a letter from a dear prayer-warrior, in a small town in North America, a Mrs K.... It read something like this:

> BELOVED CHILDREN:
> I must write and tell you what happened today. All morning I could not do my housework, because of the burden on me concerning the Three Clan Village, so finally I went to the telephone and called Mrs W.... She said that she had been feeling the very same way and suggested that we phone Mrs J... and all go to prayer. We did so, each in her own kitchen, this morning we spent in intercession for those quarrelling clans. We feel God has answered. You will know.

I consulted my diary. Night with us is morning with them. It was the very time that we felt the "astounding change" of which I had written in the circular. It was the same twenty-four hours that the clan arrows were burned!

Now these prayer-warriors were not seemingly of the earth's mighty ones. Mrs K...was delicate, had a heart condition. Mrs W...was expecting a serious operation, and Mrs J...was going blind. All three were elderly women, too frail physically to cross the small town and gather in one place, but each in her own kitchen was joined to the others in spirit, and the strength of that extra intercession, in addition to what all the prayer-helpers were sending forth, pushed the battle over the wall.

Our Lord differentiated between the strength of demons. (Matt. 17:21.) Some strongholds of Satan require more spiritual force to overthrow than others. And it is not surprising if numbers count in such battles.

I have been helped in this matter by an analogy from mental telepathy. But I do not want to be misunderstood; prayer is not mental telepathy. Science can never explain prayer, although it does profess to explain mental telepathy, and tells us that there are such things as wave-thoughts, which exercise influence upon the one to whom they are directed. Just supposing that to be true, how easy it is to see the power of missionary intercession. For wave-thoughts would emanate only from the soul and so are limited. Prayer, on the other hand, emanates from the spirit, the only part of man that can reach out and touch God as well as man. How simple, then, the power of the prayer closet: many spirits working together with God the Holy Spirit for the liberating of a human soul, or a village of souls. Thus, as man has been able to advance in his research of mental telepathy, it is not surprising that those who "by reason of use of their senses exercised to discern" can tell when they have prayed through to victory. The unseen missionary, the prayer-helper, has here an effectual weapon against the Sharp Winds from a Bitter Height, which is the last word in spiritual warfare. Remember the parabolic picture of this in Exod.

17:11-14. Joshua on the battlefield won only as Moses on the mount kept his hands of intercession lifted high. Even in that work (some think Moses a type of Christ as our Intercessor) Moses *had to have human help*. The missionary on the foreign field must likewise have other spirits to aid him with the battle in the heavenlies. Explain it as you wish, it is a fact, *and it works*.

The Lisu work has had wonderful prayer-warriors in the past; but many of them have been translated into His Presence. We are needing prayer-warrior reinforcements. And China, all China, needs them too.

> If radio's slim fingers can pluck a melody
>   From night—and toss it over a continent or sea;
> If the petalled white notes of a violin
>   Are blown across the mountains or the city din,
> If songs, like crimsoned roses, are culled from
>   thin blue air—
> Why should mortals wonder if God answers
>   prayer?
>   ETHEL ROMIG FULLER.

Chapter 10

"JES' PEBBLES"

De sunflower ain't de daisy, and de melon ain't de rose,
  Why is dey all so crazy to be sumfin' also dat grows?
Jes' stick to de place you're planted, and do de best you
    knows,
  Be de sunflower or de daisy, de melon, or de rose,
Don't be what you ain't, jes' you be what yo is.

Pass de plate if you can't exhaust and preach.
  If you're jes' a little pebble, don't try to be de beach.

U P to now, this book has been mainly about
    outstandingLisu Christians, those who could
"exhaust and preach." The biographies also have
been of those who have completed their course. It
is not safe to write of those who are still in the
running--if one had written of David, for instance,
before the Bathsheba incident, he would have been
accused of "misrepresenting." All of us are possible Davids. But I would like to say that the power
which wrought in the lives of Me-do-me-pa and
Homay, is still working in other lives just as
attractive. That power is still as potent, and you
may correctly pray for the Homays and Me-do-me-
pas still being stormed upon by the blasts of Sharp
Winds from the Bitter Height--for there are many
them. You may pray also for those who would be
Homays and Me-do-me-pas if they had their

opportunity to hear the gospel–there must be many of them, too.

There are also some who are "jes' pebbles"; and a real picture of the Lisu church is incomplete without its "pebbles."

OLD BIG

Old Big, a rough country farmer, accepted the Lord the first time he heard of Him, when La-ma-wu and his party first took the gospel to Pine Mountain Village. His hut was on the lowest level of the village, but his mansion in glory. Until he died, I never heard of his dishonouring the Lord in any way. On Sundays he used to sit up near the front, and the light on his face was never dim.

Sometimes in an audience a speaker will notice one 'face particularly because of its shining sympathy–always such a face is of untold help to the preacher. Old Big was like that–a tall, lean old man with a countenance of kindly wrinkles. He was delighted with the music and kept pressing forward until he was next to the organ and finally sat down on the same box as a prodigal boy. A favourite hymn was chosen and Old Big knew every word by heart. How his face glowed as he sang–

I shall know Him, I shall know Him,
    When redeemed by His side I shall stand;
I shall know Him, I shall know Him
    By the print of the nails in His hand.

There he sat with such a light on his face, seemingly unconscious that beside him was Prodigal, the boy who had been at fault with his daughter. When the beautiful song was ended and the voices

had dropped into silence, I could not resist leaning
across the organ and pointing a finger right at
Prodigal. "When we see the Lord, we shall be ever
so pleased, but when you see Him you are going to
be terribly afraid!" I said. And while his startled
eyes held mine I reminded him of the sin which
stood between him and God—and his head hung
down like a shot.

There is a word of St Augustine's which I like; to
me it is the only answer to Peter's, "To whom,
Lord, shall we go?" He says, "And he who loveth
Thee...goeth...but from Thee well-pleased to Thee
displeased."

Old Big was facing his Lord well-pleased, and
his wrinkled countenance was one glow of beatific
joy; but Prodigal was facing the same Lord
displeased, and his head hung so low you could
not see his face.

Sunday in Lisuland was a different day from all
the rest of the week. First of all there was a before-
breakfast service for just our own village, when
from up above us and down below us our
neighbours gathered together at the Lord's feet for
an hour or so. Then followed breakfast and after a
while folks from the other villages began to gather.
To right and left thin brown trails crawled up the
mountain's giant sides, and gradually over them
came, trickling single file, village after village of
worshippers who approached like tiny armies of
coloured ants. Immediately on arrival most of
them ran into House of Grace to shake hands with
Ma-Pa and Ma-Ma—and it used to be to hear the
victrola, but it was broken later. Almost always
one of the first of these eager greetings was from
dear Old Big, whose village is near, just down by

the Salween bank. I always looked forward to his beaming smile and loving handshake. About sixty-five years old, his kindly face was a token of "the adding up of days in which good work is done." Some others of the Lisu saints may have given us heartache or worry from time to time, but never Old Big. Behind him came his sweet, happy-faced wife. Lisu couples if they love each other never show it in public. True, the happy newlyweds sometimes cannot help letting out a beam or two, but it is not considered good form. This old couple were the exception, however, and it was lovely to watch the simple pleasure they took in each other's company. Charles named them Zacharias and Elizabeth in these latter years, for they truly "walked blameless." They were not rich, but so often, in shaking hands, an egg or two or some other like gift, was slipped quietly to their missionaries. The first-ripe corn each year was faithfully brought to us, and if they killed a pig, a bit of the pork would be sent up the hill as a gift to Ma-Pa and Ma-Ma, or to any of our missionary guests.

I still chuckle over the recollection of a visit we had some years ago from the British Consul of those parts. A very tall, dignified gentleman with a monocle, he was. Old Big heard that a foreign visitor had come to House of Grace, and supposing, of course, that it must be another new Ma-Pa, and having just killed a pig, he trotted up the hill to present the gift himself. I was not aware of it when he walked in, until I suddenly heard him say in Lisu—which His Britannic Majesty's Consul did not understand, of course—"Ma-Pa, we're so glad you've come. I've brought you a bit of pork!"

I turned around to see my elegant guest adjusting his monocle downward toward a strip of greasy pork tied in the middle with a straw for carrying, which was being confidently held out toward him with the left hand while Old Big's right was pushed forward for the expected handshake. I took in the situation in a second, and could have hugged the dear kindly old saint—but I feared the Consul felt otherwise! I quickly explained the situation—in English!—and my guest proved to be a good sport, for he shook hands with Old Big while I rescued the pork and delivered it to the care of his valet!

Because of its connection with Old Big, let me quote here from the circular which told of that Consular visit:

May 27, 1941.

"Oh, Ma-Ma, look at all the pack horses coming up the ridge! *A-bo*, they are still coming; I've never seen such a caravan in these parts. What can they be hunting?" This question took me running to the window, and as I watched and wondered I suddenly remembered a letter received the month before, telling of a proposed journey of the Tengyueh British Consul up the Salween canyon.

"The English Consul!" I exclaimed. "Whatever shall I do? How can we entertain a Consul in this bamboo shanty? Oh, John-n-n!" But the great gentleman was already coming over the trail, and John, having no time to give advice, ran out to receive him.

He proved to be a six-foot, well-built Englishman — a real gentleman. He was not a Christian, but was not a hypocrite either. He made no pretence about his standing, but said that he respected Christianity and, if anything, had a leaning toward Roman Catholicism, "because of its beautiful ritual." He was really very enjoyable and endured us for two nights and a day with all the courtesy and niceness one could wish. After he left he sent us a letter which I copy below. The "Ma" and "Ho" whom he mentions are two Lisu Christians he hired as guides from here on. This is his letter:

> H.B.M. Consulate,
> Tengyueh, Camp Chihzelo.

Dear Mrs Kuhn:

In choosing paper to use to write and thank you very much for your kindness and hospitality to me at Maliping (Oak Flat), I have been at pains to choose a large sheet which may leave some clean paper for your students.

Officially I am glad to have had the opportunity of meeting you; and privately it was a pleasure. I very much enjoyed my halt at Maliping [isn't he a good sport?] and the rest refreshed me much.

Ma-fu-yi and his friend were of the greatest help to me, and the journey, though certainly arduous, was very enjoyable. The mules made it all right, with only two minor accidents, but after the first accident...the head muleteer became frightened and hired carriers for most of the loads.

The scenery was certainly impressive; but I was equally impressed with the work that you and your colleagues have done in this part of the world. At one time travel along this route was a matter of some danger; but now wherever I went I was received with friendliness and courtesy. Even though I was obviously no missionary (I use tobacco a lot) people seemed to take great pleasure in shaking me by the hand and wishing me "*hwa-hwa*." There appeared a very real sense of companionship when Ma and Ho met other Christians and shook them by the hand. At An-a-ma-po [one of

the newly turned villages this year] many of the
locals produced well-thumbed hymn-books from
their bags and started shouting them at me, and at
night I went to sleep to the sound of hymn-singing
from the local chapel. [But I must be frank and say
that the hymn tunes were neither so musical,
beautiful or suitable to the mountains as the wilder
Lisu songs.] And while halting before starting to
climb up to Bya-lo-shih one of the coolies hired by
the muleteers produced a Lisu Hymn-book and
Catechism and a simple Chinese religious work
from his pack and passed the time by reading to
me. It was certainly most impressive.

Yours most gratefully and sincerely,

ML GILLETT

The mention of the large sheet of writing paper
is in laughing reference to a remark of mine that
we use the blank backs of all letters not private (including his!) for scribbling paper for our RSBS
students who are too poor to afford much writing
paper.

The account of the hired Lisu at Bya-lo-shih
especially thrilled me as he must have been one of
the small group there, which group first found
Christ by Luke's testimony that night in the rice-
field as we went up to Luda. "Ye know not
whether shall prosper, this or that." Only one
believed then, but others have since, though teachers seldom get to that part, it is so far away.

Old Big did not escape from the Sharp Wind of
the Munition of Rocks. At the very outset of his
Christian life he was faced with the problem of the
two wives he had taken as a heathen. That is a very
worrisome Wind: it blows up heated discussions
with relatives-in-law, and Old Big might not resort

now to his former solace of an opium pipe or drink of wine, to help endure taunting words. But somehow he was led to a solution, and somehow given strength to endure. The wife that did not love the Lord, was put away, and eventually married someone else. Safely out of that spiritually monsoon it would not be long before others blew up. Sometimes inclement weather would destroy much of their crop, their year's food; once it was a nephew hired to help him, but misbehaving. "If I dismiss him, Ma-Ma, his parents will make it hot for me. But"–and I remember how his face set–"the most important thing is *eternal life*." He felt that God required him to rule his house after a godly manner and, Wind or no Wind, he did.

In 1943 we told of Old Big's death from a fever:

> Yesterday as I took the weeping widow in my arms to comfort her, and tried to tell her how that dear, good, shining face was worshipping in heaven, this his first Sunday there, she whispered to me, "Yes, but Ma-Ma, I won't be able to see his face in chapel." And in my heart I had to add, "And so say we all." Too old to learn to read, he always sat up close to the front and with radiant countenance did his best to memorize hymns, texts and sermon outline, so that I had long regarded him as my special Sunday joy. During the week he held services in his own home for his neighbours and preached and sang from memory.

"Pebbles in a brook polish one another"–thank God for the pebbles of His Lisu church.

THE INFANT BRIGADE-AND A GOATHERD IN PARTICULAR

"Ma-Ma! The new goatherd has come!"

"Oh, all right, Homay, I'll eat supper with you all, seeing I'm alone tonight. I'll see him then. Show him his room and make him comfortable."

A new servant always meant a girding up of one's loins to attack the disagreeable. Leila Cooke once described breaking in a new cook, in words something like this: "You must teach him not to throw egg-shells behind the stove, that the sweepings of the kitchen floor will be discovered if pushed behind the door, not to throw dirty dishwater on the floor, and if he gets jam on his fingers not wipe it off on the wall." Every word of it is true. People at home have servants, too: the bottle of milk that arrives on your doorstep, pasteurized and ready to drink; the gas which comes when you turn on the jet of your cook-stove; the water in your faucets and the electric light button on your wall. In Lisuland, water has to be carried up several hundred feet of mountain on a human back, usually. Food grains must be pounded out and husked by primitive foot-mills. Salt and sugar arrive in stone-like lumps and must be granulated by hand, and so on. House-helpers are indispensable, but not always agreeable. I have always tried to receive these trials in the form of servants, however, as an answer to the old question, *What is that in thine hand?*—in other words, as human souls to influence for Christ. *I have not always been successful.* Moreover, as pointed out before, when we do meet with success, they get called into the preaching ministry and we may not but relinquish them, and start in with a raw one, probably not nearly so easy to deal with. Goatherds are not a very close contact, however, and at supper-time I was introduced.

I beheld a little fellow (looked like nine years old, but they said he was seventeen!) seated on his haunches, with his head lowered and staring at me with the glare of a little wild animal. I did not feel comfortable.

"All right," I said, as pleasantly as I could, after we had shaken hands, "let's eat. Perhaps the new goatherd will ask the blessing?"

"Nope. Won't. Can't."

I was astounded! What a beginning! There he squatted, still staring at me, this time pugnaciously, a sort of hit-me-and-I'll-bite-you look on his face. I turned to Homay. The church found servants for us usually, and only those who were Christians were allowed to enter our employ.

"Isn't he a believer?" I asked.

"Yes, Ma-Ma, though not baptized yet." She was doing her best to be sympathetic, but the corners of her mouth were curling with the desire to laugh. "He can't read or write."

"But *every* Christian knows how to pray!" I continued, dissatisfied. Then, catching the look on her face—she was ever a lover of peace—"All right, I'll pray then," I agreed, and the meal started in silence.

Diminutive in size, but not at all in thoughts of his own importance, Goatherd seemed to think that he must take care that no one took advantage of him. He used to glare at me, and snap back his answers just as viciously as a little chipmunk, so I mentally labelled him that! He did not milk any more faithfully than he pleased, either. One morning we would get a quart of milk, the next perhaps a little over a cupful—but woe betide me if I tried to point out that goats don't go dry that fast! Many times we would have dismissed him for cheekiness if it had not been that he was the only son of a widow. She was blind and needed part of his wages. So we struggled on.

A year later I decided that I would not have an eighteen year-old in my house who could not read! Goatherd must learn, so at evening I called him in, told him nicely that it was good to know how to read God's Word for himself and that I meant to teach him. But he made not the least effort to learn. His body was there, for he came each night *if called*, but that was all. An evening is difficult for a missionary to spare, and I seemed to be wasting it all. I was almost in despair. Then the Luda trip, just narrated in Chapter Nine, took us from home for three months and Victor Christianson took over the teaching of Goatherd.

The next March, when we returned to Oak Flat, Mr Christianson said, "Goatherd can read now, and is learning to sing! I've named him Amos! You'd be surprised what a nice singing voice he has!" This was as good as it was astounding. I wonder if the reason was not much due to the fact that the previous summer, when Goatherd had been very ill with typhus fever, Mr Christianson had nursed him as kindly and tenderly as if he had been a dear chum, instead of an unsatisfactory servant. Now, if this were an ordinary story, I would tell you that from now on, Love did its work and the chipmunk became a sweet saint. But these are not made-up stories. The truth is, that although Amos "allowed" us to educate him, he still often played when he should have worked (one evening he had to report four kids eaten by panthers, only the little heads left, while he had been playing) and still was saucy when it pleased him–to me at any rate. Now I will quote from letters of April, 1940.

HEAT MISTS

Heat mists come unannounced, veil all the lovely familiar mountain forms and take the colour out of life, and they are a parable, for there are times in human days when happiness seems to depart and just the drab and commonplace are left. I knew I was in for one such again, as I stood on the upper road and watched the long beloved line wend its way on to Sunset Ridge and drop out of sight over its farther edge: John, Lucius, Cath and Victor Christianson, and a wriggly tail of carriers. Without the loved faces for over six weeks what a desolate stretch lay ahead. John and Lucius were going to Chinaland because John's new appointment as superintendent of the China Inland Mission work in West Yunnan made a hurried survey necessary. Cath Christianson was going out for medical advice and Victor to hold meetings at Hollow Tree District. There was no reason for me to go, and every reason for one of us to remain, so here I was. Duty with the sparkle of companionship is a happy thing, but alone with more or less unfamiliar faces (for Homay and Dorcas had left us and Job and party were not yet back) it looked very drab.

At evening, I thought, there would be inspiration as usual at Sunset Ridge, but for the first time the Ridge failed me, for heat mists had truly and physically come and filled up all the canyons and covered with a grey dull film every outline of beauty which would please one's soul. No, no comfort anywhere without, but within? No Heat Mists can blur out Him who is our fountain within, and as perhaps some of you are facing a drab period when all the colour has seemed to depart from life I would tell you how He comforted me, for He has given peace and quiet happiness.

I have been through Heat Mists before, and I know that there are three things I must do. First, remember that this has come only to pass. How often have I thanked Dr Page for that story of his; there will be some of you who have not heard it, so here it is. An idiot boy was seeking for guidance in the old magic way of shutting your eyes, opening the Bible and diving your finger on to a spot at random. He had done it three times in different places and each time the book and finger came to "and it came *to pass* that..." He pondered anxiously, then the light broke. "Why, of course," he said to himself, "this trouble came *to pass* not to stay." So the first thing is to remember that Heat Mist days are not eternal—they have just come to pass, that is all.

Secondly, be sure that they are an opportunity for more abundant fruitfulness. That is always their purpose. It was the ugly confinement of prison which brought Luke's Gospel, Paul's prison Epistles, Bunyan's *Pilgrim's Progress*, and Rutherford's undying letters into being.

Thirdly, tears or no tears, just go on and open your eyes to see God's edelweiss. That is what Miss Carmichael calls the little happy things sent to cheer the greyness of the Heat Mist days, as the edelweiss cheers the mountain-climber at a bleak, hard place. "The bright flowers of the edelweiss waiting to be gathered among the rough rocks of difficult circumstances—and they always find, I think, that far more than the toils of the climb, they remember the places where they gathered the edelweiss of God."

On the very first day I found an edelweiss. His name is Joe (I refuse to speak of him as Joseph; he has not attained unto that yet). He is one of the two new servants that replaced Homay and Dorcas, and the breaking-in of Joe into an American cook was one of the Heat Mists which had confronted me. I suppose every missionary woman dreads the hour-by-hour trial of training a new, raw servant.

Joe is a little old man in a nineteen-year-old skin. In other words, dignity, solemn dignity, under a pimply skin, small eyes that never look straight at you—for that would not be proper; bristly hair that by no amount of water and plastering can be made to lie flat, but with an honest heart which makes up for all. Joe wants to do well. The new girl doesn't; she merely hopes to hold her job. When Joe breaks a dish he is flabbergasted. When the girl does, she tells you about it with a careless laugh and if you don't show equal lightness she sulks. We prefer them to be flabbergasted.

Well, that first day at noon, when I was trying to drown loneliness by hard work on the Rainy Season Bible School preparations, Joe came solemnly into my room with an air of gravity and mystery which made my heart sink, wondering, What has happened now? Coming up close, he cast his eyes to the northeast corner of the ceiling and said in a low tone of confidentiality, "Just set the table for one, eh?" Blessed aspirant to butlership—if I had been a heathen I would have thrown my book at him for reminding me of what I was trying so hard to forget, but being a Christian and his "Ma-Ma" I got rid of him as quickly as possible and then sat back and laughed. Joe expands to his fullest stretch beneath the glory of being the missionary's cook. You should see the swell of his chest as he sets the table in the presence of his admiring fellow villag-

ers, who know nothing of the mysteries of ta-
blecloths and cutlery! Yes, quite unconsciously, Joe
helped me over a hard place, and I am grateful for
him.

Passionate devotion to the things which are vital
delivered Paul from bitterness of soul, from anger
and ill will. Disappointments and hardships...may
be used for the perfecting of character and for the
glory of Christ.

–C R Erdman

The above thought was a blessing to me; truly
turning to things which are vital clears up self-pity
and puts the pep back into life. I decided to teach a
class in the evenings, calling in the servants as a
start. They assembled, and on looking them over I
named them the Infant Brigade, for they are all just
beginners. They do not look particularly promising. Joe was one of the first to come in. He sucked
in his breath noisily and exclaimed with a happy
little laugh, "This is unthinkable"–meaning perhaps, that now the dignity of Bible student, as well
as of missionary cook, was about to descend upon
his already burdened shoulders.

The laundress and house-cleaner is the girl mentioned above. Our beloved Homay found that she
could not take care of her baby and look after us
too, so she withdrew from our home, but not from
our hearts. Gruff-Growl's daughter delightedly
promised to take her place, but she has proved to
be not strictly honest and unless the Lord changes
her heart she will have to be dismissed. She seems
to like to join the evening classes, however, and of
course is welcome.

Next are Mule-Boy and Amos. (It costs a great
deal less to keep goats and a herd than to buy
canned milk.) Mule-Boy is Simon's younger brother
with the family hot temper, and added to it a

graceless tongue which has nearly cost him dismissal more than once. In fact, the reason he still is here is only the compassion of Christ. During our visit to Luda one day I found a Lisu Gospel in a wrong place. Opening it to find the owner I saw written inside in ill-spelled scrawl, "My beloved Testament." Mule-boy had won it as a prize at the Christmas games, and has taken to Bible study since then. This year he can both read and sing, and even applied for baptism! Not at all graciously, but with obvious interest, Amos is now a member of the Infant Brigade.

My big edelweiss of these weeks has undoubtedly been Yongpeh-Peter. As you know, Yongpeh-Peter and Yongpeh-John, converts of only a year, were sent here to learn the doctrine in hopes that they will return as evangelists to their own people so that the China Inland Mission can gradually withdraw from those parts. But both boys know how to burn charcoal, so in the day time they burn for us (Mule-Boy is kept at home to learn from them, with an eye to the future) and at night I teach them. Peter is big, twenty-five years old, plain-faced and very quiet in voice and manner. He does not impress you at all, until some day you are in a difficulty and a gentle voice beside you says, "I'll attend to that for you, Ma-Ma," and in a twinkling and without fuss or words your problem is shouldered and, in course of time, satisfactorily solved.

Others beside myself are beginning to see this. Joe runs to Peter now, when he finds it hard to decipher his growing cook-book. One morning early, while still at my devotions, I heard the shanty door swing open and two come running breathlessly in. Peter's feet arrived at my bedroom door and Joe's nose was pressed against the bamboo matting wall. A serious problem was shaking the little cook's universe. "Ma-Ma!" came his voice through the matting, "what and where is *maple flavouring?*"

"It's in the square bottle."

Simultaneously from the door and wall came a sigh of relief. "Oh, the *square* bottle!" and forthwith they turned and rushed out again. Who got to the square bottle first I do not know, but I'm sure Peter likes to be consulted. He is better with his hands than his brain. When it comes to study, Yongpeh-John is much more showy, but I praise the Lord for Peter. He was once married, but four years ago a band of Wild Lolo carried off his beautiful young wife and she has never been heard of since.

Yongpeh-John, fat, round, and pleasant, is the last member of the Infant Brigade. As he has but lately joined us I do not know him very well. Can you see these six, gathered around our table at evening time, making most awful noises in their effort to learn a new hymn; struggling laboriously with the New Testament letters, and after reading, trying to bend unwieldy minds to the task of getting thought out of those symbols as well as words? Baby lessons these, but these are foundation days. This is the kind of work that the Ma-para must do in the villages as new believers are brought in. Joe–girl–Mule-Boy–Amos–Peter –John–not very wonderful material, but Teacher Job began as Mr and Mrs Cooke's goatherd. At any rate, even though they are not lovely, shall we not take the crude new believers of His church into our hearts and prayers also?

Moses' mother made an ark of bulrushes that death might not swallow her child. Who thought that the small babe would one day shake Egypt?–*From Bishop Taylor Smith's Bible.*

If we but notice God's edelweiss He will send us more. Spoiled children are those who will not allow you to console them. You will remember that all those winter months, our leading Ma-pa-ra had been away down south. The day they were expected back they did not arrive, although we had built a flower arch of welcome for them and put wild rhododendrons in their rooms. The next night it was raining and as the Infant Brigade was in the midst of preliminary acrobatics on the phonetic scale we heard a gunshot. Immediately we were all out of the room and into the dark and rain as if we were the bullets. I called out to Joe. "You stay and mind the house" (for a thief had entered a few nights before), which, poor fellow, checked his speed and made him turn back in groaning obedience. Pushing up to the trail I could just discern other villagers emerging from their huts. A white horse was coming with someone leading it–Job! Wasn't it like him to arrive first and all alone. Oh, how good to greet again those you love!

I have told about that arrival in Homay's story. The Infant Brigade could enjoy such evenings. Slipping into the cosy circle around the fire in Luke's hut, or our own servant's shanty, they could listen while these more mature Christians talked. Very often the talk was just good-humoured storytelling of their trips and experiences, with lots of laughter interspersed. Even a small, illiterate "chipmunk" like Amos could not help but be a bit broadened by such contacts.

Amos was not accepted for baptism that year, however, as his work was so unsatisfactory. It was pointed out to him that if he really believed in his heart he was saved *then*, but that new *life* always manifests itself sooner or later, and that for the sake of those watching the church, we felt that we wanted to delay his baptism until his life more nearly matched his profession.

At the end of one month of careless work, after giving the wages to each servant I went to my room, but soon was surprised at the appearance of Amos who, with a crimson face, held out his hand to give me back his money.

"I don't want it, Ma-Ma," he said with much embarrassment. "I don't deserve it." I nearly fell over with the shock. It was the first sign of a conscience he had ever shown. Trying quickly to seize such a grand opportunity, I pressed the wages back on him, and gave him a talk on it being required in stewards that a man be found faithful, and told him that mere money will not repay the cost of faithless service.

Amos was meeker and nicer for quite a few weeks after that but gradually the old spunkiness and carelessness would return. Nevertheless, his books became very precious to the laddie; he began to take them out to the herding with him, and studied constantly. Gradually too, he began to pray in public, and a year or two later, Luke passed him for baptism.

It was in 1942, I think, that Amos decided to leave us. By that time he had saved enough money from his wages to buy a small farm and set up for himself. His blind mother and sister also lived with him and I was glad to see him ambitious to become something. I knew that he would have to work far harder on the farm than he did for us, and probably make less money, but he would be growing into a useful member of the community, so we gave him our blessing, and he left us.

Little goatherd! He had developed one of the truest and sweetest tenor voices in the whole church. Maybe when I get to heaven I shall see my once vicious little Chipmunk, with transformed, radiant, face, glorifying God among the choristers there.

ROMEO AND JULIET

It was in 1939, while visiting villages on the west bank of the Salween, that we came to one called Runaway Horse Ascent. In the little chapel there we were attracted to a sweet young girl, obviously the most spiritually-minded among the women. On inquiry we were told that she was going through a trial. One of the young men had proposed to her and she wished to accept him, but there was an ancient feud between their families, and the parents of each side bitterly refused to let the marriage take place.

"Then we must call them Romeo and Juliet!" I laughingly said, and we henceforth referred to them by those names.

Their love had persisted, and their parents' bitterness had also persisted, but Juliet said she would say *yes* to no one but Romeo. I turned to take a good look at this lad who had won such a loyalty of affection. He was not attractive. True, there was an honesty and earnestness in his eyes and a strength in the ruggedness of his face, but there was also an ugly tubercular gland on his neck.

Our first contact with Romeo left an impression on us that he was but one among many. We saw that he was manly and honest but so were (and are) many of his neighbours. One does not notice a pebble much at first.

A year passed; that winter we had spent at Village of the Three Clans, and on our way back to Oak Flat, an accident occurred which drew Romeo to our attention. Again it involved a horse-riding escapade, but not with trusty old Jasper. In descending the canyon from Three Canyons, we had met with a raging stream whose bridge was broken. Jasper and Jessie could not ford such a torrent, nor could they be expected to cross on the one or two wobbling planks which were left, and over which we ourselves had to cross, so from there on we all had to walk. After many miles, at noon the next day, we met Romeo's uncle, who pressed us to stay at his village that night.

"Only if you will get a horse for Ma-Ma to ride up the hill," said our Lisu. She's tired walking; you should not ask her to climb to your house." Thereupon the old man gave up his animal to me, but it was much smaller than Jasper. Halfway up the slope it suddenly jerked back, missed its footing, and fell over backwards with me still in the saddle. My head just missed striking a sharp rock, but my ankle was badly sprained and I had to be carried into Romeo's little shanty. There I was introduced to his sister, a sweet-faced girl about twenty years old, who was full of sympathy for me. She gave me the best bed they had, and set in to cook something for me to eat. The house was a model of neatness and cleanliness.

"I'm awfully sorry Ma-Ma's foot hurts so," she said as she worked, "but it is all in the Cross, isn't it? There must be suffering if there is to be blessing. And none of ours is to be compared to what our Lord went through for us."

I turned and looked at her. She was talking as

naturally as any other Lisu lassie would have
about where she found her firewood, but her
thoughts were those of a mature Christian! I have
never met a Lisu girl of her youth who was so
acquainted with the deeper things of God! In silent
amazement, for she talked on as she worked, I got
my foot into an easier position, then said, "Will
you tell me, little girl, how you became a
Christian?" Her answer ran like this:

"It was about six years ago whenTeacher Andrew was in these parts. Brother [Romeo] and I
both decided at the same time to leave devil
worship and to trust God. But father bitterly
opposed us; he said he would take away our share
of his land when we refused to worship the
demons and went on praying and studying the
Books, so he thrust both Brother and me out of his
house. Mother was dead, but uncle, here, had
turned Christian and he said he would let us live
on his land if we would help him in his farm work
until we could clear a farm for ourselves. We had
to work hard" - her hands were calloused and
rough - "but oh, we were free to worship God, and
Jesus has been so precious to us! We've been very
happy in this little house, and when Father
married again, we moved over here. Of course we
go over and help him now and again, when his
farm work is heavy, but we come back here to live.
We have peace here." She lifted such a bright,
serene face to mine, that I loved her on the spot.
Romeo was away from home. He had heard of the
missionary hospital in Burma where Thomas had
been helped, and where they did not ask for fees
from Christian Lisu, so he had taken all the savings
of his and his sister's (gladly given) to pay his road

expenses and had gone off to see if they could heal his tubercular glands.

The next morning, when it was time to leave, I found that Romeo's sister was one of our porters. "Oh, it's all right, Ma-Ma," she said brightly. "I am accustomed to carry heavier loads than this, and the village men are not free to go today."

When we finally parted, I had a picture on my heart of a clean young soul, determined to follow her Lord wholly no matter what the suffering. Why had not someone told me there was such a girl in those parts? Were there many more like her that I had never heard of? Was her brother, Romeo, as fine as she? "Yes," said the Lisu; "the two of them are just the same. They are good and earnest."

The next winter we took our trip to Stockade Hill and the south. I believe it was on the way down that we met Romeo on the road, coming home, fully healed. A broad, open-faced young fellow, we just sensed trustworthiness, and manliness, as we looked at him.

"No; they did not charge me a cent," he answered. "They even paid me, because I worked for them carrying water for the hospital....Yes, thank God, the gland is healed. Go in peace, Ma-Ma!"

We had to part, he going north and we to the south. I thought pleasantly of the joy of the little sister waiting to welcome him back, and of sweet Juliet's shy pleasure that her one-and-only was now free from the disagreeable sore on his neck. They would see one another in chapel, and sometimes on the mountain trails, perhaps. Then our own journey commanded our attention.

Months passed. A year or so passed. We were back at Oak Flat discussing the possibility of a girls' Bible school. "There is one girl I want to have—Romeo's sister," I said to the Lisu teacher conversing with me.

"Oh, Ma-Ma, don't you know?" he said, amazed at my ignorance. "She is dead! When Romeo got home from the hospital she was ill with a fever, and she never recovered."

"Oh," I cried, sitting back, heart-broken, "why didn't someone tell me?"

There was silence. The Lisu were puzzled at my interest. There are hundreds of girls in the Lisu church; some die every year. One cannot report everything. These white people take the strangest fancies! Romeo's sister was a good girl, but not very able at singing or writing—big things in the Lisu man's eyes. Why be so interested in *her*?

But Ma-Ma was obviously interested in that family, so they replied: "Perhaps you don't know, Ma-Ma, that Juliet is dead, too? She died before Romeo's sister did. Lots of people died from that epidemic of typhus."

Oh, poor Romeo! I was speechless. *Lest I should have sorrow upon sorrow*—the words pressed themselves in upon my numbed feelings. By this time my thoughts had stirred the group around me and all were quiet, thinking of the tragic grief of one young life—of the Bitter Wind that had blown upon one small Nest.

"How is Romeo? If I had only known, I think I would have tried to go and see him," I said. He lives across the river and about two days' journey from House of Grace, which is a long way if there is not an important reason for going.

"Oh, he's all right. He's living alone in their little hut. He does not complain, and he goes to church regularly. But his neck has started to suppurate again. It certainly is hard for him." Again a silence. "I think he's going to try to come to RSBS," said one. From then on, Romeo was definitely on my daily prayer list.

And in April, 1943, he came. His tubercular glands had inflamed, and as that disease is infectious, and the Lisu sense this and fear it, it was arranged that Romeo sleep alone and cook his own food separately. It was a joy to teach him, and his mature, experienced mind simply licked up the truths of the Word. That year we had tried splitting up the RSBS into three periods of one month each, so in August he promised to return and join us again. After all had dispersed to their homes, at the end of the April study, word gradually filtered through to us that Romeo had begun teaching his fellow villagers every night, and that they had built a little mud chapel.

August saw Romeo gather with us once more for further study, and during those few weeks God gave us a revival such as we had seldom experienced. Our little son, Daniel Kreadman, was born on August 1, so I was not able to teach that session, but the students would often come after classes and talk with me. When they spent one whole night in prayer, I was awake most of the time and with them, of course, in spirit. By the time the school closed I was up and around, and one day I had a talk with Romeo alone.

Of course he had been much on my heart. By that time our own China Inland Mission Hospital at Tali had been opened, so I wrote to them and told them of Romeo, and asked if they would take him in and treat him free of charge, in exchange for simple duties like carrying water. Their affirmative answer had just come, so with much joy I told Romeo of the new opportunity for healing.

"Thank you, Ma-Ma," he said, but without display of any great thrill. He hesitated a moment, then said slowly, "I don't think I will go, thank you."

"But, Romeo, it would mean healing for you!" His noble face was lifted up and had a faraway look in his eyes. Quietly he said, "I do not despise their kindness, nor yours, Ma-Ma. Please thank them for me. But it is this way. I believe this sickness of mine is aggravated by lack of nourishing foods, such as you white people can get. As long as I stayed near a hospital it would be better. I came home to my native diet and the old trouble came back again. So if I want to stay healed, I must stay all my life near a hospital."

Here his eyes came back from the far distance and looked straight at me. "Ma-Ma, it was good for my body, being in the Burma hospital, *but it was not good for my soul!*"

"I know. I know," I said sadly. I had been told that the native nurses there had tempted him constantly.

"And where in Chinaland would I get *food for my soul* like we have been having these past few weeks?"—and his arm pointed out to the little Bible School House up the hill from us. "No, Ma-Ma. Many thanks to them, but I will just stay here—" his eyes flooded with tears, but on his face there was a light I have never forgotten. "Yea, though my life be now at a point to be shed as wine over the burnt sacrifice—still I rejoice" *(Phil. 2:17; Arthur Way)*.

I knew he meant to give what remained of his

life to the service of God, and I stood silent, thrilled, yet with tears.

His disease was too dreaded by the Lisu to admit of a travelling ministry among them. He would not have been welcome in many homes, so he specialized on his own village. In the daytime he worked his little farm as he had strength; in the evening he taught all who would come. His village, and more especially the Village-of-Wheat-Level above it, had been notoriously "rotten" (to use the Lisu word.) Nazareth never had a more hopeless reputation. "Can any good come out of Wheat Level?" has been the cry, with tears, from its Lisu pastor's heart. But as Romeo taught a wonderful little group began to collect around him. A young girl whom we named Leah-the-second came two years in succession to our Girls' Bible School, and fine young boys came from Romeo's group to our Boys' Bible School.

Now, if I were a fiction-writer I would stop there. I do not fear the truth myself. I know the God behind it. But when God's providences take an unexpected turn, shallow thinkers make shallow and dishonouring remarks. One would expect Romeo's offering to have been "crowned with success." But God does not always deal so with His loved children. In His Word, one of the pictures which has so deeply moved me is that of Paul at the end of his course, aged, alone, in prison, writing his very last letter to faraway Timothy. He, earth's noblest, standing at the judgment seat of earth's vilest (Nero); and not only that inexplicable paradox, but the saint in his old age, after a life simply poured out for Christ, has to write. "You know that everyone in the province of Asia has deserted me." (2 Tim. 1:15). The work of his lifetime, apparently, lost. And also "At my first defence, no one came to my support, but everyone deserted me." Desertion, seeming failure, and the rattle of Nero's chain on his wrist. That is the way Paul's life ended to the shallow onlooker. Time has proved that what *seemed* like an ill-reward, has really been a wonderful reward. No one doubts now that Paul's reckless giving to his Lord was recompensed, and neither did he doubt, even under those seemingly contradictory circumstances. "But the Lord stood at my side," he wrote on. "I have...fought the *good* fight....Now there is in store for me the crown." God's *near ones* know His faithfulness.

As we were packing up to come home on furlough, a letter arrived from Romeo. It stated tersely that Leah-the-second and A-fuh (one of the boys) had sinned. It was a heartaching disappointment, but my biggest ache was for Romeo himself. He had so hoped to be a fruitful servant to his Lord. I quickly wrote back a little note of comfort. He answered with a word message which thanked us for our love, and said that he was getting weaker physically, but would go on teaching. We left the canyon, and a few months later Romeo's trials were ended for ever.

> Wait for the light and it will surely come; for even if our Heavenly Father should, in our last hours, put us to bed in the dark, we shall find it morning when we awake.–*Spurgeon*.

Morning. And *Jesus!*...Juliet!...Sister! "Jes' a little pebble"...Will his Lord say that?

THE MISSING LINK

Two days' journey to the north of Romeo's little home, the mountain ravines become truly abysmal. The Lisu there are unspeakably degraded. The strength of Satan seems unconquerable. That territory we call The Heathen Patch because it is a patch of heathenism between two areas which have largely turned Christian. For many years evangelists and prayer-partners have thrown their labours and prayers against it, only to be seemingly thrown back. Of late years the edges have started to crumble very slightly.

One day in 1943 I was handed a letter from the young evangelist in charge of that district. "Ma-Ma," he wrote, "one of the converts up here is coming to study at the April Bible School session. His name is Chi-lee. Pray for him."

That school was Romeo's first school with us, too. But of all the students expected, I was most interested in seeing our first scholar from The Heathen Patch. On assembling day his teacher proudly brought him up to shake hands. I think I must let the circular of that month describe him.

Then from farther in the deep ravines comes Chi-lee. I wonder what you would think of him? Transplanted just as he is into your parlour, you would doubtless come to the conclusion that the Missing Link had at last been found! A mop of coarse black hair chopped off without regard to order, low brow, small eyes, shapeless wide-spreading nose, protuberant jaw, dirty white garments like potato sacking, and forever scratching himself hither and yon—not fleas this time, but the itch.

"Can he read?" I asked his teacher after shaking

hands. (Wouldn't it be awful if a missionary were
the one to find the Missing Link!) "Yes, read and
write," answered his sponsor proudly. Well, that
was hopeful. Evolution monkeys can't do that.

I was preparing to teach Peter that year, and as
we had a staff of only three, we could not grade
the school. When I stood up before them, there was
Luke's intelligent face, and right beside him the
Missing Link, blinking his small eyes at me
hopefully. I had a sinking feeling for a moment.
Then inwardly I thought, *Well, I cannot hold up the
whole class for the sake of one or two. I'll just have to go
ahead, and the dear Link will have to lope along after us
as best he can.*

Chi-lee listened well, but when it came to examinations he did not get a pass. But what did that
matter? He was the first student from The Heathen
Patch, and after a decent haircut, a lesson in
washing his clothes, and sulphur ointment to
conquer the Unmentionable, he really looked
amazingly different. That was quite satisfactory
progress for just one month's study! He himself
was full of joy, and testified to blessing, so we
parted happily.

"Be sure you come again and study in August,
Chi-lee!" we called out.

"I sure will, Ma-Pa, Ma-Ma; pray for me! Stay
behind prayerfully!" and he and his party were
over the hilltop and out of sight.

There is no mail in the canyon. Letters do not
come unless someone is coming on business, and
can take them. Two months passed before I got a
letter from that district. It was from his Lisu
teacher and announced, "Chi-lee has gone back to

God," the Lisu expression for *dead*. I could not believe my eyes. Then earnest investigation discovered this.

On return to his home, Chi-lee had gathered together the young people of his village, and started to teach them what he himself had learned. The heathen were furious.

"It isn't enough that you yourself go to the White Man, and learn this doctrine that makes our demons angry at us," they railed, "but you must bring it back, and start teaching it here! Stop, or we'll kill you!"

But Chi-lee went on teaching. Then one day his house was burned to the ground; he lost simply everything. His father, afraid, refused him shelter, so he was driven into the wild jungle to live under a shelter of boughs and branches which he roughly put together. From there he wrote me of his trial, but the letter did not reach me until it was too late. The handwriting was so neat I could hardly believe he had written it himself, but his teacher said he had. The Lisu evangelist was far away at the time. Chi-lee's letter expressed no regret that his witness had cost him so much—he just stated the above facts and asked us to pray for him. But before his plea reached us, he had died from the malignant malarial mosquitoes lurking in the long grasses of the wild mountainside.

Chi-lee was fruit from our Heathen Patch territory. But there are many more great areas, and there are still other whole tribes which have never yet heard of the gospel of the grace of God. I know of one area of the Lisu tribe, about two weeks' journey from our Lisu, where live thousands of people. Some of them heard this wonderful doctrine was being preached out in Chinaland, and a little party made the trip of two or three days' journey to that missionary lady and asked her to come to tell them also. *That was ten years ago*. Ever since then, that lady (now over sixty years of age) has been trying to find someone to go to those Lisu, and up to this date no missionary has ever been resident among them. (Several made trips at various times, and report that the district truly is there and the Lisu number thousands.)

Ten years they have waited. Do you think that when they called for gospel messengers, God did not respond? It could not be. He gave His most precious Son that *all* might know and receive eternal life. I think that man did not respond. It costs something to leave loved ones and the comforts of civilization. I believe that *each generation* God has "called" enough men and women to evangelize all the yet unreached tribes of the earth. Why do I believe that? Because everywhere I go, I constantly meet with men and women who say to me, "When I was young I wanted to be a missionary, but I got married instead." Or, "My parents dissuaded me," or some such thing. No, it is not God who does not call. It is man who will not respond!

Our dear Missing Link is in heaven, and took a little fruit along with him, too. I am sure his one talent received a "Well done!" from his Master. But I am wondering what God is going to say to this *other kind of Missing Link*—the Link missing from His chain of witness to the uttermost parts! "My flock lacks a shepherd and so has been plundered and has become food for all the wild animals and...my shepherds did not search for my flock but cared for themselves rather than for my flock" (Ezek. 34:8).

Satan's stronghold towers up triumphantly. The awful abyss gapes wide beneath them. The Sharp Winds from the Bitter Height are still blowing. Oh, will you not help point out to the terrified little Nestlings, that behind them is the Cleft of the Rock, so close, so sheltering, but so *unseen* unless you and I go to them?

I S O B E L
KUHN

IN THE ARENA

OM
publishing

CONTENTS

Explaining the Title

1. Obstacles 1
2. Uncongenial Work 22
3. Secret Choices 28
4. Crossed Nature 35
5. Frustrations 44
6. Extinguished Candle-flames 70
7. Small Harassments 118
8. Taut Nerves 144
9. Seeming Defeat 158
10. Between the Scissors' Knives 182
11. Stranded at World's End 195
12. Dread Disease 218

EXPLAINING THE TITLE

1940: We were missionaries on the China-Burma border, and had just received word that, owing to new dangers from the Japanese war, our mission was not allowing school-children, whose parents lived far away, to go home for the holidays. This meant that our Kathryn, who was in the China Inland Mission school at Chefoo, would not be able to reach us. As it was more than a year since she had seen her parents, it was decided that I try to reach her. This meant travel on the Burma Road. And at one place it meant that I had to thumb a ride with a Chinese truck. I would, of course, pay for my passage, but this was the only way of procuring a vehicle at that time and place.

So that raw November day saw me standing in the middle of the road, holding up my thumb to a Chinese driver, who was careening merrily along toward me. I have always felt that womanly women did not do such things, and only desperate necessity would ever have made me willing. But a mother who wants to reach her child will go through much, so there I was, holding up my thumb to this Chinese young fellow, who drew his truck to a standstill and grinned at me. We bargained for a seat, and he doubtless never dreamed that this drab, middle-aged, white woman was cringing with humiliation inside. But I was. Reasonable or not, I have never forgotten that flush of shame.

Once quietly installed in the truck, I talked in my heart to Him who has always been my refuge. "Lord, why do I have to be put in such situations as this?" And immediately the words came: *For I think that God hath set forth us ... last ... for we are made a spectacle unto the world* (1 Cor. 4:9 KJV).

A *spectacle* — that was just how I had felt. But it would never have been necessary, if I had not become a missionary to a primitive people in those back-of-beyond places. So it was, indirectly, for Christ's sake, and the thought comforted me.

As I had to spend many hours just seated in the truck as the trip continued, I had plenty of time to ponder. It might seem absurd to some to appropriate such a wonderful verse to oneself for such a paltry trial as a few minutes of humiliation. Obviously Paul was referring to the terrible Arena experiences of his day, when Christians were thrown to the wild beasts to make a Roman holiday. And yet, as Amy Carmichael points out, our Lord stoops to our small cries as well as to our great ones.

I had cried to Him and that verse had flashed back to me like an answer. "A spectacle — for Him." Was I willing?

Through the several years which followed, years of war strain and danger, this thought kept returning to me. The different trials of us Christians of the twentieth century are like so many platforms in the world's Arena of today. The unbeliever looks on at our struggles and is only impressed or influenced if he sees the power of God working there. The purpose of the Arena experience is not for our punishment; it is that God might be revealed.

George Matheson had an Arena experience, and because of this impending calamity his fiancee broke their engagement. That alone would not make him a spectacle. But the comforting power of his God came down upon him at that dark hour, lifted him to spiritual vision, and caused him to write:

> O Love, that wilt not let me go,
> I rest my weary soul in Thee;
>
> O Light, that followest all my way,
> I yield my flickering torch to Thee;
>
> O Joy, that seekest me through pain,
> I cannot close my heart to Thee;
>
> O Cross, that liftest up my head,
> I dare not ask to fly from Thee;
> I lay in dust life's glory dead,
> And from the ground, there blossoms red,
> Life that shall endless be.

That spectacle of the brilliant, soon-to-be sightless young man, forsaken by his earthly love, yet bathed and upheld in Christ's, has halted many a sinner in his way. George Matheson's blindness has revealed God to many another. It was not given to punish Matheson. It was allowed to manifest the power of God to bring blessing to the world.

So God taught me through the years to view my own trials as platforms in today's Arena. I thought this concept was original with me, but one day my husband found that Hudson Taylor had formed the same opinion many years ago. He said: "Difficulties afford a platform upon which He can show Himself. Without them we could never know how tender, faithful, and almighty our God is." I found it so too.

From a bed of sickness I have had time quietly to review my life, and as I gazed, it seemed that my most valuable lessons have been learned on these platforms. How often I have failed Him, I do not like to think. But of His tenderness and faithfulness there was never an end. As you read, I pray that you may not focus attention on how dark the trial, but rather on the power of God that was manifested there, and *the emergence into light.*

Chapter 1

OBSTACLES

"IF you go to China, it will be over my dead body. I will never consent," was my mother's bitter remark.

I sat with my mouth open, staring at her in aghast silence. My dear mother, who had first taught me to love the Lord Jesus, who had been president of the Women's Missionary Society in the Canadian Presbyterian church for as long as I could remember, who had opened her home to the China Inland Mission for prayer meetings. My dear mother, who was all that, to be so bitter because her daughter felt called of God to be a missionary?

"If you want to do Christian work, that is fine. You could be a YWCA secretary here in Canada. That is quite a respectable position. But a foreign missionary! Only those who cannot find work to do at home or who are disappointed in love go to the foreign field," Mother continued, bitter in her opposition.

Again my mouth fell open in utter amazement. Such an appraisal of a foreign missionary call had never entered my head before. Could it be true?

It was 1924, and I had just returned from ten wonderful days at The Firs conference in Bellingham,

state of Washington. Foreign missionaries had been
there, including J O Fraser of the China Inland
Mission, who had told us how he had opened the
Lisu tribe of the China-Burma border to the Gospel.[1]
What had taken him to China? Lack of a job?
Disappointment in love? At the moment I knew
nothing of Mr Fraser's brilliant career at London
University, and I knew nothing of his private life.
But I brushed both motives aside as absolutely
incongruous. If I could know God as J O Fraser did —
if my life could be as sweetly, powerfully fragrant
with Christ as his was — I would let people attribute
these spurious motives to me if they wanted to! I had
never heard of him or his Lisu tribe before, but after
ten days of watching him and listening to him, I was
thoroughly convinced that he was one of God's great
men. I was to learn later (and how it thrilled me!) that
many of the wisest and saintliest of our times also
thought that J O Fraser was outstanding in his
generation. I was only a young girl, with just a girl's
experience of life, but I knew I had touched true
greatness when I met J O Fraser.

But there was also Dorothy Bidlake — she had
been at that conference too — a missionary candidate
going out for the first time. Why? Because she could
not get work at home? That was not true. She was a
successful secretary in the business world. Disappointed in love? Well, she surely had gotten over
it, if that had been the compelling motive. Pink-
cheeked, dimpled, blue-eyed Dorothy simply sparkled with vivacity and fun. No pining away around
her! She was enjoying every moment of life — and

---

[1]The story of this conference is told in *By Searching*, Volume I of
Isobel Kuhn's autobiography.

not forgetting who gave it. Every memory of our times of relaxation between meetings brought a grin — how I had enjoyed Dorothy!

"No, Mother." I had weighed the evidence, and I spoke with conviction. "That is not true in all cases, whatever it might have been in some."

"Well," wailed Mother desperately, "but you would be an object of charity! Just think of people passing the hat around for *my* daughter! I could never take the disgrace of it."

For the third time I was utterly astonished. What an interpretation to put on people's giving to the Lord's work on His far-flung battle line! And this from the president of the Women's Missionary Society! I myself had newly found the Lord, and giving to His service that others could have what I now enjoyed was a sweet joy to me. That it should be patronized and called *charity* filled me with resentment. I was too young to realize that my mother was deliberately exaggerating in order to dissuade her only daughter from leaving her side. But I fear there are too many church members who *do* have that view of giving to missions. So I would just like to record here that a gift to foreign missions with such a background motive is to me like offering a heap of sawdust. And I wonder if it is not also to the Lord! Whenever I receive a gift for personal use, one of the first reactions is joy that now I have some more tithe money to use for Him. The Lord Himself has said: "It is more blessed to give than to receive," and this is true of those who give for love of Him. But I do not know what joy sawdust-givers can get.

Anyway, here was my first obstacle to answering God's call. My mother was adamant and became hysterical if the conversation along this line continued. I was set to obey the Bible, and it said, "Honour your father and your mother." How could I prepare to be a missionary when my mother said it would kill her? And she would never consent.

I went to my father, who had always been an earnest lay preacher and who had offered me to God for China when I was born. Here surely I would find encouragement! But, no.

"I'm willing for you to be a missionary, but I won't help you financially," he said. "You'll have to take up Bible study somewhere. You might just as well learn to trust God for your finances *now*. Better learn such difficult lessons in America than in China. If God wants you to go, He will provide the funds apart from me. I'm not giving you a cent, so don't expect it, dear."

Of course the money had been a big obstacle when I first realized that to become a missionary I would need Bible training. Although I had been school teaching for more than a year, I had just finished paying off my college debt and so had no bank account. But I had enrolled as a night student at Vancouver Bible School and was working toward my goal as well as I could. It would of course take years to graduate from night school, and with the impatience of youth I longed to be through study and on my way to China — longed to begin my lifework!

But by 1924 God had already wonderfully overcome the money obstacle. It was the kind of experience you read about in storybooks, so I had to pinch myself to believe it had really happened, and that it had happened to me.

It was at The Firs conference of 1923 that, under the appeal of Mrs Edna Whipple Gish from South Gate, Nanking, China, I had actually surrendered my life for foreign service. In the school year that followed I had enrolled in evening Bible school and, realizing how long it would take, I had begun to pray that God would help me in this matter. Without money how could I get Bible training quickly? My parents had moved to Victoria, and I was boarding in Vancouver while teaching in the Cecil Rhodes School. I had no Christian young friends whatever (God gave me a stern but enriching lesson that year in His ability to meet loneliness). The only person with whom I could ask fellowship in prayer in this matter was a middle-aged lady missionary, retired from Formosa because of asthma. She came about once a week to pray with me and encourage me to go on in the Lord. Her name I forget — let us call her Miss F—.

In the spring of 1924 Miss Marjorie Harrison, a talented young candidate, arrived at the China Inland Mission Home in Vancouver. The eldest daughter of Dr Norman B Harrison, author and Bible teacher, Marjorie had looked forward to going to China for years and had saved her earnings so that she might be able to pay for her own outfit and passage. None of us expected to hear that this wonderfully gifted Christian worker would be turned down by the CIM Council, but her medical examination had found her far too delicate to stand pioneer life in the Far East. The CIM knew from experience that one who had bad headaches at home would find them much intensified out in China.

Marjorie took the blow like the fine little soldier she was. For years she had lived, worked, aimed, and thought of China as her lifework. This was a shattering blow. But alone in her bedroom, after the news had been broken to her, she knelt down and made a further renunciation to Him whom she loved and served. "Oh Lord," she prayed, "this money I have saved for my outfit and passage — I dare not take it back. Will you help me to find someone to go to China in my place? I will use it for that one." No one but the Lord knew of that offering of a sweet savour, and Marjorie herself had no idea how He would work to show her who was to go in her place. But she had offered. She had accepted this disappointment as from Him, and when the supper bell rang she went down quietly and took her place at the table.

Now in the Lord's arranging, Miss F— was a guest at the table that evening. She was the only person in the city who knew I was praying for funds to take Bible training in order to go to China. As the conversation perhaps touched on candidates and China, Miss F— exclaimed involuntarily, "I wish Isobel Miller could go to Bible school!"

Marjorie looked up. She had met me at The Firs conference in 1923. I was modestly dressed, and she knew I was earning a teacher's salary. She had never thought that I lacked anything.

"Why can't Isobel go?" asked Marjorie quietly. No one present knew the thought that was springing up in her heart.

"She hasn't the money," announced Miss F—. "She had a college debt to pay back, and so could not save anything. She wants to go to China, you know."

Marjorie said nothing — she was always one who did not let her right hand know what her left hand did. But after supper she inquired for my phone number, called me up, and asked me to come over and see her.

I was delighted. I had not even known that Marjorie was in the city! Merely anticipating a joyous time of fellowship with one my own age whom I had not seen for a long time, I raced happily over to the CIM home and fell on Marjorie's neck.

Soon we were alone in her bedroom and she was unfolding to me the events of that day in her life, not telling me, however, of her prayer.

I was amazed. Marjorie Harrison to be turned down by the CIM? Why, of course it must be a mistake! It could not really be a final decision! All the ignorant impetuosity of youth tumbled over my lips. I was indignant, then brokenhearted for her. I wanted to storm, to go and see someone and make him change his mind, to *do something*. But Marjorie only smiled.

Then she told me of her prayer, of Miss F—'s innocently supplying the answer, and said, "So I feel the Lord has indicated that you, Isobel, are the one whom I am to send in my place. And as you are not ready to go, I will use my passage money to send you to Bible school, if you will let me."

I was dumbfounded. Not once had I foreseen such an outcome. I suppose I tried to refuse it. To use dear Marjorie's hard-earned pennies that were to have taken her to China — this would be sacrilege. And yet I had been praying for the Lord to open a way for me to train to go out as a missionary, and here was a door almost miraculously open! Dare I refuse? Was this not the hand of the Lord?

"I don't have enough money to put you through, Isobel," said Marjorie. "I would like you to go to Moody Bible Institute in Chicago. Now I have enough to pay your train fare there and your board for the first year. I have not enough to pay your way back, nor any for pocket money — your clothes, car fare and such. You would have to trust the Lord for all that."

Well, that seemed simple. If the Lord could work so wondrously to help me the first big step, I could surely trust Him for the second and third steps.

"That is all right, Marjorie," I answered. "My biggest obstacle is my mother. She may not consent, and the Bible says to honour your parents." And so we talked together, each of us awed and blessed by the revelation of the hand of our God so fresh upon us.

It was an excited Isobel that went home that night to her lone room in the house where she boarded. I was very much awed — two girls in that big city, each not knowing the other was there: one praying to be guided as to whom to choose to go to China; the other praying for money to train to go. And God connected them by dear Miss F—.

Then Marjorie, herself a graduate of the Bible Institute of Los Angeles, had selected Moody for me. I would never have done that. A staunch Canadian, I would have chosen Toronto Bible College, if the newly opened Vancouver Bible School had been considered too small. Why Moody? So far away! Neither Marjorie nor I knew of the existence of a young man named John Kuhn. Much less did we know that he was already there. How very important it is to obey the Lord, *step by step*! We cannot know how much may hinge on one single step. The whole course of a life might be changed by just a step.

My parents, of course, were in Victoria, and I do not remember whether I wrote them my wonderful news or waited until holiday time which would give an opportunity for a face-to-face talk. Whichever it was, I was totally unprepared for my mother's excited and bitter opposition. Accept money from.

Marjorie? Why, that was *charity*! Her daughter to live on charity! Then came those amazing concepts of foreign missionaries and their support which are recorded at the beginning of this chapter.

I was in a dilemma. I had surrendered my life to the Lord and was earnestly desiring to obey Him faithfully. I felt He had called me to the China Inland Mission. (I wanted to work with a group who proved God daily as Hudson Taylor had done.) I had prayed for an opportunity to train for His service, and He had so wonderfully answered. But my mother? His Word said to obey your parents. I was too young a Christian to know that when God's Word conflicts with man's words, we are committed to obey Him. He tells us to submit to civil authorities (Rom. 13:1, 2). Yet when the Sanhedrin said, "Don't preach," and God said, "Preach," the early apostles did not hesitate to disobey that civil authority (Acts 4:19). And God's blessing was on them.

Now I would like you to watch how tenderly the Lord worked for me in this complicated matter. Not till many years later did He show me that these crises in life may be looked upon as platforms whereon we are tried. Yes, but whereon God's power is manifested "before angels and men," and very particularly *before ourselves*.

Cornelius Vanderbreggen, Jr., once said that Philippians 3:10 — "I want to know Christ and the power of his resurrection and the fellowship of sharing in his sufferings, becoming like him in his death" — is *experienced* in reverse.

1. We are given a situation wherein we choose to act as Christ would, that is, to be like Him in His death.
2. In that choice we shall meet with suffering — but

    unexpectedly discover deep, sweet fellowship with
    Him — the fellowship of His suffering.
3. In that situation His resurrection power will manifest
    itself.
4. The end of the whole matter will be that we have come
    to know Him, oh, so much better.

I was on the platform of obstacles. I had *chosen* to
be conformed to His death. Not to smash through
Mother's life in order to have my own way. Yet I
chose also to obey His call. There was suffering;
Mother's threat that I would go to China only over
her dead body lacerated me. But the third part?
Where was the power of His resurrection? The
money obstacle had been met. It was miraculous in
my eyes. Never had such a thing happened to me in
all my 22 years. But how would He change Mother?
How could He even make her willing for me to go to
Moody — the very first step?

It was the close of the summer of 1924. I had
returned home from The Firs conference, where I had
met Mr Fraser and Dorothy Bidlake, and if it was to
be Moody Bible Institute in the autumn term I must
begin to take action. I must resign teaching, for
instance, at least one month before school opened —
that was required by the school board. I must send in
application papers to Moody Bible Institute — one
did not arrive on the doorstep of an educational
institution and expect to be received immediately.
And I had the feeling that I should know before I
made a final decision whether or not Moody Bible
Institute students could work their way through
school. I had no money for incidentals, not even
enough for one term's car fare. There was no longer
time to write Moody Bible Institute for information

and await a reply, before the deadline when I must resign my position. Why had I been so stupid as not to think of this long ago?

Then came a Friday morning toward the end of July when I remember sitting in the kitchen looking at these difficulties with a feeling of despair. It seemed absolutely impossible that all these obstacles could be removed in time for me to enter Moody in September. To obtain Mother's consent alone was an insurmountable obstacle. How could I find out in time if I could work my way through Moody?

> There is a tide in the affairs of men
> Which taken at the flood, leads on to fortune,

said Shakespeare.

There is a kind of spiritual counterpart of this. When any child of God decides to step out in absolute obedience to the will of God, there will be a frantic effort by the powers of darkness to block him. Obstacles will spring up to hinder and discourage that one. The possibility of obedience will seem more and more hopeless. When things are the blackest and most discouraging is the very time *not to give up*. That kind of namby-pamby surrender will be quickly swamped. To keep looking at our difficulties will also swamp us. We need to look resolutely away from the impossibilities and *to the Lord*. His help will come, though often it cannot break through to us until the last moment. It is very important that we be ready and prepared for action up to the last split second. God does not miss even that split second. He may seem to be delayed, but He will not be too late for the expectant soul waiting in active faith.

That last-possible morning, sitting in the kitchen, with the need for a final decision pressing upon me, I

turned to Christ and in my heart said, "Lord, what
shall I do? If I don't decide this weekend I shall be
compelled to teach this autumn term."

Clear as if spoken came the answer: "Speak to your
mother again and use E—'s going to Moody." Now
my father had forbidden me to mention China or
Bible training to my mother again. Every time I had
tried to broach the subject to Mother she had become
hysterical and would take to her bed weeping and
declaring she was ill. "She is going to become a
hypochondriac if this keeps on," said my father,
"and you are the cause. I forbid you to talk to her any
more about these matters." So even to discuss the
matter of going to Moody seemed hopeless.

Now I must explain the little matter of E—. One of
my mother's "strong weaknesses" was to see me well
married. That is, she had almost a mania for wanting
to see me married to someone with a good education
and social status in life. That very summer I had had
an offer of marriage from one who seemed all Mother
wanted. He was a university graduate, very brilliant,
a fine Christian, felt called to the Lord's work, and
came from an exceptionally fine family. I deeply
respected and admired E—, but somehow just did
not love him. I had not said a final no, for the offer
was a complete surprise, and I had given such a thing
no thought. I myself did not understand why I did
not fall in love with such a fine Christian. But I did
not intend to marry without love. Mother was
indignant and impatient with me. "You are too
sentimental," she declared. "Respect is the best
foundation for marriage," and so on. Wearied with
contentions, I had just avoided mentioning E— at all.
But a few days before this Friday morning I had
received word that E— also planned to go to Moody

Bible Institute that September! I had not told Mother because I was tired of arguing with her. But now the voice had said clearly, "Speak to your mother again and use E—'s going to Moody." Just then Mother walked into the kitchen; so, casual outwardly, but heart beating furiously, I said, "I've just heard that E— is applying to go to Moody this fall. Really, Mother, I don't know why you are so against my going."

She stopped working, thought it over with surprise, then answered, "Who said I was against your going? You can go if you like — you pay your own expenses, that is all. We cannot help you. E— is a very fine young man," with much satisfaction.

I nearly jumped at that. "Mother, do you really mean that?" (How wildly my heart beat!) "Because if you do, I will write and resign from my school job."

"Yes," said Mother calmly. "You can go to Moody if you are so set on it. But I didn't say you could go to China!"

It was just as easy as that! When God's split second had arrived, the door swung open as if on well-oiled hinges. Later on Mother repented this consent, and many a stormy session ensued. But by that time I had already resigned from my teaching position, my bridges were burned behind me, and there was nothing to do but go on. I might mention too that after all, E— did not go to Moody that autumn. His relatives counselled his taking seminary training and at almost the last moment he switched from Moody to a seminary. But at the moment when I had told Mother he was going to Moody, that had been his *bona fide* intention.

Now back to that Friday morning. The obstacle of Mother's consent was gone, but there still remained the question — did Moody Bible Institute allow its students to work their way through school? My faith was not sufficient to allow me to go forward confidently without knowing this beforehand. And instead of scolding me for this lack of faith, the Lord worked wonderfully and indulgently for me.

I was sitting in a chair beside the kitchen table when the thought came, *If only I knew someone in Chicago to whom I could wire this question!* The idea that I could wire the Institute itself never occurred to me. And then a very wonderful thing happened. Suddenly I realized that I was sitting on top of a couple of magazines which someone had left on that kitchen chair. Mechanically I got up and pulled them out from under me, intending to set them in their proper place, when my eye caught a notice printed on the back of the top magazine. It ran:

Mr and Mrs Isaac Page have been transferred to the Chicago area. If anyone wishes to communicate with them, their address is ....

and there lay the full address. It was the back page of a copy of *China's Millions*. If it had fallen straight from heaven I could not have been more startled. Daddy Page! My father's dear friend. Nine years earlier he and his wife had been about to sail for China under the China Inland Mission, and they had taken their last homeside meal in our home. Daddy Page was so full of fun that I had loved him. But as he was saying goodbye, he had placed a hand on my young shoulder and said, "Isobel, I am going to pray that God will send you to China as a missionary!" My first (unspoken!) reaction was, *You mean thing!* I had no intention of going to China and still less of being

a missionary. But Daddy Page went to China, leaving
a very uncomfortable little girl behind.

Years passed, years in which I had plunged into
worldly gaiety and even lost my faith for a while.
Dimly I remembered hearing that Mrs Page's health
had failed, necessitating their return to America.
Where they were I had had no notion — now their
address was right in my hand and it was — *Chicago*.
It was so miraculous and so definitely an example of
"Prayer is the soul's sincere desire, uttered *or*
unexpressed" that I was awed, and to this day have
never lost the thrill of it.

I went immediately to the telegraph office and
wired something like this: IS IT POSSIBLE TO WORK
ONE'S WAY THROUGH MOODY BIBLE INSTITUTE? PLEASE
WIRE COLLECT. ISOBEL MILLER.

Within a matter of hours came the answer: YES,
INDEED. THE INSTITUTE EVEN HAS AN EMPLOYMENT BUREAU
TO HELP YOU FIND APPROPRIATE WORK. HOPING TO SEE
YOU. ISAAC PAGE.

By Monday morning my resignation from schoolteaching was in the post office and that bridge was
burned behind me.

And now Satan got discouraged and left me alone,
do you think? Ah, you do not know him! Dis-
couragement is not allowed in the enemy's ranks —
that is his favourite weapon against human beings!
That last month before I was to sail for Seattle and
take the train to Chicago was the keenest testing of
the whole year.

Mother tried unremittingly to make me change my
mind. My father had gotten into serious trouble
which resulted in litigation. He was roentgenologist
for a noted surgeon, Dr Ernest Hall. An unprincipled
young doctor in the same office building, jealous of

their large practice, hired false witnesses who
charged Father with privately treating two patients,
that is, practising without the surgeon's orders. Such
an offence was punishable by imprisonment or a
large fine. There had been no one else in the office at
the hour Father treated these two, so it was their word
against Father's and Dr Hall's. It had been cleverly
staged. Father's trial was docketed for the morning of
the very day when I must leave for Moody.

Now that year had come word that all Father's
savings, invested in two mining companies, had
been lost. He had lost every cent — there would be
no money to pay a fine. My brother, newly dis-
charged from the army of World War I, was unem-
ployed. That left me as bread-earner in case the
judgment went against Father — so ran my mother's
pleading. I was an ungrateful, unconscionable child
to go off and desert her at such a crisis in family
history, she said, and so on, every day.

This was my suffering on my platform of obstacles.
But the fellowship of the Lord was my daily strength
and bolster. And how wondrously His resurrection
power had worked for me and sustained me! I was
sure, now, that I was in the path of His choice for me,
and the experience of the past month had taught me
that final deliverance might not come until the very
last split second. So I must get ready in faith to go
through the door, so to speak, if it opened at the last
moment. That meant I must allow Marjorie to buy my
rail ticket east. I must arrange my student's visa
papers for entrance to the United States — not to
speak of my application papers. Financially I was
tested. Marjorie sent me my ticket across country, but
after I had paid my head tax I had practically nothing
left for food on the train — three nights and two

days. Well, I figured, If Moses fasted forty days, I could fast two or three. I did not know that I would be asked to pay a month's board in advance as soon as I reached the Institute!

But I was the Lord's child. Levi received no inheritance among the sons of Israel, for the Lord was his inheritance (Deut. 10:9). My first encouragement came from such an unexpected source. I had gone down to the boat to see Mr Fraser sail for China. In a moment when other friends were looking over the ship, Mr Fraser turned to me and said something like this: "I have been keeping two accounts, Miss Miller. One is my personal account and the other is for investing in the Lord's work. I wish to close this second account before I leave America and I find I have a few dollars left. You are going to Moody — I do not know whether you could use them or not."

I was astounded, but recognizing the hand of the Lord in it I said, "Thank you, I can!" This was the beginning of the Lord's largess.

The last painful day arrived. My boat was to leave at half-past two in the afternoon and my father was on trial in court that morning. I had to send my trunk to the boat not knowing the outcome. You can imagine the tension of those last hours. At half-past ten our phone rang. Daddy's voice came over the line, "Praise God! Fully acquitted." The Lord had vindicated my faith.

So I left on the afternoon boat for Seattle, with Mother's weeping face as my last memory. Little did I know that I was never to see her on earth again. (Just here I would like to say that Mother was really a sweet, generous woman. I feel that I failed often to be as tender with her as was her due. I was impatient that she was not more yielded to God's will. I had yet to learn the suffering, when one's affections are nailed to the cross. It was a crucifixion experience for her to be asked to give her only daughter, and she was fighting it. That was not her norm. Her neighbours and friends would all testify to the unselfishness which usually characterized Mother. It is too bad that these pages should mention her only at the time of her greatest weakness and agony.)

Before 1924 closed, Mother was in heaven, all her tears wiped away forever. She died as the result of an operation. Of course her words of prescience recurred to me and overwhelmed me with grief for a few days. Then the Lord Himself caused an old friend of Mother's to write me a letter. This was the gist of it:

"You would like to know, I am sure, that the evening before your mother was to undergo an operation, she wrote me a long letter. In it she told me that in view of the danger of the morrow's surgery she had been reviewing her life. And she said, "I have come to the concusion that all my busy WCTU and Women's Missionary Society work has been but wood, hay, and stubble. *I feel my little girl has chosen the better part in wishing to devote all her life to the Lord.* If God spares me tomorrow I shall try to be different and build with gold, silver and precious stones."

But God saw that the affectionate heart had suffered enough, so He gathered her Home to Himself. But I always felt that God *had* removed the last obstacle and that I went to China with my mother's full consent and blessing.

What a platform! Gladly would I miss the failures and faults of mine that marred its human side. But I still glory in the wonderful revelation of a tender, faithful Saviour, never deserting and never a moment too late.

It may be like an anticlimax to explain how He brought me to Chicago and started me at the Institute with my financial needs — especially the unknown ones — fully cared for, but I would like to record it to His glory.

In Seattle I found many friends waiting to cheer me on my way. And instead of the usual box of candy, *bon voyage* gift, this one and that one slipped me a little envelope with money in it. When at last the train was speeding on its way, I found I had not only sufficient for meals on the trip, but enough to pay my first month's board in advance.

Dr Page met me at the train and took me to the Institute. He waited while I registered and was assigned to my room, then took me for an ice-cream soda, eager to learn how the Lord had worked to answer his prayer of long ago. As I told him, tears of joy ran down his face.

"For nine years Mrs Page and I have prayed that you would be called to China, Isobel, even through all those years when you were going in the opposite direction. I had a church in Penticton for a while. I was there when you and the University Players Club came to town and I saw your name on the billboards as acting in *Mr Pim Passes By*. I sent a note around to the theatre asking to see you but got no answer. But we prayed on."

Although God had foreseen and provided for my first month's board in advance, I was not prepared for Moody's announcement that the first term students are not allowed to take employment. This rather staggered me, for I had need to buy some winter clothes. Chicago winters are much colder than Vancouver's, and my winter clothing was not heavy enough. Following Hudson Taylor's principles, I told no one but just went to prayer about it. When Dr Page asked me how I was getting on, I replied, "I'll not be allowed to work the first term — they say that is the ruling for everybody. I don't yet know what I will do."

His only comment was, "Well, we can pray about it." So the matter was left.

A couple of days later Dr Page came again to see me. "Put on your coat, Isobel," he said. "I've got permission from the dean to take you around the corner. There is someone I want to introduce you to." Wondering what friend of his could be living in that neighbourhood, but still glad for a break in school routine, I ran off gaily for my coat.

Down one block and up one block he led me and — into a bank! Into the manager's room he walked and said to that august personage, "I wish to introduce you to Miss Isobel Miller. Here is $100 to open a bank account for her." I have never gotten over the shock of that moment. I stuttered and stammered and the more confused I was, the more Daddy Page grinned. The matter was taken care of, and out I walked with a bank book!

Of course I remonstrated, but Daddy Page answered seriously, "Your father has given me and mine as much as this and more in years gone past. This is just a small return to him — take it that way." I knew my father did things like that, so I was comforted into accepting it. But I often wondered how a poor China Inland Mission missionary could find $100 to give away all of a sudden like that. Maybe a relative had died and left them a legacy. Some twenty years later when on a furlough I met Dr Page and decided to ask him. By this time, having been a CIM missionary myself for nearly two decades

I knew that that gift was really wonderful. So I reminded him of it and asked where he got it — was it a legacy?

I will never forget how he laughed! He threw back his head and just laughed till he cried. "No, Isobel," he said wiping the hilarious tears away. "I remember it perfectly. We didn't have any legacy. We just emptied our bank account, that was all. We figured that we were old-timers in the life of faith and you were just beginning. It would be easier for us to trust the Lord. A legacy? Oh-ho-ho," and off he went laughing again.

So the obstacles were removed, by deep but cheerful sacrifice on the part of others. It was Marjorie's mother who told me how Marjorie went without new clothes that winter in order to pay my board bill each month, for the outfit money did not last all the first year. The next year I had the full amount to work and trust for. Emergencies came and my adventures with God in the financial realm were just as thrilling as Hudson Taylor's had been. The One who proved Himself a living Saviour to the founder of the China Inland Mission was just as living and faithful sixty years later to a little new trainee. And He will be to anyone who will surrender all to Him and step out in obedience to His call.

Chapter 2

UNCONGENIAL WORK

MOODY BIBLE INSTITUTE is located in an old, crowded district of Chicago to be a witness. Needless to say, great care is taken to protect its young women students, and the Employment Bureau examines the places of work to which the Institute girls are sent. Jobs of course must be part-time and at hours that do not clash with class instruction. This narrows the field of possible employment.

I was assigned as noon-hour-rush waitress in a large wholesale house. This firm had a restaurant for its customers, but I was not sent there. I was sent into the restaurant for its employees — a servant to the servants. The employees' restaurant was decidedly second-class and, as there were about one thousand employees all wanting lunch immediately, rush-hour help was a necessity. The regular waitresses were mostly big women, six feet tall or more. They boasted that they could carry five dinners (from soup to coffee and dessert) at one time. I staggered under two. More than that, there was a shortage of dishes, especially coffee creamers. These latter were so few that there was a continual fight behind the scenes to get possession of them — for we dared not serve an order without them. It was not our work to wash dishes but in order to get possession of a creamer we had to grab a dirty one, wash it, then fill it. This of course delayed us. Every day there was this struggle to get hold of the needed creamers. I once had a manager swear at me and actually kick me because I was slow in filling his order — I was searching for a creamer, that was the only reason.

We all had to wear white uniforms. These were clean every day *but not mended*. The regular waitresses, arriving early, picked out the good uniforms and left the old torn ones to rush-hour girls. Frequently I had to wear one originally intended for one of the six-footers, so of course it came down to my toes and bulged over my shoulders. "You are made a spectacle to all men" was literally fulfilled. With a torn sleeve and apron of nightgown length I was literally a spectacle, but my sense of humour carried me over such a little matter. The inability to carry more than two dinner orders on one tray and the delay caused by the shortage of creamers were of much more concern.

The waitresses and the male cooks were obviously what is called a tough gang. They needed the Gospel if anyone did, but there was never any time to talk! We were truly rush-hour girls. Gradually the other waitresses became friendly, and one big strapping woman in particular used to greet me each day with a thunderous clap on the back and the hail: "How the h— are you today, little girl?" I braced myself when I saw the big hand stretched out to come down! But it was meant for affectionate greeting. I was glad that someone felt kind toward me, and again the ludicrousness of it brought a grin.

In the summer vacation of 1925 I went to my maternal aunt in Canada. But during the summer of

1926 I worked most of that hot season. The weather got very humid and the fumes of the kitchen were nauseating. All year I had worked there and I was tired, so the heat, the smells, and the rush began to affect me physically. There was one hot morning in July or August when I struggled into my uniform praying for strength to get through the two hours. I was feeling ill before I even started into that hot, smelly kitchen where the orders had to be filled.

Then came a moment when I was filling a coffee cup at the big boiler-like tureen. The room began to go around and I knew I was going to faint. I had a vision of falling under the open tureen, the boiling coffee streaming down on my unconscious form, so I gave a quick cry in my heart, "Lord, help me to get the tureen turned off first!" Instantly a most wonderful thing happened. I felt the Lord Himself come and stand behind my left shoulder. He put His right hand on my right shoulder and a tingle shot through me from head to foot. Healed completely, I calmly turned off the tureen and stood for half a second in deep, unspeakable worship and communion with Him. Then He was gone, and I turned to my tray. Not only had the nausea and faintness left, but a wonderful exhilaration thrilled through me. I seemed to fly rather than walk; I was lifted above all my circumstances until it seemed I was an onlooker at my own body in its ill-fitting uniform serving the tables. That exhilaration and physical refreshment lasted for days. I told no one of this experience — it was too intimate, too personal, too sacred to share with anyone.

It was no product of the imagination. I had only cried for strength to turn off the tureen, and my fainting mind certainly never pictured anything more than the mercy to faint where I would not be scalded. But much more had been given. In this uncongenial work he had revealed Himself and He had exhibited the power of His resurrection. More than thirty years have passed, but the blessing of that experience is still one of my rich treasures. Only once again did He come to me in a presence that could be felt, and that was in my early years in China.

I have hesitated to tell of this little experience lest it might stumble others who have never had such a thrilling manifestation. You are no less His because you have not had it. It is now more than twenty years since I myself have known His presence in this way, and yet I know He is still as close to me as He was then, and even dearer to me because I have had thirty more years of proving His love and faithfulness. Whether or not you have had such a manifestation of Him is not important. The important thing is — how are you acting? Are you bitter and resentful that you must live and work under such circumstances? Or are you asking to be conformed to His image, seeking fellowship with Him in this human suffering, watching for His resurrection power to be manifested, confident that you will know Him better when the discipline is past, and to be satisfied with that? The circumstance will pass in time, but the revelation you will receive of Himself, His love, and His power will enrich you forever.

Do not misunderstand me. I did not say you will be a better Christian afterward. I did not even say you would be a stronger Christian afterward. I do say you will be a richer one.

There was a sequel to my uncongenial employment. One day almost at closing time a lady came in and sat down motioning for me to serve her. She was obviously high in the employment of the company and wore expensive rings. I filled her order but had to wait until she finished her meal in order to clear the table. By that time we were alone, and she spoke to me.

"Who are you?" she asked. "I've been watching you for several weeks. Always you are sweet and smiling. And," with a grimace, "I know this place. No one else is happy here — what is your secret?"

I could hardly believe my ears. Here was the opportunity I thought could never come — quiet and leisure to give a clear testimony. Of course I told her that the Lord Jesus had saved my soul and become my life.

"I used to believe that," she answered sadly. "But no woman can go straight in this place." Being on vacation from college, I was in no hurry to return to the Institute. The result was that she once more held out her arms to Him who has vowed never to cast out any soul that comes to Him. She came to see me and enrolled as a student in the evening school. And she gave me a beautiful opal ring for a remembrance.

It would be nice to tell you that *platforms* always result in souls saved, but I have no authority to say that such fruit will be revealed to us. The Word says that we will be a *theatron* (θεατρον) to men and angels. Some of our most painful platforms may have no human witness. In that case we should remember the significant words, *and angels*. I am sure that the suffering of the saints, while its purpose is to teach us more of Himself, to develop and enrich us, also bears fruit in other lives. But that we leave with Him.

Of one thing we can be sure, our Lord is tenderly generous to us, even when we are on platforms of uncongenial tasks. All He needed to do was answer just what I asked — strength to remain standing until I got the coffee boiler turned off. It would have been more than I requested if He had merely strengthened me to stagger through those two hours without fainting. But what a wonderful "abundantly above" He gave! To give me an experience of, as it were, His physical presence, fleeter than thought in coming! To give me that inner exhilaration which lifted me above the hot humid kitchen with its nauseating odours! Observers could see only a perspiring rush-hour girl hurrying through her tasks. They could not see the blessed fellowship with Him which was within. So we may take heart when we are tempted to pity some other child of God who seems to us to be oppressed overmuch. Remember, you cannot see the inner releases the Lord is able to give.

Chapter 3

SECRET CHOICES

A PLATFORM is a very public thing, and a secret choice is an extremely private, invisible thing. How then can we think of the two together? How can there be a platform of secret choice? Well, the θεατρον (*theatron*) of I Corinthians 4:9 is any situation in which the child of God has a struggle. And a great many of these the world never sees nor even learns about. Yet the effect of that struggle often becomes noticeable to men. "Your Father, who sees what is done in secret, will reward you" works in more matters than almsgiving. The incident to be mentioned in this chapter will reveal the compatibility of this chapter's title when the situation is in the hand of the Lord.

Again we return to the days at Moody Bible Institute. I found myself one unit of a large student body — including the evening school I believe the student body numbered one thousand. I was astonished to find that among all those young people gathered together at that time, to study His Word and to train for His service, only about one hundred of them had foreign service in mind! To me it was incomprehensible. Knowing that only a small percentage of those who offer themselves for the foreign field are accepted to go, I felt that every young Christian should at least *offer* to be a foreign missionary — give the Lord a chance to say if He wanted him there or at home. As in the case of Marjorie Harrison, many earnest souls must stay home — they are enough to minister to the home needs. It would be so easy for the Lord to keep them at home; but it is impossible for the Lord to push any out. He has made this rule for Himself — He will compel no man's love or obedience. How can you know He does not want you in the far-flung battle line *if you do not offer*? I still believe that this is the reasonable attitude to take.

Though I found a meagre hundred of fellow students who were like-minded with me in this matter, I did find very choice souls among them. I received more blessing through the devotion and fire of my fellow students at Moody than I did even through my studies. I thank God for them. After graduation we scattered, and many I did not see again for twenty or thirty years. But when we did meet, what a joy to find their passion for Christ as fervent as in student days! And what a thrill to hear from their lips that *the dreams* of student days had been fulfilled by a gentle, kind Master! He had inspired our dreams and His callings had been justified.

But the Institute schedule was a busy one, especially for us who had to work our way through. There came a day when the president of our Student Volunteer band came to me exercised in soul. I was scheduled to speak at our next meeting, and he had a burden to lay upon my heart. "It is so easy, with required hours of Bible reading, to let one's own devotional time slip. And it inevitably leads to

staleness of soul. I feel that some of us are in danger
of drifting into an empty form of relationship to Him,
of missing the vital personal touch each day. Will you
pray, Isobel, and ask the Lord for a solution? And
give us a talk on it next meeting?" I accepted the
burden, and waited on the Lord. I had felt that
danger myself. For certain classes we had to read a
book of the Bible through — perhaps several times.
Why read it again for quiet time? Especially when
leisure hours were at a premium. But reading the
Scriptures for a technical grasp of the general
argument in a book, and reading it as in the Lord's
presence, asking Him to speak a word on which to
lean that day — those were two different things. One
was no substitute for the other. Yet I knew also that
some students were trying to let classwork reading
do for personal quiet time. Deadness of soul was
inevitable.

As I prayed about it, I felt a need to gird up our
loins and form a habit of putting the Lord first each
day. Habit can be a wonderful ally, but it can also be
a formidable foe. We ourselves can choose which
kind of habits to form. My attention was drawn to 2
Chronicles 29:11: "My sons, do not be negligent now,
for the Lord has chosen you (me) to stand before him
and serve him, to minister before him and to burn
incense." Using this text for exhortation, I suggested
our making a covenant with the Lord to spend one
hour a day (for about a year) in the Lord's presence,
in prayer or reading the Word. The purpose was to
form the habit of putting God in the centre of our day
and fitting the work of life around Him, rather than
letting the day's business occupy the central place
and trying to fix a quiet time with the Lord
somewhere shoved into the odd corner or leisure

moment. I had drawn up a paper with the above text and covenant promise, and asked how many would sign with me. I suggested we meet together once a month to confess any failures and to worship the Lord together.

It was a very small meeting, as it happened, and only nine signed that original covenant. I still have that piece of paper, and the reader will be interested to know that one of the nine names was John B Kuhn.

It was never my thought that this covenant become *law*. My thought was merely deliberately to form a habit which would allow the Lord to speak personally to us all the days of our lives. Although only nine signed up that first day, somehow news of it spread, and others began to join. Then — it seems as if some human beings always have to go to extremes — some signed a covenant binding them to this hour a day *for life*. I did not sign it. What about days of illness or emergency, when it might be impossible to keep an hour quietly? There was no need *to vow*; there was only need to *form a habit* of putting God first. The hour, we agreed, could be broken up into two half-hour periods, or any division needed.

The Lord blessed us. Our monthly prayer meetings to testify and encourage one another became times of wonderful fellowship in the Lord. They grew and grew in numbers. Testimonies were often funny. One fellow at a summer camp in desperation got into a canoe and pushed out into the middle of the lake — and had a blessed time. And so on. Needless to say we kindled one another. Ten years later, on our first furlough, we visited the Institute and found that this prayer group was still going on, though no one remembered when it got started or what was the origin. We did not enlighten them, but gloried in the work of the Spirit.

To keep my hour-a-day required planning. At half-past six each morning I was due in the dining room to set tables. I tried getting up at five, but my health began to fail. After various efforts I found I could maintain normal weight if I rose at half-past five. But go where to be alone? My roommate slept through until nearly breakfast time and might resent a light at such an early hour. The only place I could find where I would disturb no one was the cleaning closet! So each morning I stole down the hall, entered the closet, turned the scrubbing pail upside down, sat on it, and with mops and dust rags hanging around my head, I spent a precious half-hour with the Master. The other half-hour had to be found at the end of the day.

This is the background of my platform of secret choices. It was the evening of the Junior-Senior party. I was a Junior and had been asked to lead the devotional with which all such parties closed. I was also on the programme as Grandma in a Dutch scene, off and on all through the banquet. The week before had been so full of work and study that I had not one moment to sit down and prepare a devotional. Work in the restaurant had delayed me, and I arrived at the supper half-hour, hungry, exhausted, and without any devotional prepared. Besides this, I still had half an hour due on my quiet time! After the party we Juniors had to clean up and I would not get to my room till midnight — the day would be gone.

Here was my platform of secret choices. That supper half-hour. (1) Should I go down and eat my supper? (2) Should I skip supper and try to prepare the devotional message? (3) Should I put God first and give that half-hour to Him? The supper bell rang, and my roommate left for the dining room. I stood for a moment irresolute; then, throwing myself on my knees by my bedside I sobbed out in a whisper, "Oh Lord, I choose you!" Then again, as I just lay in His presence too weary to form words, the sense of His presence filled the room. As before, the weariness and faintness all left me. I felt relaxed, refreshed, bathed in His love. And as I half knelt, half lay there, saying nothing, but just loving Him, drinking in His tenderness, *He* spoke to me. Quietly, but point by point, He outlined for me the devotional message I needed to close that evening's programme. It was an unforgettable experience and an unforgettable lesson. *Putting Him first always pays.*

In the exhilaration of that wonder I ran down to the banquet hall (or rather the hall behind it), slipped into my costume, and went through the programme. At the end, when the devotional message was needed, I gave very simply what He had told me during supper hour. Such a quiet hush came over that festive scene that I knew He had spoken, and I was content.

More than twenty years passed. I was home on furlough and visiting the Institute. It was the day of the Junior-Senior party and a group of us were reminiscing. "One Junior-Senior party always stands out in my memory," said one. "I forget who led it but it was a Dutch scene and the devotional blessed my soul. I've never forgotten it." She had indicated the date, so I knew. I was thrilled through and through. Of course I did not spoil it by telling her who led that devotional. In God's perfect workings, the instrument is forgotten. It is the blessing of Himself that is remembered.

This is how *secret* choices can become *public*. The

choice and the struggle are not publicized — but the release of His resurrection power which comes to you on each platform is felt by others, and in that sense there is an audience. We may never know who this "audience" might be, but we do know that He gives us far more than we deserve.

Chapter 4

CROSSED NATURE

NOW that you have read of the wonderful things the Lord did for me, I fear lest some might casually think that I myself must have been a wonderful Christian to be worthy of such blessings. I must hasten to correct this easy error. I was *not* a wonderful Christian but very much "of the earth, earthy." God's blessings are not reserved for those who are worthy; they are lavishly poured out on very unworthy ones, upon those who in their innermost souls are reaching out for Him.

I have pondered the affairs of two men, David and Ahithophel. Once they were close, dear friends. Ahithophel's counsel was so wise — it was like the oracles of God. They went to the house of God together to worship. Then David sinned. Bathsheba was Ahithophel's granddaughter. Oh, what horrible sin — adultery and then the murder of Uriah! No wonder Ahithophel was estranged and angry! Either of those sins would have scandalized him, let alone both. Surely God will bless Ahithophel and not David.

But look beneath the surface. When the prophet Nathan faced David, David repented immediately. "I have sinned," he cried. And from then on, groaning under the punishments which his sins sent him, David still reached out in brokenhearted repentance to the Lord. "Do not cast me from your presence," he cried (Psa. 51:11).

Ahithophel? He became like the elder brother in the parable of the Prodigal Son. He refused to open his heart to God's grace of forgiveness, so his heart became filled with cold fury. He who had despised David's adultery counselled the same sin to David's son. He who had furiously criticized David for taking Uriah's life ended up by taking his own. So man proves he is really no better than the sinner he is so quick to condemn, and whom he refuses to forgive.

If Ahithophel had allowed God to melt his heart in forgiveness, the day would have come when Ahithophel would have seen Solomon, son of his granddaughter Bathsheba, upon the throne of David. And that great-grandson — looking at it from the merely human viewpoint — inherited Ahithophel's own wisdom. God blessed the sinner who opened his heart to correction, and God's blessing was lost to the sinner who closed his heart to the pleadings of grace and refused to forgive.

We do not receive His blessings then because we deserve them, but only when we obey His tender injunction, "Open wide your mouth and I will fill it."

I had a greedily wide mouth; but if it had been wider, I might have received more.

In October, 1928, when I sailed for China, there were eight or ten of us young women who sailed together. And on that ship were Miss Ruth Paxson and Miss Ethel Davis, also going to China. Miss Paxson's book, *Life on the Highest Plane*, was then in manuscript form and she kindly consented to give us girls an hour's Bible teaching every day while the trip lasted. Those were memorable hours! One sentence I never forgot. Standing in front of us, an experienced missionary, she looked into our faces searchingly and said, "Girls, when you get to China, all the scum of your nature will rise to the top." I was shocked. Scum? Was that not a strong word? All of us were nice girls, were we not? Scum? A bit extravagant, surely. And so I was totally unprepared for the revolt of the flesh which was waiting for me on China's shores. The day was to come when on my knees in the Lord's presence I had to say: "Lord, *scum* is the only word to describe me."

I went to China eager and hopeful to be a soul-winner. I was ridiculously, pathetically unprepared for the cost. It is true that I had expected poverty and had even tried to discipline myself for it. While schoolteaching I had chosen a boarding house that was drab and plain, with no rugs or carpets. Fond of chocolates, I decided not to buy any candy for a year at least. This puny "self-discipline" makes me laugh now. And makes me wonder how I could have been so unprepared for the ordinary missionary hardship. I do not know, but it was so.

The China Inland Mission, true to its name, reached out to the unworked interior of that great land, where by far the great majority of unevangelized Chinese were country peasants, poor people who toil and labour in mud hovels and know nothing of the luxuries of hot baths with soap, or frequent change to clean clothing. I had to learn that it costs money to be clean; I had always taken cleanliness for granted, just like sunshine.

And so, after a happy time at language school, I found myself on a country station in a farming district, with thousands of Chinese peasants in all

directions who had never been told that the death of
Christ was for their salvation. What a wonderful
opportunity! In spirit I reached out eagerly toward
them and then — the flesh revolted.

As in all eastern lands, and among our own poor
also, these toiling people had vermin on their
persons, in their homes, and in the dust of their mud
floors. Fleas jumped on me from those floors and
nibbled joyfully. There are some people whom
insects are slow to attack. Others, like myself, seem to
be an open invitation to come and feast! Sitting close
to a country woman, I was likely to carry away a
louse. And when asked to spend a night in these
homes, bedbugs walked out in regiments upon me,
not to speak of the air force — flies and mosquitoes.

Their customs were different. They had no plumbing in their homes, so dogs acted as scavengers. My
first experience of one particular custom so revolted
me that I could not eat my breakfast and had to start a
long journey with an empty stomach.

The food of the Chinese poor is different from that
of the middle classes, and I did not find it palatable at
first. The story of how I learned to eat beancurd is a
family joke now. My husband says, with eyes
twinkling, "You have to cry first — then you learn to
enjoy it!"

And the lack of privacy. I always had a room to
myself at home and unconsciously was fond of being
by myself — a student notion I suppose. To be
thronged with people hour after hour exhausted me
emotionally, and of course a woman cannot bathe
without some kind of privacy.

The constant travelling too was a source of irrita-
tion. I never did like change; I liked to get well rooted
into one comfortable spot and stay there. So the flesh

was offended on every hand, and it revolted.

My husband did not seem to mind these things so I put it down to a different disposition. Insects did not readily attack him; brought up on strong German cheeses, he did not mind if the meat served us had spoiled. He rather liked a tangy flavour! And as for crowds, he loved them. Did not like to be alone! And travelling was nectar to him; he was never happier than when on a trip.

I had been well taught in the truth of Identification with Christ. I knew that these daily irritations and disagreeable things were opportunities to die to the flesh and sin. I frantically reckoned myself dead (Rom. 6:11), still I was hindered. At a God-given impulse to put my arm around some poor old Chinese woman, the flesh would inwardly shriek, "Watch out! You'll get a louse." Everywhere selfishness and self-pity would raise their ugly heads. I knew now that the scum had risen to the surface, and only the Lord could take it away.

It was during my first term of service that Amy Carmichael's books were sent to me. I was thrilled with them, recognized her high standards as Christ's own, but was appalled at my own low level of living. In fact, her books discouraged me, for *she* never seemed to have any faults! This is the reason I am recording this chapter: to register the Lord's patience and faithfulness to one who was not naturally heroic.

Amy Carmichael said quite casually, "Everything personal had gone long ago" — meaning that the self-life was under her feet before she even began her work at Dohnavur. She had terrific battles, but they were with Satan, the Lord's own antagonist. Anything so elementary as selfishness never seems to have troubled her. So I would get discouraged and put her books on the shelf saying. "You're too high for me. I cannot attain that." But they fascinated and lured me. Even when they were shelved the sight of them would send a rapier-thrust into me:

> Let me not sink to be a clod;
> Make me Thy fuel, Flame of God!

That was really what I wanted too — I did not want to be a clod. I would fall on my knees and weep before the Lord asking for His help. And never did I feel myself spurned. He was firm in correcting me but always loving. I have never attained the place where one is beyond the temptations of self. But I want to testify to what God can do to *change* a human being, one that found she was indeed — scum.

I was delighted one day when my attention was drawn to Galatians 2:8: "For he that wrought effectually in Peter ... the same was mighty in me" (KJV). Paul is not discussing victory over self in this verse, but the Lord was when it was pointed out to me! Peter had lots of self-life to battle, and Paul was not entirely without his also. But He that wrought effectually in Peter was mighty also *in me*.

God had to first bring me to the place where I was so exercised in spirit over producing so little fruit for Him that nothing else mattered. Physical comforts did not matter if only souls could be born into His kingdom. Moreover, God brought me to the place where I was willing that the instrument He used be someone else if necessary. I was willing not to be the one used, if only He would permit me to see that souls *were* being born into His kingdom. Shortly after I surrendered that, He swung me into Lisuland where I felt "at home" for the first time in China.

And He even tenderly showed me little ways to make it easier for the flesh. Insect powders helped a bit against those tiny pests, and He showed me other ways to overcome. Some of the changes He wrought in me are even funny. Here is one.

When we were first married we were invited one hot June day to dinner at a poor Christian's home. The flies were innumerable, the hut as usual like a junk shop, and through the open door came the odours of the nearby pigsty. Into such a setting brings mine hostess a dish of large chunks of boiled pork fat! Not a bit of lean. My stomach turned over. "Oh, John," I whispered, "do I have to eat this? I'll vomit sure." With a gracious nodding smile of thanks to our hostess, John deliberately picked up a big white chunk and placed it in my rice bowl as if it were the dish delectable. At the same time he said in English, "When her back is turned, give it to the friend under the table." A mangy, mongrel dog (flea-laden for sure) had pressed up against my feet several times, so I knew whom he meant. I pushed some rice into my mouth, and at a moment when she was not looking, I tilted the chunk of fat below the table. A succulent licking of chops from below testified to the joy with which my offering was received! But believe it or not, "He who was mighty in me" gradually gave me a real liking for pork fat — considered a choice dish among the Lisu as well as the country Chinese. It took time, of course, and cooler weather! But I found it a good lubricant for the dry rice and still drier steamed corn of Lisuland, and in time learned to welcome it eagerly! I enjoyed its flavour.

My dislike for travelling was changed too. I learned to look for the beauties of God in the scenery of

which the province of Yunnan, and especially Lisuland, are so rich they are like the borderland of
Heaven. Always a passionate lover of beauty, I was
given wonderful opportunities to adore God's
thought as revealed in His creation. I keep a five-year
diary, and very often in looking back I have been in a
different spot each year on a given day, so frequent
and full of change was my life. Yet it has been joyous
and filled with happy memories. He who wrought
effectually in Peter was mighty also in me. And He
will be in you too.

> Across the will of nature
> Leads on the path of God.

But we do not need to fear. He does not desert us
when our old Adam nature must be crossed. Some,
like Amy Carmichael, get it under their feet early.
Others, like myself, try His patience painfully, but
that patience never gives way, and it never deserts.
He that wrought effectually in Peter will be mighty
also in you.

And always God will relentlessly hold you to His
highest. He wants your soul not only purged and
clean, but with a bloom upon it. Oswald Chambers
calls it *the bloom of the touch of the Lord.* He says: "The
true character of the loveliness that tells for God is
always unconscious. Conscious influence is priggish
and un-Christian. If I say — 'I wonder if I am of any
use,' I instantly lose the bloom of the touch of the
Lord."

George Matheson has a keen and discriminating
word on how this bloom, this unselfconsciousness is
best obtained. He says, "I hear thee speak of the
forgetfulness of self. Yes, my soul, but the solemn

question is the *manner* of thy forgetting. How wouldst thou forget; shall it be by death or shall it be by life? Thou canst forget thyself by chloroform; but that is not greatness; it is the unconsciousness purchased by dying.

"But I know of an unconsciousness purchased by living — living in the life of another; it is the thing called love. The branch could forget itself by being withered; it prefers to forget itself by being in the vine."

He that wrought effectually in Peter will continue to work in us until He has formed in us that unconsciousness of self *purchased by living* — that bloom of the touch of the Lord! For the love of Him, our life lost in His.

Chapter 5

FRUSTRATIONS

I HAD never felt called to the Chinese people, although I learned to love them when I got to know them. I had felt called to the group named China Inland Mission because they followed Hudson Taylor's principles of proving God: "Learn to move man, through God, by prayer alone."

But when I heard J O Fraser speak about the Lisu tribe at The Firs conference in 1924, I had a longing to go to them. I fell in love with them! Mr Fraser was secretly disappointed, I always felt, that that conference where he had poured out his heart brought only one volunteer for the Lisu, and that a girl! He was polite, of course, but not encouraging. It was not a woman's job; he himself until then had never married because he felt no woman should be asked to endure such a life.

On returning to China, to his amazement and ours, Mr Fraser was not sent back to the Lisu tribe — he never got back to them as just their missionary. D E Hoste (Hudson Taylor's successor as general director of the CIM) had plans for higher leadership. He had been watching the godliness, shrewd insight, and brilliant ability of this young electrical engineer, and coveted his influence for more than just one of

China's tribes. Mr Fraser was at least fifty years ahead of his time in his vision of the indigenous church; and his deep prayer life and abandoned consecration appealed much to our general director.

But although Mr Fraser himself did not go back to Lisuland, my call never wavered. And yet I did not dare name it a call. It was just a great longing to go to them. At Moody Bible Institute I had heard missionary challenges that drew me breathless to the edge of my seat. Especially when L L Legters appealed for the Indians of South America; I wished I were two people, one of whom could go to those neglected Indians. But I never wavered in the vision for the Lisu tribe — that came first. And yet, when at last I got to China and to Yunnan, the person who stood most in my way was Mr Fraser himself! By that time I was engaged to marry John Kuhn. But I had held John off until I knew that the Mission had designated him to the tribes of Yunnan! John himself had felt drawn to the work in the far north-west, but when the Mission assigned him to the southwest and to the tribes, it seemed to indicate that God Himself had set His seal on our marriage. So we became officially engaged.

Mr Fraser had had to come down to Shanghai during the anti-foreign uprisings of 1927 and there he met John Kuhn and loved him. He even wrote me a letter, advising me to choose John! (He knew someone else was a possibility.) By the time John was appointed to Yunnan, Mr Fraser had become superintendent of that province. An indefatigable language student himself and a brilliant linguist, Mr Fraser was thrilled at John's progress in Chinese. He began, even that early, to plan that John would some day be his assistant superintendent. There was the assignment to the tribes, but all tribal workers had to study Chinese first. Mr Fraser saw to it that John had ample opportunity to get Chinese thoroughly.

By the time I had finished the prescribed Chinese language examinations and normally could have been sent to the tribes, Mr Fraser delayed us, saying, "Isobel is not strong enough physically to endure such a hard life." Quite possibly my difficulties in adjusting to the squalor of peasant life — many other young workers simply took those hardships with joy — was at the back of his thinking. But I honestly think it was more that he did not want John to lose any of his prowess in Chinese. To learn the Lisu language, John would necessarily get a bit rusty in the previous language learned.

John himself was happy with either designation. He was willing to go to the Lisu — he had made one trip into the Upper Salween canyon which thrilled him — but he also enjoyed working with the Chinese. It was only John's wife who kept timidly bringing up this matter of the Lisu! Ten years had passed. It was 1924 when I first felt called to the Lisu and now 1933 had dawned and we were still in Chinese work. The normal time for our furlough was approaching: John had been out seven years and I five years — seven was the normal term.

Had I been called to the Lisu? Or had it been just a sentimental attraction? Desperately I took it to the Lord — blessed refuge for all troubles. One could tell Him things one would be ashamed to tell another. "I guess, Lord", I whispered mournfully, "I will just have to conclude that I mistook your guidance, and it was not a 'call' after all."

Another application to Mr Fraser had just brought the answer, "Wait until after your furlough. We will see then."

It was that spring that I had felt so discouraged with my own ministry. We had opened the beautiful little plain of Yungping to the Gospel. It was mainly Muslim in population and had not been fruitful. I had worked faithfully. There was not a hamlet or a village on that whole plain where I had not personally gone, driven off their various dogs, pushed my way into their dirty courtyards and presented my message. The women were kind and everyone was nice to me but only a mere handful of people had accepted Christ. And most of these were very poor illiterate women — too weak to call a church. It was at Yungping that I expressed my willingness to be put on the shelf, willing not to be the one He used, if only I might see Him work!

As Lisu work seemed impossible before furlough we mentally accepted the fact. We were expecting a little playmate for our two-year-old Kathryn. It was then, when hope was dead, the Lord wrought so wondrously. But it appeared a catastrophe at first glance.

In August, 1933, John went out on a long trip to discover what tribes inhabited an area we called the Triangle. Kathryn and I, with three young lady workers, were left behind in Yungping — apparently quite safe from danger. Then one day, without warning, the Yungping River flooded. It rose so silently that we were not aware of what was happening until it had almost reached the level of our downstairs room. Then began a scramble to move people who lived there to the upstairs. I was called upon to help lift one of Miss Embery's trunks to a place of safety, and humanly speaking, that did it. I suffered a miscarriage.

It was impossible to contact John, there being no post office in the mountain villages where he was. So it was not until he returned that he learned there was no baby to look forward to. I felt the loss more keenly than he perhaps, and as he turned to comfort me he said, "God must have some purpose in this, dear. We will just ask Him what it is."

Within twenty-four hours a letter from Mr Fraser was in our hands. "I want your prayers for a perplexing problem," he wrote. Then he told us of the two Lisu churches in the Upper Salween canyon which had come into being through the sacrificial pioneering of four Lisu evangelists. That trail-blazing had cost the life of one of the four. Now those two little churches were flourishing, but they were six days' journey apart and there was only one missionary couple to care for the two. Mr Fraser had written that Leila and Allyn Cooke had separated, Allyn to care for the Luda church and Leila left in charge of the Oak Flat church. "But I cannot allow this to go on," wrote our perplexed superintendent. "Leila Cooke is very brave to stay all alone in that isolated rough place, but I cannot allow husband and wife to continue in separation! Yet I have no one else to send."

John and I looked at one another — the meaning of the Lord was now clear to us. With a newborn infant it would have been well-nigh impossible for us to begin such a rough life. But our two-year-old would have a wonderful time on those wooded slopes, with someone to watch her.

John and I knew now why the baby had been taken from us. We wrote to Mr Fraser immediately, told him of my accident and of our firm belief that it was the Lord guiding us to go to the Upper Salween.

Our dear superintendent was too much of a man of God not to recognize the hand of the Lord. But his common sense still held to it that my health could not stand Lisuland.

"Go in for a trip," he wrote. "That will relieve Mrs Cooke's present stress over this opium persecution. John must interview the official and claim gently the religious freedom of this land. Isobel can judge from this trip whether she could stand it. And as Leila Cooke has not seen another white face for months, she will no doubt be overjoyed to have Isobel's company."

This was the reason for our trip into the Upper Salween in March, 1934, when Mark and other Christian Lisu friends from Goomoo fought their way over the snowy mountain and arrived the day after we did!

I was thrilled with Lisuland — by the Lord's work in salvation and by His work in creation. The Cookes lived in a flimsy bamboo Lisu shanty. But Allyn Cooke had worked and prepared a flourishing garden — beets, carrots, tomatoes, and such good food grew in abundance. Leila Cooke had brought an iron cooking-stove and a little heater, so though life was primitive in style, it was cosy. At that time they were living in Pine Mountain Village and had a site on the mountainside to themselves.

The squalor and insects of poverty and primitive living were as bad or worse than among the Chinese farmers. But to me it was much easier to endure for two reasons — beauty and privacy were obtainable. In the Chinese peasant village you were shut up to ugly drabness. If you tried to leave the village, you found yourself in their flat rice field, where of course you could not sit down and were very conspicuous.

In Lisuland the villages were also smelly and ugly, but you could stand anywhere and lift up your eyes to the most magnificent Alpine panoramas on which to feast your soul. And for privacy there were those great mountain slopes, dotted with trees, beautiful wild flowers, and picturesque rocks. In ten minutes you could be quite alone, out of sight and surrounded by breath-taking beauty. On rainy days there was the beauty of cloud-wreathed peaks.

Living conditions in tribesland were much more difficult than on the Chinese plain. There were no stores in which to buy food or furniture. The Lisu did not use furniture. A raised plank for a bed, yes. Rough cupboards or baskets to store grain, yes. That was about all. When we moved into Oak Flat district very few Lisu used tables. They ate off a board placed on the unwashed floor (which was also the roof of the cattle pen built beneath the hut). After seeing our table, many of them began to make tables for themselves; but many were the meals which I ate off the floor, before they awakened to the possible luxury of something better. I remember one occasion when we were thus eating, the family cat made dashes for our meat dish. Being on our level — on the floor — she was very successful. But Lucius, a Lisu brother who was with us, put an end to her depredations. He caught her, held her tail down with his heel a good yard off, and placidly went on eating. Pussy yowled frantically, but no more meat was lost!

So it was that we wrote Mr Fraser again, quite confident that I could stand it and would love it. Mr Fraser replied gratefully that we might move into Lisuland until our furlough. (John was in his tenth year and I in my eighth when we finally left for America.)

How thrilled we were! Frustrations last for a time, but the will of the Lord reigns in the end — I told myself jubilantly. It was exactly ten years since I had first felt the call to Lisu work. Ten years of waiting and frustration — why? Most probably because I myself had not been ready before. I needed the hard years of plodding, which resulted in little fruit, to make me so hungry for saved souls that the physical hardships would not matter. In other words, the Lord had to train me to appreciate what He was doing among that barefooted mountain tribe before He dared let me share in the work. I always said that Lisu work was physical hardship but spiritual luxury. The physical hardship was obvious to anyone. It was spiritual luxury I would not have recognized if I had gone right into Lisu work without those barren years among the Chinese peasants.

There had been some souls saved among the Chinese, but they were illiterate! Old women could never read their Bibles, and how is one to grow spiritually without feeding on the Word? (In those early years I did not know about the Chinese phonetic.) In Lisuland they were illiterate too, but the Fraser Script was so simple and easy that a bright lad could learn to read in one month! Then you can begin to open the Scriptures to that one: this I had to learn to appreciate!

The Holy Spirit blowing like a strong wind across the mountains, new converts springing up in this village and in that one — that is a luxury. Others had paid the painful price of pioneering — we merely walked into the blessing. And the Lisu with a little training could sing in parts! Oh, how my soul had been galled by the monotone singing of the Chinese peasant! This glorious love of music and keen aptitude for it was a luxury. And so on.

Those ten long years of waiting and frustration had
been needed to open my eyes to the privileges of
being allowed to share in the Lisu work. If I had gone
into the work as soon as my Chinese language exams
were passed, I would have taken the tide of blessing
for granted, the young converts eager to be taught as
the usual thing, and I might have chafed at the
physical hardships — the poor and monotonous
food, the difficulty of getting help and getting supplies and so on. My spiritual eyesight needed to be
clarified.

After permission was given to move, we were
frustrated again! John took sick. Amoebic dysentery
first, and then a hernia operation. Why, oh, why? "It
must be the devil" — my irritated flesh wanted to
blame someone, and the devil is always a handy
object. Medical attention was needed, and the new
worker just arrived at Tali was a doctor — Dr Stuart
Harverson. So to Tali we repaired.

Here we met this new missionary who had come
from a cultured well-to-do home, yet who accepted
the physical hardships not just with patience, but
with zest! Dr Harverson simply plunged into life
among the peasants with joy and abandonment. He
was a living rebuke (though unconscious of it) to my
shrinking horror of vermin, dirt, and bad smells.
And the Lord mightily blessed. As John was sick in
bed, and Dr Harverson had not yet learned Chinese, I
had to go with him on medical calls to act as
interpreter. In a few weeks I saw many Chinese
saved; as many in four weeks as I had in the whole
previous year. (It was not a Muslim community like
Yungping; still, God taught me a lesson.)

In December, 1934, we were at last ready and

allowed to move into Lisuland, taking over the
district of Oak Flat.

My pen is tempted to dwell on those happy days,
but this is the story of frustrations, and I must pursue
the theme.

Every summer in Lisuland comes the rainy season.
It had been necessary for us to leave comfortable Pine
Mountain Village and rebuild the shanty in Oak Flat
Village. Our house site was beautiful — at the edge
of a precipitous drop where no other shanties could
be built, giving us a bit of privacy. But the garden
space had been a landslide and was simply gravel.
We were not good gardeners like Allyn Cooke and,
added to that, the soil was rocky, so our vegetable
garden was a failure. Leila Cooke had joined her
husband in the Luda church six days' journey away,
so we had no senior workers to advise or counsel us.
We saw the need of visiting in the villages, staying a
week in a place and teaching the Christians. We had
to speak in Chinese at first, Lisu evangelist John or
Job interpreting for us, while at the same time we
tried to learn their language. Travelling in the rainy
season and living in leaky Lisu huts are dangerous to
the health — we never tried that again! But that first
summer in our ignorance, we did.

When little Kathryn took ill with a very high,
strange fever I wrote Dr Harveson, our nearest
medical help, for advice, but it was two months
before his prompt answer arrived! The Burma Road
had not been built in those days.

In August John decided to make a trip into Burma
to visit the beloved Goomoo group of Christians,
whom no white missionary had ever met. That
meant he would be gone about a month (seven days'
journey each way) while Kathryn and I stayed home

at Oak Flat. John took Teacher John and left Teacher Job with me so each of us had a Lisu who could speak Chinese and act as our interpreter. So we parted.

Unknown to us I had picked up erysipelas, a severe infection affecting the whole system, on our last trip among the Lisu, and John was no sooner out of reach and communication than I became ill with strange symptoms. I had never even seen, almost never heard of erysipelas. I just knew I was ill and running a fever. I could not get up. Dear Homay took care of little Kathryn, who preferred Lisu food to our American food, so she was not a worry, but I could not eat. Rice, corn, pumpkins, beans — they did not appeal. Homay kept apologizing, said it was famine year, and she could not get meat or even eggs. Powdered milk we had, and some tinned meat. But I was soon too ill to know what I should have had. Never can I forget the tender concern of the dear Lisu. Job came many times a day and offered to go for help to Paoshan where the China Inland Mission had stationed a young nurse, Kathleen Davies, with Winifred Embery. But I said no, no, Job must not disturb them. It was a rough six days to get to them; it would take several days to purchase supplies, hire carriers and pack to come. Two weeks? I would be better then! No, I said to him. Just wait and pray.

Dear Job got more anxious as I grew weaker. One morning he appeared with some oil. He anointed me according to James 5:15 and prayed over me, then sang, "The Great Physician now is near." I was deeply touched by his love, but singing was not Job's strong point, and I am afraid I chuckled after he left over the memory of that croaking effort. Still I did not get better.

Then one morning Homay walked in and

announced, "Teacher Job has gone, Ma-ma! He got up at four o'clock this morning and has gone to Paoshan to bring medical help for you."

"Oh, dear," I thought dismally. "Now Mr Fraser will say, 'I told you so. Isobel in Lisuland only eight months and medical help has to be called for!' Oh, dear!" But I was getting too weak to care. My worst discomfort was my unwashed condition. The fever made me perspire, and I had been too weak to wash myself for days. I called dear Homay and tried to explain to her what a bed-bath was. She listened incredulously, dubiously, but did her best. Soon she was back with a basin of hot water. She set it down beside the bed, dipped her plump brown hands in it, and proceeded to stroke me! That was the most she had comprehended. She knew she was not being successful and looked so grieved and anxious that I had to pretend to be satisfied in order to comfort her. I do not remember much of what happened after that.

I was told later that Job ran his feet into blisters and did the six days' journey in four. But with all that painful effort it was more than two weeks before he was able to bring the girls into our village. They could not walk those mountains, so mountain-chair coolies had to be found, and not everyone wanted to carry, on those Salween heights! The girls guessed, and rightly, that I was sleeping on boards, so they decided to bring a folding camp bed. This with other comforts had to be carried, and carriers had to be found. Job chafed at the delay these preparations took, but at last the party climbed the last mountain and reached Oak Flat Village.

It was a wonderful moment for me when my bones felt the softness of that camp bed. But I was so weak

that I collapsed when Nurse Kathleen tried to give
me a bed-bath. "This is not from erysipelas," she
said, puzzled. "This is semi-starvation. Homay,
bring me some eggs!"

"Sorry," answered that dear girl anxiously, "but
there aren't any."

"Well, kill a chicken and we will make some
broth."

Again Homay's face fell. "There aren't any chickens. This is a famine season, and no one has come to
sell anything."

There followed hard days for dear nurse.
Frustrations! In Lisuland eggs usually abounded and
chickens were the easiest meat to get. But two
months in the year these two articles are scarce —
August and September — and those were the months
in which I took sick! To shorten the story, I lived, but
with nourishing food so scarce it was decided to
carry me out to Paoshan. So, right in line with Mr
Fraser's prophecy that I would not be able to stand
mountain rigours, ten months after arrival I was
carried out again! Several months of rest and good
food restored me, and Mr Fraser gave permission for
me to return to Oak Flat for Christmas.

Orders were that a better and healthier house
should be built, then we were to go on furlough. That
gave us three more happy months at Oak Flat among
the dear Lisu and with Job. I have always felt I owed
my life to Job, as well as to Nurse Kathleen.

But why was this frustration of sickness allowed?
One cannot always discern the reason for these
things, but two are plain to us. (1) We learned that
when one member of the party was thrusting out
into Satan's territory, it was also necessary to put a
prayer guard over those who stayed at home. We

were all praying for John and his party as they
pressed into the demon-plagued territory of
Goomoo. Those prayers cleared the party's way (they
were much blessed there) so Satan, in furious spite,
struck at the unprotected home base. Both those who
go down to battle and those who stay by the stuff
need prayer-coverage. We have never forgotten this
lesson.

(2) We learned that spirit and body cannot be
divided. It is essential that one keep clean and
yielded in the spirit, but the body's needs also must
be cared for. That means bother. It means time spent
on a garden, fruit trees, and perhaps a hen coop. We
ought not to have been so totally unprepared for a
hunger season. If the Cookes, our seniors, had been
able to live with us and coach us it would not have
happened. But workers were at a premium, as I have
shown, so we had blindly to pioneer our way.

We left for furlough in March, 1936. This book with
subject matter, *platforms* — struggles of the soul —
must necessarily pass over whole stretches of sunny,
happy experiences. On this furlough we enjoyed
comradeship in the things of the kingdom so full of
joy, laughter, and fellowship with Himself that we
turn to them over and over again in our memories
with never-ceasing delight. This furlough also introduced us to the inheritance of saints which each had
gained in marrying the other. My Christian friends
were on the West Coast and John's were in Pennsylvania. Neither of us knew much about the other's
friends, and on this furlough we met for the first
time. Of my parents, only my father was alive. We
went to see him before travelling to Pennsylvania
and again at the end of furlough.

Our ticket to China was purchased and we were

packed, ready to go on a Japanese boat sailing on
Saturday at noon. Our farewell service was held in
the China Inland Mission home in Vancouver. We
said goodbye to our friends and returned to Father's
house for our last night's sleep in the homeland.
Almost as soon as we entered the door the telephone
rang. It was Mr Wilcox, our CIM secretary who had
just farewelled us!

"There has come a telegram," he said, "from Dr
Glover [our home director]. He says that since war
has broken out between Japan and China, all sailings
must be delayed."

"Then we do not go tomorrow?" said John.

"Looks like it," was the sad answer. "Miss — is
already on the boat! She got on at Seattle. Guess I'll
have to ask her to get off when it stops here
tomorrow. Too bad."

"Well, thank you, Mr Wilcox," said John. He put
the phone down and came in to face our amazed and
incredulous group. Friends were with us at the
moment.

"Well, we do not go, Belle, dear," said John quietly.

"Why not?" I was not in a mood to accept another
frustration!

"War has broken out between Japan and China.
The Mission is cancelling all passages until the
situation can be newly assessed."

"But the fighting is in the north in Manchuria, and
we are going to the far south to Yunnan! There is no
need to hold up either the Jack Graham family or us!"
I argued.

"Now, Belle, don't try to run the Mission! We must
just submit and do it happily," said John, who did
not like it when his wife produced a disconcerting
independence or when he thought she was trying to

take the lead!

But here is where my experience of obstacles on the path of God's will stood me in good stead. John had encountered no obstacles in going to China; his path had been wonderfully clear.

"All obstacles are not from the Lord," I argued in alarm at his seeming passivity. "Dr Glover gave a blanket order which is good for most of the cases. He has forgotten perhaps that two of the several families due to sail would be going south where there is not the least danger and won't be for a long time. Moreover, he probably does not know that there is a small inter-mission school for missionaries' children about to open in Kunming. He is thinking we need to take Kathryn to Chefoo, which is in the danger zone. If he knew there was a possibility of putting our children in school in the south, it would change the whole picture."

By this time our friends were taking their leave. They had promised to drive us to the dock the next morning and said that the promise would still hold good if we needed them. We said goodbye and then turned to talk it out alone.

"Phone Mr Wilcox and ask him, if you are in doubt," I suggested anxiously.

"Well, we will ask *the Lord* first," said my husband, firmly retaining his office as head of the house! "We have not had our evening devotions yet," and he reached for the Bible. We were following a certain course of reading so he opened where the bookmark lay. Then he looked up at me, his eyes twinkling, "Guess you win, Belle! Do you remember where our reading for tonight comes?"

"No."

"Psalm 91." We both exclaimed, "Wonderful.

Praise His name!"

Then John read all those words of promise for times of danger, beginning: "He who dwells in the shelter of the Most High will rest in the shadow of the Almighty" — and ending — "and show him my salvation." When we had prayed, John got up, went to the telephone and called Mr Wilcox. After explaining our thoughts, he was overjoyed when Mr Wilcox answered, "I have been thinking the very same thing. I was just about to call you. I'll wire Dr Glover immediately." It was then midnight, so we all went to bed.

But you can imagine we were up early, ears strained for the telephone. We were living at North Vancouver and it would take a good hour to motor around by the bridge to the ocean liner's dock. But it was nine o'clock before the answer came: I APPROVE: GLOVER. Oh, what jubilation! Everything was packed and ready to go, so into Betty's and George's car we piled and off we sped.

Frustrations. Those that are from the devil we must refuse in Christ's name. Mr Fraser taught us to pray, "If this obstacle is from you, Lord, I accept it. If it is from the devil I refuse it and all his works in Christ's name."

My diary tells me we sailed on August 31, 1937, with Jack and Ella Graham and their two children, on the *Hikawa Maru*. This ship could not go farther than Japan but we were assured it would be possible to trans-ship there for Hongkong.

We had some adventures in Japan, but my next "platform" occurred on September 19, when our boat pulled into Hongkong. I was thrilled and happy over the prospect of having Little Daughter in school at Kunming. John's sister, Kathryn Kuhn Harrison, and her husband were in missionary work in that big city, so our girl could stay with her uncle and aunt — so I told myself. Imagine the shock, then, to find a telegram awaiting us at Hongkong: "Send Kathryn to Chefoo with Grace Liddell." It appeared that Miss Liddell, one of our Yunnan workers, was going to Chefoo to help on the teaching staff. A safe boat had been procured, and Mission headquarters thought it a golden opportunity to get Kathryn into our China Inland Mission school. It was, of course, much better equipped and staffed in every way than the little Kunming school. But I was totally unprepared to give up my child so soon.

I knew that, in one sense, it was giving her up for life. Although our Mission planned that children join their parents when possible for holiday times, one never again could watch them grow from day to day. The parting was excruciating for me, and for hours afterward I could not sit, lie down or do anything but grieve. I pored over all I would miss in putting her to bed at night, her sweet childish ways, the likelihood she would forget me to some extent — none of the poignant details did I miss. The consequence was that I was fearfully broken up. My dear patient husband walked the streets with me at night until I was so physically exhausted that I could lie down and fall into oblivion.

Our boat out of Hongkong to Haiphong was delayed, and so there was time to spare. I remember going to a Bible class when the subject was "Praise." The teacher stood at the doorway shaking hands with us at the close. As she took my hand she looked at me very significantly and said, "The *sacrifice* of praise" (Heb. 13:15). My inward reaction was, "But you have no children!" It was true; she and her husband were childless. Nevertheless, she had planted a truth from the Word in my heart which I have never forgotten. There are times when it is sacrifice to praise Him, in the human sense. (In the light of Calvary nothing we can offer should be called sacrifice.) But since there are so few things we *can* offer Him, this should be considered a privilege.

We took a boat to Haiphong and then through French Indo-China by train into Yunnan. It was during the long hours of sitting in the train that the Lord spoke to me. He said something like this: "Well, dear, you have *indulged your grief*. You have gone over your loss minutely and by detail. The last time you would give her a bath, the last night to tuck her into bed, the last energetic bear hug from the impetuous little arms, the last sight of lovely child-hood sprawled gracefully in sleep, and so on. And now I would counsel you. What good did it do you? Emotionally you are as worn and limp as a rag. It did not profit you physically. It did not help little Kathryn at all. It was a drag on your poor husband. Of what use was it to indulge your grief?

"Next time — for this is only the first parting of many times to come — let Me counsel you to gird up your loins and try to be a soldier. There are many small helps you can use, especially in the area of the mind. Refuse to let your mind dwell on your loss. It will not make you love her less. Deliberately think of something more helpful, or anything rather than your loss. I have given you a thing called common sense — summon that to your aid. Common sense will tell you to avoid all scenes which harrow the feelings. Singing or music, for instance. Deliberately plan your goodbye so that emotion will be strained as little as possible. When you return home after the loved one has left, change the furniture of her room around so as not to stir up memories which cause useless grief. And so on."

"But," I argued, "wouldn't that make me hard? I do not want to lose the ability to feel."

"You will not," He promised. "In fact, it will go all the deeper when it is allowed to evaporate in bursts of emotion. Sublimate your feelings; rechannel your attention toward helping someone else. Amy Carmichael says, '*Help lame dogs over stiles*. There are lots of lame dogs who have stiles to face — stiles harder than yours.'"

And so He taught me! Never again did I allow myself to be so broken up over a grief. And I found that common sense *was* a good aid. Also my love and my concern for my children certainly have never become less.

That train trip is wonderfully scenic as it climbs the heights toward Kunming which is 6,000 feet above sea level, and the beauty of my dear Lord's handiwork coupled with His direct dealing with me in my heart was healing and quieting to me. I needed it, because at Kunming another blow awaited me — another frustration.

It had never entered my head that perhaps the Mission would not reassign us to Lisu work. The reader will have foreseen this long ago, but I certainly did not. Mr Fraser had prophesied I could not stand the rough mountain life physically and after only ten months of it I had to be carried out sick. Moreover, it had taken nearly two months' time from two other workers — Nurse Davies and Miss Embery — who had had to go in and help me. It was perfectly natural that the Mission should decide against our return to the Lisu. But it had never entered my

wildest imagination, and our relatives Kathryn and
Dave Harrison, seeing that, pitied me. "Whatever
will Isobel do when she hears she is not to return to
the Lisu?" they whispered to one another.

On September 27, my diary tells me, we were
called in for an interview with Mr Fraser. He told us
gently that we would be temporarily stationed at
Paoshan "with freedom to go to Lisuland on trips."
My diary also records that on that occasion he frankly
stated he wanted John as his assistant superintendent for West Yunnan. This was not disagreeable to
John. He still enjoyed Chinese work as he did Lisu,
so it was quite a happy designation for him.

Not so for me. I had always felt like a square peg in
a round hole in Chinese work — partly no doubt
because I had had to be a pioneer evangelist which
was never my forte. Bible teaching was where I felt at
home, and *mothering*. Miss Frances Brook (author of
my Goal Is God Himself, and one of my spiritual
counsellors for years) used to say that she considered
my chief gift was that of mothering the Lisu church. I
believe she was right. But there had to be converts
already born again or a little church already formed
before one could *mother* the people or break the
Word in its deeper meanings to them. I had both in
Lisuland, converts and churches. In Paoshan the
church numbered but a mere handful and Miss
Winifred Embery was mothering them very capably.
At the same time a situation was arising in the Lisu
church at Oak Flat which gave me much anxiety. My
mother wings were fluttering in alarm over the
young. On the first of October I decided to have a
special time of prayer for Oak Flat and also lay before
the Lord the soreness of my heart at being shut out of
Lisuland. I did not want to stand in the way of my

husband's promotion, but my heart seemed tied to the Lisu Christians. I must get the victory over it. For some years it had been my habit to fast and pray one morning a month for my own spiritual needs, the church's needs, and world revival. (Miss Ruth Paxson had started me on this habit.) My diary records that while I was waiting before the Lord on this occasion, some verses in Zephaniah 3 were given me.

On that day you will not be put to shame ... because I will remove from this city those who rejoice in their pride ... But I will leave within you the meek and humble, who trust in the name of the Lord ... Sing, O Daughter of Zion; ... The Lord has taken away your punishment ... The Lord, the King of Israel, is with you; never again will you fear any harm ... The Lord your God is with you, he is mighty to save ... I will rescue the lame ... At that time I will gather you; at that time I will bring you home ... when I restore your fortunes before your very eyes.

The first part of what I have quoted applied exactly to the Oak Flat situation. And the latter part I felt was God's promise to take me back into Lisu work.

I cannot tell you the joy and victory that flooded me. There have been times when the Word on which I was caused to hope was not *clearly* from Him. It might have been the product of wishful thinking. "Lord, keep your servant from presumptuous sins." On such occasions I would say, "I *think* the Lord wants me to do thus and so." But this promise was clear. There is difference. He had promised that His sheep shall know His voice, and they do. I knew that morning that God had promised to clear up the situation at Oak Flat and to take us back into the Lisu work. I *knew*, and never doubted. So the garment of praise and singing was mine although I told no one,

not even my husband. The Lord expects us to keep
His secrets until His time comes to reveal them.
Friends marvelled at my happiness as we packed to
go to Paoshan. They did not know the secret
consolations of God. This too is a part of the platform
of frustrations — the end is that we may know Him
and the power of His resurrection.

There was no Burma Road in those days — one
travelled overland stage by stage. So it was October
27 when we arrived in Paoshan. My diary records:
"Our two soldier escorts accepted Christ." Miss
Embery and the Chinese church leaders came out to
greet us and gave us a wonderful reception.

We were there just a little more than a month when
a letter came from Mr Fraser saying he must ask us to
make a trip to Oak Flat! The situation had become
acute and, if the church was to be saved from a split,
some missionary able to speak the language must go
in immediately. He would love to have gone himself
but he was too far away and tied up with other
duties. We were also to act as escort to a new Lisu
missionary, Victor Christianson, who was to stay at
Oak Flat and learn the language. Mr Fraser hastened
to add: "Remember, this is not a permanent designation. You do not need to move all your things in. But
you will need enough to set up housekeeping for a
few months. It would be good for Victor to have the
comfort of experienced seniors for a little while."

When I heard that, I slipped away to our bedroom
and carefully closed the door. I did not want to shock
my dear husband by my "unseemly levity". But
when privacy was well secured I danced with joy.
"Temporary designation!" I gloated gaily. "So says
you, my dearly beloved Super. So says you!"

He was indeed dearly beloved. He lived on the

same high plane as Amy Carmichael and his godly life coupled with brainy leadership never ceased to inspire us. But he did not know of the Lord's promise to me to send me back the Lisu.

"So says you," I continued, "but not so says the Lord!" Then, remembering what I owed to that dear Master, I dropped on my knees in worship. Really deep worship is wordless — words are too shallow to carry the weight of the heart's adoration. How wondrously He had wrought! He had promised to take me back to Lisuland and here, less than two months after arrival in Paoshan, we were on our way into Lisuland! December 13 we climbed the hill to the west of the city and set our faces toward the Salween!

Officially it was a temporary designation. We found the church much confused over the doctrine of Law and Grace and we felt that a longer period of Bible study with church leaders was needed. We suggested that the three months of the rainy season should be given to teaching. Mr Fraser was very enthusiastic about the idea and so began our first Rainy Season Bible School (RSBS for short). It was a most blessed time — thrilling proof that this was what the Lisu church needed.

Then on September 30, 1938, as we were all packed to take a long trip into Burma to the famous Goomoo church, runners came with shattering news — *Mr Fraser was dead*. He had contracted malignant cerebral malaria and never recovered consciousness. Our superintendent had gone Home to God. Personally I have never ceased to miss him. Nearly eighteen years have passed, but at crises of decision I still often think, "What would Mr Fraser do?"

With our superintendent gone, all missionaries

remained at the station where they were, so the Kuhn family just continued on in Lisuland! Mr Gladstone Porteous became superintendent for the province, but as Yunnan was such a large field he never once got west to visit us. At length, in 1940 it was decided to divide the province into east and west, and John Kuhn was made acting assistant superintendent of the west. This meant he was supervisor of Chinese as well as tribal work. From time to time a question arose as to the Kuhn family moving out to Paoshan where John would be near the telegraph office, so the matter of "temporary designation" hung over our heads for years.

After one of these times of acute questions in the matter, I was passing by a group of Lisu church leaders who are talking together, when a remark dropped into my hearing. "We would never have had Ma-pa," one deacon was saying earnestly, "if Ma-ma had not loved us so dearly." It was a remark of shrewd perspicuity, and I pondered it as I walked on. I think he was correct. And then my mind glanced back many years to that conference in 1924 at The Firs, when Mr Fraser had poured out his heart about the Lisu tribe, inwardly hoping for one of two brilliant young men who were present. He got neither, only a girl. Of what use was a girl? In God's unfathomable ways, she was to be the one who brought the needed man into the Lisu work. *Frustrations* — have much to do in conforming us into His image. Yes, suffering, but also His sweet consoling fellowship in that suffering. It reveals to us the power of His resurrection, and when He arranges a release for us that no mortal could manipulate — *we come to know Him.*

Rock of my heart and my fortress tower
   Dear are Thy thoughts to me.
Like the unfolding of some fair flower
   Opening silently.
And on the edge of these Thy ways
   Standing in awe as heretofore,
Thee do I worship, Thee do I praise
   And adore!

AMY CARMICHAEL

Chapter 6

EXTINGUISHED CANDLE-FLAMES

THE year of 1942 always stands out in my memory as my own personal experience of "the horror of great darkness." Life had been swinging along in great joy. Despite the ever-present physical trials of primitive living, the growth of the work and the delightful friendships it developed for us were sunny experiences. But with the year 1942 life turned a sharp corner. On the surface I was flung from pillar to post, emptied from vessel to vessel. But those were only what Bishop Handley Moule calls "the outward woes of our inward pilgrimage." Inwardly I was set for a much-needed crucifixion of the flesh. But to see the picture properly, the outward woes must come first.

The Sino-Japanese war had been going on all these years, but we in the South had felt it only as a distant warning bell. But in 1941 the Japanese entered Burma and before the world's startled gaze they strode through that small land as with seven-league boots. We were working the mountains of The Hump, right on the China-Burma border north of the Burma Road. At the beginning of 1942 we were utterly unconscious that the Japanese would soon be within sight and sound! Generalissimo Chiang had lost province after province to them until in 1942 he had only three left — Yunnan, Kweichow, and Szechwan. Of these three, our province of Yunnan, with its Burma Road and airlift over The Hump, provided his only route of supplies. If the Japanese got Yunnan, all China would be theirs.

Now as to my inward pilgrimage, there was an area of my life which the Lord had long needed to discipline. It was the area of the affections. I had always considered that this was one of my strong points! — a deeply affectionate nature. But the very intensity of such love has a danger — the danger of selfish possessiveness. Intense affection wants to hold on to the loved one and is unconsciously very monopolizing. Since God taught me this truth I have seen it many times in life. Such a pure love as mother love, if it becomes too possessive can blight the life of the child. "And they that are Christ's have crucified the flesh with the affections and lusts" (Gal. 5:42 KJV). I believe it is Conybeare who interprets *lust* as "a strong desire", so we may read that verse: "They that are Christ's have crucified the flesh with the affections and strong desires." I knew this truth before I came to China, but it was mere head knowledge. I did not know how to recognize it in my own life, let alone know how to deal with it. The time had come when I must learn. So in 1942 there began a systematic stripping away from me of all whom I loved.

First, my husband was called to a conference of superintendents in Chungking, and from then on events came in such a whirl that we were separated most of the year. Next, the Chefoo school, where Kathryn stayed, was captured by the Japanese, and my little girl was wrapped in silence. Just now and again did a little childish note slip through to us, proof that she was alive and well. Before that, there had been a letter from her every week. Third, Mary Zimmerman, who acted as our home secretary, duplicating our circulars and forwarding to us news of and from our friends, fell silent. Her precious mother was taken Home to be with the Lord and this sorrow was followed by a trial so disrupting that Mary just could not keep up her usual correspondence for about a year. Husband, child, friends, and then — my right hand in the Lisu work left us. It was for a very happy reason — our boy Lucius got married that year and had to set up his own home across the river. But nevertheless the very comfortable prop he had always been to me was missing. He alone had understood how much it meant to me to have a little corner where I could be private, when I had to live in a Lisu home for one or two weeks in order to hold a short Bible conference. To the Lisu mind, to be left alone is an affliction! They all sleep in the one room, two in a bed, and are gregarious by training. They would never dream of so ill-treating a guest as to give her a room to herself! Lucius did not sympathize with this queer desire of mine either, but he had learned that it meant a lot to me, and so when we travelled, in a nice way he would explain to our hostess Ma-ma's queer liking for privacy. With a merry word here and there, he would himself rig up a screen for me (if a room could not be obtained) behind which I could retire to wash and sleep. No other Lisu ever took such care of me. Of course, when I travelled with John, he did that. But now I felt stripped of every comfort indeed.

I was not so stupid but that I saw the stripping was systematic and thorough — husband, child, friends,

and then my right hand in the work. I knew it must
be the Lord trying to teach me something, but I was
too lonely and heartbroken to submit. "Lord, I was
made to love and be loved. How can I live without
someone that is mine, *very specially mine* above the
rest around me? I'd rather be dead!" So moaned the
flesh as it was being set for the crucifixion of its
inordinate affections. And with these inner desolations the outer being was flung far and wide as I am
about to relate.

The year began happily enough. In February we
held our first Bible school for girls, with a success
that astonished the Lisu church, which had always
held that women could not learn! It was a triumph
and became a yearly event.

Then in March I developed acute toothache. I tried
to pacify it with medicines but did not succeed, for it
was the Lord Himself beginning to spill me out of my
nest. The nearest competent dentist was in Kunming,
at the other end of the province! In the old days it
would have meant a thirty-day journey, but now
with the Burma Road open, it could be done in about
two weeks. Even so, it would require two weeks to
return, so I would be gone a month or more! The pain
soon settled my hesitation, however — I could not do
any work until that ripping ache stopped — so I
called for porters to carry my things and escort me
out to Paoshan. John was at the conference for
superintendents in faraway Chungking. I could meet
him at Kunming and we would return together — it
planned itself very easily in my mind.

As I was about to leave Oak Flat I received a
pleasant surprise — Lucius appeared, announcing he
was going to escort me out, leading my mule for me
over those precipitous and dangerous mountain

roads, as had been his old familiar custom. He was building his new home (for him and Mary) and Paoshan was the best place to buy good nails. He would combine his personal business with the fun of escorting me again. To me, this was really a gift from the Lord, as Lucius was a delightful chatterbox, and his witty running-gossip of church and village life caused the long hours in the saddle to pass quickly. It was also a pleasant source of information of Lisu thinking and customs. I learned much from those hours in the saddle listening to Lucius talk. Besides this, he was a past master at making Ma-ma comfortable when we camped out at night. We had four-and-a-half days' journey to go. It used to be six, but the Burma Road had cut it short by that much. March 18 we started out, so says my diary, travelling about thirty miles and camping out at night in a big airy loft over a large horse stable! March is the beginning of spring, very often, in Lisuland. The old winter brown of the mountains is flecked with the light green of bursting buds. The pale pink of wild peach trees often dots itself against that bright green and old brown, and the delicate perfume of white rhododendron makes you catch your breath with joy and hunt for more of it. Distant mountain peaks are still snow-capped and dazzling in the golden spring sunshine and the dear cuckoo bird arrives to tell the Lisu to: "Plant corn! Plant corn!"

Boy (as John and I usually called Lucius) chattered happily about his plans and Mary's,[1] and my diary records that while we journeyed I translated and taught him the chorus, "I'm feeding on the living Bread." He loved it and by the end of the trip had it

[1]Mary's story is told by Isobel Kuhn in *Stones of Fire*.

written down and ready to teach to the brothers and sisters at Olives on his return. We caught a truck at the motor road and so got into Paoshan by Saturday, March 21.

I had been dreading the Burma Road trip. There was no regular bus service to the capital city (Kunming) and the only way was to go by a Chinese merchant truck. Chinese drivers, looking for money, regularly overloaded their trucks with merchandise, and passengers were piled on top of that! You had to climb up on top of all the boxes, bundles, and bales and perch there, holding on as best you could. Often I had seen such trucks with the top actually swaying, as the driver, to save gas and so filch a few pennies for himself, coasted down hairpin curves with precipitous drops at the edge of the road. And every now and again you came across the wreck of a truck which had gone over, so·you knew your fears were not just imagination! The very thought of Burma Road travel in those days still makes one shudder. But the Lord had an unexpected kindness waiting for me. (Note this: because 1942 was the year when He had to give me a much-needed crucifixion experience, yet if you watch closely you will see He was extra kind — whenever it was possible.) I was told that two of the Generalissimo's airmen of the Flying Tigers were driving in a private car to Kunming and would take me along with them. No Chinese truck-travel, but good American drivers! Was that not a kindness? My diary notes casually, "Rangoon has fallen" — to the Japanese.

We were to leave at half-past five in the morning, so I arose about four o'clock in order to have a quiet time for my devotions. I had been up early so many mornings and travelling till dark, that I debated whether or not to skip my quiet time that day and get a little more sleep. But the habit of *God first*, formed in Moody days, stood me in good stead now. Whatever would I have done in the days ahead if I had missed that particular quiet time? For God had something particular to say to me. Yet when I lit my lamp at that early hour and turned my sleepy eyes on the portion for the day (Gen. 28) I had the feeling, "Oh, just the story of Jacob's ladder. Couldn't be anything special in that." Is it the lazy flesh or the devil that puts such thoughts into our heads? I turned my sluggishness over to the Lord in prayer first, and then as I read that old story so familiar from childhood, verse 15 sprang out of the page as if I had never read it before. "I am with you and will watch over you wherever you go." The Lord's voice came clear and unmistakable: "This is My promise to you for the journey ahead." I thought He meant just that dreaded Burma Road travel and I was grateful.

So when Lucius came up to rope my bedding for me I told him I had received a verse from the Lord and roughly translated it. His face lit up and he beamed at me: "Praise the Lord! 'I will bring you back to this land' — He's going to bring you back again!" I stared at him. Bring me back? Why, of course I intended to come back! Lucius must have missed the point. But, oh, how I had to thank the Lord later that it was Lucius who *got the point* — it was I who nearly missed it!

So I started out on the Burma Road trip with those two American air pilots. The Flying Tigers were Madame Chiang's special protégés. They were tough but brave, daring men. They were not at all thrilled to have this drab-looking, uninteresting missionary woman tagging along with them, but were considerate and kind, as American soldiers usually are. Just once were we all really embarrassed. At Yunnanyi there was a hostel so the men put up there, and got a cell for me. There was a lock on the door (Chinese inns seldom possessed such) and I locked it, fortunately. For about two o'clock in the morning a Flying Tiger arrived drunk. First thing I knew I was awakened by my door being shaken and pounded upon till I feared it must fly into bits. At the same time a drunken voice yelled, "Woman! Open zish door! I want to see zish woman!" A growl from a nearby cell proved that someone else was awake too, which comforted me. But it did not squelch the drunken ardour. "I don't care if she *is* a mishnary woman," he yelled back, "I want to see zish woman. Woman! Open zish door," and again that object was shaken till I quaked and prayed. Curses filled the air as the growler next door saw he would have to get out of bed to rescue me. Then followed a brief struggle interspersed with yells about the "mishnary woman," then finally the drunk was hauled off and shut up somewhere. The Flying Tigers were very nice to me until I tried to speak of Christ; then they became hard. They were tough and wanted to remain tough. Yet they were so kind too.

We were four days on the trip, and the fourth day the car broke down and there we were, miles from anywhere or any help — stranded. The American boys could not speak Chinese, so their idea was to wait in the middle of the road and hold up with a gun the first truck they saw, and compel help or transportation. They were disgusted with the Burma Road and its drivers. I begged them not to use guns and offered to interpret (hoping the Chinese language which I had not uséd for six years would come back to me). After an hour or so of uncomfortable experiences, a white man in a jeep appeared and offered to pick us up. He did not have room for all our baggage so I had to leave my bedding roll locked in the back of the abandoned car. The Flying Tigers (thinking they were still in America?) meant to come back and get the car and luggage, but of course when they arrived it had been plundered, so I lost my bedding roll and the clothing which was wrapped in it.

But I looked forward to the warm, hearty welcome Kay and Dave always gave us, for of course I planned to stay with my sister-in-law, although the China Inland Mission had a guest house in the capital city. Lonely and feeling ill, I pushed through the gate into the garden expecting to hear that pleasant yell of welcome as soon as someone spied me. But all was silent. Questioning, I went into the house and called. My voice echoed dismally, but no answer. From the back of the house came a patter of small feet and soon a rosy-cheeked Chinese maiden appeared. "Oh, *Yang-si-muh!*" she gave me my Chinese name, but spoke in English to me. "The Harrison family are all away in the country for meetings! But come in, I will take care of you." It was Eva, who had been left in charge of the house. Eva was the oldest daughter of a Chinese pastor who had a large family. She wanted an education, so had come into the Harrison family to help with housework or cooking while she went to high school. She was a little thing in stature and looked only fifteen whereas in reality she was twenty-one years old. People always thought Eva was a child, but she really was a very capable young woman, as I was to learn.

Eva was delighted to have company. She had now

graduated from high school, which gave her a social status so that she was above the servant class, and it was quite proper to treat her as a companion. My Chinese was so rusty that I was pleased to hear her talk English, and she, on her part, was perfectly thrilled to get all these English conversation lessons free! So English was our medium by mutual consent. She soon had me in the Harrison's own bedroom, and made me a tasty supper, for dark had fallen before we reached Kunming. It was March 27, 1942. I had made it in nine days from Oak Flat — very good time.

Now all those travelling days my tooth had not ached. Please notice that little kindness of the Lord. But I was feeling ill, looked ill, and had dizzy spells. The doctors had quite a time finding out what was wrong with me but I will explain now so you will understand. A tooth which held a bridge had become abscessed. As the tooth was dead it did not ache — that is why the poison was so hard to discover. I had pains in my head, sometimes in my face, but never in that particular tooth. Yet the poison was going through my system and I really was ill. By the time the trouble was diagnosed and the tooth pulled, gangrene had set in. Our capable dentist said if I had come to her twenty-four hours later my life could not have been saved! It was more than two weeks after I arrived in Kunming that the tooth was discovered and all that time I was getting weaker and weaker. Alone in the house except for Eva, I was too ill to study or do much but lie in bed — and with plenty of time to brood over my loneliness!

All this time little Eva was a jewel. She would bake the nicest cookies and things to tempt my appetite, and in between meals she would sit beside my bed and chatter in English! It took my mind off myself so I encouraged her, and drew her on by questions about her life, studies, friends and so on. As she answered I began to get a picture of an unselfish, hard-working young life that amazed me. She was quite unconscious of what she was revealing, for she had worked so hard that she never had time for self-consciousness. She was a Christian and the soul of honour. Meticulously careful about honesty, she leaned over backward to escape the slightest suspicion that she was misusing things that were accessible to her. For instance — the Harrison food cupboard. Every Chinese cook I had ever met helped herself freely to lard, sugar, and such things, not to speak of leftovers. But Eva never touched a thing for herself. I gave her money to buy my food and had not much appetite. To my dismay leftovers were carefully stored for me. She was one of those souls, rare in any nation, whom money does not tempt. She almost wept with chagrin when I offered her a little gift for her very loving care of me. And she was that way all the years I knew her. I have met few like her in any land. Yet with her freedom from the greed of money, she was a most wonderful bargainer! She was of Szechwan extraction, and they are noted for their ability in that line. Eva could get more out of a dollar than anyone who ever helped me.

In addition to her honesty and industry, Eva was pure. Of course she was a daughter of Christians and had spent many years in a missionary's home, but that has been true of others who had not her love for purity. I have mixed with young people in these heathen lands, and even if their conversation was purged of the usual filthy jokes of heathendom, it seldom reached the plane where a coarse or slightly shady story did not provoke a laugh. I have often been grieved and disappointed at this lack of sensitiveness to the beauty of holiness. But Eva was as chaste as anyone I ever met. One of the stories she prattled to me during those days related to a short train trip she had had alone — returning from the village to which the Harrisons had gone. "We were late getting in and dark had fallen. The train was so crowded and unpleasant that I found a spot all by myself on top of the baggage in the luggage car, but warm and cosy because it was next the engine. I was enjoying myself there when a man crawled up toward me. 'Sister, let's play together,' he said with an unclean smirk on his evil face.

"'You stay where you are!' I cried out. 'If you come one foot closer I will throw myself down under these train wheels!' He saw I meant it and with a curse he backed away. As soon as he was gone I slid down and went back into the crowded car. The conductor must have seen that man, for he came up to me, and pointing to the fellow said, 'Was that man troubling you?' The bad man gave me such a wicked look I was terrified and replied, 'Oh, no.' He would have killed me in revenge if I had told on him. People are found in Kunming with knives in their backs all the time — no one knows who has done it. But after that, the Harrisons would never let me travel alone."

I thought this little story was very revealing, and again cogitated on what a jewel this little Chinese Christian girl was. I had seen Eva in the Harrison household for years, but never realized what a fine character was under that hard-working childlike form.

As I had continued to get worse (nobody knowing it was just a tooth) the doctor wired for John to fly to

Kunming. The Chungking conference was over, but
he had been contemplating a trip to Lashio — so
reads my diary. He arrived Easter Day, April 5. By
this time the Harrisons had returned, and loving care
encircled me. But it was ten days more before they
discovered my illness came from the tooth and pulled
it, after which my strength returned rapidly.

During this time the Japanese were advancing up
Burma — the British retreating before them and
Americans evacuating. The Burmese began to flee
into Yunnan. We, at Kunming, had occasional
air-raid alarms. Then we heard that the Japanese
had taken Lashio, where John would have been if my
wire had not brought him to Kunming. Unknown to
us, the panic of the Burma Road had already begun,
and John, as superintendent, felt he should go west
to warn missionary families in isolated parts to
evacuate. None of them had radios and so might not
know of the danger. He planned to be gone only a
few days and then return to me. By then everyone
was discussing the question — would Yunnan fall?

Just a week later, news came that the Japanese had
bombed Paoshan without warning on a market day
at noon. The carnage was terrible. My diary reports
rumours that 15,000 were killed. Survivors stam-
peded on to the Burma Road in a panic to reach
Kunming. Somewhere in the midst of it was John.
Then on May 9 John himself arrived escorting Carl
Harrison (who had been at school in Tali), Leita
Partridge, Grace and Eric Cox and baby Miriam.
These latter had barely escaped with their lives. As
their truck was climbing the Salween canyon the
Japanese arrived on the opposite bank and opened
fire! They abandoned the truck and the few posses-
sions which they had hastily gatherd together on

hearing they must flee. What a story of wandering with an infant over wild mountainsides trying to find Paoshan! Then to arrive and see it in shambles! No missionary was killed for those stationed there had all fled to our station of Oak Flat, thinking the Lisu mountains would be safe.

Four days later John left again for Tali to try to get other workers out. Then reports and rumours came piling in, one after the other. One such said the Japanese were advancing on us from three directions. We knew they had reached the Salween River in the west, for they had fired on the Coxes. Another report said a column was advancing up the Mekong River from the south of us. And another column of Japanese were said to be approaching us by the railroad from Indo-China to the east. The British and American consuls began to advise that women and children evacuate north to Chengtu. Everyone said Yunnan would fall.

Not yet a naturalized American, I came under the jurisdiction of the British consul, who did not hesitate to urge me to flee north. David Harrison was not home — he was out on a preaching trip in the country. In the Kunming Harrison household were only three women — Kay Harrison, a new worker (Evelyn Gibson), and myself. Four others of our missionaries, in the China Inland Mission guest house over the way, had decided to fly out to India. The consul had told us we might evacuate to India, or travel north to Chengtu with a Royal Air Force corps who were proceeding in army trucks. The British consul was irritated that I showed reluctance to leave. "Everybody is going to have to evacuate," he said, "and trucks are going to be at a premium. By staying on now you will be virtually taking the place on a truck that should be kept for the women and children even now fleeing toward us on the Burma Road. It is selfish to stay!" What should we do? If only John would return! But John was not my source of guidance. And the Lord was absolutely silent when we prayed for direction. Experience had taught me to stay where I was until He did speak.

But the RAF convoy was leaving early on May 17. On May 16 we got word that the Japanese had *crossed* the Salween on the Burma Road. Still there was no guidance from the Lord. Stories of Japanese atrocities to women in Hongkong and Burma poured in. The irate British consul sent me word *three times in that one day*, ordering me to go on the convoy the next morning. What should we do? We decided to go. We could take only a bedding roll and one suitcase apiece. Of all one's goods — what to pack in one suitcase? Dear little Eva went crying around the house, helping us pack. If only she could go too, she wept. "But since accomodation even for British women is difficult to find — how could I ask them to make room for a Chinese girl?" said perplexed sister Kathryn. Carlie, about six years old, was with us too. Early on the morning of May 17, 1942, we three women, Carlie, and Eva arrived at the airfield where the convoy was. We were praying for Eva's future — Kay wanted her to go back to her own home. Then the Lord did a kind thing. The RAF captain came around to check on our identity, and saw Eva crying. Remember she looked like a child.

"What is she crying for?" he asked.

"She wants to come with us," answered Kay desperately, "she doesn't want to be left behind."

"Oh, she's not very big," he said compassionately, "let her get in — sure. That's O K. What's her name?"

and the miracle was accomplished.

Eva had no bedding or clothes with her, but that did not worry her. Sunshine followed showers. In beside Carlie she hopped, and the convoy began to move forward. Evelyn Gibson and I, with two RAF men, were in one truck; Kay Harrison, Carlie, and Eva in another; and I forget how many other trucks were in the convoy. We had to sit and sleep in the back of the truck. I remember that underneath me was a spare tire and a typewriter, which in turn were on top of ammunition boxes. I put Evelyn next to the wall of the truck; I slept next to her, and one of our men slept next to me. The trucks must have been small, for that was all they would hold. We ate RAF rations, and when we stopped for sleep the men had to take turns standing watch all night.

Seven days and six nights of such travel on the Burma Road! And plenty of time to think. Dust and rattle made conversation a burden. Out of sunny Yunnan into cloudy Kweichow. I had left my husband behind in Yunnan, and Evelyn had left her fiancé, Norman Charter. Sometimes I found her crying softly to herself, and that was how I felt too. But as I lay or sat there hour after hour, day after day, I was thinking. God had not told me to come — what would happen to me? Then I remembered Lucius' beaming face that last morning. "Praise the Lord, Ma-ma," he had said. "*He says He is going to bring you back!*" Genesis 28:15 was becoming a worn place in my Bible.

"Well, Lord," I conversed with Him on the way," "maybe I'm out of your will in this trip. You did not tell me to come. But you let me be pushed into it. And you gave me Genesis 28:15 that morning. That I know. Now I claim the 'wherever I go', and I claim

the promise to bring me back. *This land* must mean
Paoshan. So some day you are going to take me back
to Paoshan. Of course I don't know when. But I have
a feeling the Japanese won't get Yunnan after all. Oh,
dear, why did I ever leave! And, oh, dear, my lonely
heart —" and I twisted and squirmed with heartache.

As we passed through Pichieh in Kweichow
province, the convoy allowed us to stop and visit our
missionaries there. Sister Welzel and Sister Hierle
(German Women's *Friedenshort* Mission) were so
sweet to us but knew nothing of war conditions.
They were carrying on as usual. We met some Miao
tribesmen on the road and my heart twisted and tore
itself anew at the memory of the Lisu and how far I
was travelling from them!

Our RAF men were very good to us. A Scotsman
named Davidson sat next to me most of the time, and
he told me of the terrible carnage of Paoshan at its
bombing. They had arrived (fleeing from Burma) at
sunset of the day of the bombing and he said it was
breaking day the next morning when they finally
managed to get through — the destruction and
carnage were so terrible. The RAF had been through
all the Burma fighting, and their talk was gloomy —
China would fall, for sure.

The afternoon of the sixth day when we pulled into
Suyung, two CIM missionaries were waiting for us.
They had had a telegram from our headquarters in
Chungking saying that their accommodations and
those at Chengtu were full up — we were to get off
the convoy at Luhsien in Szechwan Province, and
stay with Mr and Mrs Arnold Lea until further notice.
We arrived there the next afternoon at half-past four
and were cordially welcomed by the Leas. Almost my
first question was, "Has Yunnan fallen?"

"Why, no," said Mr Lea in polite bewilderment. "War news seems rather good these last few days." It seems that Generalissimo Chiang had sent his crack regiment down a back road, chasing the Japanese back over the Salween River and holding them there. Yunnan was saved. And our flight had been perfectly needless.

Now I was two provinces away from Yunnan, with no possibility of getting back! Mr Lea was very cordial, but one could see that he wondered why we had had to run *so far away*! There had never been any talk of Yunnan falling in their part of the world. I was heartsick. My life seemed one wreck of desolation, and the future black. What was happening to my little girl in Japanese hands? Well, the Leas had word that the school and children were being kindly cared for by their captors. Thank the Lord for that! A matter that made us all look sober was our extreme shortage of funds. Friends at home were giving generously, but the pegged exchange gave us only 50 per cent of the true market value. If only we could play the black market the China Inland Mission would be well off, but that was illegal and the Mission could not do it. So all of us were pinched financially. This made my return to Yunnan all the more hopeless. The RAF convoy had brought us free of charge, but if I returned I must pay my own way back — and suffer all those days and days on a Chinese truck on the Burma Road! My heart fainted at the thought.

The only thing to do, counselled Mr Lea kindly, was to brush up on the Chinese language, settle down and help with the church work at Luhsien. So twice a week I went with the Bible woman to the Chinese prison. The Szechwanese dialect was very difficult for me to understand. Where the dialect I had learned pronounced a *j* sound, these people gave a *ts* sound, so that their sentences sounded full of hissings to me. Nevertheless they were needy souls, and the fellowship with Mrs Ho was real. The prison was terrible — body lice crawling up and down the walls and everywhere. We had to change our clothes each time as soon as we returned from the place. But the poor women who were shut up there had to stay! Some accepted the Lord.

The weather too was terribly hot — 100°F. (my diary reads). Kay Harrison was not as discouraged as I. She would have to come this direction anyway, in a month or so, to put Carl into a new school which the China Inland Mission was opening in Kiating, Szechwan. So she had not lost any time really, and as Chinese was the language in which she worked the adjustment of dialect was not difficult for her.

Eva, as usual, was making herself of value. She made the bread for all Mrs Lea's big household (the Coxes and Miss Partridge had joined us now) and she was also sewing Carlie's new school outfit. She was a good little seamstress and could run a sewing machine better than I could. It was a big saving for Kay to get Carlie's things made so cheaply, yet so well.

Kay Harrison had received a letter from her husband which made us all feel bad. Dave felt that those rumours that Yunnan would fall had been the devil's masterstroke. Not only had it scattered us to far Szechwan but other missionaries had flown out to India and left China entirely. His preaching band had heard the rumours also, got excited, and all had run home. "We were going to evangelize a part of the country that had been on my heart for years, and I had the best preaching band collected that ever I've had, and now — all dispersed. Refugees from the Burma Road are still piling in. Never have we had so many opportunities for service and — no missionaries! I hear that John is having a wonderful time in the west too. It is just heartbreaking that Satan has scored such a victory!"

You can imagine how this made me feel. I simply ate my heart out with grief. Even my hair went dead until someone said it looked like straw. My diary for June 4 records that Mr Lea had a talk with me suggesting that maybe I could help in the new school at Kiating. This really flattened me. It showed that Mission leaders were trying to find a place for me in the province of Szechwan. But my husband was in Yunnan! And my dear Lisu — Oh Lord, what should I do!

Never had the Lord's presence left me. Frequently He gave me comforting Bible verses, assuring me of His love. "But I'm a human being, Lord," I wailed. "It's a human touch and love that I crave so! And not just anybody's — I want *my own. My own!*"

The next day came a letter from John telling of wonderful opportunities he was having. "I do so wish you were with me, dear," he wrote. He had joined a medical unit. Cholera had broken out after that terrible Paoshan bombing and they were inoculating the refugees — hundreds of them. And hearing their stories too, of course. Hearts were bleeding and just ready for the Balm of Gilead. Then I began to question, "Lord, may I not go back?" I spoke to Mr Lea about it. He was kind but looked a bit alarmed. "You were sent here by recommendation of the British consul. They are still fighting in Yunnan. I do not see how you could return without the consul's permission — and I'm sure he'd never give it just now. Besides, there are plenty of trucks still fleeing from Yunnan but very few returning to it. I do not know that you could get conveyance there."

But I was getting more and more desperate. "*'I will bring you back to this land'* — Lord, you did promise that! Now help me get back." The next day I wrote to Mr J R Sinton, who was acting in the place of our general director those days. I told him I felt I should return to Yunnan and of the opportunities Dave and John wrote about. Then I had to wait for an answer. In the meantime another letter came from Dave Harrison saying he could see no reason why Isobel should not return! Still Mr Lea was dubious about a woman going alone on a Chinese truck all that long way, and without consular permission!

On June 13 Mr Sinton's answer arrived. He advised my waiting until my husband invited me to return. That was enough for me. The next day was Sunday and I took the morning off for fasting and prayer. It was no small thing to act without consular authority; for I had decided it would be useless to apply for it. I must just slip back without telling him. But the main thing was the *Lord's* permission. I did not doubt that He had promised to take me back to Paoshan; the point was, *when*? Was it to be now? Or should I wait for two weeks? I went out into a Chinese cemetery and there among the graves, undisturbed by spectators, poured out my heart to Him. I had four difficulties to lay before Him — the very first being an utter impossibility. Quite simply I did not have enough money for that long trip! Some gifts had come through, but our account had been very low. And I not only had the expense of getting to Yunnan, I still would have to cross almost the entire province before I reached Lisuland again! And the exchange was still impossibly low. So my requests were laid out this way.

1. Money to make the trip.

2. John's invitation — to satisfy Mr Sinton. "It would be nice to have you here," might not be recognized as an invitation in headquarters' eyes.

3. Trucks going to Yunnan. They were very few.

4. I dreaded going alone with Chinese men. A companion, Lord?

Within just a little more than 24 hours the Lord had answered all four.

Special gifts arrived in the mail.

A telegram from John arrived, urging me to join him.

Mr Lea found a convoy of three merchant trucks going back to Kunming.

Eva asked to go with me!

The money was the biggest miracle of all. Years before, John had received a legacy. Learning that a certain young Bible student had not sufficient funds to finish her course we had given her $100. She wrote us that if ever she was able, after graduation, she would repay us — but we merely laughed at that. We gave it as to the Lord and forgot about it. I had truly forgotten all about it. But the Monday after my prayer day, the mail brought two letters from this girl. These letters were written and posted *six months apart*, yet they arrived in the same mail. *And each letter contained* US $50! The marvel of it has never left me.

The gift of Eva was just as unbelievable. That previous Saturday morning as I passed through the laundry I saw Eva scrubbing some of Carlie's clothes and silently weeping. I did not know what had caused her tears and did not feel I should ask. But I did know that whatever the trouble was, her Lord could help her. So I put my arm around her and whispered, "Tell the Lord about it, dear. He can help you," and then went on my way.

When the money for my return trip arrived so miraculously, of course I ran in to tell sister Kay. Eva, sewing in the corner, heard me say I had money to take me back to Kunming! Now her tears, unknown to me, had been because there was no money *for her* to return! Shortly after I had gone back to my own bedroom, Kay appeared at my door.

"Eva says she would like to go back with you. She says she will go and work for you in Lisuland if you will take her. I have no money to pay her return expenses, and I will not need her at Kiating where I am going, so if you want her and can pay her fare, why — take her!"

I was dumbfounded. I could not believe my ears. To me Eva was a rare jewel of a helper whom nobody would ever willingly relinquish. I was afraid Kay might regret it, as soon as bank exchange righted itself and finances did not pinch us. But she said, "No, if you want Eva, take her."

I had been praying for a companion, but had wildly imagined some other white lady might by chance be going back. I had never once thought of Eva. To tell the truth, we missionaries to the Lisu did not approve of bringing Chinese helpers into tribesland. They almost always considered themselves so much better than the Lisu, and were so patronizing to them that it caused trouble. Little Eva? I still wondered if I should promise to take her to Lisuland. To Kunming, yes. Lisuland was a little different. But Eva begged to go.

"I do not want your money," she said with tearful eyes. "I will serve you for instruction in Bible,

English, and music. I want to learn to play the organ.
I do not eat much, and I have enough clothes at
Kunming to last for several years. Please take me."

"Well, I will take you to Kunming," I said. "But
there is Mr Harrison to ask also. You have been a
wonderful helper in their home. Maybe he will not
be happy that his wife has offered you to us. If he is
not happy, I will leave you at Kunming. In the
meantime you can pray about it."

The very next day Mr Lea got us our trucks. The
one we were to ride in was a brand-new one, and by
paying the truck company a little extra, we obtained
tickets for two seats in the cab beside the driver. That
meant we would not have to perch on top of baggage,
and we would not be exposed to rain or bad weather,
for it was the rainy season.

We were introduced to our driver by the company
manager, and he bowed, smiled, and was so pleasant
that Mr Lea commented on the fact. "These three
trucks are going right through," said the manager.
"They are not allowed to pick up yellow fish."

Yellow fish was the term used for a passenger
picked up illicitly on the Burma Road by truck
drivers. Their fares went into the driver's pocket
instead of into the coffers of the company who
owned the trucks. And the drivers charged what they
thought they could get — it was a nefarious traffic.

We were to leave the next morning. I prayed on
Sunday and we left on Wednesday — that is how fast
the Lord worked for me.

However we were no sooner out of sight of
Luhsien City than our driver changed his manners
toward us. All the smiles left and he became nasty.
All along the country roads he stopped and picked
up the forbidden yellow fish. At the main cities his

truck company had inspection posts. Just before arriving at these, the truck stopped and all the yellow fish had to get off and walk through the city and beyond the inspection post to the farther side, where we picked them up again. Their baggage was coolly attributed to Eva and me, who, of course, had very little. Eva and I, having bona fide company tickets, were saved all this bother. While we were still in populous Szechwan and Kweichow our driver was not too uncivil, because twice we stayed overnight in towns where the China Inland Mission had mis- sionaries living, and he saw that we had friends to whom we could have reported his ill-conduct.

But once we began to go over the lonely mountain ranges into Yunnan, our driver showed his real colours. At one isolated spot, he stopped the truck, walked out in front of us and deliberately showed us he was an immoral man. Of course we refused to look, but Eva caught my hand in terror. "Don't be afraid, dear," I whispered, "the Lord is with us." And in my heart, "The Lord promised: '*I will watch over you wherever you go*'. This is one of the *all places*." But I now knew that we had an unclean as well as unprincipled man to deal with. I feared most for little Eva, and never let her out of my sight. The driver became nastier and nastier to me, snapping savagely at any chance to order us around.

When at length we pulled out of Kweichow, where the skies were overcast all the way, and crossed the boundary into Yunnan, the sun burst forth in a golden glory lighting up the green of beautiful mountaintops. "Now I know," I said to Eva, "why they named our province *South of the Clouds*. We are south of cloudy Kweichow." And in my heart was a burst of joy to be back again in the same province, at least, with John and the Lisu.

But our worst trial lay ahead. From Kutsing we hoped to make Kunming in one day. But that morning as we gathered before the three trucks, it was raining. Some Chinese women appeared on the scene. Yellow fish? No — free passengers, friends of the drivers. To my astonishment my driver came up and said with a nasty look, "You are to get into truck number two. There is no room for her" (indicating Eva); "she can ride up in the back of my truck."

"I am very sorry," I replied politely but firmly, "but we cannot separate. And Miss Tseng must have a cab seat. We have paid for cab seats."

"Well, you can't have it!" he swore at me. "There aren't enough cab seats. These ladies" (his smirking girl friends) "are relatives high up in the company. They come first."

Then my indignation took fire.

"Look here," I said, speaking plainly (a deadly breach of Chinese etiquette), "we have paid extra for cab seats and we are going to have them and sit together. You have been taking on yellow fish. If you do not give us our seats I'll report you to your company."

Then he really got furious. I knew he was swearing at us but his words spat out of his mouth so fast and his eyes glared and snapped so that I was lost in the torrent of Chinese language. Eva, however, understood. She began to cry, "Oh, *Yang-si-muh*, you don't know what he is saying! I don't mind standing in the rain! Let me go. He says he is going to throw us out on the lonely mountainside and leave us to the wild beasts. Oh, don't make any more fuss — I'll go!" Was there ever a blacker moment? No one in Kunming knew when we were arriving, so our non-arrival would not alarm our friends there — they might wait a month without concern for us. Another foreboding fact was that I did not have consular authority to return, so how could consular protection be asked? But there is always One with us who is greater than the governments of this world. Again desperately in my heart I cried, "Lord, your promise! '*I will watch —.*'"

I had not time to finish the verse before a hand plucked my sleeve from behind and a Chinese voice whispered hoarsely, "Get into my cab, quick — both of you!" We whirled around and sprang into the cab of the second truck. The driver shot into place behind the wheel, raced his motor, and off we sped, leaving my driver still swearing and trembling with rage. We were now in a much older truck, one that had broken down several times during the trip, but as we sped along into a good lead over the other trucks, our new driver turned to me and said quietly, "Lady, never do that again! Next time you travel the Burma Road, *you travel yellow fish.*" All day long we kept in the lead and out of sight of the other trucks. And all day I prayed that this old truck would not break down again. And it did not. Another Chinese woman was with us, so that Eva had to sit on my knee or partially so. But our driver was very courteous and drove us right up to the Harrisons' door. Luckily our baggage had been placed on his truck. We were safe. "*I will watch over you.*" He had watched. He had never promised that we would not have trials.

Dave Harrison gave us a resounding welcome and soon Eva was back in her old place making us tasty meals.

A letter from Mary Zimmerman was waiting for me. This dear friend had formed the habit of writing us long, newsy letters, quoting from letters which spoke of our circulars, so that a letter from her was like a round-robin from everybody. I had so missed them: it was wonderful to be in touch again. Rain and more toothache and another visit to the dentist are recorded in my diary.

Before our flight to Szechwan province, Kay had been teaching a Bible class attended by some university students. Dave had taught this class during our absence, but he wanted to make another trip to some needy country churches. Would I please delay going west about a half-month to teach these English classes for him until he could get back? There was really no hurry for me to return to Lisuland. The missionaries from Paoshan who had refugeed to Oak Flat would teach the Rainy Season Bible School by interpretation, so the Lisu were taken care of. It was these Chinese students at Kunming who might disperse if the classes were dropped.

As for Eva, Dave was quite pleased for her to go with us to the Lisu. Since she had graduated from high school, Eva's mother had been angry at her doing servant's work in the Harrisons' home. Several times she had made it unpleasant for them, so Dave would be glad if Eva went with us. But for the next two weeks — would I stay?

It was clearly my duty. I have heard some say that the need is not the call. I do not understood that. An obvious need is a call in any branch of human life. The Good Samaritan did not need a special Bible verse miraculously shining upon him to indicate that it was God's will he help the poor fellow who had fallen among thieves. Where common sense clearly points out a duty, that is the voice of God. We do not need any other, provided a higher duty is not claiming us. For a mother to cast aside her own child in order to go and care for a neighbour's would not be God's will. She owes a higher duty to the human soul which she herself has brought into existence. Apart from that, the need is the call.

I did not want to stay in Kunming. I wanted to get to John as soon as possible. I was desperately longing for *one of my own* to put his arms around me and comfort me. But dearer than any human love is the Master's, and I could not grieve Him by disobedience. So I consented to stay, and Dave joyfully went on his trip.

The students' class began to grow. One day I was asked if I would not teach a second Bible class: the evening class was mainly evangelistic, but some of these university students were now Christians and wanted deeper teaching.

One tall young Manchurian, Jack, was especially eager. When the Japanese conquered Manchuria, Jack's school had evacuated and he with it. He had married in his early teens and when he fled from Manchuria he had a little daughter two years old. As the Japanese advanced, his college fled before them until finally they had reached Kunming. During the first few years away from home Jack had corresponded with his wife, but for some years now he had received no word from her at all. He did not know if she and the little daughter were alive or dead.

At Kunming Jack had heard of Mrs Harrison's English classes and had started to attend. Here he met the Saviour and gave his life wholeheartedly to Jesus Christ. Jack was really born again and hungry for a deeper life with the Lord. I believe it was he who asked me to begin a morning class for Christians, and I was delighted to do so. By July 7 (my diary records) I was teaching three classes, and one young man had accepted Christ as his Saviour. But when Dave came back from his trip and could take over the classes, I felt released. Then the Lord worked for us. A Friends Ambulance Unit (British) was driving to Tali and they offered to take Eva and me with them. Oh, how grateful I was that we need not travel that stretch of the Burma Road on a Chinese truck! It was still the rainy season and we needed cover. We left Kunming on July 15.

Jack came down to see us off, expressing deep thanks and saying he had been much helped. The FAU truck was delayed several hours but Jack waited all that long time with us to make sure we got off safely. I never could forget that kindness and we corresponded a bit from then on.

I would like to digress a moment to tell more of Jack. As soon as he was saved, he became burdened for his wife and her need to know the Saviour if she were still alive. He had not seen her for ten years then, and the ordinary Chinese would have laughed at the thought of loyalty to her under such circumstances. It was good Chinese custom for a man to have a concubine to travel around with him, while the legal wife was left at home. Jack was tall, good-looking and personable. He was not even sure that his wife was alive. Why be so finicky? The only reason was the command of his Lord and Master, Jesus Christ.

Seven more years of silence passed. Still Jack was clean and single. By that time he was an ordained Episcopalian clergyman and had friends who were willing to send him to America for further training. That was, to any Chinese, a tremendous temptation. Study in America was the acme of good fortune to a young Chinese of those days, and Jack was human enough to feel the pull of it. He wrote to me about it, asking prayer for guidance. "I would love to go to America," he said, "but somehow I cannot get away from the burden of my wife and family. It is seventeen years since I saw them last. My little two-year-old girl will be a young woman of nineteen now. I feel I should try to go and find them. Please pray with me, Mrs Kuhn, that the temptations of this world will not sway me but that I may do only the will of the Lord Jesus."

A few months later another letter dated from Peking. By this time the Communists were in control of Manchuria. I do not have the original letter, but in substance it ran thus:

DEAR MRS KUHN:

I decided to do the will of the Lord and go in search of my family. I resigned my position in Yunnan and came here hoping to get information as to how I might gain entrance to Manchuria. I found I could get a seat on a plane tomorrow, but it is a very dangerous procedure for a Christian to try to do this. I am afraid. Oh, pray for me that my faith may not fail!

I looked up the Christian family in this city whose address you gave me. They were very kind to me and asked me to supper. But, oh, Mrs Kuhn, why is it that so few Christians ask to have prayer with me?

I fly in tomorrow. If it is possible, I will write to you from there. If you never hear from me again, you will know it was only because communication with you was not possible.

Then followed silence — for three long years. Then through a very roundabout way, Kay received a message. "I found my family. They have become

Christians and the Lord has given us a little son." So ends one of the sweetest little idylls that I know of Christ's Round-Table Knights in China.

And now to retrace our thoughts back to July 17, 1942, and the Friends Ambulance Unit which was pulling into Tali with Eva and Ma-ma on board. (Since she was coming to Lisuland, I taught Eva to call me by the name which I loved most to hear from Lisu lips, *Ma-ma*.) I was longing to meet my husband. He had been writing to me from Tali, had approved my delay in order to set Dave Harrison free for country work, but looked forward to my joining him at Tali as soon as Dave returned. So I was all set to meet my dear husband whom I had not seen for more than two months.

Imagine the shock I felt, on arrival in Tali, to be told John had gone on to Paoshan with Dr Mei and the medical unit! I was simply shattered. "You'll never have *anyone* to love you," mocked Satan, taking advantage of my self-pity. "God is a jealous God. He doesn't want you to have anyone but Him to love you." It is very devastating to lend your ear to the Evil One. If only we could learn that he never tells the truth! Not the whole truth; a half-truth he tells, which is ever the worst of lies. God *was* loosening my hold on human love; He *was* nailing my affections to the cross. But not that my life should be without love and loved ones. Merely that the inordinate affections should become ordered and controlled. The human props on which I leaned so heavily were bound to give way sometime or other, just because they were human. And then when they gave way — how painfully I sprawled! If I could only learn to receive my loved ones, and yet not lean so heavily on them. Hold them, and yet not be so dependent on them! It was Love, and tender anxious Love, that was disciplining me. And I was learning, although with such agony.

Eva, for instance, was always watching to help me. But already I was alerted to the danger this could become. "Watch that she does not become indispensable to you," was the Lord's tender warning in my ear. "If you clutch her to your heart and she becomes as indispensable as these others, you will have all this pain to go through again, for human props will always fail, some time or other. Lean more on Me, dear. I will never fail you nor forsake you." And so in loving Eva, there was now *harnessed affection*. Always I reminded myself to live in the light of the day when I must give her up to someone else.

But I was slow to learn. The day after arrival in Tali my diary reads: "At noon I got a letter from John. He is not coming back until August! I felt so heartbroken. But then I received a letter from Girlie, *the first one in over seven months*."

This happy letter reminded me that Roxie Fraser, the dear wife of our late superintendent, would mother my little girl in internment camp, which she did. And all this time in Tali the Lord was working for me that I might not be tried above what I was able to bear (I Cor. 10:13).

I inquired about Eva and myself proceeding to Paoshan, but found a new difficulty. Tali was the last civil post. All west of Tali was in the *military zone* now, for the Japanese were still within the province. They were on the west bank of the Salween River, and the Salween canyon (Lisuland!) was now the front line of battle. No one could go west of Tali without a military pass. Even American soliders were not allowed as far as the Salween! They chafed to get there but the Chinese were jealous of the front line and would not admit them. Paoshan was only one day's journey from the Salween. John had gone through because he was attached to Dr Mei's medical unit *which was Chinese*. If American soldiers were not allowed at the Salween, how could I, *a woman*, ever get there? Please ponder that. Against it put God's Genesis 28:15 — *"and will bring you back to this land."* Oh, how I clung to that, and how I claimed it in His presence! Ten days the Lord kept me praying and claiming that verse. Now watch how wondrously He worked.

John kept writing to me, urging that Eva and I join him in Paoshan. He seemed to forget that we could not leave Tali without a military pass. At length I decided to go to the residence of General Song (head in command of the Western Yunnan front) and ask for a pass to Paoshan for Eva and me. I shrank unspeakably from asking favours of these high-ranking Chinese. My best clothes I had left stored in Paoshan — they were stolen in the looting which took place after the bombing. Expecting to stay in Kunming only a few weeks I had not brought much with me, and some of what I brought was lost in the Flying Tigers' car which broke down. Missionary friends had given me some of what they could share, but I was painfully conscious of my shabby appearance. This did not help to give me poise. I got no farther than the outer gate of General Song's estate! His soldiers looked me up and down without much respect, kept me waiting a long time, and then sent me home without any pass! I learned later that they had not even sent in my application. This is what happened when I tried to move in my own strength.

But see what happens when God moves!

That very evening an officer arrived at our China Inland Mission compound "to inform Mrs Kuhn that General Song had telephoned to Paoshan and requested that John Kuhn come to Tali — the general providing transportation!" The reason for this was not divulged at the time, but I was told to expect my husband soon.

The reason, unknown to me then, was this. Checked at the Salween bridge on the Burma Road, the Japanese had gone north up the canyon, seeking another crossing. The tribes in those parts had received and helped them. Suddenly China had awakened to the importance of possessing the friendship of these poor "earth-people" as they had for centuries termed the tribes. But in order to solicit their cooperation it was necessary to speak to the tribes and — who knew their language? The feudal lairds, of course. So these were summoned to Tali and their influence requisitioned. But it was very soon evident that they were utterly undependable — they would sell the tribes to the highest bidder. Was there no one else who spoke Lisu? Then it was that the Lord brought the missionaries to the general's mind. Hence the phone call for John. He arrived at Tali on August 4, and what a reunion it was!

That afternoon we went together to see General Song. I had a different reception this time! The officials at the gate bowed and scraped to us, and we were taken right into the beautiful mansion which was the home of the Songs. The general was very cordial to us and quickly summoned his charming wife, who spoke English well. It was then he told us frankly of his interview with the Salween feudal lairds. "Why, I found they were all opium sots!" he exclaimed. "They cared about nothing but opium. I couldn't use them, so I sent for you — will you help us solicit the friendship of the Lisu people?"

We told them we had already done so. We had told the Lisu that the Japanese would oppose their being Christians — that alone was sufficient. And it is significant to me that the Japanese won the west bank of the Salween up to the point where the Christian church became numerous. From there on they were held back, and conquered no more!

General Song told us he would give us a military escort right to Oak Flat Village! And John was to be made adviser to the Nationalist guerrilla colonel in charge of the Pienma Pass district (which was our Oak Flat church area). We were to leave in a few days.

On our last night in Tali (so it was meant to be, but we were later delayed) the Songs invited us to a Chinese feast in their home. It was a sumptuous affair, and Madame even had a lace tablecloth spread for our benefit. (Chinese custom does not use table-cloths, as their tables are beautifully polished lac-quer.) I remember one dish appeared to be roast chicken — it was brought in with wings and legs properly trussed.

"Have you seen this dish before?" asked Madame Song, who enjoyed my undisguised admiration of her cuisine. She took her chopsticks, stuck them into the breast-bone ridge of the chicken and with a flick of her finger the chicken fell open. It had been completely boned! How they ever maintained that perfect shape without any bones to hold it together is still a mystery to me!

Before the meal ended, General Song gave a command and a smartly uniformed colonel was ushered in.

"I wish to introduce you to Colonel Hsie, who will be your escort to the Salween," announced the general. Then turning to the colonel he issued crisp orders that we were to be well taken care of. It was like a dream. Not only a military pass to a point which might at any moment become front line of battle, but an escort too — and all expenses paid! Only God could do that. "*And will bring you back to this land.*" But I still had need to claim Genesis 28:15 once more, before getting there.

Dr Roots had asked permission to ride with us as· far as Paoshan, where Dr Wesley Mei's Medical Unit was still working. We were given a brand-new truck for the trip. Eva and I sat in comfort in the cab, with the driver, while Dr Roots, John, Colonel Hsie, and the soldier escort rode in the open back.

The afternoon of the second day's travel we had come to some of the famous sharp curves of the Burma Road, with unguarded precipitous drops at the edge. I do not know anything about driving, but as we whirled around these hairpin turns and gaily struck big stones lying on the rough road I thought to myself, "Guess it is all right, but this looks to me like dangerous driving." I was just wondering about it, when we struck another large stone; there was a ripping and a pounding noise. The entrails of the engine seemed to fall out — *bang! bang! bang!* Something underneath was dragging and bouncing, the brakes were broken and the wheels would not respond. The side of the road dropped away in a precipice. I heard John screaming, "Jump! Belle! Jump!" But where to? Outside of the cab door was the edge of the precipice. I just sat still and cried in my heart, "Lord, *You promised*! 'I will watch over you wherever you go, and I will bring you back to this land' — it's not Paoshan yet!" I was still quoting Genesis 28:15 when the driver somehow managed to turn the wheel in toward the steep rock bank of the mountainside and away from the dangerous edge. Then Eva and I opened the cab door and got out.

What a sight met our gaze! Soldiers were lying in the rough gravel road with heads gashed, open, bloody and groaning. Dr Roots, John, and Colonel Hsie had jumped running, of course; but the poor common Chinese soldiers, just off the farm and with no experience of trucks or modern machinery, had jumped straight. The next few minutes were busy ones. Irate Colonel Hsie was shouting orders to tie up the driver; Dr Roots was kneeling beside the wounded with his first-aid kit open. "Build a fire and boil some water for sterilizing," he called to us. A fire? — in the middle of the Burma Road? Unpractical me — I stood and gaped. It was little Eva who ran to the hillside to look for twigs, and it was she who got a fire going and boiled water in a surprisingly short time. I helped hold heads up while the gashes were bathed clean and the doctor bound them up. Straightening up to ease my back at one time, I looked over the edge of the precipice and gasped in astonishment to see, about a hundred feet down, the wreck of what once had been a truck! I called John's attention to it. "Hm," he grunted. "One has gone over here, sure enough. It's a miracle we didn't go too." Incidentally, we had a good chance to preach Christ to those poor soldiers of our escort.

Stranded on this lonely stretch of the Burma Road, six or seven miles from Wayao, the nearest village, we had nothing to eat, and darkness was approaching. Colonel Hsie was still flying around, making one of the soldiers climb a telephone pole. Soon I saw an interesting sight — a field telephone set up! He called the military headquarters at Paoshan and explained our predicament. "All right," they answered, "tomorrow a truck will come out and get you." So that night we slept in the broken truck on the road. The next day we got no farther than Wayao — a little hamlet restaurant that catered to the trade of the Burma Road. This, by the way, was where the trail to Lisuland comes out on to the motor road! But Colonel Hsie wished to go to Paoshan first, and so did we in order to buy our staple foods of flour, sugar, and so on. And so — the Lord fulfilled His promise and brought me again into that land!

Will I ever forget that vision of Paoshan, swept clean after the destruction! "How deserted lies the city, once so full of people!" were the only words that came. Now I understood why Jeremiah wept and how the lamentations flowed as he sat and beheld Jerusalem's desolations. The business section was laid flat as a ploughed field; silence reigned there, and grass was sprouting in the main street.

But Dr Mei's Medical Unit gave us a warm welcome, with opportunities to preach in the hospital and to the soldiers. Some of the Paoshan Christians still in the city were hungry for fellowship. We learned that, with the exception of one paralytic, not a Christian was killed in that awful bombing, although at least one of them was right on the main street at the time. Praying hard, she crawled under a culvert and was saved. Our hearts went out to those who were left, but God was taking care of them — army personnel were constantly coming and going, so business was good!

We were on our way to dinner with a Christian

brother one afternoon when two soldiers, sent by Colonel Hsie, came to say he had obtained horses for us to ride and to carry our goods, and we would leave tomorrow! So began a long slow trek into the Salween canyon. If we had been by ourselves we would have made better time, but Colonel Hsie was in charge and we had to delay when he chose to. It was the rainy season and often we were soaked to the skin, but we had good places to stay at night.

We stopped a day at Six Treasuries where Colonel Hsie left us. This was the home of three feudal lairds who entertained the colonel to more than food. I was invited out by the laird's ladies, to whom I preached whenever I had opportunity. That last afternoon while I was away, and Eva was alone, Colonel Hsie appeared and tried to make love to her, offering her a college education if she would go to him! Poor child! She darted past him, ran out on to the veranda, where at least she could be heard if she screamed, then faced him and told him what she thought of him. And Eva, aroused, did not mince words.

You can imagine our feelings when we returned and she told us. What a beginning for John, who was Colonel Hsie's "adviser"! Needless to say, behind our backs the colonel turned to be our enemy, but God wonderfully protected us, for he was never allowed to do us harm.

And now I was to be *home* tomorrow! By nature I disliked travel and change, and here I had been tossed from pillar to post for six weary months. I could hardly wait to get home, to my quiet bedroom by the side of the deep ravine where the birds sang matins in the morning, and the great peaks glowed back the sunset hues with their steady unshakableness at day's end. I longed to get my roots down comfortably into familiar places! And this, my last little candle-flame had to be blown out.

I had forgotten that the missionaries who had refugeed to our home from Paoshan must necessarily have changed things. With five workers in a house where John and I had been the only two, and with three of them seriously ill, the furniture had had to be changed around. Outside, home looked just as usual, but inside nothing seemed to be as I had left it, and I felt like a stranger under my own roof. It seemed as if my last little candle-flame of human love had been extinguished. The superintendency had taken my husband (no matter where we lived he would be away from home much of the time); war had taken my little girl; marriage had taken my Lisu helper; and now home was no longer home; my roots could not sink down and be comfortable. This seemed to be the last straw that broke the camel's back. To my utter shame, my inner feelings were revealed to those dear guests, and I had to apologize and ask their forgiveness. They did forgive me, but I never forgave myself.

> The sun went down in clouds,
> The moon was darkened by a misty doubt,
> The stars of heaven were dimmed by earthly fears
> And all my little candle-flames burned out:
> But while I sat in shadow, wrapped in night
> The face of Christ made all the darkness light.

ANNIE JOHNSON FLINT

And now, lest you think my dear Master was too hard on me, I want to point out some things. The difficult lessons of 1942 taught me to *fear* leaning heavily on human props. I had surrendered husband, child, friends, all I possessed, long ago. But this was something deeper. This was relinquishing *my rights* to them. This was holding them, but on the open palm of my hand.

Alice Macfarlane, principal of our language school in Yangchow and a dear warrior saint, had taught me that metaphor. She said, "Keep your treasures on the *open* palm of your hand. If you hold something tight clenched in your fist, God may have to hurt you in order to open your fingers and take it from you. But if it is offered on the *open palm* of your hand, you will hardly know when it is gone." I never found it so easy that I did not *feel* when my treasures were taken, but it did make a tremendous difference. It prevented me from collapsing or sprawling.

Hannah Hurnard in *Hinds' Feet on High Places* expresses this truth in a different way. Little Much-Afraid, says her beautiful allegory, longed to go with the Shepherd to the High Places. She goes through many trials to get there; the final and greatest is a descent into a steep canyon called the Grave. In this deep valley were an altar and a priest, and here she was asked to let the priest reach into her heart and pull out the plant called *Natural Affection*, root and branch. When I read that I nodded my head with delighted recognition. That was what happened to me in 1942 when *"all my little candle-flames burned out."*

It does not mean that after such an experience all affection is gone. Just the very opposite is true. But affection *in its natural state* is dealt with. Affection, especially with intense natures, as it comes to us from Adam, *runs to excess* if given free rein. "Those who belong to Christ Jesus have crucified the sinful nature with its passions and desires", said Paul (Gal.

5:24).

Uncrucified love runs to inordinate affection and selfish possessiveness which blights rather than blesses. Little Much-Afraid gave up the plant of Natural Affection but she had already received the plant of the Lord's love in her heart. When we allow the Lord to nail our affections to the cross (to use the Scriptural metaphor), we do not cease to love. We love even more widely, but it is a love stripped of corrupting influences. Love is not killed — only the seed of corruption in natural affection is killed.

To go back to the practical illustration. When the little candle-flames of human joy were allowed to burn out, it hurt. So when God gave me a new one, presented Eva to me, I was immediately on my guard. *Natural affection* would have prompted me so to embrace her that we became all-in-all to one another. *Crucified affection* caused me to love her but always be alert that it might never become *inordinate affection*. Always I reminded myself "The time will come that I must do without her. How should we live so when that time comes, we can each separate without being *undone*?" That is, never to let the other one become indispensable, so that when the human prop is removed, there is a painful sprawl. Never to let *home* become so indispensable that at His call I cannot give it up! This brought me into a realm of unexpected freedom and relaxation. Human loves did not cease to delight but they no longer enslaved.

Now I do not want to profess that from the year 1942 on I never again defaulted in this matter of enslaving affections. I defaulted often enough to keep me humble and totally cast upon the Lord. I cannot even sustain the lesson I learned, without His help! My own strength is entirely untrustworthy. But through the experiences of 1942 I received a wholesome *fear* of what disobedience would do to me. And that fear helped to keep me looking to Him.

Crucified affections lift you into a realm of childlike simplicity and relaxation. "Unless you become like little children, you will never enter the Kingdom of heaven" (Matt. 18:3). The little child takes each day just as it comes. He does not waste time imagining tomorrow's woes. He lives a day at a time. If today has tears, they are shed and spent; but they are not carried over into tomorrow. In the days that were to be ahead of me, I would again have partings and separations from loved ones that cost heart agony for some hours. But never again did they overwhelm me. In other words, all the suffering when my little candle-flames went out, one after the other, were worth the tears they cost, for they purchased for me a permanent freedom from sprawling spiritually, from being knocked down and overwhelmed.

In other words, it was a kind Lord, and not a vicious One who blew out my candles, systematically, one after the other. He had something better for me than earthly candles.

> But while I sat in shadow, wrapped in night
> The face of Christ made all the darkness light.

As I look back on 1942, the disappointments and heartaches are a dark blur. That which stands out was the unfailing faithfulness of my Lord. When I was kicking against the pricks, He was never impatient, never withdrew His love. Every time I cried to Him to fulfil the promise of Genesis 28:15 He responded immediately. *"The power of his resurrection"* — that is what stands out most sharply.

And the dearness of Himself — *"that I may know him."*

And now see what He was lovingly planning to give me as soon as my Job-experience had borne fruit. He did not even wait for that fruition, but gave me Eva as a foretaste. And a wonderful reception back to Lisuland from our dear spiritual children. I could not even imagine that in a year's time a little baby son with red-gold hair and snow-white skin would be cuddled in my arms. It was beyond thought that our home should be moved from Oak Flat and that I would be put down right beside Lucius and Mary in the Village of Olives. Yet that is what happened. And there I had not only Lucius and Mary, but Eva and Danny as well!

These plans of my dear Lord were all piled up waiting for me, just around the corner of the future. And He who was so lovingly dear to me will be the same to you.

Chapter 7

SMALL HARASSMENTS

UP to now we have seen the Lord making Himself known through wondrous workings. The distrustful unbeliever would call them coincidences perhaps. But the child of God, watching the exact timing, the quick reply to a sudden prayer, does not hesitate to label them "miracles". It is a miracle when you can count on it beforehand, without any knowledge of how it would possibly happen.

But there is a less spectacular platform whereon God also manifests Himself. It is one of everyday struggle with every day's small problems. Nothing breath-taking has happened. Yet at the end of the year, or after a long period has passed, as one thoughtfully reviews it, suddenly one sees it. "Look!" we say. "Wasn't it a miracle that with all that was against us, we were enabled to go steadily forward?" It is the forward pushing, despite the harassment of small trials that prick, sting, and weary one. And perhaps this is the platform which God uses most often in the average Christian's life. So we want to look at its possibilities.

The Kuhns were now back in the canyon, although John must still keep his travel circuit as superintendent of the Chinese churches along the Burma Road.

From the military point of view we were in the danger zone (civilians were not allowed past Tali City without a military pass). Some Japanese were just across the mountains from us, and some of them just across the Salween River but several days' journey to the south. Colonel Hsie and his guerrillas had prepared trenches along the east bank of the Salween. (Oak Flat Village is on the east bank but 2,000 feet above the river.) Later, the colonel and his men moved over to Village of the Olives which is on the west bank. Of course, they had spies out all the time, and no one was allowed to cross the river without a military pass. The Japanese were known to be in the area of the great pass into Burma, the vicinity of which can be seen from our porch at Oak Flat, so we were never allowed to forget them.

Our winter schedule was usually to travel among the villages holding a two-weeks' Bible study wherever we were invited. But this year of 1942 the Rainy Season Bible School had had to be shortened owing to the paratyphoid which had broken out among the staff. So they had decided to hold the third month's study in October, by which time the weather had cleared, and the missionaries had recovered. This decision, in the Lord's kind providence, gave me the opportunity of teaching our beloved RSBS student group. John was with us only for the beginning of the school, as he had to go out to Chinaland to escort Dr Mei's Medical Unit, who were coming to Lisuland for a couple of weeks' free medical ministry to the Lisu tribe.

Those days the whole world was learning from England what a boost to a nation's morale is the spirit of *blitz or no blitz, we carry on business as usual*! The Christian missionary surely should have equal courage and faith. This was the reason we decided to ignore the *danger zone* and go quietly on with our usual programme. It had a wonderfully stabilizing effect upon the whole countryside, for the Lisu were jittery at the presence of so many armed men and ready to desert their villages for caves and other places of refuge high in the mountains.

October dawned beautifully sunny, and a fine group of students assembled. But the school had barely started when word came that soldiers in a strange uniform, one hundred strong, had arrived at the stream north of Cow's Hump Village. This threw everyone into panic. The Lisu, who had never seen a Japanese, suspected every strange uniform, and these soldiers were Orientals, they declared.

My diary says it was a Saturday when this disturbing news reached us. And on Saturdays we had no classes, for our students were sent into the surrounding villages to evangelize or to conduct Sunday services. One of the Lisu came in to tell us that our Oak Flat villagers were packing up for flight. Mrs Yang and her mother had already gone to a hamlet difficult of access far in the ravine, and others had fled to their fields. Cow's Hump was a long day's march to the north of us, but Oak Flat was so close to the main road down the canyon that plunderers certainly would not pass us by.

Of course we, the white missionaries, held council together and excitement reigned. Most of the Paoshan missionaries had returned to their work. My late experience of flight into Szechwan at the mere blowings of *wind-words* (the Lisu for *rumour*) was still poignantly fresh in my mind; also, I felt God had given me a drastic lesson which said I was not to lay down my duties and flee except at *His* Word. And this was still just rumour! I had immediately gone to the Lord about this latest, and He had given me Isaiah 26:12, *"Lord, you establish peace for us."*

It was a miserable position but the Lord used the pain of that recent experience to hold me steady in an important test. I dared not run when He said to stay.

The next day, Sunday, was calm and sunny. It was the custom for Christians in the nearby villages to come to Oak Flat chapel for worship, but with this scary rumour abroad we wondered how many would dare to come! It is easy for Lisu, however, with nothing to carry to skip up the mountainside like wild goats and, if the need arises, disappear even as you look at them. So that Sunday noon saw several hundred arrive to worship. They found that we were planning for the Bible school to continue as usual. Students who had gone to villages close at hand for the weekend would be expected to report for school by Sunday evening, and everyone was supposed to be back by nine o'clock Monday morning for classes. This word, carried back home to the villages scattered over peak and ridge, had a stabilizing effect upon everyone. So it was no surprise later to hear that the students who had gone north toward Cow's Hump had returned with the news *that the strange soldiers were not Japanese*! They were Chinese from Honan province with a slightly different uniform and accent. What they were doing in the canyon was unexplained, but fears were dispelled sufficiently for classes to resume again on Monday morning.

For the next two years we had this periodic temptation to desert Oak Flat and the RSBS student group. "Business as usual? — Impossible." "Well, let us stick to it as long as we can, and then see what God does for us." Under that spirit we were to prove

Him in a quiet but thrilling way on the Platform of Small Harassments.

Life proceeded rather smoothly until the next February. The Japanese did not seem to be gaining, and Colonel Hsie crossed the Salween and talked of occupying Fort Pienma. But at the Christmas festival when I had asked for an estimate of how many girls planned to come to our yearly Girls' Bible School in February, not one would promise! Taxes were high now and war rumours unsettling. The Lisu work is indigenous, so of course the students all paid their own way, except for the wives of the evangelists, whose board was paid by the church. But even these wives would only say they "hoped" they could come! "What if they came and then the military situation deteriorated suddenly and they could not get back again across the river?" they asked. We had no answer. That could easily happen; we could only pray the Lord to restrain the enemy so that the girls of the church might have this opportunity for Bible study which came only once a year for them.

But as 1943 dawned and all seemed quiet, there came the question, "Should we prepare for a girls' school without the promise of even one scholar?" The dormitories were badly in need of repair — they were leaking and out of plumb — and the beds had disappeared. It would cost money to repair them and time to oversee the job. Who would take the responsibility of ordering it?

Charles Peterson (at this time a bachelor) was the missionary in charge of Oak Flat station in 1943. I was to assist him where I could and John also, when he was home. Charles and I prayed about it and decided to live during these war days as if life were normal. "Business as usual" was to be our motto. If

we were not to hold a scheduled school, we felt the
Lord would warn us ahead of time. If He did not say
"stop" was it not common sense to infer that He
meant go ahead? So we decided to have the dormitories repaired and, as Charles would be out in the
village holding Bible classes, I had to hire the
workmen and oversee the job.

There was also another kind of preparation
needed. Always we tried to have new hymns and
choruses translated for the girls so that they might
have an interesting contribution to make in their
home villages when they finished their studies. The
girl students would be asked to teach the other
Christians in their villages anything new there was
to be learned. It was not usual for Lisu women to
stand up and teach, so they needed strong encouragement to be induced even to try. A bright new
chorus was excellent bait, and the girls soon forgot
their self-consciousness when they discovered that
their audience was eager to learn what they alone
could teach. So both girls and the Christian villagers
were helped by the subjects taught at Girls' Bible
School.

But as the day for assembling at Girls' Bible School
drew near, the weather turned against us. Snow
clouds came down over the great peaks (12-15,000
feet high), the wind blew icy cold, and on the lower
slopes the snow turned to rain — wet, penetrating,
chill, damp. These storm spells in February sometimes continued for two weeks. The girls on the west
bank of the Salween would have over twenty miles of
mountain road to travel, besides crossing a dangerous river; they would not dare attempt it in a
snowstorm.

Saturday was assembling day and by night we had

over a dozen girls, but all from the east bank. Now our most progressive students (mentally and spiritually) were those who lived on the west bank, so you can imagine how we prayed for them to come.

Sunday continued stormy. But Monday there was a lull. It did not really clear — the sky was dull and grey all day — but at least there was no downpour. Would the girls attempt to come? We could not know until evening so we began the school with the girls we had.

You can imagine our thrill at sunset when a shout came ringing up the trail, "Girls from the west bank are coming!"

We ran to the door, and there around the edge of the mountain was a line of little dots moving down the trail toward us! Sure enough. We ran out gingerly, for the ground was too wet and slippery to allow speed, and on to the Oak Flat trail which connects with the main road up and down the canyon. There they were — their bedding and books in big bags slung over their shoulders or carried on the back with the strap placed over the forehead to distribute the weight. Mary, Lydia, Julia, Chloe — and their brothers or husbands coming on behind, carrying their grain supply! Happy smiles and handshakes. "We were afraid you wouldn't make it," was answered by a chorus of girlish exclamations as to the difficulties encountered and their determination to press through. Chatter, chatter as bare feet pattered over the muddy trails to the church kitchen where warm fires and a hot supper were waiting.

That night, for the first evening session of the school, we had thirty-three students! And what a praise service! How it pays to take one step at a time with God! What if we had not prepared the dormitories? That very night the storm descended again and kept it up for a week. God's children need courage as well as faith. Courage to begin preparations for the workings of God: clearing the deck for action, so to speak. For sometimes His door opens only for a very short period, and if one is not fully ready to enter in, it will close — perhaps permanently. There was only that one lull in the bad weather (that Monday morning) for a week or more.

With so many bright-faced girls to teach, Charles, Eva, and I swung into the schoolwork with joy and zest, despite bitter cold and sloppy mountain trails. We thought our harassments were conquered, but alas, *no*.

The second or third day of the school Charles appeared (I think we were changing classes, I coming out and he going in to teach) with a gloomy face.

"Guess what, Isobel! Old Fox's Chinese scribe is here with the *thief*! He took the whole last hour of my preparation time which I had planned to spend on this lesson I have to teach now! I'm not sure what he is after — he's down there waiting for you now. Do pray for me this hour! I did so want to give my best," and then he disappeared into the classroom.

I proceeded downhill with a sinking heart. *Fox* was the nickname we had given to the local feudal laird because of his sly ways. The "thief" was a heathen neighbour who lived over the hill from us and who had robbed us one night while we were all at church. He was a notorious robber, but as he shared his spoils with the Fox and the Fox's scribe, they protected him. We had lost about two hundred Chinese dollars in cash and some clothing — a green sweater of mine being one article. John, with some companions, had accidentally walked into a Lisu

house and found Mr Thief seated at the friend's fire
wearing *Isobel's green sweater*! He had no chance to
escape and the native official with John said, "Leave
him to me. I'll see he gets impounded — you proceed
on your journey." There was nothing else for John to
do, apparently. Usually it was not our practice to take
the Lisu to law: and fervently did I wish it had not
been done now.

I found the scribe and his retinue (dirty, greasy
half-breeds they were, who had studied Chinese and
spoke it with such a strong tribal accent that I could
hardly recognize it as Chinese, which added to my
difficulties). I too had planned to use the next hour
for study preparation. I had added some mothercraft
subjects to those usually taught in Girls' Bible School
and I needed to look up some Lisu expressions not
often used outside of a dictionary or a delivery room.
And here were these four broadly grinning men
bowing before me and apparently enjoying themselves. Moreover, it was ten o'clock, the hour such
men expect to be served breakfast! I bowed, asked
them to be seated, then turned around to call Eva.
She was right there. Her class (knitting and babycraft
sewing) was in the afternoon, so fortunately she was
free.

"Don't worry, Ma-ma," she whispered. "I saw they
intended to eat here, and I've got a meal almost ready
for them. In just five minutes!"

Was there ever such a jewel of a girl? What would I
have done without her? And wherever would she get
meat to feed them with? Their social rank was such
that they would be insulted if they were not served
meat dishes. There was no place where we could buy
meat. At the laird's castle, of course, they slaughtered
for their own use almost every day. For ourselves we

found chicken the easiest to obtain. If it was skinny we boiled it for stew and so on. But soon the meat was on the table. (Eva had mixed a bit of bacon with this vegetable, a bit of leftover chicken with that one, and today's chicken in another form made a third dish. For culinary art, Eva deserved a medal!)

Of course they ate at great leisure and I, as their hostess, could not leave them. And you do not discuss business at mealtime. I saw my first hour go, and my second hour for preparation about to be invaded, before the scribe sat back and explained his errand.

He told me he had the Thief chained and handcuffed in the village in another house. Then he began to extol Christianity — praising us with flattery that was detestable to me, knowing that he himself spurned the Lord. On and on he went, but I was baffled — what was he driving at? Did I need to sign a document accusing the Thief? I knew that Orientals do not "come to the point" as we forthright Americans like to do, but I really could not guess his purpose in praising us for our big-heartedness, our good deeds, our forgiving spirit. As the second hour was drawing to a close I determined to end it — etiquette or no etiquette!

"I'm sorry, but we have a school here this month," I explained, "and my duties call me away. Was there something you wanted me to sign?"

"Oh, no" — how very broad became the grins now. "Then Mrs Kuhn would be able to meet them this afternoon? Would she name the hour? Maybe she wished to *see* the Thief?"

Oh, no, I had no such desire. It was all a miserable business to me. But they were waiting for an answer. Four o'clock in the afternoon? At Mr Peterson's cabin? (Maybe he could help me understand their garbled Chinese.) And with that they bowed themselves out, still grinning broadly.

Now I had to catch up broken threads. The mimeograph work on the new chorus was not yet finished perhaps. Clutching at the fleeing moments so to speak, I saw one of the Lisu deacons crossing my path and called him. We talked as we climbed toward the classroom together.

"Tell me quick, Deacon A," I said, "what is the scribe here for? Has he come to return the money? Should I sign something?"

"Oh, no, Ma-ma," replied the Lisu. "The Thief invested all the $200 he stole from you in cotton cloth meaning to sell it on the market. When the Fox heard about the robbery, he just hauled in the cloth. He's got it now, down in his yamen. The scribe will get part of it, but you won't get any — and the Thief hopes to get free, that's all he'll get."

"But isn't there any justice in —?" I was still sputtering when we reached the classroom and I had to leave the deacon and go in.

We were harassed by the scribe and his men for two days and a half. Finally, the scribe felt that Mrs Kuhn was just too stupid ever to get the point: he would have to break all etiquette and be frank with her! So leaning forward he said, "Mrs Kuhn, this man's record is so bad that if I put your accusation on paper I will then have to send him across to Luchang to the Chinese government magistrate. Only that magistrate has the power to sentence to death. And he has said that if the Thief offended once more, he would have him killed. So then if you compel me to put his accusation on paper you will be the cause of his death. You're a Christian missionary. Do you want that? Christianity professes love and forgiveness."

"Oh, yes," I answered, light having been broken so clearly for me. "But Christianity does not condone sin! I will forgive him, but he should return the money he stole."

"Oh, he spent that long ago. There's none of it left," said the scribe shaking with laughter. "Isn't that so?" he inquired of his three henchmen.

Oh, how they laughed! Yes, yes, they assured Mrs Kuhn, that was all gone long ago. Not a cent of it left! He would return the green sweater, and Mrs Kuhn would magnanimously forgive him. Wonderful thing Christianity — grin, grin, grin.

By this time the Thief himself had been brought in. He squatted at my feet watching this dramatic scene with mild interest, but with absolutely no shame or repentance visible.

"Mr Y —," I said quietly (inwardly my Irish blood was boiling). "Christianity *is* a wonderful thing. I'd like to explain it a little to you, please." Silence, and four amused pairs of eyes turned on me.

"Christianity teaches that God is no respecter of persons. And He is omniscient — He knows everything, even our thoughts. *He even knows where that cloth is which the Thief here bought with the stolen money.* And when we come to die, God is going to judge each of us according to our acceptance of His Son the Lord Jesus or our rejection. He will not ask, Who is the scribe for the laird, and, Who is the thief in prison. He will ask, *Did you accept the provision I made for your salvation,* or did you reject it? If you rejected it, you will go to hell just the same as the Thief here. You will be on a level there — rejecters of the Christ of God. I earnestly exhort you not to neglect so great salvation. In the eyes of the Judge of all the earth, you are as bad as he is right now."

The atmosphere of the cabin had changed. There were no more grins, but in place of merriment four red-faced and ashamed heads hung down. The scribe muttered something about "entering the church by and by," got up, and said they must go. One pair of eyes *did* twinkle — those of the Thief. But he was looking at the scribe who carefully avoided noticing him.

I was given the green sweater, the Thief asked me to forgive him, which I did, and the four half-breeds walked out and left us at peace, at last.

How did we ever get through those days? We did not know. But when all was over, and we compared notes, we found that no classes had been cancelled. Somehow or other one of us was always able to take over the class when the scribe sent for one of us to come and talk.

The school was a real blessing as was shown by the tears that flowed down the girls' cheeks when they had to say goodbye at the end of the month. It was abundantly worth it.

The February Girls' Bible School safely accomplished, what was next on the programme for 1943? We had written down a new venture — a short Bible school for teenage boys. These are usually the family cowhands, but of course we did not wish to limit it to that class, so we just announced a Boys' Bible School in March for ten- to twenty-year-olds. At the Christmas festival we had announced it, and drew the attention of Christian families to the date set. Ploughing had not yet begun and so other members of the family would be free to watch the cattle and let the cowherd come to this school if we held it in March.

Cows and bulls are used in ploughing the steep

mountainside and often represent the investment of
the family earnings. On such precipitous slopes the
cattle can easily get to fighting and push one another
over the ridge. They must be watched all the time. In
some places at certain times of the year the cowherd
takes the cattle to a dell where the grass is luscious,
and camps out there himself, not returning home at
night. In other words, it is hard to contact these boys
for the Lord. March, 1943, we had written down as
our first attempt.

March 6 they were to assemble; on March 4 news
came that our postmaster at the town of Six Treasuries had fled and was in hiding because he feared the
arrival of the Japanese! Six Treasuries was only one
day's distance from us, south on our side of the river.
Chinese soldiers were already posted at the two ferry
crossings, waiting to destroy those ferries if the
Japanese appeared. Suppose some boys from the
west bank did come, and the boats were destroyed?
They would not be able to get back home.

To add to our harassments, the weather was rainy,
and our cook gave notice that he was leaving. His
bride of a few weeks was homesick, and Joe must go
and live with her people.

We now had had a little experience with the
platform of harassments so we plodded on as if life
were normal.

Thirty-six cowherds arrived! And Mr Yang, the
principal of the church school, decided to cancel all
classes so that his students could also attend, which
swelled the number to *seventy-six*!

Before the Boys' Bible School ended, word came
that the Japanese had arrived at Pienma Pass. Overhead aeroplanes were seen daily and sometimes even
a dog-fight! For we were right under the trail of The

Hump flights. But we finished in peace. I quote from our circulars.

We had a closing-day programme for the boys, and the four little cowherds from Lamah Village brought much applause by rendering a beautiful anthem on Psalm 24 *a cappella* and in four parts! Charles Peterson said that one small fellow stood and sang like a bishop! With all the pleasure of it, there were smiles of amusement too.

And after they got home? Lucius said that his cowherd (who had won the honour of being elected Conductor of Music for the occasion) well — his tongue went so fast and so long recounting all his wonderful two weeks at Oak Flat that no one else got a word in edgewise all evening!

So at the end of March we had that good feeling of having attained. A spiritual battle, contested at every step, but now finished — *attained*. Is there a thrill on earth to equal it? Yes, to hear that one's spiritual children are walking in the ways of the Lord is akin to it. But these are deep things that pierce far below the surface and send a glowing joy throughout one's being. They give meaning and purpose to life and they bring the thread of eternal value into the pattern, not visible before. In other words, God has revealed Himself to us afresh in small harassments and we are forever enriched by it.

Maybe the harassment is too earthly to call a platform. Not only earthly but ridiculous. These can be like the last straw on the camel's back — the culminating sting of frustration that just seems more than we can take. Yet it is so puny we dare not list it among our trials. Take, for instance, the careless laziness of our goat-herd.

Milk was a necessity, especially when Daniel Kreadman Kuhn appeared August 1, 1943. It was

soon obvious that mother's milk must be sup-
plemented. That year, in that distant corner, powdered milk or even tinned milk was out of sight in
price. The hillside was too steep for cows, so a herd
of goats furnished our milk. But never could we get a
competent goat-herd. He would only milk as much as
he felt like — 1 quart today, a cup tomorrow! He
would deny that more than a cup was to be squeezed
from the critter! Neither Eva nor I knew how to milk,
so we could not prove our point. Exasperation!

Also, he would not even herd the animals carefully. We had two billies. The older we called Hitler,
because he loved to rule and had a passion for
destruction. He became quite rumbustious as he saw
the younger billy growing up and able to hold his
own; this made him want to be first in all things.
When they were being driven home at night, the
older billy would frequently rush ahead of the herd
and make for our kitchen. Woe betide the cook if the
door were not securely fastened! Hitler would rush
in and make for the garbage pail. Being so big and
strong he was difficult to handle in that small place
where a hard kick could dent the pots or break the
bowls. But one day he waxed bolder — he found the
stairs to the grain storeroom.

I was in my bedroom working at my desk when I
heard noises. Push — bang — a yell in Chinese — a
loud whack — a squeal, then a terrific commotion.
Above it all arose Eva's voice, high with anger:
"Ma-ma! Big Goat Old Man" (she could not stop to
remember the correct English for the *older billy*, and
the name Hitler was attached to him after this event),
"Big Goat Old Man go storeroom! Make awful mess!"
When Eva got excited, English grammar flew to the
winds — nouns and verbs were mainly all that were

needed. I got up and went out to behold a spectacle.

There was Big Goat Old Man running for his life up the hill toward the refuge of his pen. After him was a blur of blue Chinese gown and a stick that ascended and descended regularly — on hair or on air — up and down it went. I laughed until I cried. He who lorded it so over the females of the goat pen was scurrying in ignominy ahead of one small dot of feminity from Chinaland. There is no question as to who won that battle!

Nor is there any question as to how harassing a messed-up storeroom can be when Bible school is in session. We must either discipline ourselves to leave it alone until we have time to sweep and tidy it, or we must give up some hoped-for leisure time and do it. In any case it leads to self-discipline and this is a place where we meet the Lord.

"*A soul well-disciplined is beyond all price*" (Knox's Translation). I have met the Lord here many times. Philippians 3:21 used to be a help to me. It says that He is able to bring everything under his control. When the hot feelings of rebellion against circumstances would storm up in my heart I have often cried to Him, "Lord, you said 'everything', that must mean me. Then control me, control this flaming resentment, O Lord, I pray." And then He would, but first He met me and it was on just such a humiliating platform — a small harassment.

The fact that the Rainy Season Bible School of 1942 had to be broken into two sessions (by the paratyphoid sickness among the white staff) gave the idea to the Lisu Church of breaking it up into three sessions of one month each for 1943. This did not prove as satisfying, but it certainly was of the Lord for that year. I had told no one but John that we were

expecting baby Danny to arrive in August; which
would of course have meant that I could not help in
teaching. But the church voted that for 1943 RSBS be
held in three sessions, April, August, and November.

Unknown to us, God was planning to call Mrs Leila
Cooke Home to Himself in May just before the RSBS at
Luda began their three months' study. Our change of
schedule enabled Charles Peterson to teach our
students in April, then go up to Luda and help teach
there for some two months or more, and still he could
be back at Oak Flat for the November session of our
school. John took the main burden of teaching our
RSBS in August but in the middle of September he
had to leave. I had no doctor's help with Danny's
advent but one of our CIM nurses, Miss Dorothy
Burrows, skilled in obstetrics, generously offered to
take her annual vacation by coming to the canyon
and playing doctor for me. She stayed with me for
more than a month after the confinement, but as she
was serving on the Tali hospital staff she had to get
back to work, and must have an escort out. (Colonel
Hsie had escorted her in — he going out for
consultation and to get new supplies.) So John
escorted Dorothy to Tali and then went on to
Chungking where the CIM Superintendents' Conference was to assemble. This left only Charles and me
for the November session of RSBS at Oak Flat.

John and my dear nurse had no sooner disappeared than harassment arrived! Danny developed
a need for a new milk formula, warning of which he
could not speak to us, of course, so he just cried — all
the time. This was the first instalment of trouble. The
circular of those days tells more:

They had left us but one day when Charles came down

with what turned out to be rheumatic fever! At the same
time our goat-herd took sick and also the girl who does the
laundry.

And the rain came down!

Then I got word that Colonel Hsie with his Number-Two
wife was coming through, which I supposed meant that we
must entertain them! What I would do without Eva's help,
I didn't know.

Charles' cabin was down the mountain from ours,
and all his meals had to be carried to him. I have
memories of trying to carry his tray down that
slippery path, the rain drizzling on me, and my
hands shaking with weakness — I was so tired from
sleepless nights with Danny. And the November
Bible school looming up on the horizon! Should we
call it off? It seemed utterly impossible that we could
hold it! Then we reminded each other that this was
beginning to be a chronic state with our Bible school
plans! Impossible to hold it! And yet God had seen
us through every time we had stepped out in faith,
and tried to do it.

As we prayed together, light came. Charles said to
me, "There is Orville Carlson at Luda. He has not
been in the work very long, but he is quick at the
language and he taught in the Luda RSBS. He could
surely help teach our November session. I helped Mr
Cooke. I'm sure they would lend Orville to us. Maybe
he could come early and help nurse me." So a
messenger was dispatched to Luda to explain our
predicament and ask for Orville Carlson. In the
meantime — well, Charles and I laugh over the
memory of one grim evening.

It was a Sunday, Eva had gone to church. I was
going to go to bed early but had a feeling that I

should go down to Charles' cabin first and see if he needed any help. He did. The rheumatic fever was getting under way now, and he was in such pain that he needed a shot of morphine. So back up the slippery path I went to sterilize the hypodermic needle. Behold, the charcoal fire in the kitchen was almost out. With much blowing and coaxing I got a few coals hot enough to boil it the ten minutes required. Then down the mountainside I went again with the pot and needle. But I had never given an injection before this as John had always done it for me. Charles was suffering yet I hated to experiment on him. I felt I must confess my inexperience to him.

"Oh, it's easy," said Charles, picking up the needle and fitting it into the syringe. "You just want to be sure there is no bubble," and to show me how, he held the syringe up, pressed the plunger and shot my carefully sterilized needle through the open window into the wet mud of the dark mountainside! I had no other needle so had to take a lantern and search for that one. Then I trudged up the mountain to our kitchen only to find that the fire was out! I forget what happened after that. Probably church was dismissed and Eva came to my rescue, for lighting charcoal fires was never where I shone! My first lesson in giving an injection!

"Oh, it's easy. All you do is — shoot it out the window!"

Small harassments; they come to everyone. What are we to do with them or *in* them? Seek a promise from the Lord. Nothing is too small but that He will respond to comfort or to guide. My diary says that His Word to me those days was Psalm 44:4: "*You are my King and my God, who decrees victories for Jacob.*"

"When did I licht ma auld lantern?" asked a

Scottish deacon. "Was it no when I was comin' frae the licht o' ma ain hoose along the dark road tae the licht o' yours? That is where tae use the promises — *in the dark places between the lichts*." Stumbling down the mountainside in the rain with a tray for a sick fellow worker — from *ma hoose tae your hoose* — that is where to use your light.

"*You are my King and my God, who decrees victories*." He does not rule out small harassments; but He does rule that they shall not *overcome* us! And they didn't.

Orville arrived in due time.

Colonel Hsie and wife Number-Two also arrived; but as he planned that she stay indefinitely at Oak Flat Village, he took over the clinic house and set her up there, with her own household establishment. They were no trouble to me.

And baby Dan's crying spells at night? I soon was using goat milk to supplement nursing him. But I could find no formula for goat's milk and as it has a heavier curd than cow's milk, Danny had much colic — that is why he cried so. But dear little Eva insisted on also lifting this burden from me. I would never *ask* anybody to take over my baby at night — that was my responsibility, I felt. But I did not have to ask. As soon as he awoke and raised his voice in protest to colic pains, Eva could hear him, for there were only bamboo walls between us. Soon there was a patter of small feet down the hall and a knock at my door.

"Give him to me, Ma-ma," says Eva's voice. "I've got the charcoal fire going and his milk is warm," and off she would trot with him. What magic she used I do not know, but in less than an hour, back she would come with a sound-asleep little bundle, comforted. She knew how to bury hot coals in a brazier and then blow them up again into a hot fire. I tried to learn how (to save Eva's self-imposed night labour) but all I ever succeeded in doing was to blow the ashes all over the bedroom, nearly choke myself with them, and completely kill whatever coals had ever been alive! At last I gave up trying and allowed Eva to make her nightly excursion down the hall. You will wonder why I did not use a vacuum flask. Ours broke and there was no place near where I could get another. So, you see, God *was* my King, and He *did* decree victories for this poor Jacob. And again He had proved that in harassments was a good place to get to *know Him*!

Before 1944 dawned, the Japanese had entered the Salween canyon! Colonel Hsie's bringing his wife to live in our village was because he foresaw this, but of course it also put us in the most dangerous limelight.

With the enemy right across the river from us (we stood and watched the town of Luchang go up in flames, as the Japanese fired it) — surely now we could not keep a normal schedule! Especially when the year's programme began with the *Girls'* Bible School. The girls would never have the faith and courage to come, would they? But the past two years of quietly carrying on our normal projects had unconsciously been training the Lisu church (as well as ourselves) in the power of God to give victory on the platform of harassments. To tell the truth, I was inwardly hoping the girls would not come! Is not that a confession?

But Charles Peterson had been sent out to civilization for a three months' sick rest, and, although my own dear John was with me this time, did he not come down with influenza! I also had a baby to care for and altogether as I faced the Girls' Bible School my courage oozed away — and I fear it pulled faith with it!

But is it not wonderful that *if we are faithless, He will remain faithful?* (2 Tim. 2:13). He knew that really and truly in the bottom of my heart I wanted that Girls' Bible School.

They came — twenty-five of them, and the bright ones from the west bank among them! And what a good time we had, despite more harassments. (Baby caught the 'flu from John and then I caught it!)

GBS was accomplished; thank you, Lord! What's next on the programme? Oh, Boys' Bible School. But this time it *truly* is impossible. (Each test became a little severer than the last one.)

John had to leave on March 9 for Chungking — yearly conference of CIM superintendents.

Charles was not yet back from sick-leave. I would be the only white missionary on the staff. Eva did not have sufficient training to teach boys (they, of course, were not interested in knitting, etc.).

And we were out of writing materials (pencils, scribblers, paper, and ink). I had ordered them, but the Japanese were on one road in between us and Paoshan (the city where we purchased our supplies) and fear that they would cross over to the only remaining road made carriers unwilling to make the trip.

Try to have a Bible school with only one teacher and possibly no writing materials? Was not that impossible? But the Lisu church surprised me. This adventuring with God was revealing a new joy and zest to them. To my astonishment I found the church leaders were *in consternation* lest Ma-ma cancel the school!

"Oh ho," I said to myself. "All right, my lads." To them I said, "I will trust God for the writing supplies, if the Lisu church will consent to set free two of the trained evangelists from their village pastoral duties to come and help me teach."

They withdrew to consult over that and returned beaming. "We consent," they said, "and we have appointed Teachers Luke Fish and Thomas Hemp to help you teach; they will be excused from other duties during March." So the school was announced.

But the enemy of souls had not exhausted his repertoire of harassments. Assembly day came and — no writing supplies; but also — *no Teacher Thomas and no boys from the west bank of the Salween*! Thomas was pastor across the river. Luke was pastor on Oak Flat Mountain where we lived. Luke and I faced each other in dismay that evening.

"It's persecution," said Luke grimly. And I had felt the same. It required a military pass to get across the river, as we have said. There had been no difficulty about this before, as John was officially personnel adviser to the general. (Colonel Hsie was now a general.) But a new personality had appeared on the scene — a Chinese small official had been sent to the west bank of the Salween to teach Chinese to Lisu young people and to recruit Lisu young men for the military school in Tali. I did not know that the granting of west bank passes to cross the Salween was now in this man's hands. But from his peculiar efforts to win over the *Christian* young people, I had suspected him of being a Red infiltrator. He was. A few years later he was executed in Kunming as a Communist spy. But this was 1943 and we had no proof of anything.

There was nothing to do but pray; behind it was Satan, and God is the only one who can deal with him. So down on our knees we went. Now I will quote from the circular of that time.

As we prayed for Thomas' release, the Lord worked!

Prepare for a surprise ... into our home here drop some *American* soldiers. (Whether they dropped from the sky or came in by the road, the censor would not let me tell you.) But after a good square American meal (the poor fellows had not seen such food, simple as it is, for a long time, and wasn't it fun "stuffing" them!) they asked if they could do anything for us, and as they have *influence*, we got them to pull the proper wire and the evening of the fifth day of school, Thomas arrived. Then blessings avalanched.

Thomas brought Lucius and three pupils with him. There had been eleven who wanted to come, but on refusal of the pass, the others had gone back home.

The morning after we welcomed them, in walk the paper and pencils!

Then, hard on their heels and without warning, in comes — Charlie Peterson.

Well, the Boys' Bible School that began with such a limp, ended with a grand leap. The influx of more teachers meant more individual attention. And the Lisu teachers got practice in doing some things they have never thought they could do. A new chorus was needed, and, as I had not time to compose one, I gave Luke a tune and told him to find the words! He produced a soldier theme and it was a great hit!

Then the task of designing a study certificate had to be laid on his shoulders too. (To get a certificate for only two weeks' study would be a joke in America, but to these boys, many of whom will never again be given the opportunity to study away from home, a certificate will be treasured all their lives.)

Lucius did the drawing, and much of the hand printing on the certificates and they were really pretty!

Charles swung right in, drilled and advised on the closing-day programme until it was one of the brightest and most interesting we have had — a glad memory to us all.

Again, on the platform of small harassments, we had met the power of the Lord and came to know His

ability to give the grace of continuance: another
school accomplished as per schedule.

RSBS in 1944 was held during the summer in
comparative quiet as the Japanese had retreated from
Pienma. (General Stillwell was cutting their supply
line.)

And autumn brought furlough for the Kuhn
family. We had served seven years since our last one,
and now came the glad news that little daughter had
been repatriated on the *Gripsholm*. Old friends of our
youth (and incidentally treasurer of the CIM in North
America), Mr and Mrs George Sutherland had taken
Kathryn into their home as if she were their own
child, but of course she was longing to see us. We
waited only until RSBS was over, as Charles could not
conduct such a big school all by himself.

As we started the long trek home to America, we
had several days of truck travel first, and this gave
time to think back over the two years just concluded.
Two years since Eva, John, and I had come into the
canyon, front fringe of battle line. It was only as I
thought back over those two years that I suddenly
saw it as a platform. In mind I watched the line of
battle swing back and forth over Pienma Pass so
close to us, and then I suddenly realized that
constantly beset with danger and harassments we
had not only been enabled to carry on our full normal
schedule *but even to see advance*.

In 1942 we began a Bible school for girls.

In 1943 we began a Bible school for boys.

In 1943 and 44 we began children's work; Eva was
the stimulus, although I had had it in mind for a long
time. As soon as she could speak a bit of Lisu she
gathered the children of Oak Flat Village together for
a Bible club every day or evening. Then we empha-

sized Bible, illustrated Bible, and taught Bible at the Girls' Bible School and the RSBS, urging them to begin Sunday schools or Bible clubs in their villages.

As I sat back in the rattling old truck and reviewed all this, I suddenly saw the harassments as a connected series, a platform on which *the power of the Lord was manifested — that I might know Him.* Yes, we had learned much more of Him as a Helper in the challenge of small daily trials.

The scary rumours of alien soldiers approaching.

Bad weather on assembling day.

A wicked and evil magistrate interrupting and requiring to be entertained, hampering our preparations for the class-room.

An undependable goat-herd and a billy called Hitler.

Sickness of a fellow worker.

Shortness of staff and non-arrival of essential supplies. Each too small and puny to form an Arena picture in itself, but each like a tiny finger clutching at our coat-tails to drag us back from victory.

The challenge of the platform of small harassments in the Arena — what is it? It is really the gladiatorial struggle with self-pity, a most unglamorous opponent: so unglamorous that he whispers to us, "I am not important! Just let me be." How many times we have lost the fight just because we *have* let self-pity *be*!

I am reminded of a lesson not only preached but *lived* by Alice Macfarlane, principal of the CIM women's language school at Yangchow in China. She was a warrior-saint who was especially successful in downing that gladiator *Self-pity*. This is the way Alice Macfarlane would flourish her sword at that fellow.

A rumour of approaching danger? Find out what God wants you to do, then deliberately put the *wind-words* aside. *Press on with your job*!

Bad weather when your students need dry trails to travel? Take your stand against the power of the air (Eph. 6:12-18) in prayer; claim the victory of Calvary over Satan (Heb. 2:14) then *press on* in preparation for the school, expecting victory.

Interrupting guests? Unhand the small clutching fingers of self-pity and reply to the voice that shrieks, "I can't do two things at once!" "Well, take them one at a time, then."

Trust God for the ability to be gracious to the stranger within your gates, but insist that first things come first. *Press on with your job*!

That goat-herd's laziness and the mess Hitler made in the storeroom? Do not let this small thing grow until it fills your thoughts. The Lord should fill your horizon always — nothing else is worthy. Clean up the mess in the storeroom or be content to leave it until you have time. But *press on with your spiritual work*.

Sickness has come down upon us and we stagger with weakness? Well, *light your lantern*. Ask Him for a promise, and *press on*.

Promised supplies are delayed? Do the best you can, and refuse to pity yourself. *Press on*.

As we do this, there may come no special vision; no special miracle of deliverance; no special intervention of Providence. But after the whole experience is over you will look back, as we did, and you will be amazed at the way you have been carried along by a Power not your own. The time will come when you will stand, look back, and gasp, "How mightily was the hand of our God with us, yet we knew it not!"

Sitting there in the old truck, I reviewed our long series of harassments during those two war years, and the thing that stood out most, fairly towered above all else, was the *goodness of the Lord* in helping me. And in my heart I whispered to Him old love-words, written first of a pure human love, but, oh, so much more applicable to the perfect Love. *"Lord, I love Thee to the level of every day's most quiet need."*[1]

That is the platform of small harassments. God meets us on that level — *every day's most quiet need.* He will have a new word, a new sweetness or a new fellowship to help us press through to victory. And when the thrill of victory dawns upon us, we will whisper, "O Lord, it wasn't in me. It was your sufficiency for every day's most quiet need."

[1]Elizabeth Barrett Browning's sonnet "How do I love thee?"

Chapter 8

TAUT NERVES

THE only way to get out of China was to fly The Hump over to India. (It was then we discovered that this famous flight went right over our part of Lisuland! Looking down, John even saw the little ferry boat at Place-of-Action.)

Into the heat and refugee crowds of India we came. World War II was still in full operation (October, 1944) and there was no passenger ship service to America. With all other civilians wishing to go home, we had to be lumped together as refugees and take what transportation the harassed authorities could provide. After some days in Calcutta and about three weeks in Bombay, we were given transportation on a troopship going to America. Our route and port of arrival were kept secret. (Even when we landed we did not know where we were until hotel placards and street signs gave us the clue!)

So on board we went. John was sent down into the hold with the civilian men and allowed up to see us for only two hours a day. Danny and I found ourselves in an officer's cabin with other women — eleven of us, bunks three tiers high, no portholes for air, and the ship's movie theatre just outside our door. They had two sittings of talkies every night so the jazz music and noise went on until nearly midnight.

Shortly after boarding, we mothers were summoned before a ship's officer for a lecture. He had probably been ordered to put fear into us, for he certainly tried his best. He told us that we were allowed on board only out of charity. This was not a passenger ship and there was no accommodation for babies. There was no baby food on board so we need not ask for it. There was no deck on the whole ship which was safe for babies — some had no railings and all had big uncovered hawse-holes through which a child could easily fall. "If your child falls overboard, the ship will not stop to pick it up. I tell you now, so you need not ask! It is up to each mother to watch her own child," he shouted to us. There was no laundry room for us, just the usual washbowls. We were to eat at officers' mess but that compelled two sittings, so that each meal must be finished within half an hour. We must line up ahead of time so as not to lose a minute in getting seated. And so on. When he finished there was not one of us who would have dared to ask a favour, which was probably his purpose.

Danny was about fifteen months old, just at the toddling stage, and the trip lasted more than a month — 36 days, I think. Waiting in line for meals three times a day, I had to carry him, heavy as he was. To set an active toddler down meant jerking him back into line all the time, just as fatiguing as holding him. He was served a plate of officers' food — big steaks and French fried potatoes, etc. It was inevitable that his tummy would get upset, and more than one night I sat rocking him lest his cries keep the others in the cabin awake. In the daytime he had to

be watched every minute lest he toddle near those
yawning hawse-holes. To keep him within sight
while I washed his diapers was another problem.
After two weeks of this I felt I was going to collapse. I
remember standing in line for dinner, feeling my
head beginning to swim and faintness coming over
me. Again I cried out in my heart, "Lord, what can I
do? Just stand till I drop?" Now the Lord could have
come and touched me as He had done in the Chicago
restaurant nineteen years before. But He did not
choose to do so this time.

A voice called at my elbow. "Well, now, look at our
poor mother carrying this big heavy boy and me
doing nothing! Here, mother, give me this young
redhead!" Two strong, friendly hands removed
Danny from my aching arms. It was a missionary
from our cabin — the Lord bless her!

"Don't know why I didn't think of this before," she
scolded herself. "Mother, from now on I'm self-
appointed nurse for Danny. Before every meal I'm
going to come and get him, wash him up, and carry
him in. And after the meal I'll carry him out. Do you
hear?"

Did I hear! She was an angel sent from heaven, as
far as I was concerned. And she kept her word. To me
this was as much a manifestation of Christ's power
as my earlier experiences. She was my "door of
escape" (1 Cor. 10:13, Way's translation). God had
used a natural means to deliver me, that is all.

The thirty-sixth day arrived at last: our big ship
was steaming up the coast of America (we still did
not know if it was the Atlantic or Pacific coast except
by guesses). Rumours that we were soon to land
were passed from mouth to mouth and war changes
in the travel habits of America were discussed.

"They say you cannot get a taxicab any more," said one.

"And none of your friends are allowed to meet the boat," said another. This alarmed me. Our money was limited; we would need to contact our mission soon after arrival.

"What shall we do?" I asked. Miss Alice Wishart, of Kashmir, was walking with me at the moment.

"Oh, the Lord will have something waiting for us," she replied easily. "He hasn't brought us all this way to desert us now."

And it was so. We were hours and hours getting through Immigration and Customs. But the Red Cross met us, provided a nurse who took Danny and cared for him — fed him, put him to bed, and watched him. Hot coffee and doughnuts were served us. We landed at ten in the morning, but it was dark before we were ready to proceed on our way. A businessman (Red Cross helper) drove us in his car from San Pedro to Los Angeles right to the door of the China Inland Mission there! I have never forgotten it. And those carefree words of Miss Wishart were to echo again and again in my heart, through many a difficult turn in life's corners in later years. "Oh, God will have something waiting for us."

It is scriptural. Psalm 59:10 (ASV): "My God with his loving-kindness will meet me"; and another version translates it, "The God whose love meets me on the way."

Among our own (the bosom of the mission family is a wonderful place), we immediately wanted to long-distance telephone our daughter, Kathryn, that we had arrived. Over the wires my voice did not sound familiar to her, and it brought the tears; but at least she had the joy of knowing we were on the same continent as she was, and would soon be speeding to her at Philadelphia. We delayed in Los Angeles only long enough to do some shopping. I was still wearing a discarded coat and beret, and so was glad we had arrived in the dark! (Just here I might digress to invite a smile. Miss Wishart met us unexpectedly in church one Sunday after our shopping expedition, and she was about to introduce me to a friend. "This is Mrs Kuhn," she began, then noticed my new coat and hat and started to chuckle. "Mrs Kuhn as she is, not as she was!" with laughter, to her friend's complete mystification!)

On the cross-country train ride, Danny cried every night, keeping everyone in the car awake. Nothing we could do pacified him. This was one of the most humiliating experiences of my life — and it did not help *taut nerves*.

Mr Sutherland had thoughtfully arranged for us to meet Kathryn alone in a little room. Our little girl, whom we had last seen at seven and a half years of age, was now thirteen and almost at full stature. We had tried to get to her once in those intervening years, but the Japanese had bombed a bridge on our only road, so we had to turn back. But at this reunion the Lord melted us all together and there was no feeling of strangeness, praise His name!

The next six months were busy in visiting and deputation work. For the most part we stayed with our relatives, the Harrisons, who were generously hospitable, as always. Sister Kay's children were no longer small, however, so her home was arranged for adults. It was beautiful, with green plants in the windows, but at such a low level that toddlers were tempted to reach out for the pretty trailing branches and pull at them. Danny had to be watched all the time.

Everybody was wonderfully kind to me and did their best to help me rest, but at the end of six months I was as taut as on arriving. That was disappointing to everybody. How *is* a person to help such a missionary anyway? When it seems that nobody understands us, we can always turn to the Lord.

"Lord, I've been home for six months and I feel as ill as when I arrived. I just cannot unknot my nerves! If we only had a home of our own — owned it, so that if Danny broke or scratched anything no one else would suffer. And, oh, if I could be alone for a while and sleep the clock around for more than one day — as many days as I needed!" What an impossible thing to ask! But quietly and gently He gave it, all of it.

John wanted to take a refresher course at Dallas Theological Seminary. None of us had ever been to Dallas, and if John was to go we must find a home there. It was war-time, when houses of any kind were hard to find. The seminary had none available.

But we now discovered that we had some money! Ten years previously, John's father had died and left him some shares in a certain company. On our previous furlough the Christian manager of that firm had asked us to leave the shares there a time longer. "The company is not paying dividends now," he said, "but I firmly believe it will pay in a few years. Holding your shares and giving me your proxy will just give me a majority vote. I like to conduct this business on Christian lines and I appreciate that majority vote. So if you will hold your shares as they are, it will do me a favour." We were delighted to do so — and almost forgot we possessed any shares. Now when we made inquiry, to our astonishment we learned their value had tripled! The Christian manager had retired and was now indifferent as to whether we sold the shares or not. If we had sold in 1936 we would have received $2,000. By accommodating him, we now received $6,000! It took our breath away — the Lord pays high interest!

Now there was hope of a place of our own at Dallas. We wrote to the seminary for the names and addresses of real estate men and then wrote them our requirements. (1) It must come within our price range of less than $5,000. (We had to reserve something for furniture.) (2) We must be able to get possession of the house by July 28.

Then to the Lord we had requests. (1) Since we had no car, can the house be near enough to the seminary so John can walk? (2) And it should be near to a high school, so Kathryn can walk. (3) It should have two bedrooms. (4) And a fenced-in back yard where Danny can be left to play.

With the exception of one, all the real estate offices replied that a place of *any* description without *any* stipulations was *impossible*, especially in the low-price bracket! House-building materials had been requisitioned for war purposes, and so many newly-married couples in the armed forces were looking for cheap homes that any available ones were snapped up before real estate offices had a chance to list them.

The one exception wrote like the others, but added that there might be a house such as we wanted available later on — the owner had not decided whether to sell or not. We wrote back to hold it for us if it was offered for sale.

About the time I had reached my extremity of

nerves that would not relax, about the time of my prayer, another letter came from the real estate office in Dallas. "If one of you came immediately the owner might be persuaded to sell," they wrote, since we offered cash down, but they could not actually promise he would.

John and I went into council. I asked to be the one to go. We knew no one in Dallas. I would go to the YWCA and here was my chance to go to bed at seven without anyone thinking me unsociable, and without any baby-twitters at half-past five the next morning announcing that *he* (bless him!) was beginning the new day. I could shop for furniture in the daytime. John was quite happy to stay behind with the children as it would give him another month with relatives and friends in his home town. Kathryn was thirteen years old and could take care of Danny — she had prayed for a baby brother! And it was summer vacation.

I had written or wired the YWCA for a room some time before, so off I went on this great adventure, my first trip to Texas. I had a good chance to witness to a young girl on the train, and walked into the YWCA in Dallas quite confident that the Lord was with me.

But it was not to be too easy. The YWCA secretary was very courteous but almost exasperated at my innocence and ignorance. Expect to have a room at the "Y" with only a week or so's advance notice? "Why, my dear," she said, "we are booked solid for months ahead. I fear I cannot even get you a hotel room. Don't you know what the war has done to America? And as for your getting a house in Dallas — I'm sorry to discourage you, but a place of any kind *without any stipulations* is like asking for the moon. I deal with people all day long, every day in the week, just like yourself. And somebody is waiting to come in now when you go out! I don't know why people cannot be told that there are no vacant houses in Dallas. Well, I will telephone and see if I can get you a room somewhere. I have already phoned nine hotels this morning and not one of them has a corner. But you are planning to stay a while. How long did you say? A month? Well, we will see."

And then she began to phone. Inside I was praying. The first two or three places were full up. Then she tried another. "Yes," she said into the phone, "she intends to stay a month. You have a room? Oh, good. She will be right over."

"Well, you are fortunate, Mrs Kuhn," said the secretary, hanging up the telephone. "It is a hotel in rather a bad part of town so I do not call on it often. It is quite a safe place itself but the neighbourhood — well, you won't plan to roam the streets at night, I take it." I assured her I would not and she gave me the address.

It was a cheap hotel, but after Chinese inns I had learned to appreciate what America might rate third class. I had a corner bedroom with a window on each side which gave a cross-draught. It was June and the days were hot. I shared a bathroom with one other person and there were good locks on all doors. A bed, bureau, desk, and chair — what else did I need? I knelt down and thanked the Lord.

It was about noon, so I got the address of the real estate company and proceeded downstairs. The registry clerk was a woman and very pleasant.

"Oh, your real estate office is just a couple of blocks away and since we are right downtown, restaurants are plentiful. Woolworths has a good lunch counter too, and it is only two blocks away."

So I started out in Dallas. After a sandwich and coffee at Woolworths I was ready for *real estate*. I was perfectly sure God was going to get us that house! But how He was to do it would just be a thrilling adventure. With this confidence I made myself known to the real estate people. A sandy-haired, middle-aged salesman was put in charge of me.

"You are very lucky, Mrs Kuhn," he said. "To get any kind of a low-priced place in Dallas, even without stipulations of any kind, is almost impossible. Of course you haven't got this place yet! But it answers your desires perfectly. It is a five-room cottage with a screened-in back porch; it is within walking distance of the seminary and also of a high school. It has a fenced-in back yard and is only half a block from the grocery and meat markets. And I think you can buy it for $4,500. The one snag is your stipulation that you get possession by July 28. The present owner has bought another place where he wishes to combine his business and home under the one roof, but he cannot get possession of it that soon, I fear. I will take you out there now, however, and we will talk with them."

You can imagine how eager I felt as we drove up to 1718 Ripley Street.

"Hm. It needs paint. John won't like its present appearance!" I thought to myself. But it was in a surprisingly quiet neighbourhood. Across the street was a small park. And the next-door houses were not too close. It had a long, covered front porch, with a baby-gate already in!

The owners were Christians and easy to talk to. I explained our purpose in coming to Dallas, and added that if we could not get possession when we needed it, it would be useless to buy.

"Well," the owners said, "we might go and live with our daughter for a month or so. We will give you an answer tomorrow."

The third day after I arrived in Dallas the cottage was ours, money paid, deed signed, and it stipulated possession by July 28! I felt I must go and tell the YWCA secretary.

"I just thought I'd like to tell you," I said, "that I have a cottage already, bought and paid for. It meets all the stipulations and conforms to all we had wanted in addition."

She fell back in her chair and went limp, staring at me. Then as my truthfulness penetrated her understanding she sat up straight and gasped, "Mrs Kuhn, you renew my faith in God." It had renewed mine too. That is the outcome of all God's platforms.

The platform of taut nerves. He allowed them to stretch and stretch and stretch — but not to snap. And when the time came that He said, "Enough," He had planned this lovely thing for us. "No discipline seems pleasant at the time, but painful. Later on, however ..."

God's later: if it is so delightful on earth what will the *later* in Heaven be?

No millionaire furnishing his mansion had half the fun I did furnishing my cottage! Of course most things I had to buy second-hand. I procured a map of Dallas from the real estate office, purchased the early morning newspaper, looked up advertisements of second-hand things; noted what I wanted, and started off in pursuit! I had no responsibilities, no time schedule to hurry me, no baby depending on my quick return, no pressure of any kind. I had asked the Lord for a piano, an icebox, and an electric washing machine in addition to necessities — and

He gave them all. Long nights of uninterrupted sleep renewed me. By the time three weeks had passed I was longing for my family to come. And, oh, the joyous day when I welcomed them to the cottage which God had so wonderfully given us!

Of Dallas days, being together in our own wee place was the outstanding joy. Next to that, for me, were the young people from the seminary who began to come to us. It started with John handing me an invitation one day to *Students' Wives Prayer Meeting*. "You are a student's wife now," he said with a grin. So I gladly went.

Of course I was the only middle-aged person present! And the bevy of lovely young womanhood that gathered for prayer simply thrilled me. Many were earning money to put their husbands through seminary; others were young mothers and home keepers. All were the Lord's children and eager to have His best for themselves and their beloved partners. We took turns in leading with a short message and it was a joy to hear them pass on blessings from His Word. I especially enjoyed the fact that I was received at first as only another unit in the group. But the fateful evening came when a newcomer recognized me as the author of *Precious Things of the Lasting Hills*, and I was hauled out of my prized obscurity and put on the inevitable pedestal of *an author*.

How I did love those girls! Even their cultural charm meant something to me. I really had to laugh at myself — I so enjoyed their beauty, their grace of movement, the refined good taste in their dress and so on. The primitive tribes, of course, although they develop spiritually and mentally, are still crude and uncouth in their social habits.

Something within me had long been starved for the refined beauty of my own kind, such as these girls showed with every movement, and I drank it all in eagerly.

Knowing the wives led to knowing the husbands. And often vice versa, as John brought in fellow students for a chat or a cup of tea and then I found out who the wife was! In but a short time after seminary began, we were having a small group come to our home every Friday night for Bible study and prayer. As I look back on them now, *every single couple of that group reached the foreign field.* Italy, Switzerland, Formosa, China, the border of Nepal, the border of Afghanistan have felt the touch of Christ through those lives! That was a real gift from God which has permanently enriched us.

John had expected a full year at Dallas Theological Seminary. But the atom bomb changed many plans. The war ended, the State Department began to issue passports to China once more. The country was still too torn up for women and children to return safely, but the China Inland Mission sent out a letter asking the superintendents to go back to China one year ahead of their families. So we had to face it. From the beginning, the motto of our married life has been *God first,* and every now and again we are challenged with it anew. It is our joy to re-proclaim it, so this time there was no argument. The Lord gave us 2 Corinthians 4:12: *"So then death is at work in us, but life is at work in you."* We felt it meant death in the sense of breaking up our family life, that the Lisu might gain spiritually.

So John sailed for China in January, 1946.

I was grateful for the extra year with Kathryn. This is a discussion of *platforms*, not really a record of family life. But I was continually grateful for the way God had fathered and mothered her in the years we had been forced apart, and very grateful for her loving companionship and help in the almost two years we were together.

When it came to leaving Dallas, the Lord again worked wonderfully. I wanted to sell the house as it stood, furniture and all. One day an elderly married couple knocked at our door. They had heard we were thinking of selling and asked how much I wanted. I said $6,100 and they paid the full amount in cash. So the Lord had given us a home of our own, practically rent-free and money enough to pay our way back to Pennsylvania! The taut nerves were relaxed by the time the return to China had come.

The platform of taut nerves is not without its own kind of suffering. It may be He has to allow us to get so desperate that we will be willing to attempt the impossible with Him, before He sends us relaxation. Whatever the reason for His allowing those circumstances it is also a place where His fellowship is found. It is a place where His power will be manifested. And the end of it is that we know Him better. *You renew my faith in God* will be the testimony of onlookers.

> Shadows and shine art Thou,
>   Dear Lord, to me;
> Pillar of cloud and fire,
>   I follow Thee.
> What though the way is long,
>   In Thee my heart is strong,
> Thou art my joy, my song —
>   Praise, praise to Thee.
>   —AMY CARMICHAEL

Chapter 9

SEEMING DEFEAT

BACK to China on a slow, small freighter we travelled, Danny and I. Kathryn we left in Philadelphia with the Sutherlands.

"Promise me not to cry, sister!" shouted the small three-year-old brother, alarmed at her tearful face as the train pulled out of the station. "Promise me not to cry!"

We sailed from Houston; there had been a longshoremen's strike and ships were still scarce, so we had no choice. The *Joseph Lee* had no railings and took forty-six days to make the passage! Miss Ruth Nowack of our mission travelled with us, and the only other passengers were a young mother and two children. Mrs Dorothy Greenwood was going to join her aviator husband in Shanghai. Our cargo was kerosene and cotton! Some of the crew wanted to back out when they heard it; but this was one reason the old boilers were not pushed very hard, making our passage leisurely.

Ruth was a great blessing to all of us. She proved an enchanting storyteller to the children, and was so unselfish in helping us mothers. We began to have Sunday school, and Mrs Greenwood asked if we could not have it every day. We did, and had Bible study with her — none of us realizing how God had tenderly arranged that she might learn to know Him before impending tragedy struck her.

The day before we landed, the door of my cabin was thrown open and in dashed beautiful Dorothy Greenwood screaming and weeping.

She had just heard over her radio that her husband had been killed when his aeroplane crashed on Christmas Day. It was sour sad privilege to care for her.

I had expected John to meet us at the Shanghai wharf, but he had been delayed; so Danny and I, arriving in the big CIM compound in bitter cold weather, had to wait. John had been touring the province of Yunnan in a survey of the tribes and had not been able to get back to civilization when he had hoped. Lucius was with him.

Jim Greenwood's crash was followed by a similar catastrophe in which Mrs Meller of the CIM and her three children were killed. Little Peter Meller had been playing with Danny the day before, so it brought it acutely home to us. In both cases the fault was not the pilots', but the careless preparation of the plane. Generalissimo Chiang ordered all planes grounded for an investigation, and our wait in Shanghai was prolonged.

The bridges which had been blown up by the Japanese were still not repaired, so transportation into the far interior was a real problem. When John finally did arrive, the matter was discussed carefully. It was decided that John and Eric Cox drive the baggage of several families (Kuhns' included) in a truck and that Danny and I go by air. The men would have to drive across China, with broken roads, half-mended bridges, and other dangers. It would be

too hard a trip for a woman and child. Eventually
Danny and I obtained space in an army freighter, a
Flying Fortress, and it was wonderful to arrive in
balmy Yunnan after the bleak cold of Shanghai.

In Kunming we had to wait for John and the truck,
but while there we had a memorable reunion with
Lucius. Eva I had left in Tali with Mrs Watson. When
the Watsons left for furlough, Eva entered Tali
hospital to train as a nurse. We would see her as we
passed through.

In returning to China this time the one thing I had
feared was travel on the Burma Road. Yet that term
the only time I had to make a long trip on it was with
my husband as driver! From Kunming to Paoshan
we rode on the truck, and for the first and only time I
thoroughly enjoyed the Burma Road. I once heard
Ruth Stull say that the dangers she had feared when
she went to South America never met her, but
dangers far worse awaited her! I had to smile,
remembering my last term in China when this had
happened also to me. So it does no good to imagine
the evils that await us! And for the unimagined ones
the Lord is sufficient, so let us be at peace.

At Tali we met Eva. She pleaded with tears to be
allowed to go back to Lisuland with us.

"But, my dear," I reasoned, "you have only a year
and a half left and you will graduate! If you leave
now you get no credit whatever."

"I don't care about credits or certificates," she
cried. "I am happy just to be with you and Ma-pa and
Danny." If it had not been for my stern lessons in
1942 about inordinate affections, I would have been
tempted to take her with us. I would sorely need help
such as hers in the days ahead. But those lessons had
left scars which protected Eva from my possessive-

ness, and though she did not see it then, I am sure she has been grateful many times since. Our dear little Eva — she is behind the Bamboo Curtain now and we never hear of her. The last word was that she was trying to get permission to study to be a doctor — so I am sure she understands now why we let her cry in 1947!

Failing to get permission to give up her nursing, Eva asked for her annual leave in order to be with us on the trip to Paoshan. Nurse Irene Neville did the same, so we had them in the truck on the next lap of the journey. And we needed them. Climbing a steep hairpin-turn ascent we came on a Chinese truck newly wrecked, with the injured perhaps dying, lying on the road beneath. We stopped, and our two nurses administered first aid to them.

At Paoshan the Christians received us joyfully. The China Inland Mission no longer had a house in that city, so we had all to live in the chapel, while John, as superintendent, tried to rent another place for the missionaries who were to arrive soon after us. As a matter of fact, our own relatives, Kathryn and David Harrison, were appointed to take charge of the Paoshan work. This was to include caring for young workers who, we hoped, would later go to the tribes. So a large house was needed. Such a one was in prospect and soon John was involved in all the slow bargaining of the East.

Seeing that it was going to be a long process (it actually took three months before John was released to come into Lisuland and join us), I asked my husband to let Danny and me go into Lisuland ahead of him. Eva had to return to the hospital; Lucius was chafing to get home (he had been gone almost a year); there would then be no one to help me supervise Danny, and only the public chapel to live in! So it was decided that Lucius escort us back into Oak Flat. Eva and Miss Neville travelled with us as far as Wayao, where the Lisu trail enters the Burma Road. Here we said goodbye, Eva weeping rebelliously, and we began the difficult over-mountain journey.

I was surprised at the desolation of the trail. Little villages where we used to stop for lunch were now deserted ghost hamlets. "There were too many robbers and brigands on the main road," explained Lucius. "The people have fled out of sight. Soldiers, disbanded far from home, have turned bandit. It is still dangerous."

We had Chinese coolies to carry us and our things and they grumbled every stage. "When we get to the Salween and meet Lisu Christians, you will be well fed and your loads carried for you," we encouraged them, but they were openly unbelieving.

Yet it was true. The last day, at the last steep 2,000-foot climb, Lisu with horses were waiting for us! Oh, what a loving jubilant reunion! Danny had a horse to himself, and two Lisu, one on each side, walked close beside to guard the delighted three-year-old. "Mummy! My horse has bells and yours doesn't!" he shouted in elation. "My horse rides bumpily." The astonished Chinese had their loads taken off their shoulders and shifted on to Lisu backs. When at the end of the climb a delicious feast of pork was given to us all, one of those men came to me, his eyes shining. "*Chen-chen, Szumu! Ni shuo-ti pu-ts'o!*" ("It is true after all, Lady, what you said!") ... We tried to witness to him of the change Jesus Christ works in human lives.

The welcome party over, we settled down to the

grim problems of re-establishment. Lucius said goodbye and departed for his own home at Village of the Olives, across the river. I will quote from our circular.

The poor old shanty (now twelve years old) was a dilapidated sight — it leaned toward the precipice very distinctly and its thatched roof had been blown off in great patches. Inside, the furniture looked rougher than even memory could recall, and everything was covered with the dust and debris of nine months' vacancy. But Ruth (Pade-John's wife; they were the caretakers) had swept the floor and had prepared lots of cold drinking water and hot water for baths! Now none of you in luxurious America can appreciate what that last meant. I record it for the benefit of the angels (and fellow missionaries) who saw our rough journey in. (The third night we slept in a hayloft, and the fourth in a deserted corn bin, and the fifth we were nearly eaten up with fleas.) So we appreciated our welcome. It was a rainy day, but the Lord mercifully held the rain off just those two hours when we had to climb — it came down wet and plenty as soon as we were in the house. That did not seem like a nice welcome, but we learned gradually that that was the *first rain for half a year* — everybody had been praying for it for months. It rained for the next two days, a token from God to the church that His blessing is connected with the reception of His messengers and His Gospel.

Among church leaders of Oak Flat Village who were a disappointment were Pade-John and Keh-deh-seh-pa.

Pade-John had once been a wonderful Christian. He had given free the land on which our house stood! So he was the natural person to be caretaker during our absence on furlough. The change in him had come after his marriage to a nominal Christian named Ruth. Ruth was pretty and came of an influential family but was utterly unprincipled. We could not lay our finger on anything, but from the first I instinctively distrusted her. I wanted to get Pade-John to break off the engagement; which rather scandalized him as he was not aware of her true character and would not believe it. But after eleven years of marriage to her, laziness, shady ways of getting money, immoral talk and laughter in the home had turned him into a hypocrite. Both of them being clever, they covered up their tracks so well that no one could get proof of what we all suspected.

Keh-deh-seh-pa had become political headman of the village of Oak Flat after Me-do-me-pa died. He had seen the power that good man received from the Holy Spirit and, like Simon Magus, coveted it. He tried very hard to become head deacon in the church, but spiritual power cannot be imitated. He was feared but not trusted.

The old thief over the hill never had been a Christian, and he had robbed us before. But the whole countryside was filled with robbers. I had been told that there were sixty of them operating within a small radius of us, and three times at night they tried to attack us. Danny and I were the only ones sleeping in the shanty, and at first I left the bedroom windows open all night as had always been my custom. Then one night (the first attempt) I was awakened by a bird call, clear and powerful, right beneath that open window. One spring, and an active fellow could be over the sill and into our room! I knew it was not a bird at that time of night, and then I heard an answering call from behind our house. I went cold all over, and could do nothing but lie there and pray. Again this one called and that one answered. I would have been comforted if only I had known that Mr Yang, Pade-John, and Joel were up and stalking them! The calls meant, "It's all up. They're after us. Let's run." Not knowing that, I lay there petrified. It was not lack of faith that the Lord could keep me! I knew that. It was not unwillingness to suffer. It was just suspense. God does allow missionaries to be killed, now and again. Would this be that?

The next morning I sent for some of the Christian men whom I knew I could trust and told them of my scare. From that day on, one of them slept in our house with a gun each night until husband John arrived. Although Oak Flat Village had its back-sliders, there were dear loyal saints around too.

When Lucius heard of our insecurity, he wrote inviting us to move our home to Village of the Olives where he lived and where he could protect me while John was away on these long trips as superintendent. But I would not consider it. The two things of which white people require such a lot were very hard to obtain at Olives — water and fuel. Olives had only one water hole and the girls often got up at three or four in the morning in order to get water for the family breakfast! All the trees near Olives had been cut down for firewood — the villagers had to go a long way to get any. And the Kuhn family, with their western ideas of frequent laundry, used a lot of both water and firewood. At Oak Flat were the Bible school dormitory buildings which had been built up during these years. I did not see how we could possibly move our station, and did not give it serious thought. *I did not even pray about it.*

John arrived from Paoshan before the Rainy Season Bible School, and that summer (1947) we had a record number of students and had to use the

Chinese schoolhouse to accommodate them. I tried to teach children's work to the evangelists. There were no such things as Sunday schools, for instance, except what Eva had begun in Oak Flat Village, and Lucius had started one in Village of the Olives. Our RSBS students carried their vision back to the villages at the end of the summer. Said one Christian woman to Jeremiah, "When the young folks came back from RSBS and gave their testimonies, I was so thrilled that I could not sleep all that night until cock-crow, for thinking of what they had said."

The rainy season passed, and John had to go out on another trip. He had no sooner gone than Danny came down with typhus fever and I was left alone to nurse him! During this time and for several more months I was the only white missionary for many days' journey in the canyon, and the church leaders brought all problems to me.

The work at Oak Flat became more and more disappointing. Caught in flagrant sin, Keh-deh-seh-pa had to be put out of office as deacon, for the Lisu church practises New Testament discipline — and he was not pleased about it.

Those in the village itself who stood with me for righteousness were slowly but steadily melting away. Mrs Yang developed tuberculosis, and her husband had to take her back to Chinaland where the food was more what she required. This not only deprived me of a Christian man in the village who would back me up, but it left the position of teacher in the Chinese school vacant. Immediately Keh-deh-seh-pa applied for the position in the name of his second son who had been studying Chinese at Tali. The boy was a profligate — Eva had heard of his dissolute doings and told me. But the one-time

Strong Man of our village, Me-do-me-pa, was now dead. To my horror the other deacons were afraid to say no — Keh-deh-seh-pa was rich and had political power! My Irish spunk arose (alas, it is always ready to push me into impetuous action!), so I said *no*, flatly, and the deacons eagerly sheltered behind Ma-ma! If Lucius had been there, or some of our fine deacons farther north, they would have led in that responsibility.

Then came a night when Keh-deh-seh-pa and his rejected son, under cover of darkness and knowing I was alone in the shanty, entered the house to threaten me. You see, I had no absolute proof of the son's sin. But God, who has mercy on his impetuous Peters, caused a poor Christian farmer to see the two sneaking through the dark; he followed them and a few minutes after their entrance (when I was petrified with fright) I saw dear Chu-fu-si-pa slip in and take a chair in the corner. He pretended he wanted to sell me some charcoal. This provided a witness to our conversation, and as they tried to trick me into statements which could be used in a lawsuit against me, the Lord gave me the answers. I knew it was the right answer when Chu-fu-si-pa would silently beam on me. Their plot failed, and a fine Christian Lisu who spoke Chinese was given the position of schoolmaster.

But from then on a subtle persecution set in — accidents happened to our goat-herd; our water supply was taken from us and we had to go to another far away, inconvenient one. Life in Oak Flat Village for a woman alone was getting dangerous. John was gone for months: five months one year, seven months another year. When my continuance in this way seemed impossible, Charles Peterson arrived back from furlough!

God was trying to uproot me, but He kept His promise: "No temptation has seized you except what is common to man. And God is faithful; he will not let you be tempted beyond what you can bear." He never let me suffer more than I could bear.

The climax came at the end of the 1948 Rainy Season Bible School. Pade-John had asked to attend that school. I was more and more doubtful of him and Ruth; they did not ring true. But I never dreamed of what they would attempt. Pade-John had been away from home that spring, and while he was gone I noticed his wife Ruth going into the bedroom of our cookboy, Jana. I ordered her off the premises (she and Pade-John lived just below us on the hill). But it was whispered about the village that she and Jana had sinned. Neither would admit it, but they were suspended from Communion.

Rainy Season Bible School of 1948 saw another splendid body of students gather. A group came from Burma! One of them had walked seventeen days in order to be present. Several came from the mid-Salween area — a rather recent development of the work.

At the end of the school, it was the custom for each student to write the staff a letter, telling what they hoped to do for the Lord during the next year. To our concern, Pade-John wrote us that he was applying for the pastorate of the mid-Salween work! Of course he got *no* for a reply. With a wife such as he had, how could a pastorate be given him? In any case we did not feel that he himself was fit for it, although he had done well as a student. But I had learned now (John had known it long before, of course) that it was dangerous to make a charge against anyone without absolute proof in black and white. It is difficult to find this kind of evidence for unspirituality. But to our surprise, Pade-John refused to admit defeat and began making preparations to go!

It was the last day of RSBS when crowds from all the surrounding villages had gathered for the closing exercises. The programme had no sooner finished than Keh-deh-seh-pa appeared with Pade-John, a large rabble of local farmers carrying clubs and, in the midst of them, Jana and Ruth roped like criminals.

"Here is where they sinned and here is where I'll have them beaten!" called out Keh-deh-seh-pa, triumphantly.

Little Danny was playing at the side of our shanty. I quickly ran to him, called a friend aside and asked her to take Danny for a walk into the ravine. Lisu beatings are brutal, and I did not want the little five-year-old to witness one. With Danny out of the way, I sped back to the shanty. Lucius met me with a face like a thundercloud.

"Don't go into your kitchen, Ma-ma," he whispered. "They have tied Jana to one wall of it and Ruth to the other. Keh-deh-seh-pa has used his civil authority as the village magistrate, and anyone who unties them will be taken to Chinese law. He says they sinned there and they will be tried there until Ma-pa signs a paper giving the mid-Salween pastorate to Pade-John!"

"But he cannot do that!" I said indignantly. "They did not sin there! Look how tiny the kitchen is. Besides, it is the kitchen of Americans!"

Lucius looked dubious. "Better go slow, Ma-ma," he counselled. "Interference with the carrying out of Chinese justice might be an ugly accusation in the

hands of an unprincipled man like Keh-deh-seh-pa.
Ma-pa is trying to reason with him. Better just pray
about it." Lucius was as indignant as I was, but much
more accustomed to the wily tricks of so-called
justice in the canyon. So I tried to pray.

Hours passed. Danny was brought back and
clamoured for his supper. I had no cook now and no
Eva. I had to go into the kitchen and prepare our
meal. I wonder if you can imagine my feelings, trying
to do that with a living human being bound to the
left wall and another bound to the right wall! I made
tea first and offered it to the prisoners. Jana refused.
He was ashamed and savage with anger. Keh-deh-
seh-pa had committed adultery only a few months
before and no one had bound *him* and dragged *him*
through the village! Ruth was brazen. Their hands
being tied behind them I had to hold the cup while
she drank thirstily. She would have chatted if I had
allowed her to! So I prepared supper, helped by Mrs
Estella Kirkman who was our guest-speaker at that
school. She had given an excellent course on children's work and she stayed with us until Christmas.

Keh-deh-seh-pa had kept John talking for hours.
This was exactly what he wanted — a huge audience
from all over the country and the white man begging
him to relent his power and *he refusing*.

On Sundays Christians from surrounding villages
came to Oak Flat for noon worship. Closing day is
always on a Sunday, so the church audience also
witnessed Keh-deh-seh-pa's revenge.

Deacon Ah-be-pa of Plum Tree Flat sent the
women and children home but he with certain
stalwart young men of his village stayed to help John.

Darkness fell. Keh-deh-seh-pa, Pade-John, and the
rabble took themselves down the mountain to eat

their dinner. The two were still tied, standing in our kitchen. Ten o'clock at night came and John ordered me to bed. Being of a sympathetic nature, the whole thing wrought on me emotionally. I went to bed but of course I could not sleep. Then I heard the rabble coming up the hill toward us. Wild shouts and loud talking rent the night. I was about to get up and dress again when Lucius' voice sounded at the door.

"May I come in, Ma-ma?"

"Yes, yes," I cried. "What has happened?"

He came in looking so dejected. He sat down in silence and just shook his head.

"What's the noise? What has happened?" I urged.

"Ah-be-pa, dear old man, decided that he would cut the prisoners loose. He said if a white man got involved in it, it might become a consular affair and spread all over the province. If he, a Lisu farmer and church official did it, it would only be judged in the canyon. So he went and cut Ruth and Jana free."

"Good. They're gone then?"

"Yes. But Ruth must have told. For Keh-deh-seh-pa's rabble got wind of it and came up the hill brandishing their clubs for revenge. They caught hold of old Ah-be-pa and you know what that would do to Caleb, Simon, and the other fellows from Plum Tree Flat who love their old deacon so! They sprang to defend him, and there was going to be a free-for-all fight when Ma-pa cried out, 'I'll sign the paper!' Then, of course it stopped."

"Oh, he didn't!" I cried, aghast.

Lucius tried to comfort me. "He did it, committing it to God, Ma-ma. It was that, or a terrible battle, and think how the Lord would be dishonoured if the heathen heard the Christians were fighting one another! For Pade-John and Keh-deh-seh-pa still call themselves Christians. The paper is not worth anything anyway. Who would have such a fellow as a pastor now? Fool that he was to do such a thing on *this day* of all days. In a week's time the students will all be back in their homes and Pade-John's Judas-trick will be known all over the land! Oh, what a fool Satan makes of his tools!" and Lucius flung his arms out wide to show the emptiness wrought.

Just then my weary husband came in. He looked at Lucius and me, then said to him, "You've told her?" He sat down and buried his face in his hands.

Defeat. How can the *power of His resurrection* be shown on such a platform? As a family we have always believed that "*All things work together for good to them that love God.*" Romans 8:28. I know that modern translations change that verse so that it does not give that promise. The translation may be changed *but the fact remains*. God does work *all things* together for good to them that follow Him in loving obedience.

I dare to say "*all things*"? I dare. That will include sin — and dishonourable defeat? Yes, but do not misunderstand me. God will never *condone* sin or dishonourable defeat. Let us take sin first.

David was never the same man after his sin; a certain fearless manliness was gone forever. He vacillated when it came to punishing his sons, and so on. The punishment of his sin was not withdrawn.

But from the moment David cried to God, "I have sinned," the fragments of the wreck of his noble life were gathered into God's hands and quietly wrought into another vessel. Not as beautiful as the first would have been. But from that moment on, for David there was hope, a future and the loving embrace of his Father's arms. A future? Some of his

writings which have most helped succeeding genera-
tions were his penitential psalms. On the Father's
bosom there is always hope.

Defeat, when it is not sin but a sort of spiritual
Dien Bien Phu, may also claim Romans 8:28. The
enemy comes in overwhelming numbers and it is
not a question of victory but of which is less
dishonourable to the dear Lord. Or perhaps we have
tried to do something for Him and it has ended in
humiliating failure. Dorothy Bidlake once said to me,
"Isobel! 'Be careful for nothing' — *not even your
failures.*" Her words came to me that night at Oak
Flat. It seemed sacrilege not to care about what had
happened that Closing Day! But the word *careful* in
the Old English sense does not mean *concerned*. Of
course we should care about success or failure.
Careful in the King James Version means *full of care*;
anxious is how Knox translates it; *fret* is Way's
translation. We are not to fret over our defeats and
failures. We are to confess them, to commit them to
Him, to seek the next step under His guidance and to
withhold judgment on that matter until God has
completed it. "Why did God ever allow this?" the
flesh cries out, aghast. I know it did in me that night.
Oak Flat Village, where we had laboured for thirteen
years — to see a scene like it witnessed that Sunday! I
was levelled to the earth in humiliation. I had still to
experience what our wonderful Lord can do *with
defeat.*

The very first thing this did was to cause us to
move. Lucius came in the next morning (he and the
other students were going home). "Well, Ma-ma," he
said, "you will have to move over to Village of the
Olives. You can never stay alone in this village now
— can you?"

"No, I would not dare, Lucius," I said sadly, "but what shall we do for water and fuel?"

"I've been thinking and I have a plan," he answered. "The wood will have to be carried a long way but I think we can burn charcoal for you. The water? Well, you know there is only a fight for the water at mealtimes. All night it flows, overflows the pool, runs off into the valley and is lost! Now if we got a bamboo pipe carrying the water, a night's flow would be enough, wouldn't it?"

"Yes, it would."

"Good. Then I'm going home to build you and Ma-pa a house on my ground next to Mary's and my big new one. Or you can share our new house if you like."

"No," I said quickly, "I'd like a place of my own."

"All right. We'll set right to work. Ma-pa," he asked John, "when do you leave on your next trip?"

"Very soon," John replied, "but I've arranged for Mrs Kirkman to stay on until Christmas and New Year. Betty Ju, the Chinese girl, will be here too."

"And if you get scared, Ma-ma," said our big-hearted Boy, "you can all come over and live with me *any time*. Do you understand? *Any time!*"

We thanked him and he left.

I was not thrilled at the prospect of leaving my long, quiet bedroom at the edge of the abyss. Lucius's farm was almost in the centre of the Village of the Olives — noise around you day and night. There was an unpleasant danger approaching Oak Flat of which none of us knew anything, but God knew. We moved our home from Oak Flat to Village of the Olives in December, 1948. Four months later, Oak Flat Village was invaded by a band of Communist brigands! They were led by a Chinese named Dai Yi-gwan, a man who was my personal enemy. (I had found him out in oppressing the poor Lisu and had stood up for the people. It took his face away and he hated me from that day on.) He was like a demon incarnate. On their way to Oak Flat Village they inquired specially if I were there! And Keh-deh-seh-pa joined hands with Dai Yi-gwan. I shudder to think what would have been my fate if God had not uprooted me and sent me across the Salween River just out of reach.

When I heard how this band had conquered the three lairds at Six Treasuries, the first question I asked was, "Did Dai Yi-gwan join them?"

"Yes," was the answer, "he was their leader to the laird at Place-of-Action."

I was told later that Dai Yi-gwan had plans to come across the river, when God again intervened. The story of how young laird Dwan captured his captors in one bloody night's carnage at Place-of-Action, and later had to order the death of his traitor-friend Dai Yi-gwan is told in *Stones of Fire*.

I heard of that death with shuddering gratitude.

Another *good thing* in our removal was that it brought us nearer to certain areas of heathen Lisu who responded to the Gospel before we were finally driven out by the Communists.

And then — listen to this! — *there was not one ill-effect of that awful affair that I can remember*. The paper John signed? It was just as Lucius had prophesied. The next morning when we awoke, a letter had been thrust under our door. It was signed by the RSBS students from the mid-Salween. It was something like this:

Dear Pastor Kuhn,

We are leaving before dawn so that Pade-John will not find out. We hear he planned to go back with us. We don't want such a man for our pastor! We know you were forced to sign that paper, but we are hurrying back to warn the mid-Salween church that it was forced from you. *We won't have him.*

Signed ...

Pade-John did not even attempt to claim that pastorate. He was feared and abhorred everywhere he went. Finally he wrote us an apology, confessing how wrong he had been! Still no one wanted him. Finally he deserted Ruth (who, lazy and idle all her life, then had to work for her living) and he went far into Burma. But you remember that summer we had had one student come seventeen days' journey to study with us. Everywhere the churches had been warned against Pade-John. The last I heard was six years later he was found digging roads in Burma for the government — but still claiming to be a Christian. Satan is a merciless master.

What of Keh-deh-seh-pa, the green bay tree (Psa. 37:35)? He never expected Dai Yi-gwan to lose and Laird Dwan to win. When that happened he fled for his life and hid in caves of the mountains. Laird Dwan moved over to Village of the Olives and one evening I overheard him next door talking to some spies he was sending across the river to hunt down Keh-deh-seh-pa. "And when you find him, *I'm going to skin him alive*," he snorted angrily. They did that in the canyon.

My heart failed me. I could not wish that for any enemy, and I started to pray that Keh-deh-seh-pa would repent so that God could deliver him. I had no faith that he would! I just prayed that way. It is unbelievable what our God can do. First we heard that Keh-deh-seh-pa had bought pardon by a huge gift to the laird and many smooth protestations that he had no idea Dai Yi-gwan, the laird's own covenant-friend, had any evil purposes in that trip, and so on and so on.

But I was totally unprepared for what happened next. My diary records that on Saturday, January 14, 1950, Keh-deh-seh-pa arrived at the Village of the Olives to confess his faults to Mr Kuhn, to ask forgiveness, to make a public apology to the whole church on Sunday and to ask to be taken back into the church! Even after having prayed for this to happen I had a hard time believing the man to be sincere. Such is the weakness of us human beings..

He was brought up before the deacon body and the two men missionaries, John, and Charles Peterson. The meeting took place in our shanty. The house at Oak Flat, which John built, was roomy; the one which the Lisu built for us at Olives had a wonderful thatch on the roof but otherwise it was small. The central room was dining room, study, medical dispensary, and guest room all in one. The deacons brought Keh-deh-seh-pa here; and Lucius, who had been typing for the church, had to pick up the typewriter and move into the next room, which was our storeroom. Kitchen, guest room, and storeroom were all the shanty contained. We slept in a loft over the storeroom. I, being a female, was never asked to meetings of the diaconate, and I had not the smallest ambition to be invited. But since they were in the central room I had to stay in the kitchen or storeroom. I did not even try to listen to their conversation, but prayed in my heart that the Lord's will be done.

After about an hour, to my astonishment, John called me in. "Keh-deh-seh-pa has made his confession to us all," he said, "but the deacons wonder if there is not something he should confess to Ma-ma too. Would you care to question him? Have you anything against him?"

It had been a humbling process and it showed on Keh-deh-seh-pa's face. But I felt that now was the golden opportunity to deal straight with the man. John, Charles, and the deacons had probably done so but it would not hurt to put it as I saw it. So I said, "I'm just afraid, Keh-deh-seh-pa, that your desire to be reinstated in the church is only to gain a respectable cloak for your late escapades."

"What escapades, Ma-ma?" he asked simply. I named several things I had heard attributed to him.

His face lit up. "But Ma-ma, I have been maligned. It was this way" — and he proceeded to explain away his crimes, with quite obvious enjoyment. He had an amazing facility for wriggling out of situations and a smoothness of explanation that sounded most plausible. I was exasperated. We were missing the point.

"That may be so, Keh-deh-seh-pa," I said, "but my concern for you is that you have never been *born again*. I have no personal animosity for you whatever. I do not hate you, in fact, I have been praying for you. I wish no confessions from you touching myself. But I would like to know your own inner state before the Lord. No amount of public confession will bring you into His kingdom, if you have never said, 'Lord, I'm a sinner and I need a Saviour.' "

He looked abashed. Then lifted his eyes to mine and said, "I believe my sins are forgiven, Ma-ma. I believe I am born again."

"Then," said I, turning to the deacons, "if the diaconate pass you for readmittance into fellowship, I will pass you too."

So saying, I left the room and went into the storeroom. Lucius, typing energetically, did not look at me, but as I passed close to him to get some potatoes, he whispered, "Strait is the gate and narrow is the way."

My mind was now on dinner and I did not get his point. To one side was a big corn bin, to another a rice bin, and then the long potato bin. Space was at a premium — did he mean that? Keh-deh-seh-pa and the diaconate were still in the next room separated only by a bamboo wall. Lucius made a gesture of impatience, beckoned me to lean closer and whispered, "*Strait is the gate.* Keh-deh-seh-pa wriggled this way, he squirmed that way; he said it was a mistake, a moment of weakness, a snare of the devil. He wanted to call it by anything but its real name *sin*. But it is a strait gate. He had to come to it. *There is no other way in.*"

I was thrilled with the spiritual insight with which Lucius had watched the poor sinner's evasions. We looked at each other, nodding our heads, and there was the moment of that wonderful fellowship that is a joy beyond anything of earth. Both Lucius and I had entered that strait gate; we knew the simple firmness of our Lord in holding man to it; we also knew the freedom and blessing of the kingdom on the inside! If only the poor sinner will shelve his excuses, knuckle down, and *enter in*!

> So little is the door — stoop low — all else must go
> But oh, how much they win, who enter in.

And so, only one year and four months after

Keh-deh-seh-pa's green bay tree triumph, he had come to apologize and confess what a failure it had been.

The platform of defeat and failure — do not fret about it. Do not quickly assume it is the end of the matter — it is not. Wait for God to work, and believe our God when He says the gates of hell shall not prevail against His kingdom.

I have often been impressed by the dramatic picture so simply disclosed in 2 Timothy 4 — the last recorded words of Paul.

He knew his life was drawing to a close. If he had used physical sight only, he would have had to say, "My lifework has been a colossal failure." He, the saintliest of men, was in chains; he was brought thus before Nero, the vilest of men. One student of Nero's life has said of him, "He was only mud and blood." Yet Nero was on the throne, and Paul the saint a prisoner before him.

"At my first defence, no one came to my support, but everyone deserted me," Paul wrote later. What a disappointment! There were supposed to be stalwart saints in Rome at that time. His dear friends had deserted him. But not all. *"But the Lord stood at my side."* Yes, there is one Friend who never fails us.

"You know that everyone in the province of Asia has deserted me" (2 Tim. 1:15). Why, Asia comprised some of Paul's most cherished fruit! Years of his life had been spent to establish those young churches. And now, in the last epistle he wrote before he died, he says they had repudiated him. Doubtless his old enemies, the Judaizers, had influenced them.

What a melancholy picture! What a way to end a life of such self-sacrifice! Himself in bonds, shortly to be condemned and executed. His friends had deserted him. His spiritual children had repudiated him. Paul, your life is a colossal failure!

"Oh, no," he says quietly, using the eyes of faith. "I have fought the good fight ... now there is in store for me the crown of righteousness." There is no defeat in those words.

And now we, nineteen centuries later, may be judges as to which saw correctly — Paul's eyes of faith, or the fleshly eye of sight? The eye of faith saw correctly.

The platform of seeming defeat and failure will conform us to His image in humility. If we wait patiently we shall some day see His power working in undreamed-of ways. And we shall *know Him; as with Paul, the Lord will stand by us and strengthen us.*

Chapter 10

BETWEEN THE SCISSORS' KNIVES

ANY Christian, who finds himself between two extremely dangerous situations, finds himself held there without possibility of escape, needs guidance from the Lord. So this chapter will touch a bit on that subject. But first, in order that the two *knives of the scissors* be understood, we must explain some things.

Politically, the canyon of the Upper Salween was governed by Chinese magistrates who worked with local feudal lairds. These lairds owned most of the mountains, and were a mixture of Chinese and tribes. On the whole they were ignorant opium smokers, and thoroughly evil. No crime was too low and bestial — they perpetrated everything. And they had so much influence they were greatly feared by the Lisu. The power of life and death was supposed to be only in the hands of the Chinese magistrate, but as these magistrates were just as unprincipled, a bribe would take care of any little overstepping of authority. Comparatively speaking, the central Chinese government knew little of what went on in the canyon. Taxes were sent to the provincial governor and the Salween was forgotten by the world — but not by the Communists. The first rule of

Communist doctrine is to unsettle the territory they wish to commandeer, by brigandage, robbing raids, and so on. They deliberately use bandits, though they may repudiate them later.

We had been settled in Village of the Olives only four months when this first step of approaching Communism manifested itself in the uprising led by Dai Yi-gwan. He was attempting to flee to the nearest Communist camp when Laird Dwan's men shot him.

By 1949 the Communists were already entrenched in the Mekong Valley (over the mountains east of Oak Flat), and in the Luda district to the north of us, and in the Salween canyon itself. But Laird Dwan's reputation for devilry and courage, coupled with his victor over Dai Yi-gwan, made them proceed toward our section of the canyon with caution.

This year of 1949 the church had changed the dates of the Rainy Season Bible School from the usual June, July, and August, to March, April, and May. Also it was held in the Village of the Olives for the first time. The Christians in this village had built a big church on Lucius' ground, and he had built a large five-room adobe house just above the church in which one hundred Lisu students were able to sleep. Thus schoolroom and dormitory were taken care of. Our bamboo shanty was next door to Lucius' new house.

We were in the midst of our three months of study when news came of the Dai Yi-gwan brigand group. We heard of the fall of Six Treasuries; the dividing of the group — one party led by Dai Yi-gwan went after Laird Dwan; the second party crossed the river to capture a smaller official at Luchang. The Chinese magistrate, who lived in Luchang, fled into Burma at their approach, and it was he, returning with a regiment of soldiers, who finally drove out this group of brigands.

Luchang is on the same bank of the Salween as
Olives and only a morning's walk away. Dai Yi-
gwan, after he had robbed Laird Dwan, intended to
cross over, join this group, and lead them on to get
us. John was away in Paoshan. He had planned to be
with us but a similar group of brigands attacked
Paoshan simultaneously with those attacking us and
John was in the besieged city for two months — he
could not get out! So Charles Peterson and I went on
with the school.

News of the brigands reaching Luchang and Laird
Dwan's unexpected victory reached us on what we
called our long weekend. When communion Sunday
occurred the students were always sent extra far
away so as to administer it in villages which seldom
had a special speaker. Thus this weekend they were
gone one day longer than usual. I remember that we
wondered if those who had gone north would dare
return to us, for it meant the brigands were only a
morning's walk away from Olives and they had sent
word they meant to come to us. Especially did I
wonder about Teacher Philemon. It so happened on
that particular weekend that he had been assigned to
his own home village of Lameh, far away and safely
high up the mountain. Would they not conclude that
RSBS would have to disband, and stay at home?

But Sunday night Philemon was one of the first
back.

"Didn't you hear the news?" I asked him. "Don't
you know the brigands are only half a day away?"

"Yes," he answered. "That's the very reason I
returned! To take care of you and Danny, Ma-ma. Are
you going to flee? Will you come to my house?"

Bless him! It was comradeship like that which

made life sweet, and knit us all together as one family.

Not one student stayed away! Pop-eyed with the excitement of what to do next, still they had all returned, so we continued our school. And then the Lord did the thing so unusual and so perfectly timed that we delight to call it a miracle. It was getting toward May, always the driest and hottest month of the year just before June when the rainy season starts. But it began to rain. Not gentle April showers but deluges day after day, day after day. In the back of our house Lucius' mother had planted a pumpkin crop, and the leaves were huge. Every morning when Danny and I awoke in the loft where we slept, we lay and listened to the *plop, plop* of heavy rain on those big leaves. This unprecedented downpour for some two weeks caused the streams, tributaries of the Salween, to swell and become raging torrents. There were several such between us and Luchang, and the brigands could not get across to us! Never could I remember such deluges day after day — it made me think of how Noah must have felt listening to such a downpour on the roof of the ark. It was miserable weather to do anything except teach the Bible! But we all grinned at one another and said, "This is God's protection."

Strange to say, before the rains became heavy, a letter from John was handed to me by a villager of Olives who had gone to Luchang to market. This letter had been *brought to Luchang by one of the brigands*. It seems he was brother to a little Christian girl in Paoshan and, hearing what her brother's gang was planning, she suggested John write me a letter and her brother bring it — otherwise we would not have known why John had not arrived! In the letter he explained they were besieged and he could not get out of the city, but was having a wonderful opportunity to witness to the frightened populace. That brother-letter-carrier was later executed in Paoshan.

One memory of those sopping wet days was that of Abraham leading the student body in soldier drills for exercise. They had to get some exercise and outside was a hopeless mud slide. Now Abraham was a Nepali who had been led to the Lord by Christian Lisu in Burma. He had been enlisted in Nepal by the Gurkha regiment, brought to Burma to fight the Japanese, and abandoned when the regiment broke up at the end of the war. Not all armies pay their soldiers' way back home when war is over!

We had a group of students from Burma that year, and Abraham was the grand solution to the problem of how to get exercise despite the rain. Lucius' big house had a long, covered porch, and there Captain Abraham marshalled his forces at the end of the day's school. While in the army he had learned that English child's game, "This is the way we march! This is the way we jump!" — followed by the action. Danny grabbed a stick for a gun and joined in enthusiastically, picking up Abraham's accent along with the game. I was dismayed to hear our little American son going around singing. "Dish is de vay ve march ... dish is de vay ve jump!" and so on.

By the time the school concluded the brigands had been driven away, and a few weeks later John was back home. But to the north of us, right in the canyon, the Communists were in charge and threatening to descend upon us. It was only their fear of Laird Dwan which held them back. Nevertheless the work of the church went on. In the autumn it was necessary for John to make a trip to Kunming for reprints of our books, the *Catechism, First Steps in Reading,* and so on. At Christmas time many would want to buy these and we were all sold out. But by Christmas there were Communist uprisings all over the province and again John was cut off from us and could not get back. This time there was no brigand-messenger by whom to send a letter, so we had no notion why he did not arrive as promised. There is no telegraph in the canyon, of course.

The story of our bloody Christmas of 1949 has been told in detail in *Stones of Fire*. I will not repeat it here except to say that the Communists chose the Christian festival for their date of "liberation." Christmas is the one time of the year when farm work is slack and Christians from all over the canyon gathered for three days of worship and celebration. This year it was to be held in Village of the Olives, and it was to Olives that the Communists came.

I was warned ahead of time by a note; besides this, Gaius, a deacon at Sandalwood Flat Village, met the band while on a trading trip. He told me they had a few armed Chinese soldiers but also they had a large number of *Lo-zi-lo-pa* with them. Now the *Lo-zi-lo-pa* were heathen Lisu robbers noted for their ruthless cruelty. The Communists, fearing Laird Dwan's cunning and machine guns (he had lately purchased some new ones to get ready for this fight), had brought the *Lo-zi-lo-pa* with them as a reserve, so to speak.

I had heard of these *Lo-zi-lo-pa* from the mother-in-law of Dateh John. Many years before she had been driving goats to market when she met a band of them. They not only stole her goats but they put her left hand on a rock and with another rock pounded it almost to a pulp. Then they tied her in the river up to her neck and left her. Wanton brutality. She showed me her hand, which dangled uselessly from her wrist for the rest of her life.

Those were the *Lo-zi-lo-pa* who were coming toward us! The note urged me not to flee, promising my safety. At the same time Laird Dwan was making his preparations. He waited until the Communists had really entered Olives; then, leading his men by cowpaths high up the mountain banks of the dell, he opened fire from ambush. Three or four were killed; the rest fled. By Christmas Eve, Olives was once more in the hand of our feudal laird, young Dwan. These were the two knives of the scissors — and we who lived in Olives were between them.

Christmas Day, Dwan and his soldiers withdrew, and then came word that the Communists planned to let loose the *Lo-zi-lo-pa* upon us, to kill and plunder as they liked in revenge for the fact that it was the headman of Olives who had apprised Laird Dwan of their arrival.

Now we were in real danger — horrible danger. Laird Dwan would not come to our rescue. He had just received word that the governor of Yunnan had turned the whole province over to the Communists! Now under Communist rule himself, he must make peace with them as best he might. He certainly would not try to defend us.

As I have said before, the mountain on which Village of the Olives stands is border country. This side is China, that side is Burma. But the road right over our mountain is such terrible climbing that no mule could go. So we usually go by way of Pienma Pass, as I could not walk such country for very long.

I knew by now that I must take Danny home to

America. He was six years old, and was beginning to understand the vile heathen speech around him. At Oak Flat we had a large front and back garden fenced in — it was fairly simple to segregate him with a few children of Christians with whom he could safely play. At Olives we were right in the centre of the village, with no fence, and no way to control which type became his playmates. One day in the kitchen Danny told me he was not going to heaven. When I asked him why not, he answered darkly, "If you want me to be Jesus' boy, don't let me outside that door!" nodding to the one door of our shanty. Then I knew I must get him away. I taught him the Calvert Course every morning, but it was impossible to imprison such a lively youngster in such a small shanty.

Of course I had inquired about getting him to our own China Inland Mission school now moved to Kuling. But it was too late. Our secretary, Mr Frank Parry, wrote me from Kunming. "The Generalissimo's planes bomb Kunming airport every day. To get to Kuling is now impossible."

So to travel as a refugee through Burma and then to America seemed my only way. Knowing that probably I would be shut up to this route I had long before written to our home director asking that he contact the American Baptist Mission in Myitkyina, promising to refund any moneys that I might need to draw from them in case I had to evacuate. I had an answer from headquarters assuring me that the letter would be sent.

I had been saving silver currency to pay the carriers we would need for that long trek through the jungle of Upper Burma. I had money enough, and was ready to flee in every respect but two. The Lord

had not told me to go. And I did not like to go
without seeing John again.

But the *Lo-zi-lo-pa* were descending upon us!
Surely that was guidance enough? It was insanity to
stay. It was now that my bitter lesson of 1942 *in
running too soon* stood me in good stead. The flesh
loves excitement. It is always ready to jump up and
run somewhere! It pushes and hurries us in to action.
The Holy Spirit does not. He is from the God of peace
and His directions are always on time.

Wait on God. The guidance will come different
ways at different times. God is not confined to any
one method, not even to using Scripture verses. I use
a Scripture calendar and the verse that morning was,
"Do not leave your post" (Eccles. 10:4). Very
appropriate. Just like an answer. But Satan could use
an appropriate calendar verse too, or a Bible verse.
Opening the Bible at random is not defended from
his manipulations.

Whatever is given must be spoken in God's voice.
And you only learn to discern His voice by experience. If you want to be able to hear it in the crises of
life you must first seek it in the common places of
life. It is not suddenly acquired.

On this occasion, with the threat of the ruthless
Lo-zi-lo-pa descending on us, I felt the verse was
from Him. And after deciding not to flee I had perfect
peace — another sign that it was His voice. If we
have made a mistaken choice the Holy Spirit will
most assuredly disturb us about it. If peace of heart
follows, we can be sure it is of Him.

And so it proved. Day after day passed in
quietness. What was happening we did not know.
As a matter of fact, the laird's messenger, asking for a
peace conference, arrived just in time to prevent the

Lo-zi-lo-pa starting out to wreak revenge.

At length the Communist representatives to the peace conference arrived and by that we knew the threat of vengeance was lifted. Again the Lisu who had promised to escort Danny and me out through Burma urged me to go. The weather was perfect for travelling. With February would come rain on the lower slopes, snow on the heights, and the Pienma Pass might close for several months. Again I was tempted to go, but again I felt a restraint in the spirit — nothing tangible; something like the light touch of a hand holding me by the shoulder, so to speak. I just had no freedom in the spirit to leave.

And then one day (January 8, 1950) without warning, John arrived! And he had brought Eva, now graduated, with him! Oh, what a wonderful reunion!

There was so much to hear and tell. John had been held up by fighting on the Burma Road. But he had with him the coveted *Catechisms* — hundreds of them — and other printed matter. I told him of my contemplated trip to America to take Danny to school. He agreed, but thought that if I went soon, before the Communists had *organized* those distant parts, I might get back in again. But before Dan and I left he suggested a February Bible school, inviting students from Luda and all over. The Cookes had now evacuated to America (Mrs Cooke had been ill) so there were no missionaries in the Luda district. To our great joy there was a hearty response and that last session of RSBS was the best one I ever knew. One hundred students gathered. And when we sent them out during the weekends, to evangelize the villages to the north, the response was almost unbelievable. Hundreds of conversions were reported each weekend. And the new *Catechisms* sold like hot cakes. The reason was an earthly one — the Communists had said that the Christians were the only honest citizens in the canyon! But at least it gave us a chance to teach the truth to these who had never given it an unprejudiced hearing before.

Little Nurse Eva went right to work on the medical side. With almost no equipment and only a very smoky charcoal fire to sterilize instruments, she did operations on sick eyes by herself, and was so successful that her fame spread far and wide. As usual she would make only a nominal charge to the Lisu for her skill — fifty cents or a dollar, I think it was.

When they brought her a capon or eggs in their deep gratitude, she turned it over to us, insisting that the family eat them with her.

At the end of the school, Danny and I had to make preparations for our departure. It would be two weeks' trekking through the jungle of Upper Burma. John offered to go with us, but with all these new converts to supervise I felt he should not come. When Lucius offered to be my escort, we decided to accept him.

The parting with Daddy was one of the hardest we had ever had. I felt myself that I would not get back, that Communism would never allow evangelistic Christianity to work under their régime. John is an optimist by nature, but when it came to saying goodbye for once he could not force a smile. We left him on a high rock jutting out from the road, biting his lips in grim determination. And we set our faces toward a trek that must take us halfway around the world. But that is for the next chapter.

The knives of the scissors are like two dangers or

two painful situations which, to human sight, must cut us in pieces when they finally meet. What is our refuge there? It must be to shut our eyes tight to the physical situation as the mere outward eye sees it. Our refuge must be to get absolutely quiet in the inner man so that God can speak, then direction will be given. The experience may be compared to tight-rope walking. The walker must be trained on easy, low ropes first. When he is trained to throw off all the glamorous outside calls and attend to that one thing, his eye on that one goal, then only he is ready to put his training to the test in the place of danger. We must learn first, today, now, in this smaller easier matter, to walk with our eyes on the Lord only. Only then can we do it victoriously under the later high tension of danger or excitement.

First I had to learn to *fear* running away before God's time had come. Then I had to learn to discern His voice from the hurry-hurry voices of the flesh, and to hold on in steadfast patience.

If I had run off to Burma when the *Lo-zi-lo-pa* scare came, see what I would have lost:

1. I would have missed seeing John.

2. I would have missed meeting Eva. (I never saw her again. She had to stay behind in China, when at length John was ordered out of the canyon.)

3. I would have missed the repentance of Keh-deh-seh-pa.

4. I would have missed that last wonderful RSBS session where hundreds of heathen Lisu were garnered in.

These platforms, or struggles in life, do not necessarily make us stronger Christians. I want to be sure this is understood. Many victories do not make a stronger Christian. It does give us an experience of

Christ's ability to help us, so the next time it is easier
to trust Him. But it is fatal to think that we have
become strong. Oswald Chambers used to say he
feared to become forty, for so many once shining
Christians seem to grow cold or flabby in their
spiritual lives at that age. Maybe it was because they
thought themselves strong and unconsciously released the flesh from the position of crucifixion.

Platforms do not make us stronger Christians or
better Christians but they do make us *richer* Christians. Rich in our inner fellowship with Him. Rich in
our confidence that He will be our Rock and our
Deliverer in the future. Rich in the relaxation of the
little child who leans back on his father's breast,
confident, secure, and satisfied.

> Oh, the deep, deep love of Jesus,
>   Love of every love the best:
> 'Tis an ocean vast of blessing
>   'Tis a haven sweet of rest.
> Oh, the deep, deep love of Jesus
>   'Tis a heaven of heavens to me;
> And it lifts me up to glory
>   For it lifts me up to Thee.

                                        S.T. FRANCIS

Chapter 11

STRANDED AT WORLD'S END

AND now we were on our way to America. First came the Pienma Pass (10,998-feet elevation). We left Village of the Olives on March 10. That night we slept among rice fields by the side of the Salween River. March 11 we climbed, pressed through the town of Luchang, and learned that the new Communist official was due to arrive the next week. He would never have allowed us to leave, of course, so we escaped just in time. The third day we were still climbing but now on the sides of the great Pienma Mountain itself. That night we slept in a hamlet called Er-tso-cho, the last house on the slopes below the Pass. And the next morning when I woke up early, to my dismay I heard the pitter-patter of rain on the roof! That meant it was snowing on the Pass, and the trail across the top would be obliterated. All that day it rained, all the next night and all the next day! My carriers, dear Christian boys, most of them farmers in Olives, began to talk about going back home. Snow will have closed the Pass, they argued. And the weather looked like a ten-day rain, after which the ground would be just right for the first ploughing. There was no use trying to get over the Pass, we must all turn around and go back to Olives!

You can imagine how I felt — and how I prayed. To go back to Olives meant that Danny would have to go through the Communist ordeal after all — imprisonment or internment, not to speak of the moral dangers from Village of the Olives, two-thirds of which was still heathen. As a matter of fact, John was allowed wonderful freedom for one year after the Communist officials arrived. Then he was "invited" out at the point of a bayonet, and forced to trek all across China, although exit through Burma would have been so easy. In desperation I prayed, "Lord, if this obstacle is from you, I accept it; if it is from Satan I refuse it." As I prayed this, an idea came to me.

"Boys," I said, "if we turn back tomorrow to Olives because of the weather, *and then* the sun came out, wouldn't you feel foolish? And you know what a loss of money it would be to me. Now let us arrange this way and pray for God's guidance. If when we wake up tomorrow morning it is not raining we will take it as a sign to start out. On the other hand, when we reach the snow line, if it begins to snow or the trail is difficult to find, I will consent to turn back with you. I know that people perish every year trying to cross Pienma Pass in times of snow, and I have no wish to endanger you or ourselves. But I have found that if we go as far as we can, God often opens up the rest of the way. Will you do it?"

They agreed, for they were all Christians and we really had wonderful fellowship together. You can imagine how I strained my ears about cock-crow that next morning! There was silence. The pitter-patter on the roof had ceased. Throwing something over me I went to the door and looked out — not promising; heavy storm clouds lay low over the hills and the air was damp, *but it was not raining*. When I went back in, I found Lucius making the fire for breakfast, so I told him to call the others to get up, that we would start out. No one looked thrilled.

"The trail will be obliterated, Ma-ma, after two days and nights of such a snowstorm," Lucius warned quietly.

"If it is, I will turn back with you," I promised, "but let us go and see." I counted much on the fact that it was not actually raining — the sign I had asked from God. So we set out. Our host at this last cabin, the last human outpost before the final climb, was loud in protestations that we would never make it — which did not help the boys to feel any happier.

As we began that climb which would take us all the morning, the sun shot forth in one golden stream upon us. But it was only for a moment, then it disappeared behind clouds and a thin drizzle of rain descended! We were climbing through dark and lonely vegetation, up and up. The rain stopped but we were among the clouds by now, which as you know, is like being in a fog. It is wet and depressing. I was riding our mule, Jasper, and Danny was being carried in a mountain chair (like a stretcher but with a seat instead of a bed) on the shoulders of Canaan and Daniel. The Lisu, usually so merry and cheerful on the road, were silent, and I was wondering if it was right for me to endanger their lives; should I call a halt and turn back? I was praying for guidance when through the fog, up above us on the rocky ascent, loomed two black figures. They spied us as we spied them and both parties shouted. The next instant they were down beside us — two Lisu heathen of the Luda district. They were returning from a trading trip in Burma and had just crossed over the Pass!

"How's the top?" our men shouted.

"The snow is deep, but we are a large party. You can find your way by our footprints if you hurry. *Ah Beh*! Didn't we first fellows have a time!" Delighted that their lives were spared, for the trail would be easy from now on, they sprang on down the slope, passing us.

"When you reach Village of the Olives, tell Ma-pa you saw us!" I called to them.

"We'll do that," they called back, then the cloud swallowed them up.

Now our men pushed upward with new vigour. Farther on two more of this Luda party met us.

"It's beginning to snow on the top of the Pass," one of them answered our eager inquiries, "but you can make it. Watch for our footprints; there is nothing else to show where the trail is."

It was now noon and all of us were hungry but we did not dare to waste time making a fire and cooking lunch. I had one slice of bread left and a small piece of cheese. This I divided with Danny when we finally arrived at the top of Pienma Pass. It usually presents a most marvellous view, with China spread out before you on the one side and Burma on the other! But now almost all was covered with snow clouds. On the China side the sun was trying to struggle through, but on the Burma side all was dark and lowering. In fact, it was beginning to snow in tiny half-wet flakes which melted immediately they touched us.

The trail over the top of Pienma Pass is but a cowpath in width. It winds back and forth on the level for a short distance before plunging down into the steep descent. We met more Luda Lisu shivering as they struggled on toward the China side, but their feet had sunk deeply into the snow, marking out the trail for us. It was God's provision. We waited until our party was all together, the slower ones catching up with us who led the way, then we began to cross the Pass. We had not gone far when Jasper suddenly sank to his stomach in snow. I had to dismount. With Samson pulling at his head, and Lucius jerking him by the tail, they finally got the mule out and on to the trail again where the snow was not so deep. I climbed on his back once more but heard a call from behind me.

"May we carry Danny pickaback, Ma-ma? We can't make it with this big awkward chair."

"All right," I called back as Jasper floundered and snorted and the snowstorm grew thicker and heavier.

So one of the Lisu carried Danny on his back and Daniel carried the empty chair. Danny had a raincoat and rubber hat on so the snow-sleet dripped off him easily. He was the most comfortable one of the whole party and cheered the rest of us by singing at the top of his voice!

As for me, the snow melted off me and ran into my galoshes. Soon my feet were in pools of snow-water and I lost all feeling up to the knees. I was soaked to the waist too, for my plastic raincoat kept slipping back off my knees.

Of course as we reached lower altitudes the snow changed to rain, the steep path became muddy and slippery. Finally Jasper could not keep his feet, but began to slide dangerously.

"You will have to get off, Ma-ma," said Samson at last. So I had to jump off, trusting that my feet would hold me up, although I had lost all feeling in them. Lucius helped me and so we continued to slip and slide in descent. It was half-past four in the afternoon before we reached the pretty valley where Pienma Village nestled. Pink peach blossoms were beginning to burst into lovely colour against the new green of spring buds, and everything was shining from the recent rain-wash.

But nobody invited us into their homes! "There are a couple of guest houses up the hill there," they said coolly and pointed to two empty shacks which did not look in very good repair. There was nothing to do but camp in them as best we could. We asked to buy some firewood but what they gave us was green and smoked badly. Our bedding was quite wet in spots and with the smoky fire we could not get it dry. But we were out of Communist China! True, we had no visa to enter Burma; we still had ten days' trek through the jungle before we came upon civilization; and even after we reached Myitkyina Danny and I would still be halfway across the world from home. There was plenty to think about. But at least we were over the Pass.

Supper over, a bed for the night was the next problem. There were no beds in the huts so we all slept on the bamboo floor around the central fireplace. Our bedding was still streaked with damp. I chose the dry spots for Danny and wrapped him up well but I had to lie down on part of the quilt and cover with none-too-dry blankets. Then the storm began again with violence. It hailed outside once and then rain came spatting down. Every now and again it spat through the leaks of the roof on to our faces, and altogether it was a depressing situation. I knew it was snowing hard on the Pass and as it blew hard all night, by morning the Pass would be closed. In other words, we were shut up to going forward. But what if I got lumbago from sleeping in damp bedding? I had caught it some years before and that time the bedding was drier than this. With lumbago I could not walk or ride a horse all day, no matter how I summoned my will power. I was helplessly cast upon the Lord.

Was I really in His will to come? This time He had given me no Bible verse on which to lean. I had asked for one but none came. It would have been so comfortable to have a Bible verse to stand upon as in my experience of 1942. This was eight years later, and God expects His children to *grow*. I believe it was D E Hoste who said that the older he grew the harder it seemed to get guidance from the Lord. I believe he meant that guidance becomes less simple. God expects us to exercise spiritual discernment, and He guides by a certain pressure on the spirit, by a still small voice, by a something so delicately intangible that unless you are carefully tuned in to His Spirit, so to speak, you can miss it widely. It requires a close and experienced walk with the Lord, so in one sense, He has a hold on us that might not be if He always supplied us with a Bible verse every time we asked for one!

When it is only a still small voice which is our guide, it is easy for Satan to throw us into confusion by causing us to question if we heard aright. It is a good plan not to go back on past guidance. Yet how patient is our Master! He does not desert us even then. I did *not* get lumbago or even rheumatism, and we had to travel in the rain more than once after that, for the storm continued. As we journeyed through the mountains Danny asked me to sing "The Ninety and Nine," for I happened to remember all the verses. And when we came to

And all through the mountains, thunder-riven,
And up from the rocky steep —

he would join in with great gusto. *"The mountains,
thunder-riven,"* seemed our daily diet!

But the road was not as bad as maybe you are
thinking. True, it took us through the jungle of
Upper Burma, but the British (when in power in
Burma) had caused fairly good roads to be cut and
maintained through to Pienma Pass, and every ten or
fifteen miles they had built rest houses. These were
simple rustic bungalows built in a clearing in the
jungle and had a native caretaker in charge. There
were beds (without mattresses or bedding; every
traveller carried his own) and a table and chair, and
the caretaker could cook a decent meal. The Japanese
had destroyed the rest houses nearer to the border,
so we did not come across any for several days. Once
we did so, however I began to feel in clover, sure of a
clean good rest at night. But before we reached these,
we arrived at a place where lived a Lisu Christian
from the Salween. We stayed at his house and the
next morning a message reached us. Mrs Kuhn was
to report to the Burmese official immediately. Knowing I had no visa to enter Burma I had to comply,
although it meant saddling Jasper and riding back up
the mountain to the official's residence. The effort
proved to be well worth it, however.

The official was a Karen and a Christian. He told
me so himself almost as soon as he had greeted me.
He gave me some good advice about what to do, in
my visa-less state. I must report to the police as soon
as I arrived at any point of importance — Myitkyina
or Rangoon. By short-wave radio he must advise the
police at Myitkyina of my approach. But he also sent

word to the American Baptist missionary in residence at Myitkyina, Rev. Herman Tegenfeldt, who perhaps would be able to meet us with his jeep; there was a motor road that would save us two days' travel if we could get a vehicle on it. I thanked the official, and our party went back down the hill and on our way.

That night as I registered at the rest house I was startled and thrilled to see in a very familiar handwriting: *Mr and Mrs Orville Carlson*. I knew the Carlsons were hoping to go to Goomoo and teach the Maru-Kachin whom Mark had led to the Lord (a thousand of them had believed before Mark died), but I had not heard for sure that they got out of Yunnan before it fell to the Communists. We had missed them by only one week, but it was a jolt of joy to know there was somebody in Burma whom I knew!

In between those rest houses the road was often cut through heavy jungle. Wild animals abounded. The fresh spoor of a tiger lay on the dew-soft earth one early morning as we started out. We all had to keep together at such times, but the Lord protected us all the way.

At last we reached the motor road and the rest house beside it. Some of our Lisu had never seen a truck, and I was hoping I could pay a driver to give them a little ride. A government rice truck drove in the very evening we arrived, and the driver had a short trip to make the next morning. He would take the Lisu with him and from there they could go on to Myitkyina on foot. They could leave their loads behind, for he would return and get us and the baggage and drive us to Myitkyina. On the strength of that promise Samson and the mountain-chair carriers asked permission to be allowed to set out on their return journey back into China. The mule could not go on the truck, someone must go back with it, and these Lisu were not interested in seeing Myitkyina anyway.

So the next morning we said goodbye to them, and cheered off the excited group who were to have their first auto ride! Lucius was the only one left with Danny and me. Imagine our chagrin when about noon we received a telephone message at the rest house saying that the truck had broken down, but as the driver had assured the Lisu other trucks would take us, the dear Lisu were not returning to us! This did leave us in a predicament — all our heavy baggage with us and no carriers! We inquired about a truck and were told they did not come frequently — perhaps one a week.

All the following morning we waited and prayed, so you can imagine our feelings when about noon we heard a motor toot down the road. We all ran out to look, and there was a red jeep with a white man at the wheel coming merrily toward us. Mr Tegenfeldt and two of his children, Alice and John! They had brought a picnic lunch, beautifully prepared by his wife. And at the sight of those fine sandwiches wrapped in waxed paper, I felt that I had reached civilization at last!

Myitkyina is perhaps the most important city in Upper Burma. It has an airport and the Irrawaddy River flows by it. Here the Tegenfeldts live and from here, with its city church and school, they also keep in touch with a large country work among the tribes. There are several other tribes which are ranked higher than the Lisu in intelligence and tribal culture. Mr Tegenfeldt supervised work in all of these.

But one of my first questions was concerning that letter which headquarters had promised to write to Mr Tegenfeldt, guaranteeing a refund of any sums of money advanced to me. No such letter had come, said Mr Tegenfeldt. I cannot tell you the dismay and alarm that filled me.

The title of this chapter may sound far-fetched to the reader but it is descriptive of my *feelings* rather than my actual condition. I was now at the other end of the world from home. I had practically no Burmese money, did not speak their language, and had no one in the whole country to guarantee me. Moreover, I did not understand the Mission's silence. It was a time of great stress among us all and mistakes were possible. I was in a turmoil of questions and I felt stranded at the end of the world.

Well, the first thing is to *cast out fear*. The only fear a Christian should entertain is the fear of sin. All other fears are from Satan sent to confuse and weaken us. How often the Lord reiterated to His disciples, "Be not afraid!" So, alone in our bedroom in the Tegenfeldts' nice home, I knelt by the bed and spread my heart before Him. I refused to be afraid and asked Him to cast such fears out of my heart.

Then I must seek *light for the next step*. I must report to the Burmese police, but after that I would need to find a way to get some money. We still had some of Grandpa Kuhn's legacy in the bank of John's home town, Manheim, Pennsylvania. I had blank cheques with me, but who would believe that I really had the money there? Would the Tegenfeldts trust me? They had never met me before and only knew that there was a Kuhn family working in the Salween canyon.

Rather timidly I asked Mr Tegenfeldt if he could cash a cheque for me — quite a large cheque, because

I found that we would have to fly to Rangoon. The railway had been bombed and there were no through trains.

"No, I don't think I can," replied Mr Tegenfeldt. "Why don't you go on the street and try to sell it?" He did not even offer to come along and guarantee me, but I found out later why he seemed so unconcerned — he knew an endorser would not be required and probably did not guess my doubts!

So, with Lucius for company, and the little book of blank cheques on a small-town bank in America, I started down the business street looking for some shop where someone might speak English! We had not gone far when a tall Hindu, bearded and turbaned, smiled and said, "Good morning!" Timidly I entered his shop and produced my book. "I am a missionary," I said. "Would you cash a cheque for me?"

"For how much?" he inquired gravely.

"For $150 American," I replied.

He took the cheque and looked at it a moment. "Is this negotiable in India?" he asked.

"Yes," I replied. "It can be cashed anywhere."

"All right," he answered, and in five minutes a roll of Burmese money was in my hand! Just as easy as that. No one had even asked to see my passport. I felt like Alice in Wonderland, as I returned jubilant to the Tegenfeldts' home. Apparently Christian missionaries are so trusted in Burma that they can cash a cheque anywhere without a guarantor! I know of no other country in the world where this can be done.

Well, so far so good. Now to get to Rangoon. Mr Tegenfeldt took me to the police and helped me with all the red tape involved. In fact, no one could have been kinder than Ruth and Herman Tegenfeldt were to us in every way.

Word had gone around that Ma-ma and Danny were in Myitkyina and a large group of Lisu came to see us, including Abraham (the Nepali), men who had been in our RSBS and others who had fled to Burma when the brigand scare was on. We had a precious time together.

But at Rangoon — where would we stay? The Tegenfeldts gave us the address of a missionary guest house where they always stayed, and I wired to inquire if they could accommodate us. But I received no answer. Lucius and another Lisu boy rode with us to the airport and it was hard to say goodbye. I felt I might never see him again on earth, and I have not.

But just before we boarded the plane, a note was handed to me by a passenger getting off it. Once we were up in the air I opened it and saw it was signed, *Eric Cox*. Oh, how I thanked the Lord! Eric had been working among the Atsi-Kachin tribe far south of us in Yunnan. (His dear wife, Grace Liddell Cox, had died on furlough.) I knew that he too hoped to go home to America to see his children, and that he planned to go via Burma, but I did not know when he was leaving. The note said that he was at the guest house when my telegram arrived and, hearing the hostess say she had no room for us, he had made arrangements for us to stay with the Bible Churchman's Missionary Society's deaf school and he hoped to meet us at the airport!

What could have been more wonderful! Psalm 59:10 (ASV): "*My God with his lovingkindness will meet me*," had been fulfilled again. I was thrilled. Maybe we could travel on the same ship with "Uncle" Eric, and Danny would have the pleasure of his companionship. Eric had been a sea officer, holding a

master's certificate, when God called him to missionary service, so there was nothing about a ship he
would not be able to teach a small boy.

But I still had an unknown adventure to go
through before we reached Rangoon.

The aeroplane was a freight plane, dirty and
uncomfortable. We had been told we would come
down only once before Rangoon, that being at
Mandalay. But, lo, and behold, we came down at
Bhamo. Danny had gotten his hand into some black
grease so I took him off the plane hoping to find a
washroom. Bhamo was a flat, hot place with some
Burmese officials standing in a group talking. Low
one-storied buildings were in the background.

Just then a jeep drove up. In it were two white
people, dust-covered and looking like — well, like
missionaries. Glad to meet my own kind I was
approaching them when they sprang and almost ran
into me.

"You're a missionary? Your name, please?" asked
the lady.

"Mrs John Kuhn, from China."

"Oh, we know your husband! He visited us at
Namkham last year. I am Grace Seagrave and this is
my brother, Gordon."

Of course I had heard of the famous Seagrave
family. I bowed and, indicating Danny's dirty hand,
was about to ask where the washroom was when Dr
Grace said, "Oh, Gordon will take him and wash him
up." Which Dr Gordon did.

All this time Dr Grace was chattering anything and
everything and coming so close to me that I instinctively backed away. I did not see at first that she was
deliberately doing this to back me to a place where
we would be alone and not overheard by the curious

Burmese official group. When she had me backed away from them and against the side of the plane she suddenly produced a letter and said, "We have had trouble at Namkham Hospital. There has been a Karen uprising and Gordon is falsely charged with helping them. Our mail is all intercepted and we cannot get our side of the affair out to our friends. We drove sixty miles today in the hope there would be someone on this plane who would take this letter for us to the American consul in Rangoon. It explains our side. Quick! Have you got a pocket in your skirt or somewhere to put it?"

Political intrigue? This was the last thing I wanted to get mixed up in — I with no visa for Burma and having to report to the police as soon as I arrived in Rangoon! I faltered in reply, praying inwardly, "O Lord, direct me what to do!" Now, unknown to Dr Grace, there was a Burmese official walking up and down behind her, watching our every move. Just as I prayed that, this official reached the end of his walk and had to turn to come back. Instead of turning towards us he turned *away* from us. In just that one second, I quickly opened the long pocketbook I held in my hand, Dr Grace popped the letter into it, and when that man resumed his guard over us, there was nothing for him to see. Dr Gordon Seagrave returned with Danny, the call came to board the plane and — we were off. But now I carried on my person that which if discovered might have put me in prison. Dr Gordon Seagrave was put in prison later over this very affair. (I understand Dr Grace died the next year.)

There were some on the plane with us who spoke English and from them I learned that there was usually a minute baggage examination at Rangoon.

But we were late getting in. When finally we arrived, only one immigration-customs officer remained and he was anxious to get home.

"Only your personal things, I expect?" he said, indicating our baggage.

"Yes, sir."

"OK. I won't ask you to open them. Passed!" and he left us. So the Lord delivered me. At a later time in Rangoon they asked to see into my pocketbook too, but by then the Seagrave letter was safely in the hands of the American consul. I delivered it into his own hand myself, and the next year when the affair came out in *Time* magazine, I had the satisfaction of knowing that at least the Seagrave side of the matter had been presented to American authorities.

And now for the BCMS deaf school where we were so kindly received by Miss Sturman and her fellow worker. Eric Cox had missed us at the airport but came around the next morning and took me to downtown Rangoon, to the police station, to the immigration offices, to the American Consulate — everywhere. He had just been through the red tape for himself so knew where the various buildings were located and how to help me.

I had hoped we could get passage from Rangoon, but learned that ships were so few I would need to book space six months ahead. The only other way out was to fly to Hongkong and try for a freighter there. Eric himself was doing this and soon had to leave us, but he promised to telegraph if there was a possibility of our getting on the same ship.

The China Inland Mission had a treasurer stationed at Hongkong, so that once there our money problems ended; we would be able to draw on him for what we needed.

The telegram came. "BOAT LEAVING SATURDAY, ERIC." We read it with a sigh for we could not possibly make it by then. Being a Canadian, I was having to go through a long process to get into the United States, including a physical examination and shots for this and for that, which had to have intervals of time in between them and could not be hurried. So we had to relinquish hope of having "Uncle" Eric on the same ship with Danny.

At length we were through and ready to fly to Hongkong. The only bookings we could get were on the Siamese Airways, and these had a stopover of one day in Bangkok.

Siam, or Thailand as it is now called, did not interest me much. It never entered my head that I would ever return there! To me it was merely a 36-hour stopover. For some unknown reason we were not booked at the same hotel as the other passengers, but were sent to the Ratanakosin — the most modern and expensive hotel in Bangkok. We arrived on the Saturday when Eric Cox was to sail out of Hongkong. The next day was April 9 — Easter Sunday!

I inquired about English church services but could get no information from the desk clerk, so we ventured forth to try and find the missionary community. Bangkok uses pedicabs, which are like rickshas except that the driver pedals a tricycle instead of walking. We finally found the American Bible Society, where Mr and Mrs Marvin Martin received us cordially and invited us to dinner. There was no English service until night, and as I wished to get Danny to bed in preparation for an early flight on Monday morning, I took him back to the Ratanakosin.

As we walked through the lobby the desk clerk called to me, "Telephone, Ma'am!" I wondered who could be calling me. It was the Siamese Airways.

"We find you do not have a visa for Hongkong for your son, Daniel, Mrs Kuhn. You may not proceed tomorrow."

"But he is only six years old! He doesn't need a visa!" I gasped.

"When you get a visa for him you may proceed, and not until then, Madame," was the short reply, and they hung up.

My face must have betrayed my feelings, for Danny pulled at my skirt asking anxiously, "What is it, Mamma? What is it?"

"You don't have a visa for Hongkong," was all I could answer, for my heart was like lead. I wanted to get out of sight and cry. Stranded in Bangkok and at the most expensive hotel! I pulled out my little cheque-book on the home-town bank. "May I pay my bills by cheque?" I asked the clerk. You should have seen the contemptuous amusement on his face!

"No, Madam. You may pay in American cash or Siamese money. We do not accept cheques."

I turned and sought the elevator and our bedroom. Once there I fell on my knees by the bed and sought the dear Lord. "O God, undertake for me!" I cried. "Whatever shall I do? I do not know a soul in this country. The Martins were kind to give us a meal but they are utter strangers. O Lord, speak to me!" and I pulled out my Bible and desperately opened it. There before me was Isaiah 65:24, "Before they call, I will answer."

"That is a very good verse, O Lord," I said, still uncomforted, "but how does it apply to us *now*?"

As I waited before Him, my memory was illumined. Why, of course! How could I have forgotten? Quickly I pulled my purse over to me and slipped back the zipper to an inner pocket. Yet, it was still there! An American ten- and a five-dollar bill. "Before they call." Our mail in China was so interrupted that we received only a few batches of it those last six months of 1949. But in two of those batches had been a card once and a note once from a lady in California who was a stranger to me. With the note she had enclosed a five-dollar bill and with the Christmas card a ten-dollar bill. Both had come through safely, although brigands and robbers abounded. I could not use them in Lisuland, so I had put them into this secret pocket of my purse for use on the trip home but had forgotten them. That lady, the giver, I never did meet, and she has ceased to be interested in us since. But the Lord surely used her to our blessing that year.

From the depths of despair I was lifted into joyous worship of Him. How wonderful to find Him *always there*, when we have unexpected need of Him! That living touch with Him is so precious; it makes Him so real; it obliterates the line between the earthly and heavenly; it is so humbling to find Him *waiting* there. Our hotel bill, by the way, was just US$10!

On Easter Monday the British consulate was open for only one hour in the morning, but time enough to obtain the visa. A visit to the Siamese Airways, and our passages for Tuesday were secured. The rest of the day was ours, and to my astonishment I found that it was a big day in Bangkok. It was the day appointed for King Bhumipol to cremate his uncle, and the ceremony was to take place in front of the Ratanakosin Hotel! From the roof garden we had a "box seat" view of it all.

A high conical platform, to which marble steps
with brass railings led, was erected in the open park
across from the hotel. The railings were hung with
lacy green ferns and the top of the platform was
roofed with gold and crimson. On the platform was
the pyre. The procession was two hours long and a
fascinating pageant in Oriental colours and splen-
dour. The body arrived in an urn which was set in a
carriage hung with gold curtains. Set to weird
Buddhist music, the chantings of the priests filled the
air and stirred the blood to excitement. All Thailand
was represented in the companies which formed the
long procession — the nobles, the priests, the police,
the armed forces with all their divisions, and so on.
Most fascinating were the cavalry whose beautiful
horses were trained to do the dead march. The king
was carried to the scene in a golden palanquin. And
when all was set, he, dressed in a white uniform,
mounted the marble stairs between the fern-hung
brass railings — up, up, and up to the pyre at the top,
where he kindled the fire. It was earth's glory at its
most dramatic, but it contained no hope for the poor
soul of the dead man, who before God's judgment
seat must stand naked in his sins. There is no hush or
reverence in a Buddhist funeral. There is only gaudy
display and loud clamour to drown out thought.

On Tuesday morning we boarded the plane for
Hongkong. A group of Chinese gentlemen got on
with us, and we found we were to come down in
Hainan. When we reached the island the co-pilot
came back into the plane and spoke to us.

"As you see, we are circling over Hainan," he said.
"We have important personnel on board and may not
come down until the reception committee has
reached the airfield." We circled for almost half an

hour! Then down we came and the Chinese passengers got out. The reception committee was there and regiments of Nationalist soldiers were drawn up all over the field. Ten days later the Communists had taken the whole island.

Hongkong at last! As we descended the gangplank we heard a shout of greeting. Looking to our right, over there behind wire netting was — Eric Cox, smiling and waving to us! And beside him Sally Harverson of old Yunnan days. But we had to go through immigration and customs first.

The immigration officer examined Danny's passport. "Oh, you are the people who were held up in Bangkok for the little boy's visa?"

"Yes, sir."

"Well, it wasn't needed. Juniors do not need a visa to enter Hongkong."

Why was it allowed? Satan trying to harass? I do not know. There are many apparently needless trials in life, but the Lord stands with us through all of them. "May you lose nothing in the furnace but your dross," said Samuel Rutherford. The Lord will preserve everything else for us.

He had even kept "Uncle" Eric for Danny's boat trip home! The boilers of the *Skauvann* had broken down and she was delayed just long enough to get us aboard. The lovingkindness of our Lord — *"Surely goodness and love will follow me all the days of my life."*

We had a great reception by wonderful friends in Vancouver, and the same from others as we passed through Seattle; then on by train to meet Kathryn at Wheaton College in Illinois.

It was wonderful to see Kathryn again — now *grown up*, with an adult mind, and the ability to share life's problems with understanding. Our fellowship rose to a new level.

We arrived just a month before commencement —
who could find a place to stay at Wheaton *then*? A
student, sensing he would fail in his exams, suddenly went home and left a bedroom vacant in the very
house where Mrs Ella Graham had an apartment! So
we had a room right near the college, and we had
meals with kind "Aunt" Ella.

A beautiful little college town in the heart of
America! Wide streets tree-shaded, with squirrels
scampering happily from branch to branch. No
air-raid alarms. No windows iron-barred against
thieves. Just peace and plenty; the beauty of spring
and gay young voices. Family life, friendships,
freedom. It was like heaven on earth; never will I
forget it!

Halfway across the world He had brought us.
Through snowy heights and wild jungle, bombed
bridges and railways; past suspicious immigration
officials with endless red-tape regulations; soldiers,
and tension everywhere. Chinese money, Burmese
money, Siamese money, Hongkong money — oh,
let's never mention the word again! He had supplied
as each need arose, but each time in a different way.

Stranded at world's end? Maybe. But if we lean
back we will find ourselves on the bosom of Christ —
sweet, familiar place.

> Sometimes on the Rock I tremble,
>   Faint of heart and weak of knee;
> But the steadfast Rock of Ages
>   Never trembles under me!

It was an enriching experience to have found Him
living and quick to bless in those strange countries

— Burma, Thailand, and Hongkong. I realized now that I had unconsciously begun to lean on the Mission for my financial needs. It had been a rude jolt to find myself cut loose and forced to trust directly. As Hudson Taylor commented (when a newspaper reporter described him as leading a hand-to-mouth existence), "Yes, but it is from God's hand to my mouth." I ended up with being so glad that it happened just that way, that I might know again the thrill of *God's hand to my mouth*.

So the platform ended, with His power having been manifested to me again, and a fresh knowledge of Himself given.

Chapter 12

DREAD DISEASE

IF the Lord tarry, there must come, some time, a last
platform. Always the flesh would pray that it might
be an easy one. But the Lord looks to the eternal
weight of glory and so He may choose otherwise
sometimes.

The story of how we were led to go to Thailand,
after John was released by the Communists, has been
told in *Ascent to the Tribes*. The beginning of this
chapter finds us there.

I think the very beginning is to be found in my
first trip in search of the tribes of North Thailand. As
we were climbing those hills on that occasion,
hindrances, annoyances, accidents kept happening
to our group until we decided they must come from
the satanic forces which had ruled the heights above
us since first human beings found their way there.
We gathered together right there on the steep
jungle-tangled mountainside and claimed the power of God over each member of our party.

It was not before, but after that prayer of faith, that
I was suddenly struck in the breast by a stick. We
were walking single file, and a fallen tree branch lay
concealed under the leaves of the path. As the young
worker in front of me unknowingly stepped on the

one end, the other end sprang up and struck me severely.

When I could recover my breath and walk on (I was last in the line), I looked to the Lord in my heart.

"Oh Lord, why did you let that happen? I thought a blow like that to a woman, fifty years of age, was likely to turn to cancer. Was I not protected by your power?"

Although I was mistaken, these thoughts came immediately.

"You *were* protected, dear. And you *will* get cancer. And I am going to take you back to America."

Now it was not *clearly* His voice. I repeat, the Lord sometimes speaks so clearly that we *cannot confound or doubt Him, or deny.* This was not that. I did not dare say that those thoughts had been from Him. The parting with the children again had been hard, so the above thoughts might have been just the wishful thinking of the mother-part of me. Therefore I did not count on it being His voice. As soon as we returned to civilization, I went to Dr Buker for examination. He felt it was just a torn ligament, so I accepted that diagnosis and went on with my work, deliberately putting all thoughts of serious trouble out of my mind.

Seven months passed, and again I was in the mountains, in quite a different part of the country and with a different group of fellow workers. We were preaching in a hamlet where I had never been before, and the headman's shanty was packed with Lisu villagers. John presented the Gospel to them, to which they listened attentively. Then he turned to me and said, "Now you preach for a while." I felt I should tell them that Christ Jesus is stronger than the demons to whom they are so enslaved. Immediately it was as if a voice said, "Better not. If you do, the demons will take revenge on *you*." But I did proclaim that anyway, for it is a truth they much needed to know: "*If the Son sets you free, you will be free indeed*." I had no sooner said it, however, than the young men all jumped up in alarm and left the house — leaving me speaking to only women and children!

When I had finished, our party departed from the village, but as we did so someone said, "Look up at that demon shrine!" On the hill above us were young men silently encircling their shrine as if on guard. It was unusual, sinister, and humiliating. "We were in their sight as grasshoppers," came to my mind as our party climbed the hill.

That night it rained and the next morning we had to return to Base Camp. All the hillsides were slippery and wet. After we had slid and descended for about an hour someone behind me called me. I turned to hear better and slipped. Down I came on a jagged stump — a nasty jolting blow *in the same place as the first blow*. But as I fell, a picture of those young men guarding their demon had flashed before me. I had not been thinking of them, for it took all my wits to keep upright on that slippery slope.

Once down the hill and into civilization I again sought medical advice. An X-ray showed nothing. I felt as if the Lord said, "The time hasn't come yet; get on with your work." And so I did. I was not haunted by any fear of the disease — I had put it deliberately out of my mind and was joyful in my work.

Over a year passed, and physically I had never felt better in my life. But one day, noticing something not normal in the area where I had twice been hit, I felt I should see Dr Buker. He looked very serious and said a biopsy should be taken immediately. To my surprise the first report came back, *non-malignant*. Naturally, John was jubilant, but personally I did not believe it was correct. It is most important, however, never to *act* on these illuminated hunches. I distinguish between the clear voice of God and mere premonitions. I do not hesitate to bank everything on the direct command of the Lord, but I would not act on a mere impression — because, simply, many of my impressions have proved to be false — mere imagination. Satan can distressingly entangle people who acted on their premonitions.

I believe there are some human beings who are psychic. That is, they have powers like clairvoyance and mental telepathy, some more, some less. The devil plays heyday with this power, of course, and tries to turn the person into a medium for spiritism. But the Holy Spirit can also use this quality to comfort or encourage the Christian who is psychic. It then takes the form of a premonition or *an illuminated hunch*. Now Satan is always ready to pounce on this and turn it to his own advantage. He will stir up spiritual pride over it; and most certainly will try to get the psychic Christian to act on it *before it is proved* whether the clairvoyance is correct or imaginary. The only safe way to use such power is to distrust it until its source is manifest. When it is clear that it is given of God then we may humbly extract from it all the comfort we need.

By now I was beginning to believe it was the Lord, not imagination, who had told me nearly two years before that I would develop cancer. But I did not let it occupy my thoughts. I merely wrote to two very dear friends about the non-malignant report. I said, "Pray that if it is wrong I may be alerted in time, and that meanwhile I may be enabled to forget it and get on with my work." That prayer was answered perfectly. Our annual Field Conference was coming very close, and I threw my energies into preparing for it. We house-cleaned every room, and all arrangements were clearly mapped out even to the menu for each day, when Dr Richard Buker appeared and informed me that a further test of the biopsy was not so optimistic and they felt I should have an operation immediately.

As it happened, a very skilful surgeon was taking a holiday in Chiengmai just those two days and had consented to operate, if I would have it the very next morning — he was leaving the next afternoon. Immediately it was as if the Lord placed a hand on my shoulder and said, *"That is it."*

I had supper guests that night so there was not much time for the flesh to brood over it and get alarmed — which was a kindness.

Just before we left for the hospital the next morning, I turned to see what verse was on my scripture calendar. It was Psalm 127:2: "For he grants sleep to those he loves." I was startled. My hunch had spoken of going to America but there had been nothing of *death* in it. Did the Lord —? But I cast it out of my mind as they honked for me to get into the jeep. Just a chance calendar verse, anyway. Or was the Lord trying to prepare me? Better not think about it now, on the way to the operation. If it was of the Lord, He would tell me again. So I went cheerfully to the ordeal.

It was most skilfully done and I had every care. Nurse Dorothy Jones of our Mission, "specialled" me and ministered most lovingly. One morning a house doctor came and stood at the foot of my bed and said, "In all my experience I've seen very few patients come through an operation like yours with so little suffering."

"Don't you think it is because I am relaxed, doctor?" I said.

"Undoubtedly. And I used you as an illustration for my class this morning. I told them that they should try to get their patients to put their faith in something outside them — Buddha for the Buddhists, Christ for the Christian — because it would bring relaxation and help them so much." Then he left.

But I lay there thinking. Good psychology, certainly — he is a clever doctor. But how perfectly impossible for a person in such a weak condition to hook his faith on to some nebulae outside himself just because it would be to his benefit if he could! That was not what I was doing! I was resting back on a private word, spoken to me two years before.

Amy Carmichael says this: "Before we reach the place where such waters must be crossed, there is almost always a private word spoken by the Beloved to the lover. That is the word which will be most assaulted as we stand within sight and sound of that seething, roaring flood. The enemy will fasten upon it, twist it about, belittle it, obscure it, try to undermine our confidence in its integrity, and to wreck our tranquillity by making us afraid, but this will put him to flight: *'I have faith in God that it will happen just as he told me.'"*

God had told Paul (Acts 23:11): "Take courage! As you have testified about me in Jerusalem, so you must also testify in Rome." This was Paul's *private word*; and when the terrible storm struck their ship, neither sun nor stars appeared in many days, and all hope that they could be saved was taken away, Paul stood on that private word. They would not perish, for God said he was to see Rome, and he said quietly, "I have faith in God." Paul was not hooking his faith on to some nebulae outside himself, but on to the word of One whom he had proved for many years. Even as Paul said, "I must see Rome," so I relaxed and lay back on the word, "This is to take me to America." But I must not yet tell anyone that. The China Inland Mission does not fly a missionary home to the United States just because she has had a serious operation. It would have to be for some special reason, and that only God should manipulate — I must keep my hands off. But I quite believed it would happen. Now nobody had as yet told me that the operation revealed malignancy; when I asked Dr Buker he just teased me and avoided a straight answer.

But after I had been home from the hospital about a week, a letter was handed to us. It contained the medical report which said it was a fast growing malignancy and the ordinary estimate would give me only a year or so to live. The surgeon had thought he saw traces of it entering the chest and he advised my flying to America immediately. This advice was being passed on to Mission headquarters, and that is how God manipulated events until His private word to me had been fulfilled.

Now I had to face the little calendar verse of the operation morning. Had it been a mere coincidence after all? Or had it been a tender preparation? Time alone will tell.

At first I was startled — I had not expected this. And it was difficult to believe! A month after the operation (which surgeons in America highly praised) I felt normal again. The specialist who examined me was inclined to be quizzical about the melancholy prognostication — he said he found no trace of malignancy left. And so I went about my work, giving it my full attention. But I was, at the same time, making discoveries. I had a new lesson set me, and it is best expressed in the words of 2 Corinthians 10:5 "... casting down imaginations ... and bringing into captivity every thought to the obedience of Christ (KJV)."

I found that imagination could give me a bad time. If I coughed, for instance, I immediately had lung cancer (although X-rays showed the chest to be clear)! If I had a toothache, then I was getting cancer of the mouth! And so on. Every tickle or twinge was instantly interpreted as related to my grim enemy. But if I asserted my right to *a sound mind* (2 Tim. 1:7), these fears left me and the twinges never developed into anything further. "For God hath not given us the spirit of fear, but of power and of love and of a sound mind (KJV)." A sound mind is our gift from God, this verse says, but we need to claim it. The American Standard Version translates that word as *discipline*. And the one includes the other, for a sound mind is necessarily a disciplined one.

Thus I was set a new lesson, or an old lesson in a new form. I had to refuse to allow my imagination to play with my future. That future, I believe, is ordered of God, and no man can guess it. For me to let myself imagine how or when the end would come was not only unprofitable, it was definitely harmful, so I had to bring my thoughts into captivity that they might not dishonour Christ.

The best way to do this, I found, was to engage in some interesting work. While still confined to bed I tried prayer and reading. As I became stronger I set about writing a book — I drew up a daily schedule that would come within the limits of what strength I had, and tried to keep it faithfully. This I enjoyed and I can say truthfully that on this platform of a dread disease there have been many months of very real happiness. It makes for health to have a goal and keep on striving for it. Of course I realize that the Lord has been especially good to me in giving me work which is so congenial and yet does not require much physical labour. But I am sure He would have different ideas and helps for others of His children who are on this same platform.

Another thing which has helped me to keep a sound mind is the gathering of the edelweiss of God. I owe this thought to Amy Carmichael. In her book *Gold by Moonlight*, she has a whole chapter on it. Edelweiss grows on barren mountain heights, and its soft beauty is a cheery surprise to the toiling climber. So Amy Carmichael likens it to the little things of joy which can always be found in any painful experience, if only we will gather them as we go along. Sound health and a normal life I cannot have while on this platform; therefore I accept the fact and do not fret about it. But this very trial has brought me unexpected joys and these I dwell on and delight in them as His kind tokens of remembrance. Letters and cards from all over the world have come to me; people I did not know existed are praying for me and they do kind things for me. Is that not delightful? That has enriched my life.

Loving friends have made it possible for us to have our own home — a little flat, and I have already had our dear son with me longer than a normal furlough would have given. I rejoice in that. Why not? The future of my loved ones, after I leave them? The Lord who has been so kind to me will not be less so to them.

> For my beloved I will not fear, Love knows to do
> For him, for her, from year to year, as hitherto;
> Whom my heart cherishes are dear
> To Thy heart too.

AMY CARMICHAEL

My bedroom is kept beautiful with lovely flowers, gifts from loving friends and relatives. That is edelweiss.

Good books are given or lent to me — edelweiss again. Dainty things to eat are brought to our door, but to enumerate all the edelweiss is hopeless. Suffice it to say, much has been given.

What of the dark valley that will inevitably come? I am told that before he died Dr Harry Rimmer wrote to Dr Charles Fuller something like this:

Next Sunday you are to talk about Heaven. I am interested in that land, because I have held a clear title to a bit of property there for over fifty-five years. I did not buy it. It was given to me without money and without price. But the Donor purchased it for me at tremendous sacrifice. I am not holding it for speculation since the title is not transferable. It is not a vacant lot. For more than half a century I have been sending materials out of which the greatest Architect and Builder of the universe has been building a home for me, which will never need to be remodelled or repaired because it will suit me perfectly, individually, and will never grow old. Termites cannot undermine its foundations, for they rest upon the Rock of Ages. Fire cannot destroy it. Floods cannot wash it away. No locks or bolts will ever be placed upon its doors, for no vicious persons can even enter that land where my dwelling stands, now almost completed and almost ready

for me to enter in and abide in peace eternally, without fear
of being ejected.

There is a valley of deep shadows between the place where
I live in California and that to which I shall journey in a
very short time. I cannot reach my home in that city of gold
without passing through this dark valley of shadows. But I
am not afraid, because the best Friend I ever had went
through the same valley, long, long ago and drove away all
its gloom. He has stuck by me through thick and thin since
we first became acquainted fifty-five years ago, and I hold
His promise in printed form never to forsake me nor to
leave me alone. He will be with me as I walk through the
valley of shadows, and I shall not lose my way when He is
with me.

Dr Rimmer has long since arrived in that City of
Gold, and I do not know how long was his passage
through the valley of shadows. But I have learned
this, from my present platform, that the spiritual is
tied down to the physical more than is apparent.
After my first operation, finding I would have long
hours just lying in bed, I said to myself, "Good. Now
I will employ this time in intercession and prayer."
But to my surprise and alarm I found I could not!
What was wrong with me? Was I backsliding? Then I
realized it. To pray for others as I was accustomed to
do required *physical* as well as spiritual strength.
When I went to gather myself together for this
concentrated work, I found there was nothing to
gather! Nothing responded to my call. I had no
physical strength with which to rally my forces. I just
had to lie there and say, "Well, Lord, I will have to
ask you to read my heart as you read the names on
the breast-plate of the high priest in days of old."

In the same way the exercise of faith requires a
physical strength that is not apparent to the well
person, nor to the sick person himself if he has never

before had the experience of physical weakness and sinking. This explains to me myself, at least, why some of the saints have seemed to find the valley of the shadows a dark place. The Lord is most certainly there with them, but the unconscious habitual use of physical strength in laying hold of this fact by faith may disconcert by its absence. To me it is not fair to judge such a person's salvation by what is seen at his deathbed. We do not take seriously what is said in the mutterings of delirium, when a person is not himself. In the same way a Christian's apprehension of Christ should be judged by his lifelong experience of Him, not by what onlookers see during the last hours when the spirit is so hampered by a weakened and dissolving physique. Friends should take comfort in the fact that Christ is there, and the dear one will be consciously in His arms the moment the spirit is free.

I have been reading the diary of David Brainerd these days, and have noticed the relation between his own physical well-being or illness and his *sense* of God's presence. They were often related. When ill in body he bemoaned his spiritual barrenness. *"November 1. Was very much disordered in body and sometimes full of pain. ... Alas! When God is withdrawn, all is gone."* Then a few days later after he was rested a bit, he writes: *"Saw more of the glory and majesty of God ... than ever I had seen before. ... Oh, how my soul then rejoiced in God!"* The spirit is not absolutely dependent on physical well-being, as I have myself proved in these pages, but it is more closely related than we are sometimes apt to allow.

Facing the end of one's earthly pilgrimage is not a melancholy thing for a Christian. It is like preparation for the most exciting journey of all. Someone sent me a tract on this subject which I give herewith. It is called "Getting Ready to Move."

The owner of the tenement which I have occupied for many years has given notice that he will furnish but little or nothing more for repairs. I am advised to be ready to move.

At first this was not a very welcome notice. The surroundings here are in many respects very pleasant, and were it not for the evidence of decay, I should consider the old house good enough. But even a light wind causes it to tremble and totter and all the braces are not sufficient to make it secure. So I am getting ready to move.

It is strange how quickly one's interest is transferred to the prospective home. I have been consulting maps of the new country and reading descriptions of its inhabitants. One (2 Cor. 12:2) who visited it has returned, and from him I learn that it is beautiful beyond description — language breaks down in attempting to tell of what he heard while there. He says that, in order to make an investment there, he has suffered the loss of all things that he owned here, and even rejoices in what others would call making a sacrifice.

Another (John 15:23) whose love to me has been proved by the greatest possible test is now there. He has sent me several clusters of the most delicious fruits. After tasting them, all food here seems insipid.

Two or three times I have been down by the border of the river that forms the boundary, and have wished myself among the company of those who were singing praises to the King on the other side.

Many of my friends have moved there. Before leaving they spoke of my coming later. I have seen the smile upon their faces as they passed out of sight.

Often I am asked to make some new investments here, but my answer in every case is "*I am getting ready to move.*"

This spirit of expectation is our dear inheritance

and right. For the Christian, death is not the dissolution of life but the *consummation*.

> The last of life
> For which the first was made,

as Browning puts it.

Or as Amy Carmichael words it, "The days of our bloom and our power are just about to begin."

> Gone, they tell me, is youth;
> Gone is the strength of my life.
> Nothing remains but decline,
> Nothing but age and decay.
>   Not so, I'm God's little child,
>   Only beginning to live.
>   Coming the days of my prime,
>   Coming the strength of my life,
>   Coming the vision of God,
>   Coming my bloom and my power!

Coming the vision of God. Christians often say that the most wonderful thing of all will be to see our Lord face to face. I have pondered that much and feel it is surely worded inadequately. To see the Lord is but a lesser thing to one who has had a close spirit-with-Spirit communion with Him all along. What matter the colour of His eyes or the shape of His face? That is not what makes Him precious. Nothing is so deeply intimate as a spirit knit with Spirit, and that we can and should enjoy right now while here on earth. I think what is meant is to be with the Lord *with the root of sin gone*. To fellowship with Him without the lazy flesh dragging us back, or unwanted thoughts of pride and self constantly staining us. To be finally rid of corruption, to worship and enjoy Him with heart purged into His own purity, *that* will be an advance over anything that is possible on earth.

And so *the platform of a dread disease becomes but a springboard for heaven*. We become like Him in His death. In the pain which is inevitably connected with the descent into the valley of shadows there will be a fellowship, even if not perceived by weakened nature. The power of His resurrection will become known as never before. And the great end, *that I may know Him*, will be granted.